ROBESPIERRE

ROBESPIERRE

By J. M. THOMPSON

Basil Blackwell

First published 1935.
This edition first published 1988 by

Basil Blackwell Ltd
108 Cowley Road, Oxford, OX4 1JF, UK

Basil Blackwell Inc.
432 Park Avenue South, Suite 1503, New York, NY 10016, USA

British Library Cataloguing in Publication Data

Thompson, J.M.
  Robespierre.
  1. Robespierre, Maximilien
  I. Title
  944'.034'0924   DC146.R6
  ISBN 0-631-15504-X

Library of Congress Cataloging in Publication Data

Thompson, J. M. (James Matthew), 1878–1956.
  Robespierre.

  Includes index.
  1. Robespierre, Maximilien, 1758–1794.
  2. Revolutionists—France—Biography. 3. France—
History—Revolution, 1789-1794. I. Title.
  DC146.R6T45   944.04'092'4   87-29909
  ISBN 0-631-15504-X

Printed in Great Britain by
T.J. Press (Padstow) Ltd., Padstow, Cornwall

CONTENTS

CONTENTS

Contents

CONTENTS

CONTENTS

CONTENTS

Contents

FOREWORD

The Fascination of Robespierre

MICHEL VOVELLE

It is now more than half a century since J. M. Thompson's *Robespierre* was first published and the book has become a classic, but is there any justification for reissuing it now? I agree this seems an incongruous question with which to begin a preface, but it is nevertheless one which we must not evade.

Almost a century ago, at the time of the first centenary, and right up until the 1920s, our predecessors confronted one another with rival heroes: Alphonse Aulard, a liberal representative of the radical historiography of the Third Republic, defended Danton, while Albert Mathiez, who had marked socialist leanings, considered Robespierre the champion of social democracy under the Revolution. Behind these emblematical figures the real clash was between two antithetically opposed conceptions of the Revolution.

Should we speak, to take up Lucien Febvre's famous phrase, of 'a history which is no longer our own'? It is true that since then the historiography of the French Revolution has tended to emphasize the history of the anonymous masses and their obscure heroes: the 'Sans Culottes' of Paris in the works of Albert Solorel/Solord, and the 'revolutionary mob' of Georges Rudé. The pantheon of official heroes, whether revered or execrated, has given way to these unknown protagonists whom we can only follow en masse and about whom we have very little factual information.

We cannot, however, ignore the recent revival of biography which looked for some time as if it were on the decline or out of fashion: in this we see signs of the collective preoccupation of our age, in search of clues to its own identity, just as it is constantly in search of 'roots'. This renewed interest in the hero, which we find in all areas of historiography, is

xiii

particularly notable in the domain of revolutionary history, where the tradition has remained strong. Saint Just, Danton, Camille Desmoulins, Mirabeau, Madame Roland and Robespierre have remained or are returning to favour in the eyes of a public which has never really lost sight of them.

This argument alone might well justify a new edition of J. M. Thompson's work of reference. But I believe that there is a further reason for renewed interest in Robespierre in particular.

A whole study could be made of Robespierrist historiography from its origins, that is to all intents and purposes from Thermidor in Year II when the 'Incorruptible' was put to death with his friends. Some of the documentation (carefully sifted and selected), the 'papers found at Robespierre's home', were published by Courbois with the hostile purpose of supporting Thermidorian propaganda. But, to mention only a few of the more significant landmarks, the discovery of another Robespierre, no longer the agent of the Terror or the bloody dictator, but the apostle of social democracy and the noblest figure of the revolution, began to crystallize in the 1840s, when Republican historiography went in search of the great man's memory: witness the collection by Lapomeraye, a socialist and a revolutionary, of Charlotte Robespierre's memories of her brother.

In opposition to the dark legend, an image, itself carefully constructed and not entirely free from the element of hero worship, began to take shape: the three thick volumes which E. Hamel devoted to the biography of the Incorruptible between 1865 and 1867 remain the chief work of reference despite their age.

The tide of interest did not slacken from this time on. I have mentioned Albert Mathiez as being in the opposite camp to Alphonse Aulard: it was he who in 1908 founded the 'Société d'Études Robespierristes', and who, in a whole series of articles and lectures fought for the reputation of his hero. His text 'Why we are Robespierrists', which was the theme of a lecture given in 1920, amounts to a profession of faith.

Albert Mathiez planned to crown his historical work with a biography of Robespierre, but his sudden death in 1932 prevented him and his articles collected under the title 'Studies on Robespierre' must take the place of the projected synthesis.

This line of work continued in the years following Mathiez's death, which saw the almost simultaneous publication of the great compositions among which J. M. Thompson's book takes its place: his two volumes were published in 1935, while Gerard Walter's equally important work appeared in 1936. These were the first erudite studies, anxious to shed light on the various landmarks and obscure corners of Robespierre's life, while each author retained his own private view or judgements of the Incorruptible: in Walter's case suppressed anti-Jacobinism which nevertheless reveals itself fairly quickly, while Thompson too is torn between genuine affectionate admiration and the severity of the judgements he delivers throughout the course of his narrative. In the final analysis what unites the approach of the British author and that of the French writer is the desire – even if unfulfilled – to move away from impassioned history, from anathema and from panegyric, towards a painstaking and erudite reconstruction of a sequence of events. Both had to take stock of the prolific literature on the subject. Walter refers to 10,000 titles, and Thompson begins his study with an annotated critical bibliography of the works of his precursors.

But can we simply bring to a close the study of a personality who never ceases to fascinate those who are interested in the Revolution? Since the 1930s new assessments have emerged, among which we must mention Jean Massin's warm defence of Robespierre (1956) as well as Max Gallo's *Robespierre, histoire d'une solitude*. But to avoid the risk of becoming repetitive, historians must try different viewpoints and different angles: Norman Hampson in his *Maximilien Robespierre*, published in 1978, used the device of a fictional discussion between the historian confronted with the Robespierre 'case' and three interlocutors (a civil servant, a militant and a pastor) who are in fact the embodiment of his own doubts and scruples. In a similar way Jean Philippe Domecq, in *Robespierre, derniers temps* (1984), departed from classical biography and allowed himself a novelist's licence to imagine and express, within a tight historical framework, Robespierre's thoughts and intimate reflections. We will quickly pass over a certain historical novel, even more recent, which quite shamelessly makes use of the licence of that genre and of creative freedom to make Robespierre a formidable erotomaniac who was prepared to go to any lengths in order to satisfy his passion for Saint Just (D. Jamet, *Antoine et Maximilien ou la Terreur sans la Vertu*). It is no longer possible to adopt a simple and straightforward approach towards Robespierre, or are these devices, some of which are used honestly, some less so, the only way to deal with the subject without falling back into the well worn paths of hagiography or anathema?

In this context J. M. Thompson's classic text retains all its value. Following step by step the different stages of Robespierre's life, from his birth to his political career, his rise and then his fall, he analyses with precision and minute attention to detail the relevant texts, the stands taken by his subject and the stakes involved day by day. His hero disconcerts him more than once, and more than once disappoints him when he encounters mediocrity where one would look for political genius and when he finds mere rhetoric where others see the flame of revolutionary passion. But while he retains a critical eye, Thompson does not seek to deny the Incorruptible quality which was recognized in Robespierre during his lifetime, the rectitude and unmeasured commitment which in his own eyes enabled Robespierre in the most dramatic moments of the Revolution to identify with the collective conscience of France, his role of echo thus transfiguring the petty and mediocre aspects of his character.

We might at times feel that this Englishman watchful for every detail passed by a little of what gives Robespierre his spark and his historical perspicacity and thus his greatness:

but its scrupulous honesty has preserved this erudite work from ageing. It remains one of the finest introductions to the complex and controversial personality of the Incorruptible.

NOTE ON REFERENCES

1. Accounts of debates and reports of speeches in the Constituent Assembly, Legislative Assembly, and National Convention, are taken, unless otherwise stated, from the *Moniteur* (*ré-impression*, 1863) and will be found under the dates given.

2. Accounts of proceedings at the Jacobin Club are taken, unless otherwise stated, from Aulard, *La Société des Jacobins* (1889–97), and will be found under the dates given.

3. The following abbreviations are used for books or periodicals frequently referred to:—

A.H. = Annales Historiques.

A.R. = Annales Révolutionnaires.

Arch. Parl. = Archives Parlementaires.

Aulard = A. Aulard, *Histoire Politique de la Révolution française* (5ᵉ *édition*, 1921).

B. and R. = Buchez et Roux, *Histoire parlementaire de la Révolution française* (1834–8).

Blanc = Louis Blanc, *Histoire de la Révolution française* (1847–).

Carlyle = Thomas Carlyle, *The French Revolution* (1837).

Carnet = *Le Carnet de Robespierre*, in Mathiez, *Robespierre Terroriste* (1921), pp. 56–78.

Charlotte = H. Fleischmann, *Charlotte Robespierre et ses Mémoires* (1909).

Corresp. = *Correspondance de Maximilien et Augustin Robespierre, recueillie et publiée par* Georges Michon (1926).

Courtois = *Rapport fait au nom de la commission chargée de l'examen des papiers trouvées chez Robespierre et ses complices, par* E-B. Courtois (1795).

Croker = Essays on the early period of the French Revolution, by the late Right Hon. John Wilson Croker (1857).

C.P.S. = Aulard, *Recueil des Actes du Comité de Salut Public* (1889–99).

Deslandres = Maurice Deslandres, *Histoire Constitutionnelle de la France de* 1789 à 1870 (1932).

Esquiros = A. Esquiros, *Histoire des Montagnards* (1847).

Fleischmann = H. Fleischmann, *Robespierre et les femmes* (1909).

Gower = *The Despatches of Earl Gower*, ed. Oscar Browning (1885).

Hamel = *Histoire de Robespierre et du Coup d'état du 9 thermidor* par Ernest Hamel (ed. Cinqualbre, 3 vols. in 2, n.d.).

Jac. = A. Aulard, *La Société des Jacobins* (1889–97).

Jaurès = Jean Jaurès, *Histoire socialiste de la Révolution française* (ed. Mathiez, 1922–4).

Lamartine = A. de Lamartine, *Histoire des Girondins* (ed. 1902).

Lav. = *Histoire nationale de la France contemporaine* (ed. Lavisse), tom. 1–2 (1920).

Le Blond = *La vie et les crimes de Robespierre . . .* par M. le Blond de Neuvéglise (1795).

Lenôtre = G. Lenôtre, *Robespierre et la 'Mère de Dieu'* (ed. 1926).

Lewes = George Henry Lewes, *The Life of Maximilien Robespierre* (ed. 1899).

Mathiez = Albert Mathiez, *The French Revolution* (E.T. of *La Révolution française,* 1922–), 1924.

Michelet = J. Michelet, *Histoire de la Révolution française* (1847–53).

Michon = Corresp. above.

N. and Q. = Notes and Queries.

Ording = Arne Ording, *Le Bureau de police du Comité de Salut Public* (1930).

Pap. inéd. = *Papiers inédites trouvés chez Robespierre, Saint-Just,* etc. (1828).

Paris = J. Paris, *La jeunesse de Robespierre* (1870).

Proyart = J. M. Proyart, *La vie de Maximilien Robespierre* (1850).

R.F. = Révolution Française.

R.H. = Revue Historique.

R.H.R.F. = Revue Historique de la Révolution Française.

R.Q.H. = Revue des Questions Historiques.

Stéfane-Pol. = Stéfane-Pol, *Autour de Robespierre: le Conventionnel Le Bas* (1900).

Tourneux = M. Tourneux, *Les sources bibliographiques de l'histoire de la Révolution française* (1898).

Tuetey = Tuetey, *Répertoire des sources bibliographiques de l'histoire de Paris pendant la Révolution* (1889).

Vellay = C. Vellay, *Discours et rapports de Robespierre* (1908).

Villiers = Pierre Villiers, *Souvenirs d'un déporté* (1802).

Walter = G. Walter, *Robespierre* (1936–).

Ward = Reginald Somerset Ward, *Maximilien Robespierre: a study in deterioration* (1934).

CHAPTER I

THE STUDENT (1758–1781)

I

MAXIMILIEN MARIE ISIDORE DE ROBESPIERRE was born
at Arras on May 6, 1758. His father was Maximilien
Barthélemy François de Robespierre, and his mother
Jacqueline Marguerite Carraut.

If there was any Irish strain in the Robespierre family; if
their name had been corrupted from some original Robert
Spiers, Robert's Peter, Rosper, Roper, Rooper, or Roth
Fitz Piers; or if there was something Hibernian in Maximilien's character or countenance which might have come
from across the Channel;[1] at any rate, the family had been
French ever since the fifteenth century. From Gilles de
Romespierres, Ronmespierre, or Roumespierre, mentioned
in 1429-31, and his grandson Guillaume, whose seal, bearing
a coat of arms, appears on a document of 1462, the family
name and home can be traced through a continuous line of
Robespierres for over 300 years. The early bearers of the
name followed many professions. Jean de Rouvespieres
(mid-fifteenth century) kept an inn at Paris; Robert was a
Prior; Jean served in the King's mounted guard; and whilst
Baudouin held ecclesiastical benefices at Cambrai and
Hesdin, by appointment of Pope Eugene IV (1431-9),
Pierre of Ruitz was a common *laboureur*, who borrowed
money from the Municipality, and carried on a small
business in the sale of timber and stone. But before long,
though now and again a younger son would turn priest or
publican, the family settled down in the suburbs of the law,
and in that district of north-east France whose corners are

[1] The tradition appears in various and sometimes absurd forms in Lewes, Hamel,
Michelet, Lamartine, Belloc, and Hayes' *Ireland and Irishmen in the French Revolution*.
Cp. N. and Q., 9th Series, I/183, 295. The earliest biography (Le Blond, 20) says that
the family originally came from Belgium.

I

formed by the towns of Douai, Cambrai, and Arras. Jean, in the early sixteenth century, was *huissier au conseil d'Artois*, and *Auditeur royal* at Bethune; his son Robert combined a clerkship with a small grocery business; his great-grandson, another Robert, was clerk, attorney, and notary-public at Harnes, Henin, and Carvin, near Lens; and Carvin remained the chief home of the family, till finally Maximilien's grandfather and father donned the barrister's gown, and enjoyed a respectable, if not very remunerative practice at Arras, the judicial and ecclesiastical capital of Artois.

The grandfather, the first Maximilien, tried to re-establish the family fortunes by marrying an inn-keeper's daughter, who brought him some house property at Arras; and he almost achieved fame when, in 1745, Charles Edward Stuart, the Young Pretender, appointed him one of the first office-holders of the Masonic Lodge with which he rewarded the town for six months' hospitality.[1] Perhaps because he became a man of property, this ancestor made little of the law, and for a long period had no more than two briefs a year. Of his sons and daughters, Maximilien's uncles and aunts, only two play any considerable part in the present history—Marie Marguerite (1735–91), afterwards Mme Deshorties, and Amable Aldegonde Henriette (1736–91), who became Mme Durut.[2]

From this respectable but undistinguished family Robespierre's father inherited a legal connexion, a scrap of property, a coat of arms, a town house, and the right to put *de* before his name. The two houses in the Place de Chaudronniers and the rue des Bouchers might bring in some 12–15,000 *livres* a year: but property and practice together meant meagre wealth to one of a family of fourteen, with eight children. It was soon necessary to repudiate the payment for an annual *obit* and weekly mass incurred under the will of an ancestress; when Marie Marguerite married, she had no dowry but her furniture; and all that the grand-

[1] The document, dated *le jeudi* 15° *jour du* 2° *mois l'an de l'incarnation* 1745, is given in A.R. 4/113.
[2] For the complete genealogy, v. A.R. 5/236. The name was spelt Roberpierre, Roberspier, Roberspierre, or Robertspier, with or without *de* (Paris, 3).

children ultimately inherited was the inadequate sum of 8,000 *livres*. Robespierre's maternal grandfather was, indeed, a brewer; but the Carraut property disappeared in the payment of debts and bequests.[1] Without money to support them, the family title and arms gave little satisfaction, and both disappeared in the early days of the Revolution.[2] Robespierre's father, the feckless heir to this fading estate, had been intended by his parents for the religious life, and began a novitiate with the Premonstratensians of Dommartin at the age of seventeen: but finding no vocation there,[3] he came home again, read law at Douai, and fell back upon the family profession of barrister, attached to the Conseil d'Artois (1756). Within two years, at the age of twenty-six, he contracted a hasty marriage with Jacqueline Carraut, daughter of Jacques-François Carraut, a brewer, of rue Ronville, and Marie-Marguerite Cornu (January 2, 1758); and Maximilien was born four months later.[4] Two daughters and another son followed rapidly—Marie Marguerite Charlotte (born on February 8, 1760), Henriette Eulalie Françoise (December 28, 1761), and Augustin Bon Joseph (January 21, 1763); till, with the birth of a fifth child which did not survive, on July 4, 1764, the mother's strength gave out, and she died on July 16, aged 29, leaving four young children, and a memory which, his sister says, Maximilien could never recall without tears.

Hitherto a fairly successful *avocat*, the widower seems now to have become almost deranged. He failed to sign the registration of his wife's death, or to attend her funeral; and four months later, deserting his family, he took up a temporary post as bailiff to the *seigneur* of Sauchy-Cauchy, near Marquion, north of Cambrai.[5] After some-

[1] Lesueur in A.R. 7/179; Vellay in R.H. 8/148. An inventory of the Carraut property was given by Lavoine in *Avenir d'Arras*, February 17, 1914.
[2] There is some doubt as to the form of the arms; v. Hamel 1/10, Paris, 6, A.R. 7/106; Mélicocq in *Annales du Nord* 3/6/72. Maximilien signed his name with the *de* as Secretary of the Assembly at the foot of the decree abolishing titles of nobility (June 19, 1790).
[3] v. Livre journalier de l'abbaye de Dompmartin (Paris, 12).
[4] For the register of marriage and baptism, v. Paris, 13.
[5] Le Blond puts his flight before his wife's death, and attributes it to *bizarrerie de caractère ou désagrément de profession à la suite d'un procès perdu*.

thing like a year's absence, he was at home again between December, 1765, when he urged his colleagues at the bar to send an address of sympathy to Louis XV during the fatal illness of the Dauphin,[1] and March 22, 1766, when he signed an I.O.U. for 700 livres to his sister Henriette. There follows another absence of two years, and a second reappearance, in October, 1768, marked, like the first, by a heartless financial expedient; for he borrows a sum of money from his widowed mother, now an inmate of the Convent of *Dames de la Paix*, upon condition of renouncing all claims to the family inheritance. A third absence is proved by two documents signed at Mannheim in June, 1770, and October 1771;[2] and a third return by the reappearance of his name on the records of the Conseil d'Artois between February and June, 1772.[3] But after that he becomes a legend. The earliest biography, written within a few months of Robespierre's death by someone in close touch with Arras, says that he first went to Belgium, then opened a school for teaching French at Cologne, and finally, disliking this work, set out for London and the West Indies, where he may still have been living in 1795. His daughter Charlotte, who probably knew more, but whose recollections were not written down until forty years later, and who had no wish to record his delinquencies, only says that he was advised to travel, and never returned: she does not know where he died.[4] After 1772, at any rate, he never reappeared at Arras, and left his young family to face the world alone.

II

When his father first disappeared, in 1764, Maximilien was six years old, Charlotte four, Henriette three, and Augustin hardly out of his cradle. When he finally deserted them, eight years later, the two girls had already gone to live with their aunts, Marie and Amable, and the two boys

[1]Letter to Baudelet, December 9 (A.H., 1924, 72).
[2]Lavoine, *La famille de Robespierre* (R.H.R.F. 8/47). Cp. Walter 1/24
[3]A.H. 1/568.
[4]Le Blond, 21; Charlotte, 188. Cp. a local biography quoted by Mathiez in A.H. 1/568; and Walter. 1/24, for proof that he was alive in 1778.

4

with their grandparents, the Carrauts. In December, 1768, Charlotte was sent to a girls' school at Tournai, where she learnt house-keeping, needle-work, and religion. In June, 1773, she was followed there by her sister Henriette.[1]

In 1766 Maximilien, who had learnt to read, and taught himself to write, went to school, at the age of eight, as a day-boy, at the Collège d'Arras, a richly-endowed foundation of the sixteenth century, whose management, since the expulsion of the Jesuits, had been in the hands of the bishop of the diocese, and of a local committee, whilst the teaching was given by secular priests; the Principal was M. Monlier de la Borère. Here, with 29 boarders and 400 day boys, most of whom belonged, as he did, to the professional classes of the district, he learnt the rudiments of Latin.[2] Charlotte, with sisterly partiality, says that young Maximilien was hard-working, serious-minded, amiable, just, and popular, and that his progress astonished his masters; but that he took little part in school recreations, and spent long hours in solitude and meditation.[3] Le Blond simply remarks that his success owed more to patience than to genius; and records the inflexibility (*raideur*) of his character. One old schoolfellow remembered him, in after years, as 'the conventional good boy'; another wrote that he had a detestable character, and an inordinate love of domination:[4] but when we notice that the favourable verdict belongs to the time of Robespierre's popularity (1793), and the unfavourable (1794) to the month after his fall, we shall not attach much importance to either. It is likely enough, in any case, that his cramped and unhappy childhood had left a mark. The death of his mother, and the desertion of his father, when he was only a child, had turned him, his sister says,

[1] Charlotte, 21.
[2] In 1919 a British officer found in a ruined cottage on the Somme, and gave to the Bodleian, a *Catalogue des Écoliers du Collège académique de l'Abbaye Royale de Saint Vaast . . . de l'année* 1764; among the names of Robespierre's schoolfellows (not all his contemporaries) are Damiens, Lebas, Legay, Lenglet, Paris, and three English names—Fleming, Ledwich and Lock. The fact that Robespierre had a schoolfellow named Damiens may have suggested the royalist legend that he was descended from Louis XV's *assassin* (v. 1/xvi).
[3] Charlotte, 21.
[4] Fleischmann, 26.

from a normally cheerful boy (*étourdi, turbulent, leger*) into a sedate and conscientious young head of his family (*posé, raisonnable, laborieux*), who spoke seriously to his younger brother and sisters, and only joined in their games to show how they should be played. His own taste was for books and birds, and it is said that his mother had taught him to make lace.[1] When his sisters paid their Sunday visits to the Carrauts they were allowed to handle his tame pigeons and sparrows; and once even to take one home; but never again, for it died of neglect; and when he went to College he left his collection of pictures and other treasures with his family, but his birds were given to a girl friend, who could be trusted to look after them.[2]

The inevitable background of this rather austere childhood was religion—religion enforced by daily prayers at the Abbey school; religion—if only the building of toy chapels —encouraged at home by the aunts, who enjoyed a reputation for piety, and by their clerical friends; and religion made magnificent in the cathedral itself, where young Maximilien is said to have played his part in the drama of the mass, *en tunique blanche*, as acolyte or server.[3]

III

The boy's progress at school was so promising that after three years, at the age of eleven, he was given a scholarship to the University of Paris. This was one of four *bourses* remaining in the gift of the Abbot of Saint-Vaast since the recent incorporation of the fourteenth-century Collège d'Arras in

[1]Charlotte, 188, Paris 17.

[2]Charlotte, 190. Hamel finds the story touching, Croker absurd. Lenôtre's discovery that no birdcages are mentioned in the Carraut bill of sale hardly proves that it is untrue. The Dehay letter (Corresp. 4) shows that Robespierre still kept canaries, twenty years later. It was doubtless this taste that suggested to his enemies the story that he used to amuse himself by cutting off birds' heads in a toy guillotine. The legend gained credence from the fact that in the summer of 1794 the *agent national* at Arras confiscated a toy guillotine, in which some children were decapitating birds and mice. (Lecesne, *Arras sous la Révolution*, 3/18.) The *Conventionnel* Lejeune was also accused of keeping a toy guillotine with which he decapitated chickens and cut up fruit for his table (R.F. 41/513). The girl friend was probably Mlle Dehay.

[3]Ward, 274; Esquiros 1/195, on the authority of Charlotte, who afterwards denied it (A.H. 1920, 153).

the Collège Louis-le-Grand, and it provided free board and teaching throughout a course of some ten years.

Robespierre's career at Louis-le-Grand began in October, 1769. This great building, with its gloomy entrance gateway on the rue Saint-Jacques, its eight quadrangles, its Hall, Chapel, and lecture-rooms, and its insufficient supply of bath-rooms and lavatories, was not unlike an Oxford college. Its 200 scholars (*boursiers*) and its increasing crowd of boarders (*pensionnaires*) and day-boys (*externes*) were under the supervision of a Principal, a Vice-Principal, and a staff of twenty-three resident masters, whilst the lecturing was done by non-resident *professeurs*.[1] There were three principals during Robespierre's ten years—Gardin du Mesnil (–1770), author of works on the principles of rhetoric, and Latin synonyms; Poignard d'Enthieuloye, who resigned, after a few years' rule (1778), with most of his staff, leaving the College heavily in debt; and Denis Bérardier, a tolerant man, with political ambitions, who threw up academic life in 1789 to become a deputy in the National Assembly. Of these, Bérardier alone seems to have influenced Robespierre. Their friendship outlasted school days; and when his old pupil Desmoulins married, Bérardier officiated, and Maximilien signed the register.

In Robespierre's time the scholars were no longer distinguished from the commoners by being differently dressed and worse fed; but they were still at some disadvantage compared with richer boys, who might live in comparative comfort, keep a servitor, and look down on the mere recipients of charity. Robespierre, one of the poorest boys in the school, was driven to save money upon clothes, in order to spend it at the barber's, or the bookshop: in 1775, and again in 1778, he had to apply to his *Préfet d'études* for a decent suit of clothes in which to present an address to Louis XVI, or pay his respects to his patron, the Bishop of Arras.[2]

But at school poverty is no bar to friendship. During his first two years in Paris, Maximilien could take refuge from

---

[1] Eymond, *Histoire du Collège de Louis-le-Grand*; Paris; Stein in R.Q.H. 102/134.
[2] Proyart 22; Corresp. 2 (April 11, 1778).

the difficulties of his new life in the rooms of his relation, M. Delaroche, a canon of Nôtre-Dame; his death, in 1771, threw the boy back on his school companions, of whom the closest seems to have been a clever and attractive boy from Guise, two years younger than himself, named Camille Desmoulins; others who afterwards made some name in the world were Fréron, Duport-Dutertre, Suleau, and a *boursier* from Noyon named Le Brun. In the days of Robespierre's power a man named Dubois wrote to remind him that they had gone up the school side by side; and the diplomatic Abbé Noel admitted to a slight acquaintance.[1]

With every motive for working, and few interests outside school, Robespierre made steady, even brilliant progress in classics. Between 1769 and 1776 the name of Ludovicus Franciscus Maximilianus Maria Isidorus de Robespierre, Atrebas (i.e., of Arras) figures six times in the annual prize-lists, for successes in Latin and Greek verse and translation; and by 1775 he was so evidently the best classical scholar of his year that he was chosen to deliver a Latin speech of welcome to Louis XVI and Marie Antoinette, when they visited the College on the way back from their coronation at Rheims: an eyewitness noticed that the King looked kindly at the boy who was one day to demand his death.[2] This proficiency, indeed, owed less to natural genius than to a capacity for taking pains. 'He was a hard worker,' says one of his teachers, 'but heavy in hand, like an ox at the plough';[3] and laboriousness became the method of everything that he undertook.

Of Robespierre's non- or post-classical studies little is known. To Hamel it seems self-evident that 'Hérivaux's favourite pupil' should write essays 'breathing a kind of Stoic morality, and a zeal for freedom,' and he transfers to Robespierre the nickname which, for his enthusiasm for Latin oratory, had been given to Hérivaux himself—'le Romain';[4] just as, in Charlotte's sisterly imagination, he 'always carried off the first prize'. More is to be learnt,

[1]Pap. Inéd. 1/154; Corresp. 449; Gower 393.   [2]Le Blond, 48; Proyart, 22.
[3]A.H. 1931, 161.
[4]Le Blond, 46. The mistake has been repeated in all later biographies.

perhaps, from a passage in his friend Desmoulins' *Révolutions de France et de Brabant*, in which, speaking of their school-days, he reminds Robespierre how, under professors who taught them to hate their own government, they learnt the love of liberty, and longed to know how France might be freed.[1] Under such influences they grew up, like many more of their generation, to read Voltaire, Raynal, Rousseau, and other authors of the Enlightenment, whose corrupting works (*mauvaises livres*) were, according to Royou, smuggled into College by the hair-dresser, or the lavatory attendant.[2] Robespierre's 'head was full of Rousseau'; and one day, not long before 1778, there was perhaps a visit to the attic in which Jean-Jacques was nearing his end. 'I saw you,' wrote Maximilien some years afterwards, 'during your last days, and the memory remains a source of joy and pride. I contemplated your august features, and saw on them the marks of the dark disappointments to which you were condemned by the injustice of mankind.'[3]

IV

What kind of character did Robespierre bear at College? There are two accounts, and they are barely reconcilable. One comes from his biographer Le Blond, his almoner Proyart, and his schoolfellow Fréron; the other from his sister Charlotte. 'He was the same at College,' says Fréron, 'as he was in later days—melancholy, morose, and liverish; jealous of his comrades' successes; never taking part in their games, but going for solitary walks, striding along, in the manner of a dreamer and an invalid. There was nothing young about him. His restless face already showed the convulsive grimaces we came to know so well. Silent, reserved, unbending, secretive, his most marked qualities were a self-centred *amour-propre*, invincible stubbornness, and fundamental dishonesty. I can't remember ever seeing him smile.

[1] Clarétie, *Camille Desmoulins*, 21 f.; B. and R. 26/271; cp. Mercier, *Tableau de Paris*, 1/151.
[2] A.H., 1931, 161; Le Blond, 37.
[3] *Dédicace à Jean-Jacques Rousseau*, v. Charlotte, 290. This composition (which internal evidence suggests dates from 1791) is the only real evidence for the incident.

If anyone offended him he never forgot it. Vindictive and treacherous, he had already learnt to dissimulate his resentment.'[1] Le Blond says that a certain Mme Mercier of Arras, when sending a son of her own to Louis-le-Grand, wrote expressing her anxiety lest he should have anything to do with 'young Robespierre (*le jeune Robespierre*), who, between ourselves, promises to turn out a bad lot'; and goes on to describe him as a silent, conceited, unpopular boy, who cared nothing for morality, and resented the practice of it by others.[2]

This evidence is highly suspect. Fréron, one of the gang which had just overthrown Robespierre, supplied his reminiscences as material for Courtois' anti-Robespierrist *rapport*. Le Blond was a Catholic royalist refugee who hated everything to do with the Revolution. Proyart was an *émigré* priest who had no reason for sparing either the apostle of the Supreme Being, or the author of his exile; and Mme Mercier's objection, if it really refers to Maximilien, and not to his younger brother Augustin, may only mean that she had been shocked by his liberal and sceptical way of talking when he spent an occasional holiday at Arras.

On the other hand, Charlotte's account of her brother's college days turns him into the conventional hero of school-boy fiction. 'I have been told,' Laponneraye makes her say, 'that he was popular both with boys and masters. . . . During the whole of his time at College his temper was so quiet and even that he never quarrelled with his companions; whilst he made himself the champion of the younger boys against the elder, spoke up for them, and even used his fists to defend them, when his eloquence was ineffective.'[3] It is always Charlotte's thesis that her brother championed the cause of the oppressed, whether against the school bully, or the injustice of the law, or the tyranny of the state. We cannot prove that she is romancing, but it is probable that the present passage is another example of this amiable apologetic.

[1]Pap. Inéd. 1/154. This is apparently the source of the unfavourable account given in *Vie sécrette politique et curieuse de M. J. M. Robespierre* (Brit. Mus.).
[2]Le Blond, 25.   [3]Charlotte, 193.

V

In one subject—that of religion—we are on firmer ground. Robespierre went to College a conventional, if not a convinced Catholic; he left it a conventional, if not a convinced sceptic. Side by side with the classical and philosophical teaching at Louis-le-Grand, and affecting it at every turn, was the Catholic system, with its daily Offices and Mass, compulsory monthly Confession, Communion (at least) at all the great Festivals, and the Retreats that opened every Academic Year. Maximilien's first term at College was marked by the death, at the age of sixteen, of a pious young scholar, J. M. L. G. Décalogue de la Perrie, the story of whose edifying life was published soon afterwards by Robespierre's almoner, the abbé Proyart, and became a classic guide to the devout.[1] In his early years at school it must have been difficult to resist the pressure of official piety, and he was at one time a fairly frequent communicant. But, as he grew up, and his experience widened, Robespierre went through a change of mind which was hardly less common then than it is now; and though he never quite shook off his clerical traditions, he admitted in after years that 'he had been a pretty poor Catholic ever since his time at College'.[2] In a highly rhetorical passage, based perhaps on Proyart's reminiscences, but coloured by his own intolerance, Le Blond thus describes this change. 'Of all the practices obligatory in an educational establishment,' he writes, 'none seemed more difficult or uncongenial to Robespierre than those of a specially religious character. . . . Prayer and sermons, services and confession, were equally hateful to him, and he did his duties in this respect with a heart full of resentment. As he could not escape attendance at religious exercises, he took part in them quite lifelessly. He held, as he was bound, the Book of Hours in his hand, but without turning the pages. When his companions prayed, his lips were closed;

[1] *L'Écolier vertueux, ou Vie édifiante d'un Écolier de l'Université de Paris* (E.T , The Virtuous Scholar).
[2] Speech at the Jacobins, 1793, v. 1/215.

when they sang, he was silent. Even in the midst of the Holy Mysteries, and at the foot of the altar bearing the Sacred Victim, where any external irreverence would have been remarked, it was easy to see that his thoughts and interests were far away from the God he was asked to adore.' When, later, as a senior, he was no longer obliged to communicate, he ceased to do so altogether. During Retreats he made no attempt to hide his boredom. If his confessor, the abbé Asseline, sometimes reduced him to tears, this unaccustomed emotion was a sign of pain rather than penitence.[1]

Conventional we have called it, rather than convinced scepticism. There is, at any rate, little evidence that, at any period of his life, Robespierre was sufficiently interested in the dogmatic side of Catholicism to think out a position for himself in isolation, or against odds: everything suggests that he was more likely to share a fashionable reaction against the orthodoxy of the previous generation—a reaction which was not inconsistent, in his case, with the survival of a genuine belief in an overruling Providence, or with the pursuit of an almost Puritanical moral discipline.

It was here that Louis-le-Grand left its most lasting mark. It may fairly be assumed that the abbé Proyart's *Vie de l'écolier vertueux* and *Modèle des jeunes gens* were seldom read by his pupils except with derision, and that the morbidly devotional life recommended by the pious author did not find much following among Robespierre's school-fellows: but the disciplinary system inculcated in his *Instruction en forme de réglement pour les maîtres de quartier* was the inescapable frame-work of their daily lives. In school as in chapel, in hall and in dormitory, alike during games and country walks, the *maître de quartier* was always in attendance, to enforce good order and good manners, and to prevent, by every means short of deliberate spying, the entrance of wolves into the fold. In school, each boy had

[1] Le Blond, 31. This change seems to have coincided with that from an oppressively pietist régime under d'Enthieuloye and Proyart to the more liberal Principalship of Bérardier, when Robespierre was just twenty.

his desk, at which he sat for work, and in which he kept his books and writing materials, his private possessions, and the *peignoir* he wore for the daily hair-dressing. It was the duty of the master to keep silence during 'prep.', to give good or bad marks for behaviour, to send in weekly reports to the Principal, and to look through the desks, from time to time, for 'bad' books or pictures. In Hall he must always be present, to enforce order and good manners, see that the senior boys waited, as they sometimes did, on the juniors, and arrange for the reading of some work of piety. At night-time he went round the dormitories, to see that every boy was in his own *alcove*, properly washed and bedded, with his clothes tidily folded up, before putting out the lights. During recreation times his duties were particularly severe. The boys were turned loose in the school garden, to play at ball games, which he must supervise, with the constant anxiety lest *des enfans pétulans* may hurt each other, *les mécontens* break the rules, or really *mauvais sujets* get together for worse purposes. Even a Décalogue might run out into the street, against rules, to see the passing of a religious procession. On holidays there would be walks, still under the eye of a master, to the *maison de campagne* attached to the school, or, as a special treat, to the Invalides, or other 'sights' of Paris; the boys might even be given extra pocket-money, to buy fruit, or to give to a beggar; but they must be kept away from river-banks, frozen ponds, eating-houses, and other dangerous places; and care must be taken to see that they do not steal fruit, damage crops, or molest the peasantry. This rigorous system, enforced for more than nine months of the year, might be resented, but could hardly be resisted; and, whilst it turned some boys into mal-contents, others became prigs.

VI

Robespierre's speech of welcome to Louis XVI so fired his literary ambitions that, about the time of his promo-tion from Rhetoric to Philosophy (January, 1776), he contemplated entering for a prize for an Encomium on Louis XII, and wrote to M. Target, a well-known Paris lawyer, asking for a copy of a recent address by M. de Saint-Lambert to the *Académie française*.[1] Two or three years later he has finished his 'undergraduate' course, and is embarking on his chosen 'post-graduate' study of Law. Once more he appeals to the leader of the Paris bar, perhaps the famous President Dupaty, for advice as to his reading. 'I want to be a lawyer,' he writes. 'I know how many qualities are needed for fame in that profession. One at least I can claim to possess—keen ambition, and an unqualified desire for success.'[2]

But what was the sequel to this letter, and exactly where and how Robespierre pursued his study of the law, remains a little obscure. Montjoie, a hostile traditionalist, asserts that when Maximilien was sixteen or seventeen (and this is, at any rate, several years too soon), 'two of his relations who were in Paris advised him to take up the study of law, and to join the Paris bar'; and that they arranged with Ferrières, a well-known barrister, to take him into his chambers for this purpose. When the time came for him to practise, the story goes on, one of Robespierre's 'benefactors' came to see Ferrières, and was told that Maximilien's performances at College flattered his abilities, that he had 'a poor head, with little sense or judgment in it', and that he had better begin his legal career at Arras, where his name would help him, rather than in Paris. So he went back to Arras, 'nursing in his heart shame, scorn, and schemes of revenge.'[3] A rather different account, but one equally tainted by dislike, occurs in Brissot's *Memoirs*, in a passage describing his own legal training in Paris. 'Before leaving the subject of Nolleau's chambers,' he writes, 'I must recall the fact that chance gave me there, as second clerk, a man who has since played an amazing part in the Convention, but against whose future celebrity I should at that time have been prepared to bet anything. Ignorant, without knowledge of any scientific

[1]Corresp. 1. But if the date is 1786 (Walter, 1/32), it must have been written by Augustin Robespierre.　　　　　　　　　　[2]Corresp. 3.　Cp. Walter, 1/33.
[3]Montjoie, *Histoire de la conjuration de Maximilien Robespierre*.

subject, incapable of conceiving or expressing an idea of any kind, he was eminently fitted for a career of dishonesty'. Now Brissot was in chambers with Nolleau *père* during the later months of 1774, and subsequently with Nolleau *fils*, and with one Aucante, who in turn inherited the practice, till 1778; whereas Robespierre cannot have begun to study law until 1778 at the earliest; whilst there is no other evidence that he did so at 'Nolleau's'. The most, therefore, that can be allowed, of this very misleading reference, is that the two young lawyers may just have met one another.[1] Again, the layer of truth, if there is any, underlying the unfavourable account of Robespierre's abilities, in which both witnesses agree, is that, though he learnt his law in Paris, he never practised there. But there was nothing un-usual or surprising in this. What he learnt from his books, and from Ferrières, was theoretical, rather than practical. It enabled him to take his degree in Law, and to have his name inscribed on the roll of the Paris Parlement.[2] But there is no safe evidence that he ever intended this for more than a formality; and within three months—too soon for any final failure of hopes in Paris—we find him admitted to practise at the Arras bar.

It may be that Lewes is justified in assuming that, during part of this period, Robespierre 'led a life of honourable poverty, seclusion, and study' in 'a small apartment *au cinquième* in the rue Saint-Jacques';[3] but in fact we have no evidence on the point; nor is there any reason to suppose that he left the College, which had been his home for so many years.

On July 19, 1781, upon a report from the Principal that spoke of Robespierre's 'outstanding abilities', his 'good conduct for twelve years', and his 'successes both at University prize-givings and in his examinations in Philosophy

[1] Brissot, *Mémoires*, 1/160. Perroud, the editor, supposes that they may have met at Aucante's when Brissot revisited Paris in 1780-2.

[2] His *diplôme de baccalauréat en droit* was dated July 30, 1780, and his *diplôme de licence*, May 15, 1781. On August 2, 1781, he was *reçu avocat au Parlement de Paris*. Croker's failure to find his name on the official list (308) might be accounted for by the fact that he never practised.

[3] Lewes, 12.

and Law', he was awarded a leaving prize (*gratification*) of the almost unprecedented amount of 600 livres;[1] and his *bourse* at Louis-le-Grand was passed on to his brother Augustin.

[1]The document is printed in Fleischmann, 26.

CHAPTER II

THE LAWYER (1781–1789)

I

FOR a short part of each year the religious discipline of Louis-le-Grand was relaxed, and, to the regret of the abbé Proyart, most of the boys returned to the corrupting influences of their homes. During this annual summer vacation of five to eight weeks Robespierre no doubt went back to Arras, where he would stay with his grandparents, the Carrauts, dine with his friend Aymé, who helped to pay his expenses at College, and see as much as he could of his sisters, when they too were at home from school.[1] But soon these happy arrangements were broken by fresh troubles that fell on the unlucky orphans. The marriage of both aunts in 1776–7, and the deaths of M. and Mme Carraut in 1775–8, threw them upon the world again. Amable, indeed, now Mme Durut, seems to have given a temporary home to the two girls; whilst, under M. Carraut's will, half the proceeds of the sale of the family brewery (amounting to 8,262 livres) were settled upon the four grandchildren, to provide for their education, and to give them a start in life.[2] But in March, 1780, before these provisions could take effect, Robespierre's younger sister, Henriette, died at school, and M. Durut tried to recover, out of her legacy, which now reverted to the estate, a debt of 800 livres that her father had never paid. Maximilien resented this action, refused assent, as co-heir, to the repayment, and determined to make himself independent of the family. For a year after his

[1] The vacation was fixed by each college to suit its own members, and usually lasted from forty to sixty days, covering vintage-time, when many of the boys could make themselves useful at home, and ending in October (A.H. 2/67).
[2] R.H.R.F. 8/147, A.H. 1/182: There seems to be a slight variation in the figures for the whole legacy and its four parts.

17

return from Paris he kept house with his sister Charlotte, who had now left school, in the rue du Saumon. But their shares of the Carraut estate, his bonus from Louis-le-Grand, and his first earnings at the bar, were not enough to finance such independence; and in the autumn of 1782 he was forced to pocket his pride, give a receipt for the tiny residue of Henriette's legacy, and accept an offer of rooms at the Duruts'.

II

Those who have known Arras only as a blackened heap of ruins, or as a reconstructed war-memorial, find it difficult to visualize the place as Robespierre knew it in 1781. One of the oldest towns of northern France, named after a pre-Roman tribe, with traditions going back to the eleventh century, and a history of successive allegiances to kings of France, dukes of Burgundy, and Holy Roman Emperors, it was still a notable centre of Church life, of politics, and of the law. Its mediæval walls, with gates, ditch, and draw-bridge; its citadel, one of the strongest in France; its Grande Place, an immense square surrounded by arcaded and gabled house-fronts; its Petite Place, shadowed by the Sainte Chapelle, the Chapelle des Ardents, and the sixteenth-century Hôtel de Ville; its narrow, winding streets under the walls of the newly-rebuilt Abbey of Saint-Vaast; and the evidences of its trade in grain, lace, and porcelain, were full of interest either for a student of human nature, or for a lover of the picturesque. Robespierre must have known every corner of the place. Born in the rue Saint-Géry, off the Petite Place, he had spent his childhood at the brewery in the rue Ronville, near the south wall. As a young lawyer he often left his temporary home in the rue du Saumon, in the same quarter of the town, to attend to his duties at the Hôtel de Ville. Between 1782 and 1789 we find him living at three other addresses—till '86 at the Duruts' house in the rue des Teinturiers, opposite the abbey, then in the rue des Jésuites (later du Collège) in the south-west quarter, and finally in the house, which still bears his name and memorial,

in the rue des Rapporteurs, near the centre of the town.[1]
But the social atmosphere in which he was immured was
almost as stuffy as the dark rooms that closed their shutters
against the noise and dust of the streets; and the liberal
sentiments of Louis-le-Grand were grafted on the narrow
interests of a provincial society. So far as one can judge,
Robespierre had little artistic or sympathetic regard for the
world round him. His adventures were inside himself, and
the people he met were hardly more than helps or hind-
rances in the pursuit of his chosen career.

III

Charlotte Robespierre has left a detailed account of the
daily routine of the household in the rue des Rapporteurs.
Maximilien was generally up by six or seven, and at work
till eight, when the *perruquier* came to dress his hair.[2] Then
a bowl of bread and milk (*laitage*), and more work till ten,
when he would dress, and walk to the Palais de Justice for
the day's cases. Some time in the afternoon followed a light
dinner, with wine mixed with water, fruit, and coffee. Then
an hour's walk, or a visit to a friend, and another spell of
work till seven or eight. The rest of the evening would be
spent with the family, or friends. Charlotte represents her
brother as 'naturally cheerful' in society, and even as
capable of 'laughing till he cried'; but he often had distrait
moods, when he would sit in a corner of the room, during
card-play or conversation, deep in thought; and sometimes

[1] The street (named from a fourteenth-century inn-sign *Au Rat Porteur*) and the
house, a rather tall building of two floors, appear in Beffara's plan of Arras (1756).
The house, which bore on its front the date 1730, belonged then, and in 1787, when
Robespierre took it, to the de Fétel family. A bill of sale of 1830 describes it as built
round a court, with cellars; on the ground floor a dining-room, sitting-room,
ante-room, and kitchen; above, bedrooms and attics. The house survived
the bombardment of 1914–8, but has since been rebuilt; and on October 14, 1923,
a tablet was placed on it, with the inscription, *Maximilien Robespierre habita
cette maison de* 1787 *à* 1789 (Paris; Lesueur, Introd. to *Oeuvres*; R.H.R.F. 7/175,
15/447).

[2] Always particular about the setting and powdering of his hair, Robespierre spent
little, at this time, on his clothes. Among the Advielle MSS. in the Arras Town
Library is a contemporary account-book of Duplessis, a draper and glove-maker in
the Petite Place. It shows Robespierre and Carnot among its customers; and Robespierre's purchases are few and inexpensive (Fleischmann, 199).

fits of absent-mindedness, such as he never outgrew.[1] His temper was equable; 'he never contradicted people, but fell in with their plans, so that his aunts said he was an angel', with 'every moral virtue', and fated to be the dupe of more designing men. An old lady at Arras told Hamel that her mother often danced with him, and found him a pleasant partner. At the same time, with all his 'amenity of manners', he showed 'energy and inflexibility' of character; he 'never deviated an inch from his principles'; and 'whilst all the world changed around him, he alone remained unshakable in his convictions'. Comparing him with his younger brother, Charlotte makes the interesting admission that Augustin, though not so hard-working, was the more talented of the two; and adds that, whilst Maximilien had more *courage civil*, Augustin surpassed him in *courage militaire*. In appearance the younger brother was 'tall and well-made', with a face 'full of nobility and good features', whereas the elder 'was of moderate height, with a delicate complexion', and a face that 'expressed kindness and goodness' and 'almost always bore a smile', but 'was not handsome in the same regular way'.

Once again a sister's portrait needs correction by a more impartial pen. Maximilien's appearance at this time, according to a legal acquaintance, 'was quite undistinguished (*commun*); he was not above middle height, he had a small head upon broad shoulders, his hair was of a light chestnut colour (*châtain-blond*), his face round, his skin slightly marked with small-pox, his nose small and short, his eyes blue, and rather sunken, his glance shifty, and his manner cold, almost repellent; he seldom smiled, and that only sarcastically.'[2]

The inconsistencies of these accounts are not, perhaps, so serious as might appear. A man who is nervous and suspicious in public may be easy and amiable at home; and the smile which an aunt thinks angelic, may strike a casual

---

[1]Once, Charlotte says, he helped the soup onto the table-cloth; and once, returning with her from a call, walked on ahead, shut himself in his room, and, when she came in, asked where she had been.

[2]Devienne, in MS. notes supplied to Paris by M. Hippolyte Renard.

acquaintance as sarcastic or hypocritical, or even be described by an enemy as a grimace.

IV

Amongst Robespierre's special friends at Arras were several young lawyers—Lenglet, Leducq, and Charamond; Devic, formerly a *professeur* at Louis-le-Grand, and now a canon at the Abbey; Aymé, another of the canons, an old family friend; Ansart, a doctor; and 'Barometer' Buissart— a lawyer, twenty years older than himself, who got his nickname from his interest in Natural Science, with whom, as well as his wife, Maximilien kept up a correspondence all through his political career.[1] Through Durut, who was medical officer to the Oratorian College, and lived, rent free, in a house close by, Robespierre resumed friendly relations with the teachers at his old school, and was sometimes invited to lecture to the boys, at the end of the school year. He chose historical subjects, and his lectures on Henri IV, Switzerland, and the Salis-Samade regiment, then in garrison at Arras, were not forgotten by those who heard them.[2]

Through the influence of Buissart, and another friend, Dubois de Fosseux, Robespierre was elected, within two years of his return to his native place, a member of the Académie royale des belles-lettres, where the thirty 'best brains' of the town and district met, sometimes amidst public applause, to read papers and hold discussions on matters of literary, legal and scientific interest. His inaugural speech (1784) was an attack on the tradition by which a criminal's family suffered for his crime; he afterwards worked it up into a prize essay for a competition at Metz. As Director of the Academy, in 1786, he delivered another oration on the Law of Bastardy, and made a complimentary speech to Mlle Kéralio,[3] in which he maintained that woman's contribution to academic discussion is the natural complement of man's; that the presence of the other sex (witness the history of chivalry) incites men to greater efforts; and in short, that

[1] R.F. 21/380.   [2] A.H. 5/470.
[3] She afterwards married Robert, editor of the *Mercure Nationale*.

the Academy should be co-educational. In 1786 he read a paper on Criminal Law, and in January, 1789, spoke at a special meeting in honour of the new governor, the Duc de Guines. His last attendance was in February, 1789.

What did membership of the Academy mean to Robespierre? It was a tribute to his abilities as a student and a speaker. It gave him social and professional status. It kept alive interests which might otherwise have been submerged in the routine of legal practice. It enabled him to form friendships which might, indeed, have been even more valuable, had not his tastes, and the urgency of the times, drawn him from the bar to politics, and made him a bitter enemy of the academic point of view.

But perhaps the most important effect of Robespierre's association with the Academicians of Arras was the fresh stimulus that it gave to his literary ambitions. Without this, he would hardly have composed the series of prize essays which, in the development of his ideas and style, form the connecting link between his Juvenilia and his later political speeches and articles. We have seen how his early aptitude for Latin oratory turned his attention to the *Éloge*, a species of composition always congenial to the academic mind, and never more so than in an age that is living on its past. Thus it was that he seized the opportunities afforded by the system of Academic competitions, and, like other clever young men of his time, made his first bids for literary fame.

v

The *Discours sur les peines infamantes*, based upon Robespierre's inaugural address to the Arras Academy, was sent in for a prize offered by the Société royale des Sciences et Arts de Metz. It was placed second by the judges, the first prize being awarded to Lacretelle. It was subsequently printed at Amsterdam; and the original manuscript, in Robespierre's own hand, can still be seen amongst the archives of the Metz Academy.[1]

[1]The British Museum copy (Amsterdam, 1785, sold by Meriquot at Paris) is nicely printed, with a wood-cut head-piece, and one or two corrections in ink,

The questions set were (1) What is the origin of the view that the shame of a crime attaches to the criminal's family, as well as to himself? (2) Is this opinion harmful? and (3) If so, what is the remedy? Robespierre's main correntions are— (1) The feeling in question is an extension of that which leads us to regard all individuals as involved in, and involving, their families and fellow-citizens. (2) Its effects depend to a great extent upon the character of the government; for instance, under a despotism, with arbitrary justice, the disgrace of crime is less than under a democracy, where justice is fairly administered. (3) On the other hand, in a democratic state the dignity of the individual is so much enhanced that he does not suffer at second hand for the disrepute of others, or he can wipe out the stain by an act of free heroism. In any case he will have been trained to despise personal feelings, when compared with the good of his country. And here we find Robespierre already expressing the faith which became the basis of his republican creed ten years later. 'The mainspring of energy (*ressort*) in a republic,' he writes, 'as has been proved by the author of *L'Esprit des Lois*, is *vertu*, that is to say, political virtue, which is simply the love of one's laws and of one's country; and it follows from the very nature of these that all private interests and all personal relationships must give way to the general good. Every citizen has a share in the sovereign power . . . and therefore cannot acquit his dearest friend, if the safety of the state requires his punishment. A man of high principle will be ready to sacrifice to the State his wealth, his life, his very self (*nature*)—everything, indeed, except his honour.' (4) The feeling in question attaches itself, like other disabilities of the feudal and monarchical order of society, only to the unprivileged classes. (5) As to the utility of this feeling, Robespierre adopts a Jewish view of Providence, and of the rewards of righteousness.

---

apparently in Robespierre's own hand. The MS. is on forty pages of blue paper, of which thirty-five are covered with writing. On p. 36 is fixed, under the seal of the Society, the letter containing Robespierre's name and motto. His letter accepting the award (400 *livres*), and saying that he intends to spend it on the printing of his Essay, may be read in A.H. 5/269, cp. 74/167.

'Of all moral maxims,' he writes, 'the most profound is that which says that honesty is the best policy. . . . Virtue produces happiness as the sun produces light. Crime results in unhappiness as certainly as filthy insects issue from the heart of corruption'; and this, he thinks, is as true of nations as it is of individuals. Crime, then, will be prevented by wise laws, and by public virtue, more effectively than by punishment, or by any social stigma attaching to the family of a criminal. (6) Robespierre paints an affecting picture of the unhappiness caused by this social stigma—had he not suffered himself from the disrepute of his father's debts and desertion?—and describes the fatal political results of putting whole families on their trial. (7) What, then, is the remedy? Not, he thinks, a wholesale change of the law; nor any extension of paternal authority, though that is 'the most powerful check on corruption'; but rather such minor reforms as abolishing the confiscation of a criminal's property, and the legal disabilities of bastards; extending the privilege of decapitation—'a punishment to which we have come to attach a sort of *éclat*'—to all classes; encouraging the King to include in his charities the distressed families of criminals; and educating public opinion by such means as the present inquiry. 'Reason and eloquence—those are the weapons with which to attack such prejudices as this; and in an age like ours they cannot fail to be successful'.

The judges who read this Essay reported that it was 'well written, but without much feeling'; they allowed that it showed 'neatness, facility, and conciseness'; but they thought that the argument needed further development in certain directions. Its interest to a biographer of Robespierre lies rather in the degree to which it anticipates the writer's later sentiments, if not his ultimate acts.

VI

In 1784, for the fourth year in succession (there had been three failures to award) the Academy of Amiens offered a prize for an *Éloge* of the poet Gresset, the graceful author of

Vert-Vert, whom Voltaire had honoured with an epigram, and Louis XVI with a patent of nobility.[1] Robespierre, encouraged by his partial success at Metz, but doubtful whether he had set about the work in the best way, consulted his friend Buissart, as he had consulted Target in earlier days, as to what form of treatment was most likely to appeal to the judges. Buissart wrote to Sellier, at that time Professor of Mathematics at Amiens, as well as Architect to the Crown, and Director of the local School of Arts and Commerce. Sellier, in reply, enclosed a *Notice sur Gresset* supplied by a M. Baron, and some stories of his own about the poet; but he did not wish it to be known that they came from him. 'The *Éloge*,' he writes, 'that will win the prize will have to be dictated by Gresset's friends; for he is never spoken of here except with veneration, and they think it a crime if one expresses any doubts as to his celebrity'. Buissart evidently passed on this advice; but though Robespierre laid on flattery as thickly as he could, he still failed to win the prize. 'O Gresset,' he wrote, 'you were a great poet, but you were also a gentleman; and, whilst praising your works, I need never be ashamed of your conduct. Religion and virtue have nothing to blush for in the praises bestowed upon your talents. . . . I have counted it a merit in Gresset', he concludes, with a canny eye on his audience, 'to have drawn upon himself the sarcasm of a number of literary men; for I have been so bold as to insist upon his virtue, upon his respect for morality, and upon his love of religion. This will doubtless expose me to the ridicule of the witty majority; but it will win me two votes which are more than a recompense—that of my conscience, and that of yours.'

Perhaps, after all, the judges cared more for Gresset's repute as a poet than as a man of virtue, and were not over-pleased with an apologia that balanced good morals against indifferent verse. Anyhow, for the fourth year in succession, no prize was awarded. The author took what comfort he

---

[1] On the ground that 'his writings had always shown respect for religion and decency' (Proyart, *Louis XVI et ses vertus*, 2/339).

could from a copy of consolatory verses by his friend Dubois de Fosseux, and published his *Éloge* anonymously the same year.[1]

VII

In 1788 there died in Paris the lawyer Dupaty, well known both as an advocate of judicial reform and as the author of books of travel, and translations from the classics. His praises were promptly proposed by the Academy of his native town, La Rochelle, as the subject for a prize; and the following year there was published an *Éloge, par M.R. . . . avocat en parlement*, the style of which, as well as previous association, suggests that its author may have been Robespierre.[2] If this was so, one passage is worth quoting, as evidence of the direction in which Maximilien's views had developed during the crisis of 1788-9, and as a foretaste of his parliamentary style. 'You,' he writes, in a commentary on Dupaty's compassion for the poor, 'you, who ask so much in return for the charity that is extorted from you by the importunity of the needy; you, who are for ever complaining about the crowd of unfortunates that wearies your eyes; learn to blush for your insensibility! Do you know why there are so many poor? It is because you grasp all the wealth in your greedy hands. Why should this father, this mother, and these children remain exposed to all the hardships of the weather, without a roof to cover them? Why are they suffering the horrors of starvation? It is because you are living in luxurious mansions, where your gold pays for every art to minister to your comfort, or to occupy your idleness: it is because your luxuries devour in a day as much as would feed a thousand men.' There is more feeling than thought in this, and it is feeling of a kind that we have not hitherto suspected in Robespierre. Yet it is not unlike his famous outburst

---

[1] The MS. is among the archives of the Academy at Arras. Hamel mentions a copy at the Louvre. For Dubois's verses, v. Lecesne, *Arras sous la Révolution*. The *Éloge* was published by Royez of Paris, and dated 1786. Robespierre sent a copy to Chapelle, one of his old masters at Louis-le-Grand (Ward, 33).

[2] It has been suggested that the author was Réaud.

against the rich clergy in the National Assembly the same year.[1]

VIII

The society in which, after all, Robespierre seems to have been most at home, was not that of the solemn Academicians, but of the æsthetic Rose-lovers. The Rosati Club had been founded a few years before his return to Arras. Its members met every 21st of June in a garden at Blanzy, by the bank of the river Scarpe and the abbey of Avesne. Sitting under a green bower of privet, ornamented with busts of Chapelle, Chaulieu, and La Fontaine, they ate and drank, and extemporized verses on the eternal themes of life and love.[2] Arras, though a small place, had some reputation for literature and art, and there was no lack of candidates for membership of so elegant a society. Of the original nine members, Legay, 'Sylva' Charamond (for they affected nicknames), Caigniez, Despretz, and Lenglet were lawyers; Carré was a *Chevalier de Saint-Louis*, Bergaigne a flower-painter, 'Berthe' Herbet the *vicaire* of Saint-Aubert, and Gignet a surgeon at the military hospital. Later members included Carnot (also an Academician) and Champmorin, officers of the Engineers, Dubois de Fosseux, Foacier de Ruzé, and Leducq (*père*), lawyers, Pierre Cot, a musician, and the Marquis de Vaugrenant, the commandant of the town garrison.

Robespierre's admission followed the usual rites. He was summoned to the bower, inhaled three times the scent of a rose, and pinned it to his coat; drank a ceremonial glass of wine and rose-water, was embraced by one of the members, and welcomed in speech and verse. Legay's address described him as 'a man who, since his first steps in the legal career, has fixed on himself the eyes of his compatriots. We admire high talents,' it continued, 'especially when, like yours, Sir, they are always devoted to a useful end; and we have followed with the highest interest the

---

[1] v. 1/50.
[2] Dumarquez, *Délassements d'un paresseux* (1790); Paris, 159.

stages of their development.' The speaker adds, with unconscious corroboration of Charlotte's account, that Robespierre has also social qualifications for admission to the
club—'the gift of making witty remarks, and of turning a
pretty verse; a taste for laughter . . . in a word, *desipere in*
loco.[1] Charamond followed with an extempore song, which
tells us nothing, except that Robespierre diluted his wine,
and that the Rosati were not all poets. Herbet followed with
a more ambitious composition, a metrical act of admission,
which, for what it says of Robespierre, and of the Rosati,
merits translation.

> Whereas there lives a lawyer, a man of many parts;
> Whereas the case is proven, he has a pretty wit,
> In epigram and irony, and all without offence;
> Whereas he likes (who doubts it) to sing, and laugh, and drink,
> And sometimes, in his leisure, walks in the sacred vale,
> Effortlessly ascending the peak of Helicon;
> We therefore, the Rose-lovers, the only of our kind,
> We devotees of pleasure, who laugh our worries down,
> And, in our happy circle, and round our pleasant board,
> Bring back the golden ages when poets joked in verse;
> To all whom it concerneth—French, English, and the rest—
> Born north or south th' Equator—Be it known that we this day,
> In this our solemn council, and emptying each in turn
> His cup, or glass, or beaker, hereby elect, *nem. con.*,
> Maximilien de Robespierre into our brotherhood.
> And when a certain month comes, a certain day and hour,
> He must forsake his mansion, be present at our board,
> And there to willing audience must sing a pretty song;
> So now, as then, we'll cheer him:—Bravo! Hip, Hip, Hurrah!

Robespierre's reply to this demand was not a song—for
he could not sing in tune[2]—but an oration, which became
an unconscious skit upon his series of prize essays, entitled
Éloge de la Rose.[3] It shows Maximilien as the young æsthete; a
rose-lover in a literary and semi-mystical way, not of the
horticultural kind. His roses are those of 'the banquets of

---

[1] Full text of the speech in Fleischmann, 46.
[2] v. the poem by Bergaigne in Paris, 187.
[3] The MS., in Robespierre's own hand, is full of erasions and corrections, and
covers 14 pages.

Anacreon, the suppers of Horace, Augustus, and Maecenas.'
He claims affinity also with the heroes and sages of Greece
and Rome.

He goes on to describe a vision of Venus vouchsafed to himself and to his companions, whom the goddess
designated as the corner-stones of a 'sublime edifice,
founded on concord and amity', and taught 'the doctrines
they were to believe, and the rites they were to perform';
and he explains how this higher love weaned its devotees
from lower pursuits: 'we now felt nothing but distaste for
all the passing pleasures of this perishable world, and the
only bond that still attached us to life was the desire to fulfil
our glorious vocation.'

It is possible that this 'precious nonsense' lay nearer to
Robespierre's real mind than some of the vote-catching
sentiments of his more serious *Éloges*. At any rate, we shall
find affinities to it in his Puritanism, his *penchant* for a dogmatic society, his 'religion of virtue', and his Platonic
courtship of the plain but earnest Eléonore Duplay.

There must, too, have been at least one occasion when
Robespierre, dressed as a peasant, joined in the rustic dances
of the village green. 'One cannot but acknowledge his
fitness for membership of the Rosati,' wrote Dubois de
Fosseux, 'when one sees him taking part in the pastoral
revels of the village, and enlivening the dancers by his
presence. See! thegod of eloquence himself mixes familiarly
with mortals, and reveals, beneath the shepherd's smock,
the gleam of his divinity.'[1]

IX

Poetry, rather than prose, however elegantly elaborated,
was the proper medium for a rose-lover; and Robespierre
soon showed himself not unskilled in light versification on
amorous or satirical themes. These *Juvenilia*, none of which
were published under his name, have been collected under
three heads: *Poésies amoureuses*, *Poésies rosatiques*, and
Poésies diverses. The first class includes a madrigal addressed

[1]Paris, 187.

to *jeune et belle Ophélie*, whom French editors imagine to have been an English girl with the improbable name of Orptelia Mondlen[1]; a *Chanson adressée à Mlle Henriette*, and *Autres chansons*, inspired by the same lady; *Vers pour le mariage de Mlle Demoncheaux*, who is addressed as *aimable Émilie, charmante amie*; a poem beginning *J'ai vu tantôt l'aimable Flore*; another addressed *A une beauté timide*, whose name is *Sylvie*; and perhaps a poem beginning *Je l'aimais tant quand elle était fidèle*, which was found among Robespierre's papers.[2]

It would be rash to look for autobiographical evidence in these ditties, which are such as most romantic young men write, at one time or another, and whose heroines are, as often as not, imaginary, were it not that Charlotte says her brother was particularly attractive to women, and that most of his letters belonging to the years 1782-8 are addressed to them.

Mlle Dehay was probably the *personne* to whom Robespierre entrusted his pet birds, when he went to College, and who afterwards presented him with a cageful of canaries. She may also have been the *jeune fille* to whom he wrote in June, '88; she was then living at Béthune, and bringing up a puppy for Charlotte—perhaps the famous dog 'Brount.'[3] The lady to whom Robespierre sends a long account of his trip to Lens is doubtless Mme Buissart; she and her children shared her husband's life-long friendship for Robespierre.[4] There was yet another lady—her name is unknown—to whom Robespierre sent a copy of a memoir which she had inspired.[5] But the name which seems most likely to belong both to Robespierre's real life and to his world of make-belief is that of Anais Deshorties. She was a daughter of his aunt Marie Marguerite's husband by a previous marriage; and Charlotte says that Maximilien fell in love with her, spoke to her of marriage, and was 'painfully affected' when he returned to Arras in 1791, and found her married to a

[1]The lines first appeared, anonymously, in two collections of verse published at Paris in 1787. They were reprinted and attributed to Robespierre in the royalist *Actes des Apôtres* (No. 5). He never denied authorship. The original MS., in his handwriting, was sold in 1845 for 500 fr. It was addressed to a lady at Arras (MS. note to Croker, 12)—perhaps Anais Deshorties (Fleischmann, 90).

[2]Stéfane-Pol, *De Robespierre à Fouché*, 54. [3]Corresp. 23, 34.
[4]Corresp. 24. [5]Corresp. 30.

son of his friend Leducq. The circumstances (if we can assume that Charlotte is wrong as to the date) fit those of the young lady to whom two letters are addressed—one (June 6, 1787) expressing undying interest in her, though she has treated him badly, and another, three weeks later, asking whether she is happy, and saying that he is not.[1] Perhaps, too, this incident is the origin of an early portrait of Robespierre which shows him with one hand holding a rose, and the other on his heart, with the motto, *Tout pour mon amie*.[2] If we knew more about this early disappointment, it might help to explain Robespierre's distrust of human nature, and especially of women.[3]

The *Poésies rosatiques* include *La Rose*, thanking the Club for his election; *Couplets chantés en donnant le baiser à M. Foacier de Rusé* (1787), *La coupe vide*, a drinking-song, in which the author makes a recantation of his temperance principles, and a poem of twelve stanzas, beginning, *O Dieux, que voi je, mes amis?* recited at the reception of Morin de Morcant.[4] The poem beginning *Loin d'ici la cérémonie* may also have been written for a meeting of the Rosati.

The *Poésies diverses* contain one or two compositions more worthy of attention. *L'Homme champêtre*, published under a *nom de plume* in 1786,[5] gives a conventionally rose-tinted picture of country life, and of the 'happy peasant':

> He's no regrets that rend, and rend again,
> No crime or fear to mar his blameless joy;
> Pictures of happiness possess his mind;
> He lives; his kin are happy; 'tis enough;
> Nothing he needs is lacking; all his days
> He tills the ground, and sings, and is alive.
> Such is true bliss, and it is his for aye.

[1]Corresp. 11, 12. cp. Fleischmann, 86.
[2]The portrait, in which Robespierre appears *très jeune, très mol, très fade* (Michelet, A.R. 1/387), is in the Saint-Albin Collection.
[3]The story of Robespierre's relations with Suzanne Forber, an Arras sempstress, invented by Montjoie, copied by Desessarts, and improved by Reybaud, deserves no credit. (Fleischmann, 81.)
[4]Texts in Fleischmann 50, 53, 329, Paris, 184.
[5]It was published in *Le Censeur universel Anglais* on August 12, 1786, over the name 'M. Drobecq', and dedicated, like the madrigal *jeune et belle Ophélie*, to 'Miss Orptelia Mondlen'.

There exist also a fragment of a satirical ode *Sur le mouchoir*, or *L'Art de cracher et de se moucher*;[1] *L'Éloge d'un magistrat humanitaire*;[2] and a poem sent with a present of game to *une jolie femme*, beginning (*apropos* of the dead hare) *Ce fameux destructeur des choux*.[3]

Mention must be made, too, of the mock-heroic ode in honour of jam tarts,

> Thanks be to him who, with unerring hand,
> Was first to fashion thus the docile dough,
> And gave to mortals this delicious dish. . .

which Robespierre inserts in a letter describing a visit to his relations at Carvin in June, 1783.[4]

More worthy of memory, perhaps, was the poem of which his sister could recall, many years afterwards, only five lines; but those were prophetic of his fate:[5]

> The just man's torment, at his final hour,
> The only pang he feels—and I shall feel—
> Is the dark breath of calumny and blame
> Breathed by a grimmer ghost than death himself :—
> The hate of those for whom he gives his life.

X

Such were the lighter interests of a young lawyer; what of his professional work?

[1]Sainte-Beuve was told by an old bookseller at Boulogne, named Isnard, who had been a teacher of Rhetoric at the Collège d'Arras in Robespierre's time, that Robespierre wrote this poem during his briefless days, but left it unrevised; and that he (Isnard) was later dissuaded from publishing it by Charlotte, who feared that it might lose her brother the few clients he had. (*Journal des Goncourts*, in A.R. 10/263.)

[2]Noticed in Charavay's Catalogue, December, 1927: 1 page 4°; thought to have been written for a Masonic function. Cp. the *cantique maçonnique* supposed to have been sung by Robespierre at a meeting of the *loge d'Hesdin* (Savine and Bournand, *le 9 Thermidor*). But there is no evidence that he was ever a mason. (v. A.H. 5/62.)

[3]v. Fleischmann, 92. This poem was communicated to *Le Chasseur illustré* in 1913. It is supposed to have been written in August, 1793: but the date throws doubt on its authenticity.

[4]The letter containing this poem was first published by Lewes in 1849. It reappears in Corresp. 5. Cp. Walter 1/61.

[5]They were inscribed on a medallion portrait of Robespierre, about 1835, and subsequently published by Laponneraye. (Buffenoir 69.) Charlotte said they were written at the time of the attempt on Robespierre's life in 1794 (v. 2/187).

On November 8, 1781, Robespierre had been presented by his friend Me. Liborel to the Conseil d'Artois, had taken the customary oath, and had been admitted to practise in the courts of its jurisdiction. Under the old judicial system, so soon to be swept away, Artois had still some 2,000 seigneurial jurisdictions, and Arras nine separate courts, in three of which—the Conseil itself, the Sheriff's Court (*Échevinage*), and the Bishop's Court (*Prévôté de l'Évêché*, or *Salle Épiscopale*)—Robespierre's work would chiefly lie. The Conseil, proud of its sixteenth-century foundation, its privileged jurisdiction (*cas royaux et privilégiés*), and its crowd of eighty *avocats* and fifty *procureurs*, met every morning in the barrack-like halls of the Cour le Comte, the ancient residence of the Counts of Flanders, whose dark and dirty passages were the resort of lovers, duellists, and other disreputable characters. The Sheriff's Court, composed of the Mayor and ten sheriffs, had civil and criminal jurisdiction within the borough. The Bishop's Court, presided over by a *Bailli* and five *Juges-avocats*, exercised 'high, middle, and low justice' in Arras, Vitry, Maroeil, and parts of twenty-six parishes.

It was a field in which a young and ambitious man, with a fine college record behind him, and a family connection with the bar, might well hope to make a living and a reputation. Those who remembered the father applauded the son's attempt to restore the family fortunes, and readily gave him a start. Me. Liborel sponsored him before the Conseil, Me. de Madre made him his secretary, and the Bishop himself, within a surprisingly short time, gave him a vacant judgeship in the Episcopal Court.[1] And though he passed at first for a ready rather than an eloquent or invigorating speaker, and had had so little practical experience that he asked his friend Devienne to 'teach him the ropes', yet he secured from the first a practice of respectable size, standing (in 1782) seventh among the local lawyers, with fifteen briefs and twenty-three appearances in court.

[1] The *brévet de la nomination* was given by Bégis in L'Annuaire de la Société des Amis des Livres, 1889 (Tourneux 3/25007).

XI

His first brief, in the case of *Bardault v. Thellier and others*
(January-February, 1782) came through Me. Liborel, and
brought him into immediate notice. 'There is no news
here,' writes Ansart from Arras to a Paris friend (February
22), 'except that a man called Robespierre, a recent arrival
from your part of the world, has just made his first appearance here, in an important case, which he pleaded throughout three hearings so well as to discourage any one who
intends to follow him in the same career. I didn't hear him
myself, but they say he left men like Liborel, Desmazières,
Brassart, Blanquart, and even the famous Dauchez far
behind him in the way he opened his case, chose his words,
and rounded off his speech. . . . One can see nobody among
the younger generation capable of putting this brilliant light
into the shade.'[1]

It was probably this early success which brought Robespierre his most famous case—that of the lightning-conductor (*paratonnerre*)—in the following year. M. de Vissery
de Bois-Valé, a retired lawyer who dabbled in Natural
Science, had erected a lightning-conductor of his own design
on the roof of his house at Saint-Omer. A neighbour, believing that the apparatus would endanger his life, went to
the Sheriff's Court, and got an order for its removal. M. de
Vissery appealed to the Council, and engaged his friend
Buissart to mobilize scientific opinion in his defence. On the
advice of Condorcet, at that time Secretary to the Académie
des Sciences, an elaborate memoir was drawn up, and the
soundness of de Vissery's case confirmed by the best legal
opinion of Paris as well as of Artois. When the case came
before the Council, Robespierre, as 'one of the most eloquent members of the Arras bar',[2] was chosen to conduct
the appeal. Cleverly widening the issue, he reminded the
court of the persecution of Galileo, Harvey, and Descartes;
gave a detailed history of lightning-conductors, from Dali-

[1] Vellay, however, would redate the letter, arguing that it refers to the *paratonnerre*
case.
[2] De Vissery to Franklin, December 10, 1782.

bard's experiment in 1752 to the latest discoveries of
Benjamin Franklin; and added impressive evidence of the
successful use of the apparatus in France and abroad. The
judges were urged to show themselves champions of
Enlightenment. They did so, and the case was won.

Robespierre got his pleadings printed, and sold them in
Paris. A complimentary copy was sent to Franklin, with a
covering letter, in which the author asserted that 'the
happiness of being useful to his country, in persuading its
judicial authorities to welcome Franklin's important discovery, was only less than the happiness of being able to
count on the favour of one whose least merit was to be the
most distinguished scientist in the world'.[1] His gratification
must have been complete when he read in the Paris press
that 'M. de Robespierre, a young lawyer of exceptional
merit, has displayed in this affair an eloquence and a
sagacity which give the highest possible impression of his
talents'.[2] But a cynic might have noted that, whilst de
Vissery was footing the bill for the publication of the victorious speeches, he had to face another prosecution, and
finally died, worn out by the unsuccessful championship of
scientific progress.

Nor did this almost Parisian fame bring Robespierre
many fresh briefs from the clerical and conservative litigants
of Arras. Indeed, in *Deteuf v. Charlon* (November, 1783), he
went out of his way to offend churchmen by a violent attack
on the morals of a certain Dom. Brognard; a mistake for
which he hardly made amends by defending his old friends
the Oratorians in *Berbizotte v. Gillet* (August, 1784). Two
years later all his sympathy with the movement for women's
rights was enlisted on behalf of an Englishwoman, Mary
Sommerville, widow of Colonel George Mercer, Governor
of South Carolina, who had been imprisoned for debt.

One other case may be mentioned, to show in what
direction public affairs and Robespierre's ambitions were
moving. Forty years before, a French soldier named Dupont

[1]Corresp. 6. The title of the work was *Plaidoyers pour le Sieur de Vissery de Bois-Valé*, etc.
[2]*Mercure de France*, June 21, 1783. Cp. Croker, 308.

had deserted, and served for more than twenty years in the armies of Sweden and Denmark. Then, hearing that a rich uncle had died, he returned home, and claimed a share of the estate. His elder brother, instead of welcoming the prodigal, threw him into prison, under a *lettre de cachet*, as a deserter. When at last he got out, and made his claim, the brother was dead, and his cousins, who had inherited the property, appealed against the court's decision in his favour. The case dragged on for years, and Robespierre had to give it up; but not before he had used the unpopular *lettres de cachet* as the text of an eloquent exposition of the ideas of 1789. 'That Infinite Being,' he declares, 'who created man for sublime ends, and who has endowed him with the appropriate faculties, fashioned him for society, as the state best fitted to develop those precious gifts, which it is at once his duty to perfect, and his privilege to enjoy. It follows that all forms of society and government, however they are named, are good only in so far as they lead to this end, and, whenever they obstruct it, are essentially vicious and useless. Such is the real basis of that social contract of which so much is said. It does not come from a free and voluntary agreement on men's part; its foundation-deeds are written in heaven, and were drawn up, from all eternity, by that Supreme Legislator, who is the source of all order, all happiness, and all justice.' There follows a disquisition on freedom; and the speech ends with an appeal to Louis XVI to come forward as the champion of the rights of the People. 'To lead men through virtue to happiness . . .; to forge the deathless chain which should unite us to God and to our fellow-men, by destroying all causes of oppression and tyranny, . . . such, Sire, is the glorious enterprise to which you have been called.'

XII

It is at first sight surprising that, after such successes as he had in the Bardault and de Vissery cases, Robespierre should never have built up more than a moderate practice. For the facts are clear. In his first year (1782), he had fifteen briefs, and made twenty-three appearances in court. In 1787, his best year, he had twenty-four briefs, and made twenty-five appearances before the Council, in addition to four before the Sheriff's Court. His average, for the nine years 1782–9, was no more than fifteen briefs and twenty-four appearances a year. How was this? His own explanation, in the bitter *Lettre adressée par un avocat, etc.* (1788), was that the older members of the Arras bar monopolized local practice, and made it almost impossible for young lawyers to get a living; and this common complaint may well have been true. Charlotte Robespierre, to whom the facts were doubtless brought home in practical form by the shortage of house-keeping money, has several things to add. First, her brother would never take up a bad case, and was therefore always on the winning side. If this was really so, it might ultimately have made him a wealthy man; but meanwhile such caution must have lost him many clients. Secondly, he always tried reconciliation before litigation, and spared his client's pocket at the expense of his own. There is an instance of this in his letter to the Abbé Touques[1]; but does not every lawyer sometimes advise a settlement out of court? Lastly, we are told that Robespierre preferred poor to rich clients, and often helped them out of his own purse, instead of charging them a fee. There is some suggestion of this, again, in the sympathetic letter to a female client, whom he advises to elevate her mind above such trifles as the delays of the Law, and 'to find in her own heart consolation for the wickedness of vile and cruel men': yet, though these were the words of a confessor, perhaps, rather than of a lawyer, they were not such as to hurt his practice.[2] Charlotte, indeed, may have every right to insist that her brother entered the legal profession with the high ideal of 'defending the oppressed against their oppressors, and pleading the cause of the weak against the strong'; there were high-minded young men in eighteenth-century France who went to the bar for philanthropic reasons, just as there were in nineteenth-century England who took Orders as

[1]Corresp. 10.   [2]Corresp. 8.

an opportunity for social reform. And, so far as Robespierre allowed such motives to decide the choice of a client, or the conduct of a case, he would be likely to damage his professional prospects.

But these are, after all, tactical errors. May there not have been deeper reasons for Robespierre's failure? Was he definitely distrusted, or disliked?

Le Blond says that he offended his colleagues by talking about his academic successes, a weakness which one of them exposed in the epigram:

> A University prizeman
> Is not a universally prized man.[1]

Nor is it to be supposed that Robespierre easily lived down the reputation for liberal and heterodox opinions which he had earned whilst still at college. Indeed, there was quite enough in his public behaviour and utterances to alienate the older and more conventional members of the bar. His conduct of the Deteuf case (November, 1783) seriously offended the judges, and drew upon him a rebuke from his old patron, Me. Liborel. In the Duhamel case (January, 1784), heard before the Sheriff's Court, he is said to have conducted the affair so badly that his friends the brothers Carnot, who were in court, supporting his client, interrupted his speech, and expressed surprise at his great reputation.[2] In the Page case, also before the Échevinage (January, 1787), the court condemned his pleadings, which had shown no mercy to the delays and injustice of the judicial system, as containing 'expressions derogatory to the authority of the Law, and of Jurisprudence, and insulting to the Bench'. The Duport case (April, 1788) caused further offence. The politician appeared too clearly beneath the lawyer's gown; and it was no accident when, the same year, Robespierre was not invited, with other Arras lawyers, to take part in a conference on legal reform. He was not in the mood to let such an offence pass, but issued an open letter

[1] *L'on peut avoir des prix dans l'Université*
Sans être, pour cela, dans l'Univers cité. (Le Blond, 58.)
[2] Memoirs of Carnot 1/96. Vellay's reasons for rejecting the story seem inadequate.

attacking his colleagues, and earned a second rebuke from Me. Liborel.[1]

Another incident, in no way discreditable to himself, showed his discontent with the system that he was supposed to be administering. He did his work as *juge-avocat* of the Bishop's Court, his sister says, 'with exemplary equity', until, one day, he was faced with the duty of passing the death sentence upon a murderer. Thereupon he came home in great distress, took no food for two days, and ultimately resigned his post, rather than do such a thing again. Here is an instance in which we are able to check Charlotte's memory; for Guffroy, who was one of Robespierre's colleagues on the bench, has also left an account of the incident. 'The elder Robespierre,' he writes, 'will remember my firmness, when we were judges together in the Salle Episcopale at Arras, and condemned a murderer to death. He can hardly have forgotten our philosophical and philanthropic discussions; nor that it cost him much more than it did me to make up his mind to sign the death-sentence'. That is to say, Robespierre did sign the death-warrant, however unwillingly (a point which Charlotte obscures), and did not resign his judgeship. There is further evidence of this; for we have his signature as judge to a document of August 26, 1788; on June 21 of the same year he joined in the refusal of the Bishop's court to register the Lamoignon decrees; and his name still appears in the Artois *Almanach* for 1790.

In any case, the incident is misunderstood if it is taken as illustrating an academic objection to capital punishment which Robespierre conveniently forgot in the days of the Terror; for the death penalty in 1794 was a gentlemanly and painless decapitation; ten years earlier it would have meant at least a clumsy and degrading hanging, and possibly the long-drawn torture of breaking on the wheel.

Here, at any rate, is a series of incidents suggesting that

[1]Robespierre's letter appeared as *Lettre adressée par un avocat au Conseil d'Artois à son ami, avocat au parlement de Douai*; and Liborel's reply as *L . . . avocat en Parlement et au Conseil d'Artois, à l'auteur d'une libelle anonyme*, etc. Cp. Vellay in R.H.R.F. 4/508.

Robespierre grew increasingly out of sympathy with his profession, and out of favour with his colleagues; it is therefore not surprising either that he failed to make more than a bare living at the bar, or that, when the opportunity came, he turned his considerable talents, and his great ambition, from law to politics, and from a provincial court to a national assembly.

For this, too, his kind of eloquence was better suited. Contemporary critics distinguished between two types of legal oratory—that of the *avocats*, who sacrificed nicety of language to the necessity of winning their case, and that of the *gens de lettres*, who cared more for rational principles than for the letter of the law, and aimed at a literary perfection of style.[1] Robespierre definitely belonged to the latter school. He always tried to go behind the text of his brief to the general principles at stake. The Page case becomes a discussion of the rights and wrongs of usury. The defence of Mary Sommerville involves the whole question of women's rights. Dupont's grievances are taken up into the national demand for a regenerated government. Everything is judged by its relation to eternal laws of absolute justice. Further, this philosophical outlook must be expressed in the language of a student and of a scholar. For Robespierre could never forget that he was a picked pupil of the best teachers of rhetoric in the country, at a time when oratory was an art valued equally in the pulpit and at the bar, and when the power of making a persuasive speech was the most valuable asset that an ambitious young man could possess. Accordingly he studies his style with as much care as he dresses his hair; writes and rewrites his speeches; looks up appropriate quotations from Bacon and Montesquieu, Leibnitz and Condillac; and (no doubt) practises declamation in his study, or on his country walks; until he is master of a style which has, among the rhetoricians of the time, few rivals, and of a delivery which, though unattractive, triumphs over his physical disabilities, and can never be ignored.

[1] Mercier, *Tableau de Paris*, 1/196.

Historians have long been aware how deep were the sources, and how complex the character of the revolutionary movement of 1789. As an intellectual and economic change it reached far back into the eighteenth century; as a reaction against a system of society it has been traced through Louis XV to Louis XIV and Richelieu; as an assertion of personal and political liberty it may even owe its origin to John Huss and the Lutheran Reformation. Nor was it the work of any one class, or the effect of any one cause. The miseries of the workers—the vast majority of the population—both in town and country gave it body and permanence. The grievances and ambitions of the *bourgeoisie*—the thrifty, intelligent, and active minority, excluded alike from government and privilege—provided it with apostles, and with a creed. But it was the privileged orders themselves— the feudal nobility, the chartered lawyers, and the dignitaries of the church—who, by their opposition to the crown, and by their dallying with reform, started a revolution of which they were to be the first victims.

To Robespierre as a provincial barrister the crisis began with the Lamoignon edicts of 1788, by which the government attempted to break down the resistance of the Parlements to its budgetary expedients. The Bishop's Court, of which he was a member, joined in the general protest against this attack upon the vested interests of the bar. Differing from most of his colleagues in his desire for judicial reform, he resented, as hotly as they did, a complete recasting of the judicial system, which would deprive the Parlements not only of some of their most profitable business, but also of the right, which they had come to regard as constitutional, of registering the royal edicts. Thus his first appearance on the revolutionary stage was as a representative of privilege, and a champion of reaction.

But the immediate effect of this resistance was to evoke and organize other and more dangerous forms of opposition to the government. The nobility, the clergy, the middle-class intelligentsia, the representatives of trade and finance,

the members of the newly-constituted provincial assemblies
—all joined in a resistance which became less and less
passive; till, in August, 1788, the government was forced
to agree that the summoning of the States-General, which
every class regarded as the remedy for its own particular
ills, should be put forward to May, 1789. At once the
separate Orders, temporarily united against the government, fell apart again. When the provincial Estates of Artois
met in December, 1788, the Commons presented a manifesto demanding, among other things, double representation for the Third Estate; and there followed a series of
memorials and counter-memorials which would have
warned wiser rulers of the difficulties before them. But this
was not all. If the States-General of 1789 were to escape
from the feudal precedents of 1614, if the national assembly
at Versailles was to be something better than a congeries of
the royalist and reactionary bodies which had hitherto
misrepresented the views of the provinces, then the whole
system of election must be reformed.

Such was the gist of the pamphlet which Robespierre now
addressed to the people of Artois—his first essay in political
controversy. His argument is that all the ills from which the
Artois people suffer are due to the provincial Estates, and
that the remedy lies in the popular election of their representatives. He writes as a politician, not as a social philosopher,
concentrating upon local grievances, as the most effective
way to win a hearing for national issues, and upon a
political remedy, as the clue to others no less important.
Thus, too, he illustrates his argument with examples that
will appeal to an Artois audience—a recent meeting of
citizens held in the Abbey at Arras; the story of a clerk who
was dismissed for taking a bribe, and afterwards reinstated;
the *corvée* to which a number of *fermiers* were subjected,
during a shortage of fuel, in the Hainault district; and
other local scandals of which he has been informed by
sympathizers with his cause.[1]

[1] *A la nation Artésienne, sur la nécessité de reformer les États d'Artois*. Robespierre
was not alone in these opinions: they recur in a series of *brochures* in the British
Museum (R. 232). Cp. Walter, 1/102.

This pamphlet might be read merely as one of the many thousands of manifestos which, on the rather ill-advised invitation of the government, were at this time flooding the provincial as well as the Parisian press. But to those who knew Robespierre and his political ambitions, it was something more—an Election Address to the Commons of Artois. This was, indeed, made clear enough in a second edition, which soon followed, and by the active part which the writer (prompted by his friend Guffroy, who was already in Paris)[1] proceeded to play in the events of the spring of 1789.

For the Revolution was now in full swing. In January appeared the royal letter convening the States-General. On March 23 Robespierre attended a preliminary meeting of all members of the Third Estate at Arras who had not met separately as members of their *corporations*, and was one of twelve elected to draw up a memorial (*cahier*) embodying their grievances and demands. About the same time he was employed by the corporation of cobblers (*cordonniers mineurs*, or *savetiers*) to draft the special *cahier* in which they complained of a too inquisitive municipality, the competition of the *compagnon* cobblers, and the commercial treaty with England, which had sent up the price of leather.[2] Soon afterwards Robespierre was elected one of the twenty-four representatives of the Third Estate of Arras to meet the representatives of the 245 constituencies comprised in the whole *gouvernement* or *bailliage*; and at this meeting he was one of the forty-nine nominated to draw up the final *cahier* of the *bailliage*.[3]

Meanwhile he had published another pamphlet, perhaps two. The *Avis aux habitans des compagnes*, issued in March, is such a cautious document, confining itself to agreed reforms, that it cannot confidently be claimed as his work.[4]

[1]Ward, 67.
[2]Paris gives a facsimile of this document.
[3]Hamel claims that it is all his work. But in fact it contains a number of demands—free annual voting of taxes, equal admission to all public offices, freedom of the press and of worship, and so on, only some of which were peculiarly his own.
[4]Guffroy, in his *Le Frank en vedette*, claimed the authorship, and Vellay is inclined to admit it (R.H.R.F. 4/508).

But no one else can well have written *Les ennemis de la patrie démasqués*—an attack upon the municipal authorities of Arras for their reactionary conduct during the elections.[1]

On April 20 the final stage of the elections was at last reached. The representatives of all three Orders met in the great nave of the abbey to hear mass, to take an oath, and to listen to patriotic speeches by Bishop Conzié and the Duc de Guines. That done, they met again separately, to verify their mandates, to draw up their *cahiers*, and to elect their deputies. When the Commons met, it was proposed by the Duc de Guines, as chairman, that they should send complimentary addresses to the other two Orders. Thereupon 'a lawyer got up, and said that there was no need to thank people who had done nothing but renounce abuses'; and the proposal had to be dropped. This uncompromising democrat was Robespierre:[2] he had already decided to stand for the people.

Four days later the Commons proceeded to the election of their deputies. Eight had to be chosen; and, as each of them was required to get a certain proportion of votes in a separate scrutiny, it is not surprising that the election lasted five days. Those ultimately successful, in the order of their election, were—Payen, Brassart, Fleury, Vaillant, Robespierre, Petit, Boucher, and Dubuisson. Four of them were *fermiers*, representing the country voters, two lawyers, and one a gentleman (*chevalier*). Four more, all lawyers, were elected as *suppléants* to fill any future vacancies.

XIV

Robespierre's enemies asserted that his election was due to intrigue. An election pamphlet by Guffroy represents him as saying, 'I have discussed the grievances of the Commons against the nobility with such angelic sweetness that I have been given the appropriate name of "the angry lamb (*l'agneau enragé*)."'[3] Another local wit, describing the

[1] v. Ward, 68, Walter 1/123
[2] He boasted of it afterwards at the Jacobin Club (April 28, 1792).
[3] *La sentinelle artésienne* (A.R. 2/243).

chosen deputies in the language of the racing stable, reserved the same word for Robespierre—*L'Enragé*.[1] Le Blond recounts how Robespierre got his relatives to canvass for him in the country villages of the district, bargained for the support of Beaumetz, and made speeches in which he played upon all the grievances of the constituency.[2] He had, at any rate, for a lawyer, shown an unprofessional activity in politics, and had made no secret of his ambition to become a deputy. Though still looking for legal appointments,[3] he had few hopes of permanent success at Arras, and the Revolution seemed to him, as it did to so many of his contemporaries, a heaven-sent invitation to Paris and fame.

On May 1 the Artois deputies appeared before the representatives of the three Orders in the hall of the General Hospital at Arras, and took an oath to carry out their duties. They set out by the next available coach for the capital.[4] Robespierre, it is recorded, was so badly off that he had to borrow from a friend of his sister, Mme Marchand, the price of his fare, and a trunk in which to pack his clothes.[5] The particulars of his meagre wardrobe were remembered, when he became famous, by the maid who packed his belongings; and he was said to have promised the humble l'Anguillette who carried his bag to the coach, that the day would come when his family would be mayors of Arras.[6]

So Robespierre set out on his political career.

[1]Fourdrin de Frévent: he describes this horse as *vicieux comme une mule . . . et n'os mordre que par derrière, crainte du fouet* (Lenôtre, 29).

[2]Le Blond, 69.

[3]A letter to Buissart, dated May 13, shows that he was then standing for the position of *procureur du Roi près la jurisdiction prévôtale* (i.e., the Maréchaussée) *de la ville d'Arras.* (A.H. 7/76.)

[4]There was a local connexion every Friday with the coach from Amiens to Paris (Lenôtre, 31).

[5]Fouché also claimed to have lent him money at this time; but he was not at Arras (Hamel, 3/571).

[6]Le Blond, 81, 77. Proyart changes the name to Lantilette. Lecesne accepts this, but says his real name was Antoine Delmotte. He was made a member of the Arras *Comité de surveillance* by Le Bon in An. II, but never became mayor. (*Arras sous la Révolution*, 2/413).

CHAPTER III

THE DEPUTY (MAY–DECEMBER, 1789)

I

VERSAILLES was crowded; and Robespierre and his fellow-deputies had some difficulty in finding rooms at the sign of the Fox (Hôtellerie du Renard), rue Sainte Elisabeth.[1] As they did not leave Arras before May 1, they can hardly have been at Versailles in time for the royal reception of the deputies on May 2. But they certainly took part in the procession of the Orders on the fourth, and in the opening session of the fifth; sharing, no doubt, to the full the mixed impressions of those days—the excitement and bewilderment of provincials in contact with the splendours of the Court, the high hopes of patriots in the first national assembly for 170 years, and the disillusionment of citizen-deputies who found themselves treated as inferiors, and their demands for constitutional reform silently set aside.

On May 6 the deputies of the Third Estate met, by royal command, in the Salle des Menus Plaisirs; and they met alone, for the other Orders had their separate accommodation elsewhere. How should they proceed? The States of 1614, their only precedent, had consisted of two privileged Orders, and one unprivileged, and the Commons had knelt when they addressed the King. The provincial assemblies of the last few years had also been tainted by their division into Orders. The example of the English Parliament—foreign, feudal, and bi-cameral—was unacceptable. 'Imagine,' wrote Mirabeau, 'more than 500 individuals, herded into one room, not knowing one another, collected from all parts of the country, without leaders, without officials, all free, all equal, none of whom had any right to give

---

[1]v. Brette, *Recueil* 2/138; Hamel 1/80: now rue Duplessis, No. 31 (Lenôtre, 33). Michon (36) wrongly identifies it with rue de l'Étang, No. 16, on the ground that Augustin Robespierre writes from this address (Corresp. 19).

orders, and none any obligation to obey them; whilst everyone, in true French fashion, was more anxious to talk than to listen to others talking!'[1] It was not until the evening of May 8 that 'certain provisional rules of procedure' enabled the assembly to get on with its work, and to decide—to do nothing.

II

The size and arrangements of the Salle des Menus Plaisirs made it most unsuitable for its purpose. The deputies sat on backless forms, covered in green cloth, and the President with the secretaries at a big central table, from which he could not address one part of the company without turning his back on the rest. The seats originally provided for the other Orders were partly filled by *suppléants*, friends or relations of deputies, and the general public, who overflowed from the amphitheatre onto the floor of the House. This confusion was, indeed, defended as contributing to the national character of the occasion. 'The ideal plan,' said Roland, 'would be for the Assembly to deliberate in the presence of the whole people; a building of vast and majestic proportions, big enough to hold 12,000 spectators', would (he thought) be a security against corruption and intrigue.[2] But such disorder was neither comfortable nor businesslike; and in July, on the proposal of the ingenious Dr. Guillotin, the seating was rearranged in semi-circular form, with the President at the end of the hall.

In any case the place was too big; 'None but stentorian lungs,' writes Arthur Young, 'or the finest clearest voices can be heard';[3] whilst the failure to adopt proper rules of procedure, or to prohibit the intervention of the public, made calm and orderly debating almost impossible.

III

At first no places were set apart for the Press, and reporters might have to stand at the door all night, if they

[1] *Lettres à mes Commettans*, No. 2.   [2] *Arch. Parl.* 64/431.
[3] *Travels in France and Italy* (ed. Maxwell), 142.

wanted a front seat in the morning. Nor were they provided with any official material, but had to rely on their notes and their memories. The President was supposed to announce the name and constituency of each speaker: but this could not always be done; or the customary uproar might make both President and speaker inaudible.

All this has to be taken into account when reading the reports of Robespierre's earlier speeches. For instance, his attack on the clergy, on June 6, was variously reported, and attributed to different speakers; so was his speech on Lally-Tollendal's motion of July 20.[1] Even when he was identified as the speaker, his name was spelt in a bewildering variety of ways—Robespierre, Robes-pierre, Robesse-pierre, Robests-piesse, Robespienne, and so on; a common variation, Robert Pierre, with or without a hyphen, led at least once to the statement that MM. Robert, Pierre, and Buzot had taken part in a debate.[2] There is no reason to suppose that his name was purposely omitted, or distorted: other speakers suffered in the same way.

It was in order to remedy such mistakes as these that it was proposed to set up a committee of the House to edit minutes of the debates; but the motion was thrown out.[3] The deputies were suspicious of anything that might encourage jobbery, or partisanship. Instead, the custom grew up of allowing speakers to submit the MSS. of set speeches, or reports of those delivered extempore, and even of printing them, as a mark of appreciation, at the expense of the House.[4]

IV

For some three weeks after its first session the assembly of the Third Estate followed a policy of masterful inactivity.

[1] v. Rouanet in A.R. 8/336, 1/163, cp. the reporting of Barère's speeches in *Point du jour* (R.F. 44/497).
[2] *Correspondance de Bretagne*, July 20, 1789.
[3] Laborde de Mereville's proposal, May 20, 1789.
[4] Mirabeau sometimes reported his own extempore speeches by writing them down after delivery. (R.F. 45/481).

The situation is nowhere better described than in Robespierre's letter to Buissart of May 24. The Commons, he says,
refuse to adopt the name, or even to recognize the existence,
of a Third Estate. They regard themselves as a part, and the
most important part, of a 'National Assembly'.[1] They wish
to give the clergy and nobles—the missing members of the
'national body'—every opportunity to join them. If they
will not, the Commons are prepared to declare themselves
alone the National Assembly, and to act as such. He explains
why, in his maiden speech of May 16, he opposed both
Rabaut's motion for the appointment of commissioners to
confer with the clergy, and Le Chapelier's suggestion of a
solemn appeal to both Orders. He was afraid that the
ecclesiastics would take advantage of a conference to
weaken the resolution of the Commons, and he thought it
was useless to appeal to a body so fixed in its pretensions as
the *noblesse*. He therefore proposed a third plan—a friendly
invitation to the clergy alone to join the Commons; if it
were accepted, a united appeal could then be issued to the
nobles, such as they could hardly refuse without alienating
the opinion of the whole nation. This suggestion, though
supported by Mirabeau on the 16th, was unfortunately
ruled out of order. If it had been made earlier in the debate,
Robespierre was assured by many of the deputies, it might
well have been adopted; for it was a clever move to divide
the forces of the Opposition. Robespierre was disappointed;
but he consoled himself with the thought that the Assembly
included 'more than a hundred citizens prepared to die for
the country', and that the deputies were on the whole
intelligent and well-intentioned. The Artois delegation, he
tells Buissart, have already won a reputation for patriotism,
and are working in close alliance with the deputies from
Brittany. He has his own opinion of Target (a disappointing
speaker), Malouet (a dangerous intriguer), and Mirabeau,
whom he at first regards with suspicion. He exposes the
plan of the nobles—to surrender certain pecuniary privi-

[1] Notice the use of this title three weeks before its formal adoption. It occurs,
indeed, in a speech by Lafayette to the Notables in 1777 (his Memoirs 1/164), and in
the *cahiers* (Deslandres, 140).

leges as a sop to the Commons; as well as that of the bishops
—to accuse them of anti-clericalism.[1]

It is remarkable that a provincial lawyer should have been
able, so soon, to form so shrewd an opinion of policies and
personalities; still more, that he should have proved himself
a parliamentary tactician of no small ability, and an orator
whose maiden speech caught the attention of the House and
of the Press. This same letter was circulated, nearly fifty
years later, among members of the Constituent Assembly
under Louis Philippe. The King asked to see it, and, after
reading it, remarked (remembering well the circumstances
of 1789), 'C'est parfaitement exact'.[2]

The Artois deputies, of whom Robespierre was now the
recognized spokesman,[3] continued, in alliance with the
Breton members, their opposition to the policy of conferences. On May 29 they were overruled; but by June 10
their judgment was vindicated, the patience of the House
was exhausted, and an ultimatum proposed by Sieyès led to
the declaration, a week later, of the National Assembly.

v

It was, no doubt, partly exasperation with these delays
which prompted Robespierre's outburst on June 6, when
the Archbishop of Nîmes appeared before the Commons,
calling attention to the miseries of the people, and suggesting a conference of all three Orders to deliberate on a
remedy. The Commons might be excused for thinking this
démarche no more than an attempt to cheat them out of their
independence. Robespierre, by no means an anti-clerical,
was so moved by the sight of a rich ecclesiastic exploiting
the needs of the poor that he broke into an extempore
harangue that thrilled his hearers. 'The clergy,' he cried,
'should be reminded of the principles of the Early Church.
The old Canons provide for the selling of altar vessels to
relieve the poor. But there is no need for such desperate

---

[1]Corresp. 16.   [2]Hamel, 1/82.
[3]*Robespierre s'était chargé de parler pour tous les autres* (*Almanach des députés*, 1790).

remedies. All that is necessary is that the bishops and dignitaries of the church should renounce that luxury which is an offence to Christian humility; that they should give up their coaches, and give up their horses; if need be, that they should sell a quarter of the property of the church, and give to the poor.'

How great was the effect of these words we know from one who heard them—Étienne Dumont, the friend and biographer of Mirabeau. 'At this speech,' he says, 'which was so well suited to the passions of the moment, there arose, not a torrent of applause, . . . but a confused murmur, which was more flattering. Everybody asked, who was the orator? He was not known, and it was only after some minutes of investigation that a name was repeated from mouth to mouth which, three years later, was destined to make France tremble. It was that of Robespierre. Reybaz, who was sitting next me, said, "This young man is not yet experienced, he is too verbose, and does not know when to stop; but he has a fund of eloquence and originality which will not be lost in the crowd." '[1] The proposed conference never took place; and not long afterwards we find the Archbishop of Paris, in an elegantly-printed Pastoral Letter, exhorting his 'very dear brethren' to subscribe to a fund for the relief of the poor opened by the *receveur du clergé du diocèse*.[2]

The only other speech of this period which may with some confidence be claimed for Robespierre is one on a motion for an address to the King (June 12), protesting against any kind of flattery in the language used by a democratic assembly to one who is more than suspected of hostility to its claims.[3]

VI

It is often said that Robespierre made no mark as a speaker in the early days of the National Assembly. The

[1]*Souvenirs sur Mirabeau* (E.T. *The Great Frenchman*, etc.) 34.; "— too verbose": the reports of the speech are mere summaries. Walter (1/135) distrists Dumont's story.
[2]Brit. Mus. F. 61*.
[3]The *Moniteur* gives the speaker's name as *N*.

evidence does not bear this out. Certainly there was nothing impressive about 'that anxious, slight, ineffectual-looking man in spectacles, his eyes (were the glasses off) troubled, careful; with upturned face, snuffing dimly the uncertain future times'.[1] 'He told me,' writes Dumont, 'that he was as shy as a child, that he always shook with fear on approaching the tribune, and that he was hardly conscious of his surroundings when he began to speak'.[2] Yet it cannot be doubted, from the reception of his speeches on May 16 and June 6, that he made a name, among the 600 of his Order, from the very start of his political career; and his friends at Arras were already receiving letters from Paris full of his praises.[3] From the first it would be clear that his opinions were of an uncompromising kind. He had secured an introduction to Necker;[4] and Mme de Staël describes how she met him at her father's house, about this time, 'when he was known only as a lawyer from Arras, and an extreme democrat. His appearance,' she says, 'was common (*ignoble*), his complexion pale, his veins of a greenish (*verte*) colour.[5] He supported the most absurd theories with a coolness that had the air of conviction; and I felt pretty sure that, in the early days of the Revolution, he had honestly adopted ideas of economic and social equality picked up in the course of his reading—ideas which his jealous and evil disposition made it a pleasure for him to adopt'.[6]

VII

The events of June and July, 1789, which form a transition from the first to the second group of Robespierre's speeches, and a turning-point in his experience, may be described in his own words.[7]

'The present Revolution,' he writes, 'has produced in a few days greater events than the whole previous history of

---

[1]Carlyle. [2] *The Great Frenchman*, 146. [3]v. Ward, 77, 98.
[4]Le Blond, 69, 75, 82: for Robespierre's connexion with Necker, cp. Walter, 1/121.
[5]Is this the origin of Carlyle's 'sea-green'?
[6]*Considérations*, 2/130. [7]Corresp. 17.

mankind.' The counter-revolutionary alliance of court and *noblesse*, backed by foreign troops, has been defeated by the firm attitude of the Commons, led by Mirabeau. The people of Paris—'a patriotic army of 300,000 men, composed of every class of citizen, accompanied by *gardes françoises*, *Suisses*, and other soldiers', has captured the Bastille, and 'punished' its governor, and the Prévôt des Marchands, for their treachery. The fear that this army might march on Versailles has 'decided the Revolution'.

Robespierre does not say what part he played in the Tennis Court oath of June 20; but his signature appears high up (forty-fifth) on the famous list, and his figure is prominent in David's symbolical picture of the scene ; he is represented pressing both hands upon his breast, as though —it was the artist's own explanation—'he had two hearts for liberty'.[1] Again, it is not from himself that we learn that Robespierre was one of the deputies chosen to accompany the King to Paris on July 17; but his account of the scene shows that it made a deep impression on his mind.[2] 'The deputies,' he writes, 'were arranged in two lines, between which the King set out in an unpretentious carriage, escorted only by a detachment of the Paris *milice bourgeoise*. The procession began at the door of the Assembly, and made its way to the Town Hall. It would be impossible to imagine a spectacle more august, or more sublime; still more, to describe the sensations it produced in minds capable of feeling. Picture to yourself (he writes to Buissart) a king whose name only yesterday the whole capital and nation held in awe, passing along, with the representatives of the people, in front of a citizen army three ranks deep, and two leagues long. He could see his own soldiers standing among them; his ears were struck for the first time with a universal shout of *Vive la nation! Vive la liberté!* As if these great experiences were not enough to occupy one's mind, the mere mass of unarmed citizens, mobilized from every part of Paris, and covering the houses, the places of vantage, and even the trees by the road-side; the women adorning the

[1]Blanc, 2/254; Lewes, 81.   [2]Corresp. 17.

windows of proud and lofty mansions, who welcomed us as we passed, and whose applause and patriotic delight added as much charm as brilliance to this national festival; these, and a crowd of other circumstances no less interesting, sufficed to engrave the image of this great event for ever on the imagination and the heart of all who witnessed it. I saw monks (he continues) wearing the cockade that has been adopted by all the inhabitants of the capital. I saw at the church-doors that we passed on our route stoled and surpliced clergy, surrounded by the crowd, vying with them in the eagerness with which they testified their gratitude to the defenders of the country.' Robespierre ends by describing the King's reception at the Town Hall, and the visit of the deputies to the Bastille, accompanied by armed citizens, and surrounded by a cheering crowd. 'I could scarcely tear myself away from this spot, the sight of which brings such feelings of pleasure and such notions of liberty to all good citizens.' A post-script adds, 'M. Foullon was hung yesterday, by decree of the people'.

Robespierre, then, shared to the full the patriotic fervour of those July days. There is evidence, too, in the post-script, and in the reference to the 'punishment' of De Launay and Flesselles, how easily, even in a lawyer's balanced mind, fervour might become fanaticism, and private crime pass for public virtue. Robespierre had, indeed, experienced, during that passage through the cheering crowds, a revelation of Rousseauism manifest in the flesh. He had heard for the first time, like Louis, the voice of the people, and thought that it was the voice of God. From this moment dates his mission. He will be an apostle of liberty, a preacher of the rights of men, a deputy for the people.

VIII

Still in his high mood of July 17, his ears still tingling with the cheers of a free people, Robespierre returns to parliamentary routine. There is a new urgency in his words, a new singleness of purpose. He sees everywhere forms of imprisoned liberty. Every debate calls him to quixotic rescues of oppressed innocence.

Lally-Tollendal—one of those who could see nothing in the popular rising but a threat to middle-class security—proposed a proclamation calling the nation to order, and confining the recruitment of the newly-formed *gardes bourgeoises* to middle-class citizens (July 20). Robespierre secured its postponement, as an insult to the people. Yet, three days later, after Foullon's murder, he supported Barnave's suggestion of a special court to deal with cases of *lèse-nation*. He could do this without compromising his principles either as a lawyer or as a Rousseauist. The Sovereign People, like the monarch it displaces, can do no wrong. Its accountability, by a convenient fiction, is transferred to its agents—a King, a council of Ministers, or a tribunal. Its moral responsibility is discounted by the rule that what is wrong at ordinary times may be right in a revolution. Nevertheless, a dangerous door was already being opened to the punitive court of August, 1792, and the Revolutionary Tribunal of March, 1793.

If the people's right to lynch whom it would was thus admitted in theory, and limited in fact, so was its freedom to say what it thought. It was debated, should the Assembly open suspicious letters confiscated in the post? (July 24.)[1] Robespierre's view was that on principle one should not violate the privacy of the post, but that when national liberty is in danger, the case is altered; 'what at other times is a crime, then becomes an action worthy of praise'. Did he think, how long will liberty last, at this rate?

It is the same on July 31 and September 5. Besenval is accused of *lèse-nation*. He has a right to liberty in the abstract. But 'the People must be assured that its enemies do not escape the vengeance of the laws': so let him be tried. The Marquis de la Salle has been arrested on a charge of removing gunpowder from the Arsenal. Robespierre protests against his unquestioned release, and says that it would be

[1] The letters were from Castelnau, French ambassador at Geneva; and one was addressed to the Comte d'Artois.

regarded by the public as a glaring example of class favouri-
tism.[1] On the other hand, there is as yet no law against
emigration: the Duc de la Vauguyon cannot be refused the
right of passage to England (August 6). Nor need proceedings be taken against local magistrates, or private citizens,
who, in an excess of democratic zeal, have seized liberty,
rather than wait for it to come to them (August 21).
Arbitrary action is only objectionable when used against the
freedom of the individual.[2]

The next issue was liberty of conscience. Its clerical
critics hoped, by debating this question on a Sunday
(August 23), when they counted on the lay deputies taking
a holiday from Versailles, to secure the rejection of the
obnoxious Article 18 of the Declaration of Rights. But
Mirabeau and Robespierre faced the storm, and after a long
and tumultuous debate arrived at the compromise:—'No
one may be interfered with on account of his opinions, even
on religious subjects, provided that he does not express
them in such a way as to disturb public order as by law
established'. Robespierre, indeed, would have gone further
towards perfect freedom; and the clergy, already antagon-
ized by his speech of June 6, could never forgive this
apostasy of a protégé of Saint-Vaast and a model scholar of
Louis-le-Grand. Their resentment expressed itself on
August 28, and was not much appeased by Robespierre's
generous attitude towards clerical salaries and pensions.[3]

After liberty of conscience, liberty of opinion. In the
debate on Article 19 of the Declaration of Rights (August
24), Robespierre, following Barère, objected to any attempt
to limit the freedom of the Press. 'There must be no compromise,' he is reported as saying: 'the liberty of the Press
must be laid down quite frankly. Free men cannot claim
their rights in ambiguous terms. . . . Freedom of the Press
is a corollary of freedom of speech'. The only safeguard

[1]Marat wrote next day: 'The acquittal of M. de la Salle has been received with
pleasure by every class of citizen except the lower orders (*le petit peuple*), who view it
with extreme suspicion.' (Rouanet in A.R. 11/62.)

[2]A magistrate at Ville-franche had failed to convoke the *corps électoral nobiliaire*;
and four citizens of Marienbourg had appointed new municipal officers.

[3]Rouanet in A.R. 10/309: cp. 1/86.

required, on the side of the State, was a legal remedy for any abuse of this liberty.[1]

So too with the Article on the *force publique*, which Robespierre helped to formulate, and which defined the army and police as serving the public, and guaranteeing the rights of men and citizens.

Finally, on August 26, came the question of taxation; and here, more than ever, Robespierre was forced to limit the rights of the individual by the rights of the state. Should not the liberty to think what one likes, and to say what one believes, carry with it the liberty to pay what taxes one wishes? No, says the apostle of freedom; for the free citizen is a member of the free state, and what is a free act of the whole body may become a compulsory act of its separate parts. 'As soon as the power to legislate is transferred to the hands of the nation, the right to impose taxes is there too; and unless the nation could force every citizen to pay them, this right would cease to exist.'

If Robespierre still had time, as in his Arras days, to 'sit in the corner, thinking', he must have been surprised to find himself moving so quickly along the path from philosophy to politics—from the abstractions of Rousseauism to the realities of revolution. It was his legal training—his quickness in finding a formula to reconcile opposites—which saved him at this time from intellectual anarchy, just as it was his clerical upbringing—his Oratorian regularity—which saved him from amoralism.

IX

Every Frenchman with any pretence to culture, said Mallet du Pan, thought that he could draw up a constitution. 'Making a Constitution is a new term they have adopted,' reports Arthur Young, 'and which they use as if a constitution was a pudding to be made by a receipt'.[2] Hardly had Mounier finished reading the first few articles

---

[1] Similar sentiments appear in M. J. Chénier's *Dénonciation des Inquisiteurs de la pensée*, published the following day (Lav. 1/131). For the progress of liberty of the Press during and after 1789, v. Tourneux in R.F. 25/193.

[2] Saint-Beuve, *Causeries du Lundi*, 4/509; *Travels in France and Italy* (ed. Maxwell), 148.

proposed by the Constitutional Committee (August 28), when a dozen deputies were on their feet with formulas and counter-formulas for defining the character of the state. Robespierre, forced by the experiences of the last month to see that there could be no liberty without order, urged the House to adopt such rules of procedure as should secure a free hearing for all, and an uninterrupted debate. He was shouted down by the clericals, and his proposals, although backed by Mirabeau, met with no success. The House was impatient of any attempt to drill its deliberations, specially upon English lines. The National Assembly was to be a political Quakers' meeting. The representatives of the people would speak when and as they were inspired. One could not rule the voice of God out of order.[1]

It was not till September 7 that Robespierre was able to get a hearing on the crucial issue of the royal veto—the first that brought out clearly the party divisions in the Assembly. The mass of opinion, as his brother wrote to Buissart, clearly echoing his views (September 5), was in favour of a veto of some kind. 'The simplest minds are fully aware that an absolute veto would paralyse the legislature: what they cannot see is that a suspensive veto would have the same effect, and would, indeed, be even more dangerous. . . . The great majority (he goes on) is for a suspensive veto: only a very small minority opposes a veto of any kind'. But this includes the Breton deputies, who 'have just received instructions not to vote for any veto; and our Artois members will follow this brave lead'.[2]

The reasons for this extreme attitude are given in the speech of September 7. The sole origin of law, Robespierre maintains, is the General Will (*volonté générale*), working, for convenience, through a National Assembly. To allow any

[1]Rouanet in A.R. 10/308. A study of the rules of procedure in the House of Commons, made by Sir Samuel Romilly, had been translated by Dumont, and presented by Mirabeau to the National Assembly. 'We are not English, and we do not wish to be English, was the answer given to him. Not the smallest attention was paid to his writing' (Dumont, 96.) Robespierre himself did not hesitate to support an interruption of the business of the day if he felt that freedom of speech was at stake (*Moniteur*, October 20, 1789).
[2]Corresp. 18.

individual to veto the decision of such an assembly is to put the particular will above the general—'a monstrous situation, both morally and politically inconceivable'. There is, no doubt, the possibility of an abuse of power; but that is much more to be feared from a hereditary king than from an elective assembly. As to the suspensive veto, it may work in England, where 'the civil laws seem to remedy the inconveniences of the political laws', and where there is no great military force in the hands of the king; but France must settle her own problems in her own way; and to keep even a suspensive veto would be to leave 'an open door for despotism and aristocracy'.[1]

Experience did much to justify Robespierre's view. The suspensive veto, as Augustin pointed out, might have worked under a bi-cameral legislature: under single-chamber government it was sure to be swept aside by the first really democratic assembly. It soon became a trap in which to catch the king.[2] Louis, who would hardly have dared to use an absolute veto, found a suspensive one well suited to his weak and dilatory ways; whilst the Assembly, always in a hurry, found delay hardly less exasperating than denial. The sequel to the rejection of Robespierre's views in September, 1789, was the tragedy of August, 1792.

If the King, in Robespierre's mind, should have no veto on the Assembly, neither should the People. In the course of his speech on September 7 Robespierre had expressed opposition to the idea of a plebiscite (*appel au peuple*). 'The people,' as he said a few days later (September 12), 'can exercise its power only through its chosen representatives; and it is right that the people should change them frequently; for nothing is more natural than the desire to exercise its rights, to make known its opinions, and to state its wishes at frequent intervals'. But this does not mean a referendum: it means a revolution.[3]

[1] Rouanet in A.R. 11/65. The speech was published as *Dire De M. Robespierre . . . contre le veto royal*, etc. Robespierre intervened twice more in the debate, which lasted till September 11.

[2] Corresp. 19.

[3] At the time of the King's trial, three years later, the referendum came up as a political move, and Robespierre rejected it for political reasons (v. 1/304).

The veto was not only to be suspensive: it was also to be declared inoperative in respect of the foundation deeds of the Revolution. Robespierre had not intervened on the famous night of August 4:[1] but his approval of what had been done then was shown by the support he gave to Mirabeau and Barnave a month later (September 14), against the royalist contention that the decrees embodying the 'abolition of feudalism' were subject, like any others, to the royal veto. His view was that these decrees were part and parcel of the Revolution, logically, if not chronologically, prior to any question of veto, and that they required no authorization on the King's part, but merely his 'sanction', or official publication.

Louis' attempt, four days later, to discriminate between the decrees roused a storm in the Assembly; and Robespierre expressed the feeling of the majority when he said, 'In constitution-making the nation only needs one will, and that is its own'. But more delays followed; and on October 5, just two months after the 'abolition of feudalism', an exasperated House heard the King's final attempt to evade the issue cheered by members of the clergy and of the *noblesse*. This was too much. Robespierre, in a speech which can only be reconstructed from fragments recorded in various journals, denounced the King's letter as an attempt to impugn the sovereignty of the people, and proposed that the Assembly should demand his instant signature to the decrees. The cheers which greeted these bold words were remarked by a royal agent present at the debate.[2] Robespierre was supported by Duport, Grégoire, and Mirabeau. His motion was carried. A deputation waited upon the King. The decrees were signed.[3]

France, for this victory, used new weapons, and Robespierre had new allies. It was on this evening of October 5

[1] But it may have been he who protested (August 3) against the description of the feudal dues as *droits légitimes* (Hamel, 1/130); and he may have joined in surrendering the rights of Artois (Ward, 80).

[2] *Bulletin du sieur de Riolles, etc.* (Tuetey 1/969) ; was this the first time Louis had heard of Robespierre since the speech of welcome at Louis-le-Grand fourteen years before?

[3] *Rouanet* in A.R. 11/196.

that the Assembly was invaded by a deputation from the crowd of women who had marched from Paris to Versailles to ask for bread, and for the decrees on feudalism; and it was Robespierre who dealt with their leader Maillard, and calmed their excitement. Nothing could be more significant of his growing influence.[1]

Three points had still to be cleared up, before the king's subordination to the constitution was secure. The first was the Civil List. Should it be made a permanent charge on the Treasury, or should it be met by an annual grant? (October 7.) Mirabeau supported the former plan; Robespierre, suspicious, as always, of the Executive, and jealous for popular control of finance, the latter; and he won his way.

The second point was the form in which the Assembly's decrees should be published. Robespierre (October 8) declared that the old monarchical formulas were no longer suitable, and that the House ought to devise an appropriate alternative. Royal proclamations were still being issued in which the King laid more stress upon *nôtre sagesse* than upon the deliberations of the Assembly, and required the Parlement to register his edicts, as though this defunct body retained its old right of remonstrance. Phrases such as *de nôtre pleine puissance*, or *car tel est nôtre plaisir*, had an odd sound in the mouth of a constitutional monarch. But what was to be done? Nothing could be more absurd than to attempt to draft new formulas in an assembly of the whole House; and it is not surprising that Robespierre's attempt to do so was ill received, and led to a temporary set-back in his parliamentary career. The *Moniteur*, in the only hostile account of a speech of his which it allowed itself during this year, reported the scene thus. 'M. Robespierre proposes an amendment, and makes a long speech upon it, in the midst of an uproar excited by divergence of opinions. He bores the House by drafting a ridiculous (*tres-plaisante*) formula, which he always tries to read out when members are

---

[1] v. Maillard's evidence before the Châtelet (*Moniteur*, 1/App.). Robespierre's intervention is not otherwise mentioned.

talking, and fails to read out when they are listening; (this formula is) "Louis, by the Grace of God, and by the Will of the Nation, King of the French: to all citizens of the French Empire: People, here is the law which your representatives have made, and to which I have affixed the royal seal"'. This exordium was recited in such a sing-song voice that a deputy with a Gascon accent rose, and remarked jokingly, 'Gentlemen, this formula is no use; we want no psalm-singing here'; and in the resulting merriment, Robespierre sat down. One would not stress this incident, had not Robespierre's biographers underestimated it. He was accustomed to being interrupted, but not to being laughed at. Deficient in sense of humour, and surer of his opinions than of himself, he shrank from ridicule; and this experience left its mark upon him.[1]

A third point remained. Arbitrary imprisonment had been abolished, but the royal prisons were still full of the victims of *lettres de cachet*. Some members thought that those illegally imprisoned should be released, others that the House should call for a return of their names, and of the charges under which they were detained. Robespierre, remembering the Dupont case,[2] was for complete and unconditional release. His policy towards the throne in all its manifestations—veto, proclamations, *lettres de cachet*—was the same—the Voltairian *Écrasez l'Infâme*. But one must not be in a hurry to infer that he had ceased to be a monarchist. Voltaire died a nominal Catholic; and Robespierre was still far from being a republican.[3]

X

The close of the session at Versailles (October 15) found Robespierre regarded, in spite of the setback of October 8, as one of the most prominent speakers in the Assembly,

[1]Rouanet in A.R., 11/208 Montlosier (*Mémoires*, ed. Lescure, 193) recounts a rather similar incident.
[2]v. 1/35.
[3]For the sequel, v. 1/80.

and as an uncompromising champion of liberty and democracy. When the House met again in the Archbishop's Palace, in Paris, a few days later (October 19), he set himself to consolidate this reputation.

The Salle de l'Archévêché 'combined almost all the inconveniences possible for its purpose',[1] and commissioners were soon appointed to find a better place of meeting. But it was not until the collapse of a public gallery, during debate, had injured four deputies, and a number of the general public, that the Assembly moved to the famous Manège.

This was a long, narrow building, standing between the walls of the Feuillants convent and the Tuileries garden. Originally built as a riding-school for Louis XV, its proportions were not much improved by shortening in 1792, and it was always excessively inconvenient for the purposes of public assembly. The President could hardly have been worse placed for keeping order, nor the speakers for being heard; for the hall was divided into two parts by raised *tribunes* in the centre of each side, so that those sitting on the right could only half see or hear those sitting on the left. The low ceiling echoed every sound; yet a speaker had to shout to make himself heard. The mephitic atmosphere, to which Vergniaud attributed the irritability of the deputies; the prevalent disorder both on the floor of the House and in the public galleries; and the general discomfort and over-crowding of the place—all played their part in disorganizing the proceedings.[2]

Whereas at Versailles there had been accommodation for some 3,000 spectators, the Manège had only two free galleries, seating some 100 each, at either end of the hall, and a third on the side opposite the President's seat, to which entry was allowed by written order. The result was constant overcrowding, and an undesirable traffic in tickets. Matters were not improved by the 'packing' of the public

[1]*Courrier de Provence*, 55/1.
[2]Brette, *Recueil*, and in R.F. 23/64 (with plan); Lintilhac in R.F. 70/289; Vergniaud's account of the difficulties of a President, *ibid.*, 70/292.

seats. In the course of 1790 the custom of placing certain persons in the galleries, whose business it was to keep order, developed into a regular system of 'claques', organized in the interest of this or that political party. By the spring of 1791 as many as 200 *claqueurs* were receiving thirty *livres* a fortnight from certain *chefs de brigade*, who arranged for their attendance in the public seats, and told them whom to hiss, and whom to applaud. They would sometimes throw missiles at unpopular speakers, or assault them when they left the House.[1]

The method of voting was at first by rising in one's place; later, by show of hands. But on important occasions, or when the majority hoped to intimidate the minority by the fear of publicity, there would be a demand for the *appel nominal*, under which each member had to express his vote by word of mouth, giving his reasons for it, if he wished, in a short speech.

The amount of intervention allowed to the public would seem intolerable in any modern legislature, and was, indeed, a serious interference with the free expression of opinion; but there was no other way in which to secure publicity of debate, or a general knowledge of parliamentary proceedings, at a time when no full or trustworthy accounts of debates were printed, and when, even in the case of an *appel nominal*, it could not otherwise be known on what side a deputy had voted.

It should be added that, in the National Assembly, as in other parliaments, an immense amount of useful work was done behind the scenes, both on committee, and in informal meetings, only some of whose results appeared in the public debates or decrees of the House.

XI

From October, 1789, until July, 1791, Robespierre lodged with a man named Imbault, or Humbert, a Jacobin,

[1] *Ordre de l'arrivée et de l'entrée à l'assemblée nationale*, in Brette, *Recueil*, 1/162; Mathiez in A.R. 2/568.

at No. 30, rue Saintonge, in the Marais quarter.[1] This part of Paris seemed to a provincial the pleasantest in which to live, 'combining, with the wealth of the capital, the friendliness of a country house, and the amenities of a rustic retreat'.[2] The road ran out north-eastwards from the centre of the city towards the old walls, now the Boulevardes; and it was a walk of nearly a mile to the Town Hall, a mile and a quarter to the Archbishop's Palace (at the south-east corner of the Ile de la Cité), and little under two miles to the Manège, or the Jacobin Club. Robespierre's 'secretary' for seven months during 1790—a penurious journalist and dramatist, named Pierre Villiers—afterwards wrote down some memories of their association, Robespierre, (he says, was very badly off at this time. True, a decree of August 12 gave him a deputy's salary of eighteen *livres* a day, with arrears as from April 27—a sum of more than 2,200 *livres*; but only part of his income was available for household expenses, since some went to his sister at Arras, and some to a mistress—'a woman of about twenty-six, who idolized him, but whom he treated rather badly', often refusing her the door. Consequently he lived so frugally, and had so few clothes, except a well-brushed olive-coloured coat, that when the Assembly, in June, 1790, went into three days' mourning for Benjamin Franklin, he had to borrow a black suit from a man four inches taller than himself. Nevertheless he constantly refused offers of help, and gifts of money. His chief friend at this time was Desmoulins, and there was talk of his marrying Adèle, the sister of Camille's wife, Lucile Duplessis.[3] Mirabeau he

[1] In his first letter from Paris, in November, 1789 (Corresp. 21), and when signing Desmoulins' marriage register in September, 1790, he gives his address as No. 30; in his advertisement of May, 1791, and his evidence before the tribunal in August, 1791, he gives it as No. 8: so does the *Liste des députés* for 1791. Villiers gives it as No. 9. Michon claims to have identified the present No. 64 with No. 38 in 1836 and No. 30 in 1790; and adds that confusion may have arisen from the fact that when streets ran through more than one section the houses might bear two numbers. That the house had a garden of some size is clear from Robespierre's speech of April 11, 1792 (v. I/1221). Walter (I/224) describes the present building (1936).

[2] *Un provincial à Paris*, 31. Long ago, it had provided a home for Ninon de l'Enclos: now it was one of the haunts of Rétif de la Bretonne (Jabarant, *Le vrai visage de Rétif*, 237).

[3] Fleischmann, 104.

admired, and would have made a bid for his friendship, had he kept less company with men of the Court.[1]

XII

The transference of the Court and the Assembly from Versailles to Paris was to have critical results both for France and for the Revolution. For France it meant the reversal of the long tradition by which, during times of political danger, Paris had been a source of disruptive movements, and national unity had sprung from the provinces. For the Revolution it meant that the rather academic programme of the political reformers could—indeed must—now be based on the practical needs of a great city. What made both these changes practicable and effective was the process which had been going on all through the eighteenth century, by which the Paris *bourgeoisie*, gradually acquiring wealth, education, and political power, had ousted the church from its monopoly of means and privilege; and by which the capital, always more of a consuming than of a producing community, had, nevertheless, through its luxury trades, and its working-class population, drawn into closer contact with the industrial centres of the provinces, and more out of touch with Versailles.

It needed no economist to be aware of this change, no sociologist to foresee its effects upon the Revolution. It must have been forced upon Robespierre's attention every time he walked to and from his lodgings in the Marais; the immense variety of life that crowded the poorer streets, from basement to attic; the business of feeding this multitude—always a preoccupation of the government—which seemed to be turning Paris into a huge provision store; the new streets and houses springing up in the suburbs—a fruit of middle-class enterprise; the great hospitals, institu-

---

[1]For Villiers' *Souvenirs d'un déporté*, v. 1/xxvi. Lewes' variations on the theme (84), and Fréron's accusations of meanness (Pap. inéd. 1/154) seem to rest on no evidence. There was included in the sale of Sardou's collection in 1909 a pencil and pastel drawing of a woman by Claude Hoin, inscribed *La dévouée Hortense Delannoye, maîtresse du traître Robespierre*. (A.R. 2/391.)

tions, and municipal departments, passing from clerical to lay control; and the varied and vivid ways in which the districts of the city were organizing their separate affairs, and co-operating in the government of the whole community.[1] True, it might have been better if these bodies had paid more attention to the immediate necessities of a crowded population. The incredibly filthy state of the streets, especially in hot weather, the piles of refuse or manure at the doors, or the slops emptied from the windows, went ignored, in the refusal to work, the disregard for discipline, and the waste of time in political gossip, which were by now becoming endemic.[2] 'All Paris,' wrote an English visitor, 'is still in a ferment. The last sound which dies away upon the sleeping ear is the rattle of the patriot drums, and the first murmur which disturbs our rest is the martial music of the national militia. . . . It is like living in a citadel besieged. In every street you are surrounded by hawkers of pamphlets with terrific titles, and every hour is startled with some new tale of terror.'[3]

Nor would Robespierre need Mercier's Juvenalian *Tableau de Paris* to warn him of the existence, particularly in the eastern and southern parts of Paris, of a huge working-class population, quite outnumbering the well-to-do, and not only destitute, diseased and ignorant, but also morally debased by a system of government whose neglect encouraged every kind of crime, and whose fear imposed ferocious and brutalizing punishments.[4]

XIII

The second day of session at Paris (October 21) saw the first shots fired in a struggle which was to alter the whole course of the Revolution—that between the middle-class and the proletariate. There was something more than the

[1]Cp. Jaurès 1/130–157.   [2]Tourneux 1/20.
[3]William Taylor, May 14, 1790.
[4]Braesch, arguing from the proportion of *ouvriers* to *patrons* in 1791, concludes that the working class numbered 293,820 out of a total population of 500–550,000 (R.F. 63/289).

usual shortage of bread, and a baker was murdered. The conventional remedy was called for—a court to punish disorder. Robespierre believed, as his brother wrote to Buissart,[1] that the shortage was the work of profiteers, who bought up bread wholesale, in order to retail it at a gain; and he maintained that the situation was being exploited by enemies of the Revolution, who hoped, by driving the Assembly into the use of force, to create bad blood between the government and the people. Martial Law, he rightly foresaw, meant class warfare. Indeed, within two years municipal troops were shooting down their fellow-citizens on the Champ de Mars, and, within four, Bailly, the author of the 'massacre', was to hear, as he mounted the scaffold, the words, 'Remember the Martial Law'.

Middle-class reaction soon took another form. What qualifications ought to be required in an elector, or in a candidate for election, for a municipal or departmental body? The Assembly was agreed on three points—French nationality, twenty-five years' age, and a month's domicile (October 22). The Constitutional Committee proposed a fourth, which could hardly be reconciled with any reading of the Declaration of Rights, and which roused violent opposition—a property qualification, which they defined as the payment of direct taxes equivalent to three days' wages, for electors, and ten days', for candidates.[2] The excuse given for thus limiting the franchise and representation was the fear of corruption; its real origin was the belief, which was pretty generally shared by political thinkers and practitioners of the time, however democratic their professions of faith, that the common people were not fit for political responsibility, and that the management of the state ought to be in the hands of men of property and education. But to Robespierre, supported by Duport and Grégoire, any property franchise appeared to be a middle-class bid for power, particularly odious on the part of legislators who

[1] Corresp. 18.
[2] When difficulties arose as to the value of a day's work, it was laid down that it should be fixed by local usage, between a minimum of 20 *sous* and a maximum of 50 *centimes* (Lav. 1/165).

had themselves been elected on an almost universal suffrage, and who had solemnly declared, only two months before, that the Law was the expression of the General Will, and that 'every citizen has the right to assist personally, or through his representatives, in drawing it up'.[1] 'Every citizen,' he therefore declared, 'has an equal claim to representation, whoever he may be. Sovereignty resides in the people—that is, it is distributed among all the individuals composing the people'; and it follows that every citizen has a right to vote—to exercise his part of the sovereignty. The case for manhood suffrage could not be more cogently put;[2] and if the speaker had only added the one word *citoyennes* to his *citoyens*, he would have been not only three years in advance of the Revolution, which did not abolish the property qualification (and then only on paper) till 1793, but also much more than half a century ahead of France, in which manhood suffrage was first achieved by the revolution of 1848, and in which women are still without the vote.

A week after this fateful division, the bourgeois majority in the Assembly took another step to secure their power. It was proposed (October 29) that no one should be eligible as a deputy in the new legislature unless he paid taxes to the value of at least one *marc d'argent* (about fifty-four *francs*, equivalent to some fifty days' work)—a qualification which would exclude one Frenchmen in three, and rule out a number of the present members.[3] The only amendment moved was one to make an exception in favour of the sons of those thus qualified; and this amendment Robespierre twice opposed (October 29, November 3), feeling, apparently, that, if the obnoxious measure were to stand, it had better be as obnoxious as possible. He carried his point,

[1]Declaration of Rights, Article VI.
[2]Jaurès (2/8, 16), in his eagerness to show that the Constituents never faced the question of universal franchise, represents Robespierre as arguing 'coldly and half-heartedly': but there is no sign of this. It is more noteworthy that he should not yet attack the prejudice which still denied the vote to domestic servants, bankrupts, actors, Protestants, and Jews. (Lav. 1/164.) Cp. 1/70.
[3]Severe as this sounds, it was liberal compared to the views of the party of the Right, who proposed a *revenu foncier* of 1,200 *livres*, hoping to make the Assembly representative of the landed aristocracy, on the English and American model (Lav. 1/164).

but the *marc d'argent* remained, as an offence to democracy for another two years.

The result of these franchise decrees was to set up a fatal distinction between what came to be called the 'active' and the 'passive' citizens—a distinction as stupid as that suggested by our phrase 'the working classes', and much more dangerous. It was reckoned (in May, 1791) that out of the total population of the country—about twenty-four millions —only 4,298,360 were 'active,' and had a vote, whilst about 2,000,000 adults were excluded from the franchise.[1] Loustalot prophesied that within ten years the *marc d'argent* would either restore despotism, or bring about a communistic revolution. He was not far wrong. In 1795, Babeuf, the prophet of communism, was indeed crushed, but by 1799 France was under the heel of Napoleon.

The immediate effect of these measures was a feeling of soreness in many parts of the country—a feeling which Robespierre, bitterly resenting the way in which the cause of the people had been betrayed, took every opportunity to exploit.[2] A 'seditious resolution' of the Metz Parlement (November 17) led to a debate, in which he attacked the conservative Vicomte de Mirabeau, whose *pasquinades revoltantes*, he considered, compromised the dignity of the House.[3] On November 18–19 he moved to increase the size of the new legislature, and of the departmental assemblies, in order to make them more democratic. He intervened in a similar sense in the matter of the Cambrai Estates (November 19) and the disorders at Toulon (December 14).[4]

He only spoke twice more before the end of the year. On December 23 he carried his principles of October 22 to their logical conclusion, and demanded the franchise for Jews, actors, and Protestants. The conservative and catho-

[1]Lav. 1/ 165.   [2]cp. Corresp. 21.

[3]Augustin to Buissart, September 5. The Vicomte retaliated on December 15, by giving the lie to Robespierre in the House, and securing the adjournment of the debate.

[4]The Cambrai Estates had passed a 'seditious decree'. On the approach of an Anglo-Dutch fleet the citizens of Toulon had armed themselves, and imprisoned some officers of the garrison.

lic orator, Maury, had declared that the profession of an actor was as infamous as that of an executioner, and that a Jew was as much a foreigner as an Englishman or a Dutchman. Robespierre's reply was an eloquent protest against anti-Semitism; whilst as to actors, he maintained that 'their virtues would reform the stage, and that the theatres would become schools of high principles, good behaviour, and patriotism'. He already foresaw the part that the stage was to play in the propagation of Jacobinism.[1]

XIV

So ended France's first year of liberty, and first six months of parliamentary government. Great things had been done: the arbitrary power of the Crown restrained, the worst of feudalism abolished, the nation armed, the sovereignty of the people established beyond recall. If there was cause for apprehension, it lay less in the resentment of the defeated aristocracy than in the oligarchical tendencies of the victorious middle-class. These tendencies were natural enough. It was popular action which had determined the issue at every crisis of the Revolution—on July 14, August 4, October 5. But the populace was ignorant, unorganized, incoherent, and unfit to rule. It would have been an act of faith beyond any reasonable expectation, if the lawyers and business men of the Assembly had shared their political rights with the labourers of the countryside and the slum-dwellers of the towns. Robespierre might have realized this. But he was not trying to be reasonable. He was fired with Rousseauism, with the memory of July 17, and with the Declaration of Rights. He had so fallen in love with liberty and equality that he wanted to see them everywhere. If he had been a member of an official Opposition, liable to be asked to govern the country better than the men he was criticizing, he would have been forced to modify his programme. Once or twice he was troubled, for a moment, by that choice between the practicable and the desirable which

[1]cp. A.H. 8/261.

torments all statesmen. But for the present, and in the main, he could be an untrammelled champion of the great democratic abstractions. In a series of nearly fifty speeches he had forced himself on the attention of the House and of the country. He might be provocative, he might be bitter; others besides Chateaubriand might find him boring.[1] But to the foodless, workless, and voteless class, to the people who suspected that the Revolution had only loosened one form of oppression to bind them under another, Robespierre already stood out as a possible leader against the new aristocracy—the aristocracy of wealth.

Travellers crossing the Swiss frontier to the little village of Genod, in the Jura, noticed by the roadside a stone obelisk, on which the inhabitants, welcoming them to a land of freedom, had recorded, in this first year of the Revolution, the names of those who deserved 'the love and gratitude of Frenchmen'. They were Mirabeau, Syeyes (*sic*), Chapelier, Barnave, Grégoire, Robespierre, Talleyrand, and Bailly. On the back were inscribed, as 'the shame of mankind,' Maury, Mirabeau *cadet*, d'Éprémenil, Malouet, and that unpopular law-court, Le Châtelet de Paris.[2]

XV

It has been questioned whether Robespierre, during 1789, was content with the limited publicity given to his views in the Assembly, or whether he may not also have written for the Press. On November 2 there appeared the first number of a paper called *L'Union, ou Journal de la Liberté*, published by the head of an English firm, T. Marshall and Co., oddly described as 'importers of foreign cloths and investigators of genealogies', for the benefit of English residents in Paris. Originally bi-lingual, it appeared, from November 13 onwards, only in French, and continued to come out in that form until April, 1790. On the authority of a statement in the royalist *Actes des Apôtres*,[3] and of a letter addressed to

[1]Lewes, 134.
[2]*Révolutions de France*, April 18, 1791. But perhaps Desmoulins invented it (Walter, 1/208).
[3]v Fleischmann, 91.

Robespierre by a man who may have been the London correspondent of *L'Union*, Hamel believed that Robespierre was the editor of this paper. But, if this had been so, would the journal have printed his name as Roberspierre, Robert-Pierre, Robers-Pierre, and Robertspierre? Would its parliamentary reports have omitted all mention of his speeches of November 18, November 21, December 8, December 9, and twice as many more between January and April, 1790? Would it have given only ten lines to his important speech of January 25, and a short and mutilated version of that of February 22? It sometimes printed extracts, provided by the speakers themselves, from Mirabeau, Duport, the Lameths, and Rabaut Saint-Étienne: would it have done less for Robespierre? In any case what qualifications had he for editing a half-English paper?[1]

XVI

Robespierre, indeed, was so fully occupied with his attendance at the Assembly, and with the preparation and publication of his speeches—always, for him, a long and laborious affair—that he had little time to give even to his family and friends, or to the affairs of his native town. Only one of his letters belongs to the five months between July 23 and the end of the year. It is addressed to his friend Buissart, and begins with an apology for not having written before. Evidently he has fallen out of touch with his constituency. 'What are they thinking and saying,' he asks, 'in Artois? What are they doing?' How is Buissart himself occupied? 'Who are now at the head of affairs?' Are the new laws being published and enforced? But he is not really interested in provincial politics. He has caught the Parisian pose, and can hardly take his mind off the work of the Assembly. Three-quarters of the letter are devoted to his own views on

[1]v. Hamel 1/218; Tourneux; Rouanet in A.R. 9/145. *L'Union* reappeared as *Journal de la Liberté* between May and August, 1790; and as *Le Surveillant* in February, 1791. The supposed London Correspondent was P. de Cugnières (Corresp. 48): the date of his letter (September 16, 1790) is subsequent to the (first) disappearance of *L'Union*.

recent legislation—the nationalization of church property, the franchise, the new Departments. He offers no immediate prospect of a return home.[1]

It was the same with his family as with his friends. Charlotte admits that she never saw him during the two years of the Constituent Assembly, though she claims that they corresponded frequently, and that she knew all he did. Augustin, who had followed his brother to Versailles early in September, and was sending Buissart the news,[2] was on bad terms with his relations at Arras, and quarrelled with Maximilien himself. At Arras he might have done something to support his sister: at Versailles he was a charge on his brother's purse. When Maximilien moved to Paris, in the middle of October, he returned to Arras.[3] Six months later he and his sister both write, saying that there are no prospects for him there, that they are very badly off, and that they would like to come to Paris. This crisis was[4] tided over, perhaps by a gift of money; for we hear no more about the proposal till June, when Augustin hints that he would like to come up with the *fédérés* of the Pas-de-Calais for the Fête of Federation on July 14. Whether he did so is not known; but some time in the summer Maximilien relented; for when next we hear of Augustin, on September 9, he is writing at his brother's desk in Paris.[5] It may be guessed that one so wedded to his career as Robespierre did not easily reconcile himself to the company of a ne'er-do-well brother, and a jealous and sentimental sister.

[1]Corresp. 21. He had not spoken in the debate on the Departments (September 29); but his letter shows that he regards this as another anti-democratic measure.
[2]Corresp. 18 and 19: both translated in Lewes, 115.
[3]Corresp. 20; undated, but apparently the fourth week in October.
[4]Corresp. 29 (April 9), 32 (undated, but apparently about the same time).
[5]Corresp. 47; received, September 9.

CHAPTER IV

The Champion of Liberty (1790)

I

There is no clear cut between the parliamentary history of 1789 and of 1790; nor any convenient halting-place short of February, 1791. It will be best, therefore, in considering Robespierre's speeches, which compose almost the whole of his life during this period, to begin by tracing the themes already announced, and partly worked out, in the first eight months of the Assembly, and to follow up their development, if need be, a little beyond the end of the year. The first of these was the question of parliamentary procedure.

Robespierre's attempt to enforce upon the House rules of debate (August 28, 1789) might recoil upon himself. On April 20, given the right to make a second speech in a debate on the game laws (*droit de chasse*), he uses it, not to propose an amendment, but to discuss the original motion, and has to be called to order. On June 17 he tries to speak after the vote has been called for, and has to stand down. A few days later (June 23), more fortunately, he secures precedence for a motion 'in favour of the people' over one 'in the interests of a hundred or so rich individuals'. On July 1 he protests against the enforcement of an old rule under which the House can refuse to hear an address of gratitude from two released galley-slaves, only to be nick-named 'The convicts' counsel' (*avocat des galériens*). A few days later a very different reception is given to Paul Jones, and an American deputation, who ask leave to take part in the Fête of the 14th; but the House has no patience with the speech in which Robespierre tries to improve the occasion; constantly interrupted, it can be reported only in fragments, and Maury's ironical proposal to print it is ignored.

On August 2 a question of procedure became one of

75

privilege. Malouet had denounced the journalistic writings of Marat and Desmoulins. Marat had replied in his paper, Desmoulins in an address to the House. Malouet launched a fresh attack. 'Is he innocent? let him prove it. Is he guilty? I will conduct the case against him, and against anyone who takes up his defence. Let him justify his conduct if he dare.' Whereupon someone replied, from the public gallery, 'Yes, I dare!' It was said that the speaker was Desmoulins himself, and the President ordered his arrest. When his action was questioned, Robespierre defended it, but urged that Desmoulins had been guilty of no crime, and might well be released. The difficulty was happily solved by his escape; and the question of privilege was not pressed. The Assembly showed similar tact in refusing, under Robespierre's advice (August 2), to accept a motion censuring a committee of the Paris Commune.[1] Here may be added a question of procedure which arose on January 11, 1791, when Robespierre opposed the reference of reports on colonial affairs to the Colonial Committee, instead of to the Assembly itself. There were, no doubt, special reasons for such procedure in colonial questions, about which the average deputy knew little; but there was also some fear that the decision of them might be taken out of the hands of the House.

That the Assembly was seriously exercised about questions of procedure at this time is suggested not only by the incidents already described, but also by Menou's suggestions for reform;[2] and by the fact that, upon one occasion, when two speakers tried to shout one another down, the *Moniteur* printed their remarks in parallel columns, as though to hint its disapproval of such a breach of decorum. And, although Robespierre's anxiety to speak had twice led him into defying the rules of debate, yet in the main he stood by his declaration of August 28 in favour of orderly procedure.

[1] A motion by Dubois and Desmeuniers to call the *Comité des recherches de la Commune de Paris* to the bar of the House, and to demand the disavowal of a Report.
[2] The *Opinion de M. Menou*, March 21, 1790, suggested that the Agenda for the next day's session should be posted up, that notice of motions should be given beforehand, and that the reports of committees should be taken point by point. (Brit. Mus. F.R. 54 (17).)

As a minority, sometimes a minority of one, he had everything to gain by it.

II

Another question which recurred throughout the year was that of the state of the countryside. Brought up in a provincial town, and educated in the capital, Robespierre had no special knowledge of country life, and only a deputy's interest in the point of view of the peasantry who had helped to elect him. He had, indeed, welcomed the relief from feudal burdens given by the decrees of August, 1789, and had taken a leading part in forcing the king to sanction them; but he had not intervened in discussions of the rights or wrongs of the peasant risings during that summer: he left that, perhaps, to the four *fermiers* who were his fellow-deputies. But now, in the spring of 1790, fresh troubles had broken out in Quercy, Limousin, Périgord, and parts of Brittany; and at Vernon a municipal officer in charge of a grain store had been rescued from a murderous mob by a young Englishman, who was rewarded with the first civic crown bestowed during the Revolution.[1] Should order be restored by force, or by conciliation? This was a point of statesmanship, not of agriculture; and Robespierre at once intervened. It was monstrous, he said, to characterize the peasantry as 'brigands', or to use force against a class more sinned against than sinning. At any rate, conciliation must first have failed.

Le Chapelier's bill for the restoration of order (February 22) was the occasion of another speech by Robespierre, to which the *Moniteur* devoted more space than it had ever before given him, and of which Desmoulins printed every word. There was no need, he maintained, for a policy of repression. 'There was never a revolution which cost so little blood, or so few cruelties.' The remedy lies in 'just laws, and the National Guard'. Let the people be free to express their will at the elections, without influence of aristocracy or army; and leave it to the armed citizens to deal

[1] Christopher Nesham. (Mathiez, *La Vie Chère*, 23.)

with the few genuine 'brigands', and to defend their homes. This speech made a deep impression upon the House, and Desmoulins described the speaker, in the Latin they had learnt together at school, as 'a philanthropist in the true sense of the word, and a great intercessor for the people'— *Hic est vere fratrum amator, hic est qui multum orat pro populo.* But the supporters of force were alarmed, and interrupted Robespierre's renewed protests against their policy the following day. Do what he could, Le Chapelier's plan was adopted, and a new extension given to the principle of martial law.[1]

It must not, however, be inferred that the Assembly was blind to the origin of the disorders it tried to suppress. Thus, some of the landlords were trying to exact compensation for their rights of *main-morte*, abolished on August 4: Robespierre proposed and carried a motion (February 27) that they should have none. Again, under an *ordonnance* of 1669 many of the *seigneurs* had seized a third part of such common lands as had been subsequently divided up. Robespierre (March 4) demanded not only the abolition of this *droit de triage*—but also the restitution of all lands seized under it during the last forty-six years. The Assembly accepted the first part of his proposal, but not the second. That he was specially interested in this question, and that he was on the whole satisfied with the result of the debate, is shown by the fact that he wrote to Buissart the same evening, telling him of the decree, and saying 'it goes further than many people thought possible'.[2]

It may be that in this matter of enclosures Robespierre's sympathy for the people blinded him to the real interests of agriculture, and therefore, in the long run, of the peasants themselves. The Revolution had brought to a head that controversy between 'small' and 'big' farming which had been going on for a large part of the eighteenth century. The members of the National Assembly, being mainly representatives of private property, showed more sympathy

[1] *Encore une loi martiale*, was Loustalot's comment.
[2] Corresp. 26.

with the 'big' farming made possible by enclosures than with the peasants' demands for a return to the old common-land system, with its corollary of antiquated and inefficient farming. The settlement of March left untouched the main transferences of land under the *ordonnance* of 1669: they were not revised till the revolution of August, 1792. The peasantry found some compensation in the acquisition of 'national property', especially under the conditions of sale allowed by the Jacobin government of 1793–4, and in the freeing of the land from many feudal burdens. But upon the whole the Revolution ended, as it had begun, by furthering the interests of the farmers. In an agricultural country, they are the ultimate gainers both by war and revolution.[1]

A few weeks later (April 21) another feudal relic—the game laws (*droit de chasse*)—was in question. The abolition of this monopoly on August 4 had resulted in an outbreak of popular sport which not only endangered the lives of travellers, but also threatened to exterminate every wild creature in the country. Merlin proposed the restoration of *la chasse*, not as a personal *droit*, but as attaching to landed property. Against this compromise Robespierre protested, partly on the principle of liberty, and partly in the interests of his constituents, the small farmers of Artois, who did not see why they should be forbidden to shoot the animals and birds which fed on their crops. He would have no game laws; only regulations to prevent sportsmen from damaging their neighbours' crops, or shooting the passer-by.

The reclamation of marshlands was another agricultural question in which Robespierre showed concern (May 1). He believed that it should be encouraged, but not by 'Grants in aid', which would only tempt speculators to reclaim unsuitable land.

Finally, we learn, from a little-known source, that Robespierre protested at the Jacobin Club (July 9) against his former patron Necker's attempt to reverse the decree of

---

[1]Bloch, *Les caractères originaux de l'histoire rurale française*; Lefebvre, *Questions agraires aux temps de la Terreur*; Namier, *Skyscrapers: essays on Agrarian revolution*, and *The peasant and the State*.

June 19, abolishing titles of nobility—a measure which had more than superficial effects upon provincial society—and scoffed at that statesman's effrontery in setting his opinion against a decree 'dictated by Wisdom herself'.[1]

Thus, though Robespierre might be out of touch with his constituents, he was not neglecting their interests, even in matters of which he had no special knowledge.

III

The abolition of *lettres de cachet* had been one of the first acts of the Revolution (August, 1789), and it had already been debated on October 12 what should be done with the victims of this system of arbitrary imprisonment. The subject came up again on January 5, March 13, and March 16. In October, Robespierre had resented any remedy that seemed to recognize or prolong an iniquitous institution. After three months' delay, he now takes a less intransigent line, demanding that those illegally arrested should be at once released, and all other cases reviewed by the Assembly. Two months later, it was still only proposed to release, in six weeks' time, men who had already spent ten months of 'the first year of liberty' in prison. 'It were better,' he exclaimed, in words which he might well have remembered in 1794, 'It were better that a hundred guilty men should be pardoned, than that a single innocent person should be punished'. But when (on March 16) it was debated what should be the maximum sentence to be inflicted upon those prisoners whose sentences on criminal charges had to be revised, he agreed with the general feeling that, in a time of revolution, such men should be kept in prison, though in no case (he thought) for more than twenty years. Here, he showed himself more merciful than the majority, who decided that those guilty of murder or arson should be re-imprisoned for life.

[1] v. Duplain's *Courrier extraordinaire* (Fribourg in R.F. 59/52). Necker's *Opinion* appeared as a supplement to the *Moniteur* of July 2. The decree had been carried by a snap vote, many thought unconstitutionally (Paroy, *Mémoires*, 186 f.)

As work on the new Constitution progressed, the question naturally came up, by what sanction should it be enforced? There were now two armed bodies in the country —the depleted ranks of the old army, and the new masses of the National Guard. But just as the sovereign power had passed from the crown to the people, so the armed control of the country had passed from the royal troops to the citizen levies; and the only real issue left was what form of oath should be exacted from these defenders of the new order. After a discursive debate (January 7), in which Robespierre argued that the National Guard should take a special oath to defend as well as to be faithful to the Constitution, it was decreed that all *milices nationales* should swear to be faithful to the nation, the law, and the king, and to maintain the Constitution and laws, 'when required to do so by the authorities'.

The franchise settlement of October[1] still rankled in democratic minds. On January 23, Robespierre was able to show that, owing to the conversion of direct taxes (upon which the franchise rested) into other forms (*vingtièmes* and *impositions foncières*), many of his Artois constituents were automatically deprived of the vote; and he secured a temporary exemption of this and some other districts so affected from the provisions of the *marc d'argent* decree. But he failed to obtain a similar favour for St. Jean de Luz (April 17); and was hard driven to explain how it was that, in spite of such concessions, there was a general unwillingness, throughout the provinces, to pay any taxes at all.[2] How keenly he felt on the whole question may be inferred from his refusal to accept the complete exemption of 'passive' citizens from taxation (October 23). He insisted, as he had always done, that the franchise was part of the natural rights of every citizen, and he would have nothing to do with

---

[1] v. 1/70.

[2] March 25, an elaborate apologia; it was not lack of patriotism (he said), but fear of national bankruptcy, and counter-revolution.

any concession that recognized the distinction between 'active' and 'passive' citizenship.

By this implacable hostility to the property franchise—Hamel calls it his *delenda Carthago*—Robespierre won fresh supporters, but also created fresh enemies. The *comité patriotique* of Lille wrote to congratulate him, and he sent them copies of his *Adresse au peuple belgique*, and other works dealing with the subject.[1] A *procureur du Roi* at Soissons expressed admiration for his patriotism, and reported 'aristocratic plots' in that town.[2] On the other hand, attempts were made to prove that he had incited his constitutents to refuse payment of taxes. Lambert, the Controller-general of finance, quoted an alleged letter of his, saying that people need not pay the duty on wine (*droits d'aide*). Robespierre repudiated the letter: it had been forged, he said, by some counter-revolutionist. The charge was revived in a more subtle way by Briois de Beaumetz, a relation of Buissart's, and deputy for the *noblesse* of Artois, with whom Robespierre had fallen out during the elections of 1789. Following an altercation in the House, Beaumetz wrote a letter accusing him of having charged the Artois people with failure to pay their taxes. This damaging perversion of the speeches of January 23 and April 17 reached Augustin, and he passed it on to his brother. Maximilien penned an indignant reply, in which, after explaining the origin of Beaumetz's misrepresentation, he asked the electors to contrast his unsullied record as a patriot with that of Beaumetz, the champion of the royalist Estates of Artois. This reply he kept back till the eve of the departmental elections in June, when he published it with good effect; and appended a testimonial from his fellow-members of the Artois deputation.

'Although M. Robespierre,' ran this document, 'needs no other testimony to his patriotism than that of his conduct, and of his public reputation, we have much pleasure in giving him proof of the esteem and affection with which he

[1] Corresp. 24 (February 12).
[2] Corresp. 25 (February 14).

is regarded by all his colleagues. . . . He has always zealously defended the cause of the people at large, and of public liberty, as well as the special interests of Artois. *Signed*: Fleury, du Buisson, Boucher, Payen, de Croix, Brassart, Charles de Lameth, *Deputés d'Artois*.'[1]

Here may be added, as not inappropriate under the head of constitutional questions, some lesser occasions on which Robespierre pursued his quarrel with the 'executive power', as the king was now called. On July 3 he moved for a reduction in the number and salaries of the managers of the Royal Lottery—an institution of which, in any case, he would have disapproved.[2] On August 22 he opposed a petition from Béarn against the sale of the Château de Pau, the birthplace of Henri IV, on the ground that nothing should be done to increase the *domaine royale*. And the following day, in a discussion on the *postes et messageries*, he carried an amendment doing away with the royal privilege, which had given so much entertainment to Louis XV, of interfering with the privacy of the post. It was consistent with this attitude that when, on August 1, a deputation was sent to the king to assure him of the attachment of the Assembly, Robespierre should propose another deputation to take part in the memorial ceremony in honour of those killed in the attack on the Bastille.

V

Of the questions whose main development belongs to the year 1790, the two most important were the church settlement, and the departmental and municipal reorganization of the country.

No part of the work of the Assembly had more serious effects on the Revolution, and none has been more generally condemned, than the Civil Constitution of the Clergy. What part did Robespierre play in it?

[1]For this *Nota* v. Brit. Mus. F. 852 (4). It is to be noticed that de Croix and Lameth take the places of Vaillant and Petit, two of the original deputies. For the controversy with Beaumetz, a confusing series of letters. v. Corresp. 33–40.
[2]v. the debate on the *tontine* (1/118).

It was partly due to the ecclesiastical atmosphere of his school and college life, as well as to his private or professional relations with the clergy, that Maximilien was at this time, and perhaps always, less anti-clerical than his brother Augustin, whose letters from Arras are full of unbalanced attacks on the church. His outburst of June 6, 1789, had been prompted by exasperation with dignitaries who misrepresented the rank and file of the priesthood, and was, in effect, a plea for a return to primitive Christianity. He was doubtless familiar with the chapter in the *Contrat Sociale* in which his hero Jean Jacques declared that Christianity, properly understood, was too unworldly to be a state religion, and in which he outlined the 'civic religion' necessary for the healthy life of society. He was convinced that church property should be employed for the good of the nation.[1]

The nationalization of church revenues, upon which the Civil Constitution was based, came up indirectly, and from an unexpected quarter. The abbé Maury proposed that the miseries of the Paris poor should be relieved by abolishing the city dues (*octroi*) on food, and by imposing a tax on luxuries. Another priest, Collaud de la Salcette, suggested the reduction of all clerical stipends over 1,000 *écus* a year, and the confiscation of the revenues of all benefices worth over 3,000 net. Robespierre supported this amendment, which so much resembled his own advice of June 6, and laid down the principle upon which the whole policy of the Revolution in this matter was based. 'Church property,' he declared, 'belongs to the people; and to demand that the clergy shall use it to help the people is merely to re-apply it to its original purpose'. In the full-dress debate on the Civil Constitution (May 31) he showed that he was prepared for a thorough reorganization of the church as a department of the revolutionary state. 'Priests,' he said, 'considered as members of society, are simply magistrates whose duty it is to maintain and carry on public worship'. It follows that all useless ecclesiastical offices, such as archbishoprics and

[1] v. a letter of Dec. 1789. Not in Michon, given by Walter, 1/241.

cardinalates, should be abolished, and only those retained which are required to meet the public need; that ecclesiastics, like other public officials, should be appointed by popular election; and that they should be paid on the same scale: and these propositions he defended in detail in the debates that followed, refusing, for instance, even to allow the clergy a share in clerical elections, lest their class vote might sully the pure expression of the popular will.

So far, Robespierre's views met with general agreement in an Assembly whose members, without any distinct animus against the church, were unconsciously reverting to the straitest Gallicanism of the Bourbons, whilst putting the people in the place of the king. But he went on to make a suggestion which was very differently received—which, indeed, the House would not even allow him to formulate —the marriage of clergy. A few nights before, at the Jacobin Club (May 26), the abbé de Cournand[1] had proposed the abolition of clerical celibacy, on the ground that it would empty the convents, make the clergy forget their property rights, and fulfil a 'law of nature'. Numbers of pamphlets both for and against clerical marriage had been appearing during the past year; and Robespierre knew that he had many of the clergy on his side. But, by making the suggestion public, he not only offended the bishops, who feared that they would have less authority over a married than over a celibate priesthood, but also alienated his own supporters in the House, who were loud in their dissent, and his constituents, few of whom were prepared for so drastic a change. Brissot, in the *Patriote français*, whilst approving the suggestion, said that it was premature, and would cause agitation among ignorant people.[2] 'Your motion for the marriage of priests', wrote Augustin from Arras, 'has given you the reputation of an unbeliever amongst all our great philosophers of Artois. . . . You will lose the esteem of the peasantry, if you renew this proposal. People are using it as

[1] He had been a *professeur* of literature at the Collège de France since 1784. He married in 1791, and published his views in a pamphlet (R.F. 58/507).
[2] A.R. 11/31 s.

a weapon against you: they talk of nothing but your irreligion, and so forth. Perhaps you had better not give it any more support'.[1] On the other hand, Robespierre had spoken what was in the minds of many of the clergy; for he received letters of congratulation from all over the country, and so many copies of monastic verse, in Latin, French, Greek, and even Hebrew, that, as he observed to his 'secretary,' Villiers, it could not be true that France had ceased to produce poets.[2]

One of these—a Latin poem on the Constitution, by the bishop of Liège—was sent him by a young priest at Amiens, whose letter reminded Robespierre of a 'solemn undertaking' he had made him some time ago to work for clerical marriage, and for a more generous provision for the religious Orders.[3] He had now redeemed the first part of his promise, without counting the risk to his own reputation: he was soon to redeem the second also. On February 19, June 22, and June 28, the House had to decide what pensions should be granted to ecclesiastics who had lost their livelihood through the reorganization of the church. With respect to ex-monks, thrown upon the world through no choice of their own, Robespierre insisted that the wealth of the suppressed Orders was immense, and that their members ought to be more generously treated.[4] Towards ex-bishops he showed little sympathy. They deserved less consideration, he said, than the common clergy, who 'have grown old in the Ministry, and who, at the end of a long life's work, have earned nothing but infirmities. The latter claim consideration as clergy; they claim it even more as paupers'.

Some minor questions arising out of the Civil Constitu-

[1]Corresp. 39.   [2]Villiers, *Souvenirs d'un déporté*.
[3]Lefetz, July 11 (Corresp. 44); translated by Lewes, 135; cp. Lebon's letter of June, 1791 (Corresp. 73).
[4]A paper published in view of the decree of June 23, 1790, gave a list of all archbishoprics, bishoprics, and abbeys, with their revenues. There Robespierre could read that his old patron, bishop Conzié of Arras, drew a stipend of 92,000 *livres*, and that the income of the abbey of Saint-Vaast was 400,000 *livres* (Brit. Mus. F. 61*). It is worth noting that the Prior of the Dominicans from whom the Jacobin Club rented its premises had, on May 31, claimed preferential treatment for his Order. (Duplain's *Courrier extraordinaire*, v. Fribourg in R.F. 58/507.)

tion had still to be settled. We find Robespierre supporting Beauharnais' proposal (September 14) that priests shall be allowed to wear 'mufti' when off duty: it would, he thought, mark their equality with civilians, and their status as national officials. We find him, again (August 28) opposing the suggestion that priests should be eligible as magistrates, on the ground that the clergy should confine themselves to spiritual functions, and that plurality of offices is bad democracy. On the other hand he is against the proposal to exempt priests from serving on juries (February 5), using the curious argument that to judge criminals is an act of benevolence towards society, and therefore not unbecoming to a minister of religion.

What can be inferred, from these incidents, as to Robespierre's attitude towards church questions? They are, at least, evidence that he had two great convictions. The first was that Christianity is a religion of simplicity and poverty. This belief had prompted his outburst on June 6: it was this that he expressed, as clearly as possible, when he said, in the debate on clerical salaries a year later (June 16), 'The poor and beneficent author of our religion advised the rich young man to divide his wealth with the poor; and his intention was that his ministers should be poor men'. His second conviction was that society needed religion, and that the State should organize a department for this purpose—that is, a church. Only, it need not create one *de novo*; for there was a national branch of the Catholic church ready to hand—a church, many of whose clergy were already working for the repudiation of the Concordat, the nationalization of ecclesiastical revenues, and popular election of bishops and clergy.[1] There was no idea as yet of a new church, or a new worship.

VI

A number of questions about departmental and municipal government came before the Assembly during 1790. What

[1] Lav. 1/185.

is Robespierre's attitude towards this essential aspect of the new regime?

His ruling instinct is for liberty; his prevailing sympathy, for the people. He objects to any prohibition of the export of corn (January 16), not as a free-trader, but as one who fears that it will hinder the circulation of grain within the country, and cause distress among the poor. He resents any attempt to snub the rather futile generosity of the *contributions patriotiques* (March 26)—free gifts of plate, jewellery, and other valuables to the Treasury. The town of Rouen asks leave for its Corporation to raise a loan for the relief of the unemployed (January 7); the municipality of Dieppe begs for assistance in dealing with local disorder (April 29). In both cases he insists that the whole body of the citizens shall be consulted.

Considerable discontent was being caused, at this time, by the presence of royal commissioners in the provinces: it was feared that they would use their power of supervising local elections to secure the appointment of royalist or reactionary candidates. When, therefore, Le Chapelier proposed to meet the objections by withdrawing the commissioners after the elections were over, Robespierre denounced what he described as an attempt to *sabotage* the machinery of the Revolution, and did so in such forcible terms that his speech was shouted down by the royalists, praised by Mirabeau, and printed in full by *Le Hérault national*.[1] Hamel may well say that it was a valuable and prophetic appeal for Government neutrality at elections.

A more troublesome and significant question was that of the reorganization of the municipality of Paris (May 3). The Constitutional Committee proposed to replace the sixty Districts into which the capital had hitherto been divided by forty-eight Sections, and to allow these sections to meet only at certain times. The Districts—electoral divisions set up by the *réglement royal* of April 13, 1789, and organized into a municipality by an *arrêté municipal* of August 30—had perpetuated themselves as political debating clubs; and they

[1] Also as a pamphlet—*Discours sur l'organisation des municipalités.*

had become 'permanent'—that is, they had maintained the right to call *assemblées générales* at any time to discuss questions of public interest; whilst their functions, especially in police matters, had been carried out by standing committees. Valuing their independence, they argued not only that 'permanence' was a corollary of the right of free assembly, but also that Paris was better governed by the direct action of the separate Districts than it would be by any joint action of their representatives. They stood, indeed, not so much for the right of the Districts to govern Paris, as for the right of each of the sixty Districts to govern itself. The proposals of the Constitutional Committee rejected both these claims. They were, in effect, an attempt to transfer the control of the National Guard from the City to the Assembly, and to put an end to the growing opposition, on the part of popular clubs and meetings, to the dictatorship of the National Government.

Robespierre, attacking the Committee's proposals from this obvious angle, found himself unexpectedly applauded by his old enemies of the Right, who found the 'permanent' sub-divisions of the capital a favourable sphere for counter-revolution; the fact being that, until the Assembly (in September, 1793) decided that poor citizens should be paid for attending their sectional assemblies, the control of these meetings fell into the hands of the well-to-do, who could afford to attend them, and of whose reactionary influence the patriots constantly complained. The sectionalism of Paris was, in fact, the same thing, on a smaller scale, as the 'regionalism' of France—that tendency of the whole to split up into self-governing parts which always threatened national unity, and which Robespierre himself and his Jacobin friends denounced, two years later, as 'federalism', the besetting sin of their Girondist opponents. Robespierre's enthusiasm for freedom had blinded him, for the moment, to this important issue, and he played into the hands of the Opposition. But the Assembly as a whole distrusted extremists, and adopted the plan of the Committee, leaving Robespierre to the ambiguous praises of the

89

press, in which Loustalot, at any rate, celebrated his 'heroic' stand for the 'sacred rights of the people'.

The full significance of this incident could not be seen at the time. If the Assembly had been able to foresee the part that would be played by the Paris Commune a year later, it might have welcomed the movement for sectionalism, instead of condemning it. The more autonomy the Sections were allowed, the more they would disagree with one another, and the less fear there would be of their combining against the Assembly. In attempting, by the *Loi municipale* of June 27, to suppress both the Commune and the Sections, the Assembly was storing up a dangerous explosive. Paris, unable to rule itself, tried to rule France. The popular interventions of July 14 and October 5, 1789, had saved parliamentary government: those of August, 1792, and May, 1793, went far to destroy it.[1]

A final group of incidents, under the general head of municipal government, may be mentioned here. It was proposed that theatrical performances should be censored by the municipal authorities (January 13). Robespierre objected. 'Public opinion,' he boldly declared, 'is the sole judge of good taste'. An election was to be held, to fill Lafayette's place as Commandant of the National Guard at Versailles. On various pretexts the election was postponed; and the popular party suspected an intrigue to foist a royalist upon them. Robespierre intervened on their behalf (June 29). He was not successful; but they remembered his help, and not long afterwards elected him to a judgeship in the local tribunal.[2]

When France was rearranged in new Departments, a capital and a cathedral town had to be found for the Pas-de-Calais. It was at first proposed that the cathedral town should be Saint-Omer (July 6). But Robespierre, supported for once by his enemy Beaumetz, got the plan held up; and finally succeeded in making his native Arras the capital both of the Department and of the Diocese.

[1]Mellié, *Les sections de Paris*; Garrigues, *Les districts parisiens pendant la Révolution française*; Foubert in R.F. 28/141.
[2]v. 1/106.

The local politics of Soissons had already troubled the Assembly. A dispute between the municipal and district authorities about the qualification for the franchise, involving the rights of a third of the voters, was reported in February. Robespierre had received private information as to the facts, and had promised to help. When, therefore, on July 20, the municipality of the town complained that the *Bailliage* had interfered with its regulation of the food supply, he intervened, supporting the right of the town to manage its own affairs. Even when, two months later, the townsfolk took matters into their own hands so far as to confiscate a supply of grain intended for Metz, he attempted to excuse them.[1] On July 22 he insisted that a deputation from Montauban should be heard at the bar of the House: it was the best way to 'ward off evils that threatened the patriots of that town'.

Thus at Rouen, at Dieppe, at Soissons, at Troyes, in Paris, at Versailles, at Montant, and (in a sense) at Arras, Robespierre stood for the right of the people as a whole, embodied in their communal government, to represent their own wishes, and to regulate their own affairs—whether loans, elections, public entertainments, or matters of police —without interference by the central government. No doubt he favoured the people partly because he feared the anti-democratic dictatorship of the Assembly. But he was also possessed by the ruling idea of freedom, and by that belief in the essential soundness of popular judgment in which he comes so near to the standpoint of nineteenth-century Liberalism.

This only makes it the more remarkable that he should have entered no protest against the most serious attack upon popular liberty made by the Assembly—the *Loi le Chapelier* of June 14. If he felt so strongly about the attempt to limit the right of petition (May 9), why did he not strain every nerve against a law which prohibited any association of working-men, and put into the hands of their employers a

---

[1]For Gouillart's letter to Robespierre, and his reply (February 14), v. Corresp. 25; R.H.R.F. 8/303.

system of penalties which 'lay heavy upon the French working-classes for seventy-five years'? True, the measure was disguised as part of a general attack on *corporations* which was entirely congenial to the Revolution; its class bias, and its economic consequences, could not be fully appreciated at a time when Labour was still so unorganized; Prudhomme and Desmoulins made no comment upon it, and even Marat saw in it a royalist and moderate attack on the nation, not a bourgeois weapon against the proletariate. Indeed, the middle-class employers themselves, who were to benefit most by the law, do not seem to have realized the significance of it. There was, in fact, little or no class consciousness on either side at this stage of the Revolution. But should not Robespierre have been more alert? Perhaps he merely shared the general neglect of economic factors. Perhaps his tendency to see all the Revolution as the work of the people blinded him more than others to the class character of this legislation. But perhaps—and this simple explanation cannot be excluded—he was not in his place at the time. He was only twice present at the Jacobins between May 31 and June 16. Illness may have kept him away from the Assembly on June 14.[1]

VII

A lawyer, whose ideas of legal reform had already offended the Arras bar, Robespierre was likely to play a large part in the reorganization of the judicial system undertaken by the Assembly during 1790 and 1791. We find him, in fact, reported as speaking more than twenty times, and upon every branch of the subject. Shall judges sit in fixed courts, or go on circuit? In what form shall their patents of institution be drawn? What is the function of a court of appeal, and how ought it to be composed? How should the Public Prosecutor be appointed? Shall the police be given magisterial powers? How should a jury be selected? Must it be required to find an unanimous verdict? Can it bring

[1] Jaurès 2/267; Soreau in A.H. 8/287; Pontlas in A.R. 4/175; Sée in A.R. 14/373.

in a verdict of 'Not Proven'? Where shall be the seat of the Supreme Tribunal? Such are a few of the problems upon which we have Robespierre's opinion; as well as some matters of wider bearing, or of local and temporary interest, which fall under the same general head. And since Robespierre's mind was of the kind that looks behind particular cases for general principles, the study of these speeches has a more than technical interest.

He was insistent upon the principle of popular election. It should be extended (he thought) to the office of Public Prosecutor (*accusateur public*); for does he not represent the national vengeance for crimes committed against the people (August 4)? And it should be made clear, in every judge's patent of office, that he holds his authority from the nation, not from the king (May 8). Courts of first instance should be fixed, but appeals should be heard on circuit (May 2).

There should be two supreme courts, Robespierre thought—one for appeal and one for political crimes. Upon the need of the first—a *cour de cassation*—there was general agreement; but Robespierre could not persuade the House to make it, not merely a legal tribunal, but also, like Napoleon's Senate, or the Supreme Court of the U.S.A., the guardian of the Constitution (May 25).

The suggestion of a supreme criminal court (*haute cour nationale*) raised more difficult questions. The case of two deputies charged with connivance in the escape of a political prisoner (August 23) brought out the fact that there was no court—certainly not, as was suggested, the unpopular Châtelet—which commanded enough confidence to deal with so serious a charge.[1] In a series of speeches (October 25, November 10, 18), Robespierre urged that there must be a supreme court to deal with charges of *lèse-nation*; it must be composed of 'friends of the Revolution' elected by the people; it must be given power to crush all political traitors; and its seat must be in Paris—'the city which has rendered

[1] The abbé Perrotin, *dit* Barmond, and Foucauld, had helped Bonne-Savardin to escape. The Châtelet, retained as part of the district police system of Paris under a decree of November 5, 1789, had gradually been ousted from its functions by the District Committees (Garrigues, *Les districts parisiens*, 56, 65).

so many services to the Revolution, and which has always been the centre of enlightenment'. Save for the last suggestion—it was considered that the Court would be more independent if it met at Orleans—his plan was adopted.

It is curious to find, in regard to both these courts, how little respect Robespierre, himself a lawyer, has for the legal point of view. The functions of the *haute cour* might, perhaps, excuse its being composed of patriotic laymen; but there would seem to have been little reason why the *cour de cassation* should not include the best lawyers in the land. Nevertheless, we find Robespierre declaring that, since its chief function is to prevent other courts from setting up a law of their own, its judges need not themselves be lawyers. 'Indeed,' he remarks (November 18), 'the word jurisprudence ought to be struck out of the French vocabulary. In a state possessing a constitution and a legislature the courts need no jurisprudence but the text of the law'. This was to anticipate the administration of justice in a modern state which has also broken down the old professional monopolies, and where 'there are special courses for magistrates, but on the whole one trusts one's class intuition'.[1] Robespierre, whether he knew it or not, was not so eager to reform the judicial system as he was to transfer judicial power from the officers of the crown, and the privileged courts, to the representatives of the people. The mere fact that it was in the hands of patriots would, he fancied, make it pure. So a way was prepared to the Revolutionary Tribunal, the Law of Suspects, and the proscriptions of 1794.

A number of questions affecting the lower courts also came up for decision at this time. It was Robespierre who proposed and carried the institution of courts-martial (*conseils de guerre*) on which officers and men sat side by side (April 28): it was unfair, he said, for officers to sit alone in judgment on their men. It was he who foresaw the failure of the family courts (*tribunaux arbitraux de parents*) by means of which the Assembly hoped to prevent litigation between

[1] Huxley, *A Scientist among the Soviets*, 24.

94

close relations (August 5).[1] It was he who opposed the granting of magisterial powers to the officers of the *gendarmerie* and *maréchaussée* (December 27), because he considered that they were unfit for such responsibility[2]—an action in which he was supported by a petition from the Jacobin Club at Marseille.[3]

There remains the jury system, which came up for discussion early in February, 1791. Robespierre, who had already made known his belief in this democratic institution,[4] intervened several times in the debates. The committee proposed majority verdicts: Robespierre, not that he had any knowledge of, or respect for English procedure, but because he had been impressed by a case quoted in his *Éloge de Dupaty*, in which the vote of one judge had prevented a serious miscarriage of justice, preferred the Anglo-American requirement of unanimity. A minority, he said, remembering Rousseau, may be right or wrong, but unanimity is a sacrament of the general will. If the old law had required a unanimous verdict, Calas would never have been condemned. If it were only to save one innocent life in a century, such a rule would still be worth having. But he did not persuade the House (February 2). Next day, dealing with the old process called *plus ample informé*, his plea for mercy was more successful, and it was decided that a man could not be twice indicted under the same charge. He was again in a minority in proposing the admission of written as well as oral evidence (January 4), the indemnification of persons wrongfully accused, and the removal of the 'feudal' formula *sur mon honneur* from the juryman's oath (February 3); but carried his point, the same day, that imprisonment was too severe a penalty for failure to surrender to a summons. As to the method of appointing juries—a question on which he had tried in vain to speak on January 20—he thought it dangerous, in a time of revolution, to leave their

---

[1] The *tribunal* was first modified into a *conseil*, and then abolished by Napoleon.
[2] The *gendarmerie* jurisdiction would also have been a check on the *accusateur public* (Lav. 1/129; cp. Michon, *Adrien Duport*, 166).
[3] Corresp. 57.
[4] April 17, 1790, *Discours de Robespierre pour l'établissement des jurés en toute matière*.

selection (as Duport proposed) to the *procureur-général-syndic*, or any other single official, and undemocratic to exclude (as Cazalès would) all but proprietors: 'We cannot have the factions (he said) . . . using the courts as a cloak for private warfare' (February 5). This last speech ranks amongst Robespierre's most ambitious efforts in oratory. He had it printed, and sent copies of it to his friends.[1]

There were, of course, protests from interested quarters against the suppression of the old courts, and the setting up of a new system. One of these, by the Parlement of Toulouse, roused a storm; for Robespierre attacked the *garde des sceaux* for bringing it up, and hinted at the collusion of the crown, in such terms that he was shouted down, and did not speak again in the House for three weeks (October 5). There was also one part of the old system—that by which an accused man could choose whom he would of the *procureurs* to defend him—which Robespierre preferred to the Assembly's proposal to licence only a limited number of counsel in each district; and one innovation—the attachment of royal commissioners to the departmental tribunals —which he successfully opposed (March 30).

VIII

An Englishman, with centuries of national training behind him, finds it difficult to understand the French theory of justice. That difficulty is less than it might be, in the present instance, because there was, in the early years of the Revolution, a tendency to reform the French judicial system on the English model—to adopt the jury, or assizes, or a parliamentary court of appeal. Yet, even so, large parts of Robespierre's policy remain puzzling. His principles are not ours. His anxiety lest the courts should be captured by political parties, or used by the crown against the people; his insistence upon the need of a special tribunal to deal with charges of *lèse-nation*; his notion that judges need have no

[1]*Principes de l'organisation des jurés;* sent to the Jacobin Club at Versailles (Corresp. 63) and to Mme Chalabre (Corresp. 60).

expert knowledge of the law; or the precautions which he thinks necessary in the appointment of jurymen;—upon what do they rest at bottom, except a conception of the state, and of the relation between the government and the law-courts, very different from any that has been held in England since the end of the seventeenth century? When he insists, as he does at every turn, upon popular control of the judicial system, he is not really coming much closer to our standpoint than did Louis XIV, or Napoleon. He by no means gets rid of that intervention of political authority which, to our minds, makes havoc of impartial justice. He merely turns the old system inside out, and replaces the influence of the crown by influence of the people. When, after abolishing the old privileged and overlapping jurisdictions, he proposes to set up a special tribunal to deal with political crimes, it is not because such cases are more difficult to decide than others, but because, in French eyes, they must be dealt with more drastically. The ordinary courts might be too fair. Again, if the judges need not be lawyers, it is because the law which they have to administer is not, like ours, a formless congeries of legal precedents, but a neatly-printed book of rules. Or, if the appointment of jurymen demands elaborate safeguards, it is because they are regarded, not as typical 'men in the street', who will be conducted by considerate counsel along familiar routes of evidence, and directed by an impartial judge at the ultimate cross-roads, but as the audience at a debate, the spectators of a drama, the referees in a judicial contest, where no evidence will be excluded, and no methods left untried, to cheat or bully them into a verdict. They must therefore, even for ordinary purposes, be specially picked men, professional experts in human nature, and, for political trials, staunch supporters of the government of the day, whose duty and right it is to secure a conviction.

Allowance being once made for this unfamiliar background, it is possible to sum up Robespierre's contribution to judicial reform as beginning and ending in the principle of popular control. It is, in fact, not a lawyer's contribution, but a politician's. He is not concerned, ultimately, with the impartial administration of justice, but with the transference of judicial power from the classes to the masses. And what this was to mean, within the next few years, can be studied in the records of the Revolutionary Tribunal.

IX

The existence of a regular army and navy side by side with a national militia was sure to lead to difficulties. One of the first was at Toulon, where, as has already been seen, the National Guard had thrown certain officers of the naval garrison into prison.[1] When the incident came up again in the Assembly (January 16), Robespierre upheld the action of the citizens against the navy under Article II of the Declaration of Rights, which included 'resistance to oppression' among the 'natural and imprescriptible' rights of man; and he subsequently opposed de Rions' request to be allowed to attend the Fête of Federation, and to take the civic oath in the name of the fleet, on the ground that his patriotism was not so certain as his courage (July 5). He showed a similar animus against military officers on May 21, suggesting that they, rather than their men, were responsible for acts of insubordination in the army; and on June 10, when he complained of attempts to stiffen up discipline. When, on August 19, the House debated the question of naval punishments, he declared that it was not only cruel, but also inconsistent with the principle of equality, that a seaman should be made to 'run the gauntlet', whilst an officer was merely dismissed the service. The result of the debate was a decree (August 22) which distinguished *peines de discipline*, inflicted by officers, from *peines afflictives*, which could be imposed only by a *conseil de justice*. Capital punishment could only be inflicted by this court. But the punishments still allowed at the discretion of the officers were severe enough to cause mutinies, and the decree was

[1] v. 1/7on. The Commandant, de Rions, had dismissed two dockyard hands for wearing the cockade of the National Guard.

rescinded only two months later (October 27). Thus Robespierre's view was vindicated; and he deserves credit for protesting against a barbarous code of punishment, which most people at this time, in England as well as France, took for granted.[1]

The whole question of army discipline came to a head this same summer in a serious mutiny at Nancy. The disagreements, to which the Revolution naturally gave rise, between 'aristocrat' officers and 'patriot' rank and file, and which had already led to disorders at Béthune, Perpignan, and other places, were accentuated at Nancy among the garrison troops, and the Swiss of Châteauvieux's Vaudois regiment, by a strong suspicion that the regimental funds were being mismanaged. In answer to the men's complaints the officers' accounts were examined; but by other officers. They sent a deputation to Paris: Lafayette threw it into prison. The methods adopted by another officer to investigate the accounts caused fresh disturbances, which Bouillé repressed by force of arms. Twenty men of the Swiss regiment were hanged, and forty-one sent to the galleys. The mutiny was over; but the methods employed to end it caused bitter dissension between the parties of order and liberty in Paris. At first the opinion of the Assembly was all for order, and Robespierre was almost alone in opposing its vote of thanks to Bouillé (September 3). But soon his protest, backed by the Jacobin Club,[2] led to popular demonstrations in favour of the 'heroes' of the Châteauvieux regiment—anticipating those which, a year later, were a prelude to the fall of the throne; and there was a revival of the wearing of the *bonnet rouge*—the sailors' cap of the galley-slaves—as a symbol of true patriotism.[3]

This was partly why, when another mutiny broke out in the Royal-Champagne regiment at Hesdin, and thirty-six men were dismissed the service, the Assembly took a more merciful view, censuring the officers, and arranging for the re-employment of their 'victims'; though motions of censure

---

[1]cp. Michon, *La justice militaire sous la Révolution*, in A.R. 14/1.
[2]A.H. 6/556.   [3]Lav. 1/244.

on the Minister of War and the Mayor of Hesdin, proposed by Salle and Robespierre, were not carried.

Discipline, whether civil or military, is foreign to a time of revolution. The Assembly of 1790, partly because it was still monarchist at heart, and partly because mutiny in the army produced a sudden feeling of insecurity, was ready to support repression. But it is not surprising to find Robespierre, and the few who, like him, were thorough believers in liberty and democracy, passionate anti-disciplinarians. History is ironical. Within three years these very men, with Robespierre at their head, were trying to enforce on army and civilians alike one of the most drastic disciplines to which France ever submitted. Were they sincere, both in 1790 and in 1793? Yes; for by liberty they meant liberty for patriots, and that might involve, for non-patriots, the prison and the guillotine; and by democracy they meant government in the name, but not necessarily in the hands of the people: a policy which was detestable under a Bourbon might be admirable under a Committee of Public Safety.

X

There remains only the important heading of foreign affairs. During 1789 the Revolution was the private concern of Frenchmen; but, with the spread of revolutionary ideas outside France, such isolation became impossible.

The first sign of the change came from Corsica, where the slow extension of revolutionary ideas, and criticisms of Paoli's regime, encouraged the Genoese to protest against the incorporation of the island in the system of revolutionary government, and to reassert claims to sovereignty which they were thought to have surrendered in 1768. Both Mirabeau and Robespierre believed that these demands would not have been made without the support of England, which had a naval interest in the island; and the House let them 'lie on the table'.[1]

[1] On April 17 a Corsican deputation, headed by Paoli, was welcomed at the Jacobins, and Robespierre, as President, delivered an eloquent oration (printed for the first time by Walter, 1/233).

This was in January. Four months later a more serious crisis arose over the dispute between England and Spain for the ownership of Nootka Sound, on the Pacific coast of North America. Montmorin, the Foreign Minister, abruptly announced that the King had ordered the mobilization of a French fleet. This sudden danger of war not unnaturally alarmed the House, and two issues became urgent: how were negotiations with foreign powers to be conducted, and in whose hands lay the right of declaring war? Speaking on May 11, Robespierre urged the House to keep the negotiations in its own hands, and to adopt a conciliatory attitude. Speaking again on the 18th, he denied that the king had the right to declare war as the representative (*représentant*) of the nation. The king, he said, 'is merely the agent (*commis*) and delegate (*délégué*) of the nation for the execution of its wishes'. When some members protested against such language, he repeated himself more politely, defining *commis* to mean the *emploi suprême* and *charge sublime* of executing the general will. His sentiment, if not his language, was that of the majority of the members; and the debate ended in agreement on the formula (May 22)— 'War can be declared only by a decree of the Legislative Body passed after a formal proposal by the king, and subsequently sanctioned by him'. This was regarded as a notable victory for the Revolution; and at the end of the session the leading Jacobins, Robespierre and Pétion among them, were escorted through the Tuileries gardens by a cheering crowd. It was noticed, and taken by some for an omen, that the young Dauphin, attracted by the excitement, appeared at a window of the palace, and clapped his hands.[1]

Still under the influence of this crisis, Robespierre saw in the proposal to send a relief ship to the distressed island of Tabago (June 30) a fresh danger of war, and drew upon himself the ironical suggestion that he had better go to the Antilles, and investigate the facts for himself. But a not dissimilar proposal, put forward a month later (July 4) by certain deputies interested in foreign trade, that the king

[1] cp. 1/107.

should be asked to commission a number of frigates for the protection of French merchant shipping, justified his fears; though he had little ground for suggesting that the situation was being exploited by enemies of the Revolution.

The case of the Avignon prisoners was of a different kind. The town of Avignon and the district of the Venaissin, with its capital Carpentras, had formed a Papal enclave within French territory ever since the fourteenth century. Their union with revolutionary France had been proposed as early as November, 1789, and the agitation was brought to a head by a revolt at Avignon, in June, 1790, by which the anti-Papal majority drove out the Cardinal-Legate, and imprisoned some of their opponents. From this movement the Venaissin stood aloof. The Assembly debated a difficult position from time to time during the year. On July 10 Robespierre opposed the release of the prisoners until the facts were fully known. On November 18 he was ready with a speech, reported at unusual length in the *Moniteur*, and subsequently printed, in which he argued for the incorporation of the disputed territory. Avignon, he declared, could not be the Pope's property; for how could any people be the property of an individual? Nor would its *réunion* to France be an instance of that 'conquest' which the Assembly had so solemnly renounced. It was their duty to accede to the request of the Avignonese; the more so as their decision would make this strategical corner of the country 'either the support or the scourge of the constitution,' either a centre of armed opposition, or 'the bulwark of France against her foreign foes'.

It was, indeed, arguable that *réunion* was the only way to prevent the spread of federal ideas in the Departments of the Midi, where royalism was never more alive.[1] Yet it was almost certain that the annexation of Avignon would cause a rupture with the Papacy, particularly undesirable at a moment when the fate of the new church settlement depended on the Pope's acquiescence. To this danger Robespierre seems to have been blinded by his zeal for

[1]Vignier in R.F. 21/424, 23/149, 26/150.

self-determination, and, perhaps also, by his dislike for the hierarchy.

Meanwhile there had been fresh rumours of war. On the very day after Marat's alarmist pamphlet, 'It's all up with us!' (*C'en est fait de nous!*) (July 26), news came that a detachment of Austrian troops had been allowed to cross French territory into Brabant, without leave of the Assembly. D'Aiguillon moved to censure Montmorin, Mirabeau the Prince de Condé. Robespierre was against both proposals. Behind Montmorin, he said, were the court and the Ministers, behind Condé the counter-revolution. Let a day be fixed for discussing the best way to deal with all enemies of the Revolution. For this attempt to widen the issue, he was congratulated by the royalist press as a defender of their hero Condé, and promised that, instead of being 'a very long-winded speaker on the revolutionary side of the House' he would in future be 'one of the pleasantest and wittiest speakers among the aristocrats'.[1]

On August 25 a Report of the Diplomatic Committee, presented by Mirabeau, proposed to confirm the 'Family Compact' with Spain, in the form of a defensive and commercial alliance. Robespierre pleaded for reconsideration, but was only able to postpone the adoption of the Report till the next day.

It may seem inconsistent with his anxiety to avoid all occasions of war that, five months later (January 28, 1791), he should be proposing and carrying measures for issuing ammunition to the National Guard, speeding up the manufacture of munitions, and prohibiting the export of war material. But this was for defence, not attack, and for the home front in Paris, not for the war on the frontiers. His apparent militarism sprang from the same source as his real anti-militarism—suspicion of the king's ministers, and of the royalist party, whom he believed to be intriguing to end the Revolution by plunging the country into war. Looking back, it is instructive to see how true he had kept, through-

---

[1] v. the satirical *Lettre de M. l'abbé Maury à M. de Robespierre* (Brit. Mus. F. 851 (19)).

out the year, to this line of policy. His enemies denounced him as a defeatist, and even his supporters regarded him as somewhat of an alarmist. At the time it might seem that they were right. But before 1791 was out, the country was on fire with militarism, and not only the king, but also the ruling party in the Assembly, was deliberately courting war as a means of political power. Never was Robespierre's prophetic insight into the national mind better vindicated.

XI

From this survey of Robespierre's parliamentary course during nearly two years, it should be possible to estimate what he had accomplished, and what he had failed to do.

He was almost always in opposition to the middle-class interests of the majority of the House; yet, by his persistence, and by his uncompromising stand for Liberal principles, he gradually secured its respect, turning a minority of one into a small group, and carrying the Assembly with him, not only in the less controversial details of legal or agricultural reform, but also in big political and moral issues. There is abundant evidence from his enemies as well as from his friends that he had made himself one of the two or three most formidable spokesmen in the House, and figures in the country.[1] But the most heaven-born orator could hardly make two speeches a week to the same audience for eighteen months on end without sometimes boring or offending them. Robespierre's presence was unimpressive, his voice harsh, his manner provocative, his evident determination to be heard on every possible occasion a cause of antagonism. He was too often interrupted by 'murmurs', or called to order, he was the central figure of too many unruly incidents, for one to suppose that the House was always pleased to hear 'this tribune of the people'.[2]

The main cause of offence, indeed, was what Robespierre

[1] e.g. quotations from the royalist *Actes des Apôtres* in Croker, 313.
[2] *M. Robespierre a paru à le tribune; mais, l'assemblée ayant temoigné quelque impatience, l'honorable membre s'est retiré, comme Jerémie, la larme à l'oeil.* (Duplain's *Courrier*, October 3, 1790, R.F. 58/507.)

said, rather than his way of saying it. His uncompromising stand for liberty and equality was hardly more disliked by those who had never accepted the first principles of the Revolution than by those who had begun to forget them. Few things are more annoying to a statesman who is doing his best to govern the country than to be told, by those who have none of his responsibilities, that he is compromising his political principles. He knows that it is half true; but he feels that, in face of what he is doing, it is relatively unimportant. The remedy suggested by English experience is to make criticism responsible by occasionally putting the critics into power. But that remedy was impossible in a single sovereign body of over a thousand members, all of whom were at once members of the Government and of the Opposition, at once responsible rulers and irresponsible critics. Robespierre could not be blamed for playing the part, to which the system confined him, of an uneasy and sometimes accusing conscience. His fellow-members had no remedy but to stop their ears, or to shout him down.

The situation might have been borne good-humouredly, if the happy and confident temper of 1789 had still prevailed. But it did not. 'You can have no idea,' writes Robespierre to his old friend Buissart, 'of the number and difficulty of the questions with which we have to deal. The patriotic deputies of the National Assembly attempted a superhuman task when they undertook to cleanse the Augean stables of the old regime.'[1] 'The Constitutional Committee,' writes Augustin, in October, 'ought to be called the anti-revolutionary Committee; it causes so much anxiety, and is so constantly attacking the patriots.'[2] 'Paris', he says again, in December, 'shows the worst symptoms of a terrible commotion. Thousands of pamphlets appear every day. . . . There is a crowd of spies in every quarter of the city, and murderers are marked off to assassinate patriots'.[3] Robespierre himself speaks of 'the calumnies by which he is plagued', and of the 'hatred of the aristocrats'. He dare not

[1]Corresp. 26 (March 4). [2]Corresp. 49 (October 17).
[3]Corresp. 51 (December 13).

write directly to his brother at Arras, lest the name 'Robespierre' on the envelope should incite his enemies to violate
the privacy of the post.[1] Augustin, for his part, fears, from
Maximilien's silence, that he may have been proscribed,
and cannot dissemble his dread lest his 'dear brother' may
be fated to 'seal with his blood the cause of the people'.[2]
For 'the capital crawls with discontent, and the Assembly
is full of Ministry men, black reactionaries (*noirs*) and
blockheads', whilst 'the proceedings of the House are nowadays so indecent and disorderly that it is impossible to take
part in them'.[3]

Even so, the undoubted change in the temper of the
Assembly, and the sharpening of the conflict between
'patriots' and 'aristocrats,' might have been faced more
philosophically, if the deputies had allowed themselves any
relaxation. But the House was now meeting twice a day,
Sundays included; there was a crowd of committees in
constant session; and four nights in the week the Jacobin
Club pre-debated or re-debated the same questions. The
crowds round the Manège, the clamour of the news-
vendors, and the noisy controversies which overflowed
from the Assembly into the cafés and clubs, added to the
wear and tear of political nerves. In a society which had few
outdoor recreations, and knew little about personal hygiene,
there were no physical reserves to aid mental strain, and
ill-temper was aggravated by ill-health.

Robespierre himself was overwhelmed with work. Besides his daily attendances at the House (where for a time
he held one of the secretaryships),[4] and the Constitutional
Committee, and the long hours he spent at his desk, composing and correcting his speeches, he had accepted, in
October, a judgeship at Versailles,[5] and was a regular
attendant at the Jacobins, where for the first fortnight of
April he was President. The functions of this last post,
alone, were troublesome enough, he told Buissart, without

---

[1] Corresp. 26, 27, 30. [2] Corresp. 40 (June, 1790).
[3] Corresp. 47 (September, 1790).
[4] He was elected, with two others, on June 19, 1790.
[5] Corresp. 49, 54. He had spoken at a Jacobin dinner there on June 20 (A.H. 2/99).

his other occupations.[1] There were also public functions of various kinds in which, as a deputy, he had to take part. We hear of him, for instance, from an independent source, as present at the Fête of Federation on July 14, 1790. 'I was standing behind His Majesty's seat,' says Saint-Priest, 'and almost cheek by jowl with that famous rascal Robespierre'.[2]

Meanwhile his private correspondence was increasing side by side with his public engagements. Not much of it has survived: but, as against seven extant letters for 1789, of which four are written by himself, we have, in 1790, thirty-three, of which sixteen are his own. They deal partly with controversies already described, such as the accusations of Lambert, or the libels of Beaumetz[3]; and partly with legal problems,[4] or the interpretation of decrees.[5] There were replies to be written to patriotic societies at Chalons, Arras, Avignon, or Marseille.[6] There were admirers who could not be offended, and editors who had to be put right.[7] There was even a correspondent from England.[8] And always, in the background, were the Arras friends and relations—the Buissarts, brother Augustin, and sister Charlotte. Robespierre, indeed, shrank from letter-writing, and put it off as long as he could: nor was there much provision for it at his overcrowded desk.[9] But it was a duty, and somehow it was done.

XII

In No. 28 of his *Révolutions de France et de Brabant*, Desmoulins described the scene of May 22 in the Tuileries gardens following the debate on the right of declaring war,[10] when the little Dauphin had been seen clapping his hands at the palace window, and went on to put a speech into Robespierre's mouth: 'Why! Gentlemen,' he said to the crowd which surrounded him, and deafened him with its

[1]Corresp. 26, 27. [2]*Mémoires*, 2/37. [3]v. 1/82.
[4]Corresp. 23. [5]Corresp. 24, 25, 42. [6]Corresp. 28, 43, 53, 54.
[7]Corresp. 46, 41. [8]Corresp. 48.
[9]*Je trouve en ce moment des plumes, de l'encre, du papier, croyez que ce n'est pas chose facile sur le bureau de mon frère.* (Augustin to Buissart, received September 9, 1790. Corresp. 47.)
[10]v. 1/101.

cheers, 'upon what are you congratulating yourselves? The decree is a bad one—as bad as it can be. Let that brat at the window clap his hands if he will: he knows what he is doing better than we do'. The moment he read this passage, Robespierre wrote to Desmoulins, declaring that he had said nothing of the kind, and that he would never have used in public the frankness (*franchise;* Desmoulins had called him *franc*) which he thought suitable in the Assembly. Desmoulins' reply was a good piece of journalistic impudence. He printed the protest in his next issue, and added this editorial note: 'If I insert this *errata* (*sic*), my dear Robespierre, it is solely to flaunt your signature before my fellow-journalists, and to give them a hint not to mutilate in future a name rendered famous by the patriotism of its bearer. There is a dignity about your letter, and a senatorial weightiness, which rather hurts me, as an old College friend. You are proud, and you have a right to be, to wear the toga of the National Assembly. I like this noble conceit, and I am only sorry that all the deputies are not as conscious of their dignity as you are. But you might at least have given an old comrade like myself something more than a nod of the head—not that I love you any the less for it; because you *are* faithful to your principles, however it may be with your friends. All the same, why this insistence on my recantation? I may have slightly altered the facts, in the story I told; but it was all to your credit; and if you never actually used the words I put in your mouth, still they certainly express your thoughts. Instead of disavowing my journalism in such dry terms, you might have contented yourself with saying, like Cousine in that charming play, *Le Mort supposé*, "Ah! Sir, you are embroidering!" You are not one of those poor creatures described by J. J. Rousseau, who hate to have their thoughts repeated, and who say what they really think before their butler or their valet, but never in the National Assembly, or the Tuileries gardens.'[1]

It cannot be supposed that the jealousy, or the resentment

[1]Corresp. 41.

with Robespierre's pride of office, which look out between
the lines of this characteristically spiteful note, were peculiar
to his old school-fellow. Evidently he was not popular in
the House. In view of this letter, it is certainly to Robespierre's credit that he took an opportunity, two months
later, to defend Desmoulins from the anger of the Assembly,
and that he was present as a witness at his marriage.[1]

Two letters apparently owe their preservation to the fact
that they were put in as evidence during trials under the
Terror. Charles Michaud was a country priest, who wrote
to his friend Robespierre asking what the rights of the
municipality were over the parish church: it could order
the removal of the squire's pew; but could it demand
accounts from the person responsible for the upkeep of the
fabric? Robespierre's reply was part of Michaud's *dossier*
when he was brought before the revolutionary tribunal set
up by the terrorist Lebon at Arras, four years later, and
helped, no doubt, innocent as it was, to send him to the
guillotine.[2] On the other hand, when Duvignau, a Bordeaux
patriot whose zeal outran his discretion, was indicted as a
Girondist, he was able to produce a letter from Robespierre
thanking him for the gift of a pamphlet, and it saved his
life.[3]

Robespierre in 1790 was not so inured to flattery as he
became in 1794. He can therefore be excused for treasuring
a letter which went far to compensate for the sneers of
Desmoulins, and the libels of Beaumetz. It was dated
'*Blérancourt près Noyon, le* 19 *août*,' and began:—'You, who
uphold our tottering country against the torrent of despotism and intrigue, you whom I know, as I know God, only
through his miracles—it is to you, Monsieur, that I address
myself.' The request that followed was no more than that
Robespierre should interest himself in a petition from a
small local town. But the letter ended with more words of

[1]Blanc, 5/150, Clarétie, 149 f., Hamel, 1/351. The first accepts, the second bowd-
lerizes, and the third indignantly rejects the story that when Bérardier's address
moved Desmoulins to tears, Robespierre sneered *Ne pleure donc pas, hypocrite.*
[2]Corresp. 42. He was executed on April 17, 1794.
[3]Corresp. 46; A.R. 5/325.

comfort. 'I do not know you,' the writer said; 'but you are a great man. You are not merely the deputy of a province; you are the deputy of the Republic, and of mankind'. The signature to this effusion—'*Saint-Just, électeur au département de l'Aisne*'—meant nothing to Robespierre; but it was the beginning of a strange man and boy affection, from which Robespierre derived new ardour and ideas for his work, and which was, perhaps, the sincerest that he ever felt.[1]

There remains the Arras postbag. Eighteen out of the thirty-three letters belonging to 1790 were written to or from Robespierre's native town. After the long silence for which he apologized to Buissart in November, 1789,[2] Robespierre seems to have made a resolution to send a report to his constituency at the beginning of every month: there are letters dated March 4, April 1, and May 1, written to Buissart as *commissaire* for the Artois deputies.[3] But then either his resolution failed, or the letters have been lost; for there is nothing more, except a formal letter of thanks for a vote of confidence, addressed to the Arras club. For the story of local events, and its bearing on Maximilien's career, we have to fall back on Augustin's readier pen, and on a single letter from Charlotte Robespierre. The latter writes on April 9 (it is evidently the chance relic of a series of letters) reporting attempts to deal with the terrible state of unemployment and destitution among the Arras poor, and saying that she has fallen out with her brother's old benefactor, Mme Marchand, now the editress of a royalist paper.[4] It was from this letter also, and from an enclosure by Augustin, that Maximilien learnt of the financial difficulties of the home at Arras, and of the desire of his brother and sister to come to Paris. Augustin is organizing a Jacobin club at Arras, and takes the opportunity of his brother's presidency of the Paris Jacobins to ask for affiliation to the mother-society.[5] He is also concerned with the

[1] Corresp. 45.   [2] v. 1/73.   [3] Corresp. 35.
[4] Corresp. 29. We know from other sources of the distress at Arras. An appeal to the Assembly by the Mayor, Dubois de Fosseux, says that there are 8,000 paupers, out of a population of 20,000, dependent on local charity (Brit. Mus. R. 232).
[5] Corresp. 32.

counter-revolutionary propaganda carried on by the religious houses in and about Arras, and with the disposal of the revenues of Saint-Vaast, which he thinks would be better applied to the relief of the poor than to the foundation of further endowments for education, such as he and his brother had both enjoyed. He is engagingly anxious for Maximilien's safety; the 'monstrous behaviour' of his enemies 'makes his blood boil, and the villains had better keep out of his way'.[1] When he has at last induced Robespierre to pay his fare to Paris, and to find him rooms in the rue Jacques,[2] he writes to Buissart the monthly reports that his brother is too busy to keep up, and seals them with the *cachet* of the Assembly.[3] We hear more, in these letters, about Buissart than about Robespierre—his ambition to be a *juge de paix*, the memoir on weights and measures he has presented to the Assembly, or his wife and children (*marmots si gentils*); much also about Augustin's efforts to find a job, and his hopes that the new *garde des sceaux* may give him a commissionership, or the Arras electors nominate him to the local Court of Appeal. But nothing comes of it. He stays on in Paris hoping against hope for some permanent occupation; and he is still there in March, 1791.[4]

The correspondence for the year ends with three letters to the *administrateurs* of Avignon. They had sent Robespierre a vote of thanks for his part in securing their political freedom, and an expression of their desire to be not only free, but also French. He replied in terms which show that, whatever his personal disappointments, he had not lost faith in the Revolution. 'Yes, Gentlemen,' he writes, 'you shall be French: indeed, your wish, and the wish of the French people, makes you so already. France covets no new territory, but free and virtuous citizens. And what country can offer them so well as yours? If Rome gave the right of citizenship to the peoples she had conquered, why should

<hr/>

[1]Corresp. 32, 34, 39.
[2]About two miles from the rue Saintonge.
[3]Corresp. 47.
[4]Villiers, who no doubt resented his sponging on Maximilien, calls him *misérable avocasseur, sans moyens, faux, ivrogne, bas, et crapuleux*.

we refuse it to our brothers, our fellow-conquerors of despotism, who design to fight by our side for the preservation of our common liberty? That is the sole policy which can make men happy. That is my profession of faith.'[1]

[1]Corresp. 53. Full text and two other letters in A.H. 3/583, 7/269.

CHAPTER V

The Successor of Mirabeau (January–June, 1791)

I

An anti-Jacobin pamphlet of 1790 describes ironically the pleasures and privileges of the common people—how they can frequent the Opéra, the Comédie, and above all the Palais Royal, where proud Jacobins point out to them the heroes of the day: 'There goes a deputy. . . . Yes, that is King Mirabeau; and that King Barnave; and that King Robespierre.' Such is the evidence of Robespierre's enemies, who had never ceased to caricature his person and speeches in the royalist press,[1] that he had, by the end of 1790, reached an eminence that would have seemed fantastic to the provincial lawyer of 1789. He faced what the new year might bring with fresh confidence in his powers; and he might well do so; for his success had been won by factors within his own control—persistent self-improvement, and unswerving support of a cause. He had no facile ability to make him careless, no charms that might cease to attract, no sense of humour to suggest a doubt as to his own importance. What could stop his career, unless it were a success that left him nothing to fight for, or the enmity of those who were bored with his incessant uprightness? 'He was the sworn foe (said Dubois-Crancé) of every kind of oppression, the fearless champion of the rights of the people. He only needed a fine presence, a voice like Danton's, and sometimes a little less presumption and pig-headedness; for these small failings often did harm to the cause he was defending. He was a proud and jealous man, but fair and upright. His bitterest critics could never accuse him of irregular conduct. His principles were austere to a fault, and

[1] e.g. *Sermon prononcé au club des Jacobins . . . par Dom Prospère—Iscariote—Honesta Robespierre de Bonne-Foi.* (Jac. 2/177.)

113

he never deviated from them a hair's breadth. Such as he had been from the beginning of his career, such he was to the end of it; and there are mighty few men to whom such praise can be given'.[1] 'He is a living commentary,' wrote Desmoulins, 'on the Declaration of Rights, and the personification of good sense'. But he does not blink the fact that Robespierre's opinions were too advanced for the majority of the House, and even applies to him the text, 'I have yet many things to say unto you, but ye cannot bear them now'.[2] On the other hand, if Robespierre had spoken less frequently, he might have carried more weight. Members noticed with resentment that he sat as close as he could to the *bureau*, so as to lose no opportunity of occupying the tribune. The Moderates of the Assembly came to calling him their Maury (after the intransigent Royalist), and welcomed his opposition, because it won them votes. Indeed, it was not in the National Assembly, but in the Jacobin Club, with its more varied and enthusiastic audience, that Robespierre was most thoroughly at home.[3]

II

Little has been said about the Jacobin Club hitherto, because the records of its proceedings during 1789 and 1790 are very scanty. But from February, 1791, they become much fuller, and its debates begin to rival those of the Assembly itself in importance.

Whilst English clubs in the later part of the eighteenth century remained primarily social, French clubs, partly influenced by them, and partly developing independently out of the earlier social and literary *salons*, took a turn towards politics and social reform. It was thus natural that the opening of the States-General in 1789 should lead to the formation of clubs for deputies. The Breton members, who were already in the habit of meeting, before they came to Versailles, were urged to carry on the practice there, in

[1] R.F. 9/704; A.R. 6/255.
[2] *Révolutions de France et de Brabant*, February 21, 1791.
[3] A.R. 6/255. The smaller building, too, suited his weak voice.

order to concert a common policy. But from their first meeting (April 30), besides an inner circle confined to themselves (*comité breton*), they also had an outer circle (*club breton*) in which other deputies might join them, to discuss matters of general interest. The meetings were held at the Café Amaury, in a large room, which some accounts place on the first floor, and others underground.[1] The outer circle included Mirabeau, Sieyès, Barnave, Pétion, Grégoire, the Lameths, and Robespierre. The proceedings were secret, and no minutes were kept, any sign of 'party' being at that time a little suspect. It was customary to discuss the agenda for the Assembly; and parliamentary incidents which seemed to happen spontaneously had sometimes been rehearsed beforehand at the club. Soon after the transference of the Assembly to Paris (October, 1789) the *comité breton* re-assembled at the Place des Victoires. By December it was drawing up rules, admitting members who were not deputies, and granting affiliation to provincial societies. Thus an outer circle grew up again, on wider lines than before; and it soon adopted a new name—*Société de la Révolution*—and occupied larger quarters at the Dominican or 'Jacobin' convent in the rue Saint-Honoré. Soon (January, 1790?) the name was changed again to *Société des Amis de la Constitution*; and finally (from September 21, 1792) to *Société des Jacobins, amis de la liberté et de l' Égalité*.[2]

A three-arched entry from the street led to an open court, in which the conventual buildings—church, cloister, library, and chapter-house—were flanked by secular dwellings. The first meeting-place of the club was the refectory; but its wall-benches and improvised seats soon proved inadequate for the crowd of members, and they gratefully accepted the monks' offer of a lease of the library—a big vaulted room above the church, containing a valuable collection of books

---

[1]The tradition accepted by Aulard is that of the first-floor room; the authority was an eye-witness, who claimed to possess the chair occupied by Robespierre. The building is now the Brasserie Muller, at the corner of Avenue Saint-Cloud and rue Carnot; over the door is a tablet recording its history (A.R. 2/382, Walter, 1/229).

[2]Aulard, *Études*, 1/4; Jac., Introd. to Vol. 1; R.F. 22/107, 36/385; some details are not yet certain.

and oriental MSS., and bearing on its walls portraits of distinguished members of the Order. Here seats were arranged in four rows down each side of the room; but these too became over-crowded; and in May, 1791, a final move was made into the church itself, whose huge vaulted nave, choir, and side-chapels, with their mediæval pictures, statues, tombs, and coloured glass, provided an ample if incongruous setting for the political debates of a new dispensation.[1]

The rules of the club show that it was meant to be a non-party society, with branches all over the country, for defending and promoting the principles of the constitutional revolution, and for discussing beforehand the agenda for the Assembly. Members could be nominated, if *députés* or *suppléants*, by two members; if not, by five. They could be censured, or expelled, for opinions contrary to those of the club, or for absence, without good cause, for more than a month. The officers were a President, a Treasurer, and four Secretaries; the President and Secretaries were generally changed every month. Meetings were held every evening at six when the Assembly was not sitting, and at least three days a week when it was. No subscription is mentioned in the rules, only voluntary contributions; but Louis Blanc is probably following a good oral tradition when he says that there was an entry fee of twelve *livres*, and a subscription of twenty-four *livres*, paid quarterly.[2] The admission of the general public was not properly regulated till October, 1791, when the choir and organ galleries were fitted with seats. It is said that on great occasions room was found for as many as 2,000 spectators. The list of members printed in December, 1790, contains 1,102 names; but both the number of members, and that of affiliated societies, varied greatly from time to time, according to the political situation. Generally speaking, the sentiments of the club were

[1]For picturesque descriptions of club meetings, v. Michelet, Lewes, Belloc. The introductions of busts of Mirabeau, Helvétius, and other 'saints' of the Revolution (cp. 1/294) can only have emphasized this oddness.
[2]This is corroborated by the accounts published by Desfieux, the Club Treasurer in 1791 (A.R. 7/37).

those of the majority in the Assembly; whilst the size of its subscription, and the method of election, excluded all but deputies, or well-to-do citizens of the middle class.[1]

III

During the first six months of 1791 the debates in the Assembly may seem to be marking time; many of their topics are already familiar, and the speakers on both sides have come to know one another's points of view so well that there is an air of unreality about their arguments, and even about their abuse. But the biographer of Robespierre cannot pass over this period, for it is that in which the deputy from Arras definitely challenges the supremacy of Mirabeau, and becomes, after his death, the most influential orator in the House.

Robespierre's first intervention in public business, after a silence of three weeks, was to defend, as he had done before, the privacy of the post (February 28).[2] His second was to oppose his old enemy Le Chapelier's bill for treating disrespect to public officials as *lèse-nation*, and thus, in effect, setting up the principle of *droit administratif*. Such proposals seemed to him an attack upon liberty, and an invitation to judicial tyranny. He was almost English in his suspicion of officialism, and in his belief in the value of public criticism. His third intervention, later in the same day, was in the matter of the *émigrés*. The stream of aristocratic emigration, which had flowed since July, 1789, leaving suspicion and unemployment behind it, had lately been swollen by the flight of the king's aunts: and there were rumours that Louis himself was planning to follow them. On this very day a Parisian mob had set out to demolish the *donjon* of Vincennes, and Lafayette, at the Tuileries, had disarmed a crowd of nobles who were suspected of covering a royal flight. That Robespierre took the incident of the *Chevaliers du poignard* seriously, and had, indeed, in some sense predicted it, may be inferred from the language in which it is

[1]Barnave's *Règlement*, February 8, 1790.   [2]cp. 1/55, 83.

described by his brother in a letter to Buissart soon afterwards.[1] But when Le Chapelier, for the Constitutional
Committee, introduced a bill for preventive measures
against emigration, the principle of liberty once more overruled the feelings of the moment; and he made a speech
which, whilst it offended the 'thirty voices'—Duport,
Lameth, Barnave, d'Aiguillon, and their friends—silenced
by Mirabeau on this occasion, won the approval of the '1789
Club' and of the Moderate press.[2] The same scrupulousness
prevented Robespierre from supporting a measure proposed
by Desmeuniers a few days later (March 3), which might
have seemed the answer to his difficulties of February 28.
Government control over local administration was to be
secured by setting up a hierarchy of district and departmental authorities, subordinated to the Ministers. Such an
organization might have obviated much of the administrative anarchy of the next few years, and ante-dated the
Napoleonic centralization. But in Robespierre's mind it
contained a threat to popular liberty which no plea of mere
efficiency could justify. The smallest electoral body (*assemblée primaire*) seemed to him invested with a fragment of the
national sovereignty, and therefore answerable to no lower
authority than a National Assembly. The compromise
finally arrived at had important consequences; for the
Revolution was likely to stand or fall, in the long run, less
by the actions of the Parisian government than by the
reactions of the provinces.

The same evening—for by now, owing to the pressure of
business, the Assembly was meeting twice a day—the abbé
Gouttes, in the name of the Finance Committee, brought
forward a scheme for a National Lottery (*tontine*), out of the
proceeds of which it was hoped not only to provide Old
Age Pensions, but also to form a Sinking Fund for the
extinction of the National Debt. This respectable gamble
had the support, both of the *Académie des Sciences*, and of
Mirabeau, whose secretary Clavière had a place on the

[1] *Mon frère avoit prédit cette horrible manœuvre* (Corresp. 62).
[2] The *Moniteur* gives a very short summary of the speech, and fails to keep its
promise of *la suite demain*.

Board of Directors, and who proposed to launch the scheme by impounding five days' stipend from every deputy. This was well enough for those who could afford it; but to poor men like Robespierre, who barely lived upon their eighteen *livres* a day, it would be a heavy sacrifice. He therefore attacked and defeated the proposal, on the double ground that lotteries were undesirable, and that the payment of deputies was a security against government by the rich.

Two days later (March 5) his clear-headedness again saved the House from a dubious commitment. The Austrian government had asked for the extradition of two men accused of forging drafts on the bank of Vienna, and the Diplomatic Committee proposed to grant the request out of hand. He urged and secured delay. 'We must be certain,' he said, 'as to what are the actual rights and duties of nations in such matters'.

He was less successful, soon afterwards (March 9), in an attack upon one of the last hiding-places of royal power. It was proposed that the *administrateurs du trésor public* should be appointed by the king. But the Treasury, he urged, almost in the words he had used in the debate on taxation eighteen months before,[1] belongs to the people, of whose contributions it is composed: it is for them, therefore, to appoint the Treasurers. For his almost solitary stand in this matter Robespierre received the rather embarrassing congratulations of a social lion-hunter, Mme de Chalabre, and an invitation to dinner.[2]

There remain two episodes which enlisted all Robespierre's sympathies—his belief in the people, his respect for the patriot clergy, his hatred of judicial oppression, and his resentment at departmental interference with local liberty.

Issy l'Évêque was a small village near Autun. In the early days of the Revolution, under the leadership of its curé, one Carion, the villagers had organized a permanent committee, a volunteer force, and a common stock of grain. The curé himself was chairman of the committee, commandant of the militia, and supervisor of the granary—'Danton

[1] August 26, 1789. [2] Corresp. 61, cp. 2/216.

in a cassock' was Desmoulins' name for him.[1] When some of the farmers complained of this regime, the magistrates of the *bailliage* arrested Carion, and sent him before the Châtelet at Paris, under a charge of *lèse-nation*. This discredited court, by way of a last gesture, threw him into prison; and he had been there seven months before the Assembly at last intervened. Robespierre, following Merle, urged that all charges should be dropped, and the curé released. The House agreed. The judicial proceedings were quashed, and Carion set free—another victory for the people.

Two days later there came up a second case involving the food shortage in the provinces, and a charge against the clergy. Two lives had been lost in a food-riot at Douai. Alquier, presenting a Report, moved to censure the municipality, and to threaten the local clergy with penalties for incitement to revolt. Douai was not far from Arras: Maximilien's brother had been at school there, and he knew the local conditions well. He protested against both parts of the proposal. But the Assembly was determined to make an example, and threw the municipal officers into prison. The only part of Robespierre's speech which succeeded was his plea for the clergy; and that won him less applause from his friends than from his enemies. Twice within three days he had championed this increasingly unpopular cause. Such indiscretion might well become, in later years, the basis for a charge of clericalism.

It was Alquier, again, who reported (April 2) on the troubles at Nîmes. This time Robespierre only expressed the hope that care would be taken to discriminate the innocent from the guilty.

IV

At eight o'clock the next morning (April 3) an event happened which was to change the course of the Revolution, and Robespierre's career. Mirabeau was dead. Robes-

[1] Jac. 2/144.

pierre had long outgrown, if not his doubt of the man's honesty, at least his disbelief in his powers. Sometimes during the last two years they had championed the same cause; more often they had been on opposite sides. But they had always respected one another as good fighters; the younger man had copied and courted the elder;[1] and the elder had been generous enough to express his praise. Now —he could do no less—Robespierre repaid part of his debt, by speaking (April 3) of 'that illustrious man, who, at the most critical times of the Revolution, showed so courageous a front against despotism', and by supporting 'with all his power, or rather, with all the feelings of his heart', the proposal for a public funeral. He also favoured the suggestion that the newly-built church of Saint-Généviéve should be used as a burial-place for great Frenchmen, and that the first to be interred there should be Mirabeau; and a measure to this effect was hurried through the House.

What were Robespierre's thoughts, as he walked with his fellow-deputies behind the star-studded trappings and the figure of Fame that adorned Mirabeau's funeral car? Did he know that he was burying not only Mirabeau, but also the Monarchy[2]—the last chance of saving the French throne? Hardly: for Mirabeau's relations with the court were as yet guessed rather than known; royalism still had a firm hold on the country; the monarchical party might even be gaining ground in the House; and the very fears expressed lest the king might be planning flight showed how essential his presence was thought to be for the success of the Revolution. No; but at least the king's cause was weaker for the loss of its chief champion. And what a change it would be in the House—that great voice and presence gone, that vast store of political knowledge closed! Who could take Mirabeau's place? Malouet wrote afterwards, and may have said at the time, that there were only two men on the Left of the Assembly who were not

---

[1] Le Blond (101) says that Robespierre sat at Mirabeau's side in the Assembly, followed him in the streets, and even copied his *coiffure*; so that the papers dubbed him *le singe de Mirabeau*.

[2] *le deuil de la Monarchie*, Mirabeau's supposed words on his deathbed.

demagogues, only two who followed their own line of conduct, irrespective of public opinion—Mirabeau and Robespierre. The death of the first left the position of the second unique. It would have needed a man much less interested in himself than Robespierre not to be conscious of this opportunity, one much less ambitious not to use it for his career. Political vistas opened up behind the coffin of Mirabeau. Where Elijah had failed, Elisha would succeed. The king's cause had really been hopeless from the beginning: the cause of the People could not fail, if it were pursued to the end. Mirabeau's advocacy had been ruined by his full-blooded amoralism: no such reproach should ever be brought against the untiring correctness of Robespierre's thin-lipped soul. He would take the other's place as the spokesman of the Assembly, the instructor of the nation, the saviour of France. And the People—the people which 'in its revolutionary consciousness, wider than all parties and all feuds, reconciled all the forces of the Revolution', and in its Popular Societies 'set side by side the bust of Robespierre the Incorruptible and the bust of Mirabeau accused of corruption',[1] would range itself under a leader, whom it had already come to recognize as the one consistent and outspoken champion of its cause.

v

Robespierre's speeches after April 3 show a new confidence, and a broader style, befitting his emancipation, and the larger canvas that the national interests now demand.

He could not have had a better occasion to open a new stage in his parliamentary career than the debate on testamentary law which took place on April 5. It was a lawyer's subject, and it enabled him to appear as the pupil and defender of his great predecessor. For one of the last acts of Mirabeau's life had been to prepare a speech for this debate;

[1] Jaurès 2/344. It is at this point, too, and with the same feeling, that Louis Blanc gives his full-length portrait of Robespierre (5/269)—'that frozen embodiment of principle', that 'reflective but marble statue of justice', whose feelings are all in his head: 'put your hand on his heart, and there is not a stir of life in it'.

and, at his own request, Talleyrand read it to the House. So delivered, the discourse seemed less an argument than an act of homage, and Robespierre had an easy task in showing that its proposals were an appropriate extension of the sacred principle of equality from persons to property.

But he added something of his own, and something significant, when he said that equality of succession is not only a law of nature, but also a means of diminishing wealth, which is an enemy of virtue;[1] for this idea is the clue to anything in Robespierre's creed which can be called socialistic. It is clear that he cannot have meant quite what we mean either by 'nature', or by 'virtue'. Indeed, to a Frenchman of 1791 almost everything was 'natural' which was opposed to the old regime, and hardly anything 'virtuous' which did not glorify the Revolution: in a word, 'natural' meant 'rational', and 'virtuous' 'patriotic'. Robespierre had in mind something like the definition with which Montesquieu prefaces his *L'Esprit des Lois*: 'what I call *vertu* in the republic is love of one's country, that is to say, love of equality. It is not a moral or a Christian virtue, but a political one; and it is as much the main-spring of republican government as reputation (*honneur*) is the main-spring of monarchies.'[2] He knew from experience the way in which men of wealth—not merely the old aristocratic landlords, but also the new middle-class plutocrats—were, for various selfish reasons of their own, opposing the advance of the Revolution. He believed that real patriotism was to be found among the poor, just because they were poor. Accordingly his 'order of nature' was the sovereignty of the common people; and his 'rule of virtue' the patriotic conduct of the poor—of those who had no interests opposed to the common weal. This way of looking at things, of course, prevented his being a socialist, in the sense of one who wishes to abolish poverty, or a communist, in the sense of one who wishes to abolish patriotism. He would only

---

[1] *Avec les grandes richesses, la vertu est en horreur.*

[2] *Avertissement*, prefixed to *Livre I*. cp. the Metz essay (1/23). Robespierre would certainly have disagreed with Voltaire's historical argument against the *vertu* of democracies (*Lettre a M. de Chevalier de R . . . X*, September 20, 1760).

redistribute wealth so far as it could be done without making the rich so poor that they could no longer be taxed, or the poor so rich that they were no longer patriotic.

VI

On April 6 began the great series of constitutional debates which characterizes this period, and Robespierre made his critical attitude clear at once by opposing the king's right to appoint ministers. He went on to insist that it was the right (*droit*) of the nation to object to bad ministers, and the duty (*devoir*) of the Assembly to demand their dismissal. Next day he opened the resumed debate with a drastic proposal. Eighteen months before, a memorable resolution, aimed partly at Mirabeau, had prevented any deputy from holding office under the crown. Mirabeau was now dead; but Robespierre believed the principle to be so important that he proposed to prolong the disqualification for four years after the dissolution of the Assembly. D'André showed the inner meaning of this suggestion when he urged that deputies should undertake never to solicit places for their friends or relations. The issue was, in fact, more than constitutional. The proposal was not merely another concession to the doubtful principle of the 'division of powers': it was also a blow struck for political purity. The poverty of many of the deputies had made the readiness with which bribes were offered and taken, and the extent to which places and emoluments were solicited by those who hoped to make a living out of the Revolution, a public scandal. Robespierre's motion was an instalment of that gospel of virtue which he already had in mind, and of which he afterwards became the apostle and martyr. He had made a similar suggestion, not long before, in the case of judges of appeal: he was soon to carry the same principle further in the 'self-denying ordinance' of May 16. The fact that the present proposal was accepted by the House was a tribute not only to its honesty, but also to his gift of leadership.

The debate went on for more than a week, and hardly a

day passed without a speech from Robespierre. He would have ex-ministers legally answerable for their actions more than three years after giving up office (April 18), and joined Buzot in trying to strengthen the machinery for calling them to account (April 10). He agreed that the allocation of functions among ministers might be left to the king; but attacked the proposal that the Minister of Justice should be empowered to supervise the judges in their application of the law, or to call them to account; for the law is its own interpreter, and the judges, representing the people, can be called to account only by the Public Prosecutor (April 9, 11). He moved to reduce the stipends and pensions of ministers, and to deprive them of the disposal of the police (*gendarmerie*—April 11, 13). So persistent were his attacks on the powers of ministers that his old enemy Beaumetz accused him of federalism. 'This systematic refusal,' he said, 'to give the government any control, however indirect, over the armed forces, is federal in principle (*un système fédératif*), and tends to destroy the unity of monarchical government (*l'unité monarchique*)'. Robespierre's friends indignantly denied the charge: but there was this much truth in it, that the extreme decentralization into which, in its reaction against the old regime, provincial administration was being allowed to lapse, did afford a foothold for risings against the central government. Lyon, Toulon, and the Vendée were very soon to prove that Beaumetz's fears were not ill-founded. But the irony of the charge was that those who accused Robespierre were, before long, to take advantage of this very system, and to fall under the charge of *fédéralisme*, whilst he was to be the organizer of a centralized regime expressly designed to defeat it. When and why Robespierre changed his mind, it remains to discover. At present, in the spring of 1791, he is still reacting against the old monarchical system. At the British Embassy, at this time, 'Robertspierre, Pethion, Buzot, and Prieur' were regarded as the leaders of 'a sett of men whose object is the total annihilation of monarchy, however limited'.[1]

[1]Gower's despatch of April 15.

VII

Hardly was the debate on ministers ended, when an incident occurred which went far to justify Robespierre's suspicions. Nine months before, the Foreign Minister had roused a storm by allowing Austrian troops to pass through French territory.[1] Now came a report of a concentration of Austrian forces on the eastern frontier. Robespierre, suddenly discovering that a democratic committee might be just as inefficient as a royal minister, threatened to move for the dismissal of the members of the Diplomatic Committee, whose business it was (Pétion asserted) to watch the movements of foreign powers.

Another reminder of the impossibility of isolating the Revolution was afforded by the recurrent problem of Avignon. Since the debate of November 18, nothing had been done towards that *réunion* which seemed to be the only solution of local disorder. Menou's collection of historical documents was not yet complete. The Diplomatic Committee was still considering its report. More serious, the Avignon question was hopelessly entangled with the church settlement. Under the Civil Constitution of the Clergy the Assembly had imposed a form of oath[2] which had two unhappy results: it split the clergy into two bodies—those who were prepared to take the oath, and those who were not; and it determined the Pope to abandon his neutral attitude, and to anathematize the Revolution.[3] So long as the Papacy held its hand, it was bad policy to press on the Avignon affair. Now that Pius had declared himself, this motive for moderation no longer existed; and Robespierre expressed the general impatience when (April 21) he demanded that the Committee should present its report as soon as possible. Meanwhile, it would be highly injudicious to accede to the Pope's request for troops to restore order at Avignon (April 28). When the report was at last pre-

[1] July 27, 1790 (v. 1/103).
[2] Decreed, November 27; accepted by the King, December 28, 1790; enforced, January 2, 1791.
[3] Papal Briefs of March 10 and April 13.

sented, on April 30, it was found to contain proposals for the annexation of Avignon, and the payment of compensation to the Papacy. Robespierre spoke three times in the five days' debate which followed, and always in favour of *réunion*; but the House, with a moderation remarkable in face of Papal provocation, decided once more for delay.[1] It was not until more than four months later (September 14), when civil war in the church had become inevitable, and foreign war was imminent upon the frontiers, that Robespierre's solution was accepted.

The interest of the Avignon affair, for a biographer of Robespierre, lies in the evidence it affords of the development of his views on church questions. There is no trace, now, of Papalism, or even of any tenderness towards Catholic scruples. The Pope is merely a temporal ruler claiming control over the people of Avignon—a control which nature and reason alike declare to be absurd. The Assembly is warned against the secular evils that may result if Avignon is left in foreign hands; but not against the religious strife which will be caused by a breach with the Papacy. The Pope, no doubt, had already anathematized the Revolution; but the vote of May 4 shows that the quarrel was not yet regarded as irremediable. It follows that Robespierre was now ready, if indeed he had not always been so, to carry the principle of the sovereignty of the people to its logical conclusion in the affairs of the church as well as of the state; and that, though he no more considered himself a Protestant than a Republican, yet he would have no scruples in attacking any prerogative of King or Pope that stood in the way of national self-determination.

Meanwhile, other questions had intervened. On April 23 the king repeated a *démarche* which he had made a year before, and sent assurances to all foreign courts that he was a free agent, sincerely attached to the new Constitution, and to the principles of the Revolution. The Assembly can hardly have known that this declaration was intended to

---

[1] At the Jacobins, the same evening, Robespierre said that, if the vote were not reversed, there would be civil war. (Jac. 2/384.)

cover the king's plans for flight, which were already far advanced, and which the incident of the attempted journey to Saint-Cloud (April 18) precipitated. But when it was proposed that a solemn vote of thanks should be conveyed to the king, Robespierre, speaking ironically, and perhaps with some prescience of Louis' treachery, said that they should not so much thank the king for any fresh adhesion to revolutionary principles, as congratulate him on the continued accordance of his sentiments with those of the nation. Whether or not the House realized this *double entendre*, it might fairly remember, a month later, the warning that it had received.

VIII

On April 27–8 there took place a long-expected debate on the National Guard. It is a curious illustration of the methods of discussion in the Assembly that Robespierre's speech on this subject should have been written in 1790, sent to the press in January, 1791, and delivered in the House in April.[1] Whatever the advantages of this arrangement for political education, it had serious drawbacks in public business; for the speech was so long (it occupied seventy-eight pages of print) that the deputies resented Robespierre's attempt to speak again; whilst (once published), it was so incapable of modification that the orator could not take advantage of those shades of opinion in the House that might have enabled him to win his case. Indeed, one is inclined to ask, did he wish to win it, or only to publish a democratic manifesto?

To Robespierre, as, indeed, to most of his hearers, the National Guard was the nation in arms. Its origin, as a citizen army evolved spontaneously from the events of July, 1789, and representing the defence of Paris against the threats of the crown, had made it a counter-weight rather than an addition to the royal army; and it must now be organized in such a way that it could neither be used oppressively by the Executive Power, nor offer temptations

[1]Corresp. 59.

to some general ambitious to make himself a new tyrant.
Accordingly Robespierre suggests various modifications of
the usual military establishment and routine. The appointment of officers should be taken out of the king's hands,
and their numbers limited. Everything should be done to
discourage professional solidarity (*esprit de corps*) among the
officers, or in the ranks; there should be no 'crack regiments' (*corps d'élite*), no decorations, no wearing of uniform
off parade. If the members of the citizen army want rewards
for their services, let them find them in 'the courage and
virtue of free men, and the sacred cause for which they were
entrusted with arms'. So far, so good. But the crux was still
to come. The Constitutional Committee proposed that the
Guard should be recruited only from amongst the 'active'
citizens. That they should do so was a foregone conclusion;
none the less, Robespierre felt bound, on principle, to
object. The National Guard, he declared, was the sanction behind the laws and the constitution. If the laws and
the constitution are designed in the interests of the whole
nation, it is for the nation as a whole to protect and enforce
them: if they are not, they are bad laws, and a bad constitution. 'Who, after all,' he cried, 'made our glorious revolution? Was it the rich? Was it the powerful? No, it was the
people alone who willed it, and who carried it through; and
that is why the people alone can preserve it'. At this, someone remarked that he was identifying 'the people (*peuple*)'
with the whole body of citizens. 'And so I do,' replied
Robespierre, and went on to claim that it was his opponents
who were trying to divide the nation, not himself. But, in
fact, this was just the weak point in his argument. In the
absence of a French word to describe something that French
history scarcely recognized, he had misused an ambiguous
term. He might have remembered that when, in the famous
debate of July 17, Mirabeau had proposed that the deputies
should call themselves '*représentants du peuple français*', emin-
ent lawyers had objected that the word *peuple* was ambiguous: to the deputies of the Commons it might suggest the
whole nation (Latin *populus*), whilst the clergy and nobility

might take it to mean the lower orders (Latin *plebs*). Robespierre shared Mirabeau's difficulty. He was quite honestly trying to combine two points of view—that from which he had seen the whole nation achieving the Revolution, and that from which he was coming to see that a part of the nation—though by far the largest and most patriotic part—would inherit it. Democracy, he held, began with a rising of the whole middle and lower class—nine-tenths of the nation—against an oppressive regime; but it would end in something not unlike the liquidation of privilege, the dispossession of the rich and powerful, and a dictatorship of the proletariate. Holding this view, he could not really use the word *peuple* in the same sense as his opponents. He and they were entirely at cross purposes; and when, later in the day, he tried to move an amendment to the motion, he was shouted down.[1]

IX

The refusal of political rights to 'passive' citizens was, by now, the deliberate intention of the Moderates who, more and more, ruled the Assembly and the state. On May 9, Le Chapelier followed up his law prohibiting associations of workmen[2] with another designed to deprive the already disfranchised class of its only other peaceable means of influencing public opinion—the right of petition. A series of articles was formulated, making the *droit d'affiche*—the right of posting bills in the streets—a monopoly of the government, disallowing any association, such as a political club, to present petitions to the Assembly, and excluding 'passive' citizens from any form of petition whatsoever. But this time the reactionaries had gone too far. Public indignation was aroused;[3] and Robespierre won assent to his declaration that 'to present petitions is the

---

[1] It was apparently apropos of this debate that Mme Roland regretted Robespierre's habit of speaking impromptu. (*Correspondance*, ed. Perroud, 2/270.)

[2] v. 1/91.

[3] Gouvion, major-general of the National Guard, wrote to Bailly, the Mayor of Paris, stating the extra precautions he had taken to prevent disorder outside the Manège. (Tuetey, 2/4098.)

imprescriptible right of every Frenchman'—a right which they had enjoyed even under despots, as Prussians had under Frederick the Great. God himself, he said, is more merciful than the framers of this bill; 'for he listens to the cry of the unfortunate, and of the sinner'. As a result of this appeal, though the ban on club petitions was not raised, the rights of 'passive' citizens remained untouched, and the *droit d'affiche* was allowed to any citizen who was prepared to put his name to his opinions. The victory was only partial; for another clause of the bill, which Robespierre and Buzot opposed unsuccessfully, gave power to municipalities to control all communal or sectional assemblies. And the real motive of the measure—fear of what the lower orders might do when organized in their sections and societies—remained untouched; for this was, in fact, a form of political action as natural to Frenchmen as parliamentary government is uncongenial. The framers of the bill already foresaw something of the struggle which was so soon to follow between the National Assembly and the Paris Commune. Robespierre himself might have taken warning; for though it was the Jacobin Club which raised him to power in 1792–3, it was his failure to carry the Sections which caused his fall in 1794.

X

This question had hardly been decided when another great debate began, on the French colonial possessions in the West Indies.

It was evident from an early date in the Revolution that the colonial question would raise unusual difficulties. On the one hand, the principles of liberty and equality were of universal application: on the other, how could they be applied to a mixed population of black natives and white settlers, of free men and slaves? Even that would be to understate the difficulties; for there were in the Antilles, at this time, not merely twelve black men to one white, and six slaves to one master, but also three intermediate classes

—*petits blancs*, or white 'beach-combers;' mulattoes, who owned a quarter of the slaves, but who were kept in a state of inferiority by the white settlers; and freed negroes. Nor could the problems of the situation be discussed coolly; for the representatives of the slave system and the white monopoly were already organized in the *Société correspondante des colons français*, or *Club Massiac*; the Moderate reformers controlled the *Comité Colonial*; and the *Amis des noirs*, founded by Brissot, Condorcet, and other Liberals, were working for the immediate abolition of the slave trade, and the ultimate suppression of slavery. Moreover, more than a year before, the Colonial Assemblies, hitherto consisting only of white men, had been thrown open to all land-owners with two years' domicile, and paying taxes, and had been asked to express their views. Thus the question, like that of self-government in India, could not be closed; and the Assembly had either to go back on its rather light-hearted challenge to the vested interests of the white settlers, or to make it good by abolishing slavery, and conferring a constitution.

It is a proof of the reputation Robespierre enjoyed that he should already have been approached by two deputations from the West Indies. On February 1, Leblond and Mathelin, representing Cayenne, asked his support against an instruction of the Colonial Committee which proposed to treat Guiana—a country two months' voyage away, and almost as large as France—as a dependency of Martinique.[1] Two months later (March 31) a deputation from the *ci-devant assemblée de Saint-Marc*, who had been refused a hearing, and thrown into prison, successfully appealed to him to bring their case before the House. It may be inferred that, in his careful way, he was studying the question, and preparing to champion the rights of the native population.

On May 7 the Colonial Committee proposed that it should be left to the *assemblées coloniales* (to which, besides white men, only free mulattoes of the second generation should be admitted) to frame laws for bettering the condi-

[1]Corresp. 56.

tion of the *hommes de couleur* and freed negroes (slaves being omitted). In his first speech on this motion, Robespierre pointed out the obvious injustice of a proposal which withdrew a measure of franchise already granted, and allowed white men to legislate for negroes (May 10). In his second he was roused by the manner in which Moreau de Saint-Méry, a champion of the settlers, spoke of the slaves, to use words which, however creditable to his feelings, did little good to himself, or to his cause. 'A single mention of the word "slave" in any of your decrees,' he said, 'is an admission of your dishonour . . . and tantamount to a constitutional decree of slavery. . . . It were better (he went on) to lose every colony we have (*périssent les colonies*) than to sacrifice our happiness, our glory, and our liberty. It were better, I say, to lose every colony, than to yield to the threats of the colonists, and to legislate in their private interests.' It was easy to twist these words, as Brissot did in his Memoirs, into the expression of a desire to get rid of the colonies at all costs. Robespierre's admirers praised his denunciation of slavery, but shook their heads over his indiscretion. That he felt deeply about the subject is shown by the fact that he left the chair, at the Jacobin Club, the same evening, to make a speech attacking Charles Lameth, and then (such at least is the report of the proceedings) used his powers as chairman to prevent him from making a reply.[1]

Robespierre's third and last intervention in the debate (May 15) was to protest against any further whittling down of the Rights of Man, of which he regarded himself as the champion. The House finally contented itself with giving mulattoes and freed negroes the same political status as white men, whilst entirely excluding slaves. Even the slave trade went on, with Government support, for another two years.[2] And so the matter remained, a singular example of the difference between the theory and practice of Freedom,

[1] *Le petit Robespierre qui avait repris la sonnette* (Jac. 2/414). For the whole debate, v. Hardy in A.R. 12/357; Saintoyant, *La colonisation française pendant la Révolution*; Elicona, *Moreau de Saint-Méry*.
[2] Government payments for the transport of slaves to the French colonies were abolished on August 16, 1792, but still continued, in respect of contracts made before that date, till August, 1793. (R.F. 54/358.)

until Robespierre's plea for justice was at last heard—in 1848.

The immediate and most important result of this debate, for Robespierre, was that he definitely broke with the 'Triumvirate'—Duport, Barnave, and Charles Lameth; and it was characteristic that he should do so for no personal reasons, but upon what was to him a moral principle.

XI

The following day Robespierre's quixotic temper prompted a gesture whose consequences were more serious than could be realized at the time. The subject for discussion was the *corps législatif* to be set up under the new Constitution; and Thouret had begun to give reasons why members of the old legislature should be eligible for the new, when Maximilien rose to a point of order. It was improper, he said, for deputies to discuss this question, for they could not do so impartially, so long as they were themselves eligible to the next legislature. He therefore proposed that they should here and now declare themselves ineligible. The idea that any member of a parliament should voluntarily exclude himself from re-election, and persuade his fellow-members to do the same, has seemed so extraordinary, that historians have suggested all kinds of ulterior motives for Robespierre's action. It has been said that he knew he would not be re-elected, and wanted company in retirement; or that he was tired of the Assembly, and wished to cover his retreat to the Jacobins; or that he intended to give up speaking for writing, and already saw himself in the editor's chair; or that he knew the post of *accusateur public* was his for the asking,[1] or even (it is his friend Desmoulins' suggestion) that he sacrificed himself, to prevent the re-election of such men as Le Chapelier, Desmeuniers, d'André, or Beaumetz. The answer to all these conjectures lies in Robespierre's speech. He is arguing from his own feelings to what he believes to be those of the whole

[1] Augustin Robespierre to Buissart, November 25, 1790 (Corresp. 51).

House. History and conscience (he thinks) both suggest that, when the legislator's work is done, he should retire. Will it be difficult to find another 720 deputies as patriotic as themselves? He does not believe it. Will there be a lack of leaders? The House will be more democratic without them. 'The only leaders we need in a legislative assembly (he declares) are Reason and Truth' (*applause*). As for the retiring members, they will do more good out of the House than in it, by carrying revolutionary principles into every corner of the country.

The effect of these arguments was overwhelming. Robespierre's motion was passed almost unanimously. A royalist deputy demanded the printing, at the public expense, of 'this sublime discourse'. 'The Assembly broke up,' reported the *Moniteur*, 'amid the applause of its own members; and the galleries emptied in silence', as though amazed at the magnanimity of its representatives.[1]

They were probably surprised themselves. Although many of them had outgrown the enthusiasm of 1789, and were finding the political atmosphere, like that of the *Manège*, increasingly mephitic; though there were some few who had no hope of re-election, and welcomed Robespierre's motion as a dignified euthanasia; yet there can have been few unaffected by the loss of public position, and of eighteen *livres* a day. What were they thinking of—their wives doubtless put the question, if they did not ask it themselves—to throw up Paris life and a political career for a mere punctilio?

The wider results of this 'Self-denying Ordinance', though serious, were probably not so momentous as is commonly supposed. During the two and a half years of the Constituent Assembly a new generation had grown up, less simple in holding the revolutionary faith, but more experienced in applying it. The embarrassments into which the Legislative Assembly fell were due less to its personnel than to its circumstances; the old members were absent, but the consequences of their acts remained. On the other hand,

[1] For a full account of the debate, v. Michon, *Adrien Duport*, 206.

the benefits which were expected to accrue from the absence of leaders, and the lessening of party strife, were not realized; and the presence of so many ex-deputies in the country, whilst contributing to the political education of the people, also lessened the prestige of the new Assembly, and created rival authorities in the *Commune*, the clubs, and the press. This need not be an unhealthy development in a country that has political experience, and a flexible constitution; but in the France of 1791, fresh from revolution, and experimenting with its first rigid constitution, it was a real danger.

Far from feeling any doubts about the wisdom of its renunciation, the Assembly proceeded, two days later, again under the guidance of Robespierre, to prohibit re-election altogether until after an interval of two years (May 18). This time, after expounding the political dangers of re-election, Maximilien went on to speak more personally than he had done hitherto about the advantages of retirement. Two years of political activity are enough, he thinks, to satisfy any reasonable ambitions. 'When a man has made good use of them, he can return with a good deal of pleasure to the bosom of his family, to meditate on the principles of legislation more deeply than it is possible to do in the bustle of business, and, above all, to recover that taste for equality which is so easily lost in high office'.

XII

This is, perhaps, the place to mention a discourse that Robespierre delivered at the Jacobin Club (May 11) on the congenial subject of the freedom of the press. He had not spoken on Sieyès' Press Law of January 20, the previous year; indeed, it was so badly received, that it never got beyond a first reading: but he may well have been aware that the first act of a really strong government would be to stop the irresponsible criticisms which, at present, could be broadcast by any publisher or pamphleteer.[1] Accordingly,

[1] For Sieyès' Law, v. Lav. 1/132; for the failure of all attempts to muzzle the press before August, 1792, v. Tourneux in R.F. 25/193.

as one who is still (but perhaps not long to be) a lover of liberty, he regards complete freedom of speech, both private and public, as the chief safeguard against tyranny. That is to say, there must be no preventive censorship, no prohibitions on an author's desk; but he does not deny that it may be necessary to have a remedial censorship, by way of punishing the writer afterwards for 'incendiary, dangerous, or seditious' sentiments. But, even so, who is to be the judge? Or what certainty is there that the Galileos and the Rousseaus will not be persecuted, and the venal scribblers go untouched? Allow perfect liberty, and (he was simple enough to believe) the press will publish nothing that is not 'as pure and serious and healthy as your revolutionary morals'. On the same principle, 'The only competent judge of personal sentiments, and the only legitimate censor of the press, is public opinion'. Freedom of speech is necessary for the criticism of public officials, and even of the law; and no remedy need be provided but the common law-courts, where complaints will be dealt with, not on any technical definition of libel, but on a general consideration of the character of the litigants.

It has not been sufficiently recognized how far Robespierre's views on this matter diverge from the French tradition, and approximate to the English. True, he believed it essential, as did every Frenchman, to call freedom of speech a Right, and to embody it in a Declaration; but his rejection of any kind of preventive censorship, and his reliance, for redress, upon the ordinary courts, are quite out of the main current of French Press Law, which fills more than 300 pages of Dalloz's *Répertoire* with government enactments attempting to control the expression of opinion.[1] One has only to study the history of the censorship under Napoleon, or the Restoration, or the Second Empire, to realize how liberal Robespierre's policy was, and how different public life in France might have been, had it been accepted.

A curious incident, in connexion with this speech, is worth recording, as an instance of Robespierre's absence of

[1] Dicey, *Law of the Constitution*, 248.

mind. The day following its delivery, he drove home at half-past nine in the evening (he could afford such luxuries now), and left the MS. in the cab, together with a treatise on Popular Societies lent him by Lanthenas. He accordingly advertised his loss, offering a reward, and expressing the hope that 'patriots will do their best' to see that the papers are found. The chief sufferer by his carelessness was Lanthenas, who had spent several months copying out his MS., and had to start the work over again.[1]

Within three weeks an incident happened which put Robespierre's views on freedom of speech to the test. On April 18 the king's attempt to leave Paris for Saint-Cloud was prevented by the people, who suspected him of attempted flight. On June 1, Montmorin, the Foreign Minister, called the attention of the Assembly to a passage in the *Moniteur* in which this incident was represented as an attempt of the royal family to escape to Brussels. Members on the Right demanded the punishment of the paper; but Robespierre objected, both on the general ground of liberty, and for the particular reason that they only had Montmorin's word for it that the report was untrue. The House as a whole agreed; and three weeks later their suspicions were justified by the flight to Varennes.

XIII

On May 27–8 Robespierre had his last say on two old topics—the *marc d'argent*, and the purity of elections. On the 30th he was faced with a new question, which touched him closely: should the *code pénal* include a provision for capital punishment? Not many years before, he had seriously considered whether he should give up a judgeship, rather than condemn a criminal to death.[2] But then it was death by torture, and involved the disgrace of the criminal's

---

[1] The advertisement appeared in *L'Orateur du peuple*, Vol. 6, No. 18, p. 152, and is given in A.R. 2/97 (another version, apparently less accurate, from *l'Intermédiaire des chercheurs et curieux*, June 20–30, 1924, is in A.H. 1/462). For Lanthenas' account, v. *Corresp. de Mme Roland* (ed. Perroud), 2/280.

[2] v. 1/39.

family: now torture had been abolished,[1] murderers were to be decapitated like gentlemen, and he had himself conducted a campaign against the incrimination of their families. He might therefore have been excused if he had changed his mind, and supported the death penalty in the single case in which it was proposed to retain it, *viz.*, when 'a party leader was declared a rebel by decree of the Legislative Body'. But Robespierre's stiff mind could admit no exception to a moral rule; and he proceeded to prove, with examples drawn from the history of Greece, Rome, Russia, and Japan, that capital punishment was unjust, irreparable, degrading, and ineffective. The House, however, thought otherwise, and retained the death penalty for political crimes, thus opening the door to the Revolutionary Tribunal, the Reign of Terror, and the recurrent proscriptions, which, up to quite recent times, have given to party struggles in France the likeness of civil war. The irony of the situation—that the opponent of capital punishment in 1791 should demand the King's death in 1793, and sanction the executions of 1794—is obvious enough now. But a man of principle, though he can be trusted for a routine consistency, is, after all, more liable than any other to radical changes of moral allegiance. There is no conduct so incalculable as that of a fanatic.

The debate on capital punishment was still proceeding, when, on May 31, the President read to the House a letter which he had received from the abbé Raynal, criticizing the work of the Assembly, and demanding the restoration of the royal prerogative. This octogenarian survivor of the Prophetic age, whose *Histoire philosophique*[2] had earned him one term of banishment under Louis XV, seemed to be provoking another; but Robespierre, who knew something of the vanity of authors, and had no wish to encourage martyrdom, suggested that Raynal's letter might be excused,

[1]Lewes (131) gives an instance of 'breaking on the wheel' as late as August, 1790.
[2]*Histoire philosophique et politique des . . . Européens dans les deux Indes*, the most advanced passages of which were due to Diderot. His present letter was encouraged by Malouet, and largely written by Clermont-Tonnerre. (Fletcher's ed. of Carlyle, 1/73.)

as the ramblings of a dotard. The Assembly need do nothing but reassert its principles, and go on with its work. The House accepted this wise advice, and resumed its ordinary business. No one knew that Raynal was the favourite reading of a Norman girl who was to murder Marat.[1]

XIV

Ever since the Nancy affair, the condition of the army had caused concern to the leaders of the Revolution. What, they asked, was the use of destroying aristocracy and royalism in the civil government of the country, if they were still rampant in its armed defences? The Jacobins, as was nowadays becoming the custom, first took up the question. On June 2 and 8, Anthoine and Roederer denounced royalism among the officers of the army. Robespierre was for drastic remedies: he would dismiss them all, and appoint new men. 'The man who does not wish or advise their dismissal,' he declared, 'is a traitor'.[2] But he feared militarism as much as royalism. 'There must be no attempt to turn our soldiers into machines.'[3]

When the question came up in the Assembly two days later, it was proposed to restore discipline in the army, not by the dismissal of officers, but by providing better training (*cantonnements*), imposing severe penalties for disorder, and demanding from every officer a written undertaking to obey and respect the Constitution. Robespierre's attack on this plan, all the more rhetorical because it was partly extemporized, won few votes, and a chance of 'purging' the army was thrown away. The creation of the National Guard had, no doubt, put it out of the power of the old army to reimpose a royalist regime. But, if Robespierre had had his way, there might have been no Bouillé or Choiseul to cover the king's flight to Varennes, no Swiss officers to defend

---

[1]A.R. 6/309. André Chénier adopted a similar tone when answering Raynal's pamphlet in the *Moniteur* of June 2 and 5 (*ibid.*). Even Malouet praised this 'remarkable improvisation' of Robespierre's (Michon, *Adrien Duport*, 220).

[2]Some enthusiast demanded that 'this maxim should be inscribed in capital letters in every corner of the Hall' (*applause*).

[3]Jac. 2/490.

the Tuileries, no Dillon to be murdered by his runaway troops; and that process might have been speeded up, by which the armies of the Directory and Empire were officered by men of their own class, co-heirs of the Revolution.[1]

Robespierre spoke only once more before the flight of the king, and that, too, was on a military question. The municipality of Brie-Comte-Robert had complained of the conduct of a detachment of *chasseurs* quartered upon the town. Robespierre took up their case, and called for an inquiry (June 18). His rather inquisitorial manner prompted one of the deputies to ask whether he was already practising for the office of Public Prosecutor, to which he had just been elected. He retorted that it was a matter of public interest. But nothing was done, even when, two months later, one of the victims of the soldiery died in prison (August 6). It would seem that Robespierre had good reason for his dread of militarism.

By the middle of June it seemed likely that the Constitution would soon be finished, and that the country would be asked to elect its new Legislative Assembly. It was proposed that the primary elections (of electors) should be held on June 12–25, and the secondary elections (of deputies) on July 5. On June 19, the Jacobins listened to an address to the electoral assemblies which Robespierre had drawn up at the request of the Correspondence Committee of the club. The electors, he tells them, will be paid (*cheers*), on account of their loss of time. Their duty will be to choose candidates primarily for their patriotism (*vertu*); but they must beware of 'deceptive appearances', and 'reject the false friends of liberty'.

XV

It is impossible to read through the debates of April-June, 1791, without feeling that Robespierre had gone far

---

[1]Pio, an Italian who had been given French citizenship, wrote to *Révolutions de France et de Brabant* (No. 81, June 15), saying that Robespierre deserved a civic crown for the stand he made on this occasion. (Hamel, 1/473, Walter, 1/277.)

towards realizing his ambition, and filling Mirabeau's place. In a series of great issues—legal, constitutional, diplomatic, military, and colonial—his carefully argued and eloquently expressed speeches had become a regular feature of public business; and he was regarded not only in the House, but also in Paris and in the provinces, as the chief exponent of revolutionary progress. If his devotion to principles sometimes made him intransigent, or difficult to work with, there were also occasions when his detachment gave him an uncanny insight, and a power of prophecy. If he was often in a minority in the Assembly, he as often expressed the views of the majority in the streets. If, in minor matters, he showed the gifts of a parliamentary tactician, it was by refusing to accept compromises in major matters that he won a reputation for political rectitude. There were some more brilliant men in public life, and many with more attractive qualities; but probably none whose future success could more certainly be foreseen. For it was founded, not only on intense application and self-culture, but also on self-identification with a society, and with a cause. 'If Robespierre's voice seems suddenly to have grown louder, it is because it is no longer an individual who is speaking, but a whole people—the members of the Jacobin clubs'.[1] Royalist pamphleteers might dub him disparagingly 'the candle of Arras', and contrast him with Mirabeau, 'the torch of Provence',[2] but his advance was already being noted, and his future greatness predicted, by foreign observers. 'The man held of least account,' wrote an English traveller, 'by Mirabeau, by Lafayette, and even by the Lameths, and all the Orleans faction, will soon be of the first consideration. He is cool, measured, and resolved. He is in his heart Republican, honestly so, not to pay court to the multitude, but from an opinion that it is the very best, if not the only form of government which men ought to admit. He is a stern man, rigid in his principles, plain, unaffected in his manners, no foppery in his dress, certainly above corruption, despising wealth, and with nothing of the volatility of

[1]Michelet, 3/4.   [2]Fleischmann, 111; Bachaumont, *Mémoires* (Sept. 2, 1765).

a Frenchman in his character. . . . I watch him very closely every night. I read his countenance with eyes steadily fixed on him. He is really a character to be contemplated; he is growing every hour into consequence'.[1]

XVI

How far can the gaps of Robespierre's political life, during the first six months of 1791, be filled up from his correspondence, or from other sources of evidence?

The extant letters during this period fall into three groups—private letters of January–February; correspondence with public bodies during April–June; and another group of private letters belonging to June.

The private correspondence shows several aspects of Robespierre, the public man. Daunou, a prominent Oratorian, asks for his help in securing the position of his Order under recent ecclesiastical legislation. One of the troubles of his busy life, Robespierre replies, is that he cannot send immediate answers even to the letters that interest him most, such as Daunou's. 'But the name of the Oratory recalls images and memories which will always be dear'; and he will do what he can. There is no clericalism in the letter, and nothing anti-clerical; simply the courtesy of equals who have memories in common, and who might become friends.[2]

A trace of the old artificiality of *Rosati* days appears in the reply to Mme Guyard, who had asked to be allowed to paint Robespierre's portrait. 'They tell me,' he writes, 'that the Graces wish to paint a likeness of me. I should be quite unworthy of such kindness, if I did not keenly appreciate its value. Unluckily a surfeit of business worries—or it may be some jealous deity—has hitherto prevented my expressing to them all the gratitude I feel; and the respect that is their due must be prefaced by the apologies I owe. I beg them accordingly to accept the one, and to inform me of the day and hour when I may present the other.' That is neatly put; and it would be pleasant to have the rest of the story.

[1] W. A. Miles to Pye, March 1, 1791.
[2] Corresp. 55; A.R. 14/428; R.H.R.F. 4/114.

It is known that Mme Labille-Guyard exhibited in the Salon of 1791 thirteen portraits of public men of all parties, and that none of them was more admired than *No.* 34, that of *l'Incorruptible*—a pastel, preserved only in Drouhin's popular engraving.[1]

Another portrait of Robespierre hung there too, as we know from a private letter, in which it is thus described: '*No.* 215. M. Boze: Portrait of Robespierre, in pastel: a marvellous likeness. Everyone, my friend, stands in front of this worthy (*respectable*) man; some offer their tribute in phrases, calling him "the incorruptible legislator", or "the friend of mankind"; and some in verses, and more verses. Among others I noticed these lines, modelled on some in the tragedy of *Tancred*:

> "To every pure-born heart how dear
> Is Maximilien Robespierre!"

M. Boze is exhibiting other portraits of little merit; but, however bad they were, one would always be grateful to him for so fine a rendering of our greatest man (*nôtre premier homme*), whom he has seen, whom he has addressed, and whom he has actually touched. Oh! M. Boze, what happy days you must have spent in his company!' Such sentimentalities are sufficient proof of the position Robespierre held in public esteem in the summer of 1791.[2]

The letter of February 14 to Desmoulins, written two months after his marriage to Lucille Duplessis, suggests other thoughts. 'May I remind M. Camille Desmoulins,' it begins, 'that neither the fine eyes nor the engaging qualities of the charming Lucile are sufficient reason for not advertising my work on the National Guard?' There is a trace of spitefulness here that might have warned Desmoulins how lightly personal claims would weigh with this man, com-

[1]Corresp. 58; Fleischmann, 110; Charavay, *Assemblée électorale de Paris*, 2/xxxiv. Mme Guyard afterwards married the painter Vincent, who gave this letter to Lord Egerton, and so it reached the British Museum. The reference to 'the Graces' gains point from the fact that Boilly, who painted Robespierre at Arras about 1783, was known as *le peintre des Grâces*.

[2]R.H.R.F. 3/131. Boze was court painter to Louis XVI. The portrait is supposed to have been in the possession of Albertine Marat, who presented it to the *Cabinet des Étampes* in Paris (A.R. 1/645).

pared with public duty. Within little more than three years the writer would be signing warrants for the arrest of his friend, and of his friend's wife, and regarding it as a patriotic act to send them both to the guillotine.[1]

Mme Guyard was not the only one of the Graces who admired Robespierre. Jeanne-Marguerite de Chalabre was a well-to-do woman of thirty-nine, with some pretensions to a title,[2] who opened a correspondence with him about this time. The first extant letter is one in which she thanks him for a copy of his speech on juries. She wants to talk to him about the political situation, and tries to tempt him to come to dinner. 'You needn't fear,' she says, a 'big party of mug-wumps: there will be nobody here but a very few—really a very few—old friends, and all of them good patriots'. Robespierre seems to have got out of this invitation; for not long afterwards she asks him again, allowing him to choose his own time. After this, there is a long gap in the correspondence; and the next letter shows the lion-hunter still pursuing her prey with flattery and admiration, in spite of his admonitions 'not to be so enthusiastic'. The only other published letter shows that, two months later again, Mme de Chalabre was attending the Assembly to hear Robespierre speak, and was on friendly terms with his hosts, the Duplays. It is not surprising that in July, 1794, she was involved in his fall, and spent nearly a year in prison. Nothing more remains, except a forlorn letter in the National Archives, in which she abjures her old friend.[3]

XVII

An important group of letters shows Robespierre's relations with several public bodies.

[1] Corresp. 59. Robespierre was not the only one of Desmoulins' friends who thought his marriage was distracting him from his political duties. (A.R. 8/567.)

[2] Fleischmann, 226.

[3] Corresp. 60, 61, 115, 123. Mathiez (*Conspiration*, 156) accepts the story that Robespierre visited her at Vanves; but it does not follow, as Sénart asserts (*Révélations*, 150) that she was his 'Cerberus', through whom many who had requests to make of him forwarded their communications. Fleischmann (236) prints another (undated) document from the Fillon Collection as a letter from Mme de Chalabre to Robespierre; but internal evidence is against this ascription.

After his intervention in the Avignon debate, and his speeches on the National Guard, both matters of special concern to them, the patriots of Marseille came to regard Robespierre as a possible champion of their own interests; so that, when Mirabeau died, the Municipality wrote, asking for his help against a decree extending the powers of the royal commissioners at Aix, and infringing on the departmental administration.[1] Unfortunately, as is explained in his letter of May 24, the matter came up in the House at a time when he was absent through illness or overwork. He apologizes for this, with a politeness that verges on flattery. There is no title, he says, that he would sooner bear than that of defender of Marseille. Its cause is the cause of all good Frenchmen. 'You and I,' he ends, 'will continue to watch over liberty and our country, and to protect them with all our power in these critical times'.[2] Another letter from the Mayor (May 27) is answered towards the end of July, with apology for delay, and with fresh expressions of devotion; and on August 10 he writes again in the same strain, enclosing a copy of his *Adresse aux français*.[3] By this time he was in correspondence with the Aix Commissioners, and hearing their side of the case, which did not agree with that of his clients at Marseille.[4] In January, 1792, the Club Thubaneau of Marseille placed a portrait of Robespierre beside those it already had of Mirabeau and Paoli; and when the Marseillais commissioners, Loys and Barbaroux, arrived in Paris in February, 1792, their first visits were to Pétion and to Robespierre, whom they reported to be as fond of Marseille as though it were his native town.[5]

Robespierre had won the respect of the Versailles patriots, as of those of Marseille, by his willingness to champion their interests in the Assembly. They had already rewarded his help in the matter of a disputed election by

---

[1]cp. 1/107. A.R. 15/113; Corresp. 65.　　　　　　[2]Corresp. 70.
[3]Corresp. 88.　　　　　　　　　　　　　　　　　　[4]A.H. 63/260.

[5]Barbaroux, *Correspondance*, February 13, 1792; Chabaud in A.R. 15/113. Robespierre's championship of Marseille was not forgotten. As late as December, 1851, one of those proscribed by Napoleon III proposed to erect on the Pic du Canigon a tower inscribed with his name, to be *le phare du Midi révolutionnaire*. (R.H. 134/148.)

making him a judge in the local tribunal.[1] On October 8 he accepted an invitation to become a member of the Versailles Jacobin club. On February 17 he sent them his speech on the National Guard: the club so approved of it that they urged their affiliated societies to support its proposals. Later, he sent them also his speeches on juries and on the *marc d'argent*; and, in reply to a request for information about the political situation at Saint-Omer, gave a testimonial to the good character of the Jacobin club there.[2]

Of greater interest and importance is the long letter of June 13, in which Robespierre explains to his friends at Versailles the motives which have led him to give up the judgeship he had held there for the last eight months, and to accept the post of *accusateur public* in the criminal tribunal of the Department of Paris. 'My appointment,' he writes, 'has at once surprised and alarmed me. It burdens me with functions that could not be less congenial to my tastes and disposition. It involves me in a whirlpool of delicate, difficult, and momentous affairs, at a moment when I am exhausted by an accumulation of tasks and anxieties. I was hoping for a position in which I might get some time to myself, and devote myself to the study and exposition of the great truths which underlie the laws and the policy befitting a free people'. If he had been ambitious for a further term of public service, he goes on, he would have preferred re-election to some future legislature. The post at Versailles offered a peaceful alternative. But it was his duty to accept the more urgent and dangerous post at the strategic centre of the Revolution. He would like, nevertheless, to keep in touch with the Versailles club, and will attend their meetings whenever he can. All this is explained at a length, and with a solemnity, which sounds disproportionate to the occasion, and which (one feels) has its origin less in the courtesy due to Robespierre's friends at Versailles than in his intense interest in himself. The seminary influence is still alive in him. The scruples he urges are those of a

[1] v. 1/106.
[2] Vaillandet in A.H. 8/49; Corresp. 63, 72.

moral theologian: his confidences are the whispers of the confessional.

As a pendant to this letter, under the same date, appears Robespierre's formal leave-taking, forwarded through the *procureur-général-syndic* of the Department.[1]

Robespierre's correspondence with Toulon runs a course parallel to that with Marseille. He had won the regard of the citizens so long ago as December 14, 1789, by upholding their action against the officers of the naval garrison. He had defended them again in the debates of June–August, 1790.[2] They rewarded him for these services, towards the end of that year, or early in 1791, by inscribing his name on the civic roll of honour (*dans les fastes de la ville*), and in the following June by giving him the title of *citoyen de Toulon*; for, as they said, 'what more perfect model of public spirit could we set before our citizens than yourself?' Robespierre replied with compliments, and presentation copies of his latest speech. He explains, as he did to the Marseillais, that only illness had prevented him attending to their interests on May 21; and he exhorts them, as the *magistrat vertueux* of a people worthy of freedom (for he has just been made Public Prosecutor) to continue firm in their support of liberty and the constitution. A month later he thanks the Toulon Jacobins for the *titre glorieux* they have bestowed upon him—presumably that of honorary member of their club; and finally, on the day on which he sends a copy of his *Adresse aux français* to the Marseillais, he encloses another to his friends at Toulon, and receives a complimentary reply.[3]

Robespierre's election as *accusateur public* took place on June 10, and was one of the last acts of the electoral assembly

[1]Corresp. 77–8 (June 13). The appointment as *accusateur public* appears in the *Moniteur* of June 19, but was doubtless settled before. The Versailles club took Robespierre's resignation well, applauding his speech on the army (July 7), supporting his stand against the Feuillants (after July 17), thanking him for his *Adresse aux français* (August 11), and keeping up a friendly correspondence with him (Vaillandet in A.H. 8/54).

[2]v. 1/98.

[3]Corresp. 64, 66, 67, 74, 80, 85, 91, 92; Parès, *Robespierre, citoyen de Toulon*. Another copy of the *Adresse* was sent to the Jacobins of Toulouse, and read there amidst 'a religious silence' (A.H. 3/584).

of 781 business men and lawyers, representing the 'active' citizens of Paris, which, since November 18, 1790, had appointed most of the personnel—judges, curés, and departmental administrators—of the new regime.[1] He was chosen by a large majority. D'André, the runner-up, was elected to the office of *substitut*, but refused it;[2] whilst Duport, who had been elected to the presidency of the court on the 9th, resigned, as he had threatened to do, rather than work with Robespierre. These refusals were expressed in terms which suggested that Robespierre stood for an attack upon the security of person and property, and was therefore unfit to hold his new post. D'André's objections were honest, but Duport's real reasons were found in private animosity: he had, it seems, never forgiven Robespierre for his proposals of May 16 and 18, or for his attitude towards the Colonial question.[3]

XVIII

There remain a few private letters belonging to June, 1791. Joseph Lebon, formerly *professeur* of Rhetoric at the Oratorian college at Beaune, was now 'constitutional' vicar of Vernois. He had written to the Assembly on November 2, 1790, saying that he was destitute, and asking that the decrees on clerical pensions might be amended to cover his own case.[4] As a fellow-countryman and acquaintance of Robespierre, he addresses him (June 3) in the second person singular, and mixes familiarity with flattery. '*Courage, mon brave ami,*' he begins; 'you have only one more step to take (he is thinking of the imminent dissolution of the Assembly), and you will leave political life almost unique among our legislators, as incorrupt as you entered it'. Knowing how busy Robespierre is, he has hesitated to write before, but now urges him to revive the proposal for clerical marriage which he had first made a year ago.[5] 'Secure,' he

[1]Charavay in R.F 18/377.
[2]D'André's Letter of June 15, 1791 (Charavay, *Assemblée électorale de Paris*, 1/612).
[3]Michon, *Adrien Duport*, 221.   [4]R.F. 64/229.   [5]v. 1/85.

says, 'the final destruction of that execrable requirement to cheat the demands of nature, which has hitherto been the ruin of morality and of the laws'. Besides, he adds, evidently with some feeling, a bachelor priest is taxed at a higher rate than a married one. He re-opens the letter to ask whether, under the *marc d'argent* decree, he is eligible for election to the new Assembly, and to suggest that, if he is not, a decree should be put through, qualifying priests who possess private means (*un patrimoine d'environ* 2000 *francs*).[1]

There will be other letters from Lebon. Their increasing familiarity and vulgarity cannot but have given rise, in Robespierre's fastidious mind, to some doubts as to the company he was keeping: but he believed the man honest and useful, and supported him, during his later exploits as a terrorist at Arras, to the last possible moment.[2]

He is on happier terms with his *cher et joieux ami*, Buissart, to whom he writes at once (June 12) with the news of his appointment as Public Prosecutor, mentioning the intrigues which nearly prevented his election, and his dislike of giving up his post at Versailles. 'I am destined,' he says, 'to lead a stormy career. I must follow it out to the end—until I have made the last great sacrifice to my country. I am in a constant state of over-work. I cannot exchange ideas with you as often as I should like to do'.

There follow two letters from a more distinguished friend, though not such a faithful one. Pétion first writes (June 15) to say that he has been nominated in place of Duport to the presidency of the criminal court, and that Buzot has replaced d'André. He would have come to see Robespierre, he adds, 'but I said to myself, I shan't find him in; he is always out to dinner'—a note on Robespierre's habits which confirms Charlotte's reminiscences.[3]

The second letter is undated, but clearly belongs to the

[1]Corresp. 73. The position of the clergy under the franchise laws was obscure. Aulard (66) can only quote Robespierre himself as suggesting that they ranked as 'active' citizens.

[2]Jacob, *Joseph Lebon*; cp. *Index*.

[3]Corresp. 79, Charlotte, 218. A letter from Robespierre to Réal (Corresp. 82) assures him that Buzot is legally qualified for election. Cp. Charavay *Assemblée électorale de Paris*, 613.

same period, when, as *accusateur public*, Robespierre had the supervision of the Paris prisons. Pétion writes, asking leave for one of his family, his friend, and his landlord, to supply medical necessities to poor prisoners—a reminder that even in these urgent times politics and philanthropy breathed the same air.[1]

XIX

The Robespierre of June, 1791, has not only more authority as a speaker and politician, but also more social poise and confidence, than six months ago. He can write as tactfully to an artist as to an ecclesiastic, to a journalist as to a *procureur-général-syndic*. He knows how to accept a citizen-ship, and how to avoid an invitation to dinner. Although he is overwhelmed with his work at the Jacobins, and in the Assembly, and must sit up far into the night composing and correcting a series of great speeches, yet he finds time to write a letter of over a thousand words to save the feelings of a suburban committee. He has, indeed, had at least one week's illness, and is wearing himself out by his con-scientiousness. He has been looking forward—and his friends with him—to the speedy completion of the Consti-tution, and to the dissolution of the Assembly, which will enable him to retire for a while into private life. Then comes the call to the judgeship in Paris, which he cannot well refuse, if only because his brother is still out of work, and which, without the strain of Parliamentary life, is not incon-sistent with some pursuit of study and authorship.

Such is the future he is planning, when the king's flight to Varennes, on June 21, transforms the whole political scene, prolongs the labours of the Assembly, postpones the Constitution, and drowns all private claims in the urgency of a national crisis. The opportunity for retirement passed, and never returned.

[1]Corresp. 83.

CHAPTER VI

THE SAVIOUR OF THE JACOBIN CLUB

(JUNE–NOVEMBER, 1791)

I

THE flight to Varennes probably had a more decisive influence than any other single event upon the course of the French Revolution. Earlier incidents—the Tennis Court oath, the fall of the Bastille, or the march of the women to Versailles—had directed its torrent in a certain direction. Now, for a year and a half, the revolution had flowed, not without an occasional spate or drought, along a fairly defined channel, and the voyager might well think himself within sight of the sea. Varennes was a sudden land-fall, damming up the stream, so that it broke through, a year later, with redoubled force, and irreparable disaster.

The monarchy, which had hitherto seemed the one familiar element in the State, the solitary link between the old France and the new, was now to become a hostile and almost foreign power, standing between the country and its destiny. The Assembly, which had come to regard itself as inspired, and supposed its laws written on tables of stone, was soon to be discredited as a middle-class caucus, and its Constitution dashed to pieces. The common people, gradually disillusioned as to all they had hoped for from a peaceful revolution, were to turn against their old representatives, and drive their new leaders into war, and a Republic.

In the course of this fourteen months' turmoil the Constituent Assembly came to an end, and the Legislative Assembly took its place. This change, with the corresponding break in Robespierre's political life, affords the first convenient halting-place; but there is no real breach in the continuous development of events towards the catastrophe of August, 1792.

II

On June 20 Robespierre had been away from Paris—perhaps visiting his Jacobin friends at Versailles. He knew no more than others did of the king's intention to escape; if he guessed that there were plans, he can have had no idea that they were so advanced. When, early on the morning of the 21st, the news went round that the royal family had fled during the night, and crowds began to flow towards the Tuileries; when, at nine o'clock, Robespierre heard in the Assembly the official version of the flight, and the accusing document that Louis had left behind; he shared the general feelings of anger and alarm; but he played his part in that calm and dignified behaviour of the deputies which did so much to prevent public panic, and to suggest the possibility of a French Republic. He had, however, by this time, become deeply suspicious of the Constitutionalists, and foresaw that the unusual docility of the House might be exploited in party interests. It was significant that, whereas Louis' memoir showed that he had fled deliberately, Bailly maintained that he had been 'carried off by the enemies of the state'; and that, whilst the king was approaching the frontier, and appealing for foreign aid, Paris was still garrisoned by royal troops, whose allegiance to the Assembly was by no means sure. Robespierre's first act, on hearing of the king's capture at Varennes, was to propose the award of civic crowns to the two citizens who had arrested him, and to Mangin, the local surgeon who had brought the news. But when, later in the evening, Thouret moved that all who had helped in the flight should be declared traitors, and that any who showed disrespect to the royal authority should be thrown into prison, he at once objected to such measures as prejudging the character of the flight, and insulting the people. That night, at the Jacobins, he showed more clearly what was in his mind. He believed that the ministers, and some others who, like Lafayette, passed for patriots, had known more than they should about the king's plans, and were exploiting the situation in the interests of reaction.[1] But that was not all; for he had come to think that there was a conspiracy afoot, not only against France, but against himself—'one man of honesty and courage prepared to unmask their plots, one man who thinks so lightly of life that he fears neither poison nor the sword, and would be supremely happy if his death contributed to the freedom of his fatherland'. Upon which (it is reported) Desmoulins cried, 'We would all give our lives to save yours!'; and the whole audience of 800 rose, and took an oath to defend Robespierre's life.

With some speakers it might be possible to regard such words as a theatrical gesture, and no more. But although Robespierre was self-centred enough to like to picture himself as a martyr, he was also too shrewd to cry 'Wolf!' unless some such animal was really in sight. And this strain in his speeches soon becomes so common as to force the inquiry whether it may have had some ground in actual fact.

For more than a year now Robespierre had been the chief butt of the aristocratic party. He speaks in April, 1790, of 'the hatred with which the aristocrats regard me', and he is afraid of their opening his correspondence.[2] Augustin's letters are full of alarms and gloomy anticipations, not only whilst he is at Arras, and imagining the worst of Paris, but also when he is living in the capital, and in constant touch with his brother.[3] This atmosphere of danger seems to dissipate itself for a while in the early months of 1791, when Robespierre has won a secure position in the country and in the House. But the king's flight may very well have seemed to him the unmasking of a fresh and more serious attack—a definite attempt to stop the Revolution, in which

[1] On June 26 an exiled Belgian patriot, named Van Miest, reported to Robespierre from London that the news of the king's flight had delighted the aristocrats, and that they were in despair at his recapture (Corresp. 81).

[2] Corresp. 27, 30.

[3] Corresp. 31, 33, 34, 40, 51. Several popular leaders had been challenged to duels (Lewes, 161).

the lives of all democratic leaders might be at stake.[1] Was he so far wrong? If the king had succeeded in reaching Mont-médy, and placing himself in the hands of Bouillé, the *émigrés*, and the Austrian army, could the thing have ended, and was it meant to end, in anything less than an armed march on Paris, the dissolution of the Assembly, and the proscription of Robespierre and his friends? 'Mr. Robes-pierre, the great *Dénonciateur*,' writes Lord Gower on July 22, 'is about to be *dénoncé* himself'; and a certain Dumas de Labrousse was reported to have said, on June 21, that he had gibbets ready to hang the members of the Assembly, and of the Jacobins, especially Barnave and Robespierre, whom he oddly regarded as 'two Protestants who had destroyed religion'.[2]

Nor were Robespierre's alarms at this crisis peculiar to himself. Such, indeed, is the impression given by Mme Roland's *Memoirs*, written in the prison to which Robes-pierre's party had consigned her, and in a mood in which she was not likely to remember her early weakness for the successful young Liberal. 'I had been struck,' she says, 'with the terror which seemed to obsess him on the day of the King's flight to Varennes. . . . I found him that afternoon at Pétion's house, saying in a tone of alarm that the royal family would never have taken this step unless they had in Paris a body of supporters ready to organize a massacre (*Saint-Barthélemy*) of patriots, and that he did not expect to outlive the day '. But Mme Roland conveniently forgot that she had written a very different account of this incident to her friend Bancal des Issarts only a few hours afterwards. 'Yesterday evening,' the letter runs, 'a number of us met, including Robespierre, and agreed that our lives hung by a thread (*nous nous considérions sous le couteau*). Each of us was preoccupied with the question, how best to serve the public weal before losing our lives, as we might in some unforeseen massacre '.[3] The Cordeliers club took the matter so seriously

[1] Robespierre had inside information as to the wholesale and arbitrary arrests which were made at the time of the 'massacre'. (Corresp. 97.)

[2] Tuetey, 2/2681.

[3] *Corresp.* (ed. Perroud) 2/306. Her letters at this time are full of praise of Robespierre.

that it sent a guard to protect Robespierre on the night of June 21.[1] It was stated on July 10 that a secret society had put a price on his head, and that he was known to have made his will, and to be expecting martyrdom at any moment. The same alarm was felt in the provinces. The Jacobin Club at Marseille wrote saying that if Robespierre or Danton, those 'apostles of liberty', were threatened, the Marseillais would fly to their defence.[2]

There was sufficient reason, then, for the scene at the Jacobins on the evening of June 21; and there is no need to accuse Robespierre either of striking theatrical attitudes, or of being the victim of a 'persecution complex'. The most that it seems reasonable to allow is that the strain of overwork and anxiety from which he was suffering may have led him to exaggerate the danger.[3]

III

Whether or not Lafayette and the Moderate leaders of the Assembly—Bailly, Barnave, Duport, the Lameths, and their friends—were privy to the king's flight, they certainly behaved as though they had made up their minds from the first how they were going to use it. From the first —witness Bailly's speech of June 21—they represented the flight as an abduction (*enlèvement*).[4] As soon as Louis' recapture was known, Thouret was ready (June 23) with a decree that suggested his rehabilitation, as though he had done nothing improper for a king. And such was, in fact, to be the official policy. No doubt this line of action could be defended in the national interests. The moderates argued that Louis restored would be a hostage for peace, whereas Louis dethroned would be a pretext for foreign intervention, and war.[5] But they had another motive which came

---

[1] Mathiez, *Club des Cordeliers*, 47.　　　　　　[2] Jac. 2/549.

[3] Dumont is romancing when he says that Robespierre hid himself for two days, and meditated flight to Marseille. (*The Great Frenchman*, 196.)

[4] Even the Jacobin Club wrote to its affiliated societies that *le roi, égaré par des suggestions criminelles, s'est éloigné de l'Assemblée nationale*. (R.F. 22/107.)

[5] v. a passage from *La Correspondance nationale*, quoted by Mathiez, 129.

nearer home. They had made up their minds that a revenge-
ful people was more to be feared than a disloyal king. Louis
was to be exculpated and restored, under the supervision of
the Constitutional party, to save the country from republicanism. Robespierre, with his usual clear-headedness, saw
through this policy, and set himself to oppose it. When
Duport proposed (June 26) that the evidence of the king
and queen, for the judicial inquiry into their flight, should
be taken by commissioners specially chosen from among
the deputies, he objected, not so much to an attempt to
save the royal feelings, as to the opportunity afforded to
misrepresent the facts. The king and queen, he said, were
at this moment no more than any other citizen and his wife,
owing an account of their conduct to the nation; and they
ought to conform to the ordinary procedure. When Muguet,
a fortnight later (July 13), in the official report on what
was now called 'Bouillé's conspiracy', proposed to indict
Bouillé and Fersen (who was well out of the country) before
the Supreme Court, but to pass over the king's responsibility, on the ground that he was beyond the reach of the
law, Robespierre boldly challenged the whole idea of inviolability. First, he says, the maxim, 'The king can do no
wrong' (such is his meaning, though he does not use the
English terms) cannot apply to private acts of the king,
but only to those for which a minister is held responsible.
But, secondly, if the king is answerable, there may still be
no court by which he can be tried. In that case, he does not
shrink from a dangerous alternative. 'The Law of Nature,'
he says, 'is prior to society, and teaches men that, when the
laws do not avenge their wrongs, they have the right to
avenge themselves'. Thirdly, Robespierre refuses to allow
distinctions of guilt between the criminals of June 21: either
they must all be convicted, from Louis XVI to Mme
Tourzel, or all discharged. Speaking again on the 15th, he
expounded his view of the kind of evidence needed in such
a trial. 'If there were actual proof of Monsieur's guilt,' he
said, 'there would be no question about returning a true
bill. . . . But it is not necessary to have proofs of guilt, in

order to commit a man for trial; suspicions (*indices*) are enough.'

The deputies, in the full swing of their reaction against the popular temper, paid little attention to these remarks: had they done so, they might have realized what a short step it might be from such doctrines to a king's trial, a Revolutionary Tribunal, and a Prairial Law. As for Robespierre himself, outvoted on July 14, laughed at on the 15th, and shouted down on the 23rd, he made no further attempt to speak in the House till August 6.[1]

IV

Indeed, his position, not only in the Assembly, but also at the club, was at this time full of difficulties. Republicanism had almost suddenly become a political issue, threatening to overturn the flimsy constitutionalism of Bailly and Barnave; and Robespierre, who never cared to hurry his decisions, had to make up his mind about it. It may be true that on June 21, when Pétion and Brissot maintained that the king's flight spelt the doom of the monarchy, and that they had better prepare public opinion for a republic, 'Robespierre, with his habitual grimace, and biting his nails, asked, What is a republic?'[2] Even if he were prepared for the idea—and perhaps he was not—it was certainly one that needed defining. The word *république* had not yet lost its Latin meaning, or its Roman associations. A Frenchman of the eighteenth century could talk of a ' monarchical republic', or of a 'republican monarchy', meaning in either case a state in which autocracy was tempered by some degree of popular representation; and republicanism in 1791 would be judged less by its theories than by its acts. When, therefore, Robespierre maintained that the king's flight had destroyed the constitutional safeguards of the crown, when he demanded the trial of the royal family and

[1]On the 14th he had unsuccessfully opposed Desmeuniers' proposal for the temporary suspension of the king's executive powers. Mme Roland was enthusiastic for the stand he made against the 'coalition' (*Corresp.* ed. Perroud 2/328).
[2]Mme Roland's *Mémoires* (ed. Barrière), 255.

its accomplices before the ordinary courts of the land, it was easy for his enemies to accuse him of republicanism.

His formal answer to the charge was made in a speech at the Jacobins on July 13. 'I have been accused,' he said, 'in the bosom of the Assembly, of being a republican. My enemies do me too much honour: I am nothing of the sort. Had they accused me of monarchism, they would have done me too little honour; for neither am I a monarchist. I will begin by observing that there are plenty of people to whom the words "monarchy" and "republic" mean absolutely nothing. The word "republic" does not mean any particular form of government: it is applicable to every form of government under which men enjoy freedom and a fatherland (*tout gouvernement d'hommes libres qui ont une patrie*); and one may be as free under a king as under a senate. What is the French constitution at the actual moment? It is not a monarchy: it is not a republic: it is both.'[1] Nothing could be clearer than this, or truer to the tradition of French thought. It was a complete answer to Robespierre's critics. Nevertheless, what his followers wanted, at the crisis of July, 1791, was not a lecture on Constitutional Law, but a lead against the constitutionalists; and that he could not quite make up his mind to give.[2] The democratic party was divided. All sections of it, indeed, wished for the definite deposition (*déchéance*) of the king, instead of the temporary suspension which was part of the Moderate plan; but they could not co-operate in the next step. The leaders of the Cordeliers Club, and many of the journalists and politicians, who, up to the end of June, had indulged in republican propaganda, thought that, once Louis was dethroned, the Dauphin should be put in his place, either under the regency of the Duc d'Orléans, or supervised by a committee of the Assembly: Marat, Danton,[3] Pétion, and Brissot, knowing the character of Orléans, and not being

[1] Jac. 3/12.
[2] Louis Blanc (5/461) thinks that Robespierre was really a republican at this time, but thought it dangerous to say so.
[3] Danton's membership of the reactionary *Bons Enfans* club made him suspect at this time. Challenged by Robespierre, he proved his patriotism, and went even further in the direction of republicanism. (A.R. 2/249.)

unwilling to assume power, preferred the second alternative. But this plan did not please republicans either of the type of Robert, the editor of the *Mercure National*, and his wife (formerly Mlle Kéralio, of the Arras Academy), or like Condorcet and Thomas Paine, the author of the republican manifesto of June 23; and this left wing was supported by a crowd of lesser men, products of the 'popular' and 'fraternal' societies, under the leadership of Hébert, Chaumette, Hanriot, and their like—men who had helped to pull down the symbols of royalty from the streets and shop-fronts on June 21, and now hoped to pull down royalty itself.

V

On July 13, when Muguet's motion for the king's suspension came before the House, crowds gathered outside the *Manège*, and clamoured for his deposition. On the 14th the Cordeliers Club presented a petition for a plebiscite to be held on this issue; but the Assembly refused to hear it. On the 15th they sent six *commissaires* to the House with a fresh address in much the same terms as that of the day before; but when they reached the House, they were informed by Pétion and Robespierre that they came too late: Muguet's decree had just been carried. They thereupon asked for something in writing which they could show to those who had sent them, and were given a letter, signed by Pétion and Robespierre, explaining that such petitions as theirs were liable to be misunderstood by the enemies of the people, and to embarrass its representatives. With this warning the commissioners went on, first to the *Amis de la Vérité*, and then, with a crowd of followers, to the Jacobin Club.[1] Here it was decided that both clubs (Jacobin and Cordeliers) should join in a manifesto calling for the king's deposition; and this was drafted the same night by Brissot, in terms which spoke of the 'replacement of Louis XIV by constitu-

[1] One of the six, Jacques Varlet, wrote an account of the affair, in an apologia of April 8, 1792 (Brit. Mus. F. 353 (3)).

tional means'—any suggestion of a republic being carefully avoided. In the course of the 16th this formula was read aloud by Danton and others to the crowds which had assembled on the Champ de Mars, and met with a good deal of criticism: the phrase 'constitutional means' (*moyens constitutionels*), in particular, was suspected of covering Orleanist or even royalist designs: but the Jacobins insisted upon its retention, as a security against a republican interpretation of the petition.[1] The same day the Assembly finally voted for the king's suspension until he should have approved the completed Constitution. This rendered the petition illegal, and the Jacobins cancelled it, while it was still at the printer's. But the extremer party in the Cordeliers refused to stop, and determined upon a fresh petition, demanding the king's trial, and the organization of what (still avoiding the word 'republic'), they called 'a new Executive' (*un nouveau pouvoir executif*). This petition was drawn up on the 'altar of the country' in the Champ de Mars the following day (July 17), and signed there by more than 6,000 persons;[2] and it was some fifty of these signatories who were shot down on the steps of the altar by National Guardsmen, under the orders of Lafayette (the Commandant), Bailly (the Mayor), and the municipality of Paris.

The 'massacre of the Champ de Mars' was never forgotten or forgiven. It opened a breach between the Constitutionalists and the Republicans, between the *bourgeoisie* and the *ouvriers*, which could not be closed even by a national war, or by the establishment of a French Republic. Both parties had put themselves in the wrong—the demonstrators, by rejecting the verdict of the General Will, as expressed by the National Assembly; and the city authorities, by using martial law against their fellow-citizens, whose disfranchisement left them no means of expressing

---

[1] v. Robespierre's speech at the Jacobins on the 16th, reported only in *Bouche de fer* (Hamel, 1/511).

[2] They included Chaumette, Sergent, Momoro, Meunier, Hébert, Hanriot, Santerre, Maillard, David, and Coffinhall. v. a detailed account of the document and signatures in Michelet, 3/206.

their views but that of public petition. The blunder, on the government side, was probably due less to policy than to panic; but it might have been defended at the time as a seasonable attempt to enforce public order. The provocation, on the side of the people, was caused by lack of unity and leadership. None of the Jacobin politicians come particularly well out of it—not even Robespierre.

He had, indeed, taken a bold decision, when he demanded the king's trial; he had begun the attack against the Constitutional party; he had accused the Assembly of betraying the interests of the nation. Yet, when the sense of the House went against him on the 15th, he drew back, and became as cautious as any Constitutionalist, telling the Cordeliers deputation that it was too late to protest, and opposing the joint petition of the 16th. During the critical hours of the 17th he was at the Jacobins, sending out delegates, like doves from the ark, to see whether the disorders of the Champ de Mars were abated, and lamenting the sad state of affairs.[1] And when the massacre was over, he had no blame for either party. 'Let us weep,' he wrote, 'for those citizens who have perished: let us weep even for those citizens who, in good faith, were the instruments of their death. Let us in any case try to find one ground of consolation in this great disaster: let us hope that all our citizens, armed as well as unarmed, will take warning from this dire example, and hasten to swear peace and concord by the side of these newly dug graves'.[2]

What is to be made of this moderation? Was it the timidity of the debating-hall politician called to translate his words into acts? Was it a strain of Arras legalism reasserting itself? Was it due to the knowledge that the Moderates were waiting for an excuse to proscribe the democrat leaders, and that any support of the petitioners of the 17th would give them what they wanted? That certainly: but it was more. It was a new fear, which the events of the last three weeks had intensified, of what might happen to the cause of liberty if the Constitution, which

[1] Jac. 3/25.   [2] *Adresse aux français.*

Robespierre had so freely criticized, were never enacted, and if a faction, which its enactment would force into retirement, were to follow up its success of July 17th by establishing an unconstitutional oligarchy. The escape from this danger, he was convinced, lay not in republicanism, or any other new regime, but in the achievement, as soon as might be, of the Constitution, and the election of a Legislative Assembly.[1] In other words, it was Robespierre's sense of the intrigues and unworthiness of the present Assembly, and of the violently partisan spirit of the clubs, which made him long for a new start in the political world, rather as his feeling of over-work and exhaustion made him long for a holiday. He was indecisive, only because no decision, under the present conditions, seemed worth making. He failed to lead, because all roads seemed equally dangerous or distasteful. He fell back on the Constitution, because that, at any rate, would bring new men to the head of affairs—men chosen by the people, to whom *liberté* and *vertu* might once more seem divine.

VI

Robespierre's moderation during the July crisis did not save him from accusations of treason. A woman who was arrested on July 19 for 'incendiary expressions' against the Assembly, the municipality, and the National Guard, 'excepted Robespierre, Reubell, Pétion, Danton, and Marat.'[2] It was said that on July 17 Robespierre's portrait had hung on the altar of the country; that there had been found among Fréron's papers a plan to make him dictator; and that the mob had cried, '*Plus de Louis XVI: nôtre roi est Robespierre!*' Wild charges are commonly flung about at such a time; and it does not seem likely that, if there had been any substance in them, they would have been passed over by the Public Prosecutor in the inquiry which he held soon afterwards, and in which, whilst blaming Pétion and Robes-

[1]*Discours sur l'inviolabilité royale.* 'The only thing to hope for at the moment is a new legislature, if you want to avoid a Long Parliament, proscriptions like those of Sylla, and a thousand incalculable horrors' (Mme Roland, July 22; R.F. 29/170).
[2]Tuetey, 2/2379; Mathiez, *Club des Cordeliers*, 137, 259; *Lettres de Bouchotte*.

pierre for a temporary flirtation with republicanism, he exculpated them from any more serious accusations.[1]

It was obvious, too, that whilst Marat, Fréron, and Desmoulins were forced to suspend their papers, whilst Brune, Legendre, and Santerre went into hiding, and Danton took refuge in L'Aube, Troyes, Arcis, and finally in England,[2] Robespierre did no more than change his lodgings, and was able to keep up his daily attendances at the Assembly and the club. He was thus enabled to guide the Jacobins during the most critical time of their fortunes.

For the immediate result of the crisis was a split in the club, many of whose members withdrew, and founded a more moderate society in the neighbouring Feuillant convent.[3] The new club, assuming the old name (*Société des amis de la constitution séante aux Feuillants*), claimed to be the rightful heir of the Jacobin tradition, and the legal owner of the club premises. This manœuvre closely resembled the foundation of the *Société de 1789* by Lafayette and his friends a year earlier: but the Duport-Lameth-Barnave party against whom that secession had been aimed were now themselves among the seceders.[4] On July 18 Robespierre proposed to meet this move by sending an address to the Assembly, pointing out that the petition of July 16 was not illegal when it was drawn up, and that it had been withdrawn as soon as the decision of the Assembly made it so. 'We are not factionists,' the address declared; 'it is useless to attempt to attach the idea of crime to the love of liberty, that sublimest of all the virtues.' On the 24th he rejected an invitation to fuse the Jacobins with the Feuillants, with rather the same feelings as he had, two years before, rejected the insidious offers of the clergy to the Commons. On August 5 the club circulated to the affiliated societies an address he had drawn up, describing what had happened,

---

[1] Aulard, 154; Mathiez, *Club des Cordeliers*, 358; A.R. 1/488.
[2] For Danton, v. A.R. 11/537; Mathiez, *Conspiration*, 130.
[3] For a list of the seceders, incomplete in the second part of the alphabet, v. *Brit. Mus.* R. 157.
[4] Michon, *Adrien Duport*, 82.

and justifying the refusal to reunite with the secessionists; and a later move for reunion, from the Jacobin side, was similarly suppressed.[1]

By thus insisting upon the continuity and orthodoxy of the club, Robespierre preserved an organization which, in the following years, was to dominate the whole course of the Revolution. The ground which the Feuillants had won was gradually regained. The new club, helped by its proximity to the Manège, by the wealth of its members, and by its use of government facilities for propaganda purposes, had, indeed, at first great advantages over the old; and all Robespierre's popularity and political strategy were needed to counter its attack.[2] But by degrees he was successful. During the first fortnight of the schism nearly 400 provincial societies had declared for the Feuillants, and scarcely a dozen for the Jacobins. But by the third week in July, when the Jacobin propaganda began to overtake that of the Feuillants, petitions were coming in for a reunion of the two societies. Before the end of the summer many provincial clubs which had wavered between Pope and anti-Pope reaffirmed their allegiance to the old society. Prieur, Grégoire, Barère, Dubois de Crancé, Talleyrand, Rabaut Saint-Étienne, and Sieyès rejoined the Jacobins. By September the club membership had risen to 700 or 800; and soon 500 new clubs in the provinces were asking for affiliation. By December Feuillant meetings were being broken up by Jacobin demonstrators; and though a group of dissentients still met from time to time, in a variety of premises, up to the summer of 1792, the schism had no life in it.

Robespierre, who had presided almost alone over this reconstruction of the Jacobin forces, was now their leader in a fuller sense than ever before. When he entered the club on November 28, he was greeted with loud applause. Collot d'Herbois, who was in the chair, proposed 'that this member of the Constituent Assembly, rightly called "the In-

[1] Jac. 3/36, 49, 64, 69, 93.
[2] By the end of August the Treasurer of the Jacobins reported a deficit of 2,000 *livres* (A.R. 7/37).

corruptible", should preside over the society'. The proposal
was carried unanimously. Robespierre took the chair, and
made a speech of thanks.[1] The honour was no less than his
patient and cautious policy deserved. Indeed, so great was
his repute at this time that the Bishop of Bourges, a venerable patriot of sixty-four, found nothing absurd in addressing him as the 'Immortal champion of popular rights', and
saying that he would be proud to merit the name of *petit
Robespierre*.[2]

VII

Meanwhile the Assembly, which had hoped to end its
work in July, was condemned to another two months'
session, and to a settlement of the difficult situation
created by the king's flight and return. Here the effects of
the July crisis were at once apparent. It was not the flight
itself, or the proofs of the king's treachery, which had most
alarmed the deputies, but the popular demonstrations, and
the threat of republicanism. Instead of using the discredit
of the crown to strengthen democratic control over the
government, it was now their aim to revise the Constitution in the king's interest, and to diminish the rights of the
people. Robespierre found himself struggling against a flood-
tide of reaction. It was the situation of 1789 over again:
except that the place of the court and the royalist party was
now taken by the 'Triumvirate' and its Feuillant supporters;
and that it no longer seemed to be a crime to conspire
against the country, but to be over-jealous for its freedom.[3]
Anyhow, tired as he is, he must fight on.

Most of the new debates are on old issues. Thus, on
August 10, we find him maintaining, as he had done more
than a year before, that the sovereignty of the people is
inalienable, and that the king cannot be the deputy, but only
the delegate, of the nation. Thus, on August 11, he delivers
a final attack upon his old enemy, the *marc d'argent*. Four
days later he makes another of his attempts to whittle down
the power of the Ministers, by opposing a motion to allow

[1] Jac. 3/364.   [2] Corresp. 98.   [3] *Adresse aux français*.

them to speak in the House. On the 18th he once more expresses his doubts about the safety of the north-east frontier. On the 22nd an attempt to revive Sieyès' Censorship Law brings him to the tribune with a fresh exposition of his belief in the freedom of the Press.

The second of these speeches needs special attention; for it was one of Robespierre's best, and was circulated by the Cordeliers Club, as a charter of democracy, all over the country. It went over the old ground of the inconsistency between 'passive' citizenship and the Rights of Man; it pointed out the abuses to which the measure would lead, the class-privileges it would introduce, the stigma it would inflict on poor patriots, the premium it would place on money-making, and the encouragement it would give to oligarchical corruption. But, with all this, it showed a new sympathy with the case of the poor, about which Robespierre had learnt much during the days of July. The poor, it said, have a stake in the country, as well as the rich. 'Yes,' the poor man might say; 'the coarse clothes which cover my body, the humble roof beneath which I purchase the right to live in privacy and peace, the modest wages with which I support my wife and children— all this, I allow, does not amount to an estate, a castle, or an establishment; perhaps, on a scale of wealth and luxury, it is worth nothing at all. Nevertheless, viewed in a human light, it has a value: for it is something of my very own, no whit less sacred than the shining acres of the rich. Why! is not my liberty, my life, the claim of protection or redress for myself, and for those who are dear to me—is not the right to resist oppression, and to give free rein to all the faculties of my mind and my affections—is not each of these first and most precious gifts of nature entrusted, as yours are, to the custody of the laws?' The rich man, it may be argued, pays more to the state. Yes, but that is only because society allows him to be rich. And if we are to press the point, what is the origin of that excessive inequality of means which concentrates all the wealth of the country in a few hands? Is it not to be found in bad laws, bad governments, and (in a word) in all the vices of a corrupt society? Or, again, are the poor so unfit for a share of power? 'Do you honestly believe that a hard and laborious life engenders more vices than softness, luxury, and ambition? Have you less confidence in the honesty of our workmen and artisans, who, by your standard, will hardly ever rank as "active" citizens, than in that of the courtier and the tax-farmer, who, on the same reckoning, will stand 600 times as high? . . . For my own part, I bear witness to all those whom an instinctively noble and sensitive mind has made friends and lovers of equality, that in general there is no justice or goodness like that of the people, so long as they are nor irritated by excessive oppression; that they are grateful fot the smallest consideration shown to them, for the least good that is done to them, and even for the evil that is left un-done; and that among the poor, and under an exterior that we should call coarse, are found honest and upright souls, and a good sense and energy that one might seek long and in vain among a class that looks down upon them.'

This speech is one that no biographer of Robespierre can lightly pass over. Its passages of genuine eloquence place him among the great orators. Its evident sympathy for the poor makes it impossible to conceive of him as a hard-hearted man, or to doubt the genuineness of his democratic professions. The sentences in which it deals with the problem of poverty are among the earliest and most important indications of his political philosophy. He is aware of the failure of society to equate merit and reward. He resents the unequal distribution of wealth. He desires better laws, better government, and a reformed society, in which the disabilities of poverty may disappear. He does not, indeed, say how this is to be brought about—whether by the universal suffrage that he desiderates, or by (what he is careful not to mention) a republican constitution. Later, perhaps, he will see his way more clearly. At present he is merely stating a profoundly difficult problem, and showing his desire to solve it.

But how many of his contemporaries went so far? How

many 'friends and lovers of equality' were ready to give political power to the poor? Can one be surprised that Robespierre's speech was regarded as a gospel of hope by the dispossessed and disfranchised classes, or that the *Société des indigens amis de la constitution* wrote to him, in almost idolatrous terms, 'we love thee, we revere thee, we bear thee in our heart'? Even the Assembly was shaken. But Thouret's tardy proposal to abolish the obnoxious *marc d'argent* was coupled with a fresh qualification for electors which robbed the concession of most of its value. A year later the revolution of August 10 swept all restrictions away.

VIII

These were old chains, which the reactionary party were trying to tighten. There were others which they sought to re-impose; and Robespierre found himself fighting against proposals to restore the king's body-guard (August 24), the royal prerogative of pardon (*droit de grâce*—September 2), and the title of 'Prince' to members of the royal family (August 25). This last was specially offensive to his democratic sense. If *Prince de Condé*, he argued, or *Prince de Conti*, why not *Count de Lameth*? 'Let us all have titles, or none.'

Charles Lameth, once Robespierre's friend, but now one of his bitterest enemies, soon found an opportunity to revenge this sneer. There had been a mutiny amongst the men of the Beauce regiment in garrison at Arras, and exceptionally severe methods of repression were proposed (August 28). The Lameths attempted to fasten upon Robespierre the responsibility for this outbreak, alleging that he had been in treasonable correspondence with the troops. In point of fact, he had kept himself informed of the whole affair through Guffroy, his old colleague of the Episcopal Court at Arras, and now *procureur-général-syndic* of the district; and it appears from their correspondence that the Jacobin Club at Arras, if not Guffroy himself, had played a mediating part between the government and the troops that

169

might easily lend itself to misrepresentation. Robespierre's
own part in the business consisted in nothing more than
procuring a hearing for the men's address to the Assembly,
and the postponement of their trial.[1] As soon as he was free
to leave Paris, he went to Arras to investigate the affair on
the spot.[2]

The last stone of the constitutional arch was put in its
place when the Assembly decided (August 30–1) that provision should be made for changing the Constitution in
case of need, not by another revolution, but through a
Constituent Assembly summoned for the purpose. In their
fear of democratic reaction, and knowing that they were
themselves going out of office, the deputies were anxious to
make revision as difficult as possible: they therefore proposed an arrangement which would involve a ten years'
moratorium for any constitutional change. Robespierre did
not oppose this; but he urged that the Constituent
Assembly should have power to review the conduct of the
legislature; for 'the sovereignty of the nation means its
ability to repress, when it wishes, any usurpation of power
by the authorities it sets up'. Thus his last word before the
final drafting of the Constitution was marked by that distrust of elected bodies which had been growing on him
during the two and a half years of the National Assembly.
Liberty was his creed; and everywhere he found it opposed
by tyranny—the tyranny of feudalism, overthrown in 1789;
the tyranny of the royal prerogative, destroyed bit by bit
during 1790 and 1791; the tyranny of the constitutional
reaction, which he hoped to see end with the dissolution of
the Assembly; and now the tyranny of Parliament, which he
feared would be inseparable from any form of representative government. A man who saw things so clearly was on
the way to complete political disillusionment; and out of
that strange things might come.

It remained only to submit the Constitution to the king.
But this simple proceeding gave rise to a long and heated
discussion, during which Robespierre delivered his last

[1]Corresp. 86, 94, 96, 99–103.   [2]v. 1/187 f.

important speech in the Assembly (September 1). Louis, he said, will accept the Constitution with delight, for it gives him so much power—'complete control of the executive; . . . the right to veto the actions of a series of national assemblies; the opportunity of influencing their proceedings through his ministers' right of entry into the House; absolute authority over his agents, the administrative bodies; power to regulate the foreign policy of the nation; finally, the use of a huge army (*armées innombrables*)[1], and of a public Treasury, swollen with all the national property which has come into his hands—forty million *livres* for his personal expenditure.[2] Why! (exclaimed Robespierre) there is not a power in the state, but it pales before the king's!' Nevertheless, nothing is to be gained by delay: let Louis be presented with the Constitution as soon as possible. 'The nation offers you (let us tell him) the most powerful throne in the universe: here are your title-deeds: do you accept it?' He is free to decline, if he likes. No one will mind; and he will be as safe in Paris as anywhere else. But let us not give him an opportunity for intrigue (in the direction of a further revision of the Constitution) by letting him leave the capital. There is a tone of exaggeration and ill-temper in this speech which shows how the recent debates had frayed the speaker's nerves. Yet it is worth remembering that Mirabeau had said essentially the same thing in his Notes to the court almost a year before.[3] The Revolution had, indeed, retrenched many of the king's prerogatives: but it had left powers enough for effective constitutional rule, had Louis known how to use them—the appointment of ministers, and their right of speech in the House; the suspensive veto; the Civil List; the nomination of administrators of the Treasury; a *garde constitutionelle*; the appointment of a quarter of the junior officers, and all the higher commands

[1]The regular army in 1791 numbered 110,000 infantry and 3,000 cavalry; the *gendarmerie*, 7,455 men; the *garde nationale* (in Paris alone), 31,000 men and 120 guns. Against these, if it came to a struggle, the king could only count on the 1,200 infantry and 600 cavalry of the *garde constitutionelle*, and a small number of *Suisses*. (Lav. 1/182.) From this one can judge Robespierre's exaggeration.
[2]The Civil List was 25,000 francs.
[3]*Correspondance entre le Comte de Mirabeau et le Comte de la Marck.*

in the army; and the initiative in declaring war. At the same time it had removed the most formidable obstacles in the way of the old autocracy—the privileged Orders, the Parlements, and provincialism; whilst it had lessened the danger of popular opposition by setting up a property franchise, excluding 'passive' citizens from the National Guard, limiting the freedom of the press, and suppressing the right of collective petition. If the inlets of royal power were less abundant than they had been, the outlets were less choked up; and a thinner stream of prerogative could run more freely.

IX

The Assembly was now near its end; but it did not have a quiet passing. The question of the colonies, last debated in May,[1] raised a fresh storm. The moderate concessions then made to the mulattoes and freed negroes had been obstructed in every possible way by the reactionary Colonial Committee. Now (September 5) came a deputation from the town of Brest asking for redress, and a violent reply by A. Lameth reopened the whole controversy. Robespierre declared that if any blame attached, it was to Lameth and Barnave, who had prevented the execution of the national decrees. At this the House was in an uproar, and there were demands for Robespierre's arrest—*A l'Abbaye, à l'Abbaye, M. Robespierre!* When quiet was restored, Robespierre contented himself with asking for an inquiry; and there the matter rested. But three weeks later reaction had its way. Barnave proposed a decree (September 24) which abrogated the concessions of May 15, and put mulattoes as well as freed negroes once more at the mercy of the white settlers. Robespierre protested, in three speeches, in the name of humanity and justice, but could not prevent the Assembly from going back on its promises, and handing over the colonies to oppression and civil war.

It was apropos of this debate that the abbé de Salamon sketched, for the benefit of his friend Cardinal de Zelada, a

[1] May 15 (v. 1/131 f).

vivid, if hostile, pen-portrait of Robespierre. 'This young lawyer', he wrote, 'is well-known for his emotional out-bursts (*emportements*), and his republican enthusiasm. He learns nothing by experience: his mistakes only make him more stubborn and opinionative, and prove that he has limited gifts and a narrow outlook. The complete failure of a political programme which the laws are beginning to proscribe has only increased his passion, which now passes all bounds. He leaps upon darts and pikes like a lion wounded in the chase. Having no more arguments or evidence to adduce, he fights with insults and slanders: he rends and bites those whom he cannot persuade. Any deputy who does not think as he does is a traitor to the country'.[1]

Nevertheless, looking back on the whole controversy, and putting aside the amenities of debate, to which others besides himself paid scant attention, Robespierre had little with which to reproach himself. Without Brissot's or Barnave's special concern in the colonial problem, he had taken it up as part of his campaign for humanity and free-dom, had made himself, in his painstaking way, an authority on the subject, and had become the chief champion of a cause which was engaging the sympathy of humanitarians in other countries as well as his own. He had not been tactful. But tact is a virtue of majorities: in a minority it is taken as a sign of weakness. On the other hand, he had not been Utopian. He had seen that it was better to fight for a limited franchise (for the mulattoes and freed negroes) which had been promised, and might be granted, than for a complete one (including all black men) which there was no possibility of securing. And this attitude was justified by the sequel. For the revolt which soon broke out at St. Domingo was aggravated both by Barnave's refusal of rights to the freed blacks (who threw in their lot with the slaves), and by Brissot's premature campaign for emancipa-tion; and the results of the Assembly's vacillating policy recoiled disastrously upon the situation in Paris.[2]

[1] *Correspondance*, 327.   [2] Hardy in A.R. 12/357; Mathiez, *La Vie Chère*, 39.

Two final incidents. On September 17 an official sent to arrest Danton followed him into a building where the Paris electors were holding a meeting; for which 'breach of privilege' the president of the electoral assembly arrested him, and threw him into prison. Robespierre upheld his action, saying that the inviolability of the Assembly extended to any place where its members were elected—a bold doctrine, which the House would not accept. Finally, on September 29, Le Chapelier, that old enemy of the people, introduced a report from the Constitutional Committee, the upshot of which was an attempt to deprive Popular Societies—the chief means of Jacobin propaganda in the provinces—of the rights of affiliation and correspondence. Robespierre naturally attacked this proposal as contrary to the constitutional guarantees of free speech and free association. This time he won his point;[1] and it was a victory of immense moment to the Revolution.

Next day (September 30) the king appeared in the House, and renewed his oath to enforce respect for the Constitution. The work of the National Assembly was done.

The crowd which waited outside the House watched the dispersal of its members with little regret. But when Robespierre and Pétion appeared—the two men, as Desmoulins said, who embodied all that was good in the Assembly—there were cries of *Vive la Liberté! Vive Robespierre! Vive l'Incorruptible!* Their heads were crowned with oak-leaves, and an enthusiastic mob dragged their *fiacre* home through the streets.[2] Even Mme Roland, writing two years later, and from a Jacobin prison, has to admit that, at this period of his career, Robespierre was almost the only invincible (*inébranlable*) champion of democratic principle in the Assembly.[3] And a play was put on at the Théâtre Molière in which Robespierre was represented on the stage,

[1] The formal *projet de décret* was adopted; but the *instruction* necessary to give it effect was allowed to lie on the table. (Michon, *Adrien Duport*, 343.)
[2] *Révolutions de Paris*, No. 116, cp. a quotation in Lewes, 208.
[3] *Mem.* (ed. Barrière), 254.

confounding Rohan and Condé by his logic and his virtue.[1]

X

Mme Roland played so large a part in the Revolution that her relations with Robespierre have a special importance. She and her husband had been in Paris, fulfilling a mission on behalf of the city of Lyon, from February 20 until the middle of September, 1791. They returned to their farm in time for the autumn vintage, and did not revisit the capital until December. Soon after her arrival at Clos de la Platière (September 27), Mme Roland wrote to Robespierre, lamenting the lack of real patriotism both in Paris and in the provinces. 'No one born with a soul,' she says, in her self-satisfied way, 'and who has kept it unstained, could look on Paris in these latter days, without lamenting the blindness of corrupt nations, and the abyss of evil from which it is difficult to rescue them'. It is, indeed (she thinks), the same everywhere: society is so badly ordered, that most men are unhappy. Here in Villefranche and Thézée (her district and parish) she meets many purely nominal patriots, 'men who like the Revolution because it has destroyed what was above them': they are monarchists to a man, and 'bridle at the mention of a Republic'. Lyon itself is 'devoted to the aristocracy: the elections are detestable, and the deputies are enemies of liberty, stock-jobbers with little or no reputation': there are no men of talent; and though 'the mass of the people never deceives itself very much or very long', yet electors, administrators, and representatives are all for sale. She ends by hoping that Robespierre will be glad to hear from her husband and herself, 'two beings whose souls were made to feel for' him, and who give their friendship only to the few who are worthy of it.[2] It is not known how Robespierre answered this effusion, or whether he acknowledged the writer's claim to spiritual affinity. But certainly his friendship with the Rolands did not long outlast their return to Paris at the end of the year.

[1]Hamel, 1/561.　　　[2]Corresp. 104; ed. Perroud 2/384; for the sequel, v. 1/223.

There has been occasion to refer, more than once, to a brochure which Robespierre composed in July, 1791, as a defence of his conduct during the weeks succeeding the flight to Varennes. This *Adresse de Maximilien Robespierre aux Français* is, as its title implies, more than an occasional pamphlet. It is Robespierre's apologia, in the full sense of the word—his confession of political faith; and it may well stand as *Finis* to the chapter of his life that ends with the Constituent Assembly.

'I am driven,' he begins, 'to defend at once my honour and my country';—they were, indeed, to him almost identical, and his principles were those of the Declaration of Rights. 'I proudly admit,' he goes on, 'that I have never considered this Declaration as an idle theory: I have regarded it as a body of judicial axioms at once universal, unchangeable, and imprescriptible, intended to be applied to all mankind. I have always thought that all my expressions of opinion, if not all the decrees of the National Assembly, ought to be logical expositions of the two principles which are the sum and essence of the Declaration— equality of rights, and the sovereignty of the nation. I have always held that equality of rights belongs to all members of the state; that the nation includes the working class (*la classe laborieuse*), and everyone, without distinction of rich or poor. I was conscious that the easiest victims of human injustice could not be excluded from the sympathy of those who were deputed to provide a remedy. I knew that I represented them as fully as any other class. And I will admit that I was bound to their cause by that imperious impulse which attracts us towards the under-dog (*les hommes faibles*); for it was this impulse, more than any reasoned knowledge of my duty, which had always claimed my sympathy for those in trouble.'

He has been accused, as a result of this partiality for the poor, of encouraging popular disorder. 'I can testify,' he replies, 'that this large and interesting class, hitherto called "the people", is the natural friend and the indispensable champion of freedom. And why so? Because it is precisely this class which is neither corrupted by luxury, nor depraved by pride, nor carried away by ambition, nor troubled by those passions which are inimical to equality. I can affirm that, whenever the French people came together—at the capture of the Bastille, at the Federation of 1790, or at the time of the flight to Varennes—I have found it true to its character—generous, reasonable, magnanimous, and moderate.' It is unfair to reproach the people as a whole with the occasional crimes of individuals. As to the sovereignty of the people, he has always held it to be a fact, not a fiction. The Assembly cannot constitutionally do anything contrary to the rights of the sovereign people; and the nation ought to have constitutional means of enforcing its will upon its representatives. An absolutely independent legislature would be 'a moral and political monstrosity'. He is not afraid of monarchy, even of hereditary monarchy, so long as the people is given its proper place, and does not humiliate itself before its 'delegate', the King.

He ends by comparing his position with that of Socrates. 'Did the Athenian philosopher cause more offence to the great people, the ecclesiastics, the sophists, and the political charlatans, than I have? Have not I too spoken ill of false gods, and tried to introduce into our modern Athens the worship of virtue, justice, and equality? . . . There is nothing that cannot be done by money, by slander, by intrigue, or by bayonets. All these weapons are in the hands of my enemies; whilst I—a simple, weak, isolated individual—have nothing on my side but my courage, the justice of my cause, and the prayers of all good patriots'.

XII

The crisis of July, 1791, brought about an important change in Robespierre's domestic life. When the Jacobin Club broke up on the 17th he was in greater personal danger, perhaps, than ever before. It was 11 o'clock at night. The members were greeted, as they came out, with threats and insults. Robespierre, arm-in-arm with Lapoype (a fellow-Jacobin), and Lecointe (in the uniform of the National Guard) had some difficulty in forcing his way through the crowd. Detachments of the municipal troops, fresh from the 'massacre' of the Champ de Mars, were still in the streets which lay between the rue Saint-Honoré and the rue Saintonge, a mile and a half away. Robespierre knew what he might expect from the men who had shot down his followers, and were imprisoning his friends. He asked Lecointe whether he knew of anyone near at hand who would put him up for the night. Lecointe suggested Maurice Duplay, a member of the club, who lived on the north side of the rue Saint-Honoré, only a few yards away; and Duplay hospitably took him in.[1] The original invitation was doubtless only for one night. But it was followed by a suggestion that Robespierre should give up his lodgings in the Marais, and take a room at the Duplays', recently vacated by Dom Gerle,[2] where he would be close to the Assembly and the club. Not long afterwards the plan was carried out.[3]

The house, No. 366, rue Saint-Honoré, which thus became Robespierre's home for the last three years of his life, is well known from a description by one of those who lived there; and this can be verified in outline by a visit to the present No. 398, which occupies the same site. The building formed three sides (north, west, and south) of a court backing onto the garden of a Conceptionist convent. The entrance, on the north side of the rue Saint-Honoré, was by an arched passage (*porte cochère*) between a jeweller's shop, named Rouilly, on one side, and an eating-house on the other: over it was a wooden eagle, like the figure-head of a ship.[4] On the ground floor were a dining-

---

[1]This is Fréron's account (Pap. inéd. 1/154). Mme Roland credits herself with an attempt to offer Robespierre an asylum, and to get Buzot to defend him at the Feuillants, and in the Assembly. (*Mem.*, ed. Barrière, 258.)

[2]The Jacobin Club list records his lodging there in 1789-90 (Alger, *Paris*, 440).

[3]On August 9 Robespierre still gave his address as rue Saintonge (Mathiez, *Club des Cordeliers*, 332).

[4]A.H. 67/39.

room and drawing-room, facing onto the courtyard, and a study and kitchen looking out on the convent garden. In the courtyard itself were two sheds for Duplay's carpentering business, and a small garden, with flower beds belonging to the children. The first floor, approached either by an outside staircase on the left as one entered the yard, or by narrow steps—little better than a ladder—from the dining-room, contained, over the south front, facing the street, a room later occupied by Charlotte or Augustin Robespierre; four rooms on the west side—those of Jacques-Maurice, Simon, Maximilien Robespierre, and M. Duplay, and on the north side Mme Duplay's room, and (presumably) those of her three daughters. The house had no second floor; but there was a cellar under the street front, and a loft under the roof. Robespierre's low-ceilinged room was very simply furnished—a walnut bedstead, with blue and white damask curtains, made out of an old frock of Mme Duplay's, a small desk, some straw-seated chairs, and a cupboard to serve as a book-case. The only window looked onto the courtyard and the carpenters' sheds, so that the room was never free from the sounds of domestic work, or the noises of hammer and saw.[1]

It is difficult not to dislike some of the characteristics and poses of 'the Incorruptible'; but here is a genuine bit of simplicity and hard living. How many authors or statesmen would be content to live and work in a tiny bed-sitting-room, overlooking a builder's yard, when they might have every comfort that success could give?

XIII

True, there were compensations. Robespierre had his books, his friends, and a refuge from people he did not wish to see.

[1] v. Mme Lebas' account in Lamartine 2/194, and Stéfane-Pol, *Autour de Robespierre*. The upshot of the Hamel-Sardou controversy about the site (bibliography in Tourneux 4/25075–8) seems to be that the present No. 398 occupies the site and follows the main plan of the old building, and that the rooms on the first floor (including Robespierre's) approximate in position to those of 1791, but that the whole structure has been rebuilt; so that only a metaphysician can say whether the new room is the same as the old.

The shelves that contained the neat MSS. of his speeches also held a small library, collected partly from personal taste, but mainly (it may be presumed) for the routine of public work. An inventory made in 1794 mentions certain periodicals which he received as a member of the Convention; correspondence with foreign powers, ministers, and the Committee of Public Safety; official papers on the foreign trade of the Republic; several French, English, and Italian grammars; half a dozen dry-titled law-books; and some works on morals and history, such as Mably, Guicciardini, Fleury, and Fénelon. Philosophy is represented by de la Rochefoucauld, Francis Bacon, and Pope's *Essay on Man*. Lastly there are some pamphlets, including *Les crimes des reines de France*, and a number of treatises on mathematical subjects.[1]

A man's library is some guide to his mind. Can we infer anything from this undeniably meagre list of books, in which law and mathematics bulk so large, whilst poetry is represented only by Pope, and fiction by Fénelon? It is worth while to compare Robespierre's library with Danton's. Some of Danton's books are the same: Guicciardini, Pope, and Fleury figure on both lists. But his is a collection of 700 volumes, in Latin, French, Italian, and English, including long sets of Rousseau, Raynal, Voltaire, Shakespeare, the *Spectator*, Buffon, and Condillac, as well as Ovid, Montaigne, Rabelais, Richardson, Boccaccio, Johnson's *Dictionary*, Adam Smith, Blackstone, and Robertson—a much richer fare. There are, of course, some good reasons for the difference. Danton was a comparatively rich man, Robespierre a poor one. Danton had a country house as well as a town lodging, Robespierre only one small room. Danton's public life was periodic, and left leisure for reading, whereas Robespierre's was continuous, and absorbed the whole of his energy. Add, that Danton could talk and write, as well as read, in English and Italian. Nevertheless, it seems fair to infer, from the books Robespierre kept by him, that he had rather deliberately turned

[1]Full details in R.F. 21/533. The titles are all given in French; but the presence of Italian and English grammars suggests that Robespierre read Guicciardini, Bacon, and Pope in the original.

his back on the unregenerate tastes of his youth, and focussed his thought on a definite and narrow field. Is it of no significance that the classic prizeman of Louis-le-Grand kept no Latin authors on his shelves, and the Arras sonneteer only a single volume of verse? Is there no evidence, in the predominance of law, history, morals, and mathematics (though the last may have been a chance 'accession') of an intentional concentration of interests? May one not also connect the reduction of Robespierre's library with his development as an orator? His forensic speeches had been noted less for their thought than for their learning. His parliamentary orations are almost bare of the allusions to classical and philosophical authors by which he marked his superiority to the common *plaideur*: they are either practical expositions of passing topics, or elaborate essays on matters of principle, in which the writer is working out a position for himself; and that, not by induction from the opinions of others, but by deduction from a few ruling convictions. He has no need, for this purpose, of the shelves full of Raynal and Condillac, of Blackstone and Adam Smith, from which Danton never succeeded in drawing a political principle. He can even do without a copy of Rousseau.[1] He has Jean-Jacques' axioms in his head. He spins the web of his thought in tough geometrical gossamer out of his own body. The pattern repeats itself, and the shape does not always fit the space it has to cover; but it is undeniably his own. He used his books: he did not let his books use him.

Two additions are worth making. There is reason to believe that after her death Robespierre came into possession of a copy of *La Henriade*, which had belonged to Marie Antoinette; and that, among the papers taken over by Courtois at Thermidor, was a Bible which he had annotated and underlined.[2]

[1] Lamartine, struck by this omission, or prompted by Mme Lebas, says that 'a volume of Rousseau or of Racine was generally open on his table'.

[2] A.R. 7/144, 2/592. The Bible was in Courtois' possession at the time of his death, but has since disappeared. A comparison with Saint-Just, also a lodger in Paris, is perhaps fairer. His library, like Robespierre's, included Republican periodicals and works on mathematics; but it was much richer in French literature; for besides Demosthenes, Cicero, Tasso in French translations, it included Rousseau, Bossuet, Pascal, Fénelon, Montesquieu, Mably, La Bruyère, and La Fontaine.

XIV

Besides his books, Robespierre had his friends.

The family circle at No. 366 in 1791 consisted of seven persons—Duplay and his wife, their three unmarried daughters, a son, and a nephew.

Maurice Duplay was a man of fifty-five, '5 ft. 6 ins. tall, with chestnut-coloured hair and eye-brows, oval face, high forehead, blue eyes, long nose, large mouth, and round chin'.[1] The son of a carpenter and builder near Vezelay, he had come to Paris, prospered in the family trade, and put his earnings into house-property, which now brought him in 15,000 livres (the equivalent of some £700) a year.[2] He was regarded, even by those who took exception to his political opinions, as 'a good father and a good husband, naturally kind and indulgent'; 'the most generous of men,' said Lebas, 'who spends all his life doing good'. To his hospitality all the Robespierres could bear witness: his honesty was proved when, after his imprisonment in 1794, he sold his house property to pay his debts. Already a Jacobin, in hope of social reform, his friendship for Robespierre soon took him more deeply into politics, and he became an elector, a commissioner for his Section, and a juryman of the Revolutionary Tribunal. Tradition says that whenever he served on the tribunal he took his duties very seriously; so that when Robespierre asked him, one day, what he had been doing there, he replied, 'I have never tried to find out, Maximilien, what you do on the Committee of Public Safety'; and the other silently shook his hand.[3]

Twenty-five years ago he had married Françoise-Eléonore Vaugeois, the daughter of a fellow-builder employed on the king's work at Choisy. Middle-aged now, still bustling about the house in her blue-striped skirt and cotton

---

[1]From his card of identity (Fleischmann, 100).

[2]He had leased No. 366 for nine years as from April 1, 1779; and again on July 1, 1783 (R.F. 36/376). He owned three houses in the rue de l'Arcade, rue de Luxembourg, and rue d'Angoulême (Hamel, 1/519).

[3]Stéfane-Pol, 75: 'improved' by Esquiros 2/388. But there was no mystery about the proceedings of the Tribunal.

stockings, but needing spectacles by the evening fire-side, Mme Duplay was a good mother and a good manager—though a little too much inclined, Charlotte Robespierre thought, to mother and manage others besides her own family. 'My mother was kind', says her youngest daughter, 'but very strict'; and Augustin Robespierre praised her for bringing up her daughters 'to be good house-keepers'.[1]

There were four daughters—Eléonore, the eldest, named after her mother, and still at home; Sophie, already married to a royalist lawyer named Auzat, and living at Issoire;[2] Victoire; and Elisabeth, who two years later became the wife of Philippe Lebas. The plain, dark-haired Eléonore was evidently the 'serious one' of the sisters, sharing her father's politics and patriotism. 'She had the soul of a man,' Robespierre is reported to have said, 'and would have known how to die as well as she knew how to love'. Some historians have inferred that he was her lover. Souberbielle, who, as the family doctor, often dined with the Duplays, and was in the best possible position to know, strongly denied this. 'They were very fond of each other', he said, 'and they were engaged to be married, but nothing immodest passed between them. Without affectation or prudery, Robespierre kept out of, and even put a stop to, any kind of improper talk; and his morals were pure'.[3] It may be that one day Maximilien took Eléonore's hand in his—the symbol of betrothal in Artois:[4] but, in spite of the episode of the rue Saintonge, everything suggests that he was at this time too devoted to his career, and to his reputation, to commit any social indiscretion, even that of matrimony. Of the other daughters, Sophie and Victoire remain almost unknown; but Elisabeth's naïve, attractive character can be read in every line of her *Manuscrit*.[5] Jacques-Maurice, the youngest child, was only thirteen in 1791, and still at school: a year later 'our young patriot', as Maximilien called him, went to

---

[1] Stéfane-Pol, 106, 296.
[2] Afterwards (Thermidor, An. II) at Lille, where Victoire had stayed with her (A.R. 12/512).
[3] Poumiès de la Siboutie, *Souvenirs d'un médecin de Paris*, 27.
[4] Esquiros 2/216, perhaps on information derived from Mme Lebas.
[5] It is printed in Stéfane-Pol, 102.

the front with Lebas. The household was completed by
Simon Duplay, an orphaned nephew of seventeen, to whom
the Duplays had given a home, and who worked at the
family business. He joined the army a year later, lost a leg
at Valmy, and was afterwards known as 'wooden-legged
Duplay'. In the warrant for his arrest at Thermidor he
appears as 'Robespierre's secretary'; but he denied this,
saying that Robespierre never had a secretary, and never
employed anyone to copy out his speeches.[1] A similar claim
was made by Villiers, and has been put forward in connexion with other names: but in point of fact, all the
extant copies of Robespierre's speeches are in his own
hand.[2]

Elisabeth's narrative shows on what friendly terms
Robespierre lived with this household, and how happy he
was there. 'Our best friend' (*nôtre bien bon ami*) she calls him,
and says, 'we loved him more than a brother'. 'He took our
part,' she adds, 'when, as sometimes happened, our mother
found fault with us. I was very young, and rather silly; but
he gave me such good advice that, young as I was, I enjoyed
listening to him. If I was upset about anything, I used to
tell him all about it. He was never censorious, but a friend,
the best brother a girl could have, a model of virtue. He had
a great regard for my father and mother, and we all loved
him dearly'. When she fell in love with Lebas, and her
parents objected to the marriage, it was Robespierre who
befriended his *Babet*, and talked them round. When Guffroy
made unwarrantable charges against her honour, it was he,
again, who comforted her. 'Poor little girl,' he said, 'cheer
up! It's nothing to worry about. Philip is very fond of you,
and it makes him happy to have his Elisabeth. Then he took
both our hands, and held them in his own, as though he
were giving us his blessing'. On his side, Maximilien told
Lebas 'what happiness it was to be living with people so

[1]Charles Nodier, who knew him, doubted his qualifications for such work
(*Souvenirs*, 291).

[2]For Villiers, v. 1/xxvi. Poumiès de la Siboutie, *Souvenirs* (336), calls Julien de
Toulouse Robespierre's secretary. Another, Bégue, *dit* Magloire, made the claim on
his tombstone, when he was buried in 1793 (A.H. 50/162). For Simon, v. Grasilier,
Simon Duplay, and A.R. 6/418, 11/113.

honest, and so devoted to the cause of freedom', whilst Augustin said that his brother had come to regard the whole family—father, mother, and sisters—as his own.[1]

Among the friends who from time to time joined this family circle were, in the early days, Pétion and the Lameths; occasionally the butcher Legendre, Merlin de Thionville, and Fouché; more often Taschereau, Desmoulins,[2] and Pio; and very frequently Lebas, Saint-Just, the painter David, Couthon,[3] and Buonarroti. The list is Lamartine's, corrected by Mme Lebas, but it is not complete; other names can be added, with more or less certainty—Pierre Vaugeois, Mme Duplay's brother, and his friend Didier, a locksmith; Gravier, a distiller from Lyon, who lodged with Didier next door; Cietti, an Italian designer of wall-papers, with whom Duplay doubtless had business relations; Lohier, the Duplays' grocer; Nicolas, the government printer, whose press was at No. 355; Franche-le-Hausse and Souberbielle, both of whom claimed the title of 'family doctor'; a Corsican cobbler from Arras, named Calandini; Boisset, the *archiviste* of the Jacobin Club; the artist Gérard, whose portrait of Robespierre hung in the sitting-room;[4] Félix Lepelletier, son of the deputy;[5] and Dom Gerle, whose compromising friendship contributed to Robespierre's fall. In addition to these, Anthoine, the mayor of Metz, lodged with the Duplays in the summer of 1792; as did also a M. de Broc, a Norman gentleman, with his wife and two small children, under an assumed name, and venturing out only after dark.[6] The list could doubtless be enlarged: it is sufficiently suggestive, as it stands, of the catholic hospitality of the Duplays, and of the variety of persons and interests with which Robespierre, in this quiet middle-class household, was brought into contact. It was a sheltered life, but it was not a narrow one.

[1] Stéfane-Pol, 120 f.
[2] Fréron says Robespierre used to laugh at Desmoulins' witticisms till he cried. (Pap. inéd. 1/154.)
[3] Couthon seems to have lodged at the Duplays' for a time in the summer of 1792 (v. 1/292 n.).
[4] A.R. 1/244.
[5] Hamel, 3/63.
[6] Poumiès de la Siboutie, *Souvenirs*, 37.

XV

It is possible to reconstruct, from the recollections of Mme Lebas and her family, several features of the Duplays' daily life[1]—the evenings in the *cabinet d'étude* when Lebas sang from his favourite Italian composers, and Buonarroti played the piano,[2] or when Robespierre read aloud, in dramatic style, extracts from Racine or Corneille, before saying good night to the company, and returning to his work upstairs; or when they all took parts, and did their best to play up to the practised declamation of the professional speakers. There were other evenings—not more than two or three a year—when Robespierre would escort Mme Duplay and her daughters to a classical drama at the Théâtre Français; or even days when it was possible for the whole family to walk in the Champs Elysées, or make an excursion into country further afield. They chose, Elisabeth says, the quietest spots, where Maximilien, accompanied by herself, her mother, her sisters, young Jacques-Maurice, and the dog *Brount*[3], liked to watch the Savoyard children dance, and would give them money—*il était si bon!* He was never so gay and happy as on these occasions, and it was generally on these evenings, when they got home, that he recited his favourite poetry. At other times he would go for solitary walks, accompanied only by his dog. But these recreations were exceptional. The Assembly commonly sat from 10 to 3 or 4, and the Jacobin Club from 6 (sometimes earlier) to 8 or 10. A hurried dinner at 5, when Mme Duplay took care not to forget Robespierre's liking for oranges and coffee[4], allowed little time for relaxation.

[1]Lamartine's account must be checked by Stéfane-Pol (97 f.); for, after submitting his MS. to Mme Lebas and her son, he failed to incorporate some of their suggestions (*ibid.* 53 f.).

[2]B. and R. 35/341. It may be only Hamel's guesswork that places the piano there.

[3]Esquiros (2/458) knows all about Brount. It was perhaps on these excursions that Robespierre exercised his talent for drawing: at any rate, there exists a sketch of an old woman 'well and carefully drawn', signed with his name (A.R. 13/510).

[4]Guffroy, a hostile witness, makes out that Robespierre was unduly fond of oranges and jam—he would eat *un pot de confitures fines* at a sitting, and take a glass or two of old wine before going to make a speech at the Jacobins. (A.R. 4/110.) Fréron, another enemy, agrees about the oranges, and says at one time he drank wine and liqueurs immoderately, but took nothing but water during the last months of his life (Pap. inéd. 1/154).

The constant business of reading reports, writing letters, composing speeches, and interviewing petitioners or politicians, made up a day's work of the most exacting kind—and one which repeated itself interminably; for there were no Parliamentary recesses, no politicians' week-ends, and no party Whips to tell a deputy when he need be in his place to vote, and when he might safely stay away. Robespierre's was a regular, temperate, and laborious life.

There came a time when Robespierre's connexion with the Duplay household was made a cause of offence; when his sister accused them of keeping him to themselves, and poisoning his mind against her; or when his enemies said that they isolated him from his followers, and flattered his conceit. But in 1791, at any rate, when party bitterness knew some limits, and men still felt some stirring of the ideals of 1789, Robespierre could hardly have done better, either for himself, or for the cause that he had at heart. His hosts were simple honest patriots of the lower middle class—the backbone of the Revolution; and the house in the rue Saint-Honoré was a perfect setting for the public life of 'the Incorruptible'. To Maximilien himself, for whom family life had hitherto such unhappy associations, the sane and friendly atmosphere of the Duplay household was just the corrective needed for a spirit in danger of introspection and embitterment.[1]

XVI

He had perhaps begun to feel this, when, some two months after his move from the rue Saintonge, the Constituent Assembly came to an end, and he was free, for the first time for many years, to take a real holiday. It would be pleasant to be able to settle down, uninterrupted, to the spell of thinking and writing that he had promised himself. But there was one thing to be done first: he must visit

[1] It is difficult to separate fact from fiction in the accounts of Robespierre's daily life: e.g., the story of the Savoyard children may have been transferred from Rousseau's *Rêveries d'un promeneur solitaire*. (Lenôtre, 242.) Did he drive out to Arthur's estate at Bercy, catch a fine pike in the fish-pond, and express compassion for the fish's death-struggles? Did he dine at Issy with Couthon, and walk in the Princesse de Chimay's park? Did he frequent the forest of Montmorency, and inhabit for a time Rousseau's *Hermitage*? (A.R. 3/386.) Not, at any rate, in 1791.

Arras. There were many reasons for this. The Artois people were his countrymen and his constituents; and he had not been among them for more than two years. Arras was his home; and there were definite questions to be settled there: the differences between the Popular Society and the Council-General of the Commune during the crisis of July; the affairs of the local Jacobin Club, which, after making him an honorary member in June, had in July sided with the Feuillants, and slandered him;[1] the 'mutiny' of the Beauce regiment, to be looked into with Guffroy;[2] the political situation, which he hoped to discuss with his friend Buissart;[3] and the future of his brother and sister, who, even now that Augustin was an *administrateur du Département*, and had returned to Arras to share his sister's expenses, found it none too easy to live in the house in the rue des Rapporteurs.[4] He accordingly wrote to Charlotte saying that he was coming home, and fixing the day of his arrival; and he arranged to travel with Pétion, who was going in the same direction.[5] However private the intention of the journey (and Charlotte is at pains to stress this) it soon turned into a triumphal progress. At Bapaume, where his brother and sister and Mme Buissart were waiting for him with a carriage, to cover the last stage to Arras, two detachments of National Guards that happened to be passing through joined with the local patriots in presenting him with a civic crown, and entertaining him at a banquet; nor were the District and Municipal authorities too proud to pay him an official visit. From Bapaume onwards his carriage was escorted by officers of the National Guard, and a fresh detachment from Arras. 'At Arras itself (such is Robespierre's own account of it) the people received me with demonstrations of affection which I cannot describe, and the thought of which still warms my heart. Every possible means was used to express it. A crowd of citizens

---

[1]Corresp. 84, 89.   [2]v. 1/169.   [3]Corresp. 76.
[4]Augustin must have returned to Arras some time between March and July.
[5]Charlotte's narrative, to do more honour to her brother, omits all mention of Pétion. Was he going to England? Mercier, *New Picture of Paris*, 1/149, says he returned from there to be Mayor of Paris.

had come out of the town to meet me. They offered a civic crown, not only to me, but to Pétion also, and in their cheers the name of my friend and companion in arms was often mingled with my own. I was surprised to see the houses of my enemies, and of the aristocrats (here at Arras they are Feuillants or Ministerialists; the rest have emigrated) lit up along the route of the procession: I could only attribute it to their respect for popular feeling'. He was, indeed, told that the municipality had opposed these demonstrations. 'If it had been the king himself,' they naïvely remarked, 'it would have been excessive: you did nothing of the kind for us, when we took office': and as soon as Robespierre reached home, they sent out constables to extinguish the illuminations. But that did not end the rejoicings: for next day the National Guards danced in the *Place*, and sang patriotic songs, and marched to Robespierre's house, 'making the air resound with acclamations extremely disagreeable to a Feuillant ear'.[1]

Written under different circumstances, or to a different correspondent, this letter might be thought complacent and conceited. But that would be to misinterpret it. Robespierre is delighted at his reception; but so he is at Pétion's: and why? Because it means popular approval of the policy for which they both stand—that of opposition to the reactionary royalism of the Feuillants; because it shows that the National Guard, which in July had been the tool of that party, is now ready to take the side of the people—a remarkable instance of the change of public opinion; and because it proves that the old ardour of 1789, which recent events had tended to extinguish in the capital, still burns brightly in the provinces. Besides, Robespierre is writing to a discreet man, who shares his views, and who will be delighted to hear of his friend's great doings in the country.

XVII

How did Robespierre spend the six weeks that elapsed between his arrival at Arras and his return to Paris? His

[1] To Duplay, October 16 (Corresp. 105).

sister says that he did not stay long in the rue des Rapporteurs, but went to stay not far away, in the country, 'in
order to enjoy the pleasures of repose' and meditation.
When he returned, he went to see an old friend who lived
a few miles away, but found him so changed and cold that
he came back deeply wounded, and never visited him again.[1]
Early in November he paid a visit to Béthune, perhaps to
see his friend Mlle Dehay. Once more, a private journey
became a public triumph. He was met some miles short of
the town by a deputation of the citizens, and conveyed for
the rest of the way in a carriage hung with flowers and
oak-leaves. He entered the town escorted by mounted
citizens, the National Guard, and a trumpeter of the local
cavalry regiment. After a midday meal, he attended a
Jacobin meeting in the Town Hall, at which women's
hands placed a civic crown on his head; and the day ended
with a public banquet. Robespierre slept three nights at the
Lion d'Or, whose landlord declared that, if he had only one
bed, and the choice lay between Robespierre and the king
himself, he would give it to Robespierre.

It is known that he also visited Lille; for at a meeting of
the local *Société populaire*, on November 24, 'the Incorruptible' was placed on the President's right, delivered a
discourse, which was much applauded, and was given the
accolade, and a civic crown. Here, too, there had been
difficulties between citizens and soldiers: but when the
commandant apologized for their behaviour, Robespierre
promised to take up their case, recommending him and his
men 'always to fix their eyes on God, the law, and the
fatherland'.[2]

But Arras must have been the main centre of Robespierre's interests; and here there seem to have been three
matters which made a special impression upon his mind.

One was the defence of the frontier. What he saw at
Arras, Lille, and Bapaume confirmed the suspicions he had
already formed in connexion with the Porentruy and Thion-

---

[1] Vellay suggests that this was Dubois de Fosseux.
[2] A.R. 12/65.

ville incidents.[1] The personnel of the National Guard, he told Duplay, was excellent; but their organization, owing to the incompetence or ill-will of the municipal authorities, was as bad as could be. They might dance in the *Place* at Arras; they might incite the country people against the 'refractory' clergy; but what use would they be, if the country were attacked by a foreign army? Robespierre returned from Arras determined to put national defence in the front of his programme, and to work against war, until the country was fit to defend itself.

Another matter on which his visit to Arras threw new light was emigration. He had hitherto maintained that it was the right of any individual to leave the country, if he would. But the sight of the inns on all the northern roads filled with refugees, and the evidence of the inn-keepers as to the number of people who, for some time past, had been crossing the frontier, led him to wonder whether, here too, liberty might not be abused, to the danger of the state.

XVIII

A third matter, to judge from the place it holds in his correspondence, exercised him even more. Hitherto, when questions of church policy came up, Maximilien, with his seminarist training, and his clerical friends, had been inclined to snub the anti-clerical outbursts of his brother Augustin, and of the Arras Jacobins. But the ecclesiastical atmosphere of his native place, which had grown remote and rather unreal during his absence in the capital, now struck a sudden chill to his Parisian mind. Arras itself, with a cathedral establishment, eleven parish churches, nine monasteries, and thirteen nunneries, was a battle-ground of clericals and anti-clericals. Three months before Robespierre's visit, the anti-clerical party had induced the departmental Directory to prohibit, for a time, public attendance at the nunnery chapels, where it was alleged that masses were said by 'refractory' priests; and a petition for the

[1] v. I/190.

expulsion of all 'non-jurors', signed amongst others by Augustin Robespierre, had been forwarded to the Assembly.[1] Opinion on both sides was deeply moved; and the clericals had recourse to time-honoured methods to work up feeling against their persecutors. They had gone so far, it was said, as to carry through the streets a Calvary, in which there were represented, by the side of the Penitent Thief, Maury, Cazalès, and other royalist deputies, and by the side of the Impenitent reviler of Christ, the revolutionary members of the Assembly, holding spear, vinegar, and *absinthe*, and crying, 'If thou art the Son of God, perform a miracle, and meet the deficit!'[2] Robespierre's arrival at Arras coincided with a fresh outbreak of propaganda. A 'miracle', he tells Duplay, 'has just been worked at the Calvary chapel. . . . While a refractory priest was saying mass, a lame man threw down his crutches, and walked'. His first reaction is that of a tolerant sceptic. He notes that the *dévot sanhédrin* of the clergy has, as a result of the miracle, vastly increased its sale of votive candles; and he chaffingly remarks, 'I don't intend to stay long in this Holy Land; I am not worthy of it'.[3] But he soon sheds this Voltairian detachment. He dines with his friend Joseph Lebon in the *presbytère* at Neuville-Vitasse, and hears all about his quarrel with his predecessor and rival, the non-juror Lebas; the parish clerk's account was that 'they talked of nothing but reforms and revolutions'.[4] Thus he began to see in the refractory priests and their followers the centre of a counter-revolutionary movement, and realized how little this danger was appreciated in Paris—always a world of its own, out of touch with the provinces. It was not for an ex-deputy, a politician on holiday, to publish alarmist opinions; but he expressed his fears in a private letter to a friend, which subsequently got into the press. 'Public affairs,' he wrote, 'are in such a deplorable condition that it is more difficult every day to do one's duty. . . . The orators of the National Assembly have gone all wrong on the question of the clergy, almost to a

[1]Paris, *Lebon*, 17.
[2]Desmoulins in *Révolutions de France et de Brabant*, No. 23.
[3]Corresp. 105.   [4]Paris, *Lebon*, 19, 39.

man. They have delivered learned orations on toleration and freedom of worship. They have envisaged merely as a question of philosophy and religion what is in reality a question of politics and the Revolution. They have failed to see that, every time an aristocratic priest makes a convert, he turns him into a fresh enemy of the Revolution. . . . I realize how little we in Paris understand the state of public opinion, or the power of the priests. I am convinced that by their own efforts alone they could restore the Monarchy, and that the court has only to leave them untouched, in the certainty that it will soon enjoy the fruit of their intrigues'.[1]

This was a remarkable declaration on the part of one hitherto reputed a friend of the clergy. The temptation to make political capital out of it, especially at a time when the new Assembly was discussing the clerical oath, and the treatment of the non-jurors, was overwhelming. The recipient of the letter immediately showed it to Gorsas, the editor of the *Courrier des 83 départements*, and extracts from it appeared within three days in that paper, and in another.[2] Robespierre at once wrote to protest. He did not deny his authorship, or the essential fairness of the extracts; but he objected to the publication of what was never intended to be more than a private expression of opinion.[3] The protest produced editorial notes, but no apologies. The *Courrier* in fact said that the person who had communicated the letter 'took a pride in having done a service to the country'.

Robespierre's opinions had, indeed, become a matter of national importance; and his visit to Arras was to bear fruit in the Jacobin church policy of the next three years, with its paradoxical mingling of official toleration and unofficial persecution. He could not have lived long in Paris without being aware of the reaction in the Assembly,

[1]Corresp. 106.
[2]The letter was dated November 4; it appeared in the *Courrier* and the *Annales patriotiques* on November 7.
[3]Corresp. 107, 108. To the editor of the *Annales* he says the printed version is *assez inexacte*, but to the editor of the *Courrier* he admits that it *n'eut pas altéré nécessairement l'esprit et le sens de la lettre.* This excludes Hamel's view that the letter was written by Condorcet. Robespierre also sent an explanation to the Jacobin Club, which was read there on November 16 (Jac. 3/248).

and the danger of political counter-revolution. But he had been too little in touch with his constituency, and too familiar with his brother's lack of judgment, to realize the danger of clerical intrigues in the provinces. He now saw that the movement against the clerical oath was becoming an ecclesiastical counter-revolution; and the discovery gave him a new feeling of insecurity, and a readiness to harbour suspicion, which embittered his outlook. He had lost many illusions in Paris: when he returned there, he left another behind him at Arras.

CHAPTER VII

THE OPPONENT OF WAR (NOVEMBER, 1791—APRIL, 1792)

I

THE cheers which greeted Robespierre's reappearance at the Jacobin Club on November 28 were more than a tribute to the man who had saved the society during the crisis of the summer and autumn. They were a sign, for those who could read it, that the ruling power in the country, which had passed two years ago from the king to the Assembly, was passing again from the Assembly to the clubs and sections of Paris. Robespierre himself had been the chief agent of this change, when, disillusioned with his colleagues, he had proposed the resolution by which they excluded themselves from the new legislature. He was, at first sight, pleased with the result. 'Unlike many people,' he told Buissart, 'I consider the new National Assembly very superior to that which preceded it'.[1]

There was, indeed, plenty of ability among the new deputies. But circumstances decreed that much of it should run to waste. The events of July had given an unexpected and difficult turn to the political situation. The electors, if they troubled to vote at all,[2] did so under the influence of the anti-republican reaction that followed the 'massacre' of July 17, and returned representatives predominantly conservative, pledged to uphold the constitutional settlement of September. Their part was in any case an inactive and undistinguished one, compared to that of their predecessors: for they had not to create, but only to carry out a Constitution; and to do so under the critical eyes of the ex-Constituents, the veterans of the Revolution, who to so great an extent controlled the press, the populace, and the purse-strings of Paris. But the position was even worse than this;

[1]Corresp. 110.   [2]v. Taine's figures in Deslandres, 1/139.

for few of those who had helped to make the Constitution any longer believed in it; and the events of the summer had not only led to an *impasse* in the relations between the nation and the king which could be ended only by republicanism, but had also created a feud between the middle-class monarchists and the lower-class republicans which was likely to render any regime unstable and transitory.

Under these circumstances it must have been clear to any shrewd observer—and none was shrewder than Robespierre—that the Assembly was no longer the main road to a political career, and that the real clash of parties and policies, in which personal reputations were to be lost or won, would take place at the Jacobin Club. Here, four nights a week, after the House had risen, the tired deputies would meet again, to face critics fresh from the popular society, the café, or the editor's chair. Here every suspicion could be aired, every rumour reported, every grievance revived, with a republican frankness which was still a little resented in the Assembly, but which was appropriate to a society that prided itself on responding to the lightest breath of public opinion. Here a piece of gossip from the street corner, or a private letter from the provinces, was enough material for a denunciation. Here was the Capitol, and here also was the Tarpeian rock of the Revolution.

In this heady atmosphere Robespierre's talents flourished. As the champion of liberal ideals, as the heir of Mirabeau, as the saviour of the club, and as the chief object of reactionary hatred, he stood almost alone. No one had a longer experience of parliamentary history, procedure, or tactics. No one had a stronger sense of party differences, or a keener scent for intrigue. The leadership which, by sheer persistence, he had forced the society to recognize, was now his by right. The easy applause of the Jacobins gave him new confidence in his powers, and lent fresh authority to his words. The normal danger of such a position was demagogy; but from this he was saved, for some time, by his opposition to the popular war policy. Meanwhile, he studied the personalities of political life; mastered the methods of 'clubocracy'; and measured the possibilities of 'direct action' in a state which was rapidly growing tired of representative government. Thus, when events justified his prevision, and the Jacobins came into power on the wave of reaction against a mismanaged war, Robespierre once more stood out as the Infallible, the Incorruptible, the Indispensable; never quite a leader of revolutionists, but a unique embodiment of the Revolution.

It is upon the Jacobin Club, therefore, that attention must be fixed during the winter of 1791–2; and Robespierre's frequent interventions in its debates, together with the increased correspondence and journalism which his greater leisure now allowed, will be the principal sources of information.

II

A good deal of Robespierre's attention was given, during these months, to the organization of Jacobinism. The experiences of the summer had shown that there were three ways in which the club could capture the power that was slipping out of the hands of the Assembly—by raising the standard of membership, by educating the people, and by influencing the elections.

As to membership, there might have been no question, but for the events of July. Originally the only qualification for admission to the club had been a personal recommendation, and the payment of a subscription. Jacobin societies in the provinces had recruited themselves from the people somewhat vaguely described as *patriotes*. Most of them came from the middle and lower *bourgeoisie*—from the people who owned a little property, paid taxes, and held liberal opinions, and from the intelligent minority which had always supported the *salons*, the Masonic lodges, and the literary or political societies in provincial towns.[1] Up to June, 1791, these Societies of 'Friends of the Constitution' followed the main advances of the Revolution, without

[1] v. Cardenal, *La province pendant la Révolution.*

any great need either to formulate their faith, or to investigate the character of their members. There were differences of opinion, no doubt, over the Church question; but these cut across the political divisions; and the king's flight discounted his stand against the clerical oath. But the events of July—the restoration of a discredited king, the reactionary amendments to an already undemocratic Constitution, and the proscription of republicanism—struck at the heart of Jacobinism. All over the country there were secessions from the Friends of the Constitution like that which formed the Feuillants in Paris. Everywhere the more radical patriots were for a time under a cloud. It was therefore natural that, when the weather cleared, and the storm passed on over the constitutionalists, those Jacobins who had stood firm during the crisis should try to define their position, and to refuse the readmission of back-sliders, or the recruitment of half-hearted believers. The winter of 1791–2 saw the beginnings of a Jacobin 'purge', or Counter-reformation, whose fruits were to be the August revolution, and the *Montagnard* dictatorship of 1793–4.[1] If Robespierre played a leading part in this unpleasing *épuration* of his followers, it need not be put down to personal malignity: it was due to the conviction, forced upon him by the events of the summer, that the patriots must either close their ranks, or be overwhelmed by the forces of counter-revolution.

Within a few weeks of his return to the club, Robespierre had declared this policy, and carried the first instalment of it. He had secured the adjournment of two applications for membership—one indefinitely (December 6). He had reiterated (December 25) his objection to any reunion with the Feuillant secession. He had won a decisive victory for the policy of the 'purge' (January 6), when he combated the proposal that ex-members of the Feuillants might be nominated for membership, and secured its unanimous rejection.

The campaign was soon extended to the provinces. At Strasbourg the popular party had broken up under a com-

[1] The Tridentine Decrees of the movement were embodied in a *Projet de réglement pour le société* (1791) (Brit. Mus. F.R. 366. Cp. a form of application for membership, *ibid*. F. 349 (20)).

bined attack by the Mayor (one Dietrich, a secessionist), the *procureur-syndic* (de Broglie), and the military. Robespierre, informed of every change in the situation by Simond, the corresponding secretary of the local Jacobins, insisted that the mother-club at Paris should come to the rescue. Dietrich was marked down for ultimate destruction; and Robespierre received a civic crown and a congratulatory address from the grateful Strasbourgers.[1]

Meanwhile, the Paris club was purging its ranks with increasing thoroughness. It was agreed, always at Robespierre's suggestion, that there should be no further admissions to membership until new rules were drawn up; that any member nominating an ex-*émigré* should be expelled from the club; and that a list of the members should be compiled and posted, showing their present professions, and the positions they had held before the Revolution; for, now that the country was upon the eve of war, both at home and abroad, it was not enough that a man should profess himself, or even behave himself as a patriot; his past conduct must be above suspicion, and his present status must conform to type.

This 'purge' was bloodless; the time had not yet come when the club door led to the guillotine. But the inquisitorial way in which it was carried out made the remedy worse than the disease. An anti-Jacobin pamphlet of August, 1791, spoke of Robespierre's 'perpetual denunciations, protestations, and slanders'. Another suggested that he had resigned the post of Public Prosecutor because he preferred to be Private Denouncer at the Jacobins.[2] The case for denunciation, and the distinction between the suspicion which justifies it, and the proof required for conviction at law, were expounded with great clarity in a pamphlet of which Robespierre himself may have been the author.[3] Besides, as an anonymous denouncer frankly remarks in a letter to Robespierre, if he were summoned to give evidence in a court of law, he would lose his oppor-

[1]Corresp. 113, 114, 118; A.R. 12/389.   [2]Brit. Mus. F.R. 366.
[3]Brit. Mus. F. 347 (23).

tunity for spying; whilst he would soon cease to reveal 'truths', if he had to substantiate them.[1] Nor was there any lack of material. The counter-revolution had infinite ramifications, and most of them led back, sooner or later, to Paris. The eighteenth century treasured no traditions of political purity, and there were few French statesmen who found it easy to refuse a bribe. So the unpleasant business went on.

III

Along with the purging of the Jacobin clubs went an attempt to educate the country in the principles of Jacobinism. It had always been the policy of the Paris society to keep the affiliated clubs in the provinces informed about crucial events in the capital, and to circulate, from time to time, propagandist literature. In 1791 there was a further extension of this plan, when an extra subscription of twelve *livres* a year was collected from some 700 members, to finance Tallien's *L'Ami des citoyens*, as a counterblast to the Feuillant *Chant du Coq*.[2] Again, one of Robespierre's last acts before going away for his holiday at Arras had been to sign a letter sent out by the society, enclosing the prospectus of an *école centrale d'expériences*, a kind of training school for Jacobin agents, to be established in Paris. The scheme included courses of lectures on morality and the Constitution, which were to be printed, and circulated to patriotic schools and societies, 'where they will be read aloud to specially summoned meetings of all the local inhabitants'. Robespierre himself was one of the twelve lecturers nominated, and one of the six who seem actually to have undertaken 'the noble work of instructing and catechizing children on the Constitution'. Robespierre's experience of school lecturing at Arras helped him now. One could, indeed, well spare some of his political speeches, if one had the Sunday morning talks he gave to the *Société fraternelle du faubourg Saint-Antoine*.[3]

A third way in which the Jacobins hoped to secure power

[1]Pap. inéd., 1/125.   [2]A.R. 7/37.   [3]Jac. 3/267, 418.

was by influencing the popular elections, which were by now so important a part of revolutionary routine. The length of time over which the simplest election might extend, whilst it made it difficult for poor patriots to vote, gave their leaders ample opportunity for lobbying. Robespierre, it may be suspected, had a liking for this kind of work: it was not a pure accident that he was accused of intriguing at the elections both to the States-General in 1789, and to the Convention in 1792. But, so far as the evidence goes, he does not seem to have done anything dishonest. For one thing, he was singularly unsuccessful in pushing his own candidatures. Few prominent persons of that time can have missed election more often than he did.[1] Nor was he much more successful with his friends. He had nothing to do with Pétion's election to the mayoralty of Paris. He specially forbore to press Danton's claims as *substitut procureur* of the commune (December 4). He opposed the suggestion of a Jacobin 'ticket' for elections to the criminal tribunal (December 27); and his friend Anthoine had to be content with a minor appointment (February 27). He was, indeed, anxious that the club should do nothing to excuse another attack by the Constitutionalists. Everything was to be gained, now that public opinion was coming round to their side, by a waiting policy. Accordingly all that was usually done, at election times, was to adjourn the club, so that those who were qualified to vote might do so, and those who were not might canvass for Jacobin candidates: indeed, in view of the small polls usually cast, this was probably effective enough.

It was doubtless the same caution which dictated Robespierre's treatment of the provocative petition presented by the departmental Directory (which included Talleyrand, Desmeuniers, and his old enemy Beaumetz), asking the king to veto the decree of November 29 against the refractory priests.[2] Their opinions might be detestable, but their procedure was not illegal; and it would be unwise for the

[1] e.g. February 15 and November 10, 1791 (*procureur-général-syndic*), June 9 and December 29 (criminal tribunal).
[2] The king did so on December 9.

club to issue any counter-petition. 'We want our enemies to realize', he said, 'that the public does not echo the opinions of the society, but the society those of the public. We want them to realize that the club is nothing but a section of the general public, and that all its energy comes from the fact that the capital is deeply imbued with revolutionary principles—that capital in whose defence it is ready to sacrifice all that it holds dearest in the world'. This declaration was of a piece with Robespierre's theory of national government,[1] and deserves attention as an essential part not merely of his party tactics, but also of his political philosophy.

IV

During the five months that lay between his return to Paris (November 28, 1791) and the declaration of war against Austria (April 20, 1792), Robespierre intervened in the debates at the Jacobin Club some sixty-five times, that is, at most of the four meetings a week. It would be possible to classify some of these speeches by subject-matter; but the whole series of debates is so bound together, in chronological sequence, by a single idea, that it is best, at the risk of some over-complexity, to follow the order of events. That single idea was war.

The keynote of everything that followed was given by Robespierre himself on the very day of his reappearance at the Jacobins. Dubois-Crancé, a keen and able patriot, read the draft of a decree that he proposed to move in the Assembly, calling upon the king to disperse the hostile mobilization of *émigrés* on the frontier. After several other members had spoken, Robespierre gave his opinion. What was it? Not a warning against war; not any expression of doubt as to the *casus belli*—the emigrants; but a demand for even stronger measures. The Assembly should not merely ask the king to act, but dictate his action: instead of an indirect threat to the puny Electors of Mayence, Trèves, and Cologne, it should deliver an ultimatum to the Emperor

[1] e.g. November 28.

himself. 'The National Assembly and the Executive Power,' he declared, 'ought to treat their foreign foes as a free people treats despots. They ought to imitate the Roman who, when commissioned in the name of the Senate to present an ultimatum to an enemy of the Republic, insisted upon an immediate reply. They ought to draw round Leopold the circle that Pompilius drew round Mithridates.' Robespierre did not persist in this bellicose mood; but at the moment this much is clear: that he is not a pacifist—for he may disapprove of a particular war, but he will not disapprove of war as such; and that he believes it is the right of the Assembly, as the people's representative, to impose its will upon the Crown. He is for a national foreign policy, and, if need be, for a national war. It is likely enough that, having only just returned to Paris, Robespierre did not as yet realize all the intrigues that lay behind the war policy of the court, or of the dominant party in the House. In proportion as he sounded them, he grew more cautious. But he never wavered from the principles that he laid down on November 28.[1]

On December 9 and 12, Carra, taking advantage of the rumour that Louis was intriguing with Leopold for the support of the throne,[2] called for a mobilization of the national forces, and a declaration of war. Robespierre, after throwing doubt on the Emperor's enthusiasm for his brother-in-law's cause, pointed out that the first result of a declaration of war would be to put all the armed forces of the country into the hands of the king, and to leave Paris at the mercy of any party that wanted to end the revolution, and establish a despotism.[3]

These fears of a royalist plot seemed likely to be realized

[1] Jaurès (3/136) thinks this speech insincere. Michon's solution (A.R. 12/357) is much as above, but he obscures the importance of the speech. Cp. the speech of April 20.

[2] Louis had in fact written to the Emperor, the King of Prussia, the Empress of Russia, and the Kings of Sweden and Spain, suggesting a conference of the Powers, backed by a threat of armed intervention, as the best way of saving his throne. (Lav. 1/337.)

[3] In an address of the Jacobins to the affiliated societies, two days before (December 10), Robespierre had denounced such a plot on the part of the Court. (Mathiez, 143).

a few days later (December 14), when the king and the Minster of War came to the Assembly, Louis to say that Leopold had promised his good offices to secure the dispersal of the emigrant forces in the Electorate of Trèves, and Narbonne to announce that within a month's time 150,000 French troops would be mobilized upon the frontier. When Biauzat at the club, the same evening, professed belief in the king's honesty, and proposed that the subject should be no further debated, Robespierre refused to be silenced. 'I shall discuss the question of peace or war,' he said, 'as my conscience dictates, and because liberty is the ruling passion of my life.'[1]

As the war fever mounted, he grew increasingly cold and careful. On December 16, Brissot, who passed for the leader of the Girondist majority in the House, and for one of the ablest speakers and writers in the club, announced the result of six months' meditation in an elaborate and eloquent plea for war. Two days later, after a crowded and exciting meeting, during which the English, French, and American flags were set up in the hall, and a *jeune citoyenne* made a patriotic speech on behalf of a deputation of female spectators, the secretary read a letter from a Swiss member of the club, offering the society a sword 'as a prize for the first French general who makes an enemy of the Revolution bite the dust;' and Isnard, who was presiding, and was always ready with a theatrical gesture, waved the sword in the air, crying, 'Gentlemen, this weapon shall be for ever victorious! The French people will utter a great shout, and every other nation will answer to its voice! The combatants will cover the earth, and every enemy of liberty will be struck off the roll of free men.' This rhodomontade moved Robespierre to protest. 'I am for war,' he said, 'as much as anyone. But it must be such a war as the nation really needs—a war in which we shall first crush our enemies at home, and then march against our enemies abroad, if any still exist. But (he went on) the court and the king's ministers also desire war . . . and the nation will have nothing

[1] Jac. 3/288.

to do with a war whose object, under a pretence of defending them, is to destroy liberty and the Constitution.' Now, Brissot knows all this; yet he says, 'Trust the government.' I say, 'Distrust it.' Distrust (*défiance*), whatever you may say, is the guardian of the people's rights: it bears the same relation to the passion of liberty as jealousy bears to the passion of love.' Or else Brissot says, 'Trust the people.' But the people has often been misled; and it is the duty of its leaders to see that it is not misled again. For this is not a war of liberation, leading to freedom, but a war waged by a despot against foreign princes, emigrants, and priests. Robespierre would rather have no such war at all; but if it must come, let it be a war of defence, in which Frenchmen can fight on their own soil, and for their own liberty. In any case, he declares, the country is not ready for war. 'Before we do anything else, we must manufacture munitions everywhere, untiringly; we must arm the National Guard, and the people, if only with pikes; we must adopt fresh and sterner methods to punish ministers whose negligence endangers the security of the state; and we must uphold the dignity of the people, and defend its rights, too frequently overlooked.' Above all, if war is inevitable, its conduct must be dictated by the people, not by the court. It must be a national war, leading to a national victory.

This defence of 'distrust,' the fruit (as he said) of 'three years' experience of perfidy and intrigue,' was cheered by the club, and circulated to the affiliated societies. Many of Robespierre's hearers were convinced for the first time of the treacherous intentions of the court, and realized that the motives behind Brissot's war policy might not be as honest as they seemed. But most people thought little of the political dangers of war, compared with its glories,[1] and found Robespierre's constant pessimism a little tiresome. Indeed, it may be doubted whether he did much service to the cause of liberty and democracy, in the long run, by a policy which could not be called defeatism only because the

[1]Salamon (Corresp. 206) notices that there are posters everywhere, with *Guerre aux émigrants!*

country was not yet at war. By suggesting distrust in one quarter, he created it in others. For it could hardly be supposed that the regime of suspicion, denunciation, and revenge which he sought to impose would easily revert to the generous and loyal spirit of 1789. The patient was undoubtedly ill; but might not a national war—as Brissot and his friends felt—give him just the stimulant he needed? Robespierre's remedy was that of a political psychoanalyst, who would cure the country by concentrating its attention on the origin of its ills. By early experience and seminary training an 'introvert,' he could see no remedy for national ill-health but self-examination, confession (without benefit of absolution), and a scrupulous moralism. Such an attitude might (and indeed did) give him a reputation for political saintliness, but it could not produce real leadership, or a permanent improvement in the national health. Not only the failure of Robespierre's own career, but also that of Jacobinism, is closely connected with the political invalidism that first showed itself in the speech of December 18.

In one passage of his speech Robespierre had compared himself, not very felicitously, to the geese on the Capitol warning Manlius-Brissot of the approach of the Gauls. Brissot's reply showed that he needed no warnings, because he was, in fact, inviting the Gauls to attack. 'Treason on a big scale (*les grandes trahisons*),' he declared, 'is fatal only to the traitor. It is just what we need.' In other words, he admits even more than Robespierre has alleged. Louis is a traitor; but he, Brissot, is 'double-crossing' him. The king's 'limited war' is to be encouraged, so that it may lead to the discredit and overthrow of the crown, and to the establishment of a Girondist regime. Even Robespierre's negative policy was better, perhaps, than such an irresponsible gamble with the resources of patriotism.

V

The year 1792 opened stormily, and it was soon seen that there was to be no truce in the Robespierre-Brissot controversy. On January 1 there was a 'scene' at the club, when Robespierre, from the chair, called Lasource, a friend of Brissot, to order, and Moreton, another *Brissotin* (as the party was now named) retorted by 'calling the chairman to fairness.' The next day Robespierre began a two days' speech (January 2, 11) expounding his whole view about the war. Though better known than that of December 18, it is not so important. Most of it reiterates the old arguments, at rather wearisome length.[1] Only in one passage is there some new material that needs attention. Brissot, who had travelled in England and America, and saw himself in the rôle of an international statesman, had pictured the coming war as a triumphant progress of revolutionary doctrine throughout the countries of Europe. 'Our generals,' as Robespierre put it, 'are to be missionaries of the Constitution; our camps are to be schools of public law; and the satellites of foreign princes, far from putting obstacles in the way of this plan, will fly to meet us, not to repel us by force, but to sit at our feet,' and to listen to the gospel of freedom. In answer to this engaging picture, Robespierre made some observations which, if they had been laid to heart, might have saved France from disillusionment, and Europe from many years of war. 'No one likes an armed missionary,' he said; 'and no more extravagant idea ever sprang from the head of a politician than to suppose that one people has only to enter another's territory with arms in its hands to make the latter adopt its laws and its Constitution. . . . Before the influences of our revolution can be felt abroad, it must be fully established at home. To expect to give freedom to foreign nations before we have achieved it ourselves, is a sure way to slavery, both for France and for the world. . . . The Declaration of Rights is not like the sun's rays, which in one moment illumine the whole earth: it is no thunderbolt, to strike down a thousand thrones. It is easier to inscribe it on paper, or to engrave it on brass, than to retrace its sacred characters in the hearts of men,

[1]Jaurès (3/155) apropos of this speech, thinks Robespierre's suspicions of the Court were not justified. Mathiez, quoting the Queen's letter of December 9 to Mercy-Argenteau, answers that they were.

from which they have been erased by ignorance, passion, and despotism.'

It says much for the good sense of the Jacobin rank and file that a speech expressing (however eloquently) such unpalatable truths was enthusiastically received. 'It will be read and re-read,' wrote Desmoulins, 'in every section, every club, and every patriotic home . . . You cannot imagine,' he adds, 'the abandon, and the conviction of truth, with which some passages of this speech were delivered: it brought tears into the eyes not only of the women in the gallery, but also of half the members in the hall.'[1]

Attempts were at last made to bring about a reconciliation between Brissot and Robespierre. On January 18 the latter had been careful, whilst criticising a passage in Brissot's paper, *Le patriote français*, to disclaim any personal attack; and two days later, whilst justifying himself, Brissot urged Robespierre to make up a quarrel which gave pleasure to no one except enemies of the state. The other made no move. Dussaulx, a veteran of the Seven Years' War who was a friend of both men, and whose age and learning commanded respect, exhorted them to be reconciled. 'After what M. Brissot has said, only one thing is needed, before the meeting adjourns—the sight of these two generous men embracing one another.' 'He had scarcely spoken (say the minutes) when Robespierre and Brissot were in each other's arms, amidst the unanimous applause of the society, which was touched by this moving spectacle.'

It was characteristic of Robespierre that he should wish no one to misunderstand a gesture which, though prompted by a real liking for Brissot, was deeply distasteful to his undemonstrative nature. Accordingly he went at once to the tribune, and explained that, in yielding to Dussaulx's suggestion, he had followed the promptings of his heart, and borne witness to his friendship for 'a man who is highly respected, and who is likely to render great services to the country'; but, he went on, 'this must not be thought to

[1]Michon, *Adrien Duport*, 112. It was this speech which prompted Mme Chalabre's letter (v. 1/145).

make any difference to the opinions every man has the right to hold on questions of public policy'; and he announced his intention of answering Brissot's speech at a later meeting. Again, when Gorsas, trying to exploit the situation in the *Brissotin* interest, stated in his paper that 'M. Robespierre gave reason to hope that he would easily come to an agreement with M. Brissot over the war,'[1] he at once wrote, repeating what he had really said, and adding, 'I shall continue to oppose Brissot's views whenever they seem contrary to my principles . . . Let our union rest upon the holy basis of patriotism and virtue; and let us fight as free men, with frankness and (if need be) with determination, but also with respect and friendship for one another.'[2]

It was in this spirit that, on January 25, the day on which the Assembly issued its first ultimatum to the Emperor,[3] Robespierre delivered the third of his speeches about the war. In this he dealt with the arguments for the good intentions of the King and his Ministers, exposed the unpreparedness of the country, and drew a gloomy picture of the future. 'Ah!' he cried, in a rhetorical peroration, 'I can see a great crowd of people dancing in an open plain covered with grass and flowers, making play with their weapons, and filling the air with shouts of joy, and songs of war. Suddenly the ground sinks under their feet; the flowers, the men, the weapons disappear; and I can see nothing but a gaping chasm, filled with victims. Fly! Fly, while there is still time, before the ground on which you stand opens beneath its covering of flowers!' This Isaiad might seem fantastic at the time; but it was remembered, before the year was out, when Brunswick's troops were almost at the gates of Paris.

VI

Robespierre seems to have been fully aware, at this time, of the danger of a purely negative policy. In the pause

---

[1] *Courrier des 83 Départements*, January 22.
[2] Corresp. 117. It appeared in the *Courrier* of January 23.
[3] On January 6 it was announced that the Elector of Trèves had undertaken to disperse the emigrants. The immediate *casus belli* was removed. This did not please the war party, which proceeded (rather as in 1870) to ask the Emperor for a statement of his peaceful intentions.

which followed his third speech on the war—he did not deal with the subject again for more than a month—he set himself to think out a constructive policy; and this he expressed on February 10, in one of the best and most important of his speeches. Treating first of national defence, he charged the government with failing to carry out several suggestions that he had already made—the arming of the people, the reorganization of the higher command, the re-enlistment of discharged soldiers, and the 'permanence' of the Sections. He called for a fresh *fédération*, at which armed citizens from every Department should take the oath of liberty or death (*de vivre libres, ou de mourir*); and for a new military spirit, unrestrained by the old ties of army discipline, and expressing itself in the free and happy ritual of patriotism.[1] Turning to the internal state of the country, of which he saw evil omens in the troubles at Avignon, the reactionary petition of the Directory, the later acts of the Constituent Assembly, and the present behaviour of the Ministers, he did not think the remedy was to be found (as some proposed) in a popular Ministry, which would be subjected to the same corrupting influences as any other, but rather in closer public control both of the Legislative and of the Executive—he would, for instance, turn the *Manège* into a People's Palace, capable of containing an immense audience; in throwing open all appointments to patriots, and none but patriots; in strong measures against speculation, profiteering, and the exportation of currency; in better conditions of service in the army; in the reform of the police system, and summary jurisdiction; and in doing something to meet the just grievances of the country population. More generally, he would push on enlightened legislation, especially in the direction of popular education, through schools, theatrical performances, and national festivals. For he believed that the heart of the people was healthy, and that, if only writers could be found to inspire, and men of wealth to finance its

[1] Pétion, he suggested, as mayor of Paris, would be the ideal leader of such a crusade.

efforts, the Revolution would yet be victorious over all its enemies.

When Robespierre left the tribune, he was acclaimed as 'the hero of the Revolution,' and copies of his speech were circulated to all the Sections of Paris. It was, in truth, a fine attempt to escape from the poisonous fumes of party politics into the fresh air of constructive statesmanship; and even a generation that has grown distrustful of the promises of would-be dictators to end the ills of society can admire Robespierre's anticipation of ideas which were partly worked out under his own influence, during the Jacobin dictatorship of 1793–4, and which have, to a larger extent, become the common property of mankind.

In spite of this temporary triumph, Robespierre had little success in his campaign against the war. On January 17 the club had circularized its branches to the effect that war was inevitable. Now, on February 24, it was proposed to send them another letter, ending, 'The majority of the society is in favour of war.' Robespierre challenged the statement, but without success; whilst his suggestion, that they should publish a summary of the arguments for and against the war, was too open-minded to please either side.

A week later (March 2) despatches from Vienna were read in the Assembly which fully justified Robespierre's suspicion of the connexion between war and counter-revolution; for they contained a passage in which the Emperor hinted that he might be driven to intervene in French affairs 'by the provocative and dangerous behaviour of the Jacobin party,' whom he described, in terms too obviously dictated from the Tuileries, as 'a pernicious sect, enemies of the most Christian King, and of the fundamental principles of the present constitution, and disturbers of the public peace.' The insult was bitterly resented by the club. Nevertheless, since capital had been made, and might still be made, out of the allegation of republicanism, Robespierre moved that the Jacobins should formally declare themselves 'Friends of the Constitution in its present form (*telle qu'elle est*).' 'I love the republican character,' he said, 'as much as anyone: I know that republics are the nursery of all great souls, of all noble and generous sentiments: but I think that we should do wisely, at the present moment, to tell the whole world that we are firm friends of the Constitution—until the General Will is sufficiently enlightened by ripe experience to proclaim its desire for a happier state'. 'For my own part,' he ended, 'I prefer the king who is ours by accident of birth and circumstances to any other whom they would like to give us'—a hit at Carra's unfortunate suggestion of the Duke of Brunswick,[1] which was applauded in all parts of the House.

Two days later Barbaroux reported 'a cloud like a man's hand'—the first sign of the storm which was to break on August 10. 'The men of Marseille,' he said, 'are on the march'; and wrote home an enthusiastic account of the reception of the news at the Jacobins. 'Robespierre was magnificent: he said that anyone who spoke against Marseille in the Assembly was an infamous traitor'.[2]

VII

Meanwhile an event had taken place which altered the whole political situation. On March 10 Brissot had led an attack on de Lessart, the Minister for Foreign Affairs. The king had given way, and replaced him by a lively member of Brissot's party, whose ambition it was to combine the parts of Mirabeau and Lafayette—General Dumouriez. A week later the appointment of Clavière, Roland, Grave, and Lacoste, gave the *Brissotins* complete control of the government. A curious situation resulted. By a constitutional experiment which was not provided for in the settlement of 1791, and which, in cleverer hands, might have been accounted a stroke of genius, the king had secured Ministers representing the majority in the Assembly; at the same time he had discredited its leaders, by transferring to them the suspicion which attached itself, sooner or later,

[1] January 4.
[2] He had recently (February 10, March 7, 14) denounced the Government's mismanagement of affairs in the Midi.

to all Ministers of the Crown. The *Brissotins* were hoist with their own petard. They had what they had coveted; they were in power. But they were doubly compromised, both because they had hoped to reach this position at the expense, not by favour of the king, and because they would now be saddled with his responsibility for the war, and, in the event of defeat, with his disgrace. They could not now draw back from a contest that they had provoked; yet they were utterly unprepared to force it to a successful issue. Dumouriez, indeed, believed in victory, and drove the new government along a path they would have liked to avoid —a path all the more dangerous, since at this very moment (March 10) the cautious Leopold died, and was succeeded by the militant Francis II. Finally, Dumouriez himself was an adventurer, whose patriotism was suspect, and whose policy might at any moment compromise his supporters.

This unnatural alliance between the *Brissotins* and the court was exactly what Robespierre had feared. But there was no need to meet trouble half-way; and when, on March 19, Dumouriez appeared at the club, wearing a *bonnet rouge*, and made a patriotic speech, he welcomed him coldly, but tactfully. When the general has fulfilled his promises, he said, and has won his victories, he will deserve our special thanks. Till then, he comes to the society as an ordinary member, to get sympathy and advice. At this, Dumouriez, who liked a gesture, even if it was not a new one, threw himself into Robespierre's arms,[1] amidst the applause of members and spectators, who 'regarded their embrace as a sign of alliance between the ministerial and popular points of view'.

There was, however, something very unreal about this scene; and the feeling found expression, as often happens, in a matter of detail. When Robespierre rose to speak, some officious person placed a *bonnet rouge* upon his carefully powdered *coiffure*. Disregarding a practice which had

[1]Gower (163) says Dumouriez's speech 'worked so strongly upon Mr. Robespierre's feelings that he could not resist embracing the minister'.

recently grown up in the club, and disdaining to follow Dumouriez's example, he threw it to the ground. This, perhaps, needed some courage[1]; but such was Robespierre's influence that when, later in the meeting, a letter from Pétion (no doubt inspired by himself) suggested the abolition of this new-fangled symbol of patriotism, the members at once put their *bonnets* in their pockets, and never wore them again.

Robespierre's critical attitude towards the new Ministry has sometimes been explained—notably by Michelet—as due to personal reasons. He was disappointed, it is said, at not being asked to join the government, and jealous of those who were. The latter explanation cannot be ignored; for he was losing the generosity with which he had welcomed Pétion's appointment to the mayoralty a few months before. But the former carries little conviction. Robespierre's quarrel with Brissot's policy, if not with Brissot himself, was too complete; and the king, who had good reason for trying to conciliate the majority in the Assembly, had no call to consider a minority in the club. It was not his personal exclusion from a government of whose policy he disapproved which embittered Robespierre's outlook during the next few months, but the knowledge that the destinies of the Revolution were at the mercy of a new Assembly, and new Ministers, who might wantonly hand over the country to a worse despotism than that from which it had so recently escaped.

VIII

This was why, when it was proposed (March 21) to circularize the Jacobin clubs, describing the *Brissotin* Ministry as a body of pure patriots, Robespierre drafted an alternative address, giving his own view of the situation. This address he read to the club five days later—at the very moment when (an unconscious proof of his worst suspicions) Marie-Antoinette was communicating to the

---

[1] Souberbielle, who was there, used to quote it as an instance of Robespierre's 'civil courage' (Blanc, 6/299).

Austrians Dumouriez's plan of campaign).[1] It was, in the main, a restatement of the familiar arguments against war: but it contained one sentence which caused a strange resentment. In spite of all the courage and patience of the people (Robespierre had written), the policy of the court would have led to disaster, 'had not Providence, which always watches over us better than our own wisdom, struck down Leopold, and disconcerted for a time the schemes of our enemies.' It might have been objected that the death of the pacific Leopold contributed little to the safety of France; but one would have thought it harmless enough to attribute his removal to Providence. Yet it was precisely upon this point that Guadet, the Bordeaux lawyer, fastened in his reply. 'I have heard the word Providence', he said, 'repeated again and again in this address: I fancy it even says that Providence has saved us in spite of ourselves. I confess I can see no meaning in such a conception; and I should never have believed that a man who has worked so bravely for three years to liberate the people from the bondage of despotism would help to put it back under the bondage of superstition.' It would have been easy to meet this sneer by disavowing any serious meaning: if Robespierre had said he had been using a conventional formula, the club sceptics would have thought no more about it. Or he might have retorted that, not so long ago, Guadet himself, speaking of the court intrigues, had said, 'Providence, which watches over the destiny of France, defeated this detestable plot,' and had professed devotion to 'that heavenly religion, which is as pure as its author, as vast as nature, and as eternal as time.'[2] But he could not do so; for he knew that he believed what he had said: and the society was suddenly embarrassed by the most shocking thing that can happen in a political debate—a profession of religious faith. 'There is nothing superstitious,' Robespierre was heard to say, 'in using the name of the Deity. I believe, myself, in those eternal principles on which human weakness reposes, before

---

[1]Letter to Mercy-Argenteau, March 26 (Jaurès, 3/236).
[2]Feb. 27, 1791 (Hamel, 1/47).

it starts on the adventure of virtue. These are not idle words in my mouth, any more than they have been to many great men who were none the less moral because they believed in the existence of God.' At this there were cries of 'Order! Order!' and a commotion (*brouhahas*): but Robespierre would not be stopped. 'No,' he went on, 'there is nothing outrageous in invoking the name of Providence, and expressing a conception of the Eternal Being who intimately affects the destinies of nations, and who seems to me personally to watch over the French Revolution in a very special way. It is a heartfelt belief; it is a feeling with which I cannot dispense. How could I ever have carried through (as I have) superhuman tasks, if I had not cultivated my soul (*élevé mon âme*)? This religious sense has more than compensated me for the loss of all the advantages to be gained by those who are willing to betray the people'.

When the question was put to the vote, Santhonax cried out 'A truce to monkery!' and the meeting ended in disorder. But many of Robespierre's hearers must have recalled this profession of faith two years later, when he brought forward proposals for the national 'worship of the Supreme Being'.

A reader of Robespierre's speeches shares the surprise of his Jacobin audience, when he is presented with this Jewish belief in a Special Providence directing the Revolution,[1] and finds that it is neither a relic of childish faith, undigested by the maturer mind, nor a grotesque that has slipped into the vacant niche of religion, but a firm and intimate conviction, the inspiration of a statesman's daily life. He did not realize before that Robespierre was a religious man. It was known that he had clerical teachers, and a seminarist training, and that he had lived most of his life at Arras, a centre of ecclesiasticism. He had been suspected, once or twice, since he came to Paris, of showing unusual sympathy for the cause of priests and monks. But it was understood that he had given up the practice of religion

---

[1] Jewish rather than Christian: or even pagan, for in one passage he substitutes Chance (*hasard*) for Providence; but anyhow a reality, not a matter of words.

while still at College; he had been heard to denounce the luxury and hypocrisy of rich churchmen; he had expressed his growing anger with the counter-revolutionary intrigues of the clergy; and although the persistence with which he championed the rights of the poor and the oppressed could not but inspire respect, it had been put down less to Christian charity than to philosophical convictions, backed by a touch of careerism. It alters one's whole view of the man, if the mainspring of his activity is a belief in a Divinity that shapes the ends of the Revolution.

Yet something of this kind is needed to explain both the passion with which the cold and *gauche* young lawyer pursues his intractable ideals, and his deep certainty that he is right, and others are wrong; for those who believe in divine guidance are generally guided where they wish to go. It is clear, in the light of this confession, how Robespierre can be Brissot's friend in society, but must be his enemy in politics—we had almost said, in religion.

The *Journal de Paris*, congratulating Robespierre on this speech, recalled the fact that a monument had recently been set up in honour of Rousseau. The allusion was just. Robespierre's religion was, indeed, the Deism that Jean-Jacques had learnt at Geneva, the centre of the League of Religions, and had put into the mouth of his *vicaire savoyard*. Like that, it was grafted upon conventional Catholicism: like that, it was the reaction of a solemn mind to a frivolous society: like that, it was a sentiment of the heart rather than a conclusion of the mind. But in two respects it was independent and original; for Rousseau's Providence, made in his own image, was a vagabond and cosmopolitan god, unconcerned with men's private affairs; whereas Robespierre's was a director of nations, and a patron of the Revolution: Rousseau's was a fair-weather deity, an object of idle and refined speculation, whilst Robespierre's was a consolation in trouble, and the inspiration of a work-a-day life. Nevertheless, the likeness of Robespierre's creed to Rousseauism is as striking as its divergence from the Voltairianism which was still fashionable among the intelligent and easy-going men of the world who were represented, on the whole, by the Girondist deputies; and it would not be fanciful to see, in this incident, the momentary unveiling of a fundamental difference of mind and outlook which separated the two great parties in the state.[1]

IX

The question of the war had now reached its last and bitterest stage. Robespierre found himself once more unscrupulously attacked in the *Courrier des 83 départements*; and failing to get satisfaction from Gorsas, the editor,[2] pursued the matter at the club (April 2). His challenge was accepted by Réal, who took advantage of a division of opinion in the galleries to attack Robespierre in bolder language than had ever been heard there. 'I accuse you,' he said, 'of stubbornness and perversity in trying to pass off as the society's opinion on the war what is in fact nothing but your own. I accuse you of practising in this club— perhaps unconsciously, and I am sure unintentionally—a tyranny which presses heavily upon every free man within its walls.' Here Réal was interrupted, and could not go on: but neither was Robespierre allowed to reply; and it was evident enough that, whilst many of the members sympathized with Réal, most of them disliked the personal character of the controversies in which the apostle of principle seemed so often to be involved.

Only one thing now gave pause to such controversies— hostility to the king. In these last weeks before the war, all the mistakes of his party were recoiling upon his head. None, save the flight to Varennes, had so painfully affected public opinion as the suppression of the Nancy mutiny. It was too late to make amends by subscribing to the relief fund in aid of the imprisoned mutineers, though Danton's motion to refuse the royal donation (March 4) was defeated

---

[1]Blanc, 6/334, f. Michelet has the same idea; but to him Voltaire, not Rousseau, is the true Frenchman, and Thermidor is a Voltairian *revanche*.

[2]Who refused to print his letter of protest (Corresp. 126).

by Robespierre.[1] The arrival of the released prisoners in Paris (April 9) was too good an opportunity to be missed, and recent differences were for the moment forgotten in the enthusiasm with which Robespierrists and *Brissotins* united to fête the victims of Bouillé and Lafayette. It was Robespierre's special aim to direct the demonstration against Lafayette. Nor is his motive obscure. It is not the Lafayette of the Nancy mutiny, or even of the massacre of the Champ de Mars, whom he is really attacking, but the prospective dictator—the man more likely than any other to use the army against the Revolution. 'Against whom,' he asks, 'do you think you have to struggle? The aristocrats? The court? No; but against a general, long since commissioned by the court, that enemy of freedom, to carry out its designs; a general who has deceived the people, and is deceiving the crown; who is a stranger to the principles of liberty and equality—nay, who is their greatest foe. We are indeed surrounded by enemies of freedom, but Lafayette is the most dangerous of them all; for he still wears the mask of patriotism well enough to hold under his banner a considerable number of the less enlightened citizens. Bouillé was not wholly to blame: he was only the agent of the court, and above all of Lafayette'; and there follows much more in the same inflammatory tone. He ends by demanding that the busts of Bailly and Lafayette shall be removed from the Town Hall, and that the 'slogan' of the forthcoming fête shall be, not, 'Down with Bouillé!' but 'Down with the tyrants'; which Merlin interpreted well enough when he corrected it to 'Down with Lafayette!' (*Lafayette seul est coupable*); and so it stood. On April 9 the released soldiers were welcomed in the Assembly, and at the club, where the Girondist Vergniaud, as President, made them a complimentary speech, and gave the *accolade* to the oldest and youngest of their number. Collot d'Herbois, anxious that the Girondins should not get all the credit of the occasion, suggested that the visitors would no doubt like

[1]The royal family contributed 210 *livres* to a fund collected by the Feuillants in the Tuileries section.

to hear Robespierre, 'who had interested himself so much in their case'; and the Jacobin orator, probably primed for the occasion, spoke of the services they had rendered to the cause of freedom, and brought up once more his suggestion for the re-enlistment of those who had been unfairly dismissed from the army.

Still determined to keep the demonstration on Jacobin lines, Robespierre intervened, within the next few days, with a fresh attack on Lafayette (April 11), a warning against the activities of bad patriots (April 13), and a proposal to associate the National Guard and the *Gardes françaises* with the coming celebrations (April 14).[1]

On Sunday the 15th, the 'Fête of Liberty' at last took place. A hundred thousand citizens paraded the streets, bearing emblems of peace and plenty, and escorting a car of freedom, mounted on the *chassis* used for the apotheosis of Voltaire, and painted by David with appropriate scenes from the lives of Brutus and William Tell; as well as two *sarcophagi* dedicated to the dead members of the Châteauvieux regiment, and of the National Guard. Two days later Robespierre proposed an inscription to commemorate the occasion as one on which 'poverty and the people triumphed with the *gardes françaises*, the soldiers of Châteauvieux, and all good citizens persecuted on account of the Revolution'; and Merlin suggested that he should apply his 'fiery spirit' to the composition of a history of the fête.

It was, indeed, generally recognized as 'Robespierre's fête.' 'M. Robespierre has given his orders,' wrote Salamon, 'and they will be obeyed.'[2] The Girondists had the consoling memory of a few speeches. The royalists could only revenge themselves by lampoons.[3] It was a forecast of what was to happen, on a more serious scale, a few months later. Yet one may well pause to ask why Robespierre not merely tolerated, but enthusiastically supported, a provocative and rather silly demonstration. His motives were not so simple

---

[1]He had already (April 8) denounced a pasquinade by 'Lieut. Oatmealbread' (Paindavoine) protesting against the fête.

[2]*Correspondance*, 389.

[3]e.g. a 'Hymn of invasion' to the metre and tune of O *filii, o filiae!* (R.F. 22/390).

as they would have been a year earlier. With love of liberty, and sympathy for victims of military despotism, was now combined a desire to discredit the war party, and to outbid the Girondins in popular favour; reasons which belong to a new Robespierre, whose nature has become narrowed and embittered by political controversy, and whose nerves have been worn by illness,[1] and by the constant strain of debate.

A foreigner visiting the Jacobins about this time was struck by the impertinence of Robespierre's manner. 'Entering the club, he would throw himself on a solitary chair near the door, cross his legs, lean back his carefully curled head, and, without taking any part in the discussion, give the impression that he owned the club, and was waiting to see whether anything turned up to interest him. His flattened, almost crushed in, features, his pale complexion, and his cunning look, made his impertinence peculiarly provocative.'[2]

Two curious incidents end this phase of Robespierre's career. On April 11 Desfieux proposed that the club should subscribe towards the cost of experiments with a new kind of gun, which was said to be capable of firing twenty-five rounds a minute. Robespierre objected, not wholly on grounds of humanity. 'I have,' he said, 'a confession to make. This same proposal was brought before me towards the end of the session of the Constituent Assembly. A demonstration was given in the garden of the house where I was then living. The invention consisted of a carbine that fired nine rounds without re-charging. When the inventor asked my opinion, I advised him to make no use of his discovery; and he has not said a word about it. I will repeat here what I told him—that a discovery of this kind, if put into the hands of a free people, can indeed give them a temporary advantage over their oppressors, but that, sooner or later, it will get into the hands of the oppressors themselves, and then it will become one weapon more for enslaving the people.'

On April 13, on the eve of the Châteauvieux fête, the

[1] v. Augustin's letter of March 19 (Corresp. 122). Robespierre only spoke once at the Jacobins between March 7 and 19.
[2] Reichardt's diary (R.F. 23/84).

Jacobin club was the scene of an incident that has special interest for Englishmen. 'Deputies from the Constitutional Society of Manchester,' so run the minutes, 'introduced by M. Robespierre, requested and obtained admission to the meeting in order to ask for the affiliation of their society.' These deputies, Thomas Cooper and James Watt, not only read an address to the club, but also took part, to the great scandal of most of their compatriots, in the public procession of the 15th.

X

What of Robespierre's correspondence during these months of political strain?

It opens (November 30) with the cheerful outlook of a man just back from a holiday, who can be equally pleased with the new Assembly, with the state of public opinion, and with his friend Pétion's election to the mayoralty of Paris.[1] But this mood does not last long. It is disturbed by gloomy letters from his brother at Arras,[2] and from Simond at Strasbourg, showing only too clearly the failure of the Paris revolution to carry the country-side along with it, now that the peasantry, rid of their feudal burdens, and in possession of the land, are growing indifferent to further progress, and dislike the new paper currency as much as the prospect of war.[3] It is disturbed also by new importunities to which Robespierre's reputation exposes him. An Englishwoman, whose name is variously transcribed as 'Miss J. Theeman Stephen', or 'Miss Freeman Shepherd,'[4] has a sum of money she wishes to place at his disposal. He had, she implies, been to see her, and had promised to accept her 'small offering'; but she now sees from her bank book that he had not done so. She will, if he likes, send another order, payable at once. The sequel is unknown. Perhaps Robespierre had been merely forgetful: perhaps he thought it wiser to refuse a contribution that might have

[1]Corresp. 110.   [2]Corresp. 111, 112.   [3]Corresp. 113, 118.
[4]Alger (*Englishmen in the French Revolution*, 54) identifies her with Harriet Augusta Freeman, the translator of Mercier, who was a boarder in the English Benedictine nunnery in Paris.

been misunderstood.[1] A little later a member of the Cordeliers club asks him to stand as godfather for his child.[2] Another admirer, who characterizes Robespierre as 'a man eminently sympathetic, beneficent, and humane,' asks for an interview in order to plead the cause of 'an unfortunate patriot.'[3] The Jacobin club at Caen thank him for services rendered to some of their compatriots.[4]

Of more importance is a letter from Mme Roland, found among Couthon's papers, and addressed to a person whom it is not difficult to identify as Robespierre. She has come back from the country (March 27), and is staying in Paris at the Hôtel Britannique. She has been delighted to receive a complimentary letter from him, and hopes he will come to see her. 'I maintain here,' she adds, 'a simplicity which (I hope) will make me worthy of your regard, although I *have* the misfortune to be the wife of a Minister. I cannot hope to contribute anything useful (she means, to the party counsels), unless wise patriots help me with their ideas and their attentions. You are at the head of my list. So please come at once. I am eager to see you, and to tell you again of my regard for you—a regard which nothing can alter.'[5] Robespierre seems to have accepted this invitation; but it led to disillusionment on both sides. There is, at any rate, among Mme Roland's papers, a significant note written to her friend Bosc, which her editor dates early in April, and which begins: 'R.b.p. is with me at my house. He asked me for an interview. I shall be alone, and shall do all I can to be uninterrupted, at seven o'clock this evening.'[6] We notice (if this is the occasion of the letter) the little deception: it was not he who had asked for the interview, but herself. She does not want to be found making overtures to one whom (in spite of her flattery) she already suspects to be a political enemy. It was, indeed, the breaking-point of their friendship. When she wrote again (April 25), war had been declared: she had made a last attempt to see Robespierre, and to win his support for the policy of her husband, and

---

[1]Corresp. 116. [2]Corresp. 119. [3]Corresp. 120.
[4]Corresp. 121. [5]Corresp. 124. [6]Corresp., ed. Perroud, 2/417.

of his friends; and he had refused to come. 'I wanted to see you,' she says, 'because I believe you have an ardent love of liberty, and a whole-hearted devotion to the public good, and because I experienced, at our last interview, the sense of pleasure and usefulness that comes to good citizens when they express their feelings, and explain their views. The more you appeared to me to disagree, on an interesting question, with men whose advice and integrity I esteem, the more important it seemed to be to bring together those who are working for the same end, and who ought to be able to agree as to the best means of achieving it. . . . It has pained me to see you convinced that, if anyone, knowing the facts, thought otherwise than yourself about the war, he could not be a good citizen.' He promised (she goes on) to give her his reasons for this attitude; why is he avoiding her? None of her friends are (as he has evidently alleged) his 'mortal enemies.' She does not receive them 'intimately.' Her Constitutionalist friends are not 'intriguers.' Time will judge between them. 'It is for you to consider,' she ends, with a feminine weakness for a spiteful postscript, 'that the verdict of time may either eternalize your glory, or condemn it to endless annihilation.'[1] It is not difficult to reconstruct from this letter the kind of reply Robespierre would have sent to a spoilt and offended woman. All his hatred of the war, all his suspicions of the new Ministry, all his hyper-sensitiveness to opposition and intrigue, would keep him from her door. The element in which she hoped to fuse public enmity and private friendship was too unreal for him. His incorruptibility—or was it his intransigence?—refused a commitment which had every worldly argument on its side, as well as some considerations of public service. And for what good end? Did he already foresee the disasters of the war, the fall of the throne, and the Jacobin supremacy? Or was he just making the choice that conscience dictated, and leaving the future to Providence, which he sometimes called Chance?

Another source of worry at this time was the position

[1]Corresp. 132, ed. Perroud, 2/418.

of his brother and sister at Arras. Augustin always had a grievance. Either the Assembly has not answered a question he asked about the criminal law, or he has failed to get a judgeship, or he cannot recover the cost of postage on a parcel, or he is short of cash, and reminds Maximilien of the obligation to support his poor relations.[1] The only thing that would satisfy them was a migration from Arras to the capital; and that was ultimately arranged.

On April 10 Robespierre wrote to Roederer, as *procureur-syndic* of the Paris Department, resigning his useless office of Public Prosecutor. He had been appointed exactly ten months before, and for eight months afterwards the court to which he was attached had never come into being. During February and March the members of the tribunal had met informally to determine their procedure; and had once or twice gone so far as to 'interrogate certain accused persons,' and to deal with 'difficulties likely to arise in starting a new form of jurisdiction.' Whether or not Robespierre disapproved of these tedious proceedings, at any rate he attended so seldom that he was rebuked by the President, Treilhard, for his laxity; and, a few days before the first formal session of the court, sent in his resignation. Treilhard was instructed to reply politely (such is his own account), but in terms which could not be quoted as evidence that Robespierre had done his duty; his letter is a model of tact. The moments, he said, unhappily only too few, during which he and his colleagues had been able to enjoy Robespierre's presence and advice, only confirmed their feelings, and made them regret all the more his resignation.[2] Hamel, indeed, claims to have found evidence in the 'dusty dossiers' of the tribunal that Robespierre took an active part in its work: but Treilhard's letter is proof that he did not. Even his admirer Barbaroux was angry, and wrote, 'M. Robespierre cannot be forgiven for resigning so important a post.'[3] But it was ridiculous to accuse him of doing so for interested motives; for he was surrendering an income of 8,000 *livres* a year, and a position

[1] Corresp. 127.   [2] Corresp. 129. Pap. inéd. 3/277.   [3] Corresp. 139.

225

of value to his party (as Barbaroux saw), which was filled up a few days later by the election of Duport—a Feuillant, and a personal enemy of his own. His resignation may have been a gesture, at a moment when his *Brissotin* opponents were helping themselves to Ministerial salaries. But in any case he wanted his whole time free for political work, and for a new venture in journalism.

The last two letters before the declaration of war deal with the affairs of the Jacobin club at Pamiers, where Robespierre's speeches had been much admired, and where his portrait had been put up side by side with that of Mirabeau. His correspondent was his future enemy, Vadier, who at this time claimed his friendship, on the ground of 'identity of principles and attachments, during the perilous course that we have so proudly run.' Robespierre may often have reflected that his friends were more compromising than his enemies.[1]

XI

On April 20 Louis XVI came to the Assembly, and proposed a declaration of war against the King of Hungary and Bohemia. It was voted almost unanimously. At Strasbourg, on the 25th, Rouget de l'Isle sang the *Marseillaise*. France was on the road to Valmy and Waterloo.

[1]Corresp. 130, 131.

CHAPTER VIII

THE DEFENDER OF THE CONSTITUTION
(APRIL–AUGUST, 1792)

I

A DECLARATION of war is generally a serious moment in the life of a people, when anything that hinders national unity is sacrificed to the one end of winning through to victory. But this was not the temper of France in April, 1792. The war did not come through a sudden crisis, carrying the people off its feet. It had been anticipated for nine months; for four it had been a constant subject of political controversy. Its very outbreak was an anti-climax. If the declaration had been made in June, 1791, it would have had all the accompaniments of a great national act—the flight of a king, a threat of foreign troops on the frontier, the destruction of emblems of royalty, a calm and united Assembly, the rush of volunteers to the colours. But the great moment had passed. The king had come back, and had been officially forgiven. Republicans had been shot down, and royalism had again become respectable. The politicians had resumed their quarrels, and the army its process of disintegration. Now that war had really come, it did not feel so near or so real as it had ten months ago. It was not a national war, engaged in hot anger, or through a sudden danger to the country. It was a war of calculation, the work of a political party, in league with self-interested financiers,[1] and a discredited court. The war-mongers, too, had done little to interest or educate public opinion, and popular propaganda had been almost confined to a fête

[1] v. the letter of the Paris banker Hottinguer to Amet, Ramus, et Cie of Havre, quoted in A.H. 2/489, and ending, 'The harm resulting from a war will be less than that of a prolongation of our present position; and when the business man has contributed his share to the country, he may be allowed to pay another share into his own account. You will understand what we mean.'

whose object was to stigmatize military discipline, and to glorify resistance to the government. The country was, indeed, in a warlike mood; but it was also, as Robespierre had seen, quite unready for war; and hostilities could hardly begin with anything but disaster.

What was a patriot to do? Suppress his private feelings, make up his quarrel with the *Brissotins*, and support the government? Or retire from public life, and trust Providence to bring France to sanity and safety? Robespierre could do neither. He was making discoveries about himself, as men do in a crisis. One was, that he could not remain on friendly terms with people of whose policy he disapproved. Another was, that he did not trust Providence to save France without his own help.

Moreover, nature had made him a man who could never take things lightly. Others, with an equal belief in first principles, might yet admit degrees of priority in their application: to Robespierre they were all alike. Others, sharing his dislike of the origin of the war, and his distrust of the men who were to manage it, might yet have closed their eyes to the past, and turned their attention to the avoidance of similar blunders in the future. Not so Robespierre. The political maze into which he had wandered seemed to be constantly doubling upon itself, and bringing him back to his starting-point. The fresh obstacles to his progress were indistinguishable from the old: now it was Louis, now Lafayette, now Guadet, now Brissot: all were enemies of liberty, of the people, of Robespierre himself (he was by no means sure of the difference between these terms); and all must be met in the same way, in the name of that Providence which overrules the national destiny. That is why Robespierre's war speeches are so monotonous, and so denunciatory. He does not believe that the situation can be retrieved by a forward-looking policy, but only by an inward and therefore also a backward-looking change of mind. It is as a preacher, not as a statesman, that he faces the issue before the nation.

Again, as he is concerned with the effect of the war

upon the French people, rather than upon French prestige, it is not the foreign front that interests him, so much as the home front. 'I agree,' he is reported as saying on April 10, 'that we ought to conquer Brabant, the Netherlands, Liège, Flanders, etc. But this must not be allowed to remain a court war, or a government war. The French people must rise forthwith, and arm itself, not only to fight on the frontiers, but also to keep a watch over despotism here at home. This is a civil war: its origin is at home; and it is the home front that we must watch'.

II

This vigilance involved Robespierre in a fresh series of those personal encounters which were becoming inseparable from the debates at the club, and which—however tiresome they may be—a biographer cannot ignore. Robespierre, at any rate, did not begin them; the attack came from the other side.

Somebody reported that an affiliated society had set up a bust of Robespierre, contrary to a resolution of the club forbidding such honours to living statesmen. Why, another speaker asked, should a bust of Lafayette, whom Robespierre had denounced, still stand in the Hotel de Ville? Théroigne de Méricourt, an ambiguous foreign adventuress, who had until recently lived an extravagant and perhaps disreputable life in circles frequented by Desmoulins, Pétion, and other friends of Robespierre, had been using his name to advertise a political club for women in the Faubourg Saint-Anthoine, and he was forced to disclaim a compromising alliance.[1] Finally, after a protest against personalities by Brissot, he was openly attacked by Brissot's friend, Guadet. 'I denounce him', he said, 'for constantly talking about patriotism, and then deserting the post (of Public Prosecutor) to which he was elected; I denounce him for becoming, either by ill-luck or ambition, the idol of the people; and

[1] Particularly as Théroigne had just been released, by special instructions of the Emperor, from an Austrian prison, and might be suspected of being a spy.

I call his attention (so the modest speaker continued) to another man, who would rather die than desert the post of duty—I mean myself'. Robespierre's immediate answer was almost apologetic. 'I know I am blamed', he said, 'for making so many speeches; but I only do it to guarantee liberty, to establish equality, and to disperse intrigue'. When these aims are attained, he will gladly retire into private life. 'Glad, because my fellow-citizens are happy, I shall spend my days in peace, and in the delights of a sweet and blessed retirement'. Nevertheless, and in spite of several expressions of opinion in the club[1] that it would be better to drop personalities, and get on with the business of the war, Robespierre insisted upon his right to make a formal reply to Guadet's charges; and one may be glad that he did, for the speech is a valuable bit of autobiography.

He begins by saying that, as an upholder of freedom of speech, he cannot complain of personal attacks: 'liberty of denunciation is the people's safeguard, and the sacred right of every citizen'. But he shows their absurdity by pointing to his actual record and reputation in public life, from the time of his protest against the Lamoignon decrees[2] to his recent campaign against the war. He describes his early stand for popular rights in Artois, the enthusiasm inspired in him by the first days of the National Assembly, and his long opposition there, in an honourable minority, to the later reaction against democracy. He takes credit for the 'Self-denying Ordinance' which excluded himself from the Legislative Assembly, and perhaps from the Ministry, in the interests of Brissot, Condorcet, and their friends. He describes himself as the saviour of the Jacobin club, in the dangerous days of 1791. And for all this he is labelled a factionist (*factieux*), or—to use a newly invented term of abuse—an agitator (*agitateur*)! He is charged with deserting his post of Public Prosecutor, though he had always said he would give it up, if at any time it interfered with the more important work of 'pleading the cause of liberty and humanity before the bar of the universe, and of genera-

[1] By Albitte, Basire, and Prieur de la Marne.   [2] v.1/39.

tions to come'. He had even been exhorted to ostracize himself, and go into voluntary exile. But what despot would give him an asylum? And how could he abandon his country at such a crisis of its fate? 'Heaven', he concludes, 'which gave me a heart full of the passion of liberty, and yet fixed my birth-place under the heel of tyrants; heaven, which prolonged my days till the reign of faction and crime, may be calling me to mark with my blood the path my country has to tread towards freedom and happiness. I grasp with delight this sweet and glorious destiny'.

This is, on the whole, the most convincing apologia for Robespierre's career. If the martyr's pose seems a trifle theatrical, if the emphasis on his own services leaves Providence too little credit, yet the essential account rings true. Robespierre had been genuinely moved by the national enthusiasm of 1789. No one had laid so deeply to heart 'that great moral and political truth preached by Jean-Jacques, that men have a sincere affection for those who really love them; that only the people is good, just, and generous; and that corruption and tyranny are the monopoly of those who disdain the common crowd'. No one could have stood by that faith more loyally in times of mis-understanding, slander, and intrigue. It does not affect this view of his character—though it may of his intelligence —if one regards Rousseau's generalization as perilously near nonsense; nor was it entirely Robespierre's fault that prophecy so often became denunciation, and principles so easily turned into personalities. There was ample precedent for it among the prophets.

Nevertheless this development was exercising the minds of patriots; and the puzzlement of Albitte, Basire, and Prieur was followed, a few days later (April 26) by a private protest from the man who, next to Robespierre himself, carried most weight in his party, with whom he had lately collaborated in a patriotic manifesto, and who had, until lately, been regarded as his greatest friend.[1] In a long letter

---

[1] Their joint *Observations sur la nécessité de la réunion des hommes de bon foi contre les intrigues* was published early in 1792 (Hamel, 2/71). They had been called 'two fingers of the same hand' (Mercier, *New Picture*, 1/148).

deploring yesterday's scene at the Jacobins, and the
'hideous human passions' that were splitting the club, and
ruining the popular cause, Pétion said, 'We have lost the
quiet energy of free men. We no longer judge things
coolly. We shout like children or lunatics. I simply tremble
when I consider how we are behaving, and I ask myself
every moment whether we can continue to be free. I cannot
sleep at nights; for my usually peaceful slumbers are
disturbed by dreams of disaster.' He goes on to say that the
chief cause of these quarrels lies in 'aggravated self-concern,
and frustrated ambition'—a phrase in which he evidently
suggests that Robespierre is jealous of his mayoralty, and
of the *Brissotin* Ministers, and is venting his disappointment
in personal bitterness.[1] 'Think this over seriously', he ends,
'and redouble your efforts to rescue us from this *mauvais
pas*'. Robespierre does not seem to have answered this
spiteful and fussy letter. At any rate, three days later Pétion
writes again, saying that the situation at the club is worse
than ever, and that he intends to raise the point there
the same evening. And so he did, in a long speech, at the
end of which the House, by passing to the next business,
prevented Robespierre from making any reply. When, a few
days later, Doppet proposed that in future all denunciations
should be dealt with by a committee, Robespierre protested
that this procedure would remove the safeguard of publicity.
'I think, as others do', he said, 'that there ought to be some
limit to a good citizen's zeal in denunciation; but if the club
were to forbid my answering the libellists who cabal against
me, I should resign, and go into retirement'; at which several
women in the gallery were heard to remark, 'And we will
go with you'. Robespierre's further attempts to answer
Brissot's attacks led to a disorderly scene, in which all the
members seemed to be on their feet at once, and which was
only closed by a conciliatory motion, impugning the
accuracy of the printed version of Brissot's indictment.

[1]So too Salamon, writing on April 30, attributes the quarrels of the Jacobin
leaders to the disappointment of 'people like Collot d'Herbois and Robespierre' at
being excluded from the Ministry.

III

But by now news was beginning to come in from the front; and, as Robespierre had anticipated, it was a story of unrelieved disaster. On May 1 it was learnt that the first two armies to take the field—that of Dillon advancing on Tournai, and that of Biron on Mons—had both broken and fled, and that Dillon had been killed by his own men. Within a fortnight several regiments went over to the enemy, a number of officers deserted or resigned, the generals refused to resume the offensive, and Grave, the Minister of War, threw up his post. All this was a terrible shock to patriotic pride. Robespierre could do no more than cry 'Treason!' with the men who murdered Dillon, denounce the generals, and reiterate his old demand for the re-enlistment of discharged soldiers.

During the week that followed, a visitor to the club might have been excused for thinking that the members had quite lost their heads: the war seemed to be forgotten in an orgy of accusation and counter-accusation. On May 2 the Girondins signalized their break with the Jacobins, and their *rapprochement* with the Feuillants, by carrying a decree against Marat. On the 6th Danjou proposed, as an 'emetic remedy' for the situation, the replacement of Louis XVI by a British prince, and was denounced by Robespierre as a madman, an intriguer, and a Feuillant in disguise. A letter from the front deploring the divisions among the Jacobins was hissed by women in the gallery. Another praising Lafayette, and attacking Robespierre, was denounced by the latter as an insult, not only to himself, but to the society. Finally the Girondin Louvet interrupted Robespierre in the middle of a speech, with charges of tyrannizing over the club. 'The only despotism Robespierre exercises here', retorted Mendoza, 'is that of virtue'; and Danton closed a discreditable scene by declaring, in similar terms, that 'M. Robespierre has never used any tyranny in this House, unless it is the tyranny of reason: it is not patriotism, but jealousy, that inspires the attacks against him'.[1]

[1] cp. Hamel, 2/112.

But though both these statements might be true, one cannot but think that the feeling against Robespierre was based on something more than mere jealousy and unreason. It is possible to be right in a wrong way; and almost impossible to attack people's principles without giving the impression that you are attacking their character. In both ways Robespierre had offended; whilst his cold rectitude exasperated the offence, and his lack of humour made him specially vulnerable to counter-attack.

He had, indeed, plenty of champions, but of an embarrassing kind. J. F. Delacroix's pamphlet in his favour, and the proposal to follow it up with a paper defending him against the attacks of the reactionary press, might have been welcome.[1] But it cannot have been altogether agreeable, for a person of Robespierre's Puritan correctness, to be supported by the gross invective of Hébert's *Père Duchesne*, or the brilliant indiscretions of Desmoulins' *Tribune des Patriotes*. As for Marat, whose advocacy would have been even more compromising—that clear-sighted and intolerant fanatic declared, in answer to an accusation by Guadet, that he had had no dealings with Robespierre, either as man or editor, except a solitary interview, when Robespierre had protested against his violence, and had been reduced to horrified silence by Marat's exposition of his editorial policy. 'Our interview', wrote the Friend of the People, 'confirmed the opinion I had always had of him—that he combined the enlightened ideas of a wise senator with the uprightness of a gentleman (*homme de bien*), and the zeal of a patriot, but that he had neither the outlook nor the audacity that make a statesman.'[2]

IV

Such considerations were of less moment when Robespierre himself became an editor. It was the natural course,

---

[1] *L'intrigue dévoilée, ou Robespierre vengé des outrages et des calumnies des ambitieux* (Brit. Mus. R.112(7)). The paper was to be called *Accusateur Public*. Prudhomme's *Révolution de Paris* had recently turned against Robespierre.

[2] *L'Ami du Peuple*, No. 648, cp. Robespierre's reply to Louvet, 1/288.

in those days, for a politician no longer in Parliament. There was so little difference between printing a speech and editing a paper, that no editorial experience, no staff, no offices or organization were required. There need only be enough manuscript ready, once a week, to fill three or four sheets of small octavo size, and sufficient cash to pay the printer's bill. There would be no great profit on the venture, but there need be no great loss. It was the means by which many of Robespierre's friends or rivals had built up, not indeed a party, but a public.[1] Hitherto he had been too busy, and too sure of an audience in the Assembly, or at the club, to feel the need of such methods. But now, isolated, driven back upon himself, and attacked by a hostile press, he determined to embark on journalism. From the middle of May, *Le Défenseur de la Constitution, par Maximilien Robespierre,* began to appear every Tuesday in its red paper cover. The editor described himself, consistently with the title of his journal, as *Député à l'Assemblée constituante*. He gave the price of a subscription as thirty-six *livres* a year, to be paid to P. J. Duplain, *Libraire, Cour du Commerce, rue de l'ancienne Comédie française*: the paper could also be obtained—it was hopefully noted—at the principal booksellers of Europe, and at every post-office. Duplain was ready to receive correspondence, news, and books for review; but anything sent through the post must be properly franked.[2]

Robespierre explained his aims in a preliminary prospectus. 'Reason and public interest', he declared, 'started the Revolution; ambition and intrigue have stopped it. It has been transformed by the vices of slaves and tyrants into a lamentable state of trouble and crisis. Most of the nation want to settle down under the auspices of the new Constitution, to the enjoyment of liberty and peace. What has prevented them? Ignorance and division'. For the public

---

[1] Carra, Condorcet, Brissot, Gorsas, Barère, Marat, Desmoulins, Robert, Tallien, Audouin, Dulaure, Lequinio, Rabaut Saint-Étienne, Louvet, Villette, Fauchet, were all editors (Fleischmann, 146).

[2] The British Museum copy, which was Croker's, contains, on the inside of the cover, advertisements of other publications on sale at the same establishment, including Delolme's *Constitution de l'Angleterre*, and Mirabeau's *Considérations sur l'Ordre de Cincinnatus*.

does not know how to get what it wants, and the enemies of the Constitution propagate discord. 'In this state of things we have only one means left by which to save the situation: we must educate the good will of patriots, and guide it towards a common end'. Robespierre enumerates five ways in which he hopes to do this—by rallying support round the Constitution, by expounding the causes and remedies of the present ills, by explaining the real nature of political developments, by analysing the conduct of public men, and by calling before the bar of public opinion those who cannot be made legally accountable. 'Placed since the beginning of the Revolution,' he says, 'at the centre of political happenings, I have had a close view of the tortuous advance of tyranny; I have discovered that our most dangerous enemies are not those who have openly declared themselves; and I shall try to render my knowledge of value for the safety of my country. I need not say (he concludes) that my pen will be directed solely by the love of justice and truth. On no other terms can one descend from the tribune of the French senate, to mount the steps of the Universe, and to speak, not to an Assembly, but to the whole human race. It may be that, when one has left the stage to sit among the audience, one can form a better opinion of the play, and of the actors. Certainly those who escape from the whirl of business breathe a purer and more peaceful air, and pass a surer judgement upon men and affairs; just as the traveller who flees from the tumult of the city, to climb the summit of a mountain range, there feels the calm of nature sink into his soul, and his thoughts widen with his horizon.'[1]

No. 1 of the *Défenseur* (May 19) is headed *Exposition de mes principes*, and begins with fifteen pages on the sense in which Robespierre is championing the Constitution. 'The Constitution which I mean to defend', so he defines his venture, 'is the Constitution just as it stands.' He knows that he will be asked, 'Why then did you attack this Consti-

---

[1] The first metaphor is natural to a confirmed theatre-goer; the second, if not a commonplace from Rousseau, may perhaps be connected with the excursion to Lens (Corresp. 5).

tution, nine months ago?' His answer is, that the Constituent Assembly, falling from its high promise, passed certain decrees,—notably those on the property franchise— which violated fundamental principles of the Constitution; and that the Legislative Assembly, which might have revised them,[1] has let them stand. These were the parts of the Constitution that he opposed. Now that there is no hope of revision, and that a new party in the state is trying to destroy the whole constitutional structure, good and bad alike, 'to erect a royal tyranny, or a kind of aristocratic regime, upon its ruins', he finds no rallying-point left but the Constitution.

He has been accused both of royalism[2] and of republicanism. 'I care no more for Cromwell', he replies, 'than for Charles I. The yoke of the Decemvirs is as intolerable to me as that of Tarquin'. Surely it is not in the words 'monarchy' or 'republic' that we shall find the solution of the great problems of society? All forms of political constitution exist for the people: if they forget this, they are no better than attempts on the life of society. He was not to blame for the republican fiasco of last July: that was the work of Brissot and Condorcet. Rally round the Constitution, then. Defend it against both the king and the factions. Put up with its imperfections till they can be remedied in a time of union and peace. 'Its faults are human, but its foundations are the work of Heaven, and it bears within itself the deathless germ of its perfection.'

Such was the defensive side of Robespierre's policy. Its offensive side was his attitude towards the war; and this he proceeded to define in the second part of his first number, entitled, *Observations sur les moyens de faire utilement la guerre*. 'The war has begun: nothing remains for us but to take what precautions we can to turn it to the profit of the Revolution. Let us make it a war of the people against tyranny, instead of a war of the court, the nobility, the plotters, and the speculators against the people. It has begun

[1] It could only have done so in defiance of the Constitution.

[2] Harmand de la Meuse (*Anecdotes*, 51) says that Robespierre edited the *Defenseur* in a royalist spirit in order to be made tutor to the Dauphin.

237

in defeat; it must be made to end in victory'. But how? First, we must look back, and see what mistakes the government made at the outset. Secondly, we must remember that this is a holy war, in the name of Liberty, Equality, and the People, and wage it in that spirit. Take the Dillon affair, for instance. Robespierre does not blame the men for killing their general: he wastes no time on talk of indiscipline—a by-product of a vile system of mechanical obedience. The remedy is not to punish the murderers, but to reform the spirit of the army, and especially of the higher command. Above all, 'it is an absolutely essential condition of success against our enemies abroad that we should make war upon our enemies at home, that is, upon injustice, aristocracy, treachery, and despotism'. Away with the idle curiosity which is only interested in battles, and idolizes the victorious general. Rather, we must guard against ambition and intrigue in our generals, as we do against treachery and peculation in our politicians, 'lest there arise in France any citizen formidable enough to make himself, one day, our master, either to hand us over to the court, and govern us in its name, or to crush both king and people, and build upon their ruins a legalized tyranny, the worst of all despotisms'.

Two features in this declaration of policy call for special comment. The first is Robespierre's repudiation of republicanism, and his attempt to saddle it upon the *Brissotin* party. This had been his policy, now, for nine months; and it is to be noted that his friend Desmoulins, in the first number of his new paper, only three weeks before, had rather abruptly adopted the same attitude.[1] The paradoxical result was that an insurrection of the people against the throne was organized in the name of the Constitution, and that republicanism was charged against the political party whose overthrow was to usher in the Republic. It was a clever manœuvre, based upon the conviction (fundamental to all Robespierre's policy) that the forces of reaction were still terribly to be feared, and that a repetition of the events of July

[1]Aulard, 181.

would be fatal to the prospects of a people's revolution.

The other comment concerns Robespierre's war policy. It is prudent; it is clear-sighted; it looks beyond the immediate struggle to its ultimate effects on the state: but it has nothing to inspire or capture the crowd, and seems to lead back into the dreary maze of denunciation and proscription from which, at any rate, the war offered a means of escape.

Moreover in one point it was certain to incur the criticism of practical soldiers, as Robespierre was well aware, when he devoted the first twenty pages of his second number (May 24) to an article entitled *Sur la nécessité et la nature de la discipline militaire*. 'Discipline', he here admits, 'is the soul of an army; without it an army ceases to exist'. But what is discipline? The soldier is also a citizen and a man; and each of his three capacities carries certain obligations. But the soldier's circle of duty falls inside the citizen's, and the citizen's inside the man's. Military discipline affects what falls within the inmost and smallest circle, but no more. Thus a soldier off duty is the equal of his officer, and can behave as any other citizen, wear the tricolor badge, sing patriotic songs, and share in popular rejoicings. Very well; but can he insult his captain, or murder his general? That was the real issue, and that Robespierre carefully avoids. In any case his concentric circles of rights and duties were far too theoretical.[1] Political experience had already shown that it was impossible to govern a state in which the rights of man were extended to every citizen. Military experience would soon show that it was impossible to control an army in which every soldier enjoyed the rights of a citizen. Nevertheless there was, underlying these exaggerations, the notion of a democratic and voluntary discipline, already applied by the Paris Sections to their detachments of the National Guard, and destined to pass, from them, into the organization of the armies of Valmy and Austerlitz.

[1] On these principles, argues Rivarol, an unfaithful wife might say to her husband, 'I was a virgin before I was a wife', or 'I belonged to myself before I belonged to you' (*Mémoires*, 237).

V

Meanwhile the course of events was hurrying on towards an end which no one could clearly foresee, but which could hardly be other than catastrophic.

On May 12 the Girondist and Feuillant parties combined to organize a *Fête de la Loi*, in honour of Simoneau, mayor of Étampes, who had been lynched by a mob when trying to carry out the decrees for the regulation of food-prices. This rather childish counter-blast to the Châteauvieux fête was ridiculed by Robespierre, who had private information as to Simoneau's local reputation, and who always refused to believe that the people could be in the wrong.[1] Indeed, the names of those who organized the fête, the crowding of the streets with soldiers, and the inscription on the emblematical 'throne of law'—*Liberté*, *Égalité*, *Propriété*—cast considerable doubt upon the democratic character of the occasion.

The disunity of the country, and the struggle between political parties, soon became the background of every debate at the Jacobins. Now Robespierre is protesting against the arrest of Merlin, Chabot, and Basire on a charge of libelling Bertrand and Montmorin;[2] now drawing up an address with Dufourny and Billaud-Varenne; now expressing sympathy with Lecointre, commandant of the National Guard at Versailles, during his imprisonment by order of the Assembly; now supporting the complaints of some villagers near Saint-Malo against their magistrates. Soon we find that the club itself is split into hostile sections. The title 'Friends of the Constitution', Robespierre maintains, has become a farce. It would be better to admit no new societies to affiliation 'until the society has restored the necessary order within its own ranks'. Indeed, so bitterly was this position felt that, on May 27, John Oswald, the representative of the Patriotic Society of Manchester,

[1] Robespierre's informant was Pierre Dolivier, curé of Mauchamp. (*Défenseur*, No. 4; A.R. 9/371. cp. Mathiez, *La Vie Chère* 66 f; and the Mauchamp petition in Tourneux 1/2204.)

[2] Denouncing this outrage, Robespierre oddly declared that 'in England the law allows a citizen to kill any policeman who tries to arrest him'.

found his eloquence received with disparaging remarks by Robespierre, and the affiliation he asked for indefinitely postponed.[1]

Three days later the sordid business of denunciation was again in full swing. The three generals of the Northern Command—Luckner, Rochambeau, and Lafayette—had agreed, at a conference at Valenciennes on May 18, to suspend hostilities. Lafayette had gone further, and treated with the Austrians for an armistice, intending to march on Paris, disperse the Jacobins, recall the royal princes and *émigrés*, disband the National Guard, and establish a Second Chamber. In one letter he had even proposed himself for a dictatorship. All this was not, of course, known to Robespierre. But the Jacobin club was in correspondence with the administrative bodies of the Departments in which fighting was going on, and would have its suspicions of what was taking place.[2] When, therefore, Rochambeau, hurrying back from the front to justify himself, threw the blame for the reverses at Mons and Tournai partly upon the Ministers, and partly upon his men, Robespierre retorted that the real fault lay with the excessive powers of the generals, and contrasted Rochambeau's desertion of his post, to come to Paris, with his own resignation of an easy job (that of Public Prosecutor) to take up the dangerous and painful task of denouncing the enemies of the country. Rochambeau, baited beyond endurance, left the hall, and his name was struck off the list of members. It was one of the first of many such incidents.

The next day appeared the third number of the *Défenseur*, with a bitter article entitled *Considérations sur l'une des principales causes de nos maux*. It began with a sentence which showed how far the events of the last nine months had distorted Robespierre's judgement. 'Intrigue', he wrote, parodying an aphorism from Pascal,[3] 'is the Queen of the world'; and 'might is right' means 'trickery is right'. To this rule, he says, the Revolution is no exception; and there

---

[1]R.F. 32/481.
[2]e.g. Corresp. 311.
[3]*L'opinion est la reine du monde, la force en est le tyran.*

would be no hope, were it not still true that 'the people is sound, the cause of mankind is holy, and Heaven is just'. The real enemies of the country, he reiterates, are not to be found in the royalist party, but amongst professed patriots; and since he holds it a duty to criticize publicly, he names Brissot and Condorcet, Guadet, Vergniaud, and Gensonné, accusing them of violating the rights of the nation, and depraving the public spirit towards despotism and aristocracy. Hamel, whilst admitting that he would have preferred his hero 'calm and stoical', thinks that a perusal of this article will 'convince the reader afresh of the clarity and depth of Robespierre's judgement'. It is rather the utterance of a man whom opposition and suspicion have so embittered that he mistakes private resentment for public duty. Its clarity and depth are accidents of its narrowness.

However, a week's holiday[1] did something to restore Robespierre's balance of mind, before the crisis created by the approach of another July 14. Servan, the new Minister of War,[2] was proposing that, in place of the usual peaceful delegations, each canton in the country should send up five volunteers, ready armed and uniformed, to take the civic oath, and to form part of a reserve army of 20,000 men encamped in the northern suburbs of Paris. This project was differently interpreted according to the hopes and fears of each political party. To the Royalists it seemed a threat against the throne—the more so, since the Assembly had recently disbanded the king's *Garde Constitutionnelle*, and had only allowed him to reconstitute a small part of his personal body-guard.[3] To the Feuillants it was a blow against the counter-revolution; to the Girondins a safeguard against the city mob; to some Parisians a bulwark against invasion, to others a menace to their independence. On the day before Servan's bill was passed by the Assembly (June 7), Robespierre at the Jacobins gave his reasons against it. Paris, he said, had nothing to fear from internal

[1]There is no sign of his presence at the club between May 30 and June 6.
[2]In place of Grave, who resigned on May 8.
[3]Decrees of May 29 and June 8.

enemies which it could not deal with by its own efforts. The proposal was a dangerous one, because the new army was evidently designed to take the place of the National Guard, and to put the capital and the country at the mercy of the reactionaries. Indeed, he thought so strongly about the matter that he put aside all his constitutional scruples,[1] and seriously discussed petitioning the Assembly to rescind its decree. 'The National Assembly being subordinate to the General Will', he now declares, 'so soon as it acts contrary to that Will, ceases to exist'. Such an argument really left no assembly to petition: it pointed straight to the remedy which was now in everyone's mind, and which, to Robespierre himself, seemed the only way of escape from a military dictatorship—the complete abolition of the present regime. But he does not seem to have realized that Servan's army might well prove just what he most desired—a safeguard for Paris against the *coup de main* of some ambitious general.

However this may be, there is evidence in No. 4 of the *Défenseur*—*Observations sur les causes morales de notre situation actuelle*—that the fear of a military dictatorship is driving Robespierre back to the first principles of revolutionism. 'The issue of the Revolution', he writes, 'is quite simple, and is unaffected by changes of form. If the old abuses persist under new names, if the new forms of government are no better than the old, if there is to be no breaking of the entail of slavery and oppression, what do I care whether we have a dictator or a king, a parliament or a senate, tribunes or consuls? The sole aim of society being the preservation of the imprescriptible rights of man, the only proper motive of a revolution should be to recall society to this holy end, and to recover these rights from the usurpations of tyranny and force'. Robespierre sees that the Revolution has declined from this high ideal, and asks why. He finds the answer in its failure to be true to 'those principles of justice and morality which lie at the root of human society'. But how is one to know what they are? They are written in the soul of man, and can be read by

[1] v. e.g. July 16, 1791.

'him who has a pure heart and a virtuous character'. This evangelical precept seems for a moment to open wide the door of salvation; but, with his curious fixity of mind, Robespierre half closes it again, by reiterating his theory that 'the people, the huge class of workers', have a monopoly of virtue. Being the least cultivated part of society, they are also, according to the gospel of Rousseau, the least depraved. In other words—and this is the heart of Robespierre's convictions—the Revolution has failed because it has not been directed by and for the common people. It is not a programme of political reform which is now wanted, but a moral reformation. And this will be achieved, not by parliamentarism, which has failed, but by the direct action of the people, working through its autonomous Sections and Communes, towards a new legislature elected on a univeral franchise.

VI

The next move towards catastrophe came from the king's side. On June 13 he dismissed the *Brissotin* Ministers, Roland, Servan and Clavière, and transferred Dumouriez to the Ministry of War. On the 15th the Assembly showed its resentment by passing a vote of condolence with the dismissed Ministers. The king retaliated by refusing his consent to the Paris camp, and to a decree against the refractory priests. On the 16th Dumouriez, finding his isolation intolerable, followed his colleagues into retirement. On the 17th the Assembly set up an emergency Committee of Twelve to deal with the crisis which was now rapidly approaching.

It was characteristic of Robespierre that, as the crucial moment drew near, he should go more and more warily, detaching himself from all political parties, disowning any definite programme, and waiting to see how the situation would develop. This is the explanation of his speech at the club on June 13. 'Since the end of the Constituent Assembly', he informs his hearers, 'I have been pretty assiduous in my attendance at this society'—as though he were not its most prominent member!—'in the belief that good citizens are not out of place in patriotic assemblies, capable of exercising a salutary influence upon the progress of an enlightened public spirit; and I have done so as one equally opposed, both to the avowed enemies and to the unavowed corrupters of democracy'. If he is not committed to the club, neither does he hold any brief for the dismissed Ministers: there are more important things to worry about. 'Our safety does not depend upon the fate of any Minister, but upon our faithfulness to principles, the progress of public spirit, and the wisdom of our laws . . . I recognize no principles but those of the public interest; I desire acquaintance with no Minister; I take no man's word as reason either for enthusiasm or for indignation; certainly not that of men who have more than once been deceived, and who, within the space of a week, contradict themselves so flagrantly'.

'*Perfide incomparable,*' is Jaurès' comment on this speech.[1] But why should Robespierre show any consideration for Ministers of whose policy and conduct he disapproved? It is more blameworthy that, at the moment when his policy is bearing fruit, he should disclaim responsibility for anything but the merest generalizations, and should pose as a privileged critic, who has never demeaned himself to the political stage. If we were dealing with anyone but 'the Incorruptible', we might credit the suggestion of sordid motives for this apparent change of front. Westermann, at his trial, alleged that he had been offered three million *livres* to join the court party on the eve of August 10th. Fabre was accused, and Danton suspected, of accepting similar bribes.[2] Robespierre afterwards hinted that attempts had been made to corrupt him too.[3] But it is difficult to believe either that he was offered the tutorship of the Dauphin, through the mediation of the Princesse de Lamballe[4], or

[1] Jaurès, 4/35.   [2] A.R. 9/398.
[3] In the Convention, Sept. 25, 1792.
[4] A.R. 7/298. The story comes from Harmand de la Meuse (v. 1/237 n.), and Seiffert, the Princess's doctor.

that court money was wasted on bribing occupants of the public galleries to applaud his speeches.[1]

No; Robespierre's policy may have been unheroic, but it was honest, and unobscure. It was to stand by the Constitution, and to trust the people, until it was clear whether the people would destroy the Constitution, or the Constitution the people. The first solution was what he hoped for, but would not openly proclaim. The second was what he feared, for it could hardly lead to anything but a military dictatorship, and the destruction of all his hopes for a popular regime; but he was not the man to designate himself as the first victim of a Fayettist proscription. Such was his reputation, that this policy, which in another might have been reckoned cowardly, passed for caution; and, as he had saved the Jacobin club by repudiating republicanism in the crisis of last July, so now a policy of masterly inactivity enabled him to save the cause of the people. Whilst other popular leaders are organizing an armed deputation to the Manège, or to the Tuileries, whilst Réal is demanding the suspension of the king, and Danton the queen's exile, he can only fall back on denunciations of Lafayette,[2] and appeal to a discredited Constitution. He plays no part in, and makes no mention of, the events of June 20—the work of certain Sections of the East End, backed by the National Guard, and abetted by his old friend and new enemy, Pétion, the mayor of Paris.[3]

However, June 20 settled nothing; whilst the king's refusal to be intimidated, and some consequential royalist demonstrations in the provinces, discredited the *Brissotins*, and transferred the initative from them to the Robespierrist Sections, and to the *Fédérés*, who were gathering in the capital for the fête of July 14. Thus Robespierre's failure to

---

[1]So Cloots, writing to a friend not long before August 10. 'Suspend the Civil List', he says, 'and both our Kings (Louis and Robespierre) will come tumbling down'. (Tuetey, 10/2477.)
[2]e.g., at the Jacobins on June 18, and in *Défenseur*, No. 6.
[3]Mathiez (153) asserts that 'by Robespierre's advice the deputies of the Mountain took no part in the demonstration'; but on what authority? The converse story, that he was seen with Pétion, Manuel, and Sillery at Santerre's house, planning the rising, rests on worthless evidence (Tuetey, 4/733).

lead, at a moment when all leadership was discredited, passed for the highest statesmanship.

A week later (June 28) Lafayette appeared in the Manège, denounced the Jacobins as 'a sect which violates the national sovereignty, and tyrannizes over the citizens', and called upon the nation to support the Assembly and the throne. This *démarche* did more credit to the general's courage than to his good sense: for, while Louis refused his help, the Jacobins throve on his accusations, and presented themselves to the people as its one hope against a conspiracy of the army, the constitutionalists, and the court. Not only so. Lafayette had shown his hand. The chances of a successful military *coup* were hopelessly compromised. Robespierre could join even with Brissot and Guadet in denouncing one who had openly declared war on the Revolution; and thenceforward devoted himself to forwarding the 'constitutional rising against the Constitution', which came to a head on August 10. Both his enemies had played into his hands.

VII

The beginning of July brought more bad news from the front. Vergniaud, for the Girondins, denounced the king's conduct of the war, demanded his deposition, and proposed the declaration of a state of national emergency (July 3). But he did not carry the Assembly with him; and a theatrical reconciliation of all parties ('Lamourette's Kiss', July 7) gave, for a few hours, a false sense of security. The same evening, however, Pétion and Manuel (*Procureur de la Commune*) were arrested by the *Directoire du Département de Paris* for their complicity in the events of June 20; and on the 11th the Assembly at last published its dramatic appeal *Citoyens, la Patrie est en danger!*, and France armed for self-defence.[1]

Now that Lafayette has been discredited, and the people are taking charge of the situation, Robespierre can adopt a more hopeful view of the war. Speaking on July 7, he

[1] The official proclamation was not till Sunday the 22nd.

admits that he had at first thought the war could not serve the cause of liberty: now he thinks it can. He had thought the country unfit to fight; and events proved him right. Now he believes that, if treacherous generals are removed, and patriots appointed in their place, victory can be secured. He announces, with more enthusiasm than logic, that there are two kinds of war—those of liberty, waged by peoples, and those of intrigue and ambition, waged by despots: the first are instantly and gloriously successful, the second futile and disastrous. This war has so far been disastrous: it is therefore of the second kind. 'We have not been able to free others (he continues, more sensibly) because we are not yet free ourselves. The universe is still in travail with liberty; we still bear the scars of our old chains'. But if we can destroy despotism at home (the inference is), defeat abroad will turn to victory.[1]

Two days later Robespierre's address *Aux Fédérés* is even more explicit.[2] Their mission, he says, is to save the state by maintaining the Constitution—not the whole Constitution as drafted in 1791, but 'such laws as protect liberty and patriotism against tyranny and machiavellianism'. And how are they to do this? His premises can lead to only one conclusion—by the overthrow of the King and of the Assembly, for and by whom the reactionary elements were introduced into the Constitution. And though he is careful not to say this, the incitement to revenge is as clearly intended as it was by Mark Antony. 'The fatal hour is striking (he writes); . . . let us march to the field of Federation. There stands the altar of the country'. But there must be no idols now, as there were in 1790—no Lafayette, no Louis XVI. 'Let us take no oath but to the country and to ourselves; and let us take it at the hands (not of the king of France, but) of the immortal King of Nature, who made us for liberty, and who punishes our oppressors'. On this spot everything recalls their crimes—this soil stained with the innocent blood they shed; this altar; this (not

---

[1] *Défenseur*, No. 8, delivered as a speech at the Jacobins on July 11.
[2] *Défenseur*, No. 9.

Champ de Mars, but) *champ de mort*, covered with a funeral pall. 'Listen, then, to the piteous cries of our murdered citizens; see the blood-stained country before your eyes; gaze on mankind crushed beneath the yoke of a few despicable tyrants; and let this spectacle inspire you with great thoughts'. What thoughts does he mean? 'Do not leave this enclosure till you have resolved in your hearts on the salvation of France and of the human race'. Could anyone doubt that for 'great thoughts' they were meant to read 'vengeance on the King'; or for 'the salvation of France and of the human race', the overthrow of the crown, and of the Assembly? And yet so sensitive was Robespierre of appearances, and so anxious to preserve his political innocence, that he denounced the *Journal du soir* for saying that he had incited the Marseillais to avenge the victims of last July, and had the author of the report expelled from the club.[1]

But if some reticence must be exercised in public, there need be none at the club. On July 13, after welcoming the Assembly's reinstatement of Pétion,[2] Robespierre followed Chabot and other speakers in warning the Jacobins that a fresh plot was being hatched. In 1789, he said, when Lafayette wanted an excuse for martial law, he had a baker murdered; in 1791 he connived at the king's flight, and hanged two men on the Champ de Mars, in order to bring discredit on the Jacobins; June 20 was another of his intrigues; and now Louis XVI is no more than the puppet and victim of a man who is equally ready to act as his valet or as his hired assassin, so long as he can remain in power. The biographer must record, however regretfully, these absurd and malicious charges. Robespierre must have known—to say nothing of the other allegations—that Lafayette could not be responsible for the murder of the baker François, or for the events of June

---

[1] Aulard (H.P. 201) takes this address as suggesting nothing more than Constitutional reform, and as silently discountenancing the demand for the king's dethronement; but (apart from other difficulties) he has to admit that this involves a change of mind on Robespierre's part before the *Pétition des Fédérés* of July 17 (v. 1/253).

[2] He had been afraid that the king might gain credit by doing this (*Défenseur*, 9/431).

20, which he had so recently denounced. That he could seriously voice such slanders shows a fevered mind. There was, after all, something which could corrupt 'the Incorruptible'—not money, not even ambition, but hatred of those whom he considered traitors to the cause.

The address *Aux Fédérés* was denounced to the Public Prosecutor; but July 14 passed off quietly, though no cheers were heard for the king, and many of the crowd had *Vive Pétion* chalked on their hats. The attack on the Tuileries was postponed. Meanwhile, Robespierre exhorts all good citizens to treat the *Fédérés* as 'friends, brothers, and deliverers'; public opinion must be organized, and the patriot forces mobilized, both in Paris and on the frontiers, for a final attack on the enemy at home and abroad.[1]

On July 20 Robespierre sent to his friend Couthon, who was taking a mud-cure for his rheumatism at Saint-Amand, a valuable account of the situation. Paris, he says, is on the edge of great events. The people are indignant at the exculpation of Lafayette, just voted by the Assembly.[2] The king's deposition is to be discussed to-day, and everything points to a night of disorder. 'The revolution is embarking', he says, 'on a more rapid course, unless it is engulfed in a military despotism and dictatorship. In the present situation it is impossible for the friends of freedom to foresee and to direct events. The destiny of France seems to be abandoning her to intrigue and chance.[3] The hopeful element in the situation is the strength of public opinion in Paris, and many of the Departments, and the justice of our cause. The Paris Sections are manifesting an energy and prudence worthy to serve as a model to the rest of the country'.[4]

A week later Robespierre is ready for the most drastic measures, accepting Camus' proposals for the 'permanence' of the primary assemblies, a house to house search for arms, and the deposition of the king, his ministers, and his generals, and adding as a corollary the general arming of

[1] Jac. 4/120, 125.　　　　　　　　[2] July 19.
[3] Destiny or Providence, hitherto identified with Chance (v. 1/215).
[4] Corresp. 149 .

the people. He is evidently prepared for another *insurrection générale*, like that of July, 1789. And it is clear, from an important speech he delivers on the 29th, that this rising is to be directed not only against the Executive, but also against the Legislature; for if it is the king who is trying to destroy the nation, it is the Assembly which is failing to save it; and if the king must be deposed, the Assembly must also be replaced.[1] There must be no repetition of what happened after Varennes.

It is significant that this speech should have coincided with the first meeting (July 26) of the *comité central des fédérés*, and with the appointment of the *bureau central des sections* (July 27)—the two bodies which organized the rising of August 10. Without being a member of either, Robespierre was evidently in touch with both. The *comité des fédérés* seems indeed to have formed, within itself, a *directoire secret*, which sometimes met in the rooms of Anthoine, mayor of Metz, a personal friend of Robespierre, and at this time lodging with the Duplays. Simond of Strasbourg, a correspondent of Robespierre, was also a member of this inner circle, until he returned home on August 8. But, after abortive attempts to bring about a rising on July 26, July 30, and August 5, the initiative seems to have passed from the *directoire* to the *bureau des sections*; and Robespierre may have been less directly informed as to the later developments of the plot.[2]

On July 30 two events were a prelude to the final crisis —the arrival of the Marseillais, and the publication of Brunswick's Manifesto. Robespierre, as *mandataire* of Marseille, can have had no illusions as to the object with which the Marseillais came to Paris. 'Frenchmen prepared

[1]One of the Brest *Fédérés* says (describing the assembly on August 8) that at this time decrees were debated by 2 or 3 members, and voted by 20 or 30. The Opposition read the papers, and paid little attention to business (A.R. 33/451).

[2]Carra, a not very trustworthy witness, after saying that Robespierre took no part in the conspirators' meetings at the *Soleil d'Or* on July 26 and at the *Cadran Bleu* on August 4, adds that, when the latter was adjourned to Anthoine's rooms the same evening, Mme Duplay was alarmed, and said, 'Did they want to get Robespierre killed?' 'It doesn't concern him', replied Anthoine; 'he has only to hide himself'. (B. and R. 16/271, cp. A.R. 12/389.)

to play Brutus' part', he calls them in a letter to Buissart, probably written the same day; and he adds, 'If they leave Paris without saving the country, all is lost. We all intend to lay down our lives in the capital, rather than shrink from risking everything in a final attempt'.[1] As to Brunswick's Manifesto, it chanced that Robespierre was in the chair when Mendoza read this document to the club,[2] and, being by now in the confidence of the committees which were planning the insurrection, he was anxious to prevent any premature move. The 'platitudes and stupidities' of the manifesto were, indeed, greeted with 'roars of laughter,' and with exclamations less of anger than of pity for the benighted ignorance and foolishness, 'at least ten centuries out of date', that characterized the document. But when, a little later, the meeting was thrown into some agitation by the sound of drums beating to quarters, Robespierre first recommended calmness, and then suspended the sitting—a piece of caution for which he was subsequently attacked in the Brissotin *Club de Réunion*, whose members doubtless felt that the control of events was being taken out of their hands.[3] On August 1 Robespierre explained a further step in the plans for the rising. The overthrow of the king and the Assembly was to be followed by the election of a National Convention, from which members of both previous Assemblies should be excluded. This body would sit for a year, and frame a new Constitution.[4] Two days later this proposal was embodied in a petition from forty-seven Sections presented by Pétion to the Assembly. It was a suggestion which, with its embodiment of the 'Self-denying Ordinance,' can hardly have come from anyone but Robespierre. Fundamentally, throughout the crisis, a 'defender of the Constitution,' he pinned his hopes now, as he had

[1]Corresp. 151.
[2]It was dated July 25, known in Paris on the 28th, and read for the first time at the Jacobins on the 30th.
[3]For the *Club de Réunion* v. Mathiez, *G. et M.*, 70.
[4]Prudhomme said afterwards (*Histoire Impartiale* (1824) 3/189) that Danton, Fabre, and Desmoulins consulted him, about the end of July, as to what step should follow the deposition of the king. Robespierre's plan for a Convention was not then his own? Jaurès (4/103) calls it *ce grand programme*.

done a year earlier, on a new National Assembly. The appeal to force, quite uncongenial to him, would thus be justified. The Revolution would pass from one stage of legality to another, through the thinnest possible veil of unconstitutionalism.

VIII

As the moment planned for the rising became imminent, there were fears lest the victims should anticipate it by flight. On August 5, with some inkling, perhaps, of Lafayette's latest plan for the king's flight, Robespierre told the club that he had been informed that the Tuileries was full of Suisses, who had been treated to drinks, and given fifteen cartridges each, with which to defend the palace against attack; meanwhile, Louis would certainly try to escape; and it was the duty of every good citizen to see that he was safely guarded. On the 8th fears were expressed lest the Assembly might transfer its sittings from Paris to Rouen or Orleans. Robespierre, however, advised the club not to be distracted by this unlikely rumour from the primary issue —that of the king's dethronement. This was his last public utterance before August 10.

There must, however, have been constant conferences with the persons immediately concerned in the rising, or likely to oppose it. In his 7th *Lettre à ses Commettans*, Robespierre reminds Pétion, how, on August 7, the latter talked to him for a whole hour about the dangers of the insurrection, and urged that it should be postponed until the Assembly had had time to discuss the king's deposition. There was also the preparatory campaign which Robespierre believed to be necessary for the success of the coming attack—educating public opinion, and working up feeling against the enemies on the home front. Here the *Défenseur* played a leading part. Now it was a *Pétition des Fédérés à l'Assemblée nationale*; now an article *Sur la fédération de* 1792; now an address from *les citoyens réunis à Paris . . . aux français des* 83 *départements*; now a disquisition *Des maux et des ressources de l'état*; and now a notice *Sur l'armée des*

Marseillais à Paris.[1] All these writings—petitions and addresses included—were apparently by Robespierre's own hand; all reinforce his point of view. Thus the *Fédérés* insist that they set out to fight the Austrians, and now they find Austria in Paris itself: 'it is in our camps, it is in the king's council, it is at the head of our armies'. Again, 'A treacherous court, a coalition of insolent aristocrats (*patriciens*, one of Robespierre's favourite words), a vile crowd of criminals of all kinds, who have the Constitution on their lips, but tyranny and assassination in their hearts— such are the enemies of the country; and it is at Paris that they must be encountered. At Paris, then, we must conquer or die: here we have sworn to remain: here is our post—the scene of our triumph, or of our tomb'.[2] But they are warned to go warily, to beware of premature violence—a trick used by Lafayette and his friends to discredit the Revolution —and to explore the possibilities of constitutional action, unless or until public opinion is ready for unconstitutional remedies.

As the days go on, Robespierre grows less cautious, and more clear. His mercurial mind moves with the rising temperature of the people. *Défenseur* No. 11 assumes that there is to be an insurrection, and discusses its scope and aim. He has now thrown over his last constitutional scruples. 'The state must be saved', he writes, 'whatever means be employed: nothing can be called unconstitutional, except what tends to its destruction.' Nor is it enough to depose the king. A bad legislature is more dangerous than a bad king, because it can count on a greater degree of popular support. Besides, it is not Louis who reigns, but the succession of intriguers who rule through him; and at the moment 'your real kings are your generals'. What is the use, then, of replacing Louis by another king, a Regent, or a Council? Or what advantage is it, if the Legislative Body becomes the Executive also? 'Despotism is still despotism, whether it have 700 heads, or one.' The only

---

[1] *Défenseur*, No. 10 and No. 11.
[2] *Défenseur*, No. 10.

remedy, then, is a National Convention, which will reform such of the present laws as are contrary to the Constitution of 1791 (he means, in its original form), and institute new provisions so simple and obvious that they will be at once adopted—depriving the Executive of the means of corruption, making the deputies answerable to the people, and abolishing any veto on legislation. Finally, when all is ready for the attack, the responsibility for it must be shifted on to the shoulders of the court; and this will not be difficult, in view of the rumours that are going round as to the arming of the Tuileries. Indeed, Robespierre has by now persuaded himself, in common with most of the popular leaders, that the contemplated rising is merely an act of self-defence against a treacherous attack on Paris by the armed forces of counter-revolution.

IX

When the work of the diplomatists ends, that of the soldiers begins; and it is unreasonable to reproach Robespierre for not marching with Santerre, on August 10, to the attack of the Tuileries. Neither did Danton. Many narratives exist of the events of that day, and it is possible to reconstruct with tolerable certainty the gathering of the *Fédérés* and Sectional Guards, the order of march, the stages of the attack, the storming of the palace, the capture or massacre of its defenders, and the retreat of the royal family to the hall of the Assembly. Eye-witnesses—one of the most vivid, an English visitor to Paris[1]—have described the scenes in the streets, the Carrousel, and the Tuileries gardens—the wrecking of the royal apartments, the stripping and burning of the bodies of the dead *Suisses*, and the home-coming of the volunteers, with scraps of royalist uniforms fluttering on their blood-stained bayonets. But the most elaborate inquiry into the horrible and heroic incidents of the day[2] has not discovered a single trace of Robespierre. His enemies afterwards accused him of

[1] Dr. John Moore, *Diary*; cp. Millingen, *Recollections of Republican France*, I/119.
[2] e.g. Mathiez, *Le dix Août* (1931).

hiding, as they had done a year ago.[1] His admirers secured him the medal that was given to all members of the Commune who had taken part in the destruction of tyranny.[2] Both were beside the mark. Robespierre probably stayed at home, as most people did that day, prompted by natural caution, and incapacity for violence. From the house in the *rue Saint-Honoré* he could see the crowds coming and going, hear the sounds of firing a street or two away, and easily keep himself informed of every turn in the events.

But in the evening the Jacobin club meets as usual; and, as usual, Robespierre is there, manuscript in hand, ready with appropriate reflections on the events of the day. It is to be noticed that he ignores the king: monarchy or republic is not, to him, the issue of the day; that problem can be left to settle itself later. Instead, he advises the people to guard against any attempt of their own representatives to exploit the situation in the interests of reaction; to demand, therefore, the replacement of the Assembly by a National Convention; to exact a decree for the dismissal and condemnation of Lafayette; and not to disarm until they have secured their liberties. Meanwhile, commissioners should be sent to every part of France, to explain what has happened; the *Fédérés* should write home to those who sent them; and the Sections 'should inform the National Assembly of the real requirements of the people, and, in order to be better informed on this head, should . . . admit to their meetings all citizens, without distinction of class'. Finally, legal steps should be taken to secure the release of all imprisoned patriots.

What is most clear in this programme is the intention of the Commune (i.e. the amalgamated Sections of Paris) to dominate the situation which its successful rising has created. This is, indeed, the clue to all the events of the next six weeks. A dethroned king, a broken Constitution, a discredited Assembly that tries to save its face by a series of illegal acts (the suspension of the king, the replacement

---

[1] e.g. Vergniaud said he hid in a cellar, and wanted to fly to Marseille (B. and R. 25/365, 369, 376).
[2] Fleischmann, 147.

of the Ministers, the summoning of a Convention, and the granting of manhood suffrage), and a newly-appointed council of time-serving Ministers—all are impotent in face of the Insurrectional Commune. The men of the hour are the men who have the confidence of the Paris crowd; obscure persons, for the most part, unknown to the historians; but they made history.[1]

Robespierre treasured amongst his papers a letter which he received from one Janegon on July 19, but which loses little of its appropriateness when read in connexion with August 10. 'All brave Frenchmen', it ran, 'appreciate with me the value of your untiring efforts in the cause of freedom. Through my voice they salute you—Blessed be Robespierre, the worthy follower of Brutus! They all rely upon your incorruptible zeal, and upon the courage which gives the noble impulses of your burning and generous patriotism so many claims to honour. A civic crown and a triumph are your due: they only await the time when civic incense rises before the altar that we shall raise to you, and that posterity will adore, so long as men realize the value of freedom.'[2]

There exists, too, a medal designed by Dupré to commemorate the revolution of August 10. with the inscription, *Régénération française—10 août*, 1792. It shows a fountain in female form with water flowing from the breasts: a patriot stoops to drink from a cup held by a standing figure; it is that of Robespierre.[3]

The image is just. Robespierre was no Moses, to strike water out of a rock, or to slay the Egyptian. He was too self-centred, too calculating, to be disobedient to the voice from the burning bush. But his very scrupulousness made him the ideal cup-bearer—the man who waited on every gift of a fickle, but on the whole French Providence, and handed it on to the Chosen People. He disliked war, as

[1] The names of the members of the *Conseil Général de la Commune* nominated on the night of August 9–10 are given in *Brit. Mus.* F. 61.*
[2] Courtois, *Rapport, pièce justificatif*, No. 24 (not in Michon's *Corresp.*). Courtois suppressed the date, and the word *civic*, to give the impression that Robespierre had been offered a royal crown (A.R. 49/65).
[3] Buffenoir in A.R. 1/457.

he disliked all violence. The statesmen who made it and the generals who waged it were, he well knew, grasping at power. Whatever its results abroad, its effects at home would transform the Revolution. The crisis of 1791 had shown that it was still uncertain whether the great national rising of 1789 would result in any permanent betterment of the lot of the people. The war of 1792, whether it resulted in victory or in defeat, might very well consummate a reaction which had already begun, and crush the newly won liberties under a military despotism. He could not force the situation: he could only wait upon its developments, and hope to retrieve something of his designs from the general disaster. His methods, indeed, were not those of a strong, or generous, or straightforward man. His bitter denunciation of the politicians who were planning and of the soldiers who were conducting the war; his use of a Constitution in which he did not believe to discredit a party working, like himself, towards its destruction; his covert incitements to a violence which he was the first to avoid and to disown; and the halo of martyrdom with which he encircled himself; make it as difficult for his biographer as it was for his contemporaries to tolerate the constant irritation of his speech and print. But the fact remains that, when the *Brissotin* government failed, and the throne fell, and every attempt at a despotism was discredited, the Insurrectional Commune, the embodiment of Robespierre's plan for a popular revolution, was left master of the state. It was not his work: it was, as he would have said, a gift of Providence, or of Chance. But no single man had hoped for it, worked for it, or talked about it, as he had; and when the slow gropings of his policy at last brought him to the point of achievement, he could deservedly be hailed, if not as a great leader of the people, at any rate as an unerring interpreter of the times.

CHAPTER IX

The Revolutionist (August–September, 1792)

I

The Insurrectional Commune, which found itself in power as a result of the insurrection of August 10, was a body of 288 members, formed by the election of six representatives from each of the forty-eight Sections of Paris. Robespierre joined this body, as a representative of the Place Vendôme Section (or *Section des Piques*), on the 11th. He had already shown, by his speech at the Jacobins the night before, that he fully grasped the significance of the victory which had been won, not merely by the nation over the king, but also by Paris over France; for the point of view of the provincial *fédérés* was soon forgotten by those who had exploited it in the interests of the Commune. He had shown, too, that he looked to the insurgents to hold the ground won, and to safeguard popular liberties, until a National Convention came into being. He was now in a position to work directly for these ends. Between August 12 and 26 he was constant in his attendance at the Commune; after that date, first as president of the *assemblée primaire* of his Section, and then as a member of the *assemblée électorale* of Paris, he was still in close touch with the leaders of the Commune.

Now for the first time he appeared, as the spokesman of popular delegations, before the legislature from which he had voluntarily excluded himself; and, seeing the state of apprehension to which the Assembly was reduced, he would have been less than human if he had not enjoyed the situation. On August 12, and again on the 22nd, he petitioned the House for the abolition of the *directoire* of the Department of Paris, which he and his friends had never forgiven for its encouragement of the royal veto, or for its

259

suspension of Pétion and Manuel.[1] But the Assembly still had independence enough to resist this demand.

Again, on August 14 Robespierre led through the House a deputation of his own Section, and proposed, in a patriotic harangue, that the space left by the demolition of Louis XVI's statue, in the Place Vendôme, should be filled by a monument in honour of the citizens who had fallen on August 10.[2] This time the deputies cheered the proposal, and in due time a statue of Liberty appeared on the site, to be followed, at not infrequent intervals, by other monuments equally expressive of the political temper of the moment.[3]

The following day Robespierre reappeared with five other members of the Commune, on a weightier errand. The moderate casualties suffered by the victors of August 10 had created a demand for vengeance that was not satisfied by the slaughter of some 800 royalists. Santerre had promised that the survivors would be brought to trial, and Pétion had said that the scope of the tribunal should be extended to all enemies of the Revolution. Yet, after several days' delay, the Assembly had merely resolved to bring the surviving *Suisses* before a court-martial. It was against this decision that Robespierre's delegation protested, demanding the erection of a special court, appointed by the Sections, and having jurisdiction, without appeal, over the whole country. 'The people,' he said, 'is reposing, but it is not asleep. It wills—and rightly—the punishment of those who are to blame.' The Assembly at first refused, but was ultimately forced, by the threat of another insurrection, to give way.

This was a dangerous as well as an ungenerous move. Even if they could not regard the *Suisses* as soldiers who

[1]v. 1/201, 247.
[2]Robespierre's original idea was to destroy the Tuileries, and erect a monument in its place (*Défenseur* 12/533).
[3]Liberty was replaced in 1806-10 by a towering Roman column, on the summit of which stood Napoleon as Caesar: in 1814 the Restoration took down Napoleon, and put up a gilt fleur-de-lys: in 1833 Louis Philippe restored Napoleon, but in a frock-coat; Napoleon III replaced a copy of the Caesarean figure; the Commune of 1871 pulled the whole thing to the ground; three years later the Third Republic put it up again.

had only done their duty in defending the Tuileries, the Parisians might have reflected that their own dead were sufficiently avenged by the victory they had won, and by the killing of more than twice as many of their opponents.[1] They showed too clearly that what they wanted was not justice, but revenge. Nor can Robespierre, who had suffered nothing in the fighting, who had made an apologia for the troops that fired on the crowd a year before, and who had hitherto found excellent arguments against recourse to special tribunals, be acquitted of pandering to the lower instincts of the people. Why did he? Probably less through concern for the punishment of royalists than through distrust of the old courts, and indignation with the attempts of the Assembly to obstruct the will of the people. But within a fortnight the prison massacres were to reflect a terrible responsibility on those who, on whatever grounds, had encouraged ideas of popular vengeance.

It may perhaps be held that Robespierre made some amends for his part in setting up a retaliatory tribunal by his refusal to act as one of its judges.[2] 'Ever since the beginning of the Revolution,' he wrote, explaining this decision, 'I have been fighting against the majority of those who are now accused of *lèse-nation*. Most of them I have denounced; and I have predicted their plots, at a time when others believed in their patriotism. I could not now act as judge over men I have opposed: I could not rightly forget that, if they were the country's enemies, they were also my own. This is a good rule in all cases: it is particularly applicable here; for popular justice ought to be worthy of the people; it should be as dignified as it is swift and formidable.'[3] This scrupulousness does Robespierre credit; but one could believe in it more, if he were less concerned with his own feelings, and more with the injustice of

---

[1] The official returns gave the number of those killed on the popular side as 376 (Tuetey, Introd. to Vol. 4). The royalist dead are given by Sagnac (Lav. 2/387) as 800.

[2] As the first judge appointed by the *corps electoral*, he would in fact have been President of the Court.

[3] From a letter to the *Courrier des 83 départements*, Aug. 24 (*Moniteur*, Aug. 28).

proceedings which, characteristically, he initiated, but did not carry out.

This was not the only judicial post that he declined. Ten days before (August 14) he had received a polite note from Danton, now Minister of Justice, asking his 'dear friend' to accept a place on the *conseil de justice* attached to the Ministry. The work would only occupy part of three mornings a week; he would have congenial colleagues (Bitonzé-Deslinières, Collot d'Herbois, and Barère); and he might regard it 'not as an appointment to public office, but simply as an additional opportunity for his heart and talents to combat the enemies of freedom, and to champion the cause of the unfortunate'.[1] Danton evidently remembered Robespierre's resignation of the post of Public Prosecutor, and knew that he would need some persuasion to accept any public appointment; but all his inducements were in vain. Robespierre was not to be flattered into accepting a post that would identify him with a transitory regime, and distract him from his immediate work for the Commune, and for the cause of the people. Besides, he was doubtless anxious to give no handle to his Girondist enemies, whom he had accused of place-seeking, and who were already crediting him with designs on a dictatorship.

II

The contest between the Assembly and the Commune soon came to a head over the question of the control of Paris. On August 13 Pétion, as mayor, informed the Commune that it was the intention of the Assembly, after ratifying the proceedings of the insurrectional body which had occupied the Town Hall on the night of August 9, to dissolve it, and to reinstate the Municipality that it had displaced. On the 17th Robespierre was commissioned by the Commune to interview Pétion, and to see whether he could be induced to give up this plan, and to co-operate

---

[1] A.H. 7/187. The minute of the letter is in Fabre's hand (Danton's secretary). It is not in Michon's *Corresp.* The appointment was actually announced in the *Moniteur* of August 22.

with themselves in various measures admittedly necessary to preserve order, and prevent counter-revolution. This interview showed that the recent *rapprochement* between the two men had not outlasted August 10, and it led to no good result. Twelve days later the Assembly took advantage of the growing indiscipline of some of the Sections to decree the suspension of the new Commune, and the holding of fresh elections to replace it by a constitutional body. The Commune refused to disperse, and there was talk of another insurrection; but Robespierre, cautious, as always, when it came to a contest with the Assembly, dissuaded his colleagues from such a move.

Three days after their interview of the 17th, Pétion sent a letter which has survived among Robespierre's papers, and which throws valuable light upon the relations between the two men. 'You know, my friend,' he writes, 'what my feelings are towards you: you know that I am no rival of yours, and that I have always given you proof of my devoted friendship. It would be idle to attempt to divide us; I could not cease to love you, unless you ceased to love liberty. I have always found more fault with you to your face than behind your back. When I think you too ready to take offence, or when I believe, rightly or wrongly, that you are mistaken about a line of action, I tell you so. You reproach me with being too trustful. You may be right; but you must not assume too readily that many of my acquaintances are your enemies. People can disagree on a number of unessential points, without becoming enemies; and your heart is said to be in the right place (*on rend généralement Justice à vôtre cœur*). Besides, it is childish to take offence at the things people say against one. Imagine, my friend, the number of people who utter all kinds of libels against the mayor of Paris! Imagine how many of them I know to have spread damaging reports about me! Yet it doesn't worry me, I can assure you. If I am not totally indifferent to what others think about me, at least I value my own opinion more highly. No . . . you and I are never likely to take opposite sides: we shall always hold the same political faith. I need not assure you that it is impossible for me to join in any movement against you: my tastes, my character, my principles all forbid it. I don't believe that you covet my position, any more than I covet the king's. But if, when my term of office comes to an end, the people were to offer you the mayoralty, I suppose that you would accept it; whereas in all good conscience I could never accept the crown. Keep well. March ahead! The times are too serious to think of anything but the public interest'.[1]

There is a strain of moral patronage, and an artificial frankness about this letter, which would warn the reader, even without the previous correspondence of April, that the friendship between the two men, whatever their party associations, was breaking down. Robespierre cannot have liked either the tactless allusions to his touchiness, or the hint that he was jealous of Pétion's position, or the suggestion that he would be glad to succeed him in the mayoralty, whilst the other might aspire, however jokingly, to a crown. Did he keep the letter through a lingering regard for its writer, or because of the damaging use that might be made, some day, of that last paragraph? Within a few months, at any rate, the breach between the friends was complete. Not only had they 'taken opposite sides'; but Pétion was printing speeches attacking Robespierre, and Robespierre retorting Pétion's ill-timed charge of jealousy[2]. Within two years Pétion was dead, and Robespierre, soon to follow him, passed (was it without a pang?) a proposal from a zealous commissioner at Bordeaux to raze to the ground the house in which the ex-mayor of Paris, a hunted refugee, had sought to hide himself from the vengeance of the Jacobins.[3]

III

Within a week of Pétion's letter, France and Paris plunged into the elections which were to decide the government of the country for the next three years. Powerless in

[1]Corresp. 152.   [2]*Lettres à ses commettans*, esp. Nos. 7 and 10.
[3]Corresp. 302.

face of the Commune and its semi-independent Sections, the Legislative Assembly, by a decree of August 11, had succeeded in enforcing the principle of indirect election, but had conceded that the electoral assemblies should be chosen by primary assemblies consisting of all citizens aged twenty-one, with one year's domicile, and able to support themselves: the distinction between 'active' and 'passive' citizens was at last swept away. The Paris Sections, unable to secure direct election, made it a condition that the electoral assemblies should deliberate and vote in public, and that their choice of deputies should be submitted to the primary assemblies for ratification. The evident object of these provisions, which were first expressed in a manifesto by Robespierre's own Section,[1] was to intimidate the electors, and to secure the nomination of deputies agreeable to the people.

The nomination of electors began on August 26, and went on till September 6—in a few cases till September 8. The *Section de la Place Vendôme* met on the 27th, to elect sixteen representatives, and the operation took four days, the sessions lasting from 4 to 11 p.m., and on one occasion all night. Robespierre presided, and was the first to be elected, with only one dissentient; among the sixteen was his friend Duplay.[2]

Great trouble had been taken by the Commune to exclude royalist or reactionary candidates. All royalist papers had been suppressed; the names of those who had met at the Sainte-Chapelle a year before to elect deputies to the unpopular Legislative Assembly were printed, as a warning to their successors; and the system of voting was by *appel nominal*, which gave full scope to intimidation. The result, to a patriot mind, was eminently satisfactory. Out of an electoral assembly of 990 persons[3] only 195 were old electors; 795 were new men. Brissot, an elector in 1790 and 1791, was passed over; the new electors included Marat as well as Robespierre.

[1] August 27; *arrêté municipal*, August 28 (Mellié, *Les sections*, 65).
[2] Robespierre was also nominated by the *Section Halles-aux-Blé*.
[3] 850 representing the Paris Sections, 140 the suburban Cantons.

Then came the second stage of the elections. The first business of the *Assemblée électorale du département de Paris*, when it met in the *Salle de l'Archévêché* on September 2, was to secure a more suitable place for its deliberations, which had to be public, and would be more likely to turn out as desired if conducted under the eyes of patriots. It was therefore agreed to ask the Jacobins for the use of their hall; and Robespierre, who had planned this move,[1] was able to report next day that permission had been granted.[2]

The next step was to take fresh precautions that the elections should go in the direction desired by the Commune. Robespierre accordingly proposed, in the name of the primary assemblies, that the electoral assembly should exclude from the right of voting any of its own members 'who had taken part in the proceedings of any unpatriotic (*incivique*) club, such as the *club monarchique*, the *club de la Sainte-Chapelle*, the *Feuillants* or their affiliated societies, or any of those who had signed the petition of the 20,000';[3] and this arbitrary over-ruling of the choice of the primary electors was carried, apparently without question. Paris was now beginning to see what liberty meant in the minds of libertarians.

It was at this same meeting that a member, whose name is not given, 'reported that charges (not specified) had been brought against M. Robespierre by a *valet-de-chambre* of the *ci-devant* king': upon which proposals were made to warn the people against listening to such calumnies against one whom Marat placed first on his list of the best citizens —*hommes qui ont le mieux mérité de la patrie*,[4] and Robespierre declared from the tribune 'that he would face with perfect calmness the swords of the enemies of the common weal, and that he would bear with him to the tomb the certainty that France would remain free, and the satisfaction of

---

[1] It is forecast in the manifesto of August 27 (Mellié, *Les sections,* 66).

[2] The Assembly adjourned for the negotiations from 1 to 5 p.m. on the 2nd. The club had refused a similar request by the *Procureur-général-syndic* only the day before; but Robespierre was able to report the success of his mission by 11 p.m. on the 3rd.

[3] A royalist protest against the events of June 20, 1792 (Mathiez, 193).

[4] Charavay, *Assemblée électorale de Paris,* 3/600.

having served his country'. It is difficult not to think that this rather silly scene was staged to forward Robespierre's candidature: for the next day he was proposed by acclamation, and unanimously adopted, as Vice-president of the assembly,[1] and two days later (September 5) he was elected at the head of the list of deputies to the Convention, on the first count, by 338 votes out of 525—a result hailed by a speaker at the Jacobins as a favourable omen for future elections.[2] The rival candidate on this occasion was Pétion, whose obvious vexation at his defeat was used by Robespierre to retort his recent charge of jealousy: everyone, he said, could see Pétion's face changing colour during the counting of the votes.[3]

This was paltry enough; but worse was to follow. On September 9 a motion was passed that the claims of individual candidates should be open to discussion; and under this system Marat was elected, after a speech by Robespierre which was widely resented. Louvet accused him of 'domineering over the Assembly by intimidation and intrigue,' of putting forward Marat against the Englishman, Dr. Priestley, whose character he had 'blackened,' and of refusing a hearing to those who wished to speak on the other side. 'I was mobbed', he said, 'by those fellows with sabres and cudgels, Robespierre's bodyguard, who always surrounded the future dictator, wherever he went. They said to me, with threats (and, remember, it was a time when assassinations were taking place) "You shall go the same way as the rest"'. From Louvet's later pamphlet it appears that Robespierre said nothing worse about Priestley than that he 'wrote books in his study,' and nothing better about Marat than that ' in order to combat Lafayette and the court, he hid himself for a year in a cellar':[4] but, according

[1]Collot d'Herbois was President, and among the Secretaries were Carra, Santerre, and Marat.

[2]But Robespierre did not get so many votes as some of the definitely republican candidates—Billaud-Varenne, Lavicomterie, Robert, Boucher, or Saint-Sauveur (Aulard, 238).

[3]*Lettres à ses commettans*, No. 10.

[4]Louvet. *A Maximilien Robespierre et ses royalistes*. Mme Roland repeats the charge of attacking Priestley (Champagneux 2/339). Gorsas (*Courrier des 83 départements*, September 10), also complained of his speech.

to the queer code of the time, while there was nothing wrong in rigging the elections in the Jacobin interest, it was highly improper to overpress the claims of a Jacobin candidate. The charge of intrigue was also made, almost inevitably, in the case of Augustin Robespierre, who was elected on September 16; but Maximilien declared that he had stood on his own merits;[1] and it was known that the poet Ronsin, who had written to ask for Robespierre's support, gained nothing by it.[2] Nevertheless, the accusation of undue influence comes from too many sides to be ignored;[3] and it can hardly be doubted that in 1792, as in 1789, Robespierre, in his eagerness to further the popular cause, overstepped the line between what was then regarded as legitimate and illegitimate canvassing.

But indeed, for this, or for any other irregularities, the system was chiefly to blame. How were either calm deliberation or independent voting possible in an election in which the majority used its power, not to outvote the minority, but to disqualify it from voting; in which the passions and controversies of the hustings were introduced into the polling booth; and in which the electors were exasperated by a method of voting that absorbed eighteen days' sessions of six or seven hours each in the selection of twenty-four candidates? Nor can it have been much consolation—though it helps to explain the persistence of the system—that electors were paid for their attendance. For, in spite of this fact, only the comparatively leisured and well-to-do could afford to take an active part in so tedious and troublesome an affair—an additional reason for the tactics employed by the popular leaders to secure the return of their candidates.[4]

IV

There were other and more serious reasons why the elections of September, 1792, could not be conducted

[1] Lebon to Robespierre, Aug. 28 (Corresp. 153); *Lettres à ses commettans*, No. 10.
[2] Corresp. 154.
[3] e.g. *Aux quarante-huit sections de Paris*, by Méhée *fils* (Charavay, 3/612).
[4] v. Méry in R.F. 67/101, 68/15; cp. Mellié, 91.

calmly or dispassionately. The days during which they were held coincided with the invasion of France by foreign troops, the massacre of 'royalists' and 'aristocrats' in the Paris prisons, and the mobilization of the national defences. The electors debated in an atmosphere now chilled by fear, and now heated by patriotic excitement; in which every friend became a hero, and every enemy a traitor to the country.

August 10 had been hailed as a victory over the Austrian vanguard in Paris; but on August 15 it was heard that an invading army had crossed the frontier, and invested Thionville. On the 26th news arrived that Longwy had surrendered, under circumstances that strongly suggested treason. Within the next few days it was known that Verdun, the last fortress between the frontier and Paris, was also threatened, that there was danger of royalist risings in Brittany and Dauphiné, and that in the Vendée fighting had actually taken place between patriot troops and royalists resisting recruitment. On September 2 a messenger from the front brought news that Verdun was now besieged, that its commandant had been summoned to surrender, and that he could not hold out for more than two days. This succession of bad news, falling upon a city already distracted by the contest between the Assembly and the Commune, and by the controversies of a General Election, drove the people almost to frenzy, and it soon became doubtful whether there was any authority in the capital capable of preserving order, or preventing outbursts of violence on the part of the Sections, either against property or persons.

On August 11 the Assembly had authorised the municipal authorities to place suspected persons under provisional arrest. On the 15th, in view of the invasion, it had prohibited the families of *émigrés* from leaving their Communes, so that they might be treated as hostages. On the 18th, and again on the 29th, it had ordered fresh arrests, both of priests, and of members of the royal household; and during the last two days of the month commissioners sent out by the Sections searched every house in the city for

269

arms, and took away some 3,000 suspects to prison. These measures may have been intended less to satisfy the demand for victims, than to save them from popular vengeance; but it was more than doubtful whether their lives were any safer under lock and key.

When the news of the siege of Verdun arrived on September 2, the Commune ordered an alarm-gun to be fired, the drums beat to arms, the city gates were closed, and the Champ de Mars was filled with a crowd of volunteers, unfit to fight, but clamouring to go to the front. About noon there was an enthusiastic scene in the Assembly, when Vergniaud, Thuriot, and Danton, representatives of both political parties, vied in patriotic appeals to arms. Meanwhile certain other feelings, sordid by-products of patriotism, had been gaining ground in the popular mind— fear of treachery, and thirst for revenge; and no one who remembered the threat of an attack upon the prisons three weeks ago[1] could doubt that the danger was far more imminent now. The special tribunal set up a fortnight before to judge the 'criminals' of August 10 had ordered only three executions, and had caused special discontent by acquitting Montmorin, the governor of Fontainebleau.[2] Public funerals of the 'victims' of the 10th had worked upon the people's nerves; and the last and most imposing of these rites, celebrated at the Tuileries on the 26th, had led to public demands for revenge. The Vigilance Committee of the Commune, reconstituted on August 30, and strengthened by the addition of Marat, was known to be sorting out the prisoners, and releasing those guilty of minor offences. Marat himself, as though to underline this policy, had put up posters, advising the volunteers not to leave for the front, until they had visited the prisons, and executed upon their inmates the justice of the people.

It was not surprising that, after all these incitements, some

[1]On August 11 the administrator of the *bureau de police* wrote to Santerre, asking for a special guard at the Châtelet, Conciergerie, and La Force, in view of threats to lynch the prisoners (A.R. 14/422).

[2]True, he was popularly confused with his brother, the ex-Minister for Foreign Affairs.

of the Sections should begin to take matters into their own hands. The *Section Poissonière* passed a motion calling for the execution of all conspirators in the prisons, as a measure of security before Paris was denuded of troops; the *Section des Arcis* resolved that the people should make sure of (*s'assurer*) the prisons; and the *Luxembourg Section*, more explicitly, that 'the prisons should be cleansed by the shedding of the blood of their inmates, before leaving Paris'. In the excitement and panic of September 2, words were soon followed by acts. In the *Luxembourg* and *Sansculottes* Sections, previously strongholds of clerical landlordism, the revolution of August 10 had led to an outburst of anger against the priests, many of whom were rounded up, and interned in the Carmes (Carmelite convent), or the seminary of Saint-Firmin. Others, arrested by the Vigilance Committee of the Commune, had been temporarily herded together at the Mairie. It was these last who were to furnish the first victims. With a provocativeness which was perhaps designed, it was arranged that they should be transferred on September 2, in carriages, and by daylight, from the Mairie to the prison of the Abbaye Saint-Germain-des-Près. About three o'clock that Sunday afternoon, when four carriages containing twenty priests arrived in front of the Abbaye, they were set upon by a mob, and nearly all murdered. The same evening an informal tribunal was established at the Abbaye under one Maillard,[1] acting on instructions from certain members of the Vigilance Committee, and the inmates of the prison were 'tried': forty-three were acquitted, and 122, including Bachmann, the commandant of the Suisses, and Montmorin, the ex-Minister, condemned to death. As soon as sentence was passed, they were hustled into the street, and cut down by ruffians armed with sabres and pikes. At the Carmes, the same night, all the imprisoned priests were put to death; more than 200 thieves and debtors were murdered at the Châtelet; and a number more, including the queen's

---

[1]He had distinguished himself once before, by leading the women's march to Versailles on October 5, 1789.

friend, the Princess de Lamballe, at La Force. On September 3 fresh massacres took place at Saint-Bernard (of convicts), and Saint-Firmin (of priests); whilst at the Bicêtre reformatory the 160 victims were boys and girls. Finally, on the morning of September 4, 'popular justice' was at last appeased by the murder of 35 female inmates of the Salpêtrière hospital. On September 2 these various institutions had contained 2,637 persons: by the 5th, at least 1,100 of them had been massacred—300 priests, 150 royalists implicated in the affair of August 10, 50 Suisses, and 600 common criminals.[1]

Whilst these things were going on, the Assembly and the Commune met as usual; and the electoral assembly was discussing the form of its entry-card, and what sort of crest it should put at the head of its note-paper. Commissioners were, indeed, sent to the Abbaye, and made speeches, but soon came back saying that they could do nothing. Santerre, the commandant of the National Guard, reported that he could not count on his men to interfere with the murderers. Meanwhile the Vigilance Committee tried to improve the occasion by sending a circular to the departmental authorities in the provinces, telling them what was being done in Paris, and urging them to do likewise; and this circular was expedited by Fabre, Danton's secretary at the Ministry of Justice. 'The circular was superfluous,' says Mathiez, and gives instances of priests and aristocrats murdered without such official encouragement at various places up and down the country between August 19 and September 12. But it at least paved the way for such crimes as that of Versailles, where fifty-three prisoners from Orleans were massacred, on their way to Paris, on September 9. On the other hand, Arras was probably not the only place where the emissaries of the Paris Commune were not allowed to publish their manifesto, and were driven out of the town.[2] As for the people of Paris, they shared in the fear or apathy of their leaders, and it was not until September

[1] v. Walter, *Les massacres de Septembre*. Caron (same title), a recent and independent study, gives the total as between 1,090 and 1,395.
[2] Jacob, *Lebon*, 50.

5–8 that some of the Sections, apprehensive for their own safety, began to pass motions about 'the protection of life and property', and to appeal for a return to sanity. The country people near the capital went on with their work as usual. They were sorry that it was necessary to kill the prisoners; but what else could one do with aristocrats who were plotting to blow up Paris, with all its inhabitants?[1]

V

It has been necessary to describe the prison massacres in some detail, in order to state fairly the conditions governing the question, what was the degree of Robespierre's responsibility? The massacres went on for at least forty-eight hours. Those at La Force and the Abbaye had the official approval of the Commune (those at the Carmes and Saint-Firmin, perhaps also at the Bicêtre, were the work of Sectional Committees). The idea that the victims were political criminals, or a danger to the state, could not be held, of more than a minority, by anyone who knew the facts. Robespierre was a member of the General Council (the executive committee) of the Commune, and of the electoral assembly; he was also one of the most knowledgeable and influential men in Paris. So far as is known, he never said a word or raised a finger against the massacres.

In the minutes of the Commune for September 2 it is recorded that, after representatives had been sent to the Abbaye and the Assembly, the king's valet-de-chambre, M. Hue, was questioned at the bar of the House as to why he had whistled the air O Richard, o mon roi! and was sent to gaol for the offence; after which 'MM. Billaud-Varenne and Robespierre described in patriotic terms the profound grief that they felt for the present state of France, and denounced a conspiracy for putting the Duke of Brunswick on the throne'. Soon Manuel returned from the Abbaye

---

[1]Malouet's evidence, in Deslandres, 1/157. The evidence for the state of opinion in the provinces, and for analogous massacres there, is carefully examined by Caron, *Les massacres de Septembre*, 153 f., 363 f.

with a lamentable account of what was going on there. No action was taken. During the evening session commissioners are twice sent to La Force—the first time to investigate, the second time 'to calm the excitement as soon as possible' (*pour hâter de calmer les esprits*). Next morning there is a request from the Quinze-Vingts Section to be allowed to hold the families of *émigrés* as hostages, and to kill conspirators: the Commune passes to the next business, remarking that the Sections may do whatever they think best. Soon afterwards Robespierre is deputed, with Deltroy and Manuel, 'to go to the Temple (where the king and queen were imprisoned), and to see that everything is quiet there'.[1] Robespierre, then, was at the Commune on both the crucial days; he was well aware of what was going on; he agreed with other leaders of the people (what other inference can be drawn from his silence?) that it was better to let matters take their course:[2] his interference with the massacres limited itself, like theirs, to some half-hearted attempts to calm the minds of the murderers. In this he did no better, and no worse, than Danton, Roland, Santerre, and others whose official responsibility was greater than his own.[3] But when he is found, two months later, defending his conduct on the double ground that he did not know what was happening, and that he could not go against the trend of public opinion,[4] one is bound to say, that the first excuse is untrue, and the second unworthy of a statesman.

Nor is that the whole count. In his speech at the Commune on September 4, delivered some hours after the massacre had begun, and subsequent to the announcement of this to the body of which he was a member,[5] Robespierre

[1] *Procès-verbaux de la Commune de Paris*, in *Mémoires sur les journées de Septembre*, 1792 (ed. Baudouin, Vol. 11).
[2] Rétif de la Bretonne, who gives an eye-witness's account of the massacre, assumes that Robespierre agreed with Danton and the Commune as to the advisability of 'emptying the prisons'. (*Nuits révolutionnaires*, 22.)
[3] For the well-known story of Danton's admission of his responsibility to Louis Philippe, v. A.R. 10/677.
[4] Speech of Nov. 5.
[5] v. *Procès-verbaux de la Commune de Paris*, (ed. Baudouin) 11/242. Ward (189) tries to show that he may not have heard of the massacre.

went out of his way to denounce Brissot, if not by name, at least in unmistakable terms, as a conspirator, and as an agent of the Duke of Brunswick; upon which the Vigilance Committee issued warrants for the arrest of Roland, Brissot, and other prominent Girondins. This could only mean one thing. Had not Danton, moved by the threat against a fellow-Minister, secured the withdrawal of the warrant,[1] the Girondist leaders would almost certainly have perished with the other prisoners. In short, a charge lies against Robespierre not merely of doing nothing to stop the massacres, not merely of condoning them as an execution of popular justice upon criminals who had escaped the law, but of trying to use them as a cloak for political assassination. Mme Roland had no doubt as to his guilt. 'Robespierre and Marat', she wrote to Bancal des Issarts on September 5, 'are holding a sword over our heads. They are doing all they can to stir up the people, and to egg it on against the National Assembly and the Council (of Ministers). They have set up a *chambre ardente*. They dispose of a small army, paid for either by money they have found at the Tuileries, or by funds provided by Danton, who is the hidden leader of the gang'. Again, on September 9, after mentioning Robespierre's election to the Convention, and the attack on Brissot, 'It is my friend Dton. who manages the whole affair: Robp. is only his puppet (*mannequin*), Mat. only carries his dagger and torch. This brutal demagogue is our real ruler; we are no better than his slaves, whilst we expect every day to become his victims'. And again, on the 11th, 'The electoral body is getting worse and worse, and Robp. is dropping the mask'.[2]

Mme Roland is, of course, a prejudiced witness; but her charge gains significance from the coincidence of the massacres with the elections. Both began on the same day, September 2. Robespierre was elected on the 5th, Danton

[1]This rests on a statement by Prudhomme, uncontradicted at the time, and corroborated by Mme Roland (Madelin, *Danton*, 169; Barthou, *Danton*, 110).

[2]Corresp. ed. Perroud, 2/434, 436. Her friend Buzot also speaks of Robespierre and Danton as responsible for the massacres. (Walter, *Marat*, 249.)

on the 6th, Marat on the 9th, the day of the massacre at Versailles. When the polls closed on the 19th, Paris was found to be represented exclusively by the candidates of the Commune, which had at worst organized, and at best allowed, the massacres. The temptation, and the opportunity, to get the leaders of the *Brissotin* party out of the way during this crisis must have presented themselves. It would be so easy to order their provisional arrest, and to disclaim responsibility for anything more serious that might follow.

This then, is the question. Behind the ruffians who murdered the prisoners at the Abbaye was the Vigilance Committee of the Commune: behind the Vigilance Committee—was there a secret understanding between Danton in the Assembly, Marat at the Commune, and Robespierre in the Election chamber? Were they agreed in condoning the massacres? Did Danton refuse to allow the proscription of Roland and Brissot, proposed by Marat and Robespierre? Can we find some other interpretation of the speech of September 2, for the police visit paid to Brissot's house, and for the story of Danton's intervention? Or must we accept the verdict of a recent investigator, that Robespierre's denunciation of Brissot was 'an act of cold and calculated cruelty, which can only be regarded as an attempt to get rid of a dangerous and embarrassing rival?'[1] Have we to deal merely with a moral cowardice that dare not interfere, or with a moral turpitude that gives the excited crowd an easy opportunity to lynch one's political enemy? Is Robespierre excusable on the plea, 'I am innocent of the blood of this just person: see ye to it'; or was his offence a less subtle, but not less detestable variant of that of David against Uriah the Hittite? It is an unpleasant choice of precedents; and it is hardly possible for any one who has admired Robespierre's courage in opposition and adversity

---

[1] Walter, *Les massacres de Septembre*, 160. cp. Prudhomme's story (4/123, given on the authority of Mandat, an eye-witness) of a meeting at the Ministry of Justice on September 3, when Robespierre objected to the proposal of a dictatorship, that 'Brissot would be the dictator'. 'It is not a dictatorship, then, that you object to, but Brissot?' 'Both!'

to feel happy about his conduct when the turn of events puts his enemies into his power.[1]

VI

On September 21 the Legislative Assembly closed the session which, to save constitutional appearances, was regarded as having been permanent since August 10, by giving a formal welcome to the National Convention, and by escorting its members in procession from the Tuileries to the Manège. The deputies at this time numbered some 750; ultimately there were as many as 903, of whom 618 were new men, who had not sat in either of the previous Assemblies. The significance of this was that the old controversies would be fought out before a new audience. The small but concentrated Jacobin party, or 'Mountain' (*Montagne*) as it was called,[2] under the leadership of the Paris *bloc*, found itself 'in Opposition' against the larger but less homogeneous 'Government' group of the Girondins, the representatives of the provincial point of view, who had been elected, for the most part, before the events of September were known in the country constituencies, and who put forward a less definite political programme;[3] whilst behind both was a mass of members, of uncertain and varying size, to whom the recent developments of party strife meant little, and who were concerned for the essential issues—the organization of republican government, and the conduct of the war. These men were critics of both parties, impatient of their quarrels, subservient to any group or policy that showed itself able to 'save the country', but capable of reasserting their independence,

[1]Robespierre always had apologists. Souberbeille, interviewed by Louis Blanc in extreme old age, said that he could never speak about the events of September without horror, and had once exclaimed in the doctor's hearing, apropos of some barbarity by the Jacobin Ronsin, 'Blood again! nothing but blood! They will end by drowning the Revolution in it, these miscreants!' (Blanc, 7/192). For Robespierre's own defence, v. 1/289.

[2]From the high seats it occupied at the end of the Hall, but not without thought of the Dispensation of Mount Sinai. (R.F. 45/544, 46/171.)

[3]Aulard, *Études*, 1/6.

and overthrowing those whom they put and kept in power.[1]

This Convention was the Sovereign People, assembled, as in 1789, to make a Constitution. There was an end, therefore, of the six weeks' dictatorship of the Commune; moreover, although the Jacobins controlled the new General Council elected in December, and the Departmental Directory re-established in January, yet they had to reckon with the independence of the forty-eight Sections, each of which regarded itself as an autonomous portion of the Sovereign People. There was an end, too, of another great source of public anxiety; for on the very day that the Convention met, news came of the victory of Valmy, and, a week later, of the retreat of the Prussian army.

It might have been thought that, with the king a prisoner, the foreign foe and attendant *émigrés* in flight, and the country waiting for its first National Government, the political factions would forego their quarrels. Far from it. A king in the Temple was to prove a greater embarrassment, if not a greater danger, than a king at the Tuileries. The Prussian retreat threw into higher relief the dangers and scandal of civil war in the Vendée. Before August 10 the issue had been, Should there be a Republic? Now the issue was, Who shall control it? A contest of opinions became a contest of interests. Before September 20 there had been parties for and against the war. Now that the war seemed to be approaching a successful end, everyone was anxious to manage it, and thought he knew how: the contest of interests became a contest of programmes. But, above all, the events of the last six weeks had made political peace almost impossible. On the one hand, the bloodshed of August 10 left behind it a feeling of hatred, and a demand for vengeance, which had not been satisfied even by the prison massacres, and which now extended beyond the king and the 'aristocrats' to politicians of the Feuillant type, who were suspected of having tried to keep Louis on

[1] For a detailed description of the House at this period, v. Dulaure, *Physionomie de la Convention Nationale* (Dauban, *Paris en* 1793, 1); and for the improved facilities given to the Press, R.F. 54/288.

the throne, and were known to favour (under the guise of republicanism) a middle-class and reactionary regime. On the other hand, the brief rule of the Insurrectional Commune seemed to the bourgeois constitutionalists, who still controlled the administration, and represented the main body of opinion in the country, to realize the worst fears expressed in July, 1791; for here were the Paris Sections, enfranchising the lowest type of the city crowd, displacing their official representatives, playing fast and loose with the municipal funds, the municipal troops, and the municipal regulations, filling the prisons by arbitrary arrest of citizens, and emptying them again by organized massacre, intimidating the deputies into passing decrees of a dangerously democratic type, and conducting the elections in such a way that Paris was represented in the Convention by a solid block of nominees of the Commune.

Thus, whilst the Jacobins, conscious of their minority in the country, organized the power of Paris to keep the Revolution moving in a democratic direction, the Girondins prepared to use their majority to crush the dictatorship of the capital. The opportunities of peace were thrown away. Not merely because the politicians would not look to the future, and forget the past, but also because the Revolution had raised fresh issues that could not be foreclosed, France was plunged into a domestic struggle which could only lead to the destruction of one party in the state, and the dictatorship of the other.

VII

As soon as the elections were over, Robespierre began to re-issue his journal, which had appeared very irregularly during the weeks preceding August 10, and had since ceased altogether. Like the Jacobin club, he chose a new title—*Lettres de Maximilien Robespierre, membre de la Convention nationale de France, à ses commettans.* Otherwise the form of the paper was unchanged, though its cover was no longer a challenging red, but a sober grey—perhaps symbolizing the scepticism with which he had by now come to regard all merely political and constitutional programmes. In the Introduction to his first number Robespierre explained that he would use this tribune, 'open, unlike that of the Convention, to all the world', to defend 'immutable maxims, principles that lie at the base of the social order, as universally recognized as they are universally violated', and to do so in a spirit of truth and reason, opposed to that of passion and party indulged in by other journals. He then went on to outline the work before the Convention, which he visualized as a supplement to that of the Constituent Assembly. 'To perfect the organization and distribution of some of the constituted authorities, on principles already laid down, to dilute (*temperer*) representative aristocracy with a few new institutions calculated to guard it from corruption, and to guarantee the rights of the Sovereign—such, perhaps, is all that the Convention can do, or expect to have to its credit'. What Robespierre contemplates here is a republican revision of the Constitution of 1791, keeping everything of value, from the democratic standpoint, in the old system, whilst debarring the Convention from radical changes, which, in view of the unexpectedly Girondist colour of the new Assembly, could hardly be favourable to popular interests. Nevertheless he must have felt that this was a rather meagre programme for a Messianic assembly, heralded by a national insurrection. He is therefore at pains to point out that political institutions, however democratic they may be, can never be entirely satisfying, and that true republicanism is that of the heart. 'Which of us', he asks, 'would care to descend from the height of the eternal principles we have proclaimed to the actual government of the republic of Berne, Venice, or Holland? . . . It is not enough, therefore, to have overturned the throne: our concern is to erect upon its remains holy equality, and the imprescriptible Rights of Man. It is not the empty name, but the character of the citizens, that constitutes a republic. The soul of a republic is *vertu*—that is, the love of one's country, and a high-minded devotion which sinks all private interests in the interest of the whole community'. It follows from this, again, that the old political tests are no longer valid. It used to be enough to divide the nation into royalists and patriots. Now that all are nominally republicans and patriots, the division lies between those who put their republicanism to base and selfish uses, and those who endeavour to achieve, through it, the happiness and *vertu* of the whole people. But how is this super-political ideal to be achieved? History, Robespierre thinks, shows that society has always been in greater danger from too much than from too little government: tyranny has been the danger, not anarchy. The great problem before the legislator is to provide enough power for effective government, without the possibility of its abuse. A constitution which secured this result would be 'the masterpiece of the human mind'. It would almost need gods, as Rousseau said, to give such laws to men. And even they might fail; for there must be something in the citizens themselves to which the legislator can appeal—something which only good laws can give them. Are we, then, fixed in a fatal circle? It would seem so. But Robespierre, again following Rousseau, sees a way out of the *impasse*, by way of the natural goodness of the people. He admits, in a passage of unusual charity and common sense, that French history and social habits have made it particularly difficult for the *bourgeoisie* to recognize the merits of the working class. But he believes that 'the first thing a legislator must recollect is that the people is good; the first thing he must feel is the need to avenge the people's wrongs, and to restore its self-respect'. There is, then, after all, a great work for the Convention to attempt. 'The temple of liberty was built the first time by hands still wearing the shackles of despotism. It must be rebuilt . . . upon the foundations of justice and equality'. And this can be done, 'if the Convention never loses sight of the fundamental truth, that its first care must be to safeguard the rights of the citizens, and the sovereignty of the people, against the very government which it is setting up'.

The conclusion is rather bleak, suggesting a constitution in the style of Sieyès, to check rather than to confer the power of government; indeed, Robespierre had little to hope from a Girondist revision of Feuillant legislation. But the interest of the article lies elsewhere—in the sense it shows of the inner meaning of the August revolution, and the vision it expresses of a regenerated democracy, of a state springing from the will of an enlightened and self-respecting people. This was a real contribution to the literature of political science, on the lines of nineteenth-century Liberalism.

VIII

Robespierre's distrust of the Girondins was soon justified. In the preliminary proceedings of September 20, Pétion, now an open enemy, was chosen first President of the Convention, and the Secretariate did not contain a single Jacobin. When the formal sessions began, no time was lost in attacking the Jacobin party;[1] and on September 25 a charge of aiming at dictatorship brought Robespierre to the tribune.[2] It was a year since he had last addressed a national assembly, and five weeks since he had made any public utterance, outside the electoral meetings and the Commune. There must have been many among his new audience who were eager to hear him speak, and to form their own opinion of his person and policy.

He opened his speech by saying that he welcomed the opportunity to defend, not himself, but his country. Yet almost at once he began to talk about himself, recalling his record in the Constituent Assembly, and describing himself as the most persecuted of all champions of the people. When he reached the 'Self-denying Ordinance' of 1791, the refrain 'I did this, and I did that' (*c'est moi qui . . . c'est moi*

---

[1]Brissot on September 22 and 23, Kersaint, Vergniaud, Lanjuinais, and Buzot on the 24th, Lasource and Rebecqui on the 25th.

[2]It was made by Rebecqui. Barbaroux defined the charge by saying that 'one day, soon after August 10, Panis designated Robespierre by name as the virtuous man who was likely to become dictator of France'. Panis denied that he had said anything of the kind (Jaurès, 6/185).

qui) led to impatient cries of 'Cut it out!' (*abrégez*). When he was able once more to gain a hearing, he went on to charge his opponents with *fédéralisme*, that is, with 'the intention of turning the French Republic[1] into a congeries of federal republics, which would always be at the mercy of civil disorder, or foreign attack'. 'Let us declare', he ends, 'that the French Republic is a single state (*état unique*) under a single system of constitutional laws. Only the certainty of the strongest possible union between all parts of France can enable us to repulse our enemies with energy and success'.

The interest of this speech is that it announces so clearly the two main themes of the contest between the Mountain and the Gironde. The burden of the charge against the one was to be Dictatorship, and against the other Federalism. To the Girondin—the representative of private property, of middle-class domination, and of the interests of the pro-vinces—dictatorship meant the intimidation of a national assembly by the clubs, the Sections, and the press of the capital; the manœuvres by which Paris had secured a Jacobin representation; and the six weeks' regime of the Insurrectional Commune, with its threats of a socialistic programme. To the Montagnard—the representative of Paris, the champion of the dispossessed and disfranchised classes, and of the parts of the country most endangered by foreign invasion—Federalism meant a denial of what Paris had done for the Revolution, the sacrifice of the political and economic rights of the people to the interests of the business man and the investor, and the break-up of that national unity without which the war could not be carried on. At present both these charges were premature, and rested on the flimsiest sort of evidence. They were, none the less, logical inferences from the two main tenden-cies of the situation; for history hinted that France, under the strain of war, would either concentrate its power in an autocracy, or dissipate it in civil strife; and, before the

[1]The phrase was just 3 days old; it had not been used in the decree abolishing royalty (September 21), but was inserted rather tentatively the following day. (R.F. 22/97.) Already it was controversial.

year was out, both charges were to find their justification—the first in the Committee of Public Safety, and the second at Lyon and Toulon.

At the moment, whilst Federalism was a remote danger, Dictatorship, as Robespierre himself had been foremost in urging, was an ever-present possibility, and the most damaging suspicion that could be attached to a political enemy. It was, in fact, so dangerous, that its effect was, as the Girondists might have foreseen, to unite their opponents. 'It is my duty in justice', said Marat, 'to declare that my colleagues, and particularly Robespierre and Danton, have consistently disapproved of the idea of either a triumvirate or a dictatorship. If any one is guilty of having disseminated these ideas among the public, it is I; for I believe I am the first political writer, perhaps the only one in France since the Revolution began, to propose a military tribune, a dictator, or a triumvirate as the sole means of crushing traitors and conspirators'; and he went on to reiterate his belief in the need of 'a wise strong man' to punish the guilty, and to save the country. Danton was less bold; but his demand for the death penalty against anyone who proposed either a dictatorship or the dismemberment of the country cleverly countered the attack; and the debate ended with the passing of a decree, not against dictatorship, but against federalism—'The French Republic', it was declared, 'is one and indivisible'.

IX

On October 5 Robespierre spoke at the Jacobins for the first time, so far as the records show, since August 17. Now that a new Assembly was in session, and the club was no longer overshadowed by the Commune, or distracted by the rival activities of the ambiguous *Club de la Réunion*,[1] the hall in the rue Saint-Honoré once more took its place as the lobby of the Manège, where deputies discussed, before and after the debates, the *acta* and *agenda* of the Convention.

[1] v. Mathiez in R.H. 148/63.

But the constitution and temper of the club were changing. It had altered its name, since September 21, to *Société des Jacobins, amis de l'égalité et de la liberté*; and it was no longer dedicated to constitutionalism. Along with this homage to Robespierrist principles, it was becoming, more and more, a party meeting-place, the headquarters of the Mountain, a society whose members must not only pay a subscription, but also acknowledge certain leaders, and conform to certain tests of political orthodoxy. Thus, on October 5, Robespierre discouraged the attendance of deputies from the provinces—Parisians were easier company; on the 12th Brissot's name was struck off the list of members; on the 15th—the day after Robespierre and Dumouriez, fresh from his victories, had embraced, amidst the applause of the members—the society issued a circular giving a Jacobin version of the August revolution, and denouncing the Girondist attacks on Robespierre; on the 28th Maximilien delivered an address on the part played by calumny in the Revolution, with special reference to d'André and Maury;[1] and on the 29th, as a sequel to Louvet's attacks on Robespierre, his name too was struck off the club. Soon the line of *dénonciation* and *radiation* begins to stretch ominously ahead; and a contemporary caricaturist is encouraged to represent Robespierre, in a chef's costume, with a *bonnet rouge* on his head and a pestle in his hand, boiling his enemies in a cooking-pot—*marmite épuratoire des Jacobins*.[2]

Meanwhile the Girondins were not inactive. They proposed to counter the hostility of the Sections by filling Paris with volunteers from the provinces; and from October 19 onwards these new *fédérés* began to arrive in such numbers that by the middle of November they numbered nearly 16,000 men. Some of them mounted guard over the Convention: others marched through the streets, singing a ditty whose refrain asked for 'Marat's head, and Robespierre's, and Danton's', and were followed by a mob to the Palais Royal, shouting 'Death to Marat and Robespierre!'[3]

[1] This was published in No. 3 of the *Lettres à ses commettans* (November 2), as *Sur l'influence de la calomnie sur la Révolution*.
[2] A.R. 1/235.   [3] B. and R. 20/184.

285

The danger of bloodshed, no less real than in July, 1791, or August, 1792, was averted partly by Marat's tact—he visited the barracks of the *fédérés* from Marseille, and asked some of them to dinner ; partly by Robespierre's exhortations to calmness,[1] and by the steps taken by Pache, as Minister of War, to send the volunteers to the front. Ultimately those who remained in Paris came under Jacobin influence, and remained to strengthen the forces at the disposal of the Mountain. The failure of this Girondist move is well illustrated by a series of letters that Robespierre received from one Aigoin of Montpellier: in June, 1792, he writes as a champion of Brissot and Lafayette; by November he is denouncing the *fédérés*, and proposing the publication of daily papers to counteract Girondist propaganda.[2]

This affair was not the only failure of the Girondist majority in the Convention to gain control of Paris. Attempts were made to capture the personnel of the municipality. Here the difficulty was to find candidates for posts which, however well paid, were decidedly dangerous. The mayoralty, which should have been filled in October, was declined in turn by Pétion and d'Ormesson, and not accepted until the end of November by the insignificant Chambon. Later elections went altogether against the Girondins. The municipal officials chosen in December included Chaumette, ex-President of the Insurrectional Commune, and Hébert, editor of the extremist *Père Duchesne*. The new Commune was as revolutionary as the old. Robespierre himself was nominated for the mayoralty, and might perhaps have had it. The post carried a stipend of 75,000 livres; but he refused to give up his work as a deputy for any other position, however important or well-paid.

X

Exasperated by these failures, the Girondist leaders launched a frontal attack against Robespierre. J. B. Louvet,

[1] Speeches of October 15 and 29.   [2] Corresp. 136, 148, 149.

a novelist and romanticist, who lived in a world where everything was unreal except his own tinsel passions, had been waved on to the political stage by the magic of Mme Roland. He was at present editor of *La Sentinelle*, an anti-Jacobin publication in poster form, financed by Roland out of police grants made from Danton's secret service fund;[1] and he was willing enough to show his gratitude to his patrons, as well as to indulge his taste for publicity, by baiting the chief enemy of his party.

On October 29 Robespierre was in the tribune of the Convention, attempting to answer attacks based upon an anonymous letter,[2] and upon suggestions of another September 2, aimed at the Girondist leaders. His old enemy Guadet was in the chair, using his position to harass the speaker; interruptions made it difficult for him to get a hearing. When at last he made some general observations on the scandal of personal intrigues and attacks in the House, Louvet suddenly intervened. 'I demand a hearing', he cried, 'to accuse Robespierre'. 'And so do we', added Rebecqui and Barbaroux. Merlin de Thionville protested that it was no time for private quarrels. Robespierre's remedy against personal attacks, Danton suggested, lay in the courts. 'If I take your advice', retorted Robespierre, 'will the Convention pay the costs of the trial?'

'If every member of the House were so touchy' . . . began Buzot, but Robespierre interrupted him, and made a rush for the tribune. At this, Rebecqui protested against his 'trying to intimidate this House by speeches, as he has succeeded in intimidating the Jacobins', and Guadet called him to order. At the end of Buzot's speech the closure was carried, and the President overruled Robespierre's claim to reply.[3]

Such was the prelude to Louvet's denunciation—the first stage of a parliamentary *corrida*, in which the victim had been goaded into exasperation by a crowd of political

[1]Perroud in R.F. 62/105. Fourcade alleged that Roland offered him 300 *livres* a month to write for this paper (A.R. 15/55).
[2]The text is in Jaurès, 6/220.
[3]There is a vivid description of this scene in Moore's *Journal*.

picadors. Now the *toreador* steps into the arena, armed with a broadsword rather than a rapier, but ready to kill.

Louvet's speech covered the whole history of the Revolution since August 10, and charged Robespierre, at every turn of events, with being the villain of the piece, arch-intriguer against the heroic Gironde. August 10, he declared, was *their* work: the Commune, inspired by Robespierre, and afterwards set itself to *sabotage* their national policy. Robespierre's party was responsible for the prison massacres, and for the exclusion of Girondist voters from the polls. Robespierre had put himself forward as the leader of the Commune, bringing false charges against Brissot and his friends, and manifestly aiming at a dictatorship. 'The authority of the Assembly', said Louvet, 'was insulted and set aside by an insolent demagogue, who came to the bar of the House to dictate its decrees, went back to the General Council to denounce its acts, and returned again to the Commission of Twenty-one to threaten it with a call to arms'. This version of Robespierre's conduct on August 12 caused such an uproar in the House that he could get no hearing for a reply. But at the end of Louvet's speech his credit was still so far undamaged that he was given a week in which to prepare a considered answer to the charges brought against him.

It was enough. The *Réponse de Maximilien Robespierre à l'accusation de J. B. Louvet*, delivered in the House on November 5, and printed both by the Convention and the Jacobins, completely demolished his enemy. It took Louvet's charges one by one, and showed how ridiculous they were. He was accused, said Robespierre, of aiming at a dictatorship: yet none but a madman could suppose that his credit in Paris, without backing of money or arms, could master the other eighty-two departments. He was accused of being a friend of Marat—Marat, with whom he had once conversed, and disagreed. He was accused of tyrannizing over the elections, when he had done no more than others did, or than the regulations allowed. He had imposed his opinions, it was said, upon the Jacobin club, especially during the last ten months: this was an attack upon the club itself, which, during that period, had expressed the true opinions of the people, and had saved the country from disaster. As to the August revolution, he cannot, indeed, claim a leading part in that victory, since he was only nominated to the Commune on the 10th; but it was the work of the Commune, not of any political party. The Commune had been guilty of illegalities? Perhaps; but what of it, at such a crisis? 'The Revolution is illegal: the fall of the Bastille and of the throne were illegal—as illegal as liberty itself!' Besides, whatever the Sections and *fédérés* did on August 10 was done in the name of the whole people; and if the end does not justify the means, at least the whole justifies the part. We are here very near the pitfalls of *droit adminis-tratif*; but Robespierre hurries on to the most serious charge against himself—that he was implicated in the prison massacres. His defence is, first, that he spent so much time, during those days, either at home, or at the electoral assembly and the Jacobins, that he knew no more of what was going on in the prisons than anyone else did, and indeed heard it less soon; secondly, that the General Council, of which he was a member, but which he had ceased to attend,[1] tried to stop the massacres, but failed; and thirdly, that, in view of the indignation caused by the loss of life on August 10, the excitement due to the approach of the enemy, and the desire of the people—for it was not a mere handful of assassins—to execute vengeance on the prisoners, no one could have prevented the massacres.

Robespierre himself must have distrusted the effect of such special pleading; for he went on as soon as possible to a rhetorical appeal which effectually distracted his hearers from the weakness of his case. 'It seems pretty certain', he said, 'that one innocent man perished; and doubtless even one is far too many.[2] One ought to weep, and we have wept, over this cruel mistake. You should weep even for the criminal victims, who fell beneath the blade of popular justice.

[1]This is a fresh untruth; v. the minutes of the Commune, 1/273.
[2]For the actual number and character of the victims, v. 1/272.

But let your grief, like everything mortal, have an end; and let us keep a few tears for tragedies that affect us more closely'—the hundred thousand victims of Bourbon tyranny. 'When you listen to Louvet's pathetic account of the death of a Montmorin or a Lamballe, you might imagine you are reading a manifesto by Brunswick or Condé'; and he goes on to denounce the 'everlasting slanderers' who wish to 'avenge despotism, insult the cradle of the Republic, and dishonour the Revolution in the eyes of Europe'. Robespierre, then, makes no apology for the massacres; rather, he takes a kind of pride in them, as the work of the people. Somehow he has persuaded himself, in spite of evidence which must by this time have been known to all, that only one of the 1,300 victims was undeservedly executed. Yet this is nothing to the moral blindness which, knowing the horrible circumstances of the death of the Princess de Lamballe, can speak of it so slightingly, or can seriously suppose that it needed Louvet's exaggerations to make the massacres a dishonour to the Revolution. All that can be said is that this blindness was not peculiar to Robespierre, and that it sprang, not from natural cruelty or insensibility, but from a fanatical belief in the justice of the people, and the rightness of the Revolution.

Robespierre ended his defence by dealing with the events of August 12, and with the anonymous letter which had opened the attack on October 29. His peroration was a renunciation of his right to make counter-accusations against his enemies, and a prayer to the effect that their 'miserable manœuvres' might be 'buried in eternal oblivion': —for a revolution which had not been dishonoured by the massacre of 1,300 defenceless prisoners might yet be disgraced by the continuance of personal attacks upon Robespierre.

Louvet, trying to reply to this speech, was refused a hearing. Barbaroux was not allowed to speak from the bar of the House. At last Barère, with his flair for expressing the sense of an assembly, moved 'that the National Convention, considering that it ought to continue its attention to the interests of the Republic, passes to the business of the day'. Robespierre naturally resented the suggestion that his grievances did not concern the state; but when those words had been dropped, the motion was accepted as a proper comment on an episode which has more interest for a biographer than for a historian.[1]

When Maximilien entered the club that evening he was greeted with applause.[2] Manuel made a speech in which he described Robespierre and Pétion as 'the generals of liberty'; and Collot d'Herbois, carried away by astronomical metaphor, spoke of the one as the 'summer star', and the other the 'winter star' of the political firmament[3]. He then went on to underline the passages in Robespierre's defence dealing with the prison massacres, in such a way as to put their meaning beyond doubt. September 2, he said, 'is the principal article of our creed of liberty'; and he appealed to Manuel, who, as a member of the Vigilance Committee, had 'co-operated' in it, to agree that it was 'a magnificent day's work' (une grande journée). 'Where', he asked, 'would liberty be, where would the Convention be, but for September 2?' (Loud applause.)

So much for an unpleasant episode in Robespierre's career.

[1]No doubt a good many members shared Garat's opinion (Mem. 69), that the quarrel was like that of the Molinists and Jansenists, 'whose whole dispute turned on the manner in which divine grace acts upon the human soul, but who accused one another of disbelieving in the existence of God'.

[2]This is the first session of the Jacobins reported in the Moniteur.

[3]Their political association outlasted their friendship. It was said (by Chabot at the Jacobins on November 7) that Mme Pétion had applauded Louvet's speech.

CHAPTER X

The Regicide (September, 1792–January, 1793)

I

When Robespierre returned to Paris in November, 1791, he left his brother and sister living together in the rue des Rapporteurs at Arras, none too comfortably, upon such allowances as he could afford them, and Augustin's stipend as a member of the Departmental Administrative Council. This post once achieved, Augustin's fortunes improved: he became President of the local Jacobin club, and a judge in the Correctional Tribunal: only his youth (he was twenty-seven) prevented his nomination as a Justice of the Peace. August, 1792, found him Procureur-Syndic of the Arras Commune, and one of the Paris deputies to the Convention.

Within a few days of his election, he set out with his sister for the capital, where they took two rooms in the Duplays' house, one of which had previously been occupied by the deputy Couthon.[1] Charlotte's arrival soon caused trouble in the Duplay household. Accustomed to keep house for her brothers, and jealous of Maximilien's dependence on Mme Duplay, she set herself to persuade him that, as an important politician, he ought to have an establishment of his own, and at last badgered him into taking rooms in the neighbouring rue Saint-Florentin, where she could keep house for him.[2] But Mme Duplay was not so easily outmanoeuvred. Robespierre fell ill, and Charlotte nursed

[1] Couthon wrote to Roland from the Duplays' address on October 4, saying he was under notice to leave his present quarters within a week, and asking for rooms in the Tuileries, whence (as a cripple) he could more conveniently attend the Manège. Roland refusing (October 8), on the ground that the Tuileries was being prepared for the Assembly (which moved there on May 10), Couthon found lodgings in the Cour du Manège. But it must be added that the *Almanach royal* for 1792 gives Couthon's address as 343, not 366 rue St. Honoré. (R.F 57/412.) The two Robespierres paid Duplay 1000 *livres* a year as from October 1, 1793, for a furnished room at the back of the house and an unfurnished room at the front (A.R. 1/345).

[2] Charlotte does not mention Augustin: did he stay on at the Duplays?

him, but said nothing. When Mme Duplay heard of it, she
went to see him, and made such a fuss that he gave way
again, and returned to the rue Saint-Honoré. 'They are so
fond of me', he said, 'and show me so much attention and
kindness, that it would be ungrateful of me to refuse'.
Charlotte still made attempts to assert her rights; but the
other woman was determined to win. One day Charlotte's
servant brought Maximilien a present of some pots of
jam—it was a weakness of his; Mme Duplay sent them back
with the message, 'I'm not going to have her poisoning
him'. This *affreux blasphème* was the end. Robespierre
remained at the Duplays, and Charlotte consoled herself by
describing them to her friends as 'a race of vipers', who used
Maximilien's name to get the best of everything at the
baker's and the grocer's, whilst ordinary people went without. By July, 1793, the position had grown so strained that
Augustin took his sister away with him on a mission to the
army of Italy. Ultimately, in May, 1794, the brothers
arranged to have her taken back to Arras.[1]

The domestic troubles of the great have always afforded
material to the moralist and the cynic. The biographer,
having no better evidence (it is true) to go upon than the
counter-accusations of two jealous women, may well be
surprised at the meekness with which Robespierre allowed
himself to be overruled, now by his sister, and now by his
friend. Probably illness and overwork were the cause,
together with a strong sense of family duty, if not of family
affection. But it can hardly be doubted that the open
hospitality of the rue Saint-Honoré was more in keeping
with his reputation, and more useful to his political career,
than the privacy of a family party.

II

The illness which led to Robespierre's return to the rue
Saint-Honoré was probably the cause of his absence from
the Convention between November 5 and November 30;

[1] v. 2/105.

and it may not be fanciful to connect this period of enforced leisure with an incident which marked his return to active life. He may well have employed his time in re-reading Rousseau and Helvétius, and in thinking out his political position. At any rate, upon his first reappearance at the club, he arranged (we may safely assume) that his friend Duplay should demand the removal of the bust of Mirabeau, which had for so many months presided over their debates, and that he should make the proposal the opportunity for a speech. The moment was well chosen; for the discovery of the 'iron safe' at the Tuileries on November 20 had revealed Mirabeau's correspondence with the king; and on this same day (December 5) the Assembly had thrown a veil over the great man's bust in the Manège, and had appointed a committee to report on his conduct, with a view to the possible extrusion of his body from the Panthéon. But many must have wondered how Robespierre would treat the memory of a man whom he had once admired. He soon showed that past associations had no value for him. Mirabeau, he roundly declared, was an 'intriguer', and a 'political charlatan', unworthy of an honour which should be reserved for 'true friends of the people'. 'I see only two men here', he went on, surveying the line of busts, 'who are worthy of our homage—Brutus and J. J. Rousseau. Mirabeau ought to come down, and so ought Helvétius; for he persecuted Jean-Jacques, and would by now have been a counter-revolutionary. I also propose', he went on, 'that all these civic crowns, bestowed for the most part upon living men, should be destroyed. We have learnt only too well, by practical experience, to be less prodigal of our tributes to living men'. These suggestions were greeted with applause both in the House and in the galleries. The crowns were torn down from the walls, and burnt to ashes. Zealous iconoclasts climbed up ladders, pulled down the busts of Mirabeau and Helvétius, and vied with one another in trampling them to fragments on the floor of the House.

This public repudiation of Mirabeau was not allowed

to pass unnoticed. Prudhomme reminded his readers that it was upon Robespierre's own proposal that Mirabeau's body had been deposited in the Panthéon, and challenged him to show that he was any less dishonest than Pétion or Manuel.[1] Robespierre at once penned a long apologia. It was the Paris Directory, he alleged, which had proposed the *panthéonisation*. He disapproved of it, as he did of Mirabeau himself; but he supported it, because it was demanded by public opinion. He expressed at the time the regret that his attitude might be misunderstood. He now admits that he was to blame, but hopes that his fault, such as it was, may be expiated by his political career as a whole, and by the persecutions he has endured in the name of freedom.

This is all very well; perhaps other statesmen, in a similar difficulty, would have made no better defence. But a comparison of the two passages—and it may be assumed that Robespierre had the speech of April 3 in front of him—suggests certain reflexions. First, the original proposal for Mirabeau's *panthéonisation* came, as he says, from the Directory, and its final drafting was due to Barnave; but the support given to it by Robespierre, as the spokesman of the Left, contributed not a little to its acceptance. Secondly, it was not necessary for Robespierre to speak at all on the motion: there were many members who did not, including, no doubt, others who acquiesced in the proposal only out of consideration for public feeling: if he really 'had always thought poorly of Mirabeau', it was needlessly misleading to praise him. For, thirdly, what Robespierre on December 5 gives as the 'substance' of his remarks on April 3 may have been what he meant by them, but could not possibly have been gathered from his actual words. His audience might have thought he doubted the appropriateness of *panthéonisation*: they could not have supposed he disapproved of Mirabeau himself. It is therefore very difficult to accept as anything but an afterthought the apologia of December 5—'I feel remorse to-day for the first time in my life; for I may have let it be believed that I

[1] *Révolutions de Paris.*

shared the good opinion of Mirabeau held by the Assembly, and by the general public'. Even supposing this true, what a paltry fault it was to need expiating by the whole of Robespierre's political life and sufferings! Would it not have been more honest to say, as Marat did, what he really thought about Mirabeau; or more dignified to admit that he had been mistaken about him, and had now changed his mind?

III

Having thus, under Robespierre's guidance, disowned allegiance to their Moderate past, and renounced all claims to earthly rewards, the Jacobins turned to face the next great issue—their struggle with the Girondins over the fate of the king.

France had now been at war for the better part of a year, and was beginning to feel the strain. The luxury trades had failed, owing to the emigration of the rich nobility, and Paris was full of unemployed artisans and domestic servants. The *assignats*—the paper currency based on nationalized church property—were already depreciating, with benefit to none but land-purchasers; whilst the level of wages failed to rise with that of food prices. Partly because the farmers would not sell it for *assignats*, and partly because it was diverted for the use of the army, flour was expensive, and the poor began to go short of bread. Soon there were demands, backed by disorderly demonstrations, for the punishment of speculators and profiteers, and for the regulation of food-prices. During the harvest season local authorities took matters into their own hands, requisitioning supplies from the markets, and commandeering labour to get in the crops. As autumn passed into winter, all these conditions were aggravated, especially in the larger towns, and many riots occurred, ending in the pillaging of shops, or the forcible fixing of prices. Nor were conditions much better in the country-side, where increasing discontent was caused by the shortage of priests and the closing of churches under the Civil Constitution of the Clergy; accompanied, in many districts, by disturbing relics, or it might be, a recrudescence, of royalism.

Preoccupied by the war, by the elections, and by their attempt to crush the Paris Commune, the Girondist majority had hitherto failed to cope with this tangled situation, and would soon be quite unable to do so. It was the moment for a new party, for a strong and comprehensive policy. The Jacobin leaders were not likely to miss their opportunity; and on December 1 Robespierre delivered an elaborate *Discours sur les subsistances*, in which he declared for a policy of regulating the supply of flour by demanding returns of stocks, forcing local sales, and prohibiting speculation. His speech was well received, and he was invited to draft a decree against *le monopole*, or the wheat-corner. That Robespierre should have been so strong for regulation shows how little he was, by this time, a slave to the principle of liberty, when it conflicted with a party programme, and how nicely he could discriminate, like his master Rousseau, between the poetry and the prose of politics. It is interesting, too, to find him differing fundamentally from his young friend (and some would say, his mentor) Saint-Just. For Saint-Just, only three days before, had declared for non-intervention: leave matters alone, he had said, and the flour shortage would remedy itself by the law of supply and demand.[1] Robespierre saw further. He argued that nature had done her part, by producing an unusually good harvest, and that, if there was still want, it must be due to artificial causes. It was useless—he had always maintained this—to enforce liberty, where the motives for it were absent; and it would be folly to allow it, where its results were manifestly unjust. Speculation in food-supplies seemed to him nothing less than brigandage and fratricide. To allow it would be to put individual liberty—the right to exploit private property—above public liberty—the people's right to live. In physiological metaphor, 'food-supplies are the blood in the veins of the people, and their free circulation is as necessary for the health of the body politic as that of blood for the human

[1] Mathiez, *La vie Chère*, 107.

frame'. If the free flow is interrupted, the obstructions, at whatever cost, must be removed.

IV

Here was one side of the new policy. The other was announced two days later, in Robespierre's first speech on the question of the king's trial. This was a matter which the Girondins had obviously mismanaged. Two months before (October 10) Robespierre's own Section had published a manifesto protesting against a Girondist suggestion that they had designs on the Temple, but saying that they and other Sections were waiting anxiously for the king's trial. Instead of meeting these demands, the government had obstructed all attempts to satisfy them. Valazé's Report of November 6, and Buzot's speech on November 13, had merely postponed the issue. But the discovery of the 'iron safe' (November 20), with its compromising correspondence, made further delay impossible. On the 21st an impartial committee was appointed to report on the papers. On December 2, delegates from the Sections called for immediate action. On the 3rd Barbaroux, for the Girondins, proposed that Louis should stand his trial.

This was Robespierre's opportunity. He opened his speech (December 3) with a declaration which went straight to the realities of the question. 'This is no question of a trial', he said; 'Louis is not a defendant; you are not judges. You are not, and cannot be, anything but statesmen, and the people's representatives. You have not to give a verdict for or against an individual, but to adopt a measure of public safety, to safeguard the future of the nation' (*un acte de providence national à exercer*). A dethroned king is a lasting menace to a republican government: if anything can make him more dangerous, it is to waste time discussing your competence, or his fate. Louis cannot be tried, for he has already been tried and convicted by the institution of the Republic: even his crimes are, from this point of view, irrelevant. There is no constitution, no law, no pact to which he can appeal. An insurrection such as that of August 10 leaves nothing standing but the law of nature, and the safety of the people. 'The king's trial is involved in the insurrection; the overthrow of his power is a verdict against him; his sentence is such as is required for the liberty of his people'. There follows a passage which might serve for the self-examination of any Terrorist: 'If we fall back upon questions of form, it is because we have no principles: if we make a point of scruples (*délicatesse*), it is because we lack energy: we make a show of humanity only because we are not really humane: we reverence the shadow of a king only because we have not learnt to respect the people: and if we have a soft spot for our oppressors, it is only because we have no pity for the oppressed'. It was particularly dangerous, he thought, to talk of leniency towards Louis at a moment when royalism was reviving in the country; and quite futile to appeal to constitutional safeguards, now that the Constitution itself had been abolished. No: the Convention must face facts, and do something to justify its high calling. 'We talk of a republic, and Louis is still alive! We talk of a republic, and the person of the king still stands between us and liberty! There is fear that our very scruples may lead us into crime; that, if we show too much kindness to the criminal, we may put ourselves in the dock'.

This is strong enough; nor is it weakened by the personal reflexions which follow. 'For my own part', resumes Robespierre, 'I detest the death penalty that your law prescribes so freely: in the assembly that you still call "Constituent" I moved for its abolition; and it was not my fault if that assembly regarded the first principles of reason as moral and political heresies. But now you propose to set aside the death penalty in the case of the one man whose death could justify it. I agree, the death penalty is, in general, a crime; and that, for the very reason that it can only be justified where it is necessary for the safety of individuals, or of the body politic. But where you have a dethroned king at the heart of a revolution which is entirely held together by just laws—a king whose very name brings the scourge of civil war upon a distracted nation; in such an event neither imprisonment nor exile can prevent his presence affecting the public welfare; and if justice, in his case, admits this cruel exception to the ordinary law, it is simply the punishment of his crimes. Such is the fatal conclusion which, however much I regret it, I cannot avoid. Because the country must live, Louis must die'. And he ends by proposing that, whilst the Queen and her accomplices are brought to trial, and the Dauphin is imprisoned in the Temple till the end of the war, Louis shall at once be declared 'a traitor towards the French nation, and a public criminal'; that he shall be executed on the spot where the 'generous martyrs of liberty' fell on August 10; and that the event shall be commemorated by a monument 'which will keep alive in the heart of every people consciousness of its rights, and detestation of tyrants, and in the heart of tyrants a salutary fear of the justice of the people'.

If Robespierre had never spoken again, this speech would prove him a great orator, for its clarity, its energy, its stark common sense. Here, at any rate, he sees his way clearly, has settled with his conscience, and feels a party behind him. The historian cannot ignore the long debates that followed; but they added nothing to this first plain statement of the case; and the ultimate decision was almost exactly that to which Robespierre pointed from the first.

The Girondins were quick to see the danger. Repeated attempts were made, on the following days, to prevent Robespierre from speaking again. When he could obtain a hearing, it was to reiterate that 'as a matter of principle, and as a corollary of August 10, the king should be condemned out of hand'. His last word was the same as his first.[1]

V

The party struggle continued throughout December, both in the Assembly, and, with added virulence, at the club. On the 7th, at the Jacobins, Robespierre delivered an

[1] v. the *Moniteur's* account of the debates of December 3-4.

attack on the Girondist majority in the Convention.
It had done nothing, he said, for the people, whilst it
was stirring up the provinces against Paris, and putting
obstacles in the way of the king's trial. What was the
remedy? Not, at the moment, violence; for, 'though insurrection is the most sacred of all duties', there must be no
repetition of August 10, or even of July 17. But the public
must be enlightened, and deputies must not allow themselves to be silenced. 'So let us all take an oath', he concludes, 'to die in the tribune, rather than to yield our place,
when they would refuse us a hearing.' This melodramatic
proposal was greeted with applause, and a dozen deputies
declared that the next time Robespierre was refused a hearing, they would perish at his side. But the practical Legendre
suggested that the best way to further their ends was for
members to be at the Assembly earlier in the morning; 'for
it is noticeable that the deputies of the Right are already
in their places, ready for any intrigue, at a time when the
patriots' seats are still empty'.

It is remarkable that, at a moment when party passion
was running so high, Robespierre should have intervened
against one Achille Viard, who had accused Roland of
treacherous correspondence with *émigrés* in England
(December 7). Was his refusal to back such a damaging
charge due to generosity, or to caution? Or are we to infer
from the fact that, as Viard was taken off to prison, 'he
smiled, and saluted Robespierre', that the scene had been
prearranged?

At any rate there was no slackening of the offensive
against Roland's party during the days that followed; and
on the 12th we find Robespierre, at the Jacobins, denouncing Roland himself as the ringleader of an attempt to
destroy the club, and its affiliated societies. It was at the
same meeting that, 'remembering (as he said) how he had
learnt at College that there were two ways of educating the
mind—first by reading good books, and secondly by reading
bad ones', Robespierre suggested that the club should open
its daily meetings with readings from the two worst papers

in Paris—the Girondist *Patriote français* and *Chronique de Paris*. Condorcet's reports of the debates in the Assembly, were likely, he thought, to prove specially entertaining. The proposal was adopted.

Next day, in the Assembly, an incident occurred which revived the quarrel between the Convention and the Commune, and illustrated the temper in which the king's trial was likely to be conducted. A deputation from the General Council requested the Assembly to order that when Louis' counsel, de Sèze, went to visit him in the Temple, he should be rigorously searched (*jusques dans les endroits les plus secrets*), for fear that he might become a channel of treacherous correspondence. This ungenerous proposal was much resented by the House, but was defended by Robespierre, on the ground that there were plots afoot to save the king, and that they must not put difficulties in the way of the Commune in dealing with 'this criminal, whom you owe it to the nation to bring to justice as promptly as possible'. At this there were cheers from the gallery, which the President rebuked as 'the vociferations of cannibals'; and the question was allowed to drop. On the 14th it was alleged that Roland had circulated a mutilated and misleading version of Robespierre's speech on the king's trial. On the 16th indignation was caused by the receipt of an address from a provincial club asking for the expulsion of Marat and Robespierre, and by a Girondist attempt to divert attention from the king by proposing the exile of citizen Égalité, as the Duc d'Orléans had recently styled himself. A general expatriation of the royal family was, indeed, a measure which Robespierre himself had in mind: they could live in England, he thought, at the expense of the nation. But the expulsion of Orléans, the least suspect of them all, might lead to that of real patriots. Had he not himself been threatened with ostracism? Three days later he designated all such proposals as a Girondist plot. When he went on to complain of attacks against himself, Mazuyer threatened to denounce him. 'I have the proofs,' he said, 'here in my hand'.

One upshot of these charges and counter-charges was a curious debate at the club (December 23) on the relative merits of Marat and Robespierre. 'Robespierre', said Robert, 'is prudent and moderate in his methods; Marat is exaggerated, and has none of Robespierre's prudence. Patriotism is not enough (*Il ne suffit pas d'être patriote*). To be of real service to the people, one must be cautious in the means used to achieve one's ends; and in this Robespierre is obviously superior to Marat': and he suggested that an expression of this opinion should be circulated to the affiliated societies. Dufourny, on the other hand, urged that Marat was one of those men of robust mind (*têtes fortes*) specially needed in a time of Revolution. The club finally decided to send out a circular 'in which a detailed account should be given of the points of likeness and unlikeness, of agreement and disagreement', between the two men, so that good Jacobins might be able to 'separate two names which they are wrong in thinking ought always to be coupled together'.

Looking back, one can agree that the caution spoken of in this debate had really been characteristic of Robespierre's policy, even in its most violent manifestations. He would state as strongly as possible the Jacobin demand for the trial, conviction, and execution of the king. He would denounce at every turn the attempts of the Gironde to evade the issue. But he would allow no attack on the Convention—the embodied will of the people; and he would avoid any demonstration or disorder that might revive memories of the republican manifesto of July 17, or of the Insurrectional Commune of August 10. There must be no excuse for anti-democratic reprisals. In this he was very wise. The party issue was still in doubt, and some good observers confidently predicted a victory for the Gironde. 'Robespierre's party is still strong', wrote the British ambassador on December 17, 'but Roland's is strengthening with Brissot's, and Pétion within these few days has considerably altered his tone . . . Roland and Brissot's party are certainly struggling to save the king, in order to humble Robespierre's party, and I myself, from everything I can learn, have not the smallest doubt but they will succeed'.[1] In reality, time was on Robespierre's side. Every delay and evasion of the issue increased the popular demand for the trial, and transferred votes from the Girondins to the Jacobins.

VI

By the third week in December no further device could postpone the trial. The official indictment had been before the Convention since December 10. Louis had been questioned on the 11th. The sequel could be no longer delayed. On the 26th de Sèze spoke for the defence, alleging the irregularity of the proceedings, and relying on the king's answers to the charges brought against him, his personal virtues, and the benefits of the earlier part of his reign. Thereafter the whole issue was opened to discussion, and an interminable debate dragged on till January 14. There were three main issues: Was the king guilty? How should he be punished? And, should there be an appeal from the Convention to the people? The first was not seriously in doubt. The second gave rise to various proposals for imprisonment or banishment which were more creditable to the hearts of those who supported them than to their heads; for Louis alive, whether in or out of France, would remain a centre of royalist intrigue. The third was the chief refuge of those who shrank from the logical result of Louis' treachery. It found some support in the inviolability of the king's person, at the time when his alleged crimes were committed, under the Constitution of 1791—an inviolability which, perhaps, could only be revoked by an appeal to the people; and it embodied a hope that the Conservative and royalist instincts still alive in the country-side might save the king's life. The only other hope—and that a forlorn one—lay in foreign intervention.

Such were the circumstances under which Robespierre

[1] Gower, 258.

delivered his second speech on the king's trial (December 28). He began by repeating the main theme of his speech of December 3. Louis had been tried and condemned already, by the national rising of August 10: it only remained to pass the sentence due to his crimes. But this, he continued, must be done at once. Delay saved Louis after Varennes, and caused the massacre of the Champ de Mars: delay might save him now, and lead to civil war. This (he continues) is the chief argument against an appeal to the people. But there is another. Such an appeal would involve a controversy, in every constituency in the country, in which royalists as well as republicans would have their say, and would be given a fresh opportunity to divide and destroy the people. 'In this so-called appeal to the people, I see nothing but an appeal from what the people has willed and done (on August 10) to those secret enemies of equality whose corruption and cowardice were the very cause of that insurrection'. No, he concludes; the nation has already spoken, by the act of deposing the king: let the Convention, as its representative, finish its work. He ends with an appeal to the independent members whose votes, he knows, will ultimately determine the issue. The so-called majority, he says, meaning the Girondins, has claimed to silence the minority (the Jacobins). 'But the only real majority here is that of good citizens. It is not a permanent body, because it belongs to no party: it changes its composition every time it gives a free vote, because its allegiance is to eternal reason and the common weal: and when, as sometimes happens, the Assembly realizes that it has made a mistake, the minority becomes a majority. For every minority has the inalienable right of uttering the voice of truth. Virtue too (he thinks) has always been in a minority here on earth', and has always suffered at the hands of successful vice. But there will always be some who prefer the fate of Sydney or Hampden,[1] of Cato or Socrates, to the prosperity of a Critias, an Anitus, a Caesar, or a Clodius; 'and if there were only fifty such in France, the thought of them would be

[1] *Ils expirèrent sur l'échafaud*, he says, not very exactly.

enough to intimidate the cowardly intriguers who seek to mislead the majority'.

If the reader is looking for an impartial discussion of the issues raised by the king's trial, he will not find it in this speech. Robespierre's way of regarding the plebiscite is, in itself, sufficient to show how partisan is his outlook: his real reason for opposing it is that it would give the Girondins an opportunity to express their views, and to out-vote the Jacobins.[1] But his partisanship is only another phase of his constitutionalism. He may seem to be putting a parliamentary victory before a verdict of the people; but this is because the Convention embodies the will of the Sovereign People. He works for a majority vote in the House, because the only alternative is a fresh insurrection. And he is shrewd enough to know that another August 10 might go against him.

The speech was so much admired that, two days later, at the Jacobins, the ordinary business of the day was suspended, the orators who had put down their names to speak gave way, and the deputations waiting to be heard were shown the door, whilst Robespierre mounted the tribune, and, amid a silence of deep attention, read it all through again. A subscription was opened to print it, and an affiliated member offered to carry copies round the provinces, expounding it as he went. When Robespierre reproduced it in his journal, he appended the hostile criticisms of Brissot and Gorsas. He could afford to. It had demolished their case.

Nevertheless the struggle was not over. Owing to further evasions by the *Brissotins*, it was not till January 14 that a vote could be taken. Meanwhile Robespierre, in face of fresh attacks by his opponents[2], advises his supporters (January 1) to keep calm, and to avoid provocation. 'If any agitator tries to rouse the people against that automaton (*machine inerte*) at the Temple', they should arrest him, and

---

[1]'A majority of the Convention', wrote Gower on December 31, 'is clearly for sparing his (the king's) life, and should it be referred to the Departments, most of them are decidedly in his favour' (270).

[2]Dauban, *Paris en 1793*, 10, 12; B. and R. 22/298; Ward, 205.

have him tried. A week later, the strength of the Girondist influence in the provinces could be gauged by the number of addresses which reached the Jacobins from their affiliated societies, protesting against the attitude of Marat and Robespierre, and sometimes demanding their expulsion from the club. La Faye suggested an address to the Departments, answering these charges. 'You call us disorganizers',[1] he would say: 'yes, we are; for we shall always regard it as our duty to disorganize despotism. . . . As for Robespierre, he shall remain a member of the society; for he has always been a champion of principles, a friend of the people, and of mankind. Nor shall we exclude Marat. We do not approve of all he says; but it needs something more than fine phrases to destroy aristocrats'.

VII

On the day that the bulk of these addresses reached the club, the *Brissotins* made their last effort in the Assembly. It took the form of a motion to abolish the 'permanence' of the Paris Sections, and so to destroy the chief support of the Jacobin party. After Salle had led the attack, Robespierre obtained possession of the tribune; but the encouragements of his followers were drowned by *Brissotin* cries of 'Order! Censure him! Lynch him!' (*à l'Abbaye!*); and soon the hall 'echoed from end to end' (it is the official account) with 'violent remarks, sarcasms, and the noise of personal altercations'. A protest against the refusal to hear Roland, 'that honest Minister whom all France reveres', was drowned by the laughter of sixty members at one end of the room; but when Robespierre tried to resume, he was met with cries of *Le scélérat*, and *Le factieux et l'impudent calomniateur!* 'He thinks it's September 2; he wants to be a dictator!' shouted Baraillon; and Chambon, 'We're not afraid of your assassins, Robespierre!' Marat's 'unacademic phrases', beginning with *f . . .* or *g . . .*, and ending in dots, increased the uproar. The President rang his bell till it broke in his hands; then, as a last resort, put on his hat, and sent the ushers round to

---

[1] *Désorganisateurs*: one of the earliest uses of what became a popular term of abuse.

announce the suspension of the meeting. Gradually order was restored, the members resumed their seats, and removed their hats, and the President censured Robespierre, the Assembly, and the public in the galleries, indiscriminately.[1] When at last he was allowed to go on with his speech, Robespierre used the opportunity to sneer at 'the virtuous Roland', as one who 'is always praising himself and his friends as models of virtue, and depicting his enemies as rascals, brigands, disorganizers, and factionists', and to accuse him of being in the pay of the bankers of London and Berlin.

It needs the blind partisanship of a Hamel to find all the fault in this scene on one side, and to characterize Robespierre's attack on Roland as couched in 'dignified and serious terms, beneath which could be traced an involuntary resentment due to a series of gratuitous insults'. An impartial reader will contrast Robespierre's demand for calm on the part of his followers with his own display of temper in the Assembly. The only defence, for what it is worth, is that Robespierre's sensitiveness made him an easy prey for political pin-prickers; and that, if he had remained silent under such attacks, it would have been interpreted, not as strength, but as weakness. Things had reached such a pass that it might really seem as though the rise and fall of personal reputations had more effect on the course of the Revolution than the serious weighing of arguments. Yet, even on the score of reputation, there was food for reflexion in the remark of an anonymous member, at the end of this debate. 'The Departments (he said) will be interested to hear that Robespierre has insulted the Minister and the President, and has been thrice called to order'.

VIII

On January 14 the final stage of the king's trial at last began. Three divisions had to be taken: first, was Louis

[1]Gower, writing on Jan. 7, speaks of the 'shameful heights' to which the debates in the Assembly are being carried. 'It far surpasses,' he says, 'any country cock-match' (273).

guilty? secondly, should there be a plebiscite? and thirdly, how should he be punished? To these there was eventually added a fourth: should the execution of sentence be postponed? In each division every one of the 700 deputies gave his decision separately by word of mouth, and could speak as long as he liked in explanation of his vote. It was not surprising that the proceedings lasted for nearly a week.

On the 14th the king was declared guilty by an unanimous vote, except for a few abstentions. On the 15th the proposal for a plebiscite was defeated by 424 votes to 287; and Robespierre's name headed the list of twelve deputies for the Department of Paris, all of whom voted *Non,* without troubling to give their reasons. On the 16th came the crucial division, on the sentence. This time Robespierre gave reasons for his vote in a speech which occupies more than half a column in the *Moniteur.* He cannot convict Louis, he says, and then not sentence him. He cannot agree to the punishment of the king's accomplices, and not of the king himself. He must be pitiless towards oppressors, because he feels pity for the oppressed; and he gives his vote, unconditionally, for the king's execution. In the end, 361 votes were cast in this sense, and 334 for detention, imprisonment in chains, or death under certain conditions. There remained twenty-six deputies who voted for death, but who wished that the question of reprieve should be considered: as, however, they did not wish their vote to be dependent upon this reservation, these twenty-six went to increase the votes for death to 387—a total definitely larger than the 361 required to give an absolute majority of those present and voting. On the following day, but before the result of the division (which had gone on all night) was known, a letter was received from the king's counsel, asking that they might be heard again. They doubtless hoped that a last-minute appeal might secure the sentence of banishment which Louis himself expected.[1] Robespierre opposed this request. They must abide, he said, by the issue

---

[1] He intended to go to Switzerland, said de Sèze afterwards (R.H.R.F. 13/160).

of the vote, whatever it might be, and not admit any fresh considerations. Neither they nor he would have acted thus, one supposes, unless it had been still uncertain which way the voting would go.

When at last the figures were known, and the President declared that the sentence of the House was death, the king's defenders were allowed to speak, and 'admitted to the honours of the meeting'. Then Robespierre spoke again (January 17). He hoped that the attempt to secure a revision of the death sentence would not be carried beyond the House. The Assembly could not go back upon its decision without endangering the whole country. 'The nation', he said, 'has condemned the king who oppressed it, not simply to execute a notable act of vengeance, but to set a great example to the world; not only to confirm liberty in France, but also to evoke it in Europe'.

The only hope for the king now lay in a reprieve (*sursis*)—an indefinite postponement of the execution. This was proposed by the Girondist leaders on January 18, and debated until the evening of the 19th.

Robespierre, increasingly anxious that no last-minute scruples should deprive the Jacobins of their victory, intervened three times on the 18th—first, to persuade Thuriot to declare against a reprieve, and to back Tallien's demand for an immediate vote; next, to suggest that the division should be taken not later than 4 a.m. on the 19th, so that the execution could still be carried out within twenty-four hours of the sentence, as prescribed by law; and thirdly (when it was clear that this could not be done) to urge that precautions should be taken against any attempt to rescue the king on the way to the scaffold. At this moment Santerre, the Commandant of the National Guard, entered the hall, to assure the House that everything was quiet, and that nothing would prevent the execution. He had a force of 5,000 men in reserve, and cannon everywhere; but they would not be needed.

The final division was at last taken on the night of the 19th, and Robespierre again headed the great majority of the Paris deputies in voting against the reprieve; it was rejected by 380 votes to 310.

IX

It is difficult to suppose that there can ever have been much fear of a successful attempt to rescue the king, though the Jacobin club, on the evening of January 20, was full of rumours,[1] and Robespierre thought it necessary to counsel 'a calm demeanour, so dignified and formidable that it will freeze with fear the enemies of freedom'. Any sympathy with royalism that still survived was effectively quenched by the murder, on the morning of the 21st, of the Jacobin Le Pelletier de Saint-Fargeau—by mistake, it was said, for the Duc d'Orléans[2]—by one Paris, formerly a member of the king's bodyguard.

At daybreak the city gates were closed. At ten o'clock the royal carriage left the Temple, and passed slowly along the Boulevardes[3] to the Place de la Révolution, surrounded by troops of the National Guard. At 10.30, amidst the rolling of Santerre's drums, and before the eyes of a vast, indifferent crowd, the king's head fell into the basket of the guillotine. The city gates were opened again, and the life of Paris resumed its ordinary course.

Among those whose minds were fixed steadily on this end, there was one more certain and active than the rest. If Louis' death was any one man's work, it was Robespierre's. Yet his fixity of purpose was not simply his own: it was that of his party, and of Paris. To the people of Paris, Louis was, as Robespierre had said, not a man on trial, but a criminal already condemned. If he were not legally executed by the Convention, he might be lynched by the mob; and no one

[1] An eloquent appeal to the people to invade the Temple, and rescue the king, was widely distributed in Paris on the afternoon of the 20th (Brit. Mus. R. 525). Devaux's trial (June 13, 1794) revealed evidence of de Batz's plan to save the king. (Fletcher, Carlyle, 2/397.)

[2] Dauban, *Paris en 1793*, 27. Rétif (*Nuits révolutionnaires*, 128) says that much more interest was taken in his death than in that of the king.

[3] Not by the rue Saint-Honoré; so the story that Robespierre had the door of No. 366 shut whilst the King passed cannot be true.

desired another September 2. Nor was this all. Behind Robespierre was Paris: behind Paris was France. True, no group of deputies voted so solidly for the king's death as that representing the capital. True, there was in the whole House a bare majority for execution. But there is good reason to think that, just as fear made some of the 380 regicides, so it was not royalism which inspired the 330 provincials to vote against death, but rather dread of responsibility (and perhaps, some day, reprisals) for so momentous an act, and dislike of the domination of Paris. The Revolution is hardly intelligible except on the assumption that France as a whole—that is, the vast majority of those who stood by the New Order begun in 1789—had persuaded themselves that Louis was a 'tyrant', and were (at the lowest) indifferent to his death.[1] In so far as he had read the national mind, and translated it into action, Robespierre had shown himself a statesman. His policy was true to the main trend of the Revolution. His instinct was right, when he made the king's death a party issue, and acceptance of it a touchstone of patriotism. Those who passed the test also entered a blood-covenant, which pledged them, as never before, to the defence of the republic. The king's head, as Danton declared, was thrown down as a challenge to all the sovereigns of Europe. Louis' execution was not only the logical solution of a very difficult problem: it was also a gesture, like the Declaration of Rights, or the demolition of the Bastille, whose significance went far beyond any immediate results that might be expected of it.

Nevertheless it was a pity that Louis had ever been brought back from Varennes; for June 21 made January 21 inevitable. The best commentary was that of a woman who wrote offering to defend Louis: 'You do not kill a king by cutting off his head, but by letting him live when he has lost his throne'.[2]

---

[1]Indifference perhaps explains the fact that the king's head still appeared on coins struck during the early months of 1793 in Paris, Metz, Strasbourg, Lyon, and Bordeaux (R.F. 59/470).

[2]Montgaillard, *Revue chronologique*, etc., 2/301.

CHAPTER XI

The Anti-Girondin (January–June, 1793)

I

It was hoped that a national act of such seriousness as the king's execution would unite the nation, and reconcile the feuds of the politicians. But the circumstances of the trial, and the murder of Le Pelletier, narrowed and embittered the feelings with which Louis' death was regarded.[1]

In his address to the Departments, on January 23, Robespierre asserted that the king's acquittal, or even his reprieve, would have ensured the success of a counter-revolutionary plot against the patriot leaders. Within a few hours of the execution, Barère was proposing, and Robespierre supporting, measures against persons guilty of harbouring *émigrés*; and Maximilien, not content with eulogizing his dead friend Le Pelletier in rhetorical and rather fulsome language, and moving for his burial in the Panthéon, was calling for an inquiry of 'republican severity' into Roland's use of public funds. On the other hand, it is significant to find him opposing, on 'principles of eternal justice', a decree for the death penalty against anyone harbouring Le Pelletier's murderer, and expressing the hope that, now that the guillotine has done its work, and Louis is dead, the Assembly will abolish capital punishment. He had never varied in his dislike of the death penalty: but he had persuaded himself that the king's case was the Great Exception: the 'tyrant' once disposed of, the rule of humanity should be reinforced. He did not have his way. His colleagues were not more cruel, but they were

---

[1] An ex-usher of the Revolutionary Tribunal with the unlucky name of Paris (that of Le Pelletier's murderer) was imprisoned for changing his name to Fabricius. After Thermidor he petitioned for release, alleging that he had been 'victimized by Robespierre and his accomplices' (Tuetey, 8/1295).

313

less casuistical. The situation was one in which any government would have hesitated to give up so powerful a weapon. Robespierre himself was soon to realize this: but he continued, to the end, persuading himself that the policy of the guillotine was exceptional and transitory.

Le Pelletier's funeral was celebrated on January 24 with even more magnificence than that of Mirabeau,[1] whilst provocative speeches and pamphlets directed the vengeance of good patriots against the Gironde. On the other side, *Brissotin* exasperation expressed itself in fresh attacks on Robespierre, 'the viper of Arras, the descendant of Damiens'; and he was held up to ridicule as an object of female devotion.[2] Even those who admitted his incorruptibility might suspect that it hid a greed for power.

II

Provoked at home, and distracted abroad, the Girondist government fell into increasing confusion. The invasion of Belgium had added England to the number of its enemies, and a coastal blockade to the causes already making for economic distress. The only methods employed by a *laissez-faire* policy to meet the financial crisis were the multiplication of *assignats*, whose value was already showing a rapid decline,[3] and the levying of contributions by victorious generals in the Rhine valley and the Netherlands, which brought in far too little cash at far too great a cost in diminished prestige, and political discontent. Wage-rates were still falling behind food-prices. The provisioning of the country, left to the law of supply and demand, was breaking down. Vast numbers of unemployed were on the edge of starvation. In these circumstances the fall of Roland on January 22 was taken as a sign that the Girondist

---

[1] v. Dauban, *Paris en 1793*, 40.
[2] Suivi de ses dévotes,
   De sa cour entouré,
   Le Dieu des sansculottes,
   Robespierre est entré. . . . etc. (Hamel, 2/373).
[3] The forging of *assignats* was debated at the Jacobins on Jan. 30 and March 1.

policy of non-intervention had failed. The field was open to any party with a constructive social and economic programme. Could the Jacobins provide this?

On February 25 there were debates on the food question both in the Convention and at the club. The Assembly, on a report from Tallien, had proposed to send troops to deal with food-riots at Lyon. Robespierre insisted that these disorders were part of a much larger discontent, whose cause was counter-revolution, working hand in hand with a coalition of foreign powers. The remedies he would employ were stronger measures against the *émigrés* and the provincial Directories. Speaking at the Jacobins the same evening, he excused the disorders that had taken place as due to the natural resentment of the poor against the rich. 'The people', he said, 'are suffering: they have not yet reaped the reward of all their labour. They are still persecuted by the rich; and the rich are still what they have always been—hard and pitiless'. We get Robespierre's view again at second-hand in a letter from Augustin to Buissart, dated February 21. 'It is a critical moment', he writes; 'The *sansculottes* at Lion (sic) are getting the worst of it, and the news is that counter-revolution is making headway there. They are trying the same game in Paris. Commodities are being hoarded, and prices are jumping up. They push intrigue to the point of carrying off bread from the bakers' shops, so that the people can't procure any. The object of this manœuvre is to turn public indignation against the Jacobins, and to start fresh calumnies against Paris. We began a counter-attack against this plot at yesterday's meeting of the Jacobins, and we have warned all the Sections to be on the look-out'.[1]

If it must be said that the Girondins failed to deal with the food question, it would be unfair not to add that there is nothing in these expressions of Robespierre's views to suggest that the Jacobins had any better policy. He seems to be obsessed with the idea of a political conspiracy; as though it were either practicable for counter-revolutionists,

[1]Corresp. 156.

315

or worth the while of foreign powers, to engineer a food-shortage, or to incite food-riots. The trouble was, in point of fact, almost wholly an economic one, and called for economic remedies. Indeed, Robespierre himself was conscious of failure, and anxious about the position of his party. Writing to Buissart again on March 6, Augustin, who was doubtless in his confidence, reports that the patriots are being reproached for their inaction. 'You have cut off the tyrant's head', they are told, 'and you could, if you liked, give the people what they want'. 'These specious complaints', he continues, 'are cooling popular confidence in the deputies of the Mountain. We are in a permanent minority. The alliances which gave us a majority for the death of the tyrant do not re-occur on all questions, and cannot be reconstructed. So-called patriots play the extremist (*font les enragés*) in certain societies, push our principles to absurdity, and discredit us by a system of disorganization, pure and simple. Things have gone so far that the Mountain is thought moderate, whilst the Right co-operates with this monstrous attempt, in order to break up and overturn everything, and so restore despotism, or something of the kind. The leader of the conspirators (Gensonné) has just been nominated President: I am afraid there will be serious trouble during the next fortnight'.[1] In the same strain, a Jacobin address to the affiliated societies drawn up by Robespierre on March 1 describes the habitual calm of the Parisians as upset by intriguers, who have taken advantage of the food-shortage to work up indignation against the Jacobins, and even to suggest that the people's troubles are due to the execution of the king.

It was no doubt absurd to suppose that the *émigrés* had anything to do with the food troubles. But they were a constant source of suspicion; and soon fresh legislation was proposed against them. Robespierre's intransigence was seldom better shown than in his opposition, under this head, to the proposal that boy and girl *émigrés*, up to the ages of

[1]Corresp. 157.

eighteen and twenty-one, should be given a further opportunity to return to France, and thus to escape proscription.

III

This stiffness was doubtless due to the situation at the front, where the French arms were entering upon a second period of defeat, destined to bring disaster to the Girondist government. For two months after Valmy almost everything had gone well with the armies of the Republic. By the end of September, 1792, Anselme had overrun Nice, and Montesquiou Savoy. By the third week in October Custine had occupied Mayence, and crossed the Rhine. The victory at Jemmappes on November 6 opened the whole of Belgium to Dumouriez's advance. But there success halted: the difficulties that Robespierre had foreseen in connexion with an occupation of Belgium, and others arising out of the annexationist policy of the Republic, made Doumuriez's position increasingly dangerous: and when, at the end of February, he attempted to invade Holland, he was forced into a retreat which ended with the defeat of Neerwinden (March 18), and the evacuation of the whole of the Netherlands.

Robespierre did not intervene at first in the debates which turned on these affairs: he was more interested in the home front, and in political warfare. But on February 6, at the Jacobins, he took up the case of some Dutch patriots, who had brought an address to the Foreign Office, reminding his hearers, by a neat historical allusion, that 'such publicity would forward the cause both of the *gueux* ('Beggars') and of the *sansculottes*.'[1]

A month later the disasters in Belgium suddenly brought the war into the centre of political controversy, and made *l'affaire Dumouriez* a trial of strength between Jacobins and Girondins, in which Robespierre could not fail to play a part. On March 8 Danton and Delacroix, returning post-haste from a political mission in Belgium, described in

[1] *Gueux:* a nickname adopted by some bodies of Netherlanders in the revolt against Spain, *c.* 1570.

alarmist terms the defeat of March 1, and urged that emergency measures should be taken. Robespierre spoke hopefully, reminding the House that things had looked worse in August, 1792, and yet Valmy followed, and Jemmappes. But the same evening, with Billaud-Varenne, he visited the Bonne-Nouvelle Section, spoke of the danger of the country, and exhorted the members to arm themselves, and to fly to the help of the Republic, and of their brethren in Belgium. On their side, the two deputies undertook to deal with enemies at home, to guard the interests of those who went to the front, to provide for the support of their relations, and to see that, whilst they were away, there was no tampering with the rights of the people. This was represented by Brissot in the *Patriote* of March 9 as an incitement to anarchy; and it was true that the meeting had ended in uproar. But, if Robespierre had given way to a temporary excitement, his indiscretion ended where it began, and he took no part in the public disorders which, between the 8th and the 10th, gave the 'days of March' the semblance of a new revolution. His own aim seems to have been to secure, by constitutional means, the reconstitution of the Committees, the arrest of certain of the Ministers, and the organization of a revolutionary tribunal. He was not unduly alarmed, as he told the Convention in an important speech on March 10, by the temporary set-back at the front—a set-back due, not to any fault of the army, but to the incompetence of the higher command. Most people seemed to think that, with a big enough army, victories were bound to follow. For his own part, he thought that much more was wanted, and particularly a centralized control of all the activities of the revolutionary state (*un régulateur fidelle et uniforme de tous les mouvements de la Révolution*)—a phrase which suggests (though the immediate context is military) that he is already thinking either of a dictator, or of a dictatorial committee. He does not distrust Dumouriez—an interesting admission in view of the sequel—and he believes (rather oddly) that a successful invasion of Holland would have been followed by a revolution in England.[1] The chief source of trouble is on the home front: 'as long as traitors go unpunished, the nation will always be betrayed'. The remedy for this state of things is to change the system of government, and to entrust the execution of the laws to a commission of proved patriots, from whose purview traitors cannot escape. (Here is the Committee of Public Safety, and the Revolutionary Tribunal.) We need a coalition government, he says, in which all parties are represented. (This was a revolutionary suggestion, unfortunately rendered impossible at the moment by party rivalry.[2]) 'We must break down the barrier between the Convention and the Executive Council, because it obstructs that unity of action which is the secret of strong government'—here, at last, is the reform which might have saved the monarchy, and the Constitution of 1791; and Robespierre, throwing over Montesquieu and the 'separation of powers', frankly admits that in this respect English practice is better than French theory. Finally there should be a propaganda department to work upon foreign opinion, and to divide the Allies—an anticipation of one of the commonest, if least edifying, expedients of modern warfare.

This remarkable speech, so full of fertile suggestions, and so prophetic of the coming Jacobin regime, was not to the taste of Robespierre's audience. The Jacobins, perhaps, thought it went too far. The Girondins could see nothing in it but a bid for personal dictatorship.[3] Its best passages are scarcely mentioned by Robespierre's most enthusiastic biographer. Yet who would not sacrifice all his personal invective, and most of his rhetorical invocations of liberty and truth, for a few more pages of reasoned and constructive statesmanship?

[1] 'Let Holland be won for liberty', said Danton at the same debate, 'and the commercial aristocracy which at present dominates the English people will rise against the government that dragged it into this war of despotism against a free people: it will overthrow a Ministry so stupid as to suppose that the old order could stifle the genius of liberty which presides over France', etc. (B. and R. 25/48).

[2] This was shown by the failure of the coalitionist Committee of Public Safety set up on March 25.

[3] *Robespierre vous a proposé un chef, un régulateur*, wrote Rebecqui, *et Robespierre n'a pas porté sa tête sur l'échafaud.*

When, next day, Danton tried to carry out one of Robespierre's suggestions, by rescinding the law which, ever since November, 1789, had made it impossible for a deputy to become a Minister, the House refused even to discuss the question. If their objection had rested merely on anti-monarchical prejudice, it would hardly have survived the death of the king: in fact, it sprang rather from democratic jealousy; the deputies disliked the idea of some of their number wielding powers and enjoying emoluments not shared by the rest. The notion of a Revolutionary Tribunal was more to their liking, and its establishment was taken in hand the same day. Those who remembered Robespierre's opposition to the death penalty, expressed so lately as January 21, and his constant championship of liberty of the press, were surprised to find him not only accepting capital punishment, but also insisting that it should apply to all crimes of counter-revolution, that is, to 'every attempt made against the security of the state, or the liberty, equality, unity, and indivisibility of the Republic', especially in the form of army risings, and of subversive literature. This was Robespierre's reaction to the national emergency. Such is the education of a statesman.

Looking back on these 'days of March', we may well wonder whether any definite plan for a change of government was afoot. Were the Jacobin leaders trying to exploit popular excitement, overthrow the Girondins, and set up a dictatorship? Was it an abortive *coup d'état?* The evidence on the whole seems to be against this hypothesis. Robespierre's first reaction to the bad news from the front is not that of a man who hopes to exploit the situation: he minimises the danger, and goes out of his way to express confidence in a Girondist general. Dumouriez, it may be said, was already plotting against the government: Danton may have been in his confidence,[1] and Robespierre had embraced him at the club: but that is slender evidence for a treasonable understanding. Robespierre's connivance in

[1]Robespierre denied this at the Jacobins on April 1. The case against him is given by Mathiez (303).

the disorders of March 8–10 is quite unproved. His speech of the 10th reads very like an essay in Political Science, and very unlike the programme of an insurrection. The Revolutionary Tribunal, the only part of his proposals to be put into practice, was an agreed concession to public opinion. Robespierre's renewed attack on the Gironde (March 13) was discounted by Marat's sneer at 'the alarms of a deputy, whose fears drive him into a frenzy of patriotism', and the failure of Maure's attempt to bring about a 'friendly exchange of views' between Robespierre and Brissot (March 17) came too late to be regarded as part of a definite movement to displace the Girondist Ministers. Robespierre's refusal to accept the advice of his Marseille friends, who counselled a policy of violence (March 22), was not a sudden decision, but part of a pose that he had been holding all through the crisis. If there was ever a plan for an insurrection, it had, by that time, failed. But the most reasonable conclusion is that, as far the leaders were concerned, there had been no plan at all.

IV

Meanwhile *l'affaire Dumouriez* had gone from bad to worse. On March 10 Dumouriez hurried back from the Dutch front, leaving his army behind him. On the 11th he issued a series of proclamations, reversing, on his own authority, the Government's policy in Belgium; and this action was followed, on the 12th, by a defiant letter to the Convention. On the 18th he was heavily defeated at Neerwinden. On the 23rd he opened negotiations with Cobourg, the Austrian commander; and on the 26th with Dubuisson, Pereira, and Proli (unofficial Jacobin agents who had been implicated in the disorders of March 8–10), about a plan to march on Paris, to dismiss the Convention, and to restore the crown.[1]

Meanwhile the Convention had once more despatched

[1] A year before, Dumouriez had warned Biron against a similar scheme, which he attributed to the Feuillant party (A.H. 1/558).

Danton and Delacroix to report on the situation at the front; and on the 26th, after an unaccountable delay on his return journey, the former appeared in the Assembly, and gave an account which seemed suspiciously moderate to those who had received, only the day before, a despatch from Dumouriez which the Committee of General Defence judged unfit for publication. So great did the alarm become, that the government—following Robespierre's lead of March 11—had resort to terrorist legislation. Emigration was made a capital crime; outlawry was decreed against anyone taking part in a counter-revolutionary rising, or wearing a royalist cockade; Vigilance Committees were set up in every Commune, with powers to disarm all suspected persons; *émigrés* were banished in perpetuity, and deprived of their property and civil rights; and any offence against the emigration laws was made punishable with death. In order to deal with a state of emergency, and to carry out these measures, the Committee of General Defence set up on March 4 was replaced on March 25 by a committee of twenty-five members of both parties, bearing for the first time the famous title of Public Safety (*Commission de Salut Public*),[1] and empowered, with the assistance of the Ministers, to propose all necessary steps for the defence of the Republic, at home or abroad. Thus another item of Robespierre's scheme for an emergency government, outlined a fortnight before, came into being. But a body of such size, which included Danton, Desmoulins, and Robespierre on one side, and Pétion, Vergniaud, and Guadet on the other,[2] could not last long; and it was replaced on April 6 by its more famous successor, the Committee of Public Safety. Its minutes show that, whilst less than half the members usually attended, Robespierre only missed two meetings during the twelve days of its existence.

Such was the background of Robespierre's speeches on national defence (March 27). The country was in the

---

[1] The choice of this name was probably due to the unauthorized formation, three days before, by certain of the Sections, of an *Assemblée centrale de salut public*. (B. and R. 25/240.)

[2] All twenty-five names are in the *Moniteur* for March 27.

same position, he told the Assembly, as the Athenians were, when Philip of Macedon was on the march against them; 'But our Philip is in London, he is at Berlin, at Vienna, nay, in Paris itself.' Ignorance of what is going on at the front, and condonation of treachery at home, have brought France into a position of defeat and danger. All this Robespierre repeats at wearisome length: he has become an expert at probing the public wound. But, for a remedy, all that he can suggest is an appeal to the people, the banishment of the Bourbons, and the trial of the queen—soporifics, rather than restoratives, designed less to deal with a public emergency than to win for the Jacobins the support of the common people.

He added nothing essential to this programme when he exhorted the club, the same evening, 'to give their whole attention to the all-important business of purging Paris of intriguers'. His preoccupation with the home front even led him to resist, on the 29th, a proposal for a mass levy of troops, and to declare that 'the source of all our trouble lies in our public officials, who are either aristocrats, Feuillants, or Moderates, and who, through wickedness or cowardice, fail to do their duty'.

This same day, four commissioners were sent to deprive Dumouriez of his command, and to put him under arrest. Instead, he seized them, and handed them over to the Austrians. Meanwhile, on the evening of the 31st, the Committee had heard from Dubuisson and his colleagues an account of their interview with Dumouriez, which gave clear evidence of his treachery, and implicated various members of the Gironde. They sat all night considering the matter; when they broke up on the morning of April 1, it was known that half a dozen warrants for arrest had been signed, and that orders had been given for the sealing of Roland's papers. In the Assembly, the same day, Robespierre, Danton, and Marat seized the opportunity for a ruthless attack on the Gironde. In the evening, at the Jacobins, Maximilien was even more outspoken. 'This morning', he said, 'Dumouriez's crimes were unmasked. A letter was read to us in which he openly declared war on the Revolution.[1] Dumouriez is a traitor. And he has accomplices here in Paris'—in the administration, in the law courts, in the post office, and elsewhere. The only remedy is 'a complete reconstruction of the government'—in other words, the substitution of a Jacobin for a Girondist regime. He follows this up (April 3) with a demand for 'a revolutionary army of all the patriots, of all the sansculottes', especially those of the *faubourgs*,[2] to disarm the suspects, and for a decree of accusation against Brissot, his colleague on a committee which he describes as composed of disguised royalists, aristocrats, and enemies of freedom.

Robespierre knew that he would not be allowed to forget the support he had himself given to Dumouriez only a fortnight ago; and he was ready with an explanation of this change of front. On March 10 (he said) he expressed trust in Dumouriez on two grounds—first, because 'three months ago he planned an invasion of Holland', and secondly, 'because his personal interests and reputation were staked on the success of the campaign'. Now he says, first, that 'if Dumouriez had started three months earlier, the expedition would have succeeded'; and secondly, that 'he believed for a moment that regard for his reputation would keep Dumouriez for a while within the bounds of duty, and that he would not make any attack on the liberty of his country till he had defeated the despots conspiring against it; and then (he thought), with his schemes all exposed, it would be easy to overturn him'. A rhetorical *volte-face* could hardly be better done. Robespierre does not deny anything he said before. He takes the same themes—the 'three months', and the 'personal reputation'—and re-orchestrates them, so that they sound quite different. As once before, in the repudiation of Mirabeau,[3] it is just possible to accept the second version as an interpretation of the first; but no one

---

[1] His letter to Beurnonville, read in the Assembly on April 2, but already known to the Committee.
[2] The partly unbuilt area between the old walls and the new customs barrier of Paris, inhabited by some of the poorest classes.
[3] v. I/294–6.

listening to the first could possibly have taken it in that sense. One admires the orator's ingenuity, but one would like the man better if he had honestly admitted a change of mind.

Once past this *mauvais pas*, Robespierre's course is easy. He accuses Dumouriez of blaming his defeat upon his troops, instead of upon his aristocratic friends, and his incompetent generals; he accuses him of feathering his nest in Belgium, and of declaring war on Paris and the Convention. But, in every charge, he is striking less at Dumouriez himself, than at his supposed accomplices, the Gironde, and especially Brissot. Brissot, in his reply, had no difficulty in showing that, whatever his responsibility for the war, at least he had nopart in a general's treachery which had proved so embarrassing to his own party; and the Assembly ended by applauding Vergniaud's comment that anyone who wasted the time of the House on such frivolous accusations should himself be considered an accomplice of Dumouriez. It is difficult not to agree.

But Robespierre would not be denied. The complete exclusion of Girondist deputies from the reconstituted Committee of Public Safety (April 5) showed that Parliamentary opinion was moving towards the Jacobin side. Answers might soon be expected to an appeal sent out to the affiliated societies to agitate for the dismissal of the Girondist deputies. The decisive moment could not be far off. Robespierre therefore spoke again (April 5) on his favourite theme of conspiracy; but in wider terms than before, suggesting that the Paris intrigues were part of an international plot.

He begins by saying that for some time past he has been studying this aspect of the question. 'Instead of generalizing about liberty, I have sadly searched for the principles which compromise it (*Tell us about it*). If you wish, I will raise part of the veil (*Raise it all*). A powerful party is plotting with the tyrants of Europe to impose a king upon us, together with an aristocratic constitution, and a sham system of representation, with two chambers'. It hopes to do this by war from without, and by factions from within. Its soul is Pitt; its body is the *bourgeoisie*, who fear for their property, and the *noblesse*, who hope to recover their privileges. Like other counter-revolutionists, these plotters know that they must flatter and pretend to champion the people, so long as they have need of their support, only to throw them over when their objects are attained.[1]

Hamel's comment on this speech is that all the facts contained in it are true, but most of the inferences false: the Girondists *had* acted as Robespierre said, but not with the intentions he supposed. In other words, there certainly were two parties in the state bent on destroying one another; but the alleged conspiracy, whether Parisian or European, whether Pitt's or Brissot's, was a controversial make-belief, a figment of Robespierre's imagination. This is a serious admission. It is not much lightened by shifting the blame onto the provocative tactics of Robespierre's opponents. It would be fairer to blame an almost intolerable situation—defeat in the north, civil war in the west, economic distress, an incompetent government, and a public life corrupted by spite, peculation, and moral cowardice. There were, in all this, so many alarming effects, and so few discernible causes, that the notion of secret agencies at work was likely to seize upon the least suspicious minds. Even the royalist Comte de Paroy thought the 'forty thousand foreigners living in furnished lodgings' in Paris were a source of danger to the state.[2]   But this does not exempt Robespierre from a special responsibility, if he deliberately exploited suspicions that he could not substantiate, in order to win a political contest. Was he sincere? His introspective habit of mind, and his experience of persecution, had predisposed him to a suspicious temper, to which the idea of conspiracy easily became an obsession. But there is little evidence that he tried to fight a mental drug-habit which was apparent enough to his friends, and can hardly have been unknown to himself. Perhaps, like other addicts, he

[1]For another expression of Robespierre's view of the 'conspiracy', v. Augustin's letter to Brissot, dated April 10 (Corresp. 162).
[2]*Mem.* 81.

could not do without the temporary feeling of freedom and power that comes with indulgence, though it is followed by lassitude and despair. Perhaps he felt the need to stimulate himself with ever-increasing doses. At any rate his bitter and suspicious temper isolated him more and more, so that when the occasion came for generosity to an opponent, or co-operation with one who differed from him, he found himself incapable of it.

V

The Girondins were shaken by these attacks, but they were not yet destroyed. Though they had lost control of the Ministry, in which Clavière and Lebrun remained their only certain adherents, and were unrepresented on the new Committee, they still commanded a majority in the Convention,[1] which went on electing Presidents representing their party, up to the end of May. The party struggle accordingly dragged on, attaching itself to almost every subject that came up for discussion, until, at the end of another six weeks, the Paris Sections once more intervened, and finally decided the issue.

The incidents of this period may be trivialities: but it is of such things that most statesmen's lives are composed; and it is seldom that one dramatic defeat brings about the fall of a government, unless its position has been undermined, long beforehand, by a series of small failures. Thus at one time Robespierre is criticizing an address to the Convention, and moving to include in it a demand for the immediate trial of Orléans, Sillery, and other traitors (April 10); at another he is complaining that the law abolishing the imprisonment of debtors has not yet been enforced (April 12 and 24); or figuring in an altercation with Pétion (April 12), which ends in counter-accusations of treachery and intended assassination. It was under the stress of the last scene that, according to one account, the generally

---

[1] Partly by sending as many Jacobin deputies as possible into the provinces, to superintend recruiting (Mathiez, 315).

heartless David rushed into the middle of the hall, unbared his breast, and cried, 'Strike here! I propose my own assassination! I too am a man of virtue! Liberty will win in the end!'

Less trivial things followed. On the 13th Robespierre opposed the reading of a proclamation by Cobourg, the Austrian general, for fear that it might corrupt patriotic minds, and moved that the death penalty should be decreed against anyone proposing negotiations with a foreign power. Danton, with more sense of international realities, followed with a motion to the effect that France would not intervene in the affairs of other countries; and this was passed, with a proviso, suggested by Robespierre, that it should not apply to 're-united' territories such as Avignon and Savoy; whilst two further resolutions were added, one affirming that the Republic would allow no interference in its own affairs, and the other (a modification of Robespierre's proposal) affirming the death penalty against any attempt to negotiate with a foreign power that did not recognize the independence, sovereignty, indivisibility, and unity of the Republic.

The debate could not continue long on this high level. Only the day before, the Girondins, in spite of a protest by Danton, had issued a warrant for the arrest of Marat; and this was now followed up by a report from the Legislation Committee, proposing Marat's indictment on charges of 'pillage, murder, and attempting to dissolve the Convention'. Robespierre, as the spokesman of the Jacobins, at once intervened. How far would he go, everybody must have wondered, in the defence of the least defensible of his party? Would he fall into a trap so obviously set to catch his own reputation? His enemies were soon disappointed; for he contrived to say as little as possible about Marat, and as much as possible about the general issue underlying the attack. 'I am quite able', he began, 'to appreciate Marat's worth; and I say that, whilst he has been guilty of some errors of fact, and some faults of style, his opponents are conspirators and traitors'. He went on to say that the indictment was obviously aimed, through Marat, at his

party, and at himself ('though I have made it my constant
endeavour not to aggravate or offend anyone'), and to
describe Marat, once more, as 'a man whose mistakes
(caricatured in this indictment as crimes) I have never
shared, and whom I regard as a good citizen, a zealous
champion of the popular cause, and wholly innocent of the
charges brought against him'. This was, on the whole,
generous as well as discreet; but the Girondins were, for
the moment, in a majority, and Marat's indictment was
decreed. When Robespierre's turn came to vote, he spoke
again at some length, contrasting the readiness of the
Assembly to impeach Marat with its failure to indict
Lafayette, Dumouriez, and other royalists.[1] It is said, on the
other hand, that, on second thoughts, he refused to sign a
Jacobin address got up on Marat's behalf by Desmoulins
and Dubois-Crancé. He knew the danger of committing
himself to paper.[2]

The Girondin success soon turned to failure. Demonstrations in Marat's favour were organized by the Commune,
and by the Jacobin Sections. A crowd of admirers followed
him to the court. The judges and jury—Jacobins to a man—
reduced the trial to a matter of form; and on April 24 he
was triumphantly acquitted. Meanwhile the Jacobins had
retaliated by attacking Beurnonville, the Girondist Minister
of War (April 13, 16), and by defeating an attempt to
use correspondence seized in the post as material for an
anti-Jacobin prosecution (April 18).

Two letters from Robespierre's post-bag show how his
followers regarded the situation in Paris at this moment.
'The treachery of Dumouriez and his friends', writes
Aigoin, 'will help the Republic more than the most resounding victories. Every day's news from Paris is as good as a
hundred pairs of spectacles for our good friends, who have
hitherto been blinded by the manœuvres of Roland, Louvet,
Brissot, Gorsas and Co.'[3] 'Paris', says Augustin, 'still
remains calm and proud, in spite of the means employed to

[1]For this speech, which did not appear in the minutes of the Convention, or in the
press, v. R.F. 32/537.
[2]Walter, *Marat*, 364.   [3]Corresp. 164.

agitate it, and thus to give the Convention a pretext for quitting this great scene of enlightenment, this burning hearth of patriotism'. The divisions in the Assembly, he maintains, are not due to personal quarrels: it is a contest of principles. 'The denunciations levelled by the Girondist intriguers against the Jacobins and the Paris Commune, along with the indictment of Marat, ought to open the eyes of the provinces, and prove that the Jacobins and the people are on one side, and on the other Dumouriez, the Girondins, and the royalists'.[1] Writing to the Popular Society at Arras the same day, he is confident that the Jacobins can turn the tables on their adversaries. 'The Jacobin society is by its very nature incorruptible. It deliberates before an audience of 4,000 persons, so that its whole power lies in public opinion, and it cannot betray the interests of the people'.[2] A party which could honestly see itself in this stained glass attitude was already assured of victory.

VI

On April 24, at the Jacobins, Robespierre pronounced an eulogy on his friend Lazowski, a rich Pole, who had thrown himself into the popular cause, and even commanded part of the artillery on August 10. At the end of his harangue, the audience, which was so crowded that one of the galleries collapsed under its weight, 'waved their hats in the air, and swore to avenge his death'. Lazowski had recently been attacked by Vergniaud in connexion with the March 'insurrection': accordingly everything was done to turn his funeral into a demonstration against the Gironde. The function, dressed by David, and set to music by Gossec, rivalled in elaboration that of Le Pelletier.[3]

Two days later a practical step was taken towards purging the government departments of 'aristocrats', when the Jacobins proposed to procure a list of all the officials of the *Administration des subsistances*. Robespierre's scruples made

[1]Corresp. 166.　　　　　　　　[2]Corresp. 166*bis*.
[3]Mme Roland retaliated by sneering at the 'affecting Jeremiads of High-priest Robespierre' (*Mem.*, ed. Perroud, 1/168).

him oppose any direct correspondence with the Minister concerned: but Marat thought such purism absurd; 'An honest patriot', he said, 'could correspond with the devil himself'. It was in the course of this debate that some one reported a fire at the Ministry of Justice, and the House was thrown into such confusion that the President had to put on his hat, and warn members against the danger of panic. 'Popular Societies', Robespierre sarcastically added, 'are not fire brigades. The person who started the report must be either a fool or a rascal', and he proposed to turn him out of the club.

May 1 was chosen by the Girondins for an anti-Jacobin demonstration. A number of young clerks and officials, of the type aimed at in the motion of April 26, had been called up for military service by the Commune. Incited by the Girondin leaders, these men marched through the streets, shouting, *Vive la loi!* and *A bas la Montagne!* On the 6th, in the Assembly, Vergniaud defended the demonstrators, and delivered an attack on the Commune. Robespierre, in his reply, alleged that some of the rioters had worn white cockades, and had cried *Vive le Roi! A bas la République!* Whatever the truth of this—and *Loi*, as Isnard said, might easily be mistaken for *Roi*—the incident became another trial of strength between Paris and the provinces, the middle-class majority in the Assembly, and the 'working-class' Commune. Knowing this, Robespierre returned to the charge on May 8, with a speech on national defence, which was at the same time an eulogy of the capital and the Commune. 'Paris', he said, 'has provided more than 50,000 men to fight either against the coalition of despots, or against the enemies on the home front. Paris is the centre of the Revolution. Paris was the cradle of liberty, and will remain its strongest bulwark. But if there is a counter-revolutionary army in the Vendée, there is also one in Paris; both must be held in check'; and he concluded for the arrest and internment of all suspects, be they lawyers' clerks or nobles, financiers, bankers, or priests. Incidentally, munitions works must be organized, and citizens who have their living to make must be reimbursed for the time they spend on guard.

These proposals he expanded into a revolutionary programme in a speech at the club the same evening. After repeating the demand for the payment of patriotic services —a fairly obvious bid for the popular vote—he proceeded to outline projects that in some respects went further than ever before in the direction of a 'dictatorship of the proletariate'. There is to be a revolutionary army, recruited through the Sections, and from the *sansculottes*, to exterminate rebels, and to overawe the aristocracy; all plotters and aristocrats are to be arrested; all *sansculottes* under arms are to be paid by the state, and fed at the expense of the rich;[1] forges for the manufacture of arms are to be set up in every public place; the Commune is to stir up revolutionary ardour; and blasphemers against the Republic are to be punished, along with incompetent generals. Finally (he adds on May 10) the ministries and military staffs must be purged of counter-revolutionaries, and their places given to 'pure patriots'.

Robespierre wished this to be regarded as his political testament. 'I have no more to say to you', he ended, with a personal appeal, which he always found effective; 'for, unless there is a revival of public spirit, and the genius of liberty makes a last effort, I can but await, in the chair of senatorial office to which the people has raised me, the moment when the assassins come to sacrifice my life'. But the assassins did not come; nor was this by any means Robespierre's last speech. On May 12, and again on May 13, whilst deprecating violence, he repeated his proposals for the arming and payment of the *sansculottes*. On the 17th, certainly with the knowledge, and perhaps with the collaboration of Robespierre, Desmoulins published that fantastic but damaging libel on their political opponents, the *Histoire des Brissotins*. On the 18th the Girondins retaliated by setting up a Commission of Twelve, packed

[1]This experiment had been made in the Hérault Department, and advocated by Chalier at Lyon (Mathiez, 317–8).

Robespierre as a young man: a late Ancien Regime lawyer in the making.
Portrait by Laville Guiard from the Musée de Versailles.
(Photo N D Roger-Viollet).

Rarissime.

LA VIE
ET
LES CRIMES
DE
ROBESPIERRE,
SURNOMMÉ *LE TYRAN;*
DEPUIS SA NAISSANCE JUSQU'A SA MORT.

Ouvrage DEDIE à Ceux qui commandent, et
à Ceux qui obéissent.

PAR

M. LE BLOND DE NEUVÉGLISE,

Colonel d'Infanterie légere.

Le Bonheur fuit la Terre où commande le Crime. P. C.

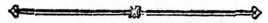

A AUGSBOURG,

Chez tous les Libraires ; et dans les principales
Villes de l'Allemagne.

M. DCC. XCV.

Avec Approbation.

The Earliest Life of Robespierre, Title Page,
from a copy in the author's possession.

Robespierre: a conventional image. Portrait by LL Boilly
from Musée de Lille. (Photo Lauros-Giraudon).

Portrait of Maximilian Robespierre. Drawing by Moreau le jeune
from Musée Lambinet, Versailles. (Photo Lauros-Giraudon).

Robespierre. Anonymous portrait from Musée Carnavalet
(Photo Lauros-Giraudon).

A Meeting at the Jacobin Club in 1791. Engraving by Masquelier in the Bibliothèque Nationale. (Photo Lauros-Giraudon).

Membership Card of the Cordeliers Club issued in the name of Robespierre's younger brother, Augustin. (Photo N D Roger-Viollet)

Robespierre in his room at the Duplays.
(Photo N D Roger-Viollet).

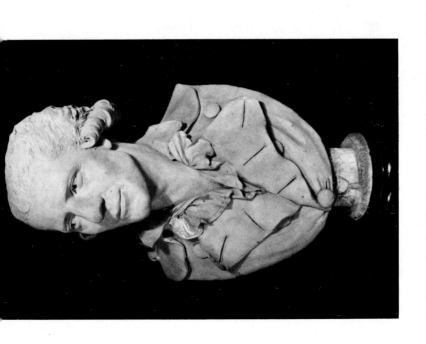

Bust believed to be of Robespierre. A characteristic example of the busts of prominent revolutionaries widely disseminated in France, especially in 1793–4. Originally in the possession of Marie-Louise of Parma, by kind permission of the Countess of Rosebery from the Collection of Lord Rosebery at Dalmeny House, Edinburgh. (Photo The National Galleries of Scotland by Antonia Reeve).

A Jacobin "Purge", "La marmite épuratoire des Jacobins." Robespierre as cook, wearing a bonnet rouge, from an anonymous cartoon of 1793, in the Bibliothèque Nationale.

The Duplays' House: Rue Sainte-Honoré, representing the arrest of Cécile Renaud, from an engraving by Duplessis-Bertaux in the Musée Carnavalet.
(Photographie Bulloz)

Robespierre Entrant dans l'appartement de Marat député assassiné le 13 Juillet 1793 par M.ᵉ
Charlotte Corday agée de 25 ans executée le 18 sur la Place de la Révolution

Il fut l'ami du Peuple il perit sa victime. — Marat au venir par un accord sublime
&tournis veslument observir vter persenel. — l'esprit de persenal et l'ame de Caton

L'AMI DU PEUPLE.

*A popular engraving depicting Robespierre discovering Charlotte Corday with the body of Marat
whom she had just murdered. A completely fictitious representation which served to link Robespierre
with the powerful revolutionary reputation of Marat. Anonymous work from the Musée du Louvre.
(Photo Lauros-Giraudon)*

Pen and Ink Drawing of Robespierre in the Convention on 9 Thermidor, by P Grandmaison.

Robespierre: drawn in the Convention with the note "eyes green, complexion pale, coats of striped green nankin, white waistcoat with blue stripes, white stock with red stripes". Attributed to Gerard. Reproduced by kind permission of Photographie Bulloz.

Warrant for the arrest of the Dantonists. Signed by members
of the Committees of Public Safety and General Defence.

Page from Robespierre's Note-book. The "Carnet" showing memoranda struck out after use.

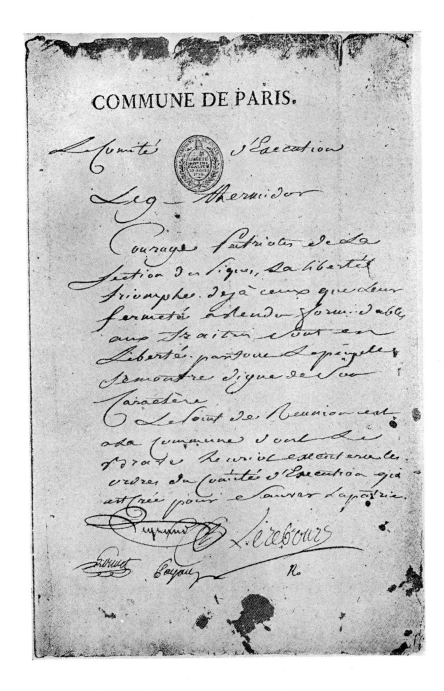

Note for the Section des Piques drafted at the Hôtel-de-Ville on the night of 9
Thermidor, announcing the release of the deputies arrested that day in the
Convention and calling for insurrectionary support. Robespierre's signature
has been interrupted – possibly by the arrival of the Convention's forces?

A dramatized and inaccurate view of the recapture of the escaped Robespierrists at the Hôtel-de-Ville on the night of 9 Thermidor. Engraving after Harriet from the Bibliothèque Nationale. (Photo N D Roger-Viollet).

ROBESPIERRE AMENÉ BLESSÉ, DANS L'ANTI-SALLE DU COMITÉ DE SALUT PUBLIC.

le 28 Juillet 1794, ou 10 Thermidor An 2ème de la Republique

During the night of 9–10 Thermidor in the antechamber of the Committee of Public Safety, Robespierre lies wounded by his attempted suicide. Engraving by Berthaut after Duplessis-Bertaux. (Photo Lauros-Giraudon).

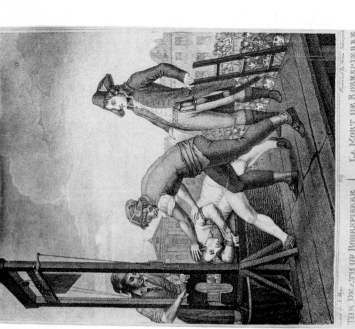

THE DEATH OF ROBESPIERRE   LA MORT DE ROBESPIERRE

English engraving of the execution of Robespierre. He is
shown struggling against the executioner, which in
reality he was in no condition to do. Engraving by James
Idnarpila after F Beys. (Photo N D Roger-Viollet).

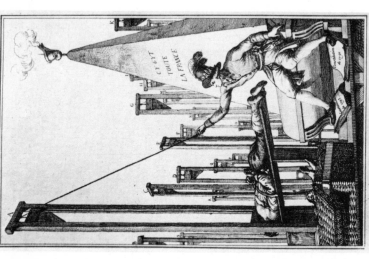

CY OT TOUTE LA FRANCE

ROBESPIERRE, guillotinant le bourreau après avoir fait guillot' tous les Francais

Anti-Robespierre Propaganda. Robespierre finally
guillotines the public executioner after having had the
whole of France guillotined. Musée Carnavalet.
(Photo N D Roger-Viollet).

with their own party, to inquire into the conduct of the Commune; and on the 24th this body issued various decrees harassing the Sections, and ordering the arrest of Hébert, Varlet, and other prominent leaders of the people.

This was the last effort of the Gironde. The moment had come for the final assault on their positions. That evening Robespierre, *à propos* of an attack on Kellermann, uttered a warning against military dictatorship. On the 25th and 26th the Commune and Sections protested against the arrest of their men, and Robespierre denounced Vergniaud; and on the 27th there was a violent scene in the Assembly which culminated in a snap vote, with the Jacobin Hérault in chair, abolishing the Commission of Twelve, and releasing the imprisoned leaders.[1]

As the crisis drew nearer, Robespierre worked himself to the edge of collapse. On the 28th he denounced Brissot as a royalist, and incited the Commune to action with a violence of language which exhausted his physical strength. Twice he had to apologize for the weakness of his voice; and at the Jacobins, the same evening, he protested that he had come to the end of his powers of endurance. 'I am no longer capable', he said, 'of prescribing to the people the means of its salvation. It is a task beyond any single man's powers— certainly beyond mine, exhausted as I am by four years of revolution, and by the heart-rending spectacle of the triumph of tyranny, and of all that is most vile and corrupt. It is not for me to point out the steps to be taken, whilst I am consumed by a slow fever, a fever of patriotism. I have had my say: I have done my duty: for the present, there is no more that I can do'.[2] The 'tumultuous applause' which drowned this peroration, showing how well Robespierre had gauged the appeal of his broken voice and look of exhaustion, need not blind one to the fact that it was safer for him, now that the insurrection was well under way,

---

[1] These measures were rescinded by the Girondists next day; but the temporary success was a signal for the popular rising that followed.

[2] According to Garat, Robespierre said to him, about this time, 'I am utterly tired of the Revolution; I am ill; the country was never in greater danger, and I doubt whether it will survive'. (B. and R. 18/339.)

to retire from any active part in it. This cautious withdrawal, at the moment when those whom he has incited are in danger of losing their heads, and it is uncertain which way the day will go, is so characteristic of him that it is difficult not to think it calculated. But it cannot be explained simply as moral cowardice. Robespierre regards himself as more than an individual: he is a public trustee for the Jacobin club, and for the cause of the people. He remembers July 17, August 10, and March 10. If things go wrong, if reaction once more triumphs, he must be in a position, as the leader of official democracy, to disown the insurrection, and to save the insurrectional machine. It was not a heroic attitude; it was, indeed, barely respectable; but it was by just such feats of balancing that Robespierre kept his foothold on the tight-rope of revolution, when others fell to the ground. Again, it is easy to call such an attitude hypocritical: but it must be realized that, in an Assembly of political play-actors, accustomed to the traditions of the bar, the pulpit, and the confessional, there were probably more who envied than who despised Robespierre for so successfully exploiting his personality. Political principle is of little account in a time of revolution.

VII

The end was now near. On May 29 a meeting of the Sections nominated an Insurrectional Committee of six, afterwards increased to nine members, to organize a popular rising on the lines of that of August 10. Early on the 31st, delegates from thirty-three *Montagnard* Sections occupied the Town Hall, and forced the Commune to put itself under the orders of this committee. Hanriot was made commander of the National Guard, and Mallarmé President of the Convention—both Jacobin nominees. When the Assembly met, to the sound of bells ringing and drums beating, it was faced by deputations demanding revolutionary measures in the interests of the common people—the impeachment of Ministers, the formation of a revolutionary army, a subsidy (raised by a tax on the rich) to keep down the price of bread, the dismissal of nobles from the higher command of the army, the manufacture of arms for the *sansculottes*, the 'combing out' of aristocrats from government offices, the arrest of suspects, the disfranchisement of all but the working classes, and public relief for the old and infirm, as well as for the families of those fighting at the front. It is clear from this programme that Robespierre's attempts to provide a constructive policy for the insurrection had not been wasted.

Barère opened the debate, in true 'trimmer' fashion, by moving to suppress the Girondist Commission of Twelve, which he had himself proposed a fortnight ago, and to give the Convention control over the armed forces of Paris. Robespierre followed. Describing this day as 'perhaps the last on which patriotism will have to fight against tyranny', he supported Barère's first proposal, but would go further, and impeach the members of the Commission. The military power he wished, naturally, to leave in the hands of the Sections. It was the clue to the whole situation.[1] During his speech Vergniaud came into the house, and was taunted with his late appearance. 'Be finished, then (*Concluez donc!*)' he replied. 'Yes, I will be finished', retorted Robespierre, 'and with you!—you, who, after the revolution of August 10, tried to compass the death of its authors; you, who have worked incessantly for the ruin of Paris; you, who wanted to spare the tyrant; you, who plotted with Dumouriez, and obstinately persecuted those patriots whose lives he was seeking; you, whose wicked reprisals have provoked, among your victims, the indignant protests that you would stigmatize as a crime!' Vergniaud was silenced, and the Commission suppressed.

But the work of the insurrection was only half done. The following evening a fresh petition was presented to the Assembly, demanding that proceedings should be taken against 27 deputies of the Gironde. June 1 passed quietly,

[1]He was reported next day as having said to a friend that 'they could not there and then secure the arrest of the deputies; but that, once the people were in insurrection, it could complete its work'. (Tuetey, 8/2771.)

and Robespierre did not intervene in the short and ineffective proceedings of the Convention. During the following night the Insurrectionary Committee arrested Clavière and (in the absence of her husband) Mme Roland, and ordered Hanriot to blockade the Assembly with armed forces, with a view to the arrest of the twenty-seven deputies. On June 2 the Tuileries was surrounded by 80,000 men. After a disorderly debate, in which all kinds of expedients were discussed, the members tried to carry the situation by a gesture, and marched out in procession, only to be driven back by Hanriot's unimaginative gunmen. There was nothing left but to submit, and to order the arrest of the leaders of the Gironde.[1] Representative government had suffered a defeat almost as fatal as that of the monarchy on August 10. It was another victory for Paris—for the Commune, the Sections, and clubs—over the growing indifference, the conservative revolutionism of the country.

VIII

On the eve of these great events Augustin Robespierre began to write to his friend Buissart, lamenting the evidences of treason, defeat, and counter-revolution: but he kept the letter open, and was able to end it with an enthusiastic account of the rising. 'Yesterday', he says, re-dating the letter, *June 1*), 'the tocsin was rung, the drums called to quarters, all the citizens took up arms, and a moral insurrection (*l'insurrection morale*) was carried out with the dignity of a great people which is worthy of freedom, and which wills that the Republic shall be saved'; and he ends with an eulogy of Paris, which, after four years' championship of liberty, has once more shown itself worthy of the nation's trust.

Such was the 'official version' of the events of May 31–June 2. Paris had saved France by destroying the Gironde. But what did this really mean? Had the Republic been in danger? Was it saved by the forcible 'purge' of the national

[1]For detailed accounts of all this, v. B. and R., 27/407, 28/4

representation? Should Paris have the credit? Various
answers were given to these questions at the time—answers
coloured, for the most part, by the passions of victory, or
of defeat: others have been added since, almost as highly
tinted by the partisanship of historians, who have either
regarded the Jacobins as patriotic heroes, or the Girondins
as martyrs to the cause of liberty. The corrective of extreme
views lies in studying, as Robespierre must have done, the
course of events since August, 1792.

Some aspects of the political struggle which culminated
in the fall of the Gironde went back to the beginnings of the
Revolution; but its essential cause lay in the events of the
six weeks during which Paris had ruled France, and the
Commune had ruled Paris. This regime might have caused
less trouble, if the revolution of August had been more
thorough. The death of the king at that moment might have
united the country. The dissolution of the Assembly might
have left the Commune in undisputed control. But the
king in the Temple was still a rallying-point for royalists,
and an embarrassment to the Gironde; whilst to the 'Rump'
of the Assembly the pretensions of the Commune were a
constant reminder of its own failure to control the situation.
The result was a series of incidents which widened the
breach between the Assembly and the Commune, as, on a
smaller scale, they broke down the friendship between
Pétion and Robespierre. The prison massacres and the
Paris elections made this breach irreparable. But it might
still, perhaps, have remained a personal and party quarrel,
had not the protagonists carried it on from the Legislative
Assembly into the Convention.

Historians have been so busy condemning Robespierre's
decree by which the Constituents excluded themselves from
the Legislative Assembly, that they have failed to remark
the much more disastrous results which followed the re-
election of so many members of the Legislative Assembly
into the ranks of the Convention. There would have been
bitterness enough, anyhow, between the majority of
country members, resentful of Parisian dictatorship, and

the small but solid block of city members, to whom the provinces stood for royalism and federalism. But when the one side include Brissot, Vergniaud, and Louvet, and the other side Danton, Marat, and Robespierre, private enmity exaggerated political differences into national issues, which could only be settled by the extermination of a whole party. The fight swayed to and fro for six months, mainly on four parts of the field—the question of the Convention guard, the king's trial, the new Constitution, and the treachery of Dumouriez; whilst all the time there was going on in the background a struggle for the capture of minor positions— mayoralties, presidencies, judgeships, ministerial appoint- ments, and membership of government committees–by which each party sought to secure a hold upon the administration. In the event, the Jacobins were everywhere successful, and the armed intervention of the people on June 2 was hardly more than the *coup de grâce* administered to an exhausted and bewildered victim.

So much is clear. The main issue of the struggle was between the Assembly and the Commune, the interests of the provinces and the interests of Paris, representative government and the dictatorship of Robespierre's 'People'. But this was not all; indeed, it was part of the Jacobin policy to distract attention from anything that might seem to be an attack upon the Convention or the Constitution. Instead, the struggle was represented as one of class, between the new bourgeois plutocracy, which had assumed the cast-off cloak of privilege, and the old poor, the age-long victims of oppression. There is, to tell the truth, little evidence that the Jacobins as a whole were less well-to-do or more democratic in their sympathies than the Girondins. The leaders of both parties came from the same class, shared the same education, and were in agreement as to nine-tenths of their political ideals. But it soon became obvious that the Revolution and the war had created economic problems, pressing with particular urgency upon the working-classes in Paris, and other large centres of population, which could not be solved by the *laissez-faire* attitude of country lawyers, and which the Parisian deputies, with their experience of semi-independent Sectional control, were more competent to attack. Whilst Roland denounced the Commune, Robespierre busied himself with drawing up a Labour programme.

Again, the conduct of the war—a war upon two fronts, at home as well as abroad—evidently needed methods of government more centralized and efficient than those of the already discredited Constitution of 1791, or any likely to be provided by a Girondist Constitution of 1793. Valmy and Jemmappes gave a respite to Parliamentary government; but when the spring of 1793 brought another period of defeat, recourse was had to the usual expedients of public panic—summary justice, and a 'war cabinet'. It was the great virtue of the Jacobins, and of none so much as Robespierre, that they were prepared to give these expedients constitutional status, and to govern the country, so long as the war lasted, by methods suited to a national emergency.

English observers believed that 'the manners of the Jacobins were more popular, their harangues less metaphysical and more level to the understandings of the vulgar, than those of their antagonists'.[1] But, though there is some truth in the view that Girondism was more idealistic, and Jacobinism more realistic, in its political origins and methods, it is also undeniable that some of the Jacobin leaders—Robespierre and Saint-Just in particular—were in a real sense just as 'metaphysical' as any of their opponents. Where their rivals saw salvation in forms of government, they saw it in national character. They attached little meaning to such words as 'republic' and 'constitution'. They pinned their faith on the natural goodness of a class which their opponents thought unfit for political power, and which they called to fulfil its destiny, rather in spite of than by means of constitutional devices, in a regime of enlightened patriotism. That was why the rising of June 2, though (with Jacobin realism) every working man who took

[1] *Annual Register*, 1793.

part in it was paid at the rate of forty *sous* a day, yet seemed to them to be a 'moral insurrection'.

The fall of the Gironde, then, was more than the defeat of a political party. It may not unfairly be said to have 'saved the Republic'—saved it from a system of government which could never win the war, from an economic policy which was helpless in the face of problems that the war had created, and from an unnatural and dangerous disunion between the capital and the country. The situation urgently required what the Girondins could never give—centralized and simplified control—a small despotic Committee, supervising all the activities of the government, legislating through a subservient Assembly, and enforcing its will by an army of travelling representatives. The Jacobins alone had the courage to face this need, and to provide an organization through which it could be met. They alone controlled the necessary driving force—the support of Paris, and of the 'people'. So Paris saved France by destroying the Gironde.

France—seldom generous towards failure—showed no sympathy to the Girondins in their fall. They, in return, showed no understanding of the causes of it. The writings of the Girondist Dispersion make melancholy reading, not only for the story they tell of suffering and persecution, but also for the evidence they afford of the pettiness, bitterness, and incompetence of their authors. The sympathy which has been so freely lavished on them has been partly due, so far as French historians are concerned, to passing reactions against Jacobinism, and to a desire to find historical precedents for nineteenth-century Liberalism; and partly, among English writers, to a chivalrous and sentimental regard for fallen greatness. Too little attention has been paid to the actual character and services of the two parties.

At the time, it was probably easier to forgive royalists, who had always opposed the Revolution, than Feuillants or *Brissotins*, who followed it half-way, and then turned their backs upon it. In denouncing the Gironde, Robespierre was denouncing men who had once been his friends, and ideas which had once been part of his own creed. The terms in which the denunciation was made were those of the tribune; the temper was that of the pulpit. There are no sins a man castigates more readily than those he once committed himself. He can think of no worse treachery than the denial of his new character. Those who have refused to follow him in his conversion are living reminders of his discredited and discarded past.

IX

The break in the course of the Revolution caused by the events of May–June, 1793, is a good moment to review Robespierre's correspondence since August, 1792. The fragments of it that remain are fewer than usual. A period of ten months provides only five letters written by Robespierre himself, and eighteen received. Bad correspondent that he was, and hourly pre-occupied with editing his *Lettres à ses commettans*, he must have written and received many more than have survived. But what can be learnt from these few?

By far his busiest correspondent is Aigoin, who keeps him posted up in the local politics of Montpellier. Two of these letters have already been mentioned.[1] It will be enough to quote one more, as an illustration of Robespierre's kindness towards a friend in trouble. 'Be sure', he writes, 'that you need never doubt the warmth of my affection (*mon tendre amitié*). Next to my country I love nothing so much as men like you. You are at one with all true friends of the Republic and of virtue in incurring a certain amount of odium. Take courage, and look to patriotism itself to console you for the persecution it has brought upon you. Count on my warm (*tendre*) devotion; but make allowance for the state of lassitude and exhaustion to which I am sometimes reduced by my disagreeable tasks. Good-bye, and give my love to all your friends'.[2]

A hurried letter to Buissart, written on the eve of August

[1] v. 1/286, 2/17.   [2] Corresp. 168.

10, asks for information about the arrest of a friend at Arras, and asks for it urgently, as though Robespierre were deeply concerned.[1] Dubois de Fosseux, not perhaps the friend he once was, encloses an address.[2] General Doraison asks for promotion for his aide-de-camp: Robespierre's intervention might go for much with the Jacobin Bouchotte, the new Minister of War.[3] Lacombe Saint-Michel describes the enthusiasm of the Corsican patriots; and encloses a subscription to the *Journal des Jacobins*.[4]

There remain two letters of special interest. On May 10 Robespierre writes to 'Fouquet de Tainville', better known to history as Fouquier-Tinville, the Prosecutor attached to the Revolutionary Tribunal at Paris, recommending one Théry as court doctor. 'You will not neglect', he ends, with what sounds less like a request than a command, 'this opportunity of doing a service to a republican'. Fouquier did not neglect it: in the margin of the letter are two notes signed by Montané, the President of the Tribunal, showing that Robespierre's recommendation was taken *en grande considération*, and that Théry was unanimously appointed to the post. Fouquier, when brought to trial after Thermidor, was at pains to prove that he had had no personal dealings with Robespierre. This letter suggests, at any rate, that Robespierre had considerable influence over the personnel of the tribunal.

There remains one document of even greater personal interest. Danton, returning from his second mission to Belgium in the second week of February, 1793, found that his first wife, Antoinette-Gabrielle Charpentier, had died a week before, and had been five days in her grave. In the violence of his grief he opened the tomb, embraced the dead body, and employed a sculptor to model the bust which may still be seen in the museum at Troyes. It was on February 15, the day following this macabre scene, that Robespierre wrote to condole with him. 'If it is any consolation', he said, 'in the midst of misfortunes which

[1]Corresp. 141.   [2]Corresp. 158.
[3]Corresp. 159.   [4]Corresp. 163.

might break down even such a soul as yours, to be certain of a warm and devoted friend, that at least I can assure you. I love you more than ever, and I shall love you till I die. At this moment I feel myself identified with you. Do not shut your heart to the voice of friendship, when it feels all our sorrow afresh. Let us weep together for the loss of our friends, and thus the sooner make the effects of our sorrow felt by the tyrants who are the authors of our misfortunes, both public and private. I had already addressed these heart-felt words to you, my friend, while you were still in Belgium. I should have come to see you before, had I not thought it right to respect the first moments of your very proper affliction. Let us embrace one another'.

'Nothing shall ever part us', Pétion had written to Robespierre only a few months before: and now he was an outlaw, hunted from cellar to attic by the emissaries of Robespierre's party. 'I shall love you till I die', says Robespierre to Danton: and a little more than a year later he was to sign the decree which sent Danton to his death. He was not a common hypocrite: he meant what he said, and was conscientious in what he did. The clues to his inconstancy are given in his own words. He loves, not Aigoin himself, but 'such men as you'; and he loves them less than his country. He condoles with Danton, not for the loss of Antoinette-Gabrielle, but of 'our friends'; and he will love him all the more when he forgets his private sorrow in vengeance on the 'tyrants' who are somehow the cause of their common misfortunes. Robespierre's affections are genuine; but they are not natural. They all stand stiffly to attention before that terrible drill-sergeant, patriotism.

CHAPTER XII

THE LAW-GIVER (APRIL–JULY, 1793)

I

A READER of the voluminous 'memoirs of the Girondist leaders might be excused for thinking not only that the insurrection of June, 1793, was the most fatal event of the Revolution, but also that it was carried through with every circumstance of ferocity. 'Couthon is thirsty'; so Vergniaud had interjected during his speech of June 2—'give him a glass of blood'. In point of fact, although a whole political party had been forcibly expelled from the Assembly, the affair had been so one-sided that not a drop of blood had been shed; the rejected members, though nominally under arrest, lived at home, dined out, and entertained their friends; and, had they been willing to accept their defeat philosophically, the whole incident might have been regarded as a friendly intimation from the Sovereign People, expressed in almost constitutional terms, that it no longer liked its old government, and wished to entrust its affairs to a new one. Nor was the Jacobin party, thus put into power, in a position to carry matters with a high hand. The Insurrectional Committee of May 30, unlike that of August 10, disappeared as soon as its work was done. The Girondist Ministers, Clavière and Lebrun, remained in office until the second and third weeks in June. Barère's proposals for dealing with the situation (June 6) included the abolition of the revolutionary committees recently charged with the supervision of suspects and the recruitment of troops, the dismissal of Hanriot, who had commanded the armed forces of the insurrection, the restoration of liberty to the press, and the provision of hostages, in the persons of members of the Convention, for the security of the arrested deputies. These measures, indeed, were felt to go too far in the way of reaction, and were soon withdrawn. 'Paris is quiet', said Robespierre: 'leave it so. The revolutionary committees are doing their work well; let them continue it. Be as severe as need be against the suspended deputies; but do not antagonize forces which, by a popular rising, have saved Paris from the counter-revolutionary troubles of Lyon, Marseille, and Bordeaux'. It had been the thesis of the Girondins that the insurgents intended to set up a dictatorship, a triumvirate, or a military despotism.[1] Nothing of the kind was or could be attempted. Meanwhile as many as seventy-five deputies had signed with impunity a protest against the removal of their Girondist colleagues; and the victorious party was not even strong enough to prevent twenty out of the twenty-nine Girondins under arrest from leaving Paris, and organizing revolt in the provinces. It was not until June 13 that Robespierre could find a majority in the Assembly to carry a resolution approving the events of May 31–June 2.

Robespierre, indeed, never doubted the significance of what had been already done, and was convinced that the time had at last come for the Jacobins to seize and organize the instruments of power. A year later there was found among his papers a memorandum in his own hand, embodying a remarkable outline of policy, which evidently belongs to this juncture. 'What we need', he writes, 'is a single will.[2] It must be either republican or royalist. If it is to be republican, we must have republican ministers, republican papers, republican deputies, a republican government. The foreign war is a fatal plague, so long as the body politic suffers from the Revolution, and from the division of wills. The internal dangers come from the middle classes: in order to defeat them, we must rally the people. Everything had been so disposed as to place the people under the yoke of the *bourgeoisie*, and to send the defenders of the Republic to the scaffold. The middle classes have triumphed at Marseille, Bordeaux, and Lyon. They would have

[1] Sénart, *Révélations*, 85.
[2] *Une volonté une.* Courtois, in his *Rapport* (*pièce justicatif*, No. 44) detached this phrase from its context, and pretended that it meant a personal dictatorship. Further details are given in another note by Robespierre (*pièce justificatif*, No. 50).

triumphed in Paris too, but for the present insurrection. This rising must continue until the measures necessary for saving the Republic have been taken. The people must ally itself with the Convention, and the Convention must make use of the people. The insurrection must gradually spread from place to place, on a uniform plan; the *sansculottes* must be paid, and remain in the towns. They must be supplied with arms, roused to anger, and enlightened. Republican enthusiasm must be inflamed by all possible means'.

This goes well beyond anything that Robespierre has previously said. It represents nothing less than a capitulation of the Jacobin party to the demands of the extreme Left. As early as May 18, Dutard, a shrewd observer, had pointed out that the Jacobins were divided into two parties, which he called the Upper and the Lower Chambers; the Upper comprising educated men, and men of property— to this Robespierre himself belonged—and the Lower consisting of 'anarchists' (of whom there were more at the Cordeliers than the Jacobins), led by Marat. The mob, he thought, would be controlled by whichever party gave it most rein. Robespierre and his friends had made deliberate use of mob violence on June 2: they could not yet throw over their ally, however uncongenial. True, their mob-rule is tinged with parliamentarism: the people is the Sovereign, directing the uncertain steps of its own representatives. But the power of the people, in the sense of the 'Fourth Estate', or proletariate, is to be absolute; and a class-war against the *bourgeoisie* is to be the undisguised means of its supremacy. Thus, on the political side, at least, Robespierre declares himself a Marxian revolutionist. Lenin himself might have penned his programme. But the test of genuine belief, in revolution as in religion, is how far the believer is prepared to go in practice. What steps did Robespierre take to realize this remarkable scheme of action?

II

A few days after the 'purge' of June 2, a deputation from Arras, conscious of backsliding, and anxious to make itself right with Robespierre,[1] congratulated the Assembly on the good work that it had begun, and exhorted it, rather patronizingly, to put an end to its 'gladiatorial quarrels'. The advice was superfluous. The leaders of the Gironde were soon pouring their invective into the ears of provincial audiences, or confiding their grievances to melancholy diaries, whilst their broken followers in the Assembly had no heart to oppose the victorious Jacobins. In a reduced and largely indifferent House,[2] there were no more 'incidents', no more personal attacks and counter-attacks, until the Jacobins fell out among themselves. Soon, too, the threat of a Girondist revolt in the provinces drew all Paris together in the defence of a Revolution specially its own, and of the unity of a country to which a capital was indispensable.

The federalist revolt, planned weeks beforehand, broke out first in the north-west, where Caen became the Girondist headquarters. Within a week it had spread south to Bordeaux. Bourges, Nîmes, Toulouse, Marseille, Toulon, and Lyon followed. By the middle of June some sixty out of the eighty-three Departments were in more or less open rebellion. For the first time in the national history it was not Paris which separated itself from France, but France which separated itself from Paris. Fortunately the twenty-two departments which supported the capital and the Jacobin regime formed a solid group in the centre and north-east of the country, and included the north-east frontier provinces: they were thus a strong base of operations both against foreign and civil foes.

Robespierre held no office, except that of deputy, previous to July 26; and his main concern, as usual, was for the home front; but his interventions during these weeks, such as they were, cannot be passed over. Thus, on June 14 he carried a vote of thanks to the Department of La Manche for its zeal in providing recruits; though he always insisted

[1]Ward, 211.

[2]Between June and October the average attendance was about 230 out of the 686 deputies still on the books; it sometimes fell to as few as fifty, and even twenty. (Lav. 2/115.)

(as, for instance, at the Jacobins on June 12) that it was useless to send more and more troops to the front, so long as their generals were incapable of using them effectively. He had more than once declared for the dismissal of aristocrat officers; yet, when the extremists of the Cordeliers club proposed to carry out this 'purge', he drew back, and secured support for a more moderate policy.[1] During the following days he is found proposing the recall of commissioners in the Vendée, the questioning of certain generals by the Committee of Public Safety (June 18), the punishment of officials of the Haute-Garonne (June 28), and the recall of a commissioner for the investigation of his charges against a general (July 24). Such measures of discipline were very necessary at a time when a national army was being increasingly recruited and commanded by amateur soldiers who were also party politicians; though there may have been no truth in the story that dissension had broken out in the armies of the Vendée and the Pyrenees between troops from Paris, who shouted *Vive la République une et indivisible!* and troops from Bordeaux, who retaliated with *Vive la République! A bas les anarchistes et les factieux!*[2] But it was very difficult to secure effective prosecution of the war against Girondism in the provinces whilst the Girondist leaders still in Paris were free to organize opposition. Accordingly, when Amar proposed (June 24) that a report should be drawn up about these men with a view to their transference to prison, Robespierre strongly supported him; though at the same time he deprecated immediate imprisonment, and did not wish to make 'these miserable individuals' into martyrs.[3] A fortnight later, Saint-Just, to whom the report had been entrusted, concluded that only nine of the twenty-eight were genuine traitors; five were accomplices; and the other fourteen no more than 'misguided persons', who might safely be allowed to resume

[1] A police spy who was present took this move as a sign of the growing breach between the Jacobins and the Cordeliers (Tuetey, 9/693).
[2] Robespierre alleged this incident in a speech of July 6. It was denied by the Girondins on the 12th, and he made no reply.
[3] Vergniaud's escape from custody prompted Drouet to propose (July 25) immediate imprisonment in the Abbaye.

their seats in the House. This moderation, which no doubt represented Robespierre's own view, was in line with the caution shown by the Jacobins, ever since June 2, in dealing with their dispossessed but still undefeated opponents; and it had its sequel in the protection that Robespierre continued to extend, during the days of his power, to the seventy-five deputies who had protested against the events of June 2. It was, indeed, a difficult and ambiguous situation, not unlike that which had existed six months before, during the king's imprisonment. The balance of power, both in Paris and the provinces, was such that, whilst the Girondins could not avenge their defeat, neither could the Jacobins consummate their victory.

III

Still, the issue was to be decided by politics, not by war. The crucial point, as Robespierre had always insisted, was the home front. Jacobinism would win the day just so soon as it could outbid Girondism in popular favour. The Jacobin leaders were well aware of this need. Accordingly the peasantry were conciliated by laws which offered *émigré* lands for sale on easy terms, allowed the subdivision of communal property in equal shares, and abolished without compensation the final relics of feudal dues. Middle-class support was won by the increase of official stipends, and by the exemption, on Robespierre's proposal, of a wide range of incomes from the forced loan, or capital levy, which was the latest method of financing the war (June 23). Most important of all, a new Constitution was hurried through the House, by which it was hoped to win over the moderate revolutionists, and to stabilize the Jacobin regime.

The Convention was a Constituent Assembly, and its main duty had always been to draw up a new Constitution, in place of that destroyed by the revolution of August 10. Within a week of its first session it had determined to set up a Constitutional Committee, and within three weeks,

without undue hurry, it had nominated nine members onto this body. But during the succeeding eight months of
the Girondist regime singularly little had been accomplished.
The invitation issued to all and sundry to submit suggestions for a Constitution (October 10, 1792), though in
accordance with the best Liberal tradition, deluged the
Committee with more than 300 projects, all of which had
to be examined. Both the original draft of the Constitution,
and the covering report by Condorcet, were of inordinate
length. It may be that these causes of delay were not
unwelcome to a party which, up to the last moments of
January, 1793, was still hoping to save the monarchy.
But they were by no means in the interest of the Girondins
themselves, whose dilatoriness lost them an opportunity
of securing constitutional status for the rights of the
provinces against Paris. On the other side, it must be
allowed that the policy of the Jacobin minority on the Committee was frankly obstructive. They did not differ from the
Girondins on details of drafting. They simply would not
have any Girondist constitution at all; since they knew
that it would be designed, in all essential matters, to put
power into the hands of the anti-Jacobin classes in the
country. It was better, as Robespierre was always insisting,
to carry on with the Constitution of 1791, until it could be
amended in a Jacobin sense. Meanwhile the country,
preoccupied with the war, showed little interest in constitutional questions; and it was not until February 15, 1793,
that Condorcet, as *rapporteur* of the Committee, brought his
draft Constitution before the Convention. It was received
without enthusiasm, and the Committee expired automatically in bringing it to birth. A fresh body of six, of
whom five were Girondins, was then appointed, and showed
a tardy zeal by making four further reports during April
and May.

The discussion of the new Declaration of Rights, which,
Robespierre had insisted, must precede the Constitution,
was based on a draft by Gensonné, and began on April 19.
A Girondist spokesman, Durand-Maillane, at once proposed

certain restrictions on the liberty of the press, hitherto guaranteed, if not always observed. Robespierre agreed, with more conviction, perhaps, than a year ago, that there were times when the greater rights aimed at by a revolution could only be secured by the sacrifice of the lesser; he could even contemplate the death penalty for writers attacking the indivisibility of the Republic, or encouraging the re-establishment of royalty—for they would be Girondins, not Jacobins. But he protested, as he had always done, against any interference with liberty of speech under normal conditions; and he carried Pétion and Brissot with him in the Declaration: 'Liberty of the press, that is to say, the right to publish one's thoughts in any way, cannot be prohibited, suspended, or limited'. Three days later (April 22) the new Declaration of Rights was adopted.

IV

Meanwhile Robespierre and a special Committee of the Jacobin Club[1] had been hard at work on the Committee's report, with the object of bringing forward counter-proposals in the Jacobin interest. On April 21 he told the club that 'the Friends of Liberty and Equality, putting aside all passion and all intrigue, ought to present the world with such a scheme for a Constitution as will silence calumny, and become the code of all nations'; and it was an instalment of this perfect plan—certain articles dealing with the right of Property—which he expounded in a notable speech in the Convention on April 24.[2]

He began by dissociating himself from any scheme for the redistribution of wealth or land. 'You must know', he said, 'that this *loi agraire*, which you have heard so much about, is simply a bogey invented by rascals to frighten fools. There was certainly no need of a revolution to teach the world that the present very unequal distribution of wealth is the source of many evils, and of many crimes: but

[1] There is among Robespierre's papers a summons to a meeting of this Committee on the first Saturday of March, 1793. (Pap. inéd. 2/123.)
[2] The notes from which Robespierre made this speech have survived, and provide a good example of his method of extempore speaking (v. R.F. 50/451).

we are equally convinced that it would be impossible to distribute it equally (*l'égalité des biens est un chimère*).[1] Personally (he went on) I think equality of wealth even less necessary for private than for public happiness. It is much more necessary to make poverty respected than to ban millionaires (*proscrire l'opulence*)'. No, the problem before the legislator is not to redistribute private property, but to insist upon the moral duties of property-owners. 'The slave-trader will tell you that the wretched creatures whom he carries overseas in the coffin that he calls a ship are his property. The country gentleman thinks the same of his plate, and of his lands. The Capet family think they have a proprietary right to degrade and oppress twenty-five million Frenchmen. None of them realize that proprietorship carries moral responsibilities (*porte sur aucun principe de morale*)'. And this (says Robespierre) is where the Declaration of Rights, as hitherto worded, fails. It defines liberty, well enough, as limited by the rights of others, but it does not carry on this conception into the right of property. One article after another guarantees the widest possible freedom in the use of property, but there is not a word to say what use of it is legitimate, and what is not; and the result is, not so much a declaration of the rights of men, as a declaration of the rights of capitalists (*riches*), profiteers, speculators, and tyrants. Robespierre accordingly proposes, as the first four articles of the section on property, the following:

Article 1. Proprietorship is the right of every citizen to use and to dispose of that portion of wealth which is guaranteed him by the law.

Article 2. The right of property is limited, like every other right, by the duty of respecting the rights of others.

Article 3. It may not be exercised so as to prejudice the safety, liberty, life, or property-rights of one's fellow-men.

Article 4. Any holding of, or dealing in, property which violates this principle is unlawful and immoral.

[1]Rétif de la Bretonne shared Robespierre's belief in a moral revolution, but thought it involved the abolition of private property (*Nuits révolutionnaires*, 24).

Having thus defined, in the first part of his speech, the nature of property, and the obligations of proprietorship, Robespierre goes on, in the second, to apply these ideas to the subject of taxation. He argues from 'eternal justice, and the nature of things', that the law which recognizes inequality of wealth must also recognize inequality of taxation; and he proposes to enact that 'Citizens whose income is only sufficient for their own support need not contribute to the needs of the state; others must contribute in proportion to their means'.[1] In any case, he would have tax-paying regarded, not as a matter of compulsion, but of charity—a duty willingly performed by the rich members of the civic family towards their poor relations.

This carries him a step further. The authors of the Declaration, he says, seem to have thought of the French nation as isolated from all others—'a human herd planted down in a corner of the globe'—and not as one of a family of nations, all of whom have a duty to help, and a right to be helped by, one another. This 'great gap' in the Declaration he proposes to fill by four more Articles, thus expressed:

Article 1. Men of all countries are brothers, and the different peoples ought to help one another according to their ability, like citizens of a single state.

Article 2. He who oppresses a single nation declares himself the enemy of all.

Article 3. Those who make war on a people to arrest the progress of liberty, and to destroy the rights of man, deserve to be attacked by all, not as ordinary enemies, but as brigands, rebels, and assassins.

Article 4. All kings, aristocrats, and tyrants, of whatever kind, are slaves in rebellion against the human race, which is the sovereign of the world, and against nature, which is the legislator of the universe.

Robespierre ended by reading out the complete draft of his Declaration, in thirty-seven Articles, amongst which those already given appeared as Nos. 7–10 and 34–37; the

[1] This clause Robespierre omitted from the version printed in his *Lettres à ses commettans*.

whole being introduced by a Preamble which claimed that 'all the crime and misery in the world are due to forgetting or underrating the natural rights of man', and which therefore provided that 'the people should always have before their eyes the foundations of their liberty and of their happiness, the magistrate his rule of duty, and the legislator the object of his mission', by 'proclaiming in the face of the Universe, and under the eyes of the Immortal Legislator, the following Declaration of the rights of men and citizens'.

This Declaration is such important evidence for Robespierre's political and social ideas, that it must be given in full.

v

THE STATE

Article 1. The object of every political association is to safeguard the natural and imprescriptible rights of men, and to develop all their faculties.

RIGHTS

Article 2. The most important rights of men are self-preservation and freedom.

Article 3. These rights belong equally to all men, whatever their physical and moral differences. Equality of rights is a law of nature (*établie par la nature*). Society, far from impairing it, guarantees it against such misuses of power as make it unreal.

FREEDOM

Article 4. Freedom is the right of every man to exercise all his faculties as he will. Its rule is justice, its limits are the rights of others, its source is nature, its guarantee is the law. The right of peaceful assembly, and the right to publish one's opinions through the press, or in any other way, are such obvious corollaries of freedom that the necessity of asserting them points either to the presence of despotism, or to recent recollection of it.

354

THE LAW

Article 5. The law can prohibit only what is harmful to society, and can require only what is useful to it.

Article 6. Any law which violates the imprescriptible rights of man is essentially unjust and tyrannical: it is not a law at all.

PROPERTY

(Here follow Articles 7–10 as given above.)

Article 11. It is the duty of society to provide a living (*pourvoir à la subsistance*) for all its members, either by procuring them work, or by assuring the means of subsistence to those who are unfit to work.

Article 12. The charity necessitated by the existence of poverty is a debt that the rich owe to the poor: it is the business of the law to settle the manner in which this debt shall be paid.

(Article 13. On taxation, as given above.)[1]

EDUCATION

Article 14. Society ought to encourage with all its might the progress of public intelligence (*raison*), and bring education within the reach of every citizen.

THE SOVEREIGN PEOPLE

Article 15. The law is the free and solemn expression of the will of the people.

Article 16. The people is sovereign; the government is its work and its property: public officials are its agents.

Article 17. No fraction (*portion*) of the people can exercise the powers of the whole; but any wish that it expresses should be respected, as being that of a part of the people, whose consent is needed to form the general will (*volonté générale*). Every section (*section*) of the sovereign assembly ought to have the right to express its will with entire freedom: it is essentially independent of all constituted

[1]p. 41.

authorities, and free (*maîtresse*) to manage its own police and its own debates. The people can change its government and recall its deputies (*mandataires*) whenever it pleases.

EQUALITY

Article 18. The law is the same for all.

Article 19. Every public position is open to all citizens, with no differentiation but that based on virtue and capacity, and with no claim but that of public confidence.

Article 20. All citizens have an equal right to share in the appointment (*nomination*) of the people's deputies, and in legislation.

Article 21. In order that these rights may not be unreal, nor equality chimerical, the state must provide salaries for public officials, and make it possible for citizens who work for their living to take part in those public meetings at which their presence is required by law, without prejudice to their livelihood, or to that of their families.

OFFICIALS

Article 22. Every citizen must religiously obey the magistrates and government agents, when they are expressing or executing the law.

Article 23. But any act infringing a man's freedom, safety, or property, whoever the agent may be, or although it be done in the name of the law—except in certain cases and according to certain forms by law prescribed—is arbitrary, and null and void. The very respect due to the law forbids submission to such an act; and if an attempt is made to enforce it, it may be resisted by force.

REDRESS

Article 24. Every individual has the right to present petitions to the depositaries of public authority. It is the duty of those to whom they are addressed to take into consideration the points raised: they have no right to prohibit, to restrain, or to punish the exercise of this right.

Article 25. The right of resisting oppression is a corollary of the other rights of men and citizens.

Article 26. When a single member of society is oppressed, the whole body is oppressed with him, and when society is oppressed, every member is oppressed with it.

Article 27. When a government violates the rights of the people, it becomes the sacred duty (*le plus saint des devoirs*) of the whole people, and of each separate portion of it, to revolt against it.

Article 28. When a citizen can no longer rely upon the state to safeguard his rights, he falls back on his natural right to defend all his rights for himself.

Article 29. In either case it is the last refinement of despotism to provide none but legal means of resisting oppression.

Article 30. In every free state it is the first duty of the law to defend social and individual liberty against abuses of authority by the government. Every institution is vicious which does not assume the corruptibility of public officials, and the goodness of the people.

Article 31. Public appointments are not to be considered as honours or rewards, but as public duties.

Article 32. Crimes on the part of the people's representatives must be severely and easily punished. No one has the right to claim an inviolability not shared by other citizens.

Article 33. The people has a right to know everything done by its deputies: they must render it a faithful account of their conduct, and submit respectfully to its judgement.

INTERNATIONALISM

(The Declaration ends with Articles 34–37, as given above.)

VI

One or two general reflexions will occur to any reader of this remarkable document. It is ill-arranged, too full in some parts, and too meagre in others. For instance, Article 2 announces that the two most important rights are self-preservation and freedom; but the Declaration goes on at once (Article 4) to deal with the latter, and nothing more is said about the former, except in Articles 25–28: there is no mention of army, police (except incidentally in Article 17), or courts of justice. Again, under the head of Freedom, the rights of public meeting and of free expression of opinion are, indeed, mentioned in passing, but liberty of conscience and worship are ignored. Or again, whilst the whole subject of franchise and representation is dismissed in two short articles (19–20), no less than ten are taken up with the means of redress against abuses of authority. In fact, the document is not the work of an orderly mind.

In the matter of expression, too, it will be noticed how often clearness, and a precise use of terms, are sacrificed to rhetoric, or to epigram. For instance, the last part of Article 4, and the whole of Articles 29–31, are out of place in a constitutional document; whilst the final Articles, 34–37, are not a declaration of rights so much as a political manifesto. In spite of his legal training, which, no doubt, paid more attention to oratory, and less to lucid exposition, than would be the case nowadays, Robespierre's intention of expressing his meaning clearly is constantly defeated by his desire to present it effectively. He shows the mind of a preacher, rather than of a legislator.

Nevertheless, this Declaration, for all its lack of balance, and its excess of rhetoric, stands out above the flood of revolutionary talk like a beacon in a tide-way. It illuminates the Revolution, and it explains the greatness of Robespierre. No one else saw so clearly, or preached so enthusiastically, the essential message which 1789 handed on to the modern world—that the object of the state is to ensure the development of all the faculties of all its members; that law and government are revocable expressions of the will of the people; that every privilege involves a duty to the society which allows it; that there is more danger to the healthy growth of a state in too much than in too little control; and that the nations of the world are a society whose members stand or fall together.

So much for preliminaries. It remains to comment on some parts of the Declaration; and to use, in doing so, a speech which Robespierre delivered in the Convention on May 10, and which was, in effect, a pendant to that of April 24.

Robespierre's doctrine of the State, upon which everything else rests, is clearly based on Rousseau's. 'Man', he begins on May 10, in words modelled on the opening sentence of the *Contrat Social*, 'Man is born for happiness and freedom, yet everywhere he is unhappy, and enslaved. The object of society (he goes on, almost repeating Article 1 of his Declaration) is the preservation of his rights, and the perfecting of his nature'. The time has come, he thinks, for society to realize its mission, and to crown an 'age of reason' by a 'great revolution', in which the state shall effectively embody the rights of man, and the laws of society shall coincide with the laws of nature. In a general way this would have the assent of all legislators and social reformers; it translates into eighteenth-century French their age-long hope that 'what is' may some day coincide with 'what ought to be'. But would they agree as to the terms of the translation? This 'natural law'—where is it at work? These 'rights of man'—upon what do they rest? Robespierre, at least, does not arrive at them by reasoning, or discover them by historical research; they come to him by an act of faith. Somehow and somewhere, he feels, there must be a natural law which is just and permanent, because all known human laws are unjust and unstable. There must be some human rights, because there are so many human wrongs. To Rousseau the poet, to Robespierre the prophet, that is argument enough. What, again, of the character of these rights? Why liberty, why equality, why (though by now he has forgotten it) fraternity? Perhaps because eighteenth-century France had suffered so long from arbitrary government, political inequality, and class war? Perhaps because, in the Paris Robespierre knew, the prosperous middle class preserved towards the poor the same attitude of disdain that they had formerly resented in the aristocracy? So far as this was so, Robespierre's Declaration is not a treatise on the theory of the State, but a political programme—as Parisian as the *Contrat Social* was Genevan, or Plato's *Republic*, for all its greater scope, Athenian. But no doubt it is by condescending to local conditions that truth, like goodness, saves the world.

If the ideal State is the first point in Robespierre's scheme of society, it soon appears, from the speech of May 10, that there is in fact only one other—the method of making it real. Everything else is subordinated to the problem, how to render the government strong enough to safeguard the rights of man, but not so strong as to violate them. Looking at French history, Robespierre is tempted to think this problem insoluble. From Clovis to Louis XVI, the nation's troubles have always come from the tyranny of government, which has put private interests before the interests of the people, and sacrificed the general will of the poor to the separate wills of rich and powerful individuals. From this he concludes again that 'the prime object of every Constitution should be to defend public and private liberty against the government itself'. If, then, the first point of Robespierre's system is an act of faith, the second is a judgment drawn from history. Now, a properly balanced treatment of the problem of power, on these lines, would be of the greatest value: unfortunately, in the remaining twenty pages of the speech of May 10, as in the almost equally large proportion of the Declaration that deals with this subject, hardly anything is said about making the government strong enough to safeguard rights; almost the whole emphasis is laid upon preventing its becoming strong enough to violate them, and devising remedies, if it becomes so. Thus Article 6 makes it impossible for the government to pass any law limiting the 'imprescriptible rights of man': indeed, it is the first business of the law to defend these rights against the government (Article 30). The government is the people's 'agent', even, in a sense, its 'property', to dispose of as it will (Article 16). Not only can the people as a whole dismiss one government, and set up another; but any portion of the people (and it is not without significance that Robespierre uses the Paris term *section*) can become autonomous, and contract out of so essential a part of government as the police system (Article 17). Citizens must, it is true, 'obey magistrates and government agents' (Article 22) when enforcing the law; but if the law violates their 'freedom, safety or property' in any way—and of this, except in certain cases, they themselves are the judges—they must refuse to do so, and may even resist by force (Article 23). Articles 26–27 make it a 'sacred duty' for the whole people to rise against a government which has violated a single right of a single citizen; and the principle of a political General Strike follows from the laws of nature (Article 28). Deputies have to render a strict account of their acts (Article 33), and are liable to prompt and severe punishment (Article 32). No wonder they are warned (Article 31) that the business of government involves no honour and no rewards: only a strong sense of duty could possibly make one undertake so thankless a task.

It is from this same point of view that Robespierre devotes the greater part of his speech of May 10 to discussing methods of limiting the power of the government. It is to be done, he thinks, not by playing off one Minister against another, nor by instituting a Tribunate, but by subdividing the offices of government, and limiting their tenure, by taking away temptations to personal ambition, by devolving unessential functions upon the Communes, by a regular system of audit, and by publicity of debates. This last, as a debater, he thinks the greatest safeguard of all. 'The whole nation', he says, paraphrasing Article 33 of his Declaration, 'has a right to know what its deputies are doing. If it were possible, the Assembly ought to debate in the presence of the whole French people; it might at any rate hold its sessions in a sumptuous edifice holding 12,000 spectators,[1] where neither corruption, nor intrigue, nor perjury would dare to show themselves, where only the general will would be consulted, and where

[1]cp. Roland's view, 1/47

no voice would be heard but that of reason and public interest'.

Robespierre himself foresees a very pertinent objection to all this. 'I may be asked', he says, at the end of his speech of May 10, 'how, with all these safeguards against officials, I am going to secure obedience to the laws, and to the government'. I reply that I secure it by these very precautions. I give to the laws and to the government every scrap of power that I take away from the governors and legislators. For the respect inspired by a magistrate depends much more upon his own respect for the laws than upon any power that he usurps from them; and the sanction (*puissance*) of the laws consists less in the armed force that lies behind them than in their harmony with the principles of justice, and with the general will. When the law is based on the public interest, the people itself is its support, and its sanction is that of all the citizens, who made it, and to whom it belongs. The army and the police are simply the people in arms, carrying out the general will, and defending the body politic against attacks from outside. The law can only clash with the general will through some fault of its own, or some misuse of it by a magistrate. A properly ordered State—that is, one in which the laws embody the general will—is peaceable and free.

An Englishman will be the last to deny that there is truth and value in a conception of the state so like that to which experience has made him accustomed. But Robespierre, just because he has no English tradition behind him, incurs the charge of working out a good principle too logically. Rousseau, despairing of just laws, had found safety in providing for changes of government by periodical revolutions. Robespierre, believing that the laws can be made expressive of the general will, reduces all government to an automatic function—the mere doing, by proxy, of what everybody wishes to be done. His elaborate precautions against misgovernment really become unnecessary. The army is the nation in arms; the government should be the nation in office. But this seems, from his experience of actual governments, too good to be true; and for the transition period, at any rate, safeguards against mis-government will be needed.

There is, underlying all this, an important assumption, another of Robespierre's debts to Rousseau—the General Will. Robespierre's State is based upon no contract, because it involves no sacrifice of interests, and no conflict of wills. Nor is it wholly Utopian, because the General Will has become a matter of experience—something which the Revolution has already shown to exist, and whose full stature its further developments are to reveal. France has already abolished royalty, nobility, and clergy. There are no social classes. We are all *citoyens*. We have all essentially the same interests. We are the People. It is true, there are still relics of royalism, of class-war, and of governmental tyranny; but they will yield to good laws, political education, and, if necessary (so Robespierre will come to see) intimidation; and then there will be one people, one faith, and one will, embodied in a peaceful and law-abiding society, in a government that realizes the rights of man, and (he was yet to add) in a church that worships the God of Nature.

There remains a difficulty which did not dismay Robespierre, because he thought it transitory. Suppose the General Will to have been disengaged from the personal interests and class hatreds that have hitherto obscured it; suppose a society reconstructed, as Robespierre perhaps saw it, on the model of the Duplay household—virtuous, democratic, united, and hard-working; how can this system be imposed upon those who may at any time disagree with it, except by violating the very rights it exists to enforce? In order that all rights may be secured, are they not all surrendered? The tyranny of an imposed government has gone; but has there not grown up in its place the subtler and more formidable tyranny of the autonomous General Will?[1] There must, at best, be a transitional period of coercion and expulsion, in order to secure unity; there must be violations of liberty in order to secure a State in which

[1] cp. Robespierre's own remarks on this, 1/243.

liberty can flourish: and how many revolutions have come safely through this period?

One final doubt, which Robespierre does not seem to have envisaged. Suppose the General Will once and for all triumphant, and every selfish interest eliminated. Where there is no clash of individual wills, has a General Will any value? Where there is no resistance, can there be any progress? Alternatively, suppose the General Will only half victorious—must there not, then, be a recurrence of crises, a movement to and fro between nationalism and individualism, the unitary and the federal State-systems? Was not history to show that the diversities of natural and social outlook could never, for long, or outside a closed area, be forced into uniformity, however Utopian?

VII

So much for the main structure of Robespierre's legislative programme. There remain certain special features that call for further comment. Hardly less important than the four Articles limiting the right of property are the two corollaries that Robespierre draws from them—State support for the unemployed (Article 11), and a progressive Income Tax[1] (Articles 12–13). The likelihood that these Articles were incorporated as a bid for popular support against the Girondins does not detract from their interest as 'the first manifestation in any French Assembly of a kind of Socialism'.[2] Robespierre is not, indeed, a Socialist, still less a Communist: he believes neither in the State ownership of wealth, nor in any plan for redistributing it. The function of the State, in respect of private property, is that of the policeman. Its first duty is to protect the individual in his use of it; its second is to protect other individuals from his misuse of it. Similarly with the problem of work and wages. These are all the property the poor man possesses; and it is as much the duty of the State to protect them as it

[1] *L'étendue de leur fortune*, in the second part of the article, is apparently to be interpreted by *les revenus* in the first part.
[2] Deslandres, 1/268.

is to protect the houses and lands of the rich. A popular Jacobin treatise had drawn the inference that refusal to work was a kind of theft.[1] Robespierre prefers the kinder conclusion that it is the business of the State to guarantee either work and wages, or subsistence for those who cannot obtain them. In doing so, he is not a political scientist, laying down an abstract theory of the duty of the State; but a philanthropist, outraged by social injustice and inequality, and believing, like any modern Finance Minister, that it is for the State to correct the balance of wealth by taxing the rich to subsidize the poor. But, as church ritual may originate in practical convenience, or social amenities in savage taboos, so the principles of modern socialism are none the worse if they derive from such unphilosophical parentage.[2]

The Article on Education (14) was no doubt meant to take some of the wind out of Girondist sails; but it is none the less interesting. We knew already that Robespierre looked to public education as a means of making the world fit for Republicans; it was not clear before, that he wished it to be given to every citizen.

· The sectionalism of Article 17 is a deliberate challenge to the departmentalism or Federalism of the Gironde. Large subdivisions (Robespierre felt) make for the disunity of the whole body; small subdivisions increase its unity. Napoleon's unitary France, like Robespierre's unitary Paris, was built upon autonomous Communes.

Robespierre's life-long devotion to manhood franchise reappears in Articles 19–20. At the same time he is realist enough to know that working men cannot put politics

---

[1] Collot d'Herbois, *Almanach du père Gérard* for 1792 (R.F. 17/434).

[2] Whilst advanced Jacobins like Buonarroti—the most important literary link between Jacobinism and nineteenth-century socialism—welcomed Robespierre's declaration as a gospel of hope for the common people, there were some extremists to whom it seemed too moderate, or at least too ambiguous. At the next meeting of the club, Boisset, a friend of Robespierre (v. 1/185) read out an alternative draft of what he called a 'Declaration of the rights of *Sansculottes*'. 'The natural rights of *sansculottes*', he began, 'are dress, food, and the reproduction of their species (*uproar and laughter*); the use and enjoyment of the fruits of the ground, the mother of us all; resistance to oppression; and an unchangeable resolve to recognize no superiors but nature and the Supreme Being'.

before their daily bread; he would therefore provide for the payment, not only of deputies, but also of electors, jurymen, and even the audience at a parliamentary debate.

Of the last four Articles (34–37) it is easy to say that they are the most rhetorical and theoretical part of the whole Declaration. Aulard stigmatizes them as 'violent, intolerant, and intolerable propaganda', and quotes Robert's criticism: 'We are not representatives of the human race, and I would rather that the French legislator forgot the universe for a moment, and thought only about his own country'.[1] Doubtless Robespierre had political reasons for adding these Articles, particularly after his disappointment of April 13: he wanted to propagate his doctrine of war against that of Brissot, and to take the wind out of Cloots's sails. But he cannot do either without generalizing, without carrying into the international sphere the conception of society which he has already extended from the family to the nation. He *is* 'thinking about his own country', but not in isolation from others. His family of peoples, all of whom regard one another as brothers, and help one another against oppression, and his 'human race, which is the sovereign of the world', as the French people is the sovereign of France, put Robespierre among the prophets of Internationalism: they are, as Mathiez claims, 'an outline of the League of Nations'.[2]

VIII

At the time when Robespierre brought forward his Declaration, the Girondist majority were already losing their hold on the House, and it was evident that they could never carry their Constitution. Within a little more than three weeks their leaders had been expelled, and their initiative, if not yet their power, had fallen into the hands of the Jacobins. Robespierre and his friends had only to take over the constitutional stock-in-trade of their rivals, and to use it to obtain popular support for a government of

[1] R.F. 18/125. [2] G. et M., 102.

national defence. On May 29, when the Convention, after a month's debate, had only passed Condorcet's Declaration of Rights, and a few scattered Articles of his Constitution, Barère proposed, in the name of the Committee of Public Safety, the appointment of a special committee of five, to produce, as speedily as possible, the essentials of a Constitution. This committee, consisting of Hérault de Séchelles as *rapporteur*, Saint-Just, Ramel, Mathieu, and Couthon, started work on June 3, and presented its report to the Convention on June 10. 'The Constitution of 1793, like the world itself, was created in six days'.[1] It was hailed as the first-fruits of the insurrection of June 2. As Robespierre said, in moving its circulation to the Popular Societies and the army, 'the mere recital of its Preamble is enough to put heart into the friends of the country, and to drive its enemies to despair. All Europe will be constrained to admire this fine monument of human reason, and of the sovereignty of a great people'.

In the debates that followed almost daily until June 23 he intervened constantly, with the competence of one who had criticized at every turn the Constitution of 1791. Thus, speaking on the Articles which abolished the *suppléant* system, and provided for fresh elections in the event of a vacancy, he thought an outgoing member need not wait to resign until his successor had been appointed (June 14). The same day, no doubt remembering how his support of the 'permanence' of the Sections had been applauded by the Right,[2] he opposed an Article which gave the Primary Assemblies wider powers of meeting. 'The intriguers and the rich', he argued, 'will spin out the meetings; the poor man will have to leave, to go to work; and they will proceed to carry any measures they like'. On the 15th it was debated whether Ministers should be elected, as deputies were, by the people, or by special bodies of electors. Robespierre, in whose eyes all Ministers were either royalists or *Brissotins*, was for marking their inferiority by indirect election. The Assembly agreed, and thus reversed one of the most

[1]Michelet, 7/206.   [2]v. 1/89.

characteristic provisions of the Girondist Constitution. But a deputy, however dignified his position, must not have impunity to plot against his country; and Robespierre was strongly opposed to a clause which provided that 'the representatives of the people cannot be called to account, prosecuted, or put on trial for any opinions which they may pronounce in the presence of the Legislative Body'. The Assembly, with the fate of the Girondist members fresh in their minds, and with a feeling that, under an increasingly one-party government, there would be less liberty of speech than before, refused to surrender their immunity; and Robespierre's proposal to reconsider the clause was thrown out. His attitude on this occasion was not forgotten a year later, when scarcely anyone doubted that the Law of the 22nd Prairial was intended to destroy the last barrier between the tribune and the guillotine.[1]

On June 16 Robespierre made two contributions to the debate. Attaching importance, as he always did, to a formula, he secured that, under the new Constitution, laws should be promulgated 'in the name of the French people', instead of 'the French Republic'—that is, in the name of the sovereign, not the government; and now nobody laughed at him.[2] Later, he objected to a loose use of the word 'representative', arguing that even the deputies themselves were mandataries, not representatives, since their decrees were without force of law until formally accepted by the people. This was not strictly accurate. Laws were subject to a referendum; decrees were not. The deputies were therefore partly mandataries and partly representatives.[3] On the 17th Robespierre intervened no less than six times. It was proposed that the Ministerial Council should have power to 'negotiate and make' treaties: remembering Nootka Sound,[4] he had the word 'make' struck out. It was proposed that it should have power to dismiss or indict the heads of the Civil Service: he opposed this, on the ground that interference from above was more

---

[1] v. 2/193 f.
[3] Deslandres, 1/284.

[2] cp. 1/61.
[4] v. 1/101.

to be feared than dishonesty from below. But this did not apply to the general supervision which he believed that public opinion ought to exercise over military as well as civil officials. Again, Hérault's Constitution had taken over from Condorcet's the proposal to submit civil disputes to arbitration: Robespierre objected that this would give the rich man (who could bribe the arbitrator) an advantage over the poor. On the question of taxation, which next came up for discussion, he admitted to a change of mind. Hitherto he had stood for the taxation of the rich, and the exemption of the poor.[1] Now, faced with the ingenious preamble to Hérault's Article—'No citizen is exempt from the honourable duty of contributing towards public expenditure'— he recognized his own sentiments,[2] and declared that to exempt the poor would be 'to vilify the purest part of the nation', and to set up a distinction between rich and poor destructive both of liberty and equality. Why deprive the poor man of the blessing attached to the widow's mite? If he is really too poor to pay anything, why should he not be given a small sum (*obole*) by the country, on condition that he returned it to the Treasury?—a suggestion that might well be taken up by modern legislators who wish to make every citizen feel the responsibility of a taxpayer.

June 18 was another full day, and Robespierre again intervened six times in the debate. Hérault had proposed that the Constitution should be revised, if need be, by a Convention sitting side by side with the Legislative Body. Robespierre thought the Legislative Body itself might do the work: but it was agreed that it should be superseded by the Convention. How long should such a Convention last? The House agreed with Robespierre that it was impossible to limit by law the exercise of the national sovereignty. If the Convention outstayed its welcome, an occasion would arise for exercising the 'sacred duty' of insurrection.

The next part of the debate has become historical. Article 4 proudly announced—it was a gesture appropriate to the

---

[1] He stood for it again, à propos of Mallarmé's 'forced loan,' on June 2.
[2] v. 2/41.

moment—that 'The French People never makes peace with an enemy in occupation of its territory'. This provoked, on the part of the Girondin Mercier, the ironical question, 'Have you then made a treaty with victory?' 'No', retorted Basire; 'but we have made a pact with death'. The Jacobins roared applause; but Mercier could see 'no real grandeur' in such 'high-falutin' ideas'. 'You have hardly any honest notions of liberty', he sneered, 'and yet you already presume to compare yourselves with the Romans'. This brought Robespierre to the tribune, burning with indignation. 'I would never have believed', he cried, 'that any deputy of the French people would dare to pronounce in this place sentiments so slavish and cowardly, or to dispute the republican virtue of the nation he represents. Where has this man discovered that we are inferior to the Romans, or that the Constitution which we are enacting is unworthy of a despotic senate that knew nothing of the Rights of Man? Where has he learnt that a people which sheds its blood for liberty is inferior to the Romans, who were the oppressors of every people'? Swayed by this eloquent improvisation, the Assembly inscribed its gesture on the statute-book.

The day's debate ended on the revised Declaration of Rights. Much had happened since the first attempt to define them four years ago. Experience had shown that they could not be so simply deduced by reason from nature as was then supposed; and political expediency demanded certain alterations in the list. To Robespierre, already engaged in the Jacobin scheme for enlightening the people, and about to present to the Assembly Le Pelletier's Education Bill, one omission was obvious, and he moved to add to the list the Right of Public Education. On the other hand, he opposed the addition of Liberty of Worship, the consideration of which had been postponed on April 19, and which he had ignored in his own list of April 27. It was not that he feared any popular relapse into superstition: but at Arras, in 1791, and now again in the Vendée, he saw religion being used as a cloak for counter-revolution. To stress liberty at such a moment was to encourage licence. Later, and under happier circumstances, he was to give State patronage to the common elements of all cults in his plan for the worship of the Supreme Being.[1] As a result of Robespierre's intervention, Hérault was asked to redraft this part of the report: but he refused to delete liberty of worship, and carried his point against Robespierre. On another matter, the institution of juries in civil cases, Robespierre also showed a change of mind. Before, he had favoured the reform; now he doubted the expediency of it, unless the jurymen were appointed by popular election.

In the final debate on the Constitution (June 23) an attempt was made to turn the Declaration of Rights into a Declaration of Rights and Duties. This, Robespierre reminded the House, was an old controversy, and the Constituent Assembly had spent three days resisting a similar proposal made by the clergy in 1789. Duties were not unimportant, but they derived naturally from rights; and it was enough that the latter should be plainly declared.

When the final vote was taken, Billaud-Varenne moved for an *appel nominal*, so that all France might know who had voted for the Constitution, and who had not; for some deputies of the Right had refused to take part in the debate. Robespierre, however, was content to express surprise and indignation at the attitude of these members; and the Assembly, which might have marked down the dissentients for proscription, preferred his more generous attitude. Its work was now done. At Robespierre's suggestion, it closed its session, and the rest of the day was given up to a popular procession through the hall of Assembly, in honour of the Constitution.

In the plebiscite which was held a month later in all parts of France not occupied by the enemy, as well as in the army and navy, 1,801,918 votes were cast for the Constitution, and 11,610 against it; but about 100,000 of the majority modified their acceptance with federal or other amendments—some thinking the Constitution too radical, and

[1] v. 2/173.

others not radical enough.[1] A month later, again, on the significant date of August 10, the announcement of the result of the plebiscite was made the occasion of one of David's most splendidly staged festivals, and the official copy of the Constitution, enclosed in a cedar casket, was carried from the site of the Bastille to the Champ de Mars, before being solemnly deposited in the Convention.

IX

The Constitution of 1793 was the work of Robespierre's party, but not of Robespierre himself. The House, as has been seen, adopted some of his suggestions, but rejected others. It is therefore hardly fair to blame him, as Aulard does, for the omission from the final draft of certain proposals which he had emphasized in his counter-blast to the Girondist Constitution two months before: they would have been as effective a bribe for popular support (were that all he meant by them) now as then: but in fact he was not in a position to dictate a policy to his party, still less to the Convention as a whole. Thus the Assembly refused to limit the right of property, as he would have done.[2] It rejected his manifesto on international co-operation, and retained Hérault's declaration of non-intervention. It inserted, against his advice, the right of liberty of worship.[3] It restored a reference to the Deity in the preamble of the Constitution, but not in the terms he would have preferred. There is, however, no reason to suppose that Robespierre was disappointed with the general results of the fortnight's work. He had told the Jacobins on June 10 that Hérault's draft of the Constitution 'provided the essential foundations of public welfare, and supplied a lofty and majestic scheme of national regeneration'; he had, during the debates, tried to add to it those 'popular Articles' it still lacked; and it was now as near as he could expect to the democratic revision

---

[1]Mathiez, G. et M. 103. Rather different figures are given by Deslandres, 1/290, and in R.F. 58/145.
[2]Deslandres, 1/274.   [3]v. 2/58.

of the Constitution of 1791 that he had hoped to see carried through by the Legislative Assembly. If he was willing to put it on one side as soon as it was enacted, it was not because he thought it bad, but because he thought it too good for the times, and judged that in the present emergency a more dictatorial form of government was required. This was the inner meaning of his speech of July 9, when he welcomed the popular acceptance of the Constitution, but warned the House against weakness. The Republic would never be safe or happy, he said, until all its enemies were punished: he left then to infer that this could only happen under the dictatorship of the Jacobin party.

X

For the moment, though not himself in power, Robespierre was loyally supporting the Dantonist government, discouraging extremist proposals that might rouse fresh excitement among the people, and defending the Committee and Ministers against attacks.[1] He was very tired, and glad to be free for a time from responsibility. 'I realize', he remarked on June 12, 'my inadequacy. I have no longer the energy to combat the intrigues of the aristocratic party. I am exhausted by four years of painful and unremunerative work. I feel that my physical and moral faculties are not up to the level of a great revolution. I give notice that I intend to resign'. At this there were general cries of 'No, No!'; and it does not seem likely that he seriously meant to do so.

But physical weariness was combining with mental discontent to give rise to new ideas of government: Robespierre was never so dangerous as when in retirement. Speaking on June 14, he said that what was needed to consummate the efforts of the government and the people was a 'centre of operations' (*point de ralliement*). 'The people as a whole', he boldly declared, 'are incapable of self-government (*ne peut se gouverner*): the centre of operations must be in Paris; and there we must concentrate the counter-revolutionaries, in

[1] v. July 8, 10, 13, 16, 24.

order to bring them under the severest penalties prescribed by law (*le glaive de la loi*)'. Here there was more than a hint of the Terror. On the same day Robespierre, once the champion of 'permanent' and autonomous Sections, is found denying freedom of meeting to the Primary Assemblies, on the ground that they may 'create an absolute (*pure*) democracy unregulated by those wise laws which might give it stability'. Two days later he opposes the admission of the general public to the meetings of committees of the Convention, not merely because the rooms are too small, but because it is enough for the public to hear the results of Committee work reported in the Convention. The same day he even surrendered one of his oldest convictions—the liberty of the press. His friend Garat had produced evidence that Girondist publications circulating in the provinces represented him and other Jacobin leaders as dictators: Robespierre at once proposed that 'the severest possible measures' should be taken to suppress 'these treacherous journalists, the most dangerous enemies of freedom'. That this speech was taken as threatening repressive action against the press in general is shown by a letter Robespierre received, two days later, from Grandville, the chief editor of Parliamentary reports in the *Moniteur*. He feels that his paper is in danger, and is at pains to point out that he has always taken the Jacobin side. When Louvet attacked Robespierre, he only gave an extract from Louvet's speech, but printed the whole of Robespierre's. During the king's trial, he gave in full the speeches demanding death, but from the rest only enough 'to preserve some reputation for impartiality'. Two months ago, when it was uncertain which way the party fight would go, he had been forced to report both sides; but no journal had been so consistently Jacobin since June 2, though this policy had lost it 1,000 subscribers in Normandy and the Midi. He hopes Robespierre will tell him, as between friends, what fault he has to find with the paper.[1] This surprisingly frank letter

[1]Corresp. 175. Another journalist, J. F. André, editor of *La révolution de '92*, wrote to the Committee of Public Safety in a similar sense, and escaped imprisonment by restarting his paper in the Jacobin interest (R.F. 13/259).

may well have confirmed Robespierre's reaction against the doctrine of liberty.

The upshot of these incidents was seen when, on June 23—the day of the enactment of the new Constitution—Robespierre proposed that the Jacobin club should put the discussion of a drastic revolutionary programme (*grandes mesures révolutionnaires*) on their agenda every day. Three days later he described Paris as the 'stronghold of liberty', and urged that it should be fully garrisoned and equipped. 'It is just as dangerous', he said, 'to demilitarize Paris as Valenciennes: the fall of Valenciennes would lose us the frontier; the fall of Paris would lose us liberty.' Later in the same debate he insists that the most effective way to combat the Girondists is not by political reorganization, but by moral reformation. 'Make laws for the benefit of the people: lay the foundations of public education: purify national morality: otherwise you will only perpetuate the crisis of the Revolution'. Here there is superimposed upon the Jacobin dictatorship and the Terror the ultimate dream of a Reign of Virtue.

XI

The Constitution, as Augustin wrote to Buissart on July 5, was not enough. 'We must have a Civil Code, and we must have a system of education. . . . The latter task is perhaps more difficult than one imagines, and the second travail (*enfantement*) will possibly be no less painful than the first'. This was no doubt Robespierre's feeling when he stood up to read Le Pelletier's Education Bill in the Convention on July 13. Le Pelletier's aim was the same as his own—to enlighten the people:[1] his ideal was the same—not instruction of the mind only, but education of the character. For this, he proposed a uniform physical, mental, and moral training for all girls from five to eleven, and all boys from five to twelve. During a transition period of four years this was to be voluntary; after that, compulsory. It

[1] 'I heard Robespierre say, in 1792, "The people will become easier to lead as the human mind acquires greater activity, light, force, and philosophy".' (Villiers, 87.)

was to be followed by a system of secondary education, for such as wished it. The cost would be borne by a graduated tax.

This scheme was too advanced for its time. Even in the modified form in which Robespierre brought it up again, on August 13, it was criticized for its expense, and for its interference with the parent's right to exploit his child's labour. The Assembly would do no more than sanction a modified system of primary schools.

The *enfantement* of an Education Bill, as Augustin had predicted, and as many Ministers of Education have found since, is a painful and difficult affair. But a beginning had been made; and the credit was largely Robespierre's.[1]

---

[1] The Assembly had refused the request of Le Pelletier's son, Félix, to be allowed to read the document, since he was not a deputy; but it paid the printer's bill (Hamel, 3/63).

CHAPTER XIII

The Decemvir (July–October, 1793)

I

THE cheers which greeted the enactment of the Constitution of 1793 had hardly died away, and the last deputation of enthusiastic Parisians was still filing out of the House, when the Socialist slum-parson Jacques Roux appeared at the bar, with a group of ragged parishioners from the Gravilliers Section. Robespierre, fearing a provocative manifesto, intervened, and he was refused a hearing. When, two days later, he reappeared at the head of a deputation from the Gravilliers and Bonne-Nouvelle Sections, he was denounced by Thuriot for promoting 'the monstrous principles of anarchy', and by Robespierre for 'trying to saddle the patriotic party with *modérantisme*, and thus to destroy public confidence in the government'.

This was the climax of a struggle which had been going on ever since the people came into power, ten months before, between the 'Upper' and 'Lower House' of the democratic party.[1] It had turned chiefly on the question, how far it was expedient to grant the demand of the poor consumers of Paris for the fixing of food-prices, and the punishment of profiteers. The *maximum*, as it was called, passed on May 4, as a concession to those whose influence might decide the issue in the coming duel between the Jacobins and the Gironde, had been sabotaged from the first by the local authorities, to whom the interests of the provincial producer were of more concern than the complaints of the city poor; the Jacobins themselves had just resisted a strong attempt to have it embodied in the new Constitution; and it was certain that, so soon as they were

[1] v. 2/34.

in a position to dispense with the support of the Paris mob, they would disown Roux and his *Enragés*.[1]

There were now, in fact, as Robespierre said on June 26, three enemies of the State—'Austria, Spain, Pitt (the royalists and *émigrés*), the *Brissotins*, and Jacques Roux'. Jacobinism was already beginning to tread that middle path between the Moderates and the Extremists which was to lead nine months later to the destruction of the factions, and the attempt to turn a party tyranny into a national government.

It was to meet this double advance of enemies on the home front that Robespierre designed the Provisional Government of 1793-4.

II

It will have been evident from the succession of incidents and debates between the beginning of June and the middle of July, 1793, that Robespierre's mind was already moving beyond the new Constitution towards a Jacobin regime less tied to parliamentary forms, and better able to deal with the double crisis of foreign and civil war. Attention has already been called to a memorandum outlining the approach to such a regime, by way of an alliance between the Convention and the armed people.[2] The time has come to signalize another writing, which seems to belong to the same period of Robespierre's career, and to carry his plans a stage further. It is called by Courtois, who published it at the end of his *Rapport*, not inappropriately, 'a kind of catechism, written in Robespierre's own hand'.

'What is our aim'? Robespierre asks himself; and answers, 'It is the use of the Constitution for the benefit of the people.

Who are likely to oppose us? The rich, and the corrupt.

What methods will they employ? Slander and hypocrisy.

What factors will encourage the use of such means? The ignorance of the *sansculottes*.

---

[1] For Roux and the *Enragés*, v. Mathiez, *La Vie Chère*, Pt. II, and Zacker, *Beshenye*.
[2] v. 2/34.

The people must therefore be instructed.

What obstacles are there to its enlightenment? The paid journalists, who mislead it every day by shameless impostures.

What conclusion follows? That we ought to proscribe these writers as the most dangerous enemies of the country, and to circulate abundance of good literature.

(The people—what other obstacle is there to its instruction? Its destitution.

When, then, will the people be educated?

When it has enough bread to eat, and when the rich and the government cease bribing treacherous pens and tongues to deceive it; when their interests are identified with those of the people.

When will this be?

Never.)

What other obstacles are there to the achievement of freedom?

The war at home and abroad.

By what means can the foreign war be ended?

By placing republican generals at the head of our armies, and by punishing those who have betrayed us.

How can we end the civil war?

By punishing traitors and conspirators, especially those deputies and administrators who are to blame; by sending patriot troops under patriot leaders to reduce the aristocrats of Lyon, Marseille, Toulon, the Vendée, the Jura, and all other districts where the banner of royalism and rebellion has been raised; and by making a terrible example of all the criminals who have outraged liberty, and spilt the blood of patriots.'

Three things are significant, in this revelation of Robespierre's mind on the eve of his accession to power—the pessimism with which he regards the state of the people, and his two recipes for victory—the employment of patriots, and the punishment of traitors. As to the first, the passage within brackets was in his mind when he made the memorandum—perhaps in July: he subsequently struck it out, either as premature, or as unsuitable for the speech or article he based upon these notes. This failure of the people to live up to its high destiny must have been Robespierre's greatest disappointment. He is realist enough to see that one cause of it is the economic distress of the poor: but to admit as much would be to play into the hands of Roux and his *Enragés*; and to find a remedy is beyond his power. So he turns aside to more congenial cures—public education, such as he hopes to provide under Le Pelletier's Bill, and a campaign against journalists and profiteers, which will strengthen the hands of the government, and win over the working-class vote.

This memorandum, then, outlines the policy which Robespierre believed necessary to save Jacobinism and the Revolution, and which he tried to embody, during the months that followed, in the 'provisional government' of the Convention and the Committee of Public Safety. It is a charter of the Terror.

III

Fresh urgency was given to the situation, and an unexpected opportunity provided for strong action, by an event which was announced on the very day that Robespierre introduced his Education Bill into the House—the murder of Marat (July 13). To the crowd Marat had long been a saint: he was now a martyr. There was an outburst of public affection, even greater than that which accompanied the death of Mirabeau. But with the politicians—less inclined than Englishmen would be to overlook a man's faults because he was dead—it was quite otherwise. Some of them had frankly detested the man and his views: others, who secretly agreed with them, had feared to be compromised if they openly co-operated with one of his sinister reputation. Besides, he was so clear-sighted, and so uncompromising, that it had been difficult to include him in any political party.

Robespierre, as the acknowledged interpreter of democracy, especially after this speech of April 13, was, more than any one, open to the charge of *Maratisme*. He was also aware—and nothing is more galling to one who thinks himself 'advanced'—that Marat regarded him as little better than a Moderate.[1] Nevertheless one would have expected a more generous attitude than that which he took up towards a man who had relieved him of the charge of dictatorship,[2] and had joined in his condemnation of the *Enragés*. In the Assembly, on July 14, he contented himself with moving that an inquiry should be held into the circumstances of the murder. At the Jacobins, the same evening, he expressed surprise that previous speakers had said so much about Marat—his poverty, his paper, and the project for a public funeral (of which he disapproved)—and so little about national safety. When that had been provided for, he remarked, it would be time enough to honour Marat as he deserved. When he went on to scoff at the idea of burying Marat by the side of Mirabeau, the club, remembering the part he had played in the earlier *panthéonisation*,[3] resented his attitude. 'Marat *shall* be buried there', cried his friend Bentabole,[4] 'whatever may be said by those who are jealous of him'. The next day Robespierre's only contribution to a series of speeches in praise of Marat was a suggestion that the society should acquire his printing-presses for its own use; and it was said that at a *fête funèbre* following the funeral he made an oration without so much as mentioning Marat's name.[5]

In Augustin's correspondence, generally a good echo of his brother's opinions, Marat's murder is first mentioned as a climax of aristocratic intrigue; but on second thoughts it is suggested that it may be useful to the Republic. For one thing, it inculpates Barbaroux, Duperrey, and other Girondins; for another, it was Marat's kind-heartedness which gave Charlotte Corday the opportunity for her crime,[6] and it is now generally known that he 'lived a

[1] v. 1/234. [2] v. 1/284. [3] v. 1/294.
[4] He was nicknamed *Marat le cadet*.
[5] So Collot d'Herbois on 9 Thermidor (Hamel, 3/61).
[6] She had obtained her interview with him by sending in the message, *Il suffit d'être malheureux pour être entendu.*

Spartan life, spending nothing on himself, and giving all he had to those who went to him for help': Danton and Robespierre, whose lives are also threatened,[1] will shine in the reflected light of Marat's apotheosis. But *panthéonisation* would spoil the good effects of this, by reviving the calumnies against Marat and his colleagues.

Thus, whilst the people mourned the loss of their greatest friend, and their severest critic, the politicians were calculating what party capital they might make out of his death. To the Jacobins it was a heaven-sent opportunity to turn popular vengeance upon their political enemies. To Robespierre himself it was the death of a rival, which brought him a step nearer to popular 'dictatorship.' The dates are significant. Marat was murdered on July 13. On the 26th Robespierre became a member of the Committee of Public Safety. On the 28th Saint-Just's report on the Girondist leaders[2] was 'revised' by Barère, with the effect that eighteen of them were now declared to be traitors, and eleven were ordered for trial. On the 30th the Revolutionary Tribunal was reorganized, so that it might do its work more efficiently. On August 2 Robespierre's friend Couthon brought an accusation against the Girondin Carra; and this was only one of a series of attacks which, by August 6, increased the number of the proscribed to fifty-five. If they were not immediately brought to trial, it was because, so long as the civil war continued, they were more useful alive than dead, as hostages for Jacobin prisoners. But their ultimate fate was already certain. Charlotte Corday's devoted crime had brought about exactly the opposite result to that which she had intended. It had completed the ruin of the Girondist party, and set the hated Jacobins firmly in the seat of power.

If Marat's murder, by removing a rival, and by rousing public indignation against the Gironde, made possible Robespierre's advent to power, it was his own action which brought him the invitation to join the Committee. From its

[1] A water-carrier was denounced on July 25 for saying, on the authority of a deputy's cook, that they had not long to live. Such is rumour, in a time of revolution.
[2] v. 2/36.

first sittings the Committee had been divided on the question of military appointments. It was the policy of Bouchotte, the Jacobin Minister of War, to dismiss royalists, and to appoint 'patriots', without much regard for their professional qualifications; and this action was backed by the Left. The Right put competence first, and political orthodoxy second. The Corsican Gasparin, the only soldier on the original committee, had resigned over the arrest of General Custine. The replacement of the experienced Biron by the incompetent Rossignol had roused a fresh storm. The Lavalette debate of July 24 challenged the policy, and indeed the very existence, of the Committee. At this point Robespierre's intervention was crucial. He knew little of military matters, and disliked military discipline: he would have modelled the whole army on the National Guard, with its officers elected from the ranks, and its easy-going methods and manners. But France was the last country, and a revolution the last moment, in which royalist and republican officers could be expected to sink their political differences in a common loyalty. If democratization were begun, it must be carried through to the logical end. This was Robespierre's contention; and popular instinct was on his side. The same day that he secured the continua-ation of Bouchotte in office (July 26), he attended his first meeting of the Committee which he had saved. The next day Saint-André proposed him for membership, in place of Gasparin.[1] He said afterwards that he had been disinclined to accept nomination. He may perhaps have doubted whether his gifts as an orator would find scope in com-mittee work, or whether the popularity he had acquired as a critic of governments might not be lost in the practice of governing. But the lure of power, and the opportunity of carrying into effect the plans he had formed for the safety of the country and the happiness of the people, soon out-weighed his scruples.

[1] *La Convention nationale décrete que le citoyen Robespierre l'ainé remplacera au comité de salut public le citoyen Gasparin, qui, à raison de sa mauvaise santé, a donné sa démission* (C.P.S. 5/393).

IV

The Convention had followed the democratic practice of the two previous Assemblies in making use of Standing Committees, both to supervise the ministries, and to prepare legislation. In addition to these, special committees were set up, from time to time, to deal with passing problems, such as education (July, 1793) or the Constitution (September, 1793). The *Commission de Douze* established in May, 1793, as a Girondist counterblast to Jacobin predominance on the Committee of General Security, formed a transition to yet another type of committee—one with a wider reference and greater powers, to deal with an emergency: there were precedents for this, too, in the *Comité des Recherches* of the Constituent Assembly, and the *Comité de Surveillance* set up by the Legislative Assembly after August 10. Such was the Committee of General Security (*Défense générale*) appointed in January, 1793, to co-operate with the Ministers in the conduct of the war. On March 25, three days after the news of Neerwinden, it was enlarged from twenty-one to twenty-five members, and given fresh powers, becoming a kind of Coalition Cabinet, including representatives of both parties in the House. On April 4 the news of Dumouriez's treachery caused a fresh crisis. The Committee itself suggested its replacement by an Executive body (*commission d'exécution*). But such a title was thought too suggestive of that assumption of executive power by the legislature which, however contrary to republican orthodoxy, was already taking place. Accordingly, on April 6, the Convention decreed that there should be set up a Committee of Public Safety (*salut public*), consisting of nine of its own members; that it should deliberate in secret; and that it should have power to supervise and direct the Ministers (*conseil exécutif*) in any measures of defence it might think necessary, on the home or foreign fronts. Between April and July, there were some changes in the number and personnel of this committee; but so well, on the whole, was its work done, that its existence was prolonged by monthly re-election. On

July 10, when Danton fell from power, the Committee was reduced to its original number of nine, who were now Saint-André, Barère, Gasparin, Couthon, Hérault de Séchelles, Thuriot, Prieur de la Marne, Saint-Just, and R. Lindet. Robespierre replaced Gasparin on July 27. On August 14, at the time of the new decrees on recruitment (*levée en masse*), Carnot and Prieur de la Côte d'Or were added, as military experts; and on September 6, in order to reconcile critics of the provincial administration, Billaud-Varenne and Collot d'Herbois.[1] Thuriot's resignation on September 20 reduced the number of the Committee to twelve; and the execution of Hérault in the following April to eleven; so it remained until Robespierre's fall in July, 1794.

Subject as it was to re-election from month to month, the Committee had no security of tenure but such as it could justify by doing its work well, and defeating its critics. Nor had it any armed force upon which it could rely; for the National Guard was under the control of the multi-sectional Commune. The fact that, under such conditions, it held its position so long, argues that its policy did on the whole meet the demands of the country. It might be minority government; but the majority showed no clear disposition to complain. It might be a dictatorship; but it saved France, and impressed Europe with the sense of a strong and consistent policy.[2]

As the Committee became permanent, its powers were enlarged. It was allowed to issue warrants of arrest (July 28); it was given unconditional grants of secret service money (August 2);[3] it nominated the members of the other committees (September 13); under the decrees of October 10th, it was entrusted with the supervision of ministers, generals, and public authorities; it could dismiss government servants, and conduct foreign diplomacy

[1]Danton and Granet were also nominated, but refused to serve.

[2]'Its formation has had an excellent effect abroad', wrote Noel from Venice to Danton on May 25. 'It is regarded a source of action, as the centre of a more dependable policy'. (R.F. 24/451.)

[3]For its ordinary expenditure it was dependent, like other committees, on the Treasury.

(December 4); and when, as a final step in this concentration of power, the *conseil exécutif* of Ministers was replaced (April 17) by twelve *commissions exécutives*, these were expressly subordinated to the Committee, and became, to all intents and purposes, a civil service under its direct control. The only department which in some sense defied this dictatorship was the police, which remained nominally under the Committee of General Security; but, in all important matters—on some twenty occasions during the year—this committee held joint meetings with its more powerful rival, and the latter alone was known as the Government Committee (*comité de gouvernement*).

Danton's committee had met twice a day, set up sub-committees, and received daily reports from the Ministers.[1] Within a few days of Robespierre's appointment, the new committee resolved to meet by eight a.m. at the latest; to begin by dealing with correspondence; then to deliberate on measures of public safety. At one o'clock they would adjourn to the Convention, and stay there till the end of the sitting, at four or five; the Committee would meet again at seven, and sit till ten. Three months later the daily conference with the Ministers did not begin till this late hour; so that it cannot have been unusual for the members to work for fifteen or sixteen hours a day. Most of them were very regular in their attendance, unless prevented by illness, or absence from Paris. Between July 26 and September 26 Barère attended sixty out of sixty-two meetings, and Robespierre only missed fourteen. But this is nothing to the regularity of attendance, if the records can be trusted,[2] during the later months of the Committee's existence. In October Robespierre missed only two meetings out of the twenty-eight for which lists of attendance are available: in

[1] R.F. 17/79.
[2] The lists of attendances are sometimes incomplete, and need to be supplemented from the signatures attached to the day's resolutions. Fresh uncertainty is introduced, if these lists 'were not made at the time of the meeting, or with sufficient care' (Aulard, C.P.S. 10/268), or if a member of the Committee present for any purpose in the Tuileries was counted as attending the Committee (Alger, *Paris*, 451). But though there are periods when the recurrence of the same names in the same order is suspicious, and one notices some obvious mistakes, there is no good reason to doubt the general trustworthiness of the lists. cp. 2/228.

November, December and January he was present at every meeting. In February and March he was absent for three weeks owing to illness, but attended on every other day; and from April till the end of June, at any rate,[1] he never missed a meeting. It does not need much imagination to realize what a strain this meant. Add that, during this same period, he attended almost daily at the Assembly, and at the Jacobins, and spoke some 160 times.

'I should like to see a picture', said Barère to David d' Angers many years later, 'of the little room in which the Committee used to meet. There nine members worked day and night, without a President, sitting round a table with a green cloth; the walls were papered in the same colour. Each of them had his special task. Often, after a few minutes' sleep, I would find a huge pile of papers in my place— reports of the military operations of our armies. . . . Round our little meeting-room we had organized our offices in the *Salle de Diane*. . . . We wanted to give a lesson in economy; we should not otherwise have done those great deeds that will astonish the world'.[2]

V

By a resolution of September 23, the Committee agreed that each of its members should take charge of a particular department of its work; that, when the Committee met, it should first deal with matters already in hand, then with deputations and correspondence, and then discuss reports, fresh questions, decrees, and measures of public safety; and that the members should take it in turns to receive petitions and deputations. But it is a little uncertain how these resolutions were carried out. Apparently, up to April 17, when the *commissions exécutives* came into being, the work of the Committee was subdivided among three *bureaux*, one of which corresponded with the travelling representatives,

[1]cp. 2/228.
[2]Esquiros, 2/383. Barère perhaps forgot that on October 4 six carriages were provided for the agents of the Committee, on June 24 another *cabriolet* and 'a well-sprung *berline*,' and that from April 22 onwards 2 *berlines* were at the disposal of members every day (C. P. S. *sub* these dates).

another supervised the execution of the laws, and a third —the *bureau de l'action*—was the central organ of government. But there must have been other sub-divisions, dealing, for instance, with war and munitions, foreign diplomacy, and police. After April 17 the Committee re-organized its work, so as to provide for the supervision of each of the twelve *commissions* by one of its members. How the work was shared out can to some extent be judged by the hand-writing of the resolutions and letters of the Committee, and by the signatures attached to them. When a draft of one of these survives in the handwriting of a particular member of the committee, it is fairly safe to assume that it belonged to his department, and that he took personal responsibility for it. The signatures are not such good evidence; for the writer of the minute did not always sign it, and those who did may sometimes have done so at haphazard, without special knowledge of the matter in question.[1] Nevertheless one may fairly argue that, if certain names are habitually attached to minutes dealing with certain subjects, those members were particularly interested in them; and this inference is a little strengthened, if the signature is the first to follow the minute. The conclusions suggested by this line of study are that there was a division of labour between members of the Committee; that it can be seen most clearly in the case of police matters, in which Robespierre and Barère are specially concerned, war and munitions, which are generally dealt with by Carnot, C. A. Prieur, and Barère, the Navy, at first Barère's department, afterwards Saint-André's, and food questions, which are in the care of Lindet. But this does not mean that there was no overlapping. Barère, for instance, ranged over several departments; and one has only to look at Robespierre's contributions to the written work of the Committee to see how unfair it would be to regard him as a specialist, interested only in a certain kind of business. Thus, out of the seventy-seven

---

[1]Carnot, on his defence, said that such signatures were a pure formality, and carried no responsibility for the measures signed; he gave instances of decrees he had signed, though disapproving of them. Aulard believes this true only in the case of unimportant matters (Aulard, *Études* 1/9).

minutes that have survived either written or signed in the first place by him,[1] forty-four deal with questions of police; but four concern the organization of the Committee, two foreign policy, eleven internal affairs, four war and munitions, one the Navy, and twelve the representatives on mission.

Indeed, like Barère, Robespierre takes part in all the work of the Committee. He makes himself responsible for administrative correspondence, for the movement of troops, for the supply of munitions, for the appointment and removal of officials, for the Paris food-supply, and for supervising plays and festivals in the capital. He deals as naturally with the site of a munitions factory, the accommodation of a provincial club, or the provision of carriages for the agents of the Committee, as with high matters of policy or police.[2]

This conclusion is borne out by the evidence of Robespierre's *Carnet*—a small notebook in which he jotted down memoranda bearing on discussions at the Committee, the Convention, or the club, between the middle of September and the end of December, 1793. The first few entries, taken as they come, deal with the following subjects: nomination of judges and jury for the Revolutionary Tribunal; reorganization of certain committees; withdrawal of commissioners from seaports; re-enactment of laws against *émigrés*; purging the civil service; providing pensions for war widows; the question of a general accused of treachery; the affair of a journalist who had attacked the government; the denunciation of an official of the Convention; an Arras man who wants a job for his son; a conspiracy reported from Strasbourg; a foreign officer deprived of his command; difficulties about recruiting for the army; military precautions against insurrection in Paris; the conduct of the siege of Lyon; denunciation of disloyal officers at Landau;

---

[1] The argument is here based only on documents subsequent to September 23, in which Robespierre's signature comes first at the foot of the minute: in the next paragraph those previous to that date are also used.

[2] v. Thompson, *L'organisation du travail du Comité de salut public*, in A.H., September-October, 1933.

the Revolutionary Calendar; affairs in the Vendée, at Bordeaux, Lyon, and Toulon; and the organization of a service of couriers for the Committee. So the notes go on, sometimes expanding into statements of policy, sometimes contracting into meagre and almost illegible jottings, or lists of names; but always showing the same wide contact with all sides of government activity. 'Robespierre not only interests himself', writes Mathiez, 'in matters of general policy, in the need of reviving public spirit, in the outwitting or suppression of conspiracy; he extends his vigilance over every branch of the administration—diplomacy and the army as much as the civil services, provisionment as well as justice, men as well as things. His wide and clear view embraces the whole battlefield of the Revolution, both front and rear, both at home and abroad'.

Mathiez goes further. 'The Robespierre of these notes', he says, 'really looks like a Prime Minister (*chef de gouvernement*). It is he who regulates the activity of the Committee, who arranges for the orderly treatment of the questions submitted to it, who provides it with a plan of work—who, in a word, organizes the new central power'.[1] But of this, it can only be said, there is no evidence, either in the *Carnet*, or in the proceedings of the Committee. Much, perhaps most, of the work of the Committee was done in the little rooms where each member dealt with the correspondence, conducted the interviews, and drafted the measures that concerned his own department. When they met together, to submit departmental questions or proposals to common discussion, they did so (as Barère says) informally, under no regular chairmanship, and with no fixed rules of procedure.[2] If Robespierre's prestige, or his comparative freedom from routine work, gave him any special influence over the policy of the government, it fell far short of that exercised (with however little constitutional recognition) by a Prime Minister, or a *Président du Conseil*.

[1] *Robespierre Terroriste*, 77.
[2] e.g. A study of the signatures attached to the Minutes suggests that most of them were supplied by the members who happened to be available at the moment.

VI

An important page of Robespierre's *Carnet*, written, apparently, in November, 1793, contains the following memorandum: 'Four essential points of government: (1) Food and provisionment, (2) War, (3) Public opinion and Conspiracies, (4) Diplomacy'. If 'Government' itself be added, Robespierre's first three months' work on the Committee of Public Safety falls under five heads.

First, what was his part in the organization of the government? In the Assembly, on August 1, Danton had proposed the plan which was to come into force eight months later, when the Council of Ministers became little more than a Civil Service working under the Committee; and Robespierre opposed it. Perhaps he scented an attempt to make the new committee unpopular, by giving it too much power; perhaps he wanted more time, in which to consider the best procedure; perhaps, as he suggested at the Jacobins on August 11, it was because he distrusted his colleagues on the Committee, and looked to the Convention and the people to save the country.[1]

A month later (August 29) Billaud-Varenne, fresh from the northern front, complained that the military decrees of the Convention were not being carried out, and proposed the appointment of a special committee to see that the Ministers did this part of their work properly. This disguised attack upon the Committee of Public Safety, made, at a moment when Robespierre was presiding over the Convention, by representatives of the Hébertist party, evidently had some weight of public opinion behind it; for though Robespierre rebuked Billaud in the House, he agreed, a week later, to add him to the Committee, along with Collot d'Herbois, another representative of the Left.

Now that the Committee had absorbed its critics, and established, by the resolutions of September 23, a method of work, Robespierre seems to have become more hopeful; and when, on September 25, a fresh attack was launched by

[1]Mathiez, (359) points out that he had just (August 9) failed to carry the impeachment of Reubell and Merlin through the Committee.

the parliamentary friends of certain cashiered generals, he intervened, deprecating such attempts to paralyse the government. After saying that he spoke as one who honoured and esteemed his colleagues on the Committee—'and you know', he added, 'that I am not prodigal in such sentiments'—he went on to describe the immense responsibilities they had to bear, and to defend their military policy. How could they do their work if they were attacked from behind? How could the Convention itself govern the country, if the Committee were discredited? And he ended by warning those who were now the accusers that they might come to find themselves accused. 'There are still some snakes in the grass', he said—but he used the word 'marsh' (*marais*), the nick-name for the Centre in the Convention—'which have not been scotched'; and in a second speech he turned upon the Douai lawyer Briez, whom it had been proposed to add to the Committee, and said that he was not fit to belong to it: instead of coming home to report the surrender of Valenciennes, he ought to have died at his post, as he (Robespierre) would have done. Members of the Committee must be above suspicion. 'I am never satisfied', he declared, with revolutionary egotism, 'unless I feel in my heart the determination to defend to the death the people's cause in all its grandeur and sublimity; unless I despise all tyrants, and every rascal who takes their side'.

It was not always easy to regulate or to define the relations between the Committee of Public Safety and other administrative bodies. In particular, the Committee of General Security was largely composed of friends of Danton, who took little pains to hide their jealousy of the more powerful committee, or to avoid trespassing upon its jurisdiction. Sometimes, as Robespierre complained at the club on August 25, both committees were trying to arrest the same person; sometimes one released a man whom the other had put in prison: but his proposals for reducing the numbers of the junior committee, and delimiting its functions, could not be carried. A little later (September 8) he was prepared to abolish it altogether. The controversy was closed (September 13) by a decree of the Convention, which ordered that in future the members of the Committee of General Security should be nominated by that of Public Safety; but the jealousy continued, and became, ten months later, a principal cause of the fall of Robespierre's party.

A note in Robespierre's *Carnet*, apparently dating from the middle of October, suggests various improvements in the 'Organization of the Committee': 'To have fixed times every day for receiving reports from the Ministers, the police, the Commandant (of the National Guard), and the Public Prosecutor, or one of the Presidents of the Criminal Tribunal. Not to admit any foreigner to the Committee, but to send them to the Ministers, or to nominate a commissioner or a secretary to interview them. To announce to the Assembly the new organization of the Committee'. Several resolutions on these lines were, in fact, adopted by the Committee on October 22—it is only surprising that they should have waited so long—and the minutes embodying them still survive, drafted and signed by Robespierre.

The casual methods of the Committee made it difficult to secure the secrecy necessary for its work. A note in the *Carnet*, apparently on October 16, speaks of 'an infamous violation of the secrets of the committee', and calls for the expulsion of 'the traitor in your midst': this was perhaps the first breath of the suspicion that, six months later, destroyed Hérault de Séchelles.[1]

In view of this evidence, it may fairly be asserted that, by the end of October, 1793, the Committee had established an effective policy and procedure, and had defeated all attempts to deprive it of power; so that there was now good prospect that the 'provisional' government would become permanent, at least 'for the duration of the war'. Nor can there be any doubt that, whatever may have been Robespierre's private feelings about his colleagues, this was his policy. He defends it in the Convention, he expands it at the Jacobins, he formulates it in schemes of work for the Committee. Yet there are already certain signs of the internal differences

[1] v. Mathiez, *Conspiration*, 158 f.

which were to prove fatal to the government in the following year—Robespierre's distrust of some members of his
own committee, his attacks on the Committee of General
Security, and his threat against the Centre of the Convention.

VII

In his *Carnet*, under the heading of 'War', Robespierre
specifies 'the manufacture of arms and ammunition, and
their distribution, plans of campaign, choice of generals,
and the employment of new troops'. In all these matters
he took an active if unprofessional interest. When he joined
the Committee, in the last week of July, 1793, the position
at the front was very bad. On the 27th the rebels in the
Vendée seized Les-Ponts-de-Cé, and threatened Angers.
On the 28th came news of the fall of Mayence, and on the
30th, of Valenciennes. In the south, which was still troubled
by the Federalist revolt, it was becoming increasingly
difficult to defend the frontiers of the Alps and the Pyrenees.
Sometimes the armies, reinforced by untrained and ill-
armed recruits, or led by aristocratic or inefficient officers,
were harassed by civilian attachés into attacks which could
only end in disaster: sometimes their operations were handi-
capped by the treachery of a disaffected province, or the
difficulties of supply. It was only gradually, and by persistence, severity, and infinite attention to detail, that the
Committee produced order out of chaos, and turned defeat
into victory. English opinion, assuming that Robespierre
was the despot his enemies averred, believed that the
French war-plans were worked out by a military committee whom he locked into a room at the Tuileries,
provided with maps, and required either to win the war or
to go to the guillotine: the ante-room was reported to be
full of aides-de-camp and couriers waiting to expedite their
orders, whilst the new semaphore system kept them in
close touch with developments at the front.[1] Robespierre's
rôle was not so dominant as this; but neither his ignorance

[1] Annual Register, 36/32.

of war nor his distaste for violence prevented his playing a large part in the military work of the Committee.

Already, in his defence of Bouchotte, the Jacobin War Minister, he had declared for the democratization of the higher command;[1] and it was he who defeated Custine's attempt to get his trial transferred from the Revolutionary Tribunal to the friendlier *comité militaire* (July 27–8). Within the next few days measures of defence follow fast— experiments with a military balloon, the strengthening of the north-east frontier, reinforcements for Corsica, daily conferences with the Military Committee, the manufacture of pikes for the infantry, and of guns for Belfort, the raising of cavalry, and the purchase of their mounts; gun- powder is ordered from Hamburg, and the construction of a *télégraphe* from Lille to Paris taken in hand; there are to be fortnightly returns of the condition of the army, and the stores; and the Paris arsenals are to be put in a state of defence. So it goes on, with increasing complexity, from day to day, and week to week.

'The only remedy', Robespierre announces one day, 'is to make a clean sweep of all the aristocrats in our armies. . . . Have no fear that we cannot replace them. Three heroes are enough to save the Republic: they are concealed in the ranks, if you want to discover them; you will find there generals really worthy of the national trust'. That was one side of his policy. Another was the speeding up of the Revolutionary Tribunal, which 'should begin the trial of those who are denounced to it within twenty-four hours of the filing of evidence'. Custine should be its first victim— Custine, who, Robespierre declares, with unpardonable exaggeration, 'has assassinated 300,000 Frenchmen in the last four years'. A third line of advance was against the 'foreign plot'. Robespierre believed himself to have evidence 'that the Cabinet of St. James, which has agents all over the Republic, and more particularly in every seaport, plays the leading part in all these plots', with the object of causing artificial famines, fresh prison-massacres, and similar troubles.[2]

[1] v. 1/71.   [2] Jac. 5/350.

On August 28 Rossignol, a typical product of Bouchotte's democratization policy, a coarse illiterate man, whose patriotism was his only claim to lead an army, was put up to make a speech in the Convention, and apostrophised from the chair by Robespierre: 'Rossignol', he said, 'we know your courage: we saw you under fire at the Bastille; and ever since that day you have marched firmly in the straight path of patriotism'. The panegyric, like Robespierre's own Presidency, was a manifesto of the new policy. The background can be filled in from a series of speeches at the Jacobins, the burden of which is the easiness of raising troops, and the difficulty of finding them patriotic generals. This attitude was, indeed, partly due to the fact that the idea of a *levée en masse* had been taken over by the Committee, rather unwillingly, from the *Enragés*,[1] and that there was some danger of the new levies being exploited by the counter-revolution. Nor could Robespierre feel quite happy about his protégé; for there followed a series of attacks upon Rossignol, which it needed all his skill to ward off.

Not long afterwards he is himself attacking Kellermann, the victor of Valmy, for the slowness of his operations at Lyon, and emphasizing, in correspondence with the national representatives attached to the armies,[2] their duty to unmask and extirpate intrigues within the higher command. That there was corruption and inefficiency among the generals cannot be doubted; but Robespierre does not seem to have considered how difficult it was for any commanding officer to do his best when criticized and attacked in public by a leading member of the government to which he was responsible. His austere patriotism left no room for *esprit de corps*.

During the Wattignies campaign Robespierre followed every development of the situation.[3] It was the touchstone

[1] It had been proposed by Lecroix on July 28, but was only adopted by the Convention, under pressure of public opinion, on August 23 (Mathiez, 360). The *Carnet* (61) speaks of a *Conspiration de la réquisition*.
[2] C.P.S. 7/377, 397.
[3] During the three months from August to October, 1793, Robespierre counter-signed only five of Carnot's military letters; on October 11, 18, and 23, he signs three of them, and in the first place, as though specially interested (*Corresp. générale de Carnot*).

of the new army system. In a speech on October 11, after making light of a set-back at Maubeuge ('a scratch on the shoulder of Hercules') he went on to prophecy the coming victory. 'To-morrow', he declared, 'will be a famous day in the calendar of the Republic. To-morrow all the forces of freedom are measuring themselves against the forces of tyranny. To-morrow will be a day of destiny for the despots of the Coalition. To-morrow a great battle is being fought upon our frontiers. We are fighting at last (he continued) under generals whom we can trust. If there is a check, if the army gives ground, it is for the whole French people to rise up and form its reserve': upon which 'loud applause broke out in all parts of the hall, and so great was the enthusiasm that every hat was raised and waved in the air, and cries of *Vive la République!* resounded on every side'. Jourdan's victory, a few days later (October 15–16), must have seemed to Robespierre a personal as well as a national triumph.

VIII

Whatever his interest in the organization of victory, it was the Home Front which remained Robespierre's chief preoccupation. In the *Carnet* he specified, under this head, three sub-divisions: censorship of the press, punishment of conspirators, and education of public opinion. 'What is needed most of all (he noted) is methodical work based on this assumption—that there are varying degrees of patriotism (*civisme ou incivisme*) in the different Departments'.[1]

'Suppress all dishonest (*imposteurs*) journalists. Circulate healthy literature'. So he had sketched his policy, apparently in October;[2] and when Prudhomme complained that he was being persecuted in the press, Robespierre proposed that he should be invited to write an article on 'the crimes of editors or journalists who are in the pay of foreign powers' (September 8). But it was easier to use political power, and public money, to support a Government press. In place of the old method of issuing occasional

[1] *Carnet*, 64. [2] *Carnet*, 69.

manifestos, like that which broadcast the *acte d'accusation* against the Girondins,[1] a regular correspondence was kept up between the Governing Committee and the representatives in the provinces; steps were taken to publish laws and official documents in Italian and German, for the enlightenment of Corsican and Alsatian patriots,[2] and it was decided to start an official journal, with the object of 'developing and spreading the principles of republican conduct and liberty, of stimulating the courage of Frenchmen against the foreign foe, of warning them against the intrigues of governments abroad, and of unmasking conspirators'. This was within a day or two of Robespierre's accession to the Committee (August 3), and it was followed a few days later by the appointment of his friends Garat and Nicolas as editor and printer of the *Feuille de Salut Public*.[3]

Another method of propaganda was soon added—the subsidization of existing journals, on condition of their supporting the government; and this was all the easier, as few of their editors could afford to refuse such a bribe. On October 9 Robespierre signed an order allotting an *émigré's* house to the printing-press of the *Anti-fédéraliste*, whose editors were his friend Payan, Fourcade, and Julien. A month later this paper, together with the *Moniteur* (now past any pretence of impartiality), the *Journal Universel*, *Père Duchesne*, and the *Journal des hommes libres*, was voted a subsidy. During the winter of 1793–4 thousands of copies of these and other publications were purchased by the government, and distributed, mainly among the troops at the front, thus securing a monopoly for the official version of events.[4]

[1] This was written and signed by Robespierre.
[2] C.P.S. 5/392.
[3] C.P.S. 5/459, 505. Aulard, *Études*, 1.
[4] The number of copies of *Père Duchesne* taken was 1,044,000, at a cost of 118,800 *livres*; of the *Journal des hommes libres*, from 2000 to 5000 (94,150 *livres*); of the *Journal Universel*, from 3000 to 5000 (58,860 *livres*); of the *Anti-fédéraliste*, 2000 (42,000 *livres*). Add, the *Journal de la Montagne*, *Rougiff*, *Le Batave*, the *Journal militaire*, and Marat's *L'ami des hommes* (up to his death); 400,000 copies of the Constitution, Rights of Man, and patriotic hymns; 58 dozen copies of Bonsel's *Entretiens du Père Gerard*; and 6000 copies of Sylvain Maréchal's *Jugement dernier des rois*—a total expenditure of 450,000 *livres* (A.R. 10/112). cp. *Vieux Cordelier* (ed. Calvet) No. 5, p. 170.

The same method was extended to the stage, which Robespierre had always regarded as a school of patriotism. On August 29 the Committee banned François de Neufchâtel's *Paméla* at the *Théâtre National*, and ordered him to submit the manuscript for their scrutiny. The play was 'cut', and put on again. But it was hardly more difficult then than it is now to evade such censorship. A few days later a Captain of Dragoons complained at the club that he had been shocked to hear reactionary sentiments on the stage; and that, when he protested, he had been arrested for a breach of the peace. Upon this, Robespierre demanded stronger measures; and the same day the theatre was closed, and the dramatist thrown into prison. Again, on December 22 a decree, drafted and signed by Robespierre, forbids the Opera to produce Bourdon's anti-clerical play entitled *Le tombeau des imposteurs*, 'or any other of a similar tendency'.[1]

Here, too, the policy of subsidies was soon tried; and Robespierre was certainly present and approving on October 8, when the Committee accepted Fauchet's scheme for the re-organization of the Opera. 'The Provisional Executive Council'—so runs this interesting document—'considering that the national entertainment called the Opera or Academy of Music is upon the point of bankruptcy; that this establishment provides a living for 1,200 *sansculotte* families; that a subsidy to it is really a loan for the good of the public; that in a free country the stage ought to be purged, and become, under government supervision, a means of public education; and that, at the same time, rich men and foreigners can be taxed for the support of the Arts; decrees that there shall be paid, out of the special funds at the disposal of the Council, a sum of 150,000 *livres*, under the head of *indemnité et secours public*, on the following conditions: (1) that the Management of the Opera shall be reconstituted, and modelled on principles of economy and patriotism, (2) that the Management shall

[1] It included a celebration of High Mass, caricaturing Catholic worship. Similar bans were placed on Maréchal's *La fête de la Raison*, and a farce called *La Sainte Omelette* (R.F. 59/278).

purchase republican works, (3) that none but patriotic plays shall be produced, (4) that the *répertoire* shall be purged, (5) that one performance every week shall be given free of charge, for and on behalf of the people, and (6) that the Management shall find employment in various subordinate posts at the Opera for the relatives of volunteers who are serving at the front'; and there is more on the same lines.

The statue of Liberty, Mirabeau had thought, should show one hand resting on a column inscribed *égalité des hommes*, and the other holding a sword between the pages of the book of the law—not young Liberty rousing a people against its oppressors, but Liberty full grown, existing by the austere execution of the laws.[1] In like manner Robespierre, now in power, interprets the principles that he laid down whilst still an irresponsible critic. Liberty may be temporarily 'veiled' (he had said) in the name of public security. There is no complete repression, not even an organized Censorship: but both in the press and on the stage counter-revolutionary propaganda is banned, whilst 'healthy literature'—that is, books or papers putting the government view of things—is encouraged and subsidized. The methods of dictatorship, like the ideals of liberty, are much the same at all times, and all the world over.

IX

The repression of rebels—the second activity on the Home Front outlined in Robespierre's *Carnet*—meant the prosecution of the civil war, and the destruction of the last elements of Girondism or Federalism in the provinces. Here it would not be enough to conquer the rebellious cities of the south—Lyon (October 9), Bordeaux (October 16), and Toulon (December 19); the countryside, too, was widely and deeply disloyal, organizing itself in various ways and degrees against the capital; Normandy and Brittany in the north-west, centred in Caen; the Garonne valley in the south-east, especially Bordeaux; the southern coastal

[1] R.F. 2/999.

districts, from Montpellier and Nîmes to Marseille; and eastwards, the Lyonnais and the Franche Compté.

As regards the towns, the presence of his brother Augustin with the army of the Alps during the summer and autumn of 1793 kept Robespierre informed of every turn in the situation at Marseille, Lyon, and Toulon. Panis, too, a member of the notorious Vigilance Committee of August, 1792, passed on advice of unexpected leniency as to the treatment of the rebels. Lyon, it was suggested, is like Caen: the common people are not ill-disposed: why not make terms with them first, and deal with the agitators afterwards?[1] Augustin put the same point in another way when he said that the hot-headed southerners were quite different from the phlegmatic northerners, and had been too easily corrupted by counter-revolutionary agitators. It would therefore be useless and dangerous to punish the people indiscriminately, or to encourage patriots to denounce one another.[2] Perhaps, as Couthon suggested, the people of that part of France were 'temperamentally slow-witted', and 'the fogs of the Rhône and Saône fuddled their brains'.[3] It was no doubt this consensus of opinion in favour of discrimination between leaders and led which, coinciding with his own inclination to believe the best of the common people, inclined Robespierre towards mercy; so that, whilst he urged Ysabeau and Tallien to 'punish the traitors and royalists promptly and severely',[4] he believed that the *sansculottes* of Bordeaux had 'remained faithful to the unity of the Republic', and showed his disapproval of the terrorist policy of Fouché at Lyon, and Carrier at Nantes.

Counter-revolution, in any case, could not be ended by the punishment of a few large towns. It was a widespread disease, and needed preventives as well as antidotes. There must be doctors and remedies everywhere. 'It will be necessary', notes Robespierre, apparently in November, 'to

---

[1]Corresp. 180 (August 6). The suggestion came from a letter to Danton by a third party, unnamed.
[2]Corresp. 190.   [3]Pap. inéd. 1/361.
[4]Corresp. 219 (P.S. in Robespierre's own hand).

despatch all over the Republic a small number of strong commissioners, armed with sound instructions, and above all with good principles, in order to restore public opinion to unity and republicanism: this is the only way to bring the Revolution to an end in the interests of the people.[1] It will be the special business of these commissioners to discover and make a list of the men who are fit to serve the cause of freedom'. On another page he adds: 'There should be 120 commissioners—two for each army, and two for each two Departments. It will be best', he goes on, with his usual caution, 'to put one strong man along with another whose patriotism is less assured; to reappoint or change them all pretty frequently; to give them all general instructions; and to keep up an active correspondence with them, on a single plan, but adapted to the needs of the different districts'.[2] The records of the Committee include many references to the activities of these commissioners, the 'national agents,' who, together with the representatives on mission, formed a civilian army of inspectors keeping the government informed as to every branch of the administration, and every member of the official personnel. If the network of correspondence between the two Committees (for that of General Security was also concerned) and the generals, Presidents, judges, agents, and commissioners all over the country had been as complete in fact as it was in theory, it would have provided a system of centralized control more than Napoleonic in its completeness.

X

The almost inevitable background of such a system was a method of denunciation, a penal code, and a summary tribunal; for it is certain that the policy of intimidation called the Terror was directed quite as much against the agents of the government as against its enemies, and was intended to enforce those republican virtues which were not so innate in patriots as, on Rousseauist principles, they

[1]Robespierre, then, regarded the Terror as transitional. What terrorist does not?
[2]*Carnet*, 72.

should have been. In this part of the Committee's work, there can be no question, Robespierre was pre-eminent. 'To purge the revolutionary committees', he notes, 'we must have a list of all their members, with their names, social position, and addresses . . . In particular, we must know about the President and Secretary of every committee. . . . Secondly, we must make a revised list of counter-revolutionary agitators in each district, . . . and take proceedings against them all. Thirdly, we must track down all deputies who are at the head of the conspiracy, and get hold of them at all costs; all, without exception, must be promptly punished. Finally, we must have a circumstantial list of all the prisoners, and decree that those who have given asylum to conspirators or to outlaws shall suffer the same penalties as they do'.[1] These were not idle threats: every page of the records shows with what energy and ruthlessness disciplinary measures were carried out.

Take some typical instances, between August and October, 1793, in which Robespierre was specially involved. Carra, editor of the *Annales patriotiques*, whose republican professions alternated with relapses into royalism, found himself denounced (August 2) for intriguing with Dumouriez, and proposing to offer the throne of Louis XVI to the Duke of York. His attempts to defend himself were silenced by Danton from the chair, Robespierre overwhelmed him with abuse, and a decree was carried ordering him for trial. Thibault, 'constitutional' bishop and representative of the Cantal, was attacked (August 5), for a protest he had made against the arrest of certain commissioners; it was of no avail that he had been a good Robespierrist at the time of the August revolution, and the king's trial; he is now an agent of a 'criminal faction' engaged in royalist propaganda, and must answer for it, like the rest. A few days later (August 8) Simonne Evrard, the 'widow' of Marat, appears at the bar of the Convention, and delivers a harangue, in a style suspiciously like that of Robespierre, denouncing the *Enragé* leaders, Roux and Leclercq, for

[1] *Carnet*, 72.

carrying on a journal under the name of *L'Ami du peuple*. Robespierre proposes the printing of this speech, and an inquiry into the conduct of the two men. A fortnight later Roux was in prison. A deputation from the *Société des femmes révolutionnaires* is snubbed by Robespierre (September 15) for asking for the release of a prisoner. Its reply, insufficiently polite, is reported to the Jacobins. Robespierre notes laconically in his *Carnet*: *Dissolution des f.r.r.* (*femmes républicaines révolutionnaires*). A deputation from the Departmental Directory of Seine et l'Oise, complaining of the punishment of three of its members, is sent away with a warning against federalism (September 17). A report from Julien de Toulouse on the situation in the south (October 14) is denounced by Robespierre, in a speech 'burning with energy and patriotism', because it criticizes the government policy at Lyon. 'I see men from the bosom of the Mountain', he cries, 'assassinating the memory of the heroes of liberty. . . . Their memory must be avenged. Either these monsters must be unmasked and exterminated, or I must perish'. The dilemma was not obvious; but the speech was greeted with 'prolonged and universal applause'. When, however, the Hébertist Brichet moved for Julien's arrest, Robespierre, always resentful of any attempt to improve upon (*renchérir*) the government policy, cooled down, and was content with the rejection of Julien's report.

The corollary drawn from the punishment of backsliders was the approval of tried patriots. Thus when Hanriot, the Jacobin commandant of the National Guard, complained of accusations against his patriotism (September 11), Danton declared that his conduct on June 2 had 'saved 30,000 lives; his eyes (he said) had blazed like gunpowder; and anyone who saw him that day must know that he is the soul of freedom'. 'History', added Robespierre, 'will sanctify the glorious days in which he served liberty and his country'. Again, D'Aubigny, who had once suffered at the hands of the Rolandists, and had lately been given an appointment in the Ministry of War, was acquitted of a charge of theft brought against him by Bourdon de l'Oise.

Robespierre, with an appeal from D'Aubigny in his pocket, came to the Assembly, and demanded his public rehabilitation (September 30).[1]

Another corollary followed—the innocence of the people. The main concern of the government was to discipline its own agents—administrative officials and officers of the army. It was Robespierre's profound faith that, whilst corruption and counter-revolution had their home in the governing classes, the mass of the common people were sound patriots. Thus when, on August 7, Royer read to the club an address from 'the emissaries of all sections of the people gathered for the great meeting of Frenchmen in Paris on August 10', Robespierre seized the opportunity to point the moral. This address, he said, gave the lie for the fourth time to the hopes of their enemies. The people stood firm in July, 1789, in August, 1792, in June, 1793; and they stand firm to-day. To another deputation (August 28), headed by an old man of eighty-three, who said that it was the proudest and happiest day of his life, Robespierre declared that 'this touching spectacle' ought to be 'proclaimed in the face of all Europe as an example of liberty, equality, and virtue', and that, when they heard of it, 'oppressed patriots would dry their tears'. It was on occasions such as these that Robespierre, playing almost automatically, by now, the rôle of leader of the people, recaptured some of the thrill of his earlier performances, and felt again the mystic faith that had inspired him when he marched through the Paris streets in July, 1789. There is no reason to suppose that his cold and fastidious nature ever liked the touch or smell of the crowd. But so far as reason, imagination, and sentiment could take him, he went whole-heartedly; and he thus gained more insight into the character of the *sansculottes*, if not more social intimacy with them, than most of his class.

XI

It was this knowledge which saved him from an error which was beginning to lose the government much of its

[1]Corresp. 207.

popular support. He was, indeed, as bitter as any of his colleagues against the 'refractory' priests; and when the Assembly debated (July 24) whether to imprison them in France, or to exile them either to Italy, which Danton described as 'the home of fanaticism', or to South America, where Basire thought they would get on well with the 'savage hordes' of Guiana, he voted for the latter country. But the Paris Commune, and certain government agents up and down the country, were pursuing a policy of repression, not merely against those priests who had refused to take the civil oath, or who were suspected of counter-revolution, but also against Catholic beliefs and practices as such. There was Fauré, for instance, a representative on mission at Nancy, who reported that he had composed a *Hymne sur les ci-devant Saints*, and had had it sung, 'with excellent effect', to the tune of the *Marseillaise*.[1] In spite of one or two indiscretions, the Convention as such had never given its approval to active and provocative anti-clericalism. This, indeed, was particularly offensive to the Arras tradition in Robespierre's mind; and he clearly foresaw that it would alienate the Catholic instincts of the peasantry, who might join in the plundering of a church, or in a masquerade of the Mass, but would dislike and despise those who had led them into it. Accordingly he missed no opportunity of protesting against an intolerance which he found both impolitic and distasteful. It was during his Presidency of the Convention (August 25) that a deputation in favour of compulsory education put up a small child to ask that, 'instead of preaching to them in the name of the so-called Deity, their teachers should instruct them in the principles of equality, the Rights of Man, and the Constitution'. Infant atheism was not to the taste of the Assembly, which showed its disapproval by 'a movement of indignation'. Again, André Dumont, whilst on a mission in the Somme, wrote to the Committee, announcing with some complacency the closing of churches, and the burning of images: at Boulogne, he announced, a 'black Virgin', famous for its

[1]C.P.S. 8/545, 609.

miraculous powers, had been successfully reduced to ashes, amidst cries of *Vive la Montagne*.'[1] He received in reply (October 27) a letter which Robespierre signed, and which certainly expressed his views. 'It appears to us', said the Committee, 'that during your recent activities you have shown too much violence towards the objects of Catholic worship. Part of France, especially in the south, is still fanatically religious. One must be on one's guard against giving the dishonest counter-revolutionists, who are trying to kindle civil war, any possible justification for their slanders against us. We must not afford them an opportunity for saying that we are violating liberty of worship, and attacking religion itself. It is right to punish seditious or unpatriotic priests: it is wrong to proscribe priests as such'.[2] The warning was disregarded, an insurrection led by the priests broke out at Amiens, and Robespierre noted in his *Carnet* that it would be necessary to replace Dumont by 'a wise and patriotic representative'.[3] It may be added, as an instance of toleration, that, rather than offend religious scruples, the committee gave instructions that Anabaptists, who had a conscientious objection to bearing arms, should be employed as navvies or drivers, or might even purchase complete exemption from military service.[4]

XII

The chief anxiety of the Committee, with respect to the population as a whole, lay in the perennial problem of the food supply. In Robespierre's notebook, *Subsistances et approvisionnmens* is the first of the 4 *points essentiels du gouvernement*; and it is divided into the two heads of Home Production—*Moiens de connoître conserver et répartir celles qui sont dans l'intérieur*, and Foreign Imports—*à en faire venir de l'extérieur*. The early meetings of the Committee, before the

[1]B. and R. 31/146.
[2]C.P.S. 8/58. In his *Compte Rendu*, four years later, Dumont had the impudence to publish the only complimentary sentence of this letter, and to suggest that the Committee had approved of his policy (R.F. 27/241).
[3]*Carnet*, 76.   [4]C.P.S. 6/24.

harvest of 1793, were largely occupied with this question; and Robespierre's interest in it is shown by the number of decrees which he signed on the subject, making grants for the provisionment of Paris,[1] or arrangements for the purchase of grain. It was not long before the Convention itself had to deal with the discontent caused by food-shortage and food-prices. A petition from the Paris salt-merchants (July 31) was, on Robespierre's suggestion, referred to the Committee. During his Presidency (August 26) a deputation from Vincennes complained of lack of bread, and displayed a black loaf, which, they declared, was all they could get. Robespierre replied that 'aristocracy, avarice, and tyranny' were plotting together to starve the people, but that they must trust the Convention—poor comfort, perhaps, but the language with which deputations have to be content all the world over. A few days later (September 4) Chaumette, *procureur* of the Commune, made a speech at the bar of the House, warning the deputies that the city was in a state of agitation owing to food-shortage and other troubles; and a petition was presented by a large body of citizens. 'The Convention', Robespierre replied, 'is deeply concerned for the miseries of the people. It will consider your demands'. But what could be done, beyond what the Committee was already doing?

That Robespierre was specially active in this matter is further suggested by two letters which have survived among his correspondence. One is from a firm of American merchants, Gregory and Livingstone (*Grégorie et Levingston*) dated October 25. They have already submitted to the Committee (they say) an offer to supply grain at a certain price, but have had no reply. Hearing that Robespierre 'shows great activity in dealing with everything that comes before him', they first call upon him, and then (failing to find him) write, enclosing a copy of their offer.[2] The other is from one Flachet, dated November 24, offering to supply the Republic with five million *quintaux* of grain.

[1]This question was dealt with eleven times between August 7 and November 2.
[2]Corresp. 234.

Secrecy, he says, is so important in such an affair that he can only approach one member of the Committee, and has chosen Robespierre as 'a recognized patriot'.[1]

If activity and patriotism could have solved the food problem, all might have been well; but something more was needed. The breakdown of the attempts to fix food prices, by the *Maximum* laws of May 4, August 25, and September 11; the failure of Garin, though he had once been a baker himself, to control the bread-supply of Paris; the impracticability of the scheme for national grain-depots (*greniers d'abondance*); the impossibility of requisitioning enough corn to feed both the civilian population and the army; and the unpopularity of such expedients as public bakeries, and food cards; brought about fresh agitations among the Paris poor, led at first by Roux and Leclerq, and soon taken up, partly from political ambition, and partly in order to increase the circulation of his paper, by Hébert, the editor of *Père Duchesne*. The 'labour demonstration' of September 4 showed that economic grievances were turning into an attack on the government; and Robespierre, who had no special quarrel with either Hébertists or *Enragés* on social or economic grounds, was forced to envisage them as political rivals, and to suspect their alliance with the royalist, the foreigner, and the counter-revolutionary. The result was that, whilst economic necessity drove him on, *faute de mieux*, into a more thorough and systematic scheme of price-fixing—the *maximum général* of September 29— political necessity required that it should be backed by force, and that the guillotine should be used against anyone who exploited the crisis to discredit and overthrow the committee.[2]

XIII

Thus every road of the Committee's activities seemed to lead to the same place—the site of a Revolutionary

---

[1] Corresp. 270.
[2] cp. Mathiez, *La Vie Chère*, Pt. II, Ch. 8–9, Pt. II, Ch. 1. The fourth of Robespierre's divisions of Government—diplomacy—is dealt with below, 2/112 f.

Tribunal and of a guillotine. Where the pen of the law ended its work, the sword of the law (*le glaive de la loi*) took it up; and there might have been inscribed on its blade, with as much truth as on the cannon of the old regime, *ratio ultima regum*—'the final argument of our rulers'. The priest, the spy, the profiteer, the half-hearted general, the food-hoarder, the dishonest contractor, the political agitator, or the *ci-devant* noble in correspondence with the enemy, soon found, as Mirabeau had said, that it was only a step from the Capitol to the Tarpeian Rock. Intimidation did not end counter-revolution; the constant and increasing stream of convictions by the tribunal was to show, not merely how wide-spread the disease was, but also how futile was the remedy. But it kept active disloyalty within limits, and persuaded a number of lazy and dishonest officials into some show of disinterested energy.

Robespierre's concern for the efficient working of this system is evident enough in the pages of his *Carnet*. 'The Revolutionary Tribunal is not working well', he notes, perhaps early in October. About a month later there are two entries, 'Organization of the Revolutionary Tribunal', and 'Revocation of the decree setting up Revolutionary Tribunals everywhere': he approved of the policy of centralizing the trial of all political offences in Paris, where procedure and penalties could be standardized, and the Committee could keep in close touch with this part of its work. Again, late in December, 'The Revolutionary Tribunal must be supervised, and its organization re-formed'.

There was, indeed, good reason for Robespierre to be dissatisfied with the Tribunal. Its record during the early months of its career was not reassuring to a Jacobin. It had, no doubt, acquitted Marat; but it had also dismissed charges against a number of generals. In the La Rouerie trial it had acquitted more than half the accused men. Montané, the President of the court, had, it was said, shown favour to Charlotte Corday, and to the *assassins* of Léonard Bourdon. Custine's trial had proved that the judges were liable to be swayed by public opinion in favour of a popular general. It was essential that the Tribunal should be reorganized, in the sense of being brought under the direct control of the Committee, with a view to the trial of the Queen, and of the Girondist leaders, which would be undertaken as soon as the government felt confident enough for such a gesture. An important instalment of this plan was carried through early in September, when the court was divided into four sections, sitting concurrently, and all judges and jurors were appointed by the two Government Committees. Yet, as is evident from Robespierre's notes, this was not enough; and he remained dissatisfied until the Law of Suspects (September 17), the Police Law (April, 15–18, 1794), and the Law of the 22nd Prairial (June 10), swept away the last obstacles to a Jacobin purge.

By the middle of October everything seemed propitious for the trial of the Queen, and of the Girondins. In that of the Queen, Robespierre does not seem to have taken any special interest. It was a concession to popular feeling, and an act of national rather than Jacobin vengeance. There is on record only his angry protest against the stupidity of Hébert's charges—charges made, not against the queen, but against the mother; and it was a protest prompted, not by any generous feelings, but by considerations of party policy. 'That idiot Hébert!' he is reported to have said, 'It's not enough that she should be a Messalina; he must make her an Agrippina', and turn public sympathy to her side.

The trial of the Girondins, on the other hand, concerned Robespierre closely: it had become essential to his policy ever since the events of June, and the federalist revolts in the provinces. Thus, when Amar introduced into the House his Report on the *Brissotins* (October 3), he opposed a vote by *appel nominal*, hoping to carry the day by non-party acclamation. On the other hand, not from pity, but from caution—to make the condemnation of the leaders more sure, whilst retaining a hold over the rank and file of the party—he prevented the extension of the proscription to the seventy-three signatories of the protest against the proceedings of June 2.[1]

When the trial came on (October 24), it soon developed into a public debate, which showed some signs of going in favour of the defendants. Finally, steps had to be taken to secure a conviction which was essential for the continued existence of the government. On October 29 Osselin, on behalf of the Jacobins, proposed a decree to closure the trial. Robespierre called it 'too vague', and suggested an alternative. 'Here is one', he said, 'which reconciles the interests of the accused men with the safety of the country. I propose to enact that after three days' hearing the President of the court shall ask the jury whether they have enough evidence to satisfy them (*si leur conscience est assez éclairée*): if they say, No, the trial is to proceed until they are in a position to bring in a verdict'. The proposal was carried. At first the jury demurred; but the same evening they agreed to a unanimous verdict of 'guilty'; and the next day the Girondins were dead.

It was at this time that a patriot general, writing to the Minister of War, headed his letter with the invocation of an unusual but seasonable Trinity of republican deities; *Liberté, Egalité, Guillotine.*[2]

[1] His correspondence during the succeeding months is full of appeals from these men (Corresp. 213, 228, 229, 232).
[2] R.F. 25/273.

CHAPTER XIV

THE INTERPRETER (NOVEMBER, 1793–FEBRUARY, 1794)

I

IN Robespierre's life, as in the course of the Revolution, long periods of conflict are separated by short interludes of recuperation. One such was in October, 1791, at the end of the Constituent Assembly. Here, at the end of October, 1793, is another. Two years ago, Robespierre had been hoping to retire into private life, but was prevented by the need of combating the war policy of the *Brissotins*. August, 1792, had given no such breathing-space, because it had been followed almost at once by the Jacobin-Girondin contest in the Convention. June, 1793, had begun the destruction of the Gironde, and the establishment of a Jacobin dictatorship. Only now, after five months' struggle, had this purpose been achieved. The Girondist leaders executed, and the queen dead, there was no fixed centre for conspiracy, at home or abroad. Wattignies had removed the immediate danger on the frontiers: at Bordeaux, Lyon, and Marseille civil rebellion had been crushed, though not yet punished. The Committee of Public Safety, by energy, subtlety, and intimidation, had made itself necessary to the country. The Jacobin party, claiming a monopoly of patriotism, had set up a government which, whatever its failure to solve the deeper problems raised by the Revolution, at least secured an unity of administration and an output of national energy such as France had never known before. It was possible, for the first time since the autumn of 1791, to look round, and to take stock of the situation.

The pause is clearly marked in Robespierre. From the beginning of November, 1793, there is a notable falling off in the number of his speeches in the Assembly, and at the club. He reserves himself, and concentrates his energy, for a fresh series of detached discourses, such as he has not had time to think out, or to compose, during the agitations of the last two years, and the strain of editorship. The intervals between these great speeches are, no doubt, filled with the routine of committee work, which grows no lighter with the lapse of time. But, for a while, the feeling of personal strain and friction is happily gone; and Robespierre has an opportunity to show what use he can make of freedom and power.

II

One of the first results of his new position was a vast increase in his correspondence. Of the 468 letters so far collected, 179 belong to the first four years of the Revolution, and 289 to the last twelve months, when Robespierre was a member of the Committee. Few of these are written by himself—it soon became unsafe to keep them; and not many of those he received are of great personal interest. But, such as they are, they give the best evidence for the daily background of his thoughts and acts.

From Amiens comes a note from Joseph Lebon, recommending for promotion, with characteristic coarseness, Hulin, one of the 'heroes of the Bastille'.[1] The secretary of the Paris Commune sends a medal in commemoration of August 10, as 'an act of homage to the Incorruptible Robespierre'.[2] An officer asks for re-employment in the army, addressing him as 'Founder of the Republic, who coverest its cradle with the aegis of thine eloquence'.[3] L. A. Félix, a writer on literary and political subjects, has arrived at Paris, after four years spent in a 'philosophical hermitage' at the foot of the Alps. He has admired Robespierre from a distance, and wants to make his closer acquaintance.[4] An ex-soldier, now a corporal of the National Guard, sends a donation towards the expenses of the war.[5] André Dumont writes to introduce a person (unnamed) with a plan (not des-

[1]Corresp. 181.　　　　　　　　　　　　[2]Corresp. 182.
[3]Corresp. 185.　　　　　　　　　　　　[4]Corresp. 186.
[5]Tuetey, 9/1509.

cribed) which he believes 'is likely to be of great value to the country'.[1] The deputy Beffroy is anxious to impress on Robespierre his fears about royalism in the army.[2] A series of letters from Westermann supplies information as to the progress of operations in the west, and tries to explain away his failure by the quarrels of the generals, and the incompetence of Rossignol.[3] There is corroboration of this view in an unsolicited and perhaps 'inspired' complaint from Sandoz, another of the western commanders[4]; and not long afterwards it was thought advisable to recall Robespierre's protégé. If Rossignol was one of the failures of the new system, Hoche was one of its greatest successes. He was, it is true, suffering at this time from a feeling that he had been passed over for promotion; but a letter to Robespierre recalling his services at the time of Dumouriez's treachery, and more recently at Dunkirk, resulted in his appointment a month later to the command of the army of the Moselle.[5] There follow two letters from Cusset, a a deputy who, despite a keen scent for conspiracies, had to be recalled from the front on charges of drunkenness and incompetence.[6] Payan, one of the editors of the *Anti-fédéraliste*, asks that his reporter may be admitted to a debate in the Convention, and have access to the correspondence of the Committee.[7] Aigoin, an old correspondent, writes from Toulouse introducing the bearers of a resolution on monetary policy.[8] The Lyon affair accounts for two letters—one from Simond, denouncing Dubois-Crancé, and another from Pressavin, a Lyon surgeon, protesting against Robespierre's recent denunciation of him at the Jacobins.[9] Delalande, writing on the same day, is an informer, who has discovered that the mistress of Perrochel, a federalist leader in Calvados, is in hiding in Paris, and in secret communication with the rebels.[10]

These are private letters. Almost in the same class come a

[1]Corresp. 193.
[2]Corresp. 194; R.F. 22/86.
[3]Corresp. 196, 198, 202.
[4]Corresp. 211.
[5]Corresp. 203; B. and R. 27/75.
[6]Corresp. 205, 212.
[7]Corresp. 206.
[8]Corresp. 210.
[9]Corresp. 216, 225.
[10]Corresp. 226.

few reports from representatives on mission, addressed to Robespierre personally, but intended for communication to the Committee. This was a not unusual practice, when the writer had any special policy or point of view which he thought Robespierre might be willing to support. Thus Augustin writes—naturally enough, to his brother—urging the need of differential treatment of counter-revolutionists in the Midi;[1] Jullien, in a series of letters, describes the steps he has taken to forward Jacobinism in Normandy and Brittany, and makes interesting suggestions as to the best methods of propaganda;[2] and Lebas, with or without his colleague Saint-Just, reports on measures to be taken with regard to Strasbourg, and the army of the Rhine.[3]

III

One of these missions—that of Augustin to the army of Italy—has special importance for a biographer of Robespierre. Writing to Buissart on July 20, he mentions his appointment, and adds, egotistically enough, 'It is a difficult mission: I have accepted it for the good of the country, for I believe that I shall be able to do her good service, if only by destroying the slanders with which my good name has been assailed'. With him went Ricord, deputy for Var, and—a cause of fresh 'slanders' against Augustin—Ricord's wife. It seems to have occurred to him, as a happy solution of the domestic difficulties of the rue Saint-Honoré, that his sister Charlotte might complete the party; and so it was arranged. But the experiment was not a success. The two women quarrelled irretrievably. Mme Ricord, says Charlotte, was 'the most frivolous and thoughtless woman in the world' and fell out with her because she found her 'a severe and uncompromising witness'. Witness of what? Of nothing less, if one is to believe Barras—and Charlotte is too modest to write plainly—than a liaison between Augustin and Mme Ricord.[4] When protests would not avail, that

[1] Corresp. 190. [2] Corresp. 199, 200, 201, 209, 231, 235.
[3] Corresp. 237, 254.
[4] Barras adds that Augustin had as a rival in Mme Ricord's favours a young artillery officer named Buonaparte.

416

wicked woman (Charlotte says) forged a letter from Augustin, ordering his sister back to Paris under a charge of 'aristocracy', and so secured a free field for the intrigue. However this may be, Charlotte returned to Paris some weeks ahead of her brother; and when he too arrived, relations between the Robespierres, the Ricords, and the Duplays became so strained that, to avoid public scandal, it became necessary to arrange for Charlotte's return to Arras. For this purpose, use was made of Joseph Lebon. Summoned from Cambrai on May 14, 1794, and arriving in Paris on the 17th, he set off again with Charlotte, and reached Arras, by Cambrai, the next day.[1] It was hardly tactful to employ such a man as Lebon; but it was absurd to suppose, as Guffroy pretended to, that there was any intention of having her imprisoned, let alone executed, by the Arras tribunal. That Charlotte resented her exile is shown by the fact that, after a visit to Lille, she reappeared in Paris, a month later, under the escort of Guyot, an old enemy of Lebon. After a heated interview with Augustin, which drove him into temporary refuge with the Ricords, she wrote, probably with the help of Guffroy, a rather hysterical letter complaining of his attitude towards her, and saying that she was going to live away from her brothers in an obscure part of the city, where her presence would no longer be an embarrassment to them.[2] She was still living in this retirement at Thermidor.[3] The quarrel with her brothers doubtless saved her life.

Maximilien's own part in this affair remains obscure: but it was his reputation that was threatened both by his brother's misconduct and by his sister's lack of self-control; and it must have been with his consent that Charlotte was sent back to Arras, and by his choice that her escort was his friend Lebon. He was the more nervous about scandal at this moment, as other attacks were being made upon

---

[1]Darthé to Lebas, May 19 (Pap. inéd. 1/149).
[2]Fleischmann in A.R. 3/321: Corresp. 423, 454. Confronted with her letter in later years, when Courtois was using it to damage Maximilien's reputation, Charlotte denied that she had written it; but the MS. remains to refute her.
[3]But she was at Arras again in the spring of 1795 (Le Blond, 19).

his *ménage*. Guffroy had spread a story against the virtue of Elizabeth Duplay; Mme Duplay was accused of being a spiteful gossip; and a malicious note had appeared in one of the papers calling the attention of the police to the fact that, though *maîtrises* had been abolished by law, Maurice Duplay still described himself, on a signboard outside his premises, as *Maître Menuisier*.[1]

IV

The official correspondence of the Committee, during November and December, 1793, adds something to previous evidence as to Robespierre's contributions to government policy. When the patriots at Marseille are urged (November 4) 'to prevent aristocracy, even under the mask of Popular Societies, from usurping the authority of the nation, and trying to resuscitate federalism', and when they are told to 'distrust the appearances of patriotism under which the counter-revolutionists and intriguers of the south so cleverly disguise their criminal plots', it is hardly possible to mistake Robespierre's touch. When Carnot's instructions for the Rhine campaign are sent to Saint-Just and Lebas (November 2), the representatives attached to that front, they are accompanied by a covering letter from Robespierre, which illustrates very well his attitude towards the military side of the committee's work. 'I have not forgotten for a moment', he writes, 'either the Rhine army or the two commissioners. I have pressed for all the necessary measures, and I have reason to believe that nothing has been neglected. The Committee has adopted a plan which seems to me very well conceived, and informed by the same idea as that which has succeeded so well with the northern army. The plan is a bigger and a bolder one than any mere defence of different sections of the front by detached bodies of troops: it is a wiser scheme, and the only one likely to achieve our ends. Carnot, who presented the idea to us, has already written to you to explain the details. In a few days' time we shall be sending him to explain our ideas to you more

[1] *Le Batave*, September 2, 1793 (A.R. 8/429).

clearly, if you have not entirely grasped them. We count greatly upon the energy you have infused into the army, and upon your personal activity. For my own part, I have no doubt of success, if you are careful to carry out our plan'. Is there a spice of patronage here, in the way in which a plan, evidently drawn up by Carnot, becomes 'our idea', 'our plan', and 'we' are prepared to 'send' him to explain it? Or was this merely the routine of a committee, all of whose members shared a common responsibility? Robespierre's hand may be traced again in a circular to the Popular Societies (November 13) instructing them to draw up lists of patriotic citizens worthy of public office, excluding any persons who are 'cold, egotistical, or indifferent to the republican revolution'; for such men 'would have been condemned to death by the law of Athens: in our country they are condemned to political death by public opinion'. And it was doubtless Robespierre's influence which obtained the Jacobin club a grant of 100,000 *livres* (November 15), 'in order to meet its various needs, and to put it in a better position to serve the Republic, and the progress of the Revolution'.

Robespierre's special interest in religious policy is further illustrated by another important letter to the Popular Societies, the minute of which exists, written and signed by himself. 'There has been an outbreak of religious troubles (he says): it is your business to minimize their effects—you Popular Societies, the fires in which public opinion is forged, strengthened, and purified. You have done everything for the fatherland: it expects everything of you. It calls you now to be, as it were, the teachers of a new system of education. . . . The more violent the death-struggles of fanaticism, the more careful should we be in our treatment of it. We must not give it fresh weapons, by using force instead of education. Lay this lesson to heart: conscience cannot be dictated to (*on ne commande pas aux consciences*). Some people are superstitious in good faith, partly because they have weak intelligences, and partly because, in the rapid transition from superstition to truth, only a few have thought out and seen through the super-ficial prejudices, while the rest hang back, and need encouragement to join in the advance. If you intimidate them, you are only asking them to retreat. They are moral invalids, who must be encouraged, if they are to be cured: a compulsory remedy will only turn them into fanatics.' This very sensible advice shows what a mistake it would be to identify the Committee or the Convention with the 'de-christianizing' policy of Hébert and Chaumette in Paris, or of such men as Fouché, Dumont, or Faure in the provinces.

But if admonition failed, Robespierre was prepared to use force. A letter to Hentz (December 10) signed in the first place by Robespierre, authorizes him to arrest members of the *société populaire* at Lille, who have been guilty of 'revolutionary exaggerations, especially in matters of public worship'.[1]

v

Robespierre's known insistence on religious toleration encouraged individuals to send him private information. Four days after signing the letter to Hentz he received a long letter from Jérôme Gillet, near Lyon, saying that attacks upon liberty of worship were giving rise to civil war everywhere, and that those who once blessed the Revolution were now cursing it.[2] Godefroy, deputy for l'Oise, wrote from l'Eure et Loire, complaining that some members of patriotic committees were 'propagating atheis-tical principles', and that 'the decree on liberty of worship ought to be enforced'.[3]

Another serious cause of scandal was the conduct of the republican troops in the war against the rebels. Early in November Robespierre received a letter from one Bouverey, a captain in the western army, saying that he has no ob-jection to a reasonable amount of killing and looting, conducted in an orderly way; but that, ever since the army entered the Vendée, the troops have killed and plundered whom they would, and no attempt has been made to stop

[1]Corresp. 278.   [2]Corresp. 284.   [3]Corresp. 307.

them.[1] Why did this man write to Robespierre, unless it was because he had a reputation for mercifulness as well as for tolerance?

The same question arises in connexion with the ferocious vengeance taken on the rebels at Lyon. Here, in addition to the official despatches he heard at the Committee,[2] Robespierre received private letters from Collot d'Herbois, in one of which he informs his 'colleague and friend' that he has been putting rebels to death at the rate of several batches of twenty a day; but that he finds this procedure too slow, and is devising a system of mass-execution. Soon afterwards came an anonymous letter, denouncing the *fusillades des Brotteaux*, in which many innocent people, including *sansculottes*, and members of the National Guard, were said to have perished. This time Robespierre acted. Collot d'Herbois returned to Paris under suspicion, bringing with him, as an apologia for his conduct, the head of the Jacobin 'martyr', Chalier. Robespierre had not answered his letters, and was only prevented from showing his open disapproval of the massacres by fear of playing into the hands of the 'Indulgents', who were using the excesses at Lyon as a weapon against the government.[3]

Robespierre's private correspondence during November and December contributes something further to the background of his ideas. Herman, whom he had brought from the Criminal Court at Arras to succeed Montané in the Presidency of the Revolutionary Tribunal in Paris, writes formally, and rather brusquely, to ask for the revision of a sentence, and to approve of Dumas' proposals for the reorganization of the court.[4] Darthé, ex-mayor of Vermanton, addressing him (either from flattery or friendship) in the second person singular, remarks (November 19) that, a year ago, Robespierre was supported by such men as Mirabeau, Pétion, and Roederer: now, he goes on, 'I can

[1]Corresp. 250.
[2]Some of these were found among his papers (Pap. inéd 1/313, 323, 326).
[3]It is curious to find that, during the height of the Terror at Lyon, Pilot, one of the republican agents, carried out a commission there for Robespierre, purchasing him several pairs of Lyon silk stockings (Pap. inéd. 2/210).
[4]Corresp. 262.

see no one but yourself still sound in the midst of corruption; and I say to myself, Robespierre has always been, and will always be regarded as the corner stone of the proud edifice of our Constitution. Please God that, in completing your work, you trust no one else to carry out your designs'.[1] Here the eulogy outsteps prose, and the letter ends with four lines of verse. Robespierre kept it: most politicians would do the same. Boisset writes (November 22) to protest against his expulsion from the Jacobins.[2] Bouchotte, the Minister of War whom Robespierre had consistently defended, sends him a letter of complaints about the War Office from the deputy Ysabeau (November 2), with his answer, point by point, in the margin. 'I try', he says, 'to keep out of controversy. Few people are fonder of democratic methods than I am; that is why I don't particularly care for my present job. I only took it from a sense of duty; and I have stuck to it for the same reason'. But he would not mind if someone else had his place.[3] An honest, overworked man: he had complained to Marat a year before that he had no time to do anything but speak in monosyllables, and sign his name.[4] Chambon La Tour asks justice for his friend Randon against a sentence of Robespierre's *Section des Piques*.[5] Beffroy again demands an interview.[6] Gay-Vernon, a 'constitutional' bishop and deputy, intercedes for a friend in prison.[7] Sergent, of the Vigilance Committee of the Commune, asks that his brother-in-law, 'a *sansculotte* full of honesty and courage', but incapable of high command, may be transferred from the army of the west to that of the north.[8] Was this modesty, or fear that he might share the punishment of other officers for the mismanagement of the campaign in the Vendée? Faure, the anticlerical deputy on mission at Nancy, complains of his policy being overridden by Saint-Just and Lebas—a waste of paper and ink, for when he writes again, he is in prison.[9] Gillet, from Lyon, sends fresh evidence of anti-clericalism.[10]

[1]Corresp. 263. [2]Corresp. 265. [3]Corresp. 268.
[4]R.F. 44/183. [5]Corresp. 269. [6]Corresp. 271, cp. 2/103.
[7]Corresp. 273. [8]Corresp. 274. [9]Corresp. 276, 337, 427.
[10]Corresp. 275, 307.

Nicolas, the government printer, and a friend of Robespierre, complains that the Departmental Vigilance Committee, of which he is a member, has been unfairly dissolved.[1]
There is another batch of letters from Jullien, now at 'Port Liberty' (L'Orient), where he says that strong measures will be needed to prevent the place following Marseille and Toulon into counter-revolution.[2] From Augustin Robespierre comes at last (December 18) news of the capture of Toulon. He is setting out at once for Paris, with the details, but is so excited by his baptism of fire that he must tell his brother all about it. 'I am quite overcome', he says, 'to find myself a hero—so they tell me; otherwise I should not believe it. I went into action with the troops: I never so much as noticed cannon-balls, bullets, or bombs: I only saw the redoubt we had to seize. The redoubt! It is ours! Forward, comrades! Courage! And I found myself at the foot of the redoubt before I knew where I was'.[3] Charlotte was right when she said that her younger brother had 'military courage'.

This account of Robespierre's correspondence may well end with two letters illustrating the suspicions and delusions which fogged the revolutionary mind, and made it so hard for a statesman to keep a level head. Soulavie, a diplomatic agent at Geneva, sends, along with a budget of accusations against generals, business men, the rich, and the priests, a special warning about Kellermann, who is said to be looking for an opportunity to betray his country to the Emperor, and a rumour that there is a plot afoot to fill the cellars of the Convention with gunpowder, and to blow the deputies sky-high.[4] Gravier, writing about the same time from La Meurthe, denounces a crowd of *ci-devants*—a notary, a canon, an actress from the Opera, an usher, a mayor, an official of the War Office, a drunken *Chevalier de Saint-Louis*, a baron, and Comte D***.[5]

The individual value of such letters may not be great; but the total effect they produce is important. Even during

---

[1] Corresp. 279.   [2] Corresp. 280, 295, 297.   [3] Corresp. 287.
[4] Corresp. 303.   [5] Corresp. 304.

the weeks of comparative rest from parliamentary strife, when Robespierre was trying to take stock of the situation, and to think out a policy for the government, he was being distracted by constant complaints and appeals, and battered by contradictory suggestions, coming from all parts of the country, and from all kinds of correspondents. He was one who disliked taking another man's advice almost as much as he disliked following another man's lead. His mind and character were of a narrow, angular type, all his own. But they were, though he might not know it, little more than a mould, into which ideas must be poured from outside, and left to solidify. It was his habit to prevent a rival from doing something, and then to do it himself. Accordingly, it was, to a great extent, by what he learnt from his correspondents, as well as from what he heard in the Committee, or at the club, that he formed the shapeless material of the Revolution into a government, a programme, and a creed. His greatness, such as it was, lay less in giving out than in taking in. He represented the Revolution: he did not refashion it. He copied its movements as faithfully as a shadow—sometimes going ahead of it, and sometimes following behind, but always impotent to alter its course.

VI

The first of Robespierre's set speeches, as the interpreter of the Jacobin government, dealt with the international relations of the Republic (November 17). The second great offensive of the French armies, begun, after the disasters of the spring, in the Netherlands, and on the Rhine, had been crowned, three weeks earlier, by the victory of Wattignies. Meanwhile the objective of the Revolutionary campaigns had passed almost insensibly from defence to 'reunion', and from 'reunion' to conquest. The habit of war had grown upon a country which was becoming every day more like an armed camp. The people wanted more victories, the Committee more prestige, the Treasury more loot. Politically and economically (it was discovered) war could be made to pay. The rulers of the Republic were preparing not only the troops with which Napoleon was to conquer Europe, but also the policy by which he was to justify his conquests. How would Robespierre view this situation?

He began with an easy contrast, calculated to win the sympathy of his hearers, between the 'prodigies of reason' from which the Revolution had sprung, and the 'crimes of tyranny' which had in vain tried to arrest its advance. He took as an instance of this the intrigues of the British government, which had hoped, by putting the Duke of York on the throne of Louis XVI, to secure the French ports, and the French colonies; and then, mistress of the seas, 'to force America to return under the domination of George'. But Pitt (he said) completely misunderstood the Revolution. 'Too immoral to believe in republican virtues, and too poor a philosopher to take a step into the future, George's minister was behind the times: the age was hurrying towards liberty, and he would turn it back to tyranny and barbarism'. Not content with this fantasy on Pitt's foreign policy, Robespierre ridicules his home policy, as an attempt to impose a royal despotism upon a liberty-loving nation of traders. But Pitt's plans for an Anglo-French monarchy were foiled by the Jacobins, and by the Republic; and when he could do no more he forced France into war.

At this point Robespierre shifts the aim of his invective onto the Girondists, who are accused of 'saving the Prussian despot and his army' (the retreat from Valmy), of 'soaking the soil of Belgium with the purest blood of France' (at Neerwinden), and of 'betraying to the enemy (in the retreat from Belgium) our treasure, our stores, our arms, and our defenders'. And by this roundabout route he reaches his real subject—the relations between the French Republic and the various foreign powers.

Three countries are still friendly—the Americans, who have never forgotten that the French people helped them to gain their freedom; Turkey, the natural ally of France against their common enemy, Austria; and Switzerland, which, in spite of some justifiable grievances, has refused to join the coalition against its nearest neighbour. The friendship of other nations, Robespierre believes, can be won by a frank statement of French policy. 'That is the advantage of a great Republic. Its most effective diplomatic weapon is its honesty. An honest man can open his heart and home to his fellow-citizens without fear: a free people can reveal to other nations the fundamental principles of its policy'.

There follows a sketch of the situation of these hitherto hostile or neutral powers—England and Holland plotting for the partition of French colonies, and French trade; Prussia and Austria, 'like two brigands, fighting over the spoils of a murdered traveller', but sinking their differences in Poland to help in the attack on France; Spain bribed to join the Coalition by an offer of territory in the Pyrenees, and Sardinia by the hope of annexing Dauphiné and Provence; the Italian states cowed under the 'press-gang domination' of England; Sweden neutral, since the death of that 'modern Agamemnon', Gustavus III; and Russia, a country which, combining 'the ferocity of savage tribes with the vices of civilization', has withdrawn from the Coalition only to extend its territory in Poland and Turkey, at the expense of Prussia and Austria.

From this cursory survey of the international situation Robespierre draws some interesting conclusions. 'The universe', he asserts, 'requires our survival'. Were France dismembered or destroyed, the whole political world would dissolve. 'Take away this powerful and necessary ally, this guarantee of the existence of the small states against the great tyrants, and all Europe is in chains'.

But that is not all. The fate of England herself is in French hands. 'Whatever anyone may say, the only real powers are those which command the land. The moment such a power chooses to cross the interval which separates it from a purely maritime power, the latter will cease to exist'. But not only is England's territory at the mercy of a continental invader; her political liberty also depends upon that of her neighbour across the Channel. How could the English reform movement, deprived of the moral support of the Revolution, carry on its struggle against 'a despotic minister', who is attempting to smother reason, enchain thought, and oppress the British nation? The last part of the speech becomes increasingly vague and rhetorical. Robespierre assures his audience that not liberty only, but philosophy and humanity—indeed, civilization itself—depends upon the continued existence of the Republic; and that, if they do their part, it must survive, were the whole of Europe leagued against it; for 'the French Republic is as invincible as reason, and as immortal as truth'.

The world-wide publication of this harangue was, in the opinion of Robespierre's hearers, no more than it deserved; for it made an immense impression, and gave its author the reputation of being the greatest statesman of the Republic. The official *Feuille de Salut Public*—certainly no impartial organ—spoke of 'the grandeur of its ideas, the depth of its political principles, and the sublimity of its republican eloquence'.[1] A modern reader will hardly subscribe to this verdict. The speech, for all its eloquence, contains no constructive programme. Robespierre is content to divide Europe into states which are friendly to France, and states which are hostile: he makes no suggestion as to how the friends are to be cultivated, or the enemies reconciled. France's right to exist—or rather, the impossibility of the world existing without her—is an axiom beyond need of proof, not the working hypothesis of a diplomatic system. This is rhetoric, not statesmanship.

Yet it is interesting to notice Robespierre's anticipation of ideas which reappeared, ten years later, as the basis of Napoleonic diplomacy. Such are the certainty that England is the arch-enemy, the belief in the superiority of land to sea-power, or the delusion that France is the champion of the small nations, and the bulwark of European freedom. It would be tempting to suppose that Bonaparte owed these notions to his friendship with the Robespierres; but they

[1]Vellay, 275.

were, in fact, commonplaces of contemporary politics, which Robespierre turned into a party manifesto, and Napoleon into the conquest of Europe: for both men owed their success (different as it was) to the power of reading and translating what was in the popular mind.

VII

It is an indication both of Robespierre's concentration on matters of high policy, and of the transference of political interest from the Convention to the Committee, that he is only once recorded as having spoken in the House during November, and twice at the club. When he intervened, it was against the Hébertists and the *Enragés*, the extreme Left of the republican party. Hébert had accused Duquesnoy, a deputy on mission, of hampering Jourdan's operations. The generals, Robespierre replied (November 9) could now be trusted, and those who criticize the Committee on the score of its military policy can only intend to embarrass and overturn the government. 'The fact is', he declared, 'that they want our places. Very well, let them have them. (Cries of 'No, No!' on all sides; and 'Stay where you are!'). I should like to see *them*, day and night, probing the wounds of the state, studying the needs of the people, and devoting their whole life to the national welfare. . . . It is not merely patriotism, or enthusiasm, or an ingrained love of freedom that sustains our efforts; it is reason, which will make the Republic immortal; where reason reigns, the people is sovereign; and such an empire is indestructible'. Robespierre's audience may not have known what he meant; but they applauded the fine phrases; and two days later, Hébert retracted his remarks about Duquesnoy, and gave him, in the presence of the whole club, a fraternal embrace.

But the 'purge' (*épuration*) was now, once more, the order of the day. The sectional clubs and popular societies, Robespierre had declared (November 9) ought to be carefully weeded out; and a beginning was made (November 18) by striking the Popular Society of Montbard off the list

428

of affiliation. 'We want no 10th of August patriots', declared Robespierre, 'still less patriots of May 31 (he meant, those who shout with the biggest crowd). Even to-day every royalist poses as a republican, and every *Brissotin* as a *Montagnard*'. Party strife had, indeed, so warped his judgement that obvious opposition hardly seemed worth his attention; whilst the more patriotic a man appeared to be, the more he should be suspected of counter-revolution.

Of all these masked enemies, the one of which he was most suspicious was anti-clericalism—the more so, since his study of the foreign relations of the Republic had shown him how it was interpreted abroad. This was what lay behind an important debate at the Jacobins on November 21. As a result of Robespierre's speech of the 9th, rumours were going round that the government intended to arrest certain deputies of the Opposition. Chabot, on the 10th, had claimed the common right of every man to be heard in his own defence, and had reminded those who now threatened force that they might become the victims of their own weapon—'To-day (it was being said) it is so-and-so's turn, to-morrow it will be Danton's, the day after, Billaud-Varenne's, and we shall finish with Robespierre'. Now, four days after Robespierre's speech on foreign relations, Hébert and Momoro revived this issue; and Robespierre, in a long harangue against the anti-clericals, did nothing to dispel their fears.

Fanaticism, he said, was no longer a serious enemy; to insist upon it, as they did, was to distract the country from its real dangers. The Convention had no intention of proscribing Catholic worship; its policy had always been to encourage, and, if need be, enforce toleration. 'He who tries to stop the saying of Mass is a worse fanatic than the priest who says it'.

But that is not all. Anti-clericalism, he declares, has, in some of these men, turned into Atheism. Now a philosopher or a private individual may think what he likes about atheism; 'but for the public man or the legislator to adopt such a system of thought would be utter insanity. The

National Convention detests atheism. It is no author, or metaphysician: it is a representative body charged with the duty of securing respect for the character as well as the rights of the French people. It was not without significance that it published the Declaration of Rights in the presence of the Supreme Being.[1] It will be said, perhaps, that I am a narrow-minded man, a prejudiced person, a fanatic. As I have already said, I do not speak as a private individual, or as a systematic philosopher, but as a representative of the people. Atheism is aristocratic. The conception of a great Being who watches over oppressed innocence, and punishes successful crime, is democratic through and through. . . . I have been a poor sort of Catholic ever since my College days; but I have never cooled in my friendship for, or failed in my championship of my fellow-men. Indeed, I have only grown more wedded to the moral and political ideas which I have just expressed. "If God did not exist, it would be necessary to invent him"[2]. . . . The French people pins its faith, not on its priests, nor on any superstition, or any ceremony, but on worship as such—that is to say, upon the conception of an incomprehensible power, which is at once a source of confidence to the virtuous and of terror to the criminal'.

This was not the first time, as Robespierre reminded his hearers, that he had used the tribune of the Jacobin club for a discourse on religion. But the speech on Providence had been an impromptu, in answer to a personal attack, and without a sequel;[3] this speech on atheism was a deliberate manifesto, the declaration of a programme, which began by purging a club, and ended by overthrowing a government. Like all Robespierre's statements about himself—a subject which he had carefully studied, and in which he had become an expert—this speech was intended, and must be taken, in all seriousness. It completes the self-revelation of the speech on Providence. It shows us the last state of a man whose mind has been swept and garnished. The old devils of Catholic superstition were banished when Robes-

[1] A reference to the preamble of the Declaration.
[2] From Voltaire's *Epître à l'auteur du livre des Trois Imposteurs.*   [3] v. 1/215.

pierre was at College; but the new devils of Providence and Retribution were not really more enlightened than the old —they were only more unreal. Robespierre was soon to find, and to find to his cost, that to the people religion still meant the priest and the mass—something they could touch and see—and not a faith without any material embodiment, and refuted by their daily experience. He made the mistake, in religion as well as in politics, of crediting the people with a capacity for general views that it did not possess. He thought, when the crowd lynched a royalist, or plundered a grocer's shop, that it was trying to express its faith in liberty and equality, whereas it really wanted loot and blood. He imagined that when priests married, or their congregations sang hymns to the Supreme Being, they were professing a preference for 'those philosophical principles which are common to all religions'; whilst these were only surface movements—concessions to natural instinct, and to patriotic convention—hardly disturbing the depths of Catholic conviction. He was led further into error by confusing politics and religion, and assuming that there must be theological states of mind corresponding to aristocracy and democracy—the one (atheism) as bad as the rich, and the other (theism) as good as the poor. It was the mistake of an earnest mind, limited by its very idealism, and arguing from evidence derived from introspection, instead of from knowledge of the world.

VIII

The speech of November 21, followed by the expulsion from the club of three 'atheists'—Dubuisson, Desfieux, and Pereira—gave a fresh impetus to the industry of *épuration*. On Nov. 29 Guiraud, impugned by Robespierre, saved himself only by volunteering information about suspicious gatherings at the *Mairie*. On December 1 Taschereau was challenged to prove his innocence before the committee. Two days later, Danton himself was accused.

Five weeks before, Danton had left Paris for his new wife and his country house at Arcis. His indolent mind and self-indulgent nature easily tired of that close application to politics, and that strained attitude of patriotism, which was now required by the rules of Jacobin orthodoxy. With finer intuitions and impulses than Robespierre, and with far greater powers of leadership, he was a child of nature, who thought nothing human alien to the Revolution. To his generous but unfastidious taste, the natural frontiers of morality were as far-flung as those of the Alps and the Pyrenees, which he grandiloquently claimed for France. He wanted Frenchmen to enjoy the Revolution, as he enjoyed good books, good food, and a comfortable fireside; and he was not censorious of the means by which security, either public or private, might be attained. Robespierre was perhaps jealous of the facility with which, during his two short tenures of power, Danton mastered the political, military, and diplomatic situation. He certainly disliked his defective sense of responsibility, and his easy-going ethics. He thought he did not take the Revolution seriously. The five weeks covering the death of the Girondist leaders, and the concentration of power in the hands of the Jacobin committee, had inaugurated a new regime, and a new Revolutionary ideal, which left little room for either the virtues or the vices of a Danton. Jacobinism was becoming a cult that called for devotees, not prophets; a machine, which men of lesser gifts could manage. Creative ability was not encouraged outside the Committee. But Danton could not be dwarfed: he must either dominate the scene, or disappear from it. His return to Paris on November 21 was due to some such feeling, combined, perhaps, with a chivalrous desire to stand by old associates who were threatened by the Committee's new campaign for political purity,[1] and with a dislike for the increasingly dictatorial and inquisitorial temper of Robespierre and his colleagues. But he did not come as a personal enemy. Antipathetic as he was to Robespierre, their characters represented two sides of Jacobinism, and their alliance still seemed necessary, if the party was to make headway against extremists whom

[1]Chabot, Delaunay, and Basire had been arrested on November 18.

they both hated. Nor was Danton the man to realize how easily Robespierre's public conscience would override the claims of personal friendship. Re-reading the letter of February 15,[1] he could surely count on the support of one who 'loved him more than ever, and would love him till he died'?

Danton's first speeches, after his return (November 22, 26, December 1) were directed against the 'atheists', and the 'de-christianizing' policy of some of the government agents; but the Hébertist critics of the Committee were quick to perceive that they also contained a veiled attack upon those extreme measures of punishment which they were urging upon it, and which it was not strong enough to refuse. Accordingly, on December 3, the Hébertists launched a full attack upon him; in reply, Danton demanded a committee to examine the charges made against him. This was Robespierre's opportunity; and those who remembered a similar occasion, six months before,[2] must have wondered whether his championship of Danton would be any less ambiguous than his defence of Marat. They were right; for the speech which followed must have given Danton some uncomfortable moments, and made him more than uneasy as to the future. Danton's conduct, Robespierre was heard to say, needed public discussion; and if no one else was prepared to take the lead, he would do it himself. He began by scouting the more palpably absurd charges against him, such as that he was an *émigré* (he had been for a time in England), or that he had wished to make himself regent for 'Louis XVII'. He went on to admit that he thought Danton had shown too much leniency towards Dumouriez and the *Brissotins*. He agreed that all patriots were alternately accused, as Danton was, or flattered, as he was, for sinister motives. And he ended by giving Danton a public testimonial which sounded more like a public warning: 'I may be wrong', he said, 'but I think that as a family man he deserves nothing but praise. As to politics, I have this to say. One difference of opinion between us led to my watch-

[1] v. 2/30.　　　　[2] v. 2/16.

ing him carefully, and sometimes with indignation. But if he did not always agree with me, was I to fear that he was betraying the country? Not at all; he always seemed to be serving it zealously'. The scene ended with Danton in the arms of the President of the Club, amid 'the most flattering applause'. But his punishment was only postponed.

IX

Two days later, in a speech of calculated rhetoric, Robespierre defended the religious policy of the government against the attacks of those foreign powers which were trying to make political capital out of its supposed 'attack on the church'. The *Réponse aux rois ligués* is in part a mere *tu quoque*—'the crimes of which they accuse us are their own'—and in part a tiresome catalogue of abuse. But it contains passages of rather turgid eloquence which anticipate the nationalistic manifestos of some modern governments. 'Your masters tell you'—so he addresses an imaginary audience of Europe—'that the French people has proscribed all religion, and substituted the worship of men for that of God. It is a lie. The French people and its representatives respect the liberty of every religion, and prohibit none. They honour the virtues of the martyrs of the human race, but without idolatry or exaggeration. They abhor intolerance and persecution, under whatever cloak they are concealed. They condemn alike the follies of superstition, the crimes of fanaticism, and the extravagances of philosophy falsely so called'. Again, there is justifiable pride in Robespierre's summary of the achievements of the Revolution. 'All the tyrants' armies in Europe driven back, in spite of five years of treason, conspiracy, and civil discord; faithless deputies executed side by side with the last of our despots; the immortal tables of the law, on which the people's representatives inscribed with their own hand, amidst the thunders of a second Sinai, the social compact of Frenchmen; the equality of all men in the eye of the law; every notable criminal trembling before the judgement-seat;

resourceless innocence finding at length, to its amaze, a refuge in the courts; patriotism triumphant, in spite of every vice that slavery taught us, and all the perfidy of our foes; the people showing itself strenuous and prudent, formidable and fair, responding to the call of reason, learning to discern its enemies even under the mask of patriotism, and flocking to the colours to defend the magnificent fruit of its courage and virtue—such is the expiation we offer to the world, whether for our own mistakes, or for the crimes of our foes'.

In such rhapsodies Robespierre was at his best. He was less happy in the attack on English political life with which he thought fit to end his speech. 'Do you, sublime Parliament of Great Britain, tell us of *your* heroes! You have an Opposition; but with you it is the patriots who are in opposition, and the despots who carry the day; the minority which criticizes, and the majority which is corrupt. Vile and insolent people! Your so-called representation is for sale; you know it, and admit it. You settle your government by the Englishman's favourite maxim: the talents of your deputies are a commodity, like the wool of your sheep, or the steel in your workshops. And *you* dare to talk of morality and freedom!'

Whatever warrant Robespierre may have had for these words in the hoary corruptions of the Parliamentary system, it needed an exceedingly hopeful eye to discern political purity and freedom in the working of the Law of Suspects, or of the Revolutionary Tribunal. But Robespierre might at least claim the decree on liberty of worship, promulgated two days after his speech, as marking, once and for all, official disapproval of the 'de-christianizers'; and the great decree setting up Revolutionary Government, voted on December 4, was nothing less than a working Constitution, which might well seem to place the governing committee in an unassailable position. The Republic had its quiver full of arrows, and could speak with its enemy in the gate.

X

Still busy with his reports, and with the work of the Committee, Robespierre made few appearances in the Convention before the end of the year. But he was more often seen at the club. Thus, on December 9, he warned the Jacobins against granting certificates of *civisme* too easily: 'The foreigner who creeps amongst you', he said, 'disguised in a *bonnet rouge*, to fix a dagger in your heart, is no less culpable than the Austrian slave who plunges his murderous bayonet into the breast of a defender of freedom. . . . Moderation is a more dangerous weapon than any bayonet'. On December 12 Billaud-Varenne and Robespierre himself emerged unscathed from the process of *épuration* amidst 'the most flattering applause'. Robespierre improved the occasion by making an attack upon the German 'Baron', Anacharsis Cloots, a rich cosmopolitan adventurer, who, after writing a book on the evidences for Mahometanism, had thrown himself into the anti-clerical campaign; and he did it so effectually that Cloots was expelled without a hearing. A little later (December 23) he attacked Philippeaux, the friend of Danton; and took the opportunity to deny the slander that warrants for arrest had ever been issued by himself, or any other single member of the committees. There were fresh rumours, too, of plots against the government; and he found it advisable to add that 'if ever a section of the people, misled by a few men, tried to dictate to the Convention, we, who are no longer *Brissotins*, or aristocrats, would know how to behave with real republican courage, and, far from flying like conspirators, would await death in our senatorial seats'.

Robespierre, in fact, had not the slightest intention of awaiting death: he was already planning to forestall it, by the overthrow, and, if need be, the execution of his enemies. The attacks upon Cloots and Philippeaux were preliminary to the great drive which was now in preparation against the extremists both of the Right and of the Left.

In this campaign the part played by 'de-christianization'

was soon overshadowed by the scandal of the India Company. This undertaking, founded, under the patronage of Louis XVI, for the promotion of trade with the East Indies, had soon became a centre of flourishing investment. Calonne himself was involved in a scandal caused by the speculations of the Abbé d'Espagnac; and, during the Jacobin-Girondin struggle of 1791, it had been asserted that the Girondist leaders frequented not only the *salon* of the virtuous Mme Roland, but also that of the wealthy Mme Dodun, the wife of one of the Directors of the Company. In the summer of 1793, Joseph Delaunay, deputy for Maine et Loire, and a member of the Finance Committee, had secured the suspension of the company on charges of evading taxation, exporting gold, and so depreciating the paper currency. Placed on a committee to liquidate the affairs of the company, he soon realized that money could be made by arranging for the liquidation to be carried out by the company itself on favourable terms, including a large commission to himself and his associates—Chabot, Fabre, Basire, the Baron de Batz, and Julien de Toulouse. In order to carry this transaction through the Assembly, a decree was falsified, over the signatures of Fabre and Delaunay. About October 12, Fabre, who, as a friend of Danton, was also threatened by the Hébertists, felt so insecure that he began to 'turn king's evidence', and denounced a number of 'foreigners', 'financiers', and corrupt (*pourris*) politicians. Chabot, following suit, soon found himself, along with Delaunay, Basire, and Fabre's victims, in prison; whence he wrote the despicable series of letters preserved in Robespierre's correspondence.[1]

By December 25 the chief figures in the India Company scandal were already in custody; but the ugly suspicions it had started were spreading far and wide, affecting not only the *pourris* and the *Enragés*, but also the Moderates, and the party of 'clemency'. Danton himself was in danger.

This moment seemed to his indiscreet and irrepressible

---

[1] v. Mathiez, *Conspiration de l'étranger*, and *Compagnie des Indes*: for Chabot's letters, *Corresp.* 268, 281–2, 285–6, 290–1, 298–9, 318, 344, 357–8.

friend, the *enfant terrible* of Jacobinism, Camille Desmoulins, an appropriate one for launching a new paper, named, after the now discredited rival of Robespierre's club, the *Vieux Cordelier*, and dedicated to the dangerous cause of *modérantisme*. The first number of this journal appeared on December 5, two days after Robespierre's 'warning' to Danton. Robespierre had seen the proof-sheets, and accepted an editorial dedication to himself and Danton, as 'two friends' of the editor. Its ostensible object was to attack the *Enragés*; but its real purpose was to put forward, indirectly and tentatively, Danton, the 'veteran Cordelier', as Robespierre's rival, and his policy as an alternative to that of the Committee. The second number (December 10) took the form of an attack on Cloots, whom Robespierre himself was to denounce two days later. But this was a feint: the real objective was shown when, in the Convention, on December 14 and 15, attempts were made by Bourdon de l'Oise and others to remove Bouchotte, the Jacobin War Minister, and certain members of the Governing Committee. At this moment, too (December 15), appeared Desmoulins' third number, the proofs of which had not been submitted to Robespierre. He thought, perhaps, that he was safe, because, only the day before, he had survived his scrutiny at the club, and had received a certificate of republicanism from Robespierre, coupled only with the advice 'not to be so versatile'. But his comparison of the Law of Suspects and the terrorist regime with the worst days of the Roman Empire, and his suggestion that the government had let themselves be misled by extremists, could not expect to pass unchallenged. It was not humanity which inspired him, but mischievousness: his aim was not to moderate the government, but to overthrow it.[1]

XI

For ten days the Committee held its hand. Then, on December 25, Robespierre came to the tribune, to reassert the policy of the government, and to warn intriguers that

[1] c.p. *Vieux Cordelier*, (ed. Calvet) 136.

no concession would be made either to extremists or to reactionaries.

The government, he begins by saying, the guardian of the Republic, has adopted Caesar's motto—'nothing has been done, so long as there remains anything to do'. It is comparatively easy (he goes on) to defeat the external foes of the country: the real difficulty is to deal with the 'eternal intrigues' of the civil enemies of freedom. He is aware that committee government is being attacked in the name of the Constitution of 1793, for which it is a provisional substitute. He warns these critics to clear their minds of constitutional cant, and to consider the needs of the situation. 'The object of a revolutionary regime is to found a republic; that of a constitutional regime is to carry it on. The first befits a time of war between liberty and its enemies; the second suits a time when freedom is victorious, and at peace with the world'. France has not yet reached this second stage. What follows? 'Under a constitutional regime, little is needed but to protect the individual citizen against abuse of power by the government; but under a revolutionary regime the government has to defend itself against all the factions which attack it'; and in this fight for life 'only good citizens deserve public protection, and the punishment of the people's enemies is death'. In other words, there is to be no relaxation, but rather a tightening up of the rule of discipline and intimidation.

Against whom is this fresh campaign directed? 'We have to steer our course', Robespierre says, 'between the two reefs of weakness and rashness, reaction and exaggeration: for reaction (*modérantisme*) is to moderation (*modération*) what impotence is to chastity, and exaggeration (*excès*) is to energy what a craving for drink (*hydropsie*) is to a healthy thirst'. Nor is there much to choose between the two extremes; 'whether you shoot too far, or not far enough, you will equally miss the mark'. There is a striking resemblance between the apostle of federalism and the preacher of a universal republic.[1] The *procureur-général* of humanity[2] gets

[1] Cloots.　　　　　　　　　　　　　　　[2] Cloots again.

439

on famously with the friend of kings. There is much in common between the vestmented priest and the fanatical prophet of atheism.[1] A democratic baron[2] is own brother to an *émigré* marquis at Coblenz; and sometimes there is less difference than one would suppose between the red cap of patriotism and the red shoe of aristocracy.

Having thus, by implication, involved Hébert and Cloots, Danton and Desmoulins, in the crimes of England and Prussia, Robespierre comes at last to the real point of his speech—the declaration of a severer policy of intimidation, of an intensification of the Terror. 'The Committee has noticed', he says, 'that the law is not prompt enough to punish the more prominent criminals. The punishment of a hundred minor and obscure scoundrels is less useful to the cause of freedom than the execution of one master conspirator'. The Committee therefore intends to make new regulations for the Revolutionary Tribunal, which will enable it to work more quickly and efficiently. Lastly, to counteract any unpleasant impression left by this announcement, and as a bid for popular support, it proposes to increase by one third the grants to disabled soldiers, war widows, and their children, and to set up a permanent body to watch over their interests.

The general policy underlying this speech is clear enough. The Committee, threatened by attacks from the extremists on one side, and from the reactionaries on the other, saw that its safety lay in appealing to the Paris 'people', organized in their Sections and in the Commune. To them a policy of clemency would be a sign of weakness, and the opening of the prisons a return to the old regime of the aristocrat and the priest. On the other hand, there was nothing the extremists promised them that the government itself, were it so minded, could not give. The Committee could out-manoeuvre both parties of its rivals by the policy of the strong hand (which France never resents) bearing gifts to the poor. It therefore resolved to stand firm, and to invoke the Sections, as in August, 1792, and June, 1793, to defeat

[1]Hébert, or Chaumette.   [2]De Batz.

factions which, under the guise either of patriotism or of humanity, were trying to oust it from control.

Its members, indeed, were not quite unanimous. On the day following Robespierre's speech, Barère, always ready with a conciliatory gesture, proposed the appointment of a special committee to examine the grounds upon which arrests had been made under the Law of Suspects, with a view to the liberation of such *sansculottes* as had been unjustly imprisoned. This was an amendment to a suggestion already made by Robespierre (December 20) for an informal committee of two to review certain 'hard cases'; it involved a publicity which he was anxious to avoid, and it bore the appearance of a concession to the party of clemency which might be misinterpreted: he therefore opposed it, and secured its rejection. The enemies of the Committee doubtless noticed this early indication that there were differences of view among its members. But the secrecy in which much of its work was now done, and the mechanical way in which its measures were approved by a skeleton Assembly—Robespierre, for instance, spoke only twice in the Convention during the month following his speech of December 25— gave few opportunities to take advantage of this weakness.

XII

Early in the new year (January 5, 1794) a scene at the Jacobins opened a fresh stage in the struggle against the 'factions'. Augustin Robespierre, lately returned from his triumphs at Toulon, took the opportunity of an exchange of accusations between Collot d'Herbois, Hébert, and Desmoulins to say that when he was last in the club it had been dealing with matters of public policy; now it seemed to be given over to private quarrels. His patronizing tone earned a rebuke from his brother. Collot, said Maximilien, was perfectly justified in his charges, and it was for those whom he accused to exculpate themselves. 'For my part', he remarked, with more truth of fact than of intention, 'I am accusing no one. . . . I only wish to get at the truth'. Two days later, defending Boulanger, of the National Guard,[1] Robespierre once more complained of intrigues against the Mountain, and appealed to public opinion against Philippeaux, Bourdon, and Fabre, who had failed to submit themselves to the scrutiny of the club.

When, later on the same day, Desmoulins faced his critics, it was with apologies on his lips, and fear in his heart. He had been under a misapprehension, he said, when (in the last number of his paper) he had praised Philippeaux; he no longer knew where he stood. Robespierre rose; and everyone in the hall must have known that it was a critical moment in the lives of the two men. How would he treat his old school-friend, his fellow-Jacobin, and, until the last few weeks, his public admirer and champion? Would he accept the fifth number of the *Vieux Cordelier*, which had appeared that very day, as the apologia it was evidently intended to be? He soon showed that neither sentiment nor excuse would be allowed to affect his judgement. The latest number of Desmoulins' journal, he declared, would rejoice the hearts of the aristocrats. Desmoulins himself was 'a spoilt child, whose good disposition had been corrupted by bad company', and he must show proof of his penitence by giving up his present friends. Not only so: to complete the humiliation of public confession and penitence, he moved that the offending writings be solemnly burnt on the floor of the house. 'Burning', retorted Desmoulins, remembering his Rousseau, 'is no argument'. It was an unlucky reminder, and it cost him his life. Maximilien suddenly dropped his half friendly tone, and denounced him openly. 'But, Robespierre', he stammered, realizing his danger, 'I don't understand you. How can you say that my paper is only read by aristocrats? It has been read by the Convention; it has been read by the Mountain. . . . You condemn me here, in the club: but haven't I been to your house? Haven't I read you my numbers, and begged you, in the name of friendship to help me with your advice, and to tell me the line of policy I ought to follow?' 'You

[1] He had temporarily succeeded Hanriot as its commander-in-chief on May 17.

442

didn't show me all your numbers', replied Robespierre; 'I only saw one or two. Not wishing to be involved in a quarrel of any kind, I preferred not to read the rest. If I had read them, I should have been accused of dictating them'. Here Danton intervened. Desmoulins, he said, must not mind the lectures (*leçons un peu sévères*) that Robespierre had given him. They were meant in a friendly way.

But were they? When, on the following day, Momoro proposed to read out No. 5 of the *Vieux Cordelier*,[1] Robespierre intervened. There was no need, he said, to read any more. 'Our opinions must be already made up. You can see in Camille's writings revolutionary principles side by side with the maxims of a thoroughly pernicious reaction (*modérantisme*). In one passage he raises the courage of patriots, in another he feeds the hopes of aristocrats. . . . He is a fantastic mixture of truth and falsehood, of statesmanship and absurdity, of sensible ideas and of selfish and chimerical designs. In my view (Robespierre continues) Camille and Hébert are equally wrong'. One represents the party which attacks the state by proposing 'ultra-revolutionary' measures, the other that which does so by proposing measures that are 'citra-revolutionary': both aim at discrediting and dissolving the Convention. But they will not succeed. 'I assure all faithful *Montagnards* (such is Robespierre's peroration) that victory lies within our grasp. There are only a few serpents left for us to crush (*Applause, and cries from all parts of the hall, 'They shall be crushed!'*) Let us not trouble about this or that individual, but only about the country'.

There is no sign here of a lingering friendliness towards Desmoulins. Robespierre speaks as a man who has closed his mind to personal considerations. He had tried to treat Camille as a penitent; he now regards him as a relapsed heretic. Perhaps he would have been more patient with him, had he not been shocked, within the last few days, by the discovery that another prominent Jacobin, the ex-actor and dramatist, Fabre d'Eglantine, who had been

[1]Nos. 2 and 3 had already been read.

posing, throughout the India Company affair, as the one righteous man, and whose judgement he had been following at every turn of a troublesome inquiry, was no better than a speculator, a forger, and a hypocrite.[1] The double disillusionment was an injury not only to his idealism, but also to his self-respect. Fabre, who had been present during the attack on Desmoulins, made a movement to leave the club. The sight was too much for Robespierre's self-control. 'As for this fellow', he said, turning suddenly upon him, 'who never appears without a lorgnette in his hand, and is so clever at expounding theatrical plots, let him explain himself here, and we will see how he comes out of it!' Fabre protested that there was no charge to answer; but there were cries of 'Off with his head!' (*à la guillotine*), and on Robespierre's motion his name was struck off the club —as was, two days later, that of Camille.

Desmoulins had only his clever and spiteful pen to blame for his fall. He was untrustworthy through and through. Even his penitence was a pretence. When he was arrested, two months later, there were found, among his papers, the uncorrected proofs of a 7th number of the *Vieux Cordelier*. In it he attacked Robespierre's doctrine that the Republic should be founded on virtue—'If all the citizens are virtuous, what need is there of a Republic?'—and asserted that, even if the Committee were composed of the wisest and best statesmen in the world, it could not expect to go uncriticized.[2] It is natural to blame Robespierre's hardness towards an old friend. But it is one thing to agree to differ on an academic issue, and quite another thing to overlook a political attack because your opponent was at school with you, or you attended his wedding, or he had once supported your policy in his paper. Accident and interest, not sympathy of mind, had brought Robespierre and Desmoulins together. One now stood for the government—what he regarded as the national government—of his country: the other was deliberately setting himself in opposition, at a

[1] Mathiez, *Conspiration*, 39 f.
[2] A.R. 2/622. The passage was suppressed by subsequent editors of the *Vieux Cordelier*. For evidence as to survival of parts of later numbers, v. R.F. 51/408.

time when the overthrow of the Committee was likely to
lead to anarchy and disaster. It would be surprising if,
under the circumstances, Robespierre had acted otherwise.
. . . But who would not like him better, if he had?

XIII

Signs are not wanting that, after the expulsion of
Desmoulins, Robespierre began to tire of an inquisition
whose victims were his own friends, and that he was
looking for a way by which the purging of his party might be
raised from a matter of personalities to one of principles.
'I want the people', he said on January 10, 'to discuss
intrigue, and not individual intriguers'. It had been remarked
of his pleadings, whilst he was still a young barrister at
Arras, that he was never happy unless he could generalize
the issue, and turn his brief into an example of a philosophical principle. It was still the same with his political
speeches. He was interested, as his eighteenth-century
Providence was interested, not in individuals, but only in
classes. As a pope may extract, from the works of a school
of biblical critics, a philosophy of which none of them are
aware, and call it Modernism, so Robespierre descries a
common element among the various ideas of his political
opponents, and calls it a conspiracy. Then the process is
reversed: individual Modernists are disciplined, or ex-
communicated; individual conspirators are expelled from
the Jacobin club, or sent to the guillotine. But it makes
a considerable difference, to the judgement passed upon this
procedure, whether it is pursued by the recognized head of
an age-old and highly organized society, or by the unac-
knowledged leader of an emergency committee, fighting for
a policy which he only half understands. In the latter case
the line between orthodoxy and unorthodoxy becomes
almost arbitrary. It is sufficiently true in theology that what
is heretical to-day becomes orthodox to-morrow: in
politics—certainly in revolutionary politics—it may equally
well happen that what is orthodox to-day will become

heretical to-morrow. Robespierre's pontifical anathema was little more than an *ipse dixit*. He was an Inquisitor without a Creed.

He was conscious of this weakness: it laid him open, at every turn, to the charge that he was aiming at personal dictatorship—a charge which he knew to be untrue. 'Anyone who has such an ambition nowadays', he declared on January 10, 'must be mad as well as wicked. Yet this is the moment chosen to repeat the charge Louvet brought against me in the Convention. Because I have exercised one twelfth part of the authority of the Committee of Public Safety, they call me a dictator! . . . The only dictatorship to which I plead guilty is that of Le Pelletier, and that of Marat (*Applause*). . . . Don't misunderstand me (he goes on): I don't mean to compare myself with either the one or the other; I am not yet a martyr for the cause of the Revolution. But my dictatorship is the same as theirs, because I share with them the threat of assassination'. At this there was renewed applause: the speaker could always win sympathy by referring to designs upon his life.

XIV

Robespierre was preoccupied, during these weeks, with the home and foreign policy of the government. The first he was to embody in a great speech early in February: the second showed itself, during January, in some further remarks that he permitted himself on the subject of England. On December 28 he had characterized a British note to the Swiss Cantons as 'a disgraceful document, illustrating the crimes of kings'. A week later (January 7) he asked that a day should be set aside for the discussion of the English government; but it was not till the 28th that he obtained his opportunity. A week before, at the Jacobins (January 21) the anniversary of Louis' execution had been celebrated by burning portraits of the kings of France and Prussia on the floor of the House, and stamping their ashes underfoot; and a committee, including Robespierre, had been instructed to draw up an 'indictment against all kings', for international distribution. It was in this spirit that he expounded the policy of the government towards England.

He began by deprecating abuse. 'It is useless', he said, 'to speak to the English people. All we desire is that they should be attentive witnesses of our debates, of our republican virtues, and of our military prestige. In order to win appreciation from another people, one must allow for its weaknesses, and speak in terms it can understand. You are mistaken (he goes on) if you think that the English people are as moral and as enlightened as yourselves. On the contrary, they are two hundred years behind you. And they hate you, because for some centuries the policy of their government has been to arm the English against the French, and to use war as a means of defeating the Opposition. It does not follow that the English people will never have a revolution: they will, because they are oppressed and ruined. The revolution will be the work of the French fleet; it will come about because the British Ministry is corrupt; and Pitt will be overthrown, because, whatever may be said about his inflated reputation, he is an imbecile'. Later in the debate Robespierre deprecated any attempt to dissociate the British people from their government, and went on to denounce them under a series of heads. 'As a Frenchman', he ended, 'and as a representative of Frenchmen, I hereby declare that I hate the English people (*applause*), and that I shall do all I can to make my fellow-countrymen hate them more. Let them make what they can of it! My sole hope is in our soldiers, and in the deep dislike which Frenchmen have for England. . . . Were they to destroy their government, perhaps we might yet be friends. Meanwhile, we shall see whether a nation of shopkeepers (*un peuple of marchands*) is as good as a nation of farmers (*un peuple agriculteur*), or their few ships as powerful as our fertile acres. There is one thing more despicable than a tyrant— it is a nation of slaves (*applause*). . . . They say—and it is perfectly true—that George is half-witted (*imbécile*): his agents are completely so. They say Pitt is corrupt: *a fortiori* his employees. There is an Opposition—good luck to it! When Parliament meets, we shall see what it can do. If it votes the Address, then the English people are not worth the trouble of governing; we need not concern ourselves any more with such a despicable race. . . . The best thing would be to plunge it again beneath the ocean from which it arose'.

Though Robespierre, who never in his life moved outside Paris and Artois, had no first-hand knowledge of England—or, indeed, of any other foreign country—he can hardly have been ignorant of our traditional policy of security in the Channel, or of our new feeling against a 'nation of cannibals', which had driven the pacific Pitt into war. If he preferred boasting and abuse to information (which he could easily have acquired) and argument (which would better have become a responsible statesman), it was because his object was to exploit patriotic feeling in favour of the government's policy of continued war against England; and this partly to distract attention from troubles nearer home, and partly just for the reason he ascribed to Pitt, 'as a means of defeating the Opposition'. But it is worth notice that, only a few days before he delivered this speech, Robespierre had received a letter from an Englishman living at Boulogne,[1] who, doubtless aware of his constant championship of the West Indian negroes, declared himself an enemy of the British constitution, on the ground that Pitt and Parliament had failed to secure the abolition of the slave-trade, and who went on to say that he looked to French influence to bring about a revolution in England. True, this correspondent deprecated public abuse of the English people, for 'every people, even that to which I belong, is good at bottom': but it is pretty evident that, whilst he neglected this advice, Robespierre took the rest of the letter to heart. He may also have seen the report recently communicated to the Committee, in which an escaped French prisoner, who had spent six weeks at Portsmouth, and four days in London, described the lamentable

[1] N. S. J. Patterson (*Corresp.* 325).

state of affairs in England—he had (he said) heard the *Ça ira* sung in the streets at night, and seen the words '*House to let*' scrawled on the walls of Buckingham Palace.[1] Upon such evidence Robespierre was ready enough to say, if not to believe, that the government of England was in the hands of imbeciles, and that upon the appearance of a French fleet in the Channel her people would rise in revolution.

There were, no doubt, good reasons why Robespierre and his friends should have been unwilling to negotiate for peace with England. Any form of peace policy was discredited, in their eyes, by its association with Danton's regime at the Foreign Office. The country had caught the war fever, which, unless it was exploited by the Committee, might be captured by their rivals; war had by now become a financial necessity, and the government could not pay its way without loot. Thus Robespierre had come, by insensible steps, and with who knows what prickings of conscience, to champion the policy of keeping his party in power by a war of conquest and confiscation—a party which he had created, only two years before, by denouncing the origins of this very contest.

Holding to the belief that Robespierre was, before all else, a man of principle, it is not difficult to see how he may have persuaded himself that the only hope for the future of the Revolution, and therefore for the great truths of liberty and equality embodied in it, lay in a Jacobin dictatorship, and that anything was justifiable that seemed necessary to keep the Committee in power. Scrupulousness, after all, is a form, though a high form, of selfishness. The more Robespierre sank his innate and excessive self-regard in the aims of his club, his committee, and his country, the less value he attached to the ideals which had monopolized the allegiance of a non-party man, a free-lance in Opposition. It is a development familiar enough in political life; and it will be judged good or bad according as the historian (if he feels it his business to judge at all) gives higher value

[1] R.F. 16/328.

to the free life of the individual or to the trammelled life of the body politic.

XV

It is one of the paradoxes of Robespierre's life that, lacking 'military courage', and despising military discipline, he yet drilled himself for the moral campaign with a more than military strictness. Political life seemed to him a battlefield: the Committee was a General Headquarters from which he directed operations; the tribune a front line, under fire. With every thought directed to making himself efficient, he had no pardon for those less thorough than himself. A political Loyola, he envisaged the state as a militarized church, and its citizens as members of an Order, living under a semi-monastic rule. This was the idea that inspired the great speech delivered in the Convention on February 5, and published under the title: *Rapport sur les principes de morale politique qui doivent guider la Convention nationale dans l'administration intérieure de la République.*

Robespierre begins by remarking that, after a haphazard course, the Revolution is at last settling down on definite lines, under a government that has character and a policy. 'But what', he soon asks, 'is our aim?' and answers that it is 'the peaceful enjoyment of liberty and equality, and the reign of that eternal justice whose laws are engraved, not on marble or stone, but in the hearts of every man— whether of the slave who forgets them, or of the tyrant who denies their truth. We desire (he goes on) an order of things in which all base and cruel feelings are suppressed, and all beneficent and generous sentiments evoked by the laws; in which ambition means the desire to merit honour, and to serve one's country, in which rank is the offspring of equality; in which the citizen obeys the magistrate, the magistrate the people, and the people the rule of justice; in which the country guarantees the well-being of every citizen, and every citizen is proud to share in the glory and prosperity of the country; in which every soul grows greater

by the constant sharing of republican sentiments, and by
the endeavour to win the respect of a great people; in which
liberty is adorned by the arts it ennobles, and commerce
is a source of public wealth, not merely of the monstrous
opulence of a few households. We want to substitute, in
our country, morality for egoism, honesty for love of honour, principles for conventions, duties for decorum, the
empire of reason for the tyranny of fashion, the fear of
vice for the dread of unimportance: we want to substitute
pride for insolence, magnanimity for vanity, the love of
glory for the love of gold: we want to replace "good company" by good characters, intrigue by merit, wit by genius,
brilliance by truth, and the dullness of debauch by the
charm of happiness. For the pettiness of the so-called great
we would substitute the full stature of humanity; in place
of an easy-going, frivolous, and discontented people create
one that is happy, powerful, and stout-hearted; and replace
the vices and follies of the monarchy by the virtues and
the amazing achievements of the Republic'.

So Robespierre dreams it all, in the small room over the
carpenter's shop in the rue Saint-Honoré—almost the only
dreamer now, after four years of revolution. But is it more
than a dream, or the expression of it anything but poetry?
Can such miracles (*prodiges*) as he envisages be achieved by
laws and regulations, even under republican government,
even among a free people? He believes they can. With a
democracy all things are possible, provided only that it is
firmly based on *vertu publique*, that is, on 'love of one's
country, and of its laws'. 'It was that which accomplished
such miracles in Greece and Rome, and which can produce
in republican France results still more astonishing'. Why so?
Because French democracy is reinforced with something
which was missing from the democracies of the ancient
world: 'The French are the first people in world-history
to establish a real democracy, by inviting all men to share
equality, and the full rights of citizenship'. It follows that
the first rule of political conduct must be to maintain
equality and *vertu*, by adopting 'every measure that tends

to arouse love of the country, to purify morality, to edify souls, and to direct the passions of the human heart towards the public welfare'. Conversely, 'a bad man, a bad citizen, and a corrupter of morals are all counter-revolutionists'.

Here Robespierre is transferring to politics that easy dichotomy which has already appeared in his scheme of society. There all rich people were bad, and all poor people good: here all bad men are counter-revolutionists; and it follows, not (indeed) logically, but intuitively, that all good men are patriots, and all patriots good men. Very soon these propositions appear as the basis of all Robespierre's beliefs.

'Virtue', he goes on, 'is a natural quality of the people', and a wise government will 'trust the people, and be severe upon its own agents'. This maxim, he thinks, would be sufficient, in a time of peace. But when the Republic is beset by traitors within and foes without, another rule must be added, and it is this: 'Manage the people by argument, and the enemies of the people by intimidation'. There follows the famous passage: 'If the basis of popular government in time of peace is virtue, its basis in a time of revolution is both virtue and intimidation—virtue, without which intimidation is disastrous, and intimidation, without which virtue has no power'.[1] Their close relationship is explained thus: 'Intimidation is merely justice—prompt, severe, and inflexible. It is therefore an emanation of virtue, and results from the application of democracy to the most pressing needs of the country'. Intimidation, no doubt, has generally been the weapon of tyrants: but the new despotism takes this weapon out of the tyrant's hand, and turns it against himself, in the name of the hitherto defenceless people.

Robespierre is now back on his favourite ground—the war on two fronts against enemies at home and abroad; the inadequacy of the present courts for dealing with traitors; and the contrasted political parties whom the government has to fear. 'The internal enemies of the French people',

---

[1] 'Intimidation' not 'terror'; for *terreur* is used transitively, and means, not feeling fear, but making people afraid.

he declares, 'are divided into two factions, like two army corps. They march by different roads, and under flags of different colours; but they march to the same *rendez-vous*—the disorganization of popular government, the ruin of the Convention, and the triumph of tyranny. One of these factions urges us to weakness, and the other to excess. One would turn Liberty into a Bacchante, and the other into a prostitute'.

There follows a passage in which Robespierre describes, with the minuteness of a John Law, the whole character of the counter-revolutionist, reserving, like some of the best moralists, his harshest sentence, not for open wickedness, but for the vice that disguises itself as virtue; for the political hypocrite; for 'the aristocrat who founds popular societies, the fanatic who attacks Catholicism, the royalist who cheers republican victories, the noble who professes a love of equality, and the tyrant who scatters flowers on the tomb of the defenders of freedom'. But how is one to distinguish the true patriot from the false, when the latter adopts so perfect a protective colouring? Robespierre's answer, again, comes from the best moral tradition: 'By their fruits ye shall know them'. 'Ask them to act: they talk. Ask them to deliberate: they are all for instant action. The country is at peace: they oppose every change. It is at war: they would reform everything. You propose measures against sedition: they remind you of Caesar's clemency. You propose to rescue patriots from persecution: they urge the severity of Brutus. The country needs peace: they display the spoils of victory. It requires war: they praise the pleasures of peace'. So he goes on, with a hundred instances—and each is a bitter footnote to the personal controversies of the time.

'What is the remedy (he ends) for all these ills? There is only one, and it is the development of the great source of energy (*ressort*) in the Republic—*vertu*'; *vertu* identified, as always, with the sovereignty of the people, and with the Jacobin dictatorship. That 'virtue is powerless without intimidation' is, for the moment, ignored: all that Robespierre demands is that the principles of political morality which he has expounded 'shall be proclaimed, both within the Republic, and without'.

It would be easy to criticize this speech—to complain of its vague idealism, tolerable enough in 1789, but tedious in 1794; to object that it ends without a single practical proposal; or to urge that, just as Robespierre was so obsessed by the idea of a 'foreign plot' that he under-estimated social and political factors in the situation which were almost, if not quite, independent of outside influence, so, in his moral earnestness, he missed the importance of economic causes, and economic remedies. But it is to be presumed that he knew his audience, and had calculated the effect of his appeal. It had, in fact, for all its idealism, two quite practical aims. One was to secure a vote of confidence in the government: and to do this it was best to confine oneself to high-sounding generalities, and to avoid controversial detail. The other was to convey a warning to the two parties of suspects: and here it is to be noted that the apparently vague and rhetorical phrases in which Robespierre denounces the counter-revolutionists are full of hints and references which were intelligible enough to his audience. Hébert, Chaumette, Fabre, and Danton could not fail to see themselves depicted, however much he might assert that all the characters described in his *Serious Call* were entirely imaginary. This was Maximilien's way of attacking crime without attacking the criminal. He persuaded himself that, by mentioning no names, he had raised denunciation to the level of political science.

The allusiveness of Robespierre's style—partly a trick of contemporary rhetoric, and partly the natural method of one whose moves on the political chessboard were always oblique—has enabled fellow-idealists to compare this speech to the Sermon on the Mount,[1] whilst admirers of Jacobin statecraft see in it nothing but a preamble to the 'socialistic' Laws of Ventôse, and to a regenerative Terror.[2] There is no need to choose either of these views to the

[1] B. and R. 31/267. [2] Mathiez, G. et M. 119.

exclusion of the other. The inconsistency between an almost Christian ideal of society, and a programme of political terrorism, had ceased to be apparent to Robespierre. Philosophy cannot explain this: it can only turn away from a state of mind that ought not to have existed, leaving its study to the practitioner in mental pathology. To history, whose function it is to describe, the paradox is an incentive to further investigation.

I

AFTER Robespierre's speech of February 5, corroborated
by that of Saint-Just on February 26, no one could doubt
that the constructive policy of the Jacobin government
involved the destruction of the opposite and opposing
factions of extremists and reactionaries. During the two
months that followed his declaration of policy, Robespierre,
as his habit was when discussion passed into action, retired
from the front line, and left the contest to take its course.
He did not intervene in the debates in the Convention
between February 10 and March 15, and in fact only made
four speeches there previous to the trial of the Dantonists.
His appearances at the club were hardly more numerous.

This temporary retirement was made the easier by the
bad state of Robespierre's health. Already, in the third
week of January, he had been absent from the club long
enough for inquiries to be made about him; and in the
middle of February a fresh indisposition led to a question
by a woman in the Gallery, and the despatch of a deputation
to make inquiries at his lodgings. His friends started a
rumour that he had been poisoned—no doubt by those
pernicious 'factionists'; a number of Sections sent representatives to ask after his progress; and police spies reported
that, whilst members of the well-to-do classes appeared
delighted at the news, the *sansculottes* shook their heads,
and said, 'If he dies, all is lost'.[1] On the other hand, Robespierre's enemies took the opportunity to spread discreditable rumours about him. His occasional visits, perhaps at
this time more frequent or more prolonged, to his brother-
in-law Vaugeois at Choisy, where he was sometimes joined

[1] A.R. 2/82.

by Jacobin friends, were magnified into secret conferences, or disreputable debauches. Others said that he was so alarmed at the Hébertist revolt that he was only with difficulty prevented from fleeing the country, and taking refuge in America.[1] In point of fact, his correspondence shows no clear sign of absence from Paris. Fréron, writing on February 29, counts on finding him there;[2] and Gravier's letter of March 10,[3] though not inconsistent with a short absence from Paris, was followed by Robespierre's re-appearance at the Jacobins three days later, at the Committee on the 14th, and at the Convention on the 15th. He was still far from well. 'Would to God', he said, in answer to the cheers of the club, 'that my physical strength were the equal of my moral fortitude! I might, then, this very day, confound the traitors, and call down national vengeance on every guilty head'.

II

Robespierre's recovery from illness cannot have been hastened by the evidence which was accumulating of the failure of the Revolution in the provinces, and the progress of counter-revolutionary intrigue. A series of letters from Jullien, the most independent and sensible of the Committee's agents, told him that Lorient was the only patriotic place in Brittany; and that in Morbihan fanaticism and reaction reigned almost unchecked. He heard of new laws disregarded, assignats refused, recruitment derided, and instances not unknown of cries of *Vive le Roi!* and the wearing of the royal cockade. Carrier's crimes at Nantes were so notorious that Jullien, not content with sending Robespierre a catalogue of his misdeeds, implored his father-in-law to use his personal influence to secure his recall.[4] From Strasbourg it is reported that 'Everything is wrong: the aristocrats are raising their heads again, the assignats are depreciating, the country people refuse to accept them, and taxation grows

[1]The 'Dropmore Spy,' v. Mathiez, *Conspiration*, 147, 173, 176, 197, cp. 2/219.
[2]Corresp. 353.   [3]Corresp. 355.
[4]Corresp. 309, 312, 319, 327, 331, 332, 339. Pap. inéd. 3/52.

heavier every day'.[1] From Calais comes evidence that the north is not much better than the west or the east. There are only twelve or fifteen real patriots in the place. 'Public spirit is corrupted by bribery and intrigue'.[2]

Nor could Robespierre derive much comfort from his more private correspondence: so many of the writers seemed to be either flatterers or knaves. Duquesnoy, indeed, was an honest man, who only wished to return to work as soon as he was fit.[3] But the wretched Chabot was still writing his cringing appeals from prison. Amans, in the Luxembourg, was already composing those vile denunciations of fellow-prisoners, which Saint-Just used, three months later, to secure the condemnation of the Dantonists.[4] Cousin, a non-commissioned officer for whom Robespierre had found a place in the Alpine Legion, is now wallowing in the blood of the rebels of the Vendée, but is tired of fighting, and would prefer a Staff job nearer home.[5] A group of Girondist prisoners in La Force express regret for their 'mistakes', and promise, if allowed to return to the Convention, to give proof of their patriotism.[6] Boisset, who has lost his position as *archiviste* of the Jacobins, and has been expelled from the club, puts the blame onto Nicolas, the government printer, with whose prices he had found fault, and quotes Mme Duplay herself as authority for his accusation.[7] This was to attack Robespierre's confidence in his home and his friends. Even Buissart's last letter from Arras complained of the law regulating food prices, which was impossible of application, and saw no escape from a new 'aristocracy of shop-keepers', except in a system of municipal trading.[8]

If there was any lull in the storm of denunciation and 'purging', it was not because the supporters of the government were by now all 'pure patriots', but because it was becoming a favourite plan with the Opposition to discredit the government by associating it with these and other unpopular forms of extreme revolutionism. And so, instead

---

[1]Corresp. 321.   [2]Corresp. 311.   [3]Corresp. 316.
[4]Corresp. 317.   [5]Corresp. 320.   [6]Corresp. 322.
[7]Corresp. 323.   [8]Corresp. 330.

of leading the attack, Robespierre must now appear for the defence. Charges brought against Amand Conédic, or the Marseille commissioners, are, at his suggestion, 'referred back'. When Brichet proposes a series of provocative measures—the invasion of England, the trial of the imprisoned Girondins, and the expulsion of the Centre party from the Convention—Robespierre denounces his attempt to out-Jacobin Jacobinism, and has him expelled from the club. When Léonard Bourdon proposes that the Popular Societies shall conduct a scrutiny of all public officials, he declares that this is 'Pitt's system', and that Bourdon is no better than a pickpocket filching his neighbours' goods while their comrades are on the scaffold.

Robespierre, then, was unwell, and discouraged. Counterrevolution was making headway in the provinces. In Paris the lengthening bread-queues were sufficient evidence of the government's failure to deal with the economic situation. Worse, the Committee itself was divided; for, whilst Robespierre reacted against extreme measures, Collot d'Herbois was taking up the cause of Carrier, supporting the terrorist regime at Lyon, and trying to bring about an alliance between the Jacobin and Cordeliers clubs; and every move towards a policy either of more or of less severity exasperated differences of opinion within the government, and was seized on, by one or other of the factions outside it, as evidence of weakness or of tyranny.[1] All that the government could hope was that the Extremists would go too far, and put themselves in a position where they could be crushed by a coalition between the government and the reactionaries.

III

So it happened. Encouraged by the apparent weakness and divisions of the Committee, Hébert and Momoro ranged the Cordeliers club by the side of the Independent opposition of Ronsin and Vincent, the *Enragés*, led by Jacques

[1] Benjamin Constant's letters in December, 1793, and January, 1794, speak of a decline in Robespierre's popularity and power (A.R. 3/96).

Roux, and Carrier, the disgraced terrorist. All of these, whatever their personal grievances, could join in representing Robespierre and his majority on the Committee as 'Sleepifiers' (*endormeurs*), whose refusal of drastic measures was lulling the country into a false security. They could plan another insurrection, on the lines of that of June 2, to rid the Convention of the amphibious Centre, the 'marsh-frogs' (*crapauds de la marais*), whose monotonous croakings of consent kept the Committee in power. The conspirators hoped, through Collot, to divide the Committee, through Pache, the Mayor of Paris, to neutralize the Commune, and through Hanriot, to obtain the help of the National Guard. Early in March posters appeared, calling for the dissolution of the Convention, and the setting up of a dictatorship. At the Cordeliers, on March 4, Hébert preached insurrection, and the table of the Rights of Man was covered with black crêpe until the people should have regained its freedom. The factionists had, in a way, chosen their time well. Not only Robespierre, but also his friend Couthon was ill, and away; and three other members of the Committee—Billaud-Varenne, Prieur de la Marne, and Saint-André—were absent on mission. But they had miscalculated the balance of forces in Paris. Their untimely attack on the Centre threw this party onto the side of the Committee. Out of the forty-eight Sections, only one answered Hébert's appeal for an insurrection. Hanriot and Pache refused to move. Saint-Just's decree of February 28, announcing a scheme for confiscating the goods of proscribed persons, and distributing them to the poor, showed that the Robespierrist party in the government had a social programme more definite and far-reaching than anything proposed by Hébert or Jacques Roux.[1]

On March 12 there was a momentous meeting of the Committee, strengthened by the return of Robespierre, Couthon, and Billaud-Varenne, at which it was decided to proceed against the factions. The next day Saint-Just, for the Committee, read a report in the Convention, denouncing

[1] v. Mathiez, 451.

both reactionaries and extremists, giving the government emergency powers, and enacting the death penalty for a widely-defined range of offences against the state. The same evening Ronsin, Vincent, Hébert, Momoro, and others implicated in the affair were arrested. Carrier was not touched—Collot saw to that—and it was thought wiser to ignore the evidence against Pache and Hanriot; but the opportunity was taken to get rid of Chaumette, Gobel, and Cloots, for their part in the anti-clerical campaign; and of a group of 'foreign agents'—Kock, Proli, Desfieux, Dubuisson, and Pereira. At the trial, a week later (March 21), twenty prisoners appeared in the dock under a general charge of conspiracy: it was the first example of that convenient travesty of justice called a *fournée*, or 'baking by the batch'. All except one—a police spy—were found guilty, and were executed three days afterwards. It was a victory for the government, which, though it had no particular remedy for the ills of the moment, had at least shown that it would not tolerate the intervention of rival practitioners.

Between the arrest and trial of the Hébertists Robespierre made several speeches, stressing the international aspect of the plot (March 16), and warning the public that the fall of the Extremists would be followed by an attack upon the Reactionaries (March 20). If anyone supposed that he felt some compunction in sending the Hébertists to their death, or that he saw anything unfair in denouncing them while their case was still *sub judice*, these speeches would quickly undeceive him. There was no intention on the part of the government, and no expectation on the part of the public, of a 'fair trial'. The defendants were 'conspirators': they had failed: their lives were forfeit. The court would do little more than legalize their assassination. Robespierre was consenting unto their death.

IV

The move against the Reactionaries, anticipated alike in Robespierre's speeches and in Saint-Just's report, was set in motion as soon as the Extremists were safely under lock and key. On March 6, three days after the arrest of the Hébertists, a report on the India Company affair came before the Committee of General Security. The same evening, at the Jacobins, Robespierre hinted that Léonard Bourdon might yet find his name on a proscription list—another was evidently in preparation. On the 17th Simond and Hérault de Séchelles were arrested. On the 21st—the day on which the Hébertist trial began—Robespierre, criticizing a speech by Tallien, said that the government was taking energetic and successful measures against its enemies, and stated pretty plainly that the Reactionaries would soon follow the Extremists to the dock and the guillotine.

It was on the same day, perhaps, that, after much hesitation, and many discussions at the Committee, he was at last persuaded by Billaud-Varenne and Collot d'Herbois to consent to the proscription of Danton. When it was first proposed, as Billaud himself later admitted,[1] he had violently opposed it, and had charged him with trying to destroy the best patriots. But he had changed his mind. Characteristically, he persuaded himself that it was not Danton the man, Danton his old school-fellow, Danton the saviour of France in 1792 and 1793 that he was condemning, but the typical Reactionary, the rallying-point of a party, who happened to bear that name. The repugnance with which a less scrupulous or a lower-principled man might have come to such a decision, he hardly felt. He had carried patriotism, he fancied, to a height at which it transcended all personal considerations. What in a weaker man might appear as heartlessness was, in him, only another proof of incorruptibility. If he still hesitated, it was not from pity, but from caution. His alliance with Danton, he may have reflected, inspired confidence in the stability of the Committee, and in the continuity of its policy, especially amongst foreign observers. Noel, Danton's Venetian correspondent, had written on January 16 that the rumour of his quarrels with Robespierre was 'the last straw at which drowning kings clutched'.[2]

---

[1] In his accusation against Robespierre at Thermidor: v. 2/257.   [2] R.F. 24/465.

Danton, too, was still a power with the people, and, however carefully the trial were conducted, his eloquence might secure an acquittal, more damaging to the government than any charge of ingratitude. What at last determined Robespierre to proceed may have been the election, on March 21, of Tallien and Legendre, both associates of Danton, to the Presidency of the Convention and of the Jacobin club. If the Committee did not strike soon, the Opposition might prove too strong for them. As for Desmoulins, he had thrown away his chance of repentance; and the notion that Robespierre treated him with particular treachery, 'never speaking so kindly to him as on the eve of his arrest',[1] is refuted by Desmoulins' own words to a friend, shortly before his arrest: 'I am done for: I have been to call on Robespierre, and he has refused to see me'.[2]

During the week following the execution of the Hébertists the Committee made its plans, and made them carefully: there must be no blundering of the executioner's axe. A list of 'conspirators' was drawn up. The *fournée* was to include, besides Danton and Desmoulins, Philippeaux and Westermann (implicated in *l'affaire Dumouriez*); Hérault de Séchelles, Delacroix, and Fabre d'Eglantine, all of whom had played leading parts in the Opposition; the men implicated in the India Company scandal—Fabre came under this head too, along with Chabot, Delaunay, and Basire; and (as before, and for the same reason) a group of 'foreign agents'—D'Espagnac, Diederichsen, Gusman, and the brothers Frey.

V

So far it is just possible to defend Robespierre's action, on the ground that the removal of these men was necessary for the continuance of the Jacobin government, without which the country could not be saved from anarchy and disaster. But can any defence be found for his next move? Having willed the end, he seems to have argued that

[1] So Riouffe, who met him in prison.
[2] Joseph Planche told the story to Quicherat, and he to Carteron, a friend of Hamel (Hamel, 3/473).

he was justified in willing the means. Yet it is difficult to read without distaste, and even disgust, the *Notes*—unluckily for his reputation, they have survived—which he supplied to Saint-Just for the revision of his speech of denunciation against Danton and his accomplices.[1]

The remarks on Fabre, which come first, are excusable, in so far as the man had played a double game, and had done his best to bring others to the scaffold. But there follows a passage about the *Vieux Cordelier* which, in view of Robespierre's connexion with that paper, can only be called disingenuous. 'Fabre', he writes, 'inspired Desmoulins. The title of their paper was meant to win public support for the leaders of a clique which concealed its plots under the name of Veterans of the Revolution. Danton corrected the proofs: he admits that he made alterations in the text'. *Who would suppose that Robespierre himself had read the first two numbers in proof, and passed them for publication?*[2]

Robespierre next turns to Desmoulins, whom he describes, fairly enough, as 'fitted by his vanity and his quick imagination to become the henchman of Fabre and Danton'. But he seems to shrink—as well he might—from denouncing a personal friend, and admits that Desmoulins' previous eulogies of Mirabeau, Lafayette, and other discredited revolutionists were made in good faith, and have been expiated by subsequent denunciation.

The bulk of the *Notes*, however, deal with Danton; and here is the crux of the charge against Robespierre. Eight months before, in a public defence of Danton, he had described him as a man 'against whom no one has the right to bring the lightest reproach, and whom no one will discredit without first proving that he himself has more energy, more ability, and more patriotism'.[3] What does he say now? The charges must be examined one by one.

(1) Danton and Fabre (he says) lived with Lafayette and the Lameths. *Four years had made this patriotic association a*

---

[1] They are reprinted, with a critical Introduction and Notes, in Mathiez, *Robespierre Terroriste*; also at the end of Stephens' *Orators of the French Revolution*.
[2] Italics are used throughout this passage for comments.
[3] B. and R. 28/410.

crime. Mirabeau compensated Danton for the loss of a legal salary, and during Mirabeau's lifetime Danton 'never said a word against him'. *Danton was not a member of the National Assembly; he had no call to speak against Mirabeau, nor had Mirabeau any need to buy his silence.*

(2) Robespierre remembers dining with Danton in the first months of the Revolution, when Danton blamed him for not co-operating with Barnave and the Lameths. *Did counter-revolution, then, begin so early?*

(3) Danton set himself to copy Fabre's talents as an actor, but only made himself ridiculous when he produced theatrical tears in the tribune, and at Robespierre's house. *Here Robespierre corroborates the story of an eleventh-hour attempt to reconcile him with Danton.*[1] *But if Danton wept, what a cruel turn he gives to it!*

(4) Danton's 'black ingratitude' is shown by his treatment of Desmoulins. When the *Vieux Cordelier* was published, he claimed liberty of the press in its favour; but when he met Robespierre on the occasion just mentioned, he spoke disparagingly of Desmoulins, and attributed his faults to a shameful private vice. *What of Robespierre's own treatment of Desmoulins?*

(5) Danton's plan is to 'break' men, when he has no further use for them; but he never attacks a real conspirator. *He was an easy-going man, who chose his friends for their manners, not their morals.*

(6) When he was Minister, Danton enriched Fabre at the expense of the Treasury. *This charge probably comes near the truth.*[2]

(7) Danton released Duport and C. Lameth, implicated in the 'massacre of the people' on August 10, 1792, and opposed Robespierre's plan for 'preventing Brissot from renewing his plots'. *Danton's stand against the attempt to involve Brissot in the September massacre was surely to his credit.*[3]

(8) Danton was to blame for the escape of the Prussians

[1] Hamel's story (2/334) is taken from Prudhomme and D'Aubigny: Mathiez (*Robespierre Terroriste*, 95) refers to Barras' *Mémoires*.
[2] v. Mathiez, *Autour de Danton.*
[3] v. p. 1/274 f.

after Valmy. *He sanctioned Dumouriez's policy of negotiation, which led to the unhampered withdrawal of the Prussians. But could anything else have been done?*[1]

(9) When Robespierre demonstrated to Danton the campaign of slander prosecuted by Roland and the *Brissotins*, he replied, 'What do I care? Public opinion is a prostitute; and it is all nonsense to talk of posterity'. He laughed at the word *vertu*, and used to say, as though it were a joke, that there was no sounder *vertu* than that which he practised every night with his wife. How could a man (this is Robespierre's comment) so alien to every idea of morality, be a champion of freedom? *It is impossible to add anything to a comment that reveals so much about Robespierre.*[2]

(10) Danton surrounded himself with rascals, and openly tolerated vicious living. He once remarked that 'the severity of our principles frightened people away from the patriotic party'. *Mathiez's researches have gone far to justify the first part of this charge: the second brings out the moral issue between Robespierrism and Dantonism.*

(11) 'One must not forget Robert's tea-parties, at which Orléans mixed the punch, and Danton and Wimpffen made up the party'. *Puerilities.*

(12) Danton was responsible for Orléans' election to the Convention. *It was no crime then.*

(13) Danton's reputation for patriotism is unmerited. At the beginning of the Revolution he showed a bold front; but he was soon in league with Mirabeau and the Lameths (*see No.* 1). Nothing more was heard of him till the Champ de Mars affair, when he was responsible for a petition that caused the death of 2,000 patriots (*gross exaggeration*); he retired to Arcis, and lived peaceably there, whilst his friends were in prison (*Robespierre threw over the petitioners, and went free*); was it because he was a secret accomplice of the government? He repeated this 'cowardly desertion' on other occasions. During the Legislative Assembly he said nothing; during the Jacobin-Girondin

[1] v. Mathiez, 222.
[2] cp. Couthon's remark on Charles James Fox. *Fox est l'être du monde le plus vil et le plus immoral, et que peut on espérer d'un homme sans moeurs?* (R.F. 51/315.)

struggle he remained neutral; at first he was for the war; afterwards he pretended to take Robespierre's side, but said to his friends, 'If he wishes to perish, let him; we have no call to share his fate.' *This apparently refers to Danton's attitude at the time of Louvet's attack, at the end of October,* 1792. Danton played no part in the rising of August 10; he was dragged from his bed to attend his Section, and made eloquent speeches when it was all over. *Compare Robespierre's own record.* In the Convention he disavowed Marat, refused to say a word in defence of Robespierre (*for the facts, see* 1/284), and was always trying to conciliate the Girondins. He never spoke energetically, except about himself; he threatened vengeance on his private enemies, and proposed peace. His abuse or silence during crucial debates could only be explained as due to his fatness, and to his amours. But he was keen enough when it came to the defence of Dumouriez, or the eulogizing of Beurnonville. He distracted public attention from the conspirators by concentrating it on the levying of troops—*a singularly mean version of Danton's patriotic campaign to 'save the country' in* 1793. He wanted to save the King's life, but was intimidated into voting for his death. He loathed the revolution of May 31, and tried to compromise it by demanding the head of Hanriot. *He had asked for an inquiry into his conduct.* When this attempt failed, he pretended he had never meant it seriously, and, meeting Hanriot in a tavern, treated him to a drink, saying, 'Let's have a glass together, and think no more about it!'

After this, Robespierre abandons his consecutive commentary on Danton's career, and returns to detached notes.

(14) Danton did all he could to save Brissot and the Girondins. *See No.* 7 *above.*

(15) He wanted to dissolve the Convention, and to establish the Constitution of 1793. *Here Robespierre attributes to Danton, Delacroix's speech of August* 11, 1793.

(16) Danton once said to Robespierre, 'What a pity it is we can't cede our colonies to the Americans; it would be a good way of making them our allies'. Later, he and Dela-

croix got a decree passed which resulted in the loss of the colonies. *Delacroix's motion of February 5, for the abolition of slavery, was supported by Danton. Had Robespierre really forgotten the stand he himself made on this very ground? Apparently others had not; for Saint-Just made no use of this note in his denunciation of Danton.*

(17) Robespierre has been 'assured' that, in March, 1793, when Dumouriez was planning his *coup* against the government, Danton went to Pache, and proposed an insurrection, adding that, if money were needed, he 'had his hand in the Belgian Treasury'. *An absurd charge.*[1]

(18) Danton proposed a general amnesty, and the dissolution of the Convention. *When Danton made the first suggestion, on August 2, 1792, the Convention was not yet in existence.*

(19) Danton's activities on March 8–10, 1793, played into the hands of Dumouriez. *See Nos. 13, 17.*

Such were the grounds upon which Robespierre was prepared to send Danton to the guillotine. Neither separately nor cumulatively do they amount to anything like proof of the charge of conspiracy. No impartial court could have taken them seriously. But the tribunal which was to try Danton was not impartial; nor did it require evidence or proof, in the accepted meaning of those terms. Robespierre knew this. He realized—he had realized all along—that if it came to a conflict of evidence, or (what was less easily avoided) a conflict of speakers,[2] it would be difficult to secure a conviction. He calculated that the only thing to do was to rake up anything that could be found to Danton's discredit—even if it were only club-gossip, or the casual remarks of an indiscreet talker—and to attribute unpatriotic motives to every act of his political career.

By a convenient fiction it was assumed that anyone who had associated with the 'heroes' of the early Revolution shared the stigma of treachery attached to them by later revolutionists. In this view, all the Constituents, except

[1]Even Kerr (*The Reign of Terror*, 356) admits this, while claiming that 'the other charges are, so far as they go, exact'.
[2]A French trial includes a debate (*débats*).

a small party of extreme democrats, all the members of the Legislative, except the minority which opposed the war, and all the deputies in the Convention who did not actively support the Jacobin government, could be accused of counter-revolution. Indeed, it would not have been difficult to make out an indictment against the Incorruptible himself, from the known facts of his relationship with Mirabeau, Dumouriez, and other 'counter-revolutionists', hardly less damning than that which he brought against Danton. Gensonné, in fact, did so. He pointed out that Robespierre was for a long time a friend of the Lameths; that in 1791–2 he was on close terms with Pétion, Buzot, and even Roland; that he proposed the *panthéonisation* of Mirabeau; and that he was no less and no more responsible than Danton for the misdeeds of his fellow-Jacobins. The assumption underlying such charges is, Gensonné concludes, 'destructive of the first elements of society'.[1]

Again, there had been a series of political crises—the Flight to Varennes, the Massacre of the Champ de Mars, June 20, August 10, the September Massacres, the King's trial, the treachery of Dumouriez, the 'insurrection' of March 10, and the revolution of June 2—at each of which charges and counter-charges had been hurled to and fro so recklessly that no man's reputation was free from suspicion. Nothing was easier, then, than to create prejudice against any politician whom it was hoped to discredit and destroy. Danton, with his casual habits, his liking for low company, and his moral indifferentism, was an easy prey. He boasted that 'they dared not attack him': but he was probably the only man who thought that, if they did, he would escape the scaffold.

This, then, is the charge—that Robespierre deliberately used any means he could lay hands on, regardless not only of his personal relations with an old associate, but also of common fairness and truth, to prejudice Danton in the eyes of the Convention and of the Tribunal, and so to secure his conviction. It would be no defence to prove,

[1]Pap. inéd. 2/435, an autograph note found among Robespierre's papers.

that 'Danton was behind all the intrigues of the profiteers, as he was behind all the intrigues of the counter-revolutionists'.[1] Perhaps he was. The question is whether the specific charges made in the *Notes* are either true or relevant; and the evidence is that, almost without exception, they are not. It is no defence to say that the *Notes* are no worse than Desmoulins' *Histoire des Brissotins*, or Fabre's *Questions* on the Hébertists: Fabre and Desmoulins never put themselves on a moral pedestal. It does not exculpate Robespierre to maintain that, whilst the specific charges against Danton are 'either unlikely, or unproved, or contradicted by known facts', the general indictment showed 'undeniable insight' into his real motives, and was justified by the subsequent discovery that he was in the pay of the Court.[2] It was not the true insight, but the untrue accusations, which secured the conviction. Unfortunately for Robespierre, the *Notes* still exist, written in his own hand. Their object and meaning are quite unambiguous. The reader can form his own opinion of them, and of their author.[3]

VI

Armed with Robespierre's *Notes*, Saint-Just completed his Report, and laid it before a joint meeting of the two committees on March 30. All but two of those present— Rühl and Lindet—signed the warrant for the arrest of the Dantonists. Robespierre's signature is one of the last: it is said that he urged the postponement of the arrest until after the Report had been read in the Convention, but that he was overruled by Vadier's remark, 'If we do not guillotine them, they will guillotine us'.[4] The warrant was executed the same night.

The next day Saint-Just appeared in the tribune, and read out his Report, in a sententious, expressionless voice, one hand motionless, holding the manuscript, the other emphasizing his theme with a monotonous gesture 'like

[1]Mathiez, *Robespierre Terroriste*, 116. [2]B. and R. 32/103.
[3]cp. A.R. 5/23, a supposed letter from Danton to the Queen, which Robespierre may have used against him.
[4]A.R. 1/101.

the movement of the blade of a guillotine'.[1] When he had finished, Legendre asked that Danton should be allowed to answer the charges against him at the bar of the House. It was incredible, he said, that the man who had saved France in 1792 could now be a criminal. Fayau took a safer line. Trust the government, he said, and do not treat Danton differently from other accused persons. This gave Robespierre his cue. 'The question before us', he said, 'is whether or not the interests of a few ambitious hypocrites are to prevail over the interests of the French people. . . . No one asks nowadays what any individual and his friends claim to have done at a particular epoch or crisis of the Revolution; what matters is the record of their political career as a whole': for, just as Robespierre believed one could attack crime without attacking criminals, or a party without attacking its members, so he thought one could condemn a man's whole career without condemning the separate parts of it—a very convenient theory for the prosecution. Legendre, he went on, had spoken as though some special privilege attached to Danton's case, over and above Desmoulins', or Delacroix's. But no: 'We will have nothing to do with privilege: we will have no idols here' (*prolonged applause*). Danton's case is not different from that of Brissot, Pétion, Chabot, Hébert, Fabre, or any other pretended patriot who has tried to sow discord between the Committee and the Convention, or to cast doubt on the justice of the Revolutionary Tribunal.

The implication was obvious. Danton's case was not *sub judice*: he was already condemned. But Robespierre did not feel quite so confident as he professed to be. The Public Prosecutor and the judges could be trusted; so, up to a point, could the paid jurymen, specially picked for the occasion. There were to be no witnesses, and few documents, to embarrass them with niceties of evidence. They would decide by their patriotic feelings, and by the demeanour of the accused. But the Dantonists might make counter-charges—such as Delacroix had already outlined in a letter

[1] Barras, *Mémoires* 1/155.

from prison,[1] and in a memoir to the Committee—against members of the government. And there was always an incalculable element in republican justice: the trial being by question and answer, nothing, short of physical violence, could prevent Danton and his friends from turning their replies into speeches, and perhaps so working on the minds of the jury and the public as to secure an acquittal.

These fears, in fact, were very nearly realized; for Danton's indignation gave him fresh powers, and word began to go round that this trial, like Marat's a year ago, might, after all, turn to the discomfiture of the government. The critical moment came at the end of the second day's hearing, when Danton was making his defence with dangerous eloquence, and in a voice that could be heard, through the open windows of the court, on the far bank of the Seine. What was to be done? The court was hastily adjourned. A day's respite was obtained by interpolating into the middle of Danton's defence the hearing of charges against less prominent prisoners. Fouquier-Tinville, the Public Prosecutor, anxious to deal fairly by the prisoners, but conscious that he would lose his post if he failed to secure a conviction,[2] wrote to the Committee, asking what he should do. Fortunately for the government there came at this moment a report from the Luxembourg that a plot was being hatched among some of the prisoners to escape from custody, massacre the members of the Committee of General Security, and rescue the accused Dantonists.[3] At a time when prison warders were open to bribery, and in a district which had been specially active in the prison massacres of September, 1792, and whose Sectional and Popular Societies might at any moment get out of hand,[4] this story did not seem quite fantastic; and Saint-Just was able to use it so as

[1] Corresp. 364.
[2] Desmoulins was a relation of his (B. and R. 34/403); and at one moment during the trial the Committee gave orders for his arrest, and Herman's (the President), on the ground that they were not showing sufficient firmness (Mathiez, 464).
[3] The report came from a prisoner named Laflotte, and implicated (among others) Arthur Dillon. There is independent evidence of a letter from Dillon to his brother, asking for his co-operation in such a plot. (Mathiez, *Corruption parlementaire*, 182.)
[4] Corresp. 362: Robespierre had received this warning only a fortnight before.

to induce the Convention to pass a decree under which 'any person accused of conspiracy who resisted or insulted national justice' was at once deprived of the right of defending himself (*mis hors des débats*).[1] This decree was read in court the next day. When the prisoners protested, they were immediately disbarred. Some of the jury were already convinced that Danton was 'an implacable enemy of the Republic'.[2] Such of them as still hesitated were 'persuaded' by a secret document communicated to them, out of court, by the President and the Public Prosecutor.[3] Thereupon they found all the prisoners guilty, except one. On the evening of April 6 fourteen were sent to the guillotine. A few days later, a fifteenth, Lulier, was reported to have stabbed himself in prison.

VII

It had been Robespierre's part, during the trial, to keep public opinion resolute for the punishment of the 'conspirators'. At the Jacobins, on April 5, he demanded that the club should discuss no other subject, and that members should be invited to give any evidence they could against the prisoners. Arthur, who was to have been one of the witnesses at the trial, but who was not called, because the jury had already made up their minds, retailed his evidence. Couthon and others followed. Attacks were made on Dufourny, and, on Robespierre's motion, he was expelled from the club. By such means Jacobin opinion was held straight on its course, and a Jacobin jury could have little doubt either as to where its duty lay, or as to what treatment it might expect, if it failed to do it.

Whilst he thus hardened Jacobin opinion against the Dantonists, Robespierre steeled his own heart against their personal appeals. Delacroix, who thought, like Chabot, that his best hope lay in turning king's evidence, wrote to him, as 'an austere republican, an enemy of conspirators

[1] B. and R. 32/187. [2] Poumiès de la Siboutie, *Souvenirs*, 26.
[3] Madelin, *Danton*, 310.

and traitors', denouncing prominent members of the governing committees—Vadier, Vouland, Amar, David, Collot d'Herbois, and Barère—whom he had reason to think might be out of favour with Robespierre.[1] Lulier reminded Maximilien that he had been a member of the Commune of August, 1792, Public Prosecutor, and *Procureur-général-syndic*; with such a record of republican service, he had never been an intriguer; indeed, he remarked, with a *sancta simplicitas* which illuminates other careers besides his own, that he 'never knew an hour beforehand what he was going to write, or say'. In the margin of the letter may still be read a note in pencil: 'Arrested for the Hébert affair: stabbed himself in prison.'[2] From Deforgues came a long apologia for his political career; it was only through Robespierre, he said, and in Robespierre's interests, that he had had any dealings with Danton: he had never even asked him to dinner without asking Maximilien too; and had often acted as peacemaker between them. A tactless and vain appeal.[3] Desfieux wrote to the Revolutionary Committee of the Section Le Pelletier, asking them to intercede with Robespierre on his behalf.[4] More moving than any of these, to a modern reader, are the letters from Lucile Desmoulins, and from her mother, Mme Duplessis, begging Maximilien to spare Camille. The older woman reminds him of the evenings they had all spent together, of the pleasure with which he had taken little Horace (Lucile's child) onto his knee, and played with him, and of the hope he had once had of becoming her son-in-law.[5] 'Robespierre', writes the young wife, 'how can you really carry through this fatal design, suggested (it must be) by the vile beings who surround you? Have you forgotten a friendship that Camille can never recall without feelings of emotion (*attendrissement*)? What wrong has my Camille done'?[6]

Why did they all appeal to him? Because he was powerful?

[1]Corresp. 364.   [2]Corresp. 366.
[3]Corresp. 370.   [4]Tuetey, 10/2465.
[5]Fleury, *Camille Desmoulins* 2/285; for *son-in-law* v.1/65.
[6]Corresp. 372. The letter was unfinished, and never reached Robespierre.

Because he might be moved to pity? As for power, the thing had gone too far for recall. As for pity, fanatical patriotism had hardened his heart. The answer to all the letters was the same—death.

Robespierre, throughout this time, acted with the same open-eyed ruthlessness that he had shown during the trial of the king. He saw, with the terrible clarity of a fanatic, that the line of advance marked out for his party was the strait way leading to salvation, and that the broad and tempting paths on either hand could lead only to damnation. By destroying the bodies of the heresiarchs he might, like any inquisitor, save the souls of their heretical followers. Now at last he was free to lead all Frenchmen along the path of the Elect, by way of 'Virtue, without which intimidation is disastrous', into the Promised Land of liberty, equality, and the untrammelled sovereignty of a good and wise people.

At last! But if he had looked back, he might have noted with alarm an ominous sequence of events, following one another at shorter and shorter intervals, like the banks of a river that slide more rapidly past as the voyager nears the edge of a great cataract. Four times, now, the Revolution had made a fresh start: four times a party had been put into power: four times the new regime had broken down: and each period of grace had been shorter than the one preceding it. The rule of King and Commons, set up in July, 1789, had lasted till the Flight to Varennes, and the Massacre of the Champ de Mars—two years: the rule of the Feuillant party, with a *Brissotin* interlude, from July, 1791, to August, 1792—one year: the rule of the Girondist Convention from September, 1792, to June, 1793—eight months. Since then the Jacobins had ruled; but only by removing one rival after another. The Girondists had been sacrificed in October, just five months after the revolution that was to make France safe for Jacobinism: and now the Hébertists, at less than five months interval, and the Dantonists, only a fortnight later, had been destroyed, to make way for Robespierrism. What expectation of life remained for this last survivor of a doomed dynasty? A contemporary rhymer pointed the moral:

Fifteen victims, one by one,
Crossed the fatal Acheron:
Last among them, proud Danton
Hung back in the rear, alone.
'You there, step up!' cried old Charon,
'What are you waiting for? Come on!'
'I'm waiting', he said, 'for friend Couthon,
For Saint-Just, and for Robespierre'.[1]

VIII

When Danton died, Robespierre was within a month of his thirty-sixth birthday. He was still, according to modern ideas, a young man; but ill-health and overwork had so aged him that it is difficult to find the debonair mouldings of the Salon portrait of 1791 in the sharpened profile of the Grandmaison sketch, or the tired, suspicious eyes of the portrait attributed to Greuze.[2] He was not an old man; but he had talked so often of martyrdom, and had been so near assassination, that he can hardly have counted on a long future in which to finish his life's work.

The Revolution, too, might well seem to have aged prematurely. Into five years the French people had crowded the experiences of two centuries. They had passed from a seventeenth-century absolutism of king, church, and nobility, into a nineteenth-century constitutional monarchy controlled by the middle classes; and from that to the dictatorship of a political party whose methods have become a model for the twentieth century. They had known civil war and foreign invasion, famine and unemployment. The national administration had at one time been left to the vagaries of local opinion, and at another dragooned by every resource of a centralized bureaucracy. The army had been broken in pieces, and reorganized; the church split into two parts—one powerless and the other persecuted;

[1]Tourneux, 1/4278.   [2]v. illustrations facing pp. 101, 228.

society from top to bottom had been overturned, wealth redistributed, and the very geography of the countryside, with the memories and habits of centuries, rearranged. These changes had come too rapidly. Though there were still outbursts of energy and enthusiasm, they had become spasmodic. The country as a whole was nervous and exhausted.

The Revolution had come about because the institutions of the old regime lagged at least half a century behind the social and political ideas of the middle class. Five years of revolution had resulted in fresh institutions, which were nearly fifty years ahead of that same middle-class opinion; for it is one thing to design a house, and another thing to live in it. The shifting of the political, economic, and social weight of the country from the privileged to the un-privileged classes had produced unanticipated stresses, and time was needed for the foundations to settle down. Perhaps, if the Revolution had been allowed to work itself out in a time of peace and economic prosperity; perhaps, if the king and his party had been better advised and served, or if the Papacy had taken a wider view of the interests of the church, the fresh order of things might have been better assimilated, before the new France came into inevitable conflict with the old Europe. But, in fact, the incompetence of the royal policy, the hostility of the Pope, the economic unrest, and the premature war had set problems which the men of 1792 and 1793 were quite unable to solve.

This was not from lack of ideas, or from any unwilling-ness to legislate. Five years of demolition and reconstruction found the French people (metaphorically speaking) better housed, better lighted, and better supplied than in the almost medieval days of Louis XV. An age of political inventions had, within a few years, carried a new power into every corner of the country, and invented a complicated apparatus for applying it to the needs of daily life. But Frenchmen of the eighteenth century were, on the whole, without the education or aptitude to exploit these oppor-tunities. They did not know how to use the popular elections, committee government, trial by jury, and other devices with which their legislators supplied them. And the politicians themselves—the trustees and distributors of the new power —seemed quite unable to agree as to how it should be applied. In a word, the machinery of government had been, almost miraculously, modernized, but there was no corresponding capacity to govern, or to be governed.

A Frenchman is, perhaps, too ready to judge his rulers by their gestures. The regime of the Committee of Public Safety, like that of Napoleon, has gained too much credit in its own country by its Roman rhetoric, its resounding victories, and its show of efficient centralization. The national effort of 1793 and 1794 was, indeed, magnificent; but its successes at home, like its victories abroad, were won by wasteful and inefficient means. The fixing of food prices, the prosecution of hoarders and profiteers, and the purchase of supplies from abroad, could not hide the fact that the economic life of the country had broken down. The regularity with which the Paris prisons were filled with disloyal officials, dishonest contractors, and defeated generals, was striking evidence of the all-seeing eye of the central committees; but counter-revolution and corruption were only driven underground; whilst the efforts of national agents and travelling deputies to standardize the administration, and to secure obedience to the laws, were constantly thwarted by the ignorance or obstinacy of local authorities, who had grown accustomed, during four 'years of liberty', to doing things in their own way. The Jacobin government, indeed, was like the French road-system. It extended in straight lines from the capital of the country to the great cities on the circumference, and where there was a road there was a law. But the roadless spaces, which became wider, the further one travelled from Paris, were often untouched by the central government, and sometimes openly hostile to it. There were schemes of finance, schemes of poor relief, and schemes of education; but, like the currency, they were on paper, and hopelessly depreciated. Destitution was widespread, and the rural population remained little less superstitious, the town mobs little less debased, than they had been under the old regime.

The failure of the Revolution to remedy these disorders was, in part, due to circumstances which it inherited from the past, or which were for other reasons out of its control. But something must be attributed to the political incompetence of the class which the Revolution had put into power. They had at their command most of the forces which were so successfully exploited by Napoleon a few years later—a peasantry ready to support any regime which secured them their land, and a middle class demanding nothing so much as security of property and *rentes*; a people in arms, jealous to defend the Revolution, and a new social system which made it possible to use everything French, and every Frenchman, in the service of the nation. If they failed to profit by such an opportunity, it was largely because they were ignorant of the economic factors which affected the situation, and honestly thought that social evils were remediable by decree, tribunal, and guillotine. But they had also two failings of a more personal kind—factiousness and lack of prestige.

Factiousness was a failing which nearly all the politicians attributed to their opponents, without being conscious that they shared it themselves. It was due partly to a political inexperience which had not yet matured into organized parliamentary parties, and partly to that clearness of mind which makes it more natural for a Frenchman to stress the differences than the likenesses between his views and those of his opponent.

The other failing was all the more serious because it arose out of the very nature of the Revolution, and was at present beyond cure. Partly owing to the progress of Liberal ideas, and partly through the failings of the last two Bourbons, the French people had ceased, by 1789, to have any real respect for their rulers. The foundations upon which such respect had once rested—noble birth, ecclesiastical office, great houses and estates, or political privilege— were soon undermined. How was that prestige to be re-

479

created, without which all government becomes either anarchy or despotism? It was no solution of this problem to substitute the rule of wealth for the rule of rank. Democracy fails, unless it embodies a respect for such qualities of mind and character as fit men to rule, and a method of government that enables them to do so. In the single-chamber system which had been felt, quite naturally, to be the proper expression of the sovereignty of the people, these conditions were not present. The prestige of the National Assembly passed away with it; and the after-glow of royal dignity which for a moment touched Louis' guillotine shed no light on the seven hundred who cast lots for his raiment. Power went to the clever writer, the eloquent speaker, the popular club-man, or the organizer of public demonstrations. These men had their personal followings, based on sympathy rather than faith, and resembling less our political parties than the 'publics' which support our favourite actors. Their utterances were applauded, but their orders were not obeyed. The larger groupings, supported (except in the case of the Paris deputies) by no clear party vote in the constituencies, had little coherence, and commanded little loyalty. It was indeed, the merit of the Jacobins that they saw through the pretences by which the Girondins persuaded themselves that their misgovernment represented the will of the people, and that they frankly used force instead of persuasion, until such time as the country might be fit for genuine democracy. But there was, in fact, too little difference, except in clear-sightedness, between themselves and those whom they displaced. They might be able to keep order more effectively, just because they had learnt, whilst in opposition, how to obstruct it—much as Michael Collins' Republican Army of 1921 could deal with Irish rebels more effectively than the 'Black-and-tans'. But they were essentially the same kind of men as the Girondins, and they commanded no obedience but that of fear or greed from the disorderly crowds whom they had once incited to insurrection, and whom they were now compelling or bribing to behave like virtuous and law-abiding citizens.

It was to Robespierre's credit as a statesmen, though as a politician it proved his undoing, that he could never wholly reconcile himself to this Jacobin realism. He was too shrewd not to see why the Girondins had failed, and to profit by their failure. He was sufficiently out of humour with his old Liberal abstractions to be willing to sacrifice liberty on the altar of national safety; nor was it easy to see how else his party could remain in power. But he held stubbornly to his belief in the supremacy of spiritual values. The science of government, to him, was *politique morale*— politics tinged with ethics. The basis of good government was the *vertu* of the governors, and of the governed. Any regime that aimed merely at material prosperity, or that contented itself with forcing obedience, instead of winning co-operation, could at best be only a transition to the enlightened self-government of a free and virtuous people.

He had never abandoned this faith: but perhaps, as the overlying strata of experience wore away, the old beliefs of his youth reappeared, and he turned back, as tired administrators will do, with a mind that had lost some of its power of fresh thought, to the Rousseauized Catholicism of Louis-le-Grand. Like an investigator who has found a chemical compound with which he can change his personality at will, he indulges once and again in terrorist orgies which he really detests, confident that he can at any moment restore the regime of reason and virtue. So the Girondins are destroyed; and Hébert; and Danton. But each time the return to sanity proves more difficult; the craving for violence returns at shorter and shorter intervals; the reign of virtue seems, not less desirable, but harder to achieve. Still, he comforts himself, it cannot be the formula which is failing; it must be that the ingredients are impure. And so, after infinite research, and with every precaution science can suggest, he will stake all upon a final experiment.

IX

During the month that lies between the execution of Danton (April 6) and the speech inaugurating the worship of the Supreme Being (May 7) Robespierre's demeanour may be studied, as that of a man who is preparing himself for the greatest moment of his career.

He does not appear much in public. He intervenes only twice in the Convention, and five times at the club. But it is to be noticed that it is always on disciplinary or police matters, involving the expulsion of two members from the Jacobins,[1] and the centralization of political trials in Paris.[2] This preoccupation with questions of punishment is equally noticeable in the proceedings of the Committee during the same period. Joint meetings with the Committee of General Security—always a sign of public emergency—follow thick and fast. The arrest of the Dantonists had been carried through in this way on March 30: on April 1 another combined meeting ordered that of Deforgues; another, on the 4th, that of Lucile Desmoulins; and another, on the 5th, that of Dufourny. Then there was a pause; but it was a joint decision of the 12th which liberated Viennot, another of the 14th which released Le Roy and Wastard, and arrested Voulland, and another of the 15th which released Moreau, and arrested Beretère. Always Robespierre was present, and signed the decrees.

The subjects dealt with at the ordinary meetings of the Committee were, of course, more varied; but it is to be noted that, although Robespierre is generally present, he now signs few decrees, except those dealing with police matters, official appointments, and the army. The destruction of the 'factions' has in no wise diminished his belief in the need for punitive methods. On the contrary, the policy of the Committee is to take advantage of its victory to crush all opposition, and to enforce its will upon every part of the administration; and this programme, prefaced by a speech by Collot d'Herbois at the Jacobins on April 10, is rigidly enforced during the weeks that follow. New officials are appointed—trusted patriots; the Popular Societies, the heirs of the independent spirit of the Paris

[1] Fion on April 8, Gentil on April 15.
[2] Speeches in the Convention, April 16 and 18.

Sections, are virtually suppressed; Ronsin's Revolutionary Army—the last hope of armed resistance to the government —is disbanded; the Jacobin press is heavily subsidized; and many of the Representatives on Mission, whose vagaries have embarrassed the Committee, are recalled. The transference of all political trials to Paris, following Saint-Just's Report of April 15, put an end to the unregulated excesses of some of the provincial tribunals, and standardized the punishment of counter-revolution. At the same time all ex-nobles and foreigners, with a few exceptions, were banished from Paris, and from any seaport, or fortified town in the war area. And, in order to concentrate control more effectively, the six Ministries, which had long lost any real independence, were now transformed into twelve Commissions, and became a bureaucracy working under the direct supervision of the Committee.

It is often urged that the need for a policy of intimidation passed away with the military successes of the autumn of 1793 and the spring of 1794, and that no kind of justification for it remained after the decisive victory of Fleurus on June 26. It may be answered that this argument lays too much stress on the military situation at the frontiers. The foreign front and the home front were so closely related, that a victory or a defeat in either sphere had immediate results upon the other. But efficiency and patriotism must flow from the centre to the circumference, from the heart to the limbs of the body politic; and the necessity of discipline at home did not cease, just because vigilance abroad could be relaxed. That was what had happened, under the Girondist regime, during the winter of 1792, and it had led to the disasters of the spring of 1793. If the successes won under the Jacobin government were to be consolidated, the Terror must go on. The opposite policy—the policy of 'clemency', in support of which the Dantonists had lost their lives— rested upon a falsely optimistic view of the state of the country, in which, in fact, corruption was still widespread, and counter-revolution assumed a hundred forms. Only the Jacobin government, as the sequel was to show, stood between the great national effort of 1794 and the neurotic anarchy of the Directory. The Committee might well be excused for thinking that it was necessary to guard against the reaction that would follow victory, and to keep the national spirit up to the high level that had won it the fear, if not the respect of the world.

Robespierre, certainly, was under no illusions as to the state of the country, or the need of continued vigilance. His own brother, sent on a fresh mission to Haute-Saône, had taken with him a new mistress, named La Saudraye, the Creole wife of a literary man, and had quarrelled with a series of government agents—Bernard des Saintes, Lejeune, and Duroy; so that Maximilien's post-bag was full of personal charges and counter-charges; whilst, as background to these unedifying disputes, he read of food troubles in the provinces, venereal disease in the army, committees full of false patriots, militant anti-clericalism, and other causes of scandal.[1] The only comfort to be derived from Augustin's letters was the recommendation of certain sound and able patriots, of whom one was 'a man of outstanding merit, a Corsican', named Buonaparte.[2]

From Jullien, too, came disquieting news as to the war in the Vendée, where the generals co-operated in nothing but treachery, sacrificed the lives of their men in ill-judged operations, and covered up their embezzlement of public funds by pretending that the military chest had been captured by the enemy.[3] These views were corroborated by officers who doubtless wished to escape punishment for the mismanagement of the campaign. One of them described the burnings, massacres, and other horrors that had become commonplaces of a civil war, and insisted that the punishment of Ronsin and Vincent—the leaders of counter-revolution on the home front—would do more

---

[1] Corresp. 340, 346–8, 351, 367, 371. Mathiez's account of the mission (*Autour de Robespierre*, 13 f.) is unduly favourable to Augustin.

[2] Corresp. 371. Perhaps from jealousy, Augustin ignores Bonaparte's success at Toulon, four months before; but Maximilien had heard of it through Saliceti's letter to the Committee (R.F. 26/374).

[3] Corresp. 339.

good than a whole army corps of reinforcements.[1] When Robespierre received this letter, Vincent and Ronsin were already on their way to the guillotine: perhaps he kept it as evidence of what he was always saying—that political operations in Paris were as necessary to national victory as military operations at the front.

x

It was with a mind full of such troubles, and upon a stage crowded with all the implements of intimidation, that Robespierre came forward, on May 7, 1794, after three weeks' absence from the Convention,[2] with his proposals for the inauguration of a State religion.

It is not certain how he had come to think that such was the remedy needed, or that this was the moment to apply it. Some historians have held that the worship of the Supreme Being was no more than a piece of political opportunism. Robespierre, they say, knew that the sceptics and ex-Catholics of the Convention thought religion necessary for the common people. Mathieu the educationist and Danton the opportunist had proposed it. Let a form of worship be devised in which Catholics and sceptics, Deists and nature-lovers, philosophers and philanthropists might all find something to their liking—a Lowest Common Multiple of religion. It would not matter whether it were true, so long as it was successful.

But this is too simple an account of Robespierre's state of mind. He was always something more than an opportunist. He might lend himself to the convenience of the moment; but it would be because he had convinced himself that it expressed something true for all time. It must be remembered, too, that he had been brought up as a Catholic, and had retained more than he was aware of the Oratorian outlook. Political experience had driven him, during the last five years, to discard many of the Liberal abstractions

[1]Corresp. 360.
[2]His name does not appear in the *Moniteur* between April 18 and May 7.

which overlaid his earlier beliefs; and it was not unnatural
that this return towards authoritarianism should have
extended also to his religious ideas. Faced by a spiritual
bankruptcy which saw no remedy but atheism or anti-
clericalism, he was in the mood to remember that both
Mably and Rousseau (recently canonized by the Revolution)[1]
had declared that a State could not exist healthily without
religion.[2] His attitude in the Constituent Assembly had
not been noticeably different from that of most of his
fellow-deputies, who officially patronized 'the religion of
the majority of Frenchmen', and whose personal views were
of a vaguely theistic type. But upon occasion he had shown
an unusual degree of sympathy for the priests, or an
embarrasingly sincere belief in divine guidance. Then had
come the experience of clerical plots against the Revolution,
and he had been driven into a policy of retaliation. More
lately again he had been impressed by the disruptive effects
of the anti-clerical movement, and had been shocked by the
vulgar excesses of the worship of Reason. Yet, much as he
disliked Hébert, Fouché, and Chaumette, he was not
unwilling to build upon their mistakes. Jullien had recently
written from Bordeaux[3] urging the establishment of 'Republican festivals': they would be specially effective, he thought,
in attaching female enthusiasm, too ready to waste itself
on political hero-worship, to the service of the State.
A hundred instances, up and down the country, showed
how often the government had offended, or failed to
exploit, the religious instincts of the common people.
Worse than this, certain acts of the Convention, such as the
Republican Calendar,[4] the decrees allowing the suppression
or union of parishes (November 6), or the official recognition of Gobel's abjuration (November 7), and of the Feast
of Nature at Nôtre Dame (November 10), might seem to

[1]Rousseau's *panthéonisation* was decreed by the Convention on April 14.

[2]It is said that, some days before Robespierre's speech of May 7, Saint-Just's
attention was called to Mably's remarks on State religion, and that he was much
struck by them (A.R. 1/345).

[3]Corresp. 378 (April 19).

[4]Robespierre, no doubt, had heard how it was celebrated by a fête at Arras
(Michelet 8/185).

have committed it to a 'campaign against the church', of which most of its members disapproved, if only because of the discredit it brought upon the Revolution in the eyes of foreign observers, and the obstacles it put in the way of co-operation with Catholic revolutionists in the Netherlands.[1] When the *Comité des Sociétés populaires* petitioned that no citizen should be forced to contribute to clerical salaries (November 6); when Léonard Bourdon proposed a public procession with church ornaments as a protest against superstition (November 8), and the *Sections Gravilliers* and *de l'Unité* performed anti-clerical masquerades at the bar of the House (November 12, 20); when the Convention itself accepted a copy of Cloots' *Certitude des preuves de Mahométisme*, and proposed to erect a statue to the clerical sceptic, Jean Meslier; then there was a reaction, and it was headed by Robespierre.

Perhaps the incident that brought home the danger to him most acutely was his friend Couthon's essay in blasphemy, when he deposited on the table of the House the 'precious blood' of Billan, and remarked that, though he had carried it for some days on his person, 'it had neither cured his paralysis nor withered up his hand'. The support which he now gave to Robespierre's religious campaign was perhaps in the nature of amends for this conduct.[2]

No time was now lost. It was noticed that, in his report on the political situation, on November 17, Robespierre had interpolated a passage condemning the anti-clerical demonstrations as part of a foreign plot. On November 21 he declared the religious policy of the government to be (1) freedom of worship, so long as it led to no breach of public order, (2) the right of *communes* to move for the suppression of public worship in their localities, and (3) the necessity of belief in a Supreme Being. In the *Manifeste aux Rois* of December 5 he repeated his warning against attacks on the church; and the following day the Com-

[1] Braesch in R.F. 55/505.
[2] R.F. 51/255, 311. cp. Lambert, *Essai sur la vie politique de Couthon*. Couthon had been as 'clerical' as Robespierre himself, till convinced of the dangers of the 'nonjuror' movement.

mittee promulgated a decree on liberty of worship which won the approval both of anti-clericals such as Prud-homme, and of atheists such as Sylvain Maréchal. But as this was still capable of misinterpretation, and was in fact used, in different parts of the country, as an excuse both for 'fanaticism', and for the persecution of priests, there grew up a demand, especially amongst the National Agents and Representatives on Mission, for a more positive and comprehensive policy. It was this demand which the Committee endeavoured to meet by promulgating the *Culte de l'Être Suprême et de la Nature*.

As to Robespierre's own part in this project, it is to be noticed that, however forward he might be, he represented the views of the Committee; however clerical he might be, he could do no more than regulate anti-clericalism; and that not only Rousseauism, but also the forms taken by the cult of revolutionary patriotism, pointed to the necessity of some religious creed and worship as the basis of civic life. It follows that, when Robespierre comes forward on May 7 with his proposals for the worship of the Supreme Being, he is not enforcing a purely personal programme; he is not preaching a return to Catholicism, but defining an official substitute for it; and this cult is no new-fangled worship, but a revised form of the religion of patriotism, hitherto imperfectly expressed by Feasts of Federation, Law, Liberty, Nature, Reason, and the like.

It may safely be added that Robespierre put forward this policy with special enthusiasm, as something more than the political expedient that some members of the Committee thought it; for to him it seemed a genuine declaration of faith in the spiritual meaning of the Revolution. That, indeed, was why he could use such bitter language against Hébert, Chaumette, and the rest, whose alarming experiments in civic religion—a deliberate caricature of Catholicism—seemed to the inexpert eye to bear a singular resemblance to the reasonable and uncontroversial proposals of the Committee. 'Atheists' he called them: quite unfairly, in theology, for they were no more so than he was; did not

Maréchal himself welcome the cult of the Supreme Being? But fairly enough in fact, for their intentions had never been religious, and his were.[1]

The title under which Robespierre proposed to address the Deity was not one of his own invention. The 'Supreme Being' (*l' Être Suprême*), an *alias* for God not unfamiliar to philosophic ears, had been introduced into the Preamble of the Constitution of 1793 by one Pomme, who was by no means a Robespierrist; Robespierre himself would have preferred the phrase, 'Immortal Legislator'. When the Committee first decided upon its religious policy, it was Couthon, not Robespierre, who announced it in the House. The scheme of worship that Robespierre presented on May 7 was based upon proposals made by Mathieu, and its festivals filled up the outline of Fabre's Republican Calendar. What was personal and original was the passion with which Robespierre's faith invested the Report. Louis Blanc records the tradition that upon this one occasion all his nervous mannerisms disappeared, and that there was no trembling of his limbs, no twitching of his features, no drumming of his fingers on the desk, as he spoke on the subject nearest his heart. He had not hesitated, in face of Guadet's mockery, to declare his belief in a Providence that watched over the affairs of France. Why should not all Frenchmen do the same? He had insisted, in speech after speech, that the mainspring of democracy was *vertu*, an idealized patriotism. Why should not that faith be embodied in the national festivals which were becoming so popular a form of propaganda? The people, he firmly believed, was virtuous at heart. But could its *vertu* live without religion? He felt that his own *vertu*, of which he was abundantly aware, was not moral opportunism, but sprang from something more consistent and permanent than the shifting modes of conduct he saw around him. In the rare moments of quiet which were still left him—when walking in the country, perhaps, or when alone in his room at night—he found something which gave fresh confidence to his

[1] v. e.g. a passage from his *Lettres à ses Commettans* quoted by Lewes, 274.

increasingly anxious isolation. What was it? Himself writ large? Robespierre, the Incorruptible, striking this noble pose, or uttering that resonant platitude? Robespierre the prophet? Robespierre the martyr? Or was there something beyond—a greater personality, into which his own might be absorbed—a Supreme Being, alone worthy of the worship of a free and virtuous people?

XI

The 'Report on the relations between religious and moral ideas and republican principles' was delivered in the Convention on May 7. Robespierre's reputation, both as statesman and orator, was by now so great that the occasion was less like a parliamentary debate than the first performance of a new play by the dramatist of the hour. The undiscriminating came to applaud anything he said, so long as it sounded well; the critics were there to interpret his message, and to lay up his indiscretions in their heart—for it was hardly safe to disagree openly. The speaker himself was fully aware of what was expected of him: never had his periods been so polished, or his antitheses so well pointed.

He began, as his habit was, with a wide survey of the world. Was there, he asked, any such thing as human progress? 'Nature tells us that man is born for freedom: the experience of centuries shows us man enslaved'. Liberty and virtue glimmer here and there in the long night of despotism and crime. Yet the world has changed, and has improved. Civilization has taken the place of savagery: crops grow where there were once forests: the sea has been conquered, America discovered, the sting of lightning extracted from the sky.[1] The travels of La Pérouse, the science of Newton, the art of David, prove our progress in the mastery of nature.

But as much more remains to be achieved. 'Human reason is like the globe we live on: whilst one hemisphere is sunlit, the other is still plunged in darkness. The nations of

[1] Robespierre liked to remember his part in the *paratonnerre* case (v. 1/34).

Europe have made astonishing advances in art and science; but they seem of be ignorant of the first notions of public morality. They know everything except Right and Duty'. Why is this? It is because hitherto the rulers of the world, intent upon power, have crushed the 'stern philosophers and friends of mankind', who might have caused political discontent, and have encouraged the soporiferous arts of 'the geometer, the painter, and the poet'. The remedy for this is obvious. 'The art of government has hitherto been the art of cheating and corrupting the governed: it must be changed into the art of enlightening them, and making them better'. The ruler must sink his private interests in the happiness of the country, and defend humanity, where once he oppressed it. The citizen must be led by good institutions along the path of social morality—'the one and only foundation of civil society'. The Revolution, Robespierre asserts, is just such a regime: it is 'a transition from the reign of crime to the reign of justice': and that is why it has been so bitterly attacked by despotism from without and conspiracy from within.

So far Robespierre has circled in the sky: now he swoops on his prey. The latest and most dangerous form of conspiracy, he says, is that which attacks patriotism, morality, and religion by disguising itself in their dress. Hébert, Danton, and their associates—he does not name them, but it is clear whom he means—made patriotism impossible, by the exaggeration of their demands; discredited morality, by preaching what they never practised; and caused a reaction towards superstition, by attacking the church. Robespierre's denunciation of these 'wolves in sheeps' clothing' may have been modelled upon the famous passage which some zealot, with more sense of rhetoric than Christian charity, added to the Sermon on the Mount, with its constant refrain of 'Woe to you, Scribes and Pharisees, hypocrites!' The Pharisee was the greatest enemy of early Christianity, because he seemed to be a better Jew than the Christian. The only thing to do was to denounce him as a 'hypocrite', that is, an actor—one whose life was

491

quite different when he was off the stage. The most dangerous enemy of the Revolution, says Robespierre, is not the
priest or the royalist, but the politician who makes broad
his patriotic phylactery, and loves the chief seat in the
Convention, and at the club, in order to make money,
embarrass the government, and provide foreign powers
with an excuse for attacking the country. For this is the
head of the indictment: since the anti-clerical campaign
began, Pitt, who helped to incite it, has been able to work up
fresh indignation against the Revolution as an enemy of
religion.

It is in order to meet this insidious conspiracy, and to
reassure Europe, that Robespierre has come forward with
his proposals for a national recognition of religion.
Atheism—such is his summary name for rationalism and
anti-clericalism[1]—has (he declares) no pragmatic value; and
there follows a rhetorical denunciation of those who try to
persuade men that 'their destinies are directed by a blind
force, which punishes at haphazard, now virtue, and now
crime, and that their souls are no more than a faint breath,
dissipated at the door of the tomb'. What nature suggests,
and what men imperiously demand, is the existence of a
God, and the immortality of the soul. Even if these beliefs
were fictions, they would be 'the grandest conceptions of
the human mind'. But the metaphysical question may be
left to the philosopher. It is for the statesman to realize
that 'everything which is useful to the world, and produces
good results, is true'. Solon had his oracles, Socrates his
familiar spirit, Rousseau 'spoke enthusiastically of the
Deity, and painted the charms of virtue in vivid colours'.
It is for the French Republic to complete the political
revolution by initiating the spiritual revolution which this
great prophet foretold, and to declare its belief in the
existence of a Supreme Being, and in the immortality of
the soul.

Robespierre foresees the objection, that his proposal will

[1]Gobel, who had renounced his bishopric, and Chaumette, who believed himself
to be as good a Rousseauist as Robespierre, had both been executed as 'atheists'.

play into the hands of the priests. No, he says; the new worship will be a fatal blow to 'fanaticism'. 'When compulsion and persecution cease (as he intends that they shall), all sects will merge themselves in the universal religion of Nature'. The priests have disfigured God, by making him in their own image, or in the image of their royal masters. 'Nature is the true priest of the Supreme Being: his temple is the universe; his worship, virtue; his feasts, the happiness of a great people assembled under his eyes, to renew the pleasant ties of universal brotherhood, and to present the oblation of sensitive and pure hearts'.

But the priests are so far right (Robespierre allows) in that they have stood for the necessity of a ritual, and of a corporate worship. A declaration of belief is not enough. It must be inculcated by education—a State education, designed to produce, not gentlemen (*messieurs*), but citizens; and it must be enforced, like the religion of ancient Greece, by great public ceremonies. 'A system of national festivals would be the most persuasive bond of fellowship, and the most powerful means of regeneration'. There should be general feast-days for the whole Republic, and special feast-days for separate localities; festivals for anathematizing tyrants, and festivals for celebrating the heroes of patriotism; festivals of Liberty, Equality, and Humanity; a feast of Glory, a feast of Misfortune; and a whole group of feasts, which, as Maximilien looks back on his sad childhood, seem the most necessary of all, in honour of family happiness.

In his peroration Robespierre returns to the political and personal considerations which, as things were, it was impossible to ignore. He knows that the government's proposals will be denounced by their critics as reactionary, and that he is risking his own reputation in putting them forward. He therefore exhorts the Convention to defy such risks, and to promote a measure which will revive the national character, and command the respect of all Europe. For himself, it may be that he is already marked down for martyrdom. But, before drinking the hemlock, he hopes at least to have the satisfaction of saving the Republic. 'We may carry the fame of our arms', he says, 'to the ends of the universe; but what is the use, if passions that we might have checked devour the vitals of our country? We must distrust the transports of success. Formidable in the hour of defeat, and modest in the moment of victory, let our prudent and virtuous conduct assure us domestic happiness and peace. There lies the real end of all our labours: there lies the task which is at once the most difficult and the most heroic'.

Robespierre then recited the proposed decree. At once a political expedient and a declaration of personal faith, it is one of the crucial documents for a judgement of the statesman, and of the man.

XII

DECREE

Article I. The French people recognizes the existence of the Supreme Being, and the immortality of the soul.

Article II. It recognizes that the best way of worshipping the Supreme Being is to do one's duties as a man.[1]

Article III. It considers that the most important of these duties are: to detest bad faith and despotism, to punish tyrants and traitors, to assist the unfortunate, to respect the weak, to defend the oppressed, to do all the good one can to one's neighbour, and to behave with justice towards all men.

Article IV. Festivals shall be instituted to remind men of the Deity, and of the dignity of their state.

Article V. These festivals shall be named after the glorious events of our Revolution, the virtues which are most dear to men, and most useful, and the chief blessings of nature.

Article VI. The French Republic shall celebrate every year

---

[1] *Devoirs de l'homme*, the complement of *Droits de l'homme*, missing from the Preamble to the Constitution of 1793.

494

the anniversaries of July 14, 1789, August 10, 1792, January 21, 1793, and May 31, 1793.[1]

Article VII. It shall celebrate, on successive *décadis*, the following festivals:[2] The Supreme Being, and Nature; the human race; the French people; the benefactors of mankind; the martyrs of freedom; liberty and equality; the Republic; the liberty of the world; patriotism; hatred of tyrants and traitors; truth; justice; modesty; glory and immortality; friendship; temperance; courage; good faith; heroism; impartiality; Stoicism; love; conjugal fidelity; fatherly affection; mother-love; filial piety; childhood; youth; manhood; old age; misfortune; agriculture; industry; our ancestors; posterity; happiness.

Article VIII. The Committees of Public Safety and of Education are instructed to present a scheme for the organization of these festivals.

Article IX. The National Convention invites all those whose talents are worthy of serving the cause of mankind to the honour of assisting in the establishment of these festivals by submitting hymns or civic songs, or anything else likely to contribute to their beauty or utility.

Article X. The Committee of Public Safety shall award distinction to such works as appear to it calculated to achieve these objects, and shall reward their authors.

Article XI. Freedom of worship is confirmed, in the terms of the decree of 18 *frimaire*.

Article XII. Any meeting of aristocrats, or any that contravenes public order, shall be suppressed.[3]

Article XIII. In the event of troubles caused by or arising out of any form of public worship, all those who excited them by fanatical preaching or counter-revolutionary suggestions, and all those who provoked them by unjust or uncalled-for acts of violence, shall be equally punished, with all the rigour of the law.

[1]The destruction of the Gironde is celebrated, not that of the 'factions': the latter was too recent, and was regarded as a corollary of the former.

[2]There are thirty-six of them, one for every 'tenth day' in the Republican Calendar.

[3]Aristocrats are in the same position under the new regime as Jews and Protestants under the old.

Article XIV. A separate report shall be prepared, dealing with the detailed arrangements consequential upon the present decree.[1]

Article XV. There shall be celebrated, upon the 20th *prairial* next,[2] a national festival in honour of the Supreme Being.

[1] A suggested form of service in honour of Modesty can be found in R.F. 3/415; and specimen invitations to a rehearsal and performance of music for a *décadi* service in R.F. 6/102.

[2] The *Moniteur* misprinted this as 2 *prairial*, and misled some historians (Aulard, 490).

CHAPTER XVI

The 'Dictator' (May–June, 1794)

I

The applause which greeted Robespierre's Report on religion was, perhaps, a tribute to the apprehension with which he was regarded, rather than a sign of enthusiasm for the proposal he had put forward. His friends secured it full publicity. Couthon demanded that it should be placarded on every wall of Paris, and translated into every known language, so that all the world should know what Frenchmen really believed; and this was done. Payan wrote that 'it contained ideas which were great, novel, and sublime', and 'proved that the government would never rob the people of the comforting dogmas of the existence of God, and the immortality of the soul'. Moreover, he succeeded in persuading the Commune to pass an important vote of congratulation.[1] Sylvain Maréchal himself, the Apostle of atheism, gave the new decrees an enthusiastic welcome, and composed a hymn in honour of *l'Être Suprême*.[2] Lequinio's approval at the club was somewhat less welcome: it was pointed out that he was the author of two books disproving the existence of the Supreme Being. Still, beneath much that was merely conventional in the addresses of congratulation which flowed in from all parts of the country, and not a little that was due to a desire to curry favour with an all-powerful committee, it was possible to discern a sober and patriotic belief in a policy which transformed the Revolution into a church, and made Paris, in Cloots' phrase, 'the real Rome, the Vatican of Reason'. The first article of the new profession of faith was accordingly inscribed in letters of gold on the *ci-devant* 'Temples of Reason', and the Report was read aloud in these buildings

[1] Corresp. 395.   [2] A.H. 1/212.

497

on three successive *décadis*. No 'fanatical' bishop, with incense and holy water, could have taken more pains to purify Paris from the reproach of false worship, and to re-dedicate it to the true religion.

But it was soon noticed that the new cult flourished chiefly in those parts of the country where ecclesiastical reaction, or the fear of foreign invasion, gave special point to a religion of patriotism; and that an unaccountable difficulty was found in distinguishing the worship of the Supreme Being from those 'atheistical' cults which it was designed to supersede. Many people must have felt, like Mercier's errand-boy, that 'there was no longer a God, but only Robespierre's Supreme Being'.[1] Gradually, as the charms of patriotism faded, the claims of Catholicism re-asserted themselves; and it was not Robespierre's *Culte*, but Napoleon's *Concordat*, that met the ultimate needs of the country.

That Robespierre himself was not satisfied with the reception of his proposals, and suspected attempts to dis-credit them by exaggeration, is shown by a debate which took place at the Jacobins on May 15. Jullien de la Drôme, after moving an address of thanks to the Convention, had gone on to propose that any citizen who did not believe in the Deity should be banished from the Republic. Robes-pierre, well knowing that the malicious suggestion had Rousseau's authority behind it, nevertheless opposed it as needless and provocative. Virtue, nature, and truth, he declared, need no extrinsic support. It is enough that the decree is accepted by the French people, and approved by the world at large. The slanders of a few conspirators cannot prevail against it. 'There are some truths (he said) which must be tactfully presented; and such is that pro-fessed by Rousseau, that one ought to banish from the Republic those who do not believe in the Deity. This principle would inspire too much fear among a crowd of decadent half-wits. I do not want to proscribe the crowd, but only (*it was a threat to Jullien*) actual conspirators against

[1] Mercier, *New picture*, 2/334.

498

freedom. I am for letting this truth remain where Rousseau wrote it: I am against putting it into practice'. 'We want', he added later in the debate, 'to consolidate the foundations of virtue and patriotism, but we have no desire to become persecutors'.

II

History shows many instances of dubious policies rehabilitated, and of unpopular rulers restored to favour, by attempted assassination. Perhaps the Worship of the Supreme Being would have remained, like the Laws of Ventôse, a paper programme, had it not been for two incidents which followed close upon the speech of May 7. On May 23, when Collot d'Herbois came home at night, he was fired at, *faute de mieux*, by a man named Admiral, who had been waiting about all day in the hope of shooting Robespierre. The pistol twice missed fire, and the only person wounded was a locksmith who ran to Collot's assistance. The following evening, at 9 p.m., a girl named Renault called at the Duplays', and asked to see Robespierre. When told that she could not, she remarked that, as a public official, it was his duty to be accessible: under the old regime it had been easy enough to obtain audience of the king. She was asked, would she prefer a king? Yes, she replied, she would give her life for one. Such suspicious behaviour ended, not unnaturally, in her arrest. It was then found that she had left at a *limonadier's* shop a basket containing a change of linen, and that she had in her pocket two knives. Further questioned, she said that she had asked for Robespierre because she 'wanted to see what a tyrant looked like'. She had no intention of employing the knives against him; but the change of linen was for use in prison, where she fully expected to be sent. The impression left by the mass of evidence, relevant and irrelevant, accumulated by the police, is that the girl did intend to stab Robespierre, but that she would never have succeeded in doing so, being, indeed, no Corday, but a poor half-witted creature, looking for notoriety.[1]

[1] Tuetey, 11/2300, the best account of the evidence.

In spite of rigorous inquiry, no connexion could be traced between Admiral and Renault, or between either of them and the various 'conspiracies' already known to the police. Nevertheless it was an alarming fact that two attempts should have been made to assassinate the high priest of the revolutionary religion; and no surprise need be felt either at the congratulations which Robespierre received on his escape, or at the prestige which it gave to the new cult. Robespierre himself, as might have been expected from his demeanour in July, 1791, and May, 1793, took the matter very seriously. Fouquier-Tinville, who went to see him the same evening, was offended by his 'despotic' manner;[1] and he so far communicated his alarm to the Committee that they allowed him to write a rather hysterical letter to his friend Saint-Just, saying that 'liberty was exposed to fresh dangers', and requesting him to return at once to Paris. Next day, in the Convention, Barère put the blame of the affair on England, whose crimes he denounced to the extent of nine columns in the *Moniteur*, and ended by proposing that in future no quarter should be given to British or Hanoverian troops. Robespierre himself followed with an emotional speech, of which the refrain was that, when every other method fails, the enemies of France have recourse to assassination. 'Slander, arson, poison, atheism, corruption, starvation, and murder—they have been prodigal in every sort of crime: but there still remains assassination, assassination, and again assassination.[2] . . . Let us rejoice, then (he goes on), and render thanks to heaven, that we have served our country so well as to be judged worthy of the tyrants' dagger. For us too there are glorious risks to run! City life is as full of danger as the battlefield: we have nothing to envy our brave brothers in arms: we pay twice over our debt to the fatherland!' This was an ingenious way of increasing the prestige of the intended victims, whilst putting aside the unpleasant thought that terrorism might recoil upon its authors.

[1] Mathiez, *Autour de Robespierre*, 142.
[2] His hearers may have contrasted Danton's *de l'audace, de l'audace, et toujours de l'audace.* The "no quarter" proposal was taken up by Robespierre. v. 2/242.

The scene at the Jacobin club, the same evening, verged on hysteria. 'At this interesting session'—so runs the official record—'the whole Society, and all the citizens in the galleries, welcomed with emotion and enthusiastic applause two of the most fervid champions of the people's rights, whom the wickedness of the British government had marked down as companions to Marat and Le Pelletier. But the God of free men watched over them: the aegis of Providence was their shield and buckler. . . . As they enter the hall, every eye is fixed upon these precious men, every heart goes out to greet them, and shouts of liveliest joy demonstrate the interest they inspire'. It is hardly possible to translate this rubbish into English, or to imagine any normal statesman, or Assembly, making so much out of so slight a danger. But for three years now Robespierre had been thinking and talking of himself as marked down for murder; and at last it had happened. For three years he had been idolized as the prophet and, it might be, the martyr of the Revolution; and now it seemed to be justified —at the very moment when he was staking his political career upon the worship of a friendly and protecting deity. It would in any case be a mistake to suppose that the Jacobins overlooked the practical advantages to be derived from the incident. Robespierre himself, speaking again at the club on the 15th, was quick to point the moral. 'I feel myself freer', he said, 'than ever I was from the mischances of mortal life. The tyrant's crime and the assassin's steel have made me more formidable to the enemies of the people. My mind turns more than ever to the unmasking of traitors. We swear, by the daggers stained with the blood of the martyrs of the Revolution, that we will exterminate to the last man the villains who would rob us of happiness and freedom'. The 'unanimous and prolonged applause' which greeted this threat was taken as warrant for an intensification of the Terror.

Robespierre's friends and flatterers were not slow to follow the lead of the club, and of the Convention. 'Worthy representative of the people', wrote a female admirer, within a few hours of the attempted assassination, 'what labours you have accomplished! How quick your progress towards immortality! I render thanks to the Supreme Being, who has watched over your life'.[1] The actors of the Théâtre de L'Égalité expressed their 'distress and alarm' at the news of the attack.[2] Daillet, a friend of Augustin, advised Maximilien to be more careful in future, not to walk out alone, nor to admit any but friends to his room.[3] Another correspondent warned him against accepting an offer of apartments in the *palais national*: it would make assassination more easy.[4]

If others thought differently about the affair, few of them dared say so. When Rousselin proposed the voting of 'civic honours' to the locksmith who had come to the help of Collot, Robespierre seems to have scented an intrigue to minimize his own part in the affair, and he was turned out of the club.

The sequel to the affair showed to what an extent the motives of fear and revenge could degrade a national government. After a month's delay, during which the excuse of public indignation against the 'assassins' disappeared, a *journée* of unprecedented dimensions advertised the impotence of a regime whose only weapon was the guillotine. With Admiral were arraigned several friends, innocent of his crime; by Renault's side in the dock stood her father, her brother, and her aunt, whose only fault—relationship to a criminal—was one which Robespierre and the Revolution had declared not to exist;[5] there were added a schoolmaster who had abused Robespierre, a man who had criticized the arrests, a woman who had not protested against or reported the critic, an aristocratic lady who kept a gambling-house, four suspect police officers, a group of bankers, and the mistress of the Hébertist Baron de Batz, along with her little servant-girl, Nicolle.

[1] Corresp. 407.
[2] Corresp. 409. Hamel (3/530) says that the marginal comment on this letter, *Flatteurs*, is not, as generally thought, in Robespierre's hand, but in that of Courtois.
[3] Corresp. 411.
[4] Corresp. 420. Couthon had recently been given rooms in the Tuileries (v. 1/292).
[5] v. 1/22 f.

On June 17, clad in the *chemises rouges* of 'parricides'—for had not two of them perhaps intended to kill the 'father of the Revolution?'—fifty-four persons were sent to the guillotine. When Nicolle was strapped to the plank, there were indignant cries of 'No children!' But Robespierre had stopped his ears.[1]

III

If Pitt had really troubled himself to direct the crazy designs of Admiral and Renault, he could have done nothing better calculated to further the policy of the Committee—a reign of virtue based upon intimidation. When the next opportunity came for appointing a President to the Convention (June 4), Robespierre was elected by the largest number of votes ever cast in the House. As President he pontificated at the inaugural festival of the Supreme Being on June 8, and on June 10 sat in the chair whilst his friend Couthon introduced a method of justice which could at last keep pace with the guillotine.

The scene of June 8 has often been described, and can be reconstructed in some detail from contemporary prints. No function in the course of the Revolution was so carefully rehearsed, or staged so successfully. Robespierre's *assassination* had obscured Léonard Bourdon's: his fête must put Hérault's in the shade.[2] Based, perhaps, on Rousseau's *Lettre sur les spectacles*,[3] it was David's *chef d'oeuvre*, and resembled one of his crowded canvasses—every figure properly placed, every gesture true to the classical tradition; but the whole composition, to modern taste, utterly lifeless and unreal. It began, on a morning of almost miraculous beauty,[4] in the Tuileries gardens, where the representatives of the people, and the national deputies in their new official dress—blue, with tricolour sashes—wearing swords, ribbons, and plumed hats, and carrying bouquets of flowers,

[1] cp. Kerr, *The Terror*, 451.
[2] Bourdon was attacked and wounded on March 16, 1794 (B. and R. 25/177); Hérault de Séchelles had presided at the Festival of Nature on August 10, 1793.
[3] Ward, 301.
[4] v. Nodier, *Mémoires*, 288; he was there.

fruit, and corn, listened to an oration by Robespierre in praise of Theism, and watched him set fire to an effigy of Atheism, out of whose ashes emerged an image of Wisdom, slightly scorched by the flames. After another speech pointing the moral of this ceremony, and the singing of a hymn,[1] there followed a procession to the Champ de Mars, in which Robespierre's dark blue suit and two bouquets, as he marched at the head of the Convention, were a trifle too conspicuous.[2] On the Champ de la Réunion, as it was now called, stood an artificial mound—a symbol of the Mountain —topped by a tree of Liberty: beneath this the deputies took their seats, and surveyed the crowd below. Patriotic songs were sung, and a hymn to the Supreme Being: swords were raised in the air, guns were fired, and the people fell into each other's arms, with cries of '*Vive la République!*' When all was over, the procession returned to the Tuileries, and the day ended with athletic sports. Contemporary witnesses assert that half a million of people—almost the whole population of Paris—were present at the fête, and remark that the sun shone upon the scene with a brilliance never vouchsafed to the festivals of the old religion. In the provinces, too, the day was celebrated with equal enthusiasm, and at papal Avignon it was crowded with peasantry, who 'showed their obvious delight to see that there was still a God'.[3]

June 8, in the old Calendar, was Whitsun Day; and all over the Christian world the faithful were meeting to celebrate the gifts of Pentecost—'love, joy, peace, long-suffering, gentleness, goodness, faith, meekness, temperance'. Robespierre doubtless remembered this, and the days when he had been 'a pretty poor Catholic'. Did he expect the New Dispensation to replace the old, or the Mountain of the Champ de Mars to out-top those of Sinai and Galilee? Perhaps. But more than preaching had been needed to establish the old religion, and more than preach-

---

[1]Not, as often stated, A. Chénier's hymn, the words of which had been thought unsuitable (R.F. 43/348, and subsequent controversy).
[2]*Robespierre portoit seul un habit bleu foncé* (the other deputies wore *bleu-barbeau*). *Il avoit un bouquet sur le coeur, et un bouquet énorme à la main.* (Nodier, *Mémoires* 289.)
[3]Letter of Moureau in B. and R. 35/189.

ing would be needed to propagate the new. He had spoken constantly of martyrdom. If he really meant it, now was his opportunity. Had he devoted himself, all political ambition put aside, to a campaign for republican virtue and religion, he might have become the first martyr of a new church, instead of the last victim of an old ambition. 'Had he even had the wit to open the prisons, and to proclaim the reign of clemency, he would have erected for himself at once a throne and an altar'.[1] But he had lost the patience that believes persuasion is better than compulsion, and mercy stronger than revenge. He could no longer dissociate virtue from terror. He had discovered three times in succession how much easier it is to get rid of an enemy than to argue him round. His thoughts, during the ceremony of June 8, were less likely to be fixed on the cross than on the guillotine. Though he held his head high, and there seemed to be a smile of unaccustomed sweetness on his smooth and sallow face,[2] he complained afterwards—and he may have been aware at the time—of the 'heavy sarcasms' and 'indecent invective' that Bourdon was airing at the expense of the fête, and of his own part in it.[3] He knew that, in spite of superficial enthusiasm, there was strong feeling, both in the Convention, and among the general public, against the 'new religion'. So faith, like virtue, would have to go hand in hand with intimidation. And he was already drafting, with his friend Couthon, a punitive decree which, to the uninstructed mind, might seem quite incongruous either with a reign of virtue, or with the worship of a Supreme Being.

IV

The Law of the 22nd Prairial (June 10) was a logical consequence of the decrees of April 16 and May 8, which had suspended the revolutionary Courts in the provinces, and brought all political cases for trial to the capital; it was at the same time a corollary of the Laws of Ventôse,

---

[1]Mercier *New picture*, 2/413. [2]Nodier, *Mémoires*, 289.
[3]Courtois, *Rapport*, No. 51.

which made such centralization doubly desirable. Paris soon overflowed with suspects awaiting trial. On April 29 it was reported that its forty prisons contained 6,921 prisoners: by June 11 the number had risen to 7,321, and by July 28 to 7,800.[1] No Revolutionary Tribunal could work fast enough to prevent the ship of state sinking under such a sea of crime. What was to be done? Precedents had been created at Lyon, Marseille, and elsewhere, by republican agents, who had extemporized new forms of justice to deal with exceptional situations. At Orange, in particular, there had been set up, by decree of the Convention, a Commission of Five, which, by dispensing with the usual formalities of counsel and witness, had succeeded in condemning to death, within two months, 332 out of the 591 persons brought before it.[2] Robespierre had been the intermediary between Maignet, who asked for this court, and the Committee, which allowed it. The Report and decree had been drawn up by Couthon, and approved by Robespierre. The minute giving effect to it, and the subsequent instructions to the Commissioners, were both in Robespierre's own hand.[3] It was therefore natural that the Committee should look to this precedent, and should entrust Robespierre and Couthon with the duty of adapting to the needs of Paris a plan which had worked so well in the provinces.

There can be no doubt—it was implicitly admitted by those who were most anxious to disprove their part in it[4]—that the decree of the 22nd Prairial expressed in principle the views of the whole Committee. But, for reasons which have never been satisfactorily explained, it was drafted, and presented to the Convention, without having been submitted again to the Committee. The other committee—that of General Security—which might have been thought equally concerned with a vital alteration of judicial procedure, was not consulted at all. True, this committee had not been consulted about the decree of May 22, regulating the

[1] Ording, Le bureau de police, 160.
[2] Pap. inéd. 2/373; B. and R. 35/171, 178, 183.
[3] Corresp. 389, 395; Ording, 178.
[4] Barère; Réponse to Le Cointre's charges (R.F. 34/169).

two Commissions, though these were legally under the control of both committees; and it is possible that on both occasions the Committee of Public Safety was pursuing a deliberate policy of taking police matters out of the hands of what it liked to regard as a subordinate body. On the other hand, Robespierre and Couthon specially resented the failure of this committee to organize the Popular Commissions provided for under the decree of April 16, and may have been personally responsible for the refusal to consult it about the Prairial Law.[1] Their failure to submit these proposals to their own committee is more difficult to explain. Did they really think the details of the law so uncontroversial that they need not be referred to their colleagues, who had accepted the principle of it? Or, knowing there was something in the draft to which they feared objection would be taken, did they hope to face the Committee with a *fait accompli*? The first hypothesis, though it was, according to Barère, the account given by Robespierre when challenged by the Committee next day, is hardly credible to anyone who examines the decree from an impartial point of view: yet it has to be remembered that the Committee was fanatical enough to approve, and the Convention powerful enough to enforce, as a New Model of Republican justice, replacing the scandals of the old regime,[2] a law which denied to prisoners the help of counsel, made it possible for the court to dispense with witnesses, and allowed no sentence except acquittal or execution; a law which, at the same time, defined crimes against the state in such wide terms that the lightest indiscretion might bring one within the article of death. To any right-minded or merciful man such procedure must seem a travesty of justice. But suppose five years of revolution, and two years of foreign and civil war; suppose a country whose courts had always been an instrument of government rather than a refuge for the oppressed; suppose a state of public opinion in which

[1]Mathiez (*G. et M.*, 209) thinks this was the only charge against Robespierre and Couthon.

[2]v. a passage in Robespierre's draft of the decree (R.H.R.F. 6/160), and Couthon's speech introducing the law (Lambert 227).

it was believed that the expression of counter-revolutionary ideas, even by a prisoner in the dock, might lead to a political assassination, or a defeat at the front; suppose a system of trial already firmly established in which the feeling of the court was so much against the accused that no one dared defend them, in which (as Robespierre himself put it)[1] 'the prosecutor is the whole nation, and the witness is the universe', and in which professional jurymen prided themselves on their flair for distinguishing traitors, as their ancestors had recognized witches, without recourse to written or oral evidence;[2] and it is just possible to understand how Robespierre might see nothing controversial in the Law of the 22nd Prairial.

The other hypothesis is better documented, but raises even more disturbing questions. The new decree contained, as it very well might, a clause cancelling previous legislation on the same subject. Did Robespierre and Couthon know that this clause abolished an immunity which had hitherto protected deputies from the guillotine? The Constitution of 1791 had declared that 'The national representatives are inviolable, and cannot be arrested, charged, or convicted for anything they may have said, written, or done in the exercise of their functions as representatives'; if they were arrested under a criminal charge, the Assembly could veto proceedings against them.[3] Substantially the same words were incorporated in the Constitution of 1793,[4] though recently, since neither Constitution was now in force, the Convention had decreed (April 1) that 'notwithstanding the inviolability of a representative of the French nation, the Assembly shall send up for trial any of its members who are strongly suspected of complicity with the enemies of liberty, equality, and republicanism'. Thus, though a snap vote of the House might send any of its members before the Tribunal, no external or subordinate body could do so. Was it likely that the deputies could be

[1] Pap. inéd. 2/3.
[2] A letter by Payan (Pap. inéd. 2/370) shows how little sympathy a suspect was likely to get from a patriotic juryman. cp. Anatole France, Les dieux ont soif.
[3] Cap. I, Sect. V, Art. 7-8.　　　　　　　　　　　　　　[4] Art. 43-4.

persuaded or tricked into surrendering this last vestige of their rights? Yet, if Robespierre and Couthon had no such intention, why did they introduce the measure so suddenly, and try to force it through the House unamended? For, as soon as it had been read, several members asked for an adjournment, that it might be examined; and Robespierre objected, saying that the law was an answer to four months' demand from the Convention and the Tribunal for the removal of acknowledged defects in revolutionary justice, and pooh-poohing the idea that the Committee would ever entertain designs on the privileges of the House. He would not even accept the suggestion that the non-controversial parts of the measure, which alone were needed for the better working of the tribunal, should be passed, and the rest postponed: he insisted that the whole should be voted, clause by clause, here and now: and so it was. The next day (June 11), as soon as the House met, and before the members of the Committee had arrived, the deputies, to secure themselves, passed a cautiously worded motion asserting 'that the exclusive privilege of the National Representation to impeach and try its own members is one of which it cannot be deprived'. Robespierre, realizing how much feeling lay beneath this motion, might well have treated it as due to a misunderstanding, and have let the matter drop. He preferred to take it as intentional provocation. On June 12th Couthon moved its rescindment, saying that the Committee had never intended any attack upon parliamentary privilege, and Robespierre himself described the whole incident as an attempt to sow discord in the Assembly. When there were factions, he said, the Mountain was the party of patriots: now that the factions have been destroyed, the Convention, the Mountain, and the Committee are all one (*c'est la même chose*); and every patriotic deputy is a member of the Mountain—a sentiment of which the representatives showed their unanimous approval. But it appears, he went on, that this concord is not complete; for there are still two parties in the Convention—'the good and the bad, the patriots and the counter-revolutionaries'; there are still 'a few intriguers', who are trying 'to carry with them a part of the Mountain, and to make it the head of a new faction'. Bourdon protested that he had no such intention, 'I never mentioned Bourdon's name', retorted Robespierre; but he went on to describe the 'intriguers' in terms which fully justified the fears of the deputies. When Charles Delacroix and Merlin de Douai tried to exculpate themselves, they gathered that their case was not much better than Bourdon's. When Tallien intervened, he was denounced by Robespierre and Billaud-Varenne in terms which made it clear that he at least was on the list of the proscribed.

It is difficult to read these debates without feeling that Robespierre's attitude was both suspicious and provocative, and that the deputies' interpretation of it was the only natural one. As to the question whether, in fact, he had or had not intended to destroy their immunity, his manner might be either that of a person discovered cheating at a political card-party, or that of an honest man who is righteously indignant at being accused of such conduct. But it is clear—and this is the essential point—that the Prairial Law *was* aimed at certain deputies, as well as at outsiders; and it is therefore probable that its framers had hoped to clear the way to proscription by destroying the immunity. It also follows that Robespierre and Couthon had good reason for keeping the details of the decree to themselves, until they could present the Committee with a *fait accompli*. Their colleagues, who might shrink from the means employed to procure it, would hardly hesitate to use a heaven-sent opportunity to get rid of their political rivals.[1]

It is painful, when there has been so much to admire in a statesman, to be asked to find him guilty on such an unsavoury charge of political intrigue—particularly so, when the occasion coincides with that of his highest professions of virtue and religion. To such shifts had Robespierre been

[1]Ording, in the most recent study of the evidence (*Le bureau de police*, 178), tries to avoid this conclusion by showing that the decree was aimed only at those prisoners whose property it was hoped to confiscate under the Laws of Ventôse. (Buchez and Mathiez also adopt this defence.) But Robespierre's own speech, and the debate, point the other way.

reduced, not by weakness, but by power, not by personal spite, but by patriotic hatred, not by private vices, which he had starved out of his life, but by public virtues, which he had artificially fed into monstrous and distorted shapes.

V

It was at once a cause and a symptom of this disease that Robespierre should have become more than ever engrossed, at this time, in police affairs. The decree of April 16 had made it the duty of the Committee to supervise 'all the authorities and public agents co-operating with the administration', 'to exact a severe account from all such agents', and 'to prosecute any of them who shall be found taking part in plots, or perverting the powers entrusted to them against the cause of liberty'. In virtue of this last clause the Committee set up a *Bureau de surveillance administrative et de police générale*, or Visitatorial Board.[1]

This procedure was regarded by the members of the Committee of General Security as an infringement upon their rights, and some of them did not hesitate to describe it as an instance of Robespierre's 'Dictatorship'. 'That popular tyrant', wrote Vadier, after Thermidor, 'had usurped our powers, and nullified them, by overruling them. His despotic direction of the Jacobin Club, and of its provincial branches, had corrupted its principles, and encouraged him to strengthen his authority by means of a so-called *Bureau de Police*, over which he presided, with Couthon and Saint-Just as his coadjutors. He had the face to carry on this committee in the same building as the Committee of General Security (the Hôtel de Brionne), and it was there that these Triumvirs drafted decrees in virtue of which persons whom we had released were arrested, and persons whose arrest we had ordered were set at liberty'.[2]

Robespierre often heard such charges before his fall.

[1] Its comparatively mild connotation nowadays need not exclude this translation of a title which has no exact English equivalent.

[2] *Bibl. Nat. Fond français, nouvelles acquisitions*, No. 20804, quoted by Ording, 32.

In his apologia of 8 Thermidor (July 26, 1794), he gave his own account of the Board; and the two versions provide material for a judgement as to the actual facts. 'During the absence of one of my colleagues', he said, 'I was put in temporary charge (*momentanément*) of a Visitatorial Board recently organized in quite a small way (*récemment et faiblement*), by the Committee of Public Safety. My short term of office (*courte gestion*) was limited to the drafting of some thirty decrees, either to liberate persecuted patriots, or to put under preventive arrest (*s'assurer de*) certain enemies of the Revolution. Would you believe it? The mere expression *police générale* has been used as an excuse to make me personally responsible for all the operations of the Committee of General Security, and for all the crimes of my enemies'.

What are the facts? The Visitatorial Board began its work on April 23—three months before the date on which Robespierre described it as a 'recent' creation.[1] The only evidence as to whether it was organized 'in a small way' is an official minute of June 20, in which the Committee of Public Safety, 'considering that it is a matter of public importance to organize the *Bureau de Police* definitely and effectively' (*définitivement et solidement*) divides it into a central office and four sub-sections, nominates a director, two assistants, and ten other officials, and orders the staff to attend daily from 8.30 a.m. to 3.30 p.m. (some of them also in the evening), and to do their work 'thoroughly and correctly' (*avec la plus sévère exactitude*). Whatever, then, may have been true of the early days of the Board, Robespierre's description of its later developments is highly misleading.

What of his own part in the work of the Board? Every day it dealt with a great mass of correspondence—letters and reports from all parts of the country, containing information about representatives, agents, local authorities, the economic state of the provinces, and suspicious characters of all kinds, from deputies plotting counter-revolution to cut-throats

---

[1] It apparently had rooms on the third floor of the Pavillon de l' Égalité—not, as Vadier says, in the Hôtel de Brionne (Ording, 37).

who might have designs upon the lives of patriots. This correspondence was sifted out by the sub-sections—one for each geographical area of the country—and submitted in the form of a daily report to the chairman of the Board. Now, a number of these reports may still be seen, annotated in the margin with such remarks as *arrêter*, *traduire à Paris*, *examiner*, *renvoyer à Carnot*, and the like. From April 23 to 28 these notes are in Saint-Just's hand: some on April 28, and all between that date and May 31 are written by Robespierre: on June 1 there are notes in both hands: from June 2 to 29, again, they are all Robespierre's: on June 30 both hands reappear: afterwards there are only occasional reports, some annotated by Saint-Just, and some by Couthon. Thus Robespierre's 'temporary' charge of the Board 'during the absence of one of his colleagues' (Saint-Just was, in fact, away at the front for nearly two months),[1] turns out to have run continuously from April 28 to June 30, and to have covered two out of the three months of its existence—precisely, be it noted, its active period, following the re-organization of June 20. During this time he read and annotated at least sixty reports, containing some 1,700 separate items, besides signing many more than the thirty *arrêtés* whose authorship he admits. Here again, then, it can only be said that his own account of his part in the work of the Board is definitely misleading.

What of the last month of the Board's activities? After June 30 there are no more notes by Robespierre. But it does not follow that he ceased to concern himself with the work. He had latterly arranged to have a portfolio full of papers brought from the office to his house every morning; and, after Saint-Just returned from the front at the end of June, and took charge of the Board, he 'frequently came to see Robespierre, and went upstairs to his room without speaking to anyone else'.[2] It is therefore highly probable that Robespierre's interest in, and influence upon, the

---

[1] From April 29 to May 31, and from June 6 to 28.
[2] Evidence of Simon Duplay; v. Mathiez, *Autour de Robespierre*, 175. One of the extant Reports is endorsed: 'To be returned to Lejeune (*chef principal* of the *bureau*), at the *Bureau de police*, from citizen Robespierre'. (Ording, 42.)

work of the Board continued up to the time of his fall. The point is important, because it was precisely during this period of Robespierre's ostensible retirement from the Board that the executions for which it shared responsibility with the Committee of Public Safety reached their most terrible proportions.

How, in fact, was this responsibility distributed? After Robespierre's fall, the surviving Terrorists tried to shoulder it all onto him. But an examination of the actual minutes of the Board[1] shows that some of its *arrêtés* were either drafted or signed in the first place by other members of the Committee of Public Safety—not Robespierre, Couthon, or Saint-Just; that others, signed in the first place by one of these three, were counter-signed by other members of the Committee of Public Safety; whilst a third group has no such counter-signatures. The inference is that the Visitatorial Board habitually reported to the Committee of Public Safety, and that most of its *arrêtés* were signed, if not drafted, by members of that body. The suggestion that the Triumvirate, or Robespierre personally, dictated the policy which, between the beginning of May and the end of July, sent some 1,800 persons to the guillotine, breaks down. The responsibility lay with the Committee of Public Safety as a whole.[2]

As to Vadier's suggestion that the Visitatorial Board usurped the functions of the Committee of General Security, the examination of a number of typical cases shows that the Committee of General Security continued, throughout the period under discussion, to carry out by far the greater number of arrests, without any interference from the Board; that the supervision of government officials (in accordance with the resolution of June 20) was the only business taken out of its hands by the Board; and that all important or political charges were dealt with by one or both of the Governing Committees. There were, admittedly, a few instances of overlapping; but on the whole the Board

[1] Containing 121 out of its 464 *arrêtés*.
[2] Louis Blanc was the first historian to notice this; v. Lewes, 329.

kept to its subordinate function of preparing business for the committees of Public Safety and General Security.

VI

What of the Revolutionary Tribunal—the final argument of the terrorist regime? Between April 1, 1793, and June 10, 1794 (the date of the Prairial Law), it passed 1,254 death sentences: between June 10 and July 27 it passed 1,258— as many in these nine weeks as in the previous fourteen months. The Prairial Law was Robespierre's work; so, judging from its date, was the reorganization of the Visitatorial Board on June 20; for at that time he was in sole charge of it. Between April 28 and June 30 it was he who read and annotated the daily reports made up by the Board, and drafted or signed a considerable proportion, at any rate, of the *arrêtés* it submitted to the Committee of Public Safety—of which, again, he was a leading member. What, then, was his personal responsibility for the resulting executions? Is it true, as was afterwards asserted by Barère and his friends, that 'Dumas and Coffinhall, the Presidents of the Revolutionary Tribunal, were at Robespierre's house every morning, concocting their plans', and drawing up lists of victims which transformed decrees of national justice into an arbitrary proscription?[1] Certainly Robespierre interested himself in the personnel of the court more than impartiality might require; but the Tribunal was an instrument of government, not of justice, and must be in the hands of men who could be trusted to convict. Of the Presidents, Herman stands first, and Dumas second, on the list of proved patriots in Robespierre's private papers. Herman was a contemporary and fellow-townsman, a distinguished member of the Arras bar, whom Robespierre had brought in to succeed Montané, and whom he described as 'an enlightened and upright man, fit for the highest posts'.[2] Amongst the jurymen, whom Robespierre is said

---

[1] R.F. 34/73. Dumas succeeded Herman: Coffinhall was his assistant. Fouquier-Tinville at his trial also said that Dumas visited Robespierre every day.
[2] Pap. inéd. 2/11, cp. Paris, *Lebon*, 82.

to have chosen with the greatest care,[1] were his host, Duplay, and his friends Nicolas, Girard, and Renaudin. Simon Duplay became assistant director of the *Bureau de Police*; its doctor was also a nominee of Robespierre.[2]

But this is far from proving that Robespierre used the Tribunal for his own ends. If he had wished to do so, would it not have been necessary to control Fouquier-Tinville, the Public Prosecutor? As to this, Fouquier's own evidence—given, no doubt, at a time when he was anxious to disown relations with Robespierre, but never contested, and generally accepted as trustworthy—is of the greatest importance. At first, he said at his trial, he was under the orders of the Committee of General Security; but soon after the establishment of the Revolutionary regime (December, 1793) he was sent for by Robespierre, and blamed for not reporting to the Committee of Public Safety; and after the fall of the Hébertists (March, 1794) his visits to this Committee became more frequent. Twice only was he received by Robespierre alone; all his other dealings were with the members as a whole. All his prosecutions were based upon instructions given and papers supplied at these conferences. He never provided Robespierre personally with the daily lists of persons to be tried. The only time he went to Robespierre's house was on the day of the attempted assassination by Admiral; as for Couthon or Saint-Just, he did not even know where they lived. This evidence is corroborated, in its main contention, by certain letters in which the Committee of Public Safety asks Fouquier to provide it with lists, or reports.[3]

It may fairly be concluded that the charge against Robespierre of going behind the back of the Committee, and using the Tribunal for his own ends, is untrue. But it must also be admitted that, through his direction of the Visitatorial Board, his daily interviews with Dumas (if Fouquier's corroboration of that story is to be given the same value as the rest of his evidence), and his personal contacts with

[1]So Le Cointre (Mathiez, *G. et M.*, 209).   [2]Corresp. 169.
[3]Ording, 155. Barère's statement that the Committee of Public Safety disowned the proceedings of the *Bureau de Police* is manifestly untrue (Mathiez, *G. et M.*, 157). ·

members of the court, he was in a position which laid him open to such charges. That he was fully conscious of this, is shown by the misleading apologia of 8 Thermidor; but he was not the first or the last statesman to minimize his share in a discredited policy or institution; and it need not be inferred that he had been guilty of anything worse than indiscretion.

VII

Some further evidence may be drawn from the notes which Robespierre added in the margin of the reports of the Visitatorial Board. A Revolutionary Committee at Lunéville denounces a cobbler for seditious language. 'Why denounce suspects', is Robespierre's comment, 'instead of arresting them?' Should members of the same family be allowed to live together in the same internment camp (asks Herman)? His answer is, 'No'. The Revolutionary Committee of Tartas excuses itself for failing to send in a return of prisoners, on the ground that the person charged with the duty has been drowned, and a number of documents lost. 'Inform the Committee', writes Robespierre, 'that the death of one of its members makes no difference to its responsibility, and that its explanations are unconvincing'. A suspected person has been put under custody in his own house. 'Such persons ought to be put in prison'. A correspondent who describes himself as a *procureur de district*, and encloses a letter from a *procureur-général-syndic*, is reminded that both titles are incorrect. A person calling himself the 'President of the commune of Exmes' asks whether the law against 'external signs of worship' covers 'the crosses women wear round their necks'. 'There is no such thing in the Republic as a President of a commune', is the annotation; 'this man's letter had better be sent to the *commissaire de police générale*, to find out whether he is a rascal or a madman'.

Along with these instances of the rather pedantic severity with which Robespierre thought it necessary to treat the agents as well as the victims of the government, are others which prove that he could show a reasonable clemency, and that he was careful not to commit himself unless he knew the facts of a case. He often asks for explanations (*éclaircissements*), or a further report (*me présenter cette affaire*). One marginal note is written out three times before it satisfies him. Names, facts, documents, must be supplied. Denunciations must be precisely expressed. In a few instances, where the reports preserve marginal notes by Robespierre and Saint-Just on the same case, the younger man calls for instant arrest, the older, with characteristic caution, for further information. It is not, therefore, surprising, though it explodes the myth of the terrorist methods of the Board, that out of 775 notes by Robespierre, Saint-Just, and Couthon, only 229 should be found ordering arrest, or reference to the Tribunal, or transference to Paris.[1]

VIII

Another charge made against Robespierre by the Thermidorians was that the emissaries of the Committee of Public Safety were his secret agents, through whom he tyrannized over the Departments. No such question could have arisen in connexion with the Representatives on mission. But, after the organization of centralized committee government in December, 1793, most of these semi-independent 'pro-consuls' were withdrawn, and replaced by subordinate agents, with more definite instructions, and more limited powers. Some of these men used to address their reports, or to send them with covering letters, to individual members of the Committee. But there is no evidence that these reports were not communicated to the other members. Nothing could be more straightforward than the conduct of Étienne Lambert, the shepherd friend of Saint-Just, who goes round the provinces in his peasant's smock and *sabots*, and sends in his secret reports to the Committee.[2] Rousseville, appointed to report on ex-nobles

[1] Ording, 83. For an earlier use of these reports, v. Dauban, *Paris en 1794*, 364.
[2] Ording, 140.

living in the suburbs of Paris, was responsible for a good many warrants of arrest issued by Robespierre: but there is no suggestion that they were not sanctioned by the Committee.[1] Demaillot made his reports to the Visitatorial Board, and had direct dealings with Robespierre, as the head of this department: but he was appointed by the Committee, and regarded as its agent.[2] Garnerin, Vieille, and Pottofeux were personally known to Robespierre and Saint-Just—no more.[3] Leymerie, another 'agent of the Committees', writes more than once to Robespierre, and asks him to consult Couthon and Amar about his case; but there is no secrecy.[4] The only person who might be suspected of 'secret agency' is Jullien; his reports, addressed to Robespierre personally, were, in fact, published by Courtois just to give such an impression. But there is nothing in them which might not be, and (doubtless) was not communicated to his colleagues.[5]

It was Courtois, again, who tried to give colour to another charge, by printing, as though they were part of Robespierre's private papers, a number of reports by Guérin about the movements of some of his personal enemies. Guérin was at the head of an *espionnage* department, which he organized secretly under the orders of the Committee of Public Safety. He and his assistants went about Paris collecting information at the street-corners, and in the cafés, which they embodied in daily reports to the Committee. It was only by omitting the word *citoyens*, with which these reports began, or by altering it to *citoyen*, that Courtois could give the impression that they were addressed to Robespierre personally.[6] Here, then, is another charge that cannot be proved.

IX

Nevertheless, when all allowances have been made, and the grosser slanders of Robespierre's enemies set aside,

[1]Ording, 142.   [2]Ording, 143.   [3]Ording, 144.
[4]Pap. inéd. 1/357.   [5]Ording, 146.
[6]Ording, 149; Schmidt, *Tableaux*, 2/123. Sénart (*Révélations*, 156) says Héron and Taschereau were spies of Robespierre. Barère (*Mem.* 1/92) adds Mme Taschereau.

there remains the inescapable fact that it was under a judicial system which he initiated and helped to direct that a government of which he was, perhaps, the most influential member, perpetrated the worst enormities of the Terror. Whatever reasons of policy or public danger might excuse the normal activities of the Revolutionary Tribunal, no defence is possible for the wholesale massacres, or *fournées*, in which, on fifteen days between April 20 and July 26, of the second year of the Republic, and the fifth of Liberty, 540 persons, at an average rate of thirty-six a day, were sent to the guillotine.

These *fournées* fall into two groups—those of April, May, and June, all of which, except two (April 20 and 24) belong to the time when Robespierre was in charge of the Visitatorial Board, and those of July, the so-called 'prison conspiracies', when it was in the hands of Saint-Just, with occasional help from Couthon—the two men who were Robespierre's special supporters on the Committee of Public Safety. Almost certainly all the *fournées* were ordered by the Committee, acting upon Reports from the Board. Robespierre, therefore, bears a double responsibility. All the trials, except the first three, were carried out under the provisions of his law of 22 Prairial. The mass execution of Admiral, Renault and the fifty-two other 'parricides' on June 17 was an act of personal vengeance in which he at any rate acquiesced. His signature appears on documents dealing with two of the 'prison conspiracies'—that of June 16, when thirty-six inmates of the Bicêtre were executed, and that of July 7, when no less than sixty prisoners from the Luxembourg were sent together to the scaffold. Here he acquiesced in the highest degree of injustice; for the proscription lists were drawn up on information, often of the flimsiest kind, provided by prison spies, or by prisoners who hoped to escape punishment by denouncing their fellows; and at the 'trials' little or no attempt was made to substantiate the charges, whilst the admission that one was a priest or an aristocrat was equivalent to a death-sentence. Again, the chief responsibility for organizing the prison evidence, and for drawing up the lists of prison 'conspirators', falls on Robespierre's friend Herman, at this time director of the *commission d'administrations civiles*; and though Herman affirmed at his trial that he had only been to see Robespierre twice during the eight months that he was President of the Tribunal, and three times during the four months that he directed the *commission*,[1] yet it may fairly be assumed that they took the same view of this matter. On all these grounds, Robespierre's responsibility seems to be beyond question.

One further consideration. Herman was, by all accounts, an 'enlightened and upright man', whom everybody respected, and with a distinguished legal career behind him; yet he could lend himself to these travesties of justice, these outrages to common humanity. In other words, whilst the evidence goes to show that Robespierre was fully responsible for the terrorist policy and procedure, it also suggests that his case does not stand alone. The moral problem raised by his conduct cannot be isolated from that of the Terror as a whole.

Perhaps, indeed, it is not a moral problem so much as a psychological, or even a medical one. Robespierre's and Herman's ancestors, not many centuries back, were sensible and kindly men; but under stress of religious fanaticism, or fear of the powers of evil, they had burnt witches and heretics at the stake. Robespierre and Herman were sensible and kindly men; but under the stress of fanatical patriotism, and fear of conspiracy, they persuaded themselves that it was reasonable to put to death, with slight concessions to legal appearances, hundreds of their fellow-countrymen. Moral scruples, they felt, should not be allowed to obscure a moral principle.[2] That *vertu* about which Robespierre spoke so beautifully became, in practice, a patriotism 'beyond good and evil', changing the habits of thought (perhaps altering the grey matter of the brain) in such a way that a terrorist became as incapable of distinguishing right from wrong—not to say cruelty from humanity—as a

[1] Ording, 166.   [2] *La petite tue la grande morale* (Mirabeau).

blind man is of distinguishing night from day. Virtue could not reascend its throne until the reign of *vertu* was ended. There could be no public morality until someone was found to say, 'Patriotism is not enough'.

X

It is likely enough that a sixteenth *fournée* would have been added to the series, if Robespierre had not, for once, impeded the course of revolutionary justice. Why he did so, and with what result, matters so much for the crisis of his story that the Théot case demands more detailed treatment than it would otherwise deserve.[1]

During the years immediately before the Revolution, popular credulity had revenged itself upon the philosophic rationalism and formal churchmanship that passed for religion by running after false prophets and charlatans. Fashionable society frequented Mesmer, Saint-Martin, and Cagliostro; persons of humbler origin or slenderer means patronized Suzette Labrousse, the girl Brohne, or Catherine Théot. This old prophetess—she was already eighty-three when the outbreak of the Revolution gave her a fresh vogue —had been noted for her piety whilst still the servant-girl of a convent. In middle age she came to believe that she was 'the Virgin who would receive the child Jesus, who was coming to earth, carried by an angel, to bring peace to the world, and to receive all the nations'. Ten years before the Revolution she had been sent to the Bastille, for a letter to the clergy of Paris denouncing their errors, and prophesying the coming of the Messiah; and had been kept in confinement as a lunatic till 1782. Now, living with, and exploited by a widow Godefroy, she announced that the succession of 'Moses, Solomon, the Prophets, and the Apostles' would end with 'the mother of the Saviour', who (his plans slightly revised) would descend, amid flashes of lightning, near the Panthéon and the School of Law, and would put an end to the reign of anti-Christ. Meanwhile, with

[1] v. throughout, Mathiez in R.F. 40/481, and *Autour de Robespierre*, 129; R.F. 48/258, for another 'mystic', Madeleine Schweitzer.

the help of an ex-monk and ex-Constituent, Dom. Gerle, the gatherings at the widow's house were given a more ecclesiastical flavour: séances became services, and an initiation ceremony was introduced, which involved liturgical kissing, and the sign of the cross. The new cult became popular. Soldiers came for charms that would make them invulnerable, invalids for miraculous cures, young people for love-philtres, and hysterical or inquisitive women to enjoy the latest sensation. In January, 1794, Chaumette, as *procureur* of the Paris commune, raided the house, but took no action against the prophetess. Three months later, when Robespierre was starting his campaign for the worship of the Supreme Being, some discontented member of the Committee of General Security hit upon the Théot affair as a good opportunity to bring his religious policy into contempt. Agents of the Committee appear to have visited the prophetess, turned her thoughts in the direction of Robespierre, and induced her to dictate—for she was illiterate, and partly paralysed—a letter in which she claimed that Maximilien's mission was foretold by the prophet Ezekiel, called him her dear minister, and congratulated him upon the honour he had rendered to her son, the Supreme Being. Such language was hardly more extravagant than the flattery to which some of Robespierre's correspondents had by now accustomed him;[1] and when it was found that Dom. Gerle carried a certificate of *civisme* signed by Robespierre, and had been badgering him for an official appointment, it was felt that there were enough ingredients for the manufacture of an effective 'scandal'. On May 12, only five days after Robespierre's Report on religion, the Committee of General Security ordered the arrest of Théot and her accomplices. Vadier's report on the case was timed for June 15, the octave of the Festival of the Supreme Being, when Robespierre was still President of the Convention. The prophetess's name was changed from Théot to Theos (God), and the most was made of

[1] *Je vous regarde comme le Messie que l'Être éternel nous a promis pour réformer toute chose*, wrote Chauvet, on June 17 (Corresp. 437).

every absurd and unsavoury element in the case.[1] Robespierre, whose correspondence had recently included several anonymous letters accusing him of dictatorship, and threatening him with the fate of Danton,[2] took alarm, and used all his influence on the Committee of Public Safety to prevent the case coming into court. This, ten days later, he succeeded in doing, although it involved overruling the decision of the Convention on April 16. Fouquier-Tinville was sent for at 1 a.m. on June 27, and informed by Robespierre himself that the trial would not take place. 'He, he is opposed to it', was Fouquier's report to Vadier and his friends. Robespierre was only just in time. One of the accused persons was packing up his clothes, to go to the Conciergerie. Fouquier himself, in close touch with the conspirators, was already preparing his indictment against Robespierre.[3]

XI

The matter could hardly end with the quashing of the trial. The same day, Payan, Robespierre's chief supporter on the Commune, wrote expressing his concern about the case, and urging that a counter-attack should be undertaken.[4] His suggestion was that the Committee of Public Safety should itself present an impressive report, calculated to overshadow that of Vadier, and to restore its prestige amongst the members of the Committee of General Security, some of whom were only half-hearted supporters of Vadier and his friends. This report should, he thought, denounce fanaticism, suppress such superstitious sects as the Théotists, organize public festivals, and attack those who, like Bourdon and his accomplices, were corrupting public morality. This should be done at once: there could not be a

[1]Vadier cleverly kept back (or did he afterwards invent it?) the letter implicating Robespierre personally, and produced it for his *coup de grâce* on July 27 (v. 2/258.)

[2]Corresp. 434, 460-1.

[3]R.F. 40/509; Mathiez, *Autour de Robespierre*, 142; R.H.R.F. 11/338.

[4]Payan's view of the seriousness of the situation is corroborated by Buonarroti (Mathiez, *Corruption*, 286).

better opportunity for striking down the conspirators. Robespierre and the Committee (he says) have so far centralized the government only on its physical or mechanical side; what they have now to do is to use this machinery to unify and standardize public opinion.[1] In other words—such is the upshot of a significant letter—the worship of the Supreme Being is at present only a cult: it must become a church. The surest method of government (as many dictators have noticed) is not physical intimidation, but intellectual enslavement.

How far Robespierre was prepared to accept Payan's wider ideas, or to embark upon the policy they implied, it is impossible to tell; for within a month he was dead. Hitherto he had always said that there was no intention to enforce the new cult, or to interfere with other expressions of religious belief, provided they did not involve political counter-revolution.[2] But this purpose need not have excluded a compulsory system of moral and religious education, on the lines laid down by Le Pelletier.[3] What, however, Robespierre evidently seized upon in Payan's letter, with a terrorist's pathetic belief that it was really for the last time, was the suggestion that the moment had come to get rid of Bourdon and his group of 'conspirators'. This became the programme of his speech of 8 Thermidor;[4] and it was the attempt to carry it out which, by a process of natural retribution, cost him his life.

XII

Cécile Renault had said, when arrested outside Robespierre's room, that she wanted to see what a tyrant was like. She had been brought up, no doubt, to think of tyrants as kings, who sat on thrones, and wore golden crowns. It must have been difficult to associate tyranny with a dandified little lawyer, who lived up a builder's yard, and drove to the Convention in a hired cab. Yet the ingredients of

[1] Corresp. 443.
[2] e.g. his answer to Lequinio on May 15 (v. 2/185).   [3] v. 2/63.
[4] v. its *rapide tableau de toutes les factions* (2/249).

despotism—flattery and fear, are easily come by, and the thing itself is sometimes more effective for the absence of a conventional background.

The house in the rue Saint-Honoré had been, to Robespierre's admirers, the ideal setting for a champion of the people: it was becoming, for his enemies, the sinister refuge of a would-be dictator. 'As long as he stayed at Humbert's', said one, 'he was accessible to patriots, and to his friends; but once he went to live at the Duplays', he gradually became invisible. They shut him out from society, they worshipped him, they intoxicated him, and they exalted his pride to the point of perdition'.[1] 'His room', according to another, 'was a pretty boudoir, in which his own likeness was repeated in every form, and by every art—in paintings on the right-hand wall, in engravings on the left; his bust at one end of the room, and his bas-relief at the other—not to mention half a dozen small engravings of his portrait on the tables'.[2] Another described how he had been to see Robespierre, found him just out of the hands of the hairdresser, with his face covered with powder, had to stand by, unnoticed, while he finished his toilet, and went away without a word or a look.[3]

All this was gross exaggeration. Lacante may have been turned out of the house at a time when visitors were not wanted;[4] but when Ouvrard came on an errand of mercy, introduced by Elisabeth Duplay, Maximilien invited him to share his meal, and advised him how to proceed.[5] The pleasant story of the Norwegian sea-captain, Nicolay Linde, who used to describe two interviews with him in 1793, is apocryphal in parts, but may be evidence that he could be both accessible and genial.[6] The supposed secrecy of Robespierre's ménage was, in fact, nothing more than the precautions taken by his hosts to save him from the importunity of people who were not his friends, or from the

[1]Fréron (Pap. inéd. 1/154). [2]Barbaroux, *Mémoires* (ed. Dauban), 358.
[3]Barras, *Mémoires*, 1/148. [4]Lenôtre, 109.
[5]A.R. 5/693. cp. the story of Mme de Trémond (R.H.R.F. 1/49).
[6]A. H. 5/457. It represents Robespierre as suffering from gout. Cp. Millingen, *Recollections of Republican France*, 281–5.

attacks of those who, as more than one incident had shown, might become his assassins.

But the old calm was gone. The whole Duplay household were involved in the fortunes of their guest. The father, unable to let his house-property, had lost money, and had been forced back into the carpentering business. The mother was worried by the political situation, and by quarrels between Robespierre's Jacobin associates,[1] of whom Buissart disapproved.[2] Even Anthoine was said to have abused her hospitality by spreading stories at Metz to the discredit of Robespierre and his friends.[3] Both daughters' affections were being sacrificed on the altar of public duty; for Maximilien was too busy to think of marrying Eléonore, and he had sent Philip Lebas off to the front on the eve of his union with Elisabeth.[4]

As for his own work, it was becoming every day more difficult, and more dangerous. It is doubtful whether, even now, he employed a secretary; neither Simon Duplay, who disowned the title, nor Bégue, *dit* Magloire, who claimed it,[5] seem to have been more than occasional amanuenses. The evidence of Robespierre's manuscripts suggests that he wrote what had to be written himself, and corrected his own proofs, always laboriously, but sometimes with a passion for destruction which struck out whole passages with an untidy network of dark lines, and sometimes with a cautious constructiveness which erased and substituted words, one at a time.[6] Both methods were equally characteristic of the man.

It is likely enough that nowadays, when Robespierre went from his lodgings to the Convention or to the club, he was accompanied by one or more of his friends; but the notion that these men were organized, or armed—a 'volunteer bodyguard of *Tappe-durs*, let us say *Strike-sharps*, fierce Patriots with ferruled sticks'[7]—finds little or no ground in

[1]Letter of Mme Duplay (*Pap. inéd.* 3/230). [2]Ward, 137
[3]B. and R. 22/298. [4]Stéfane-Pol, *Autour de Robespierre*, 127.
[5]A.H. 9/163. Cp. 1/184n. [6]Stéfane-Pol, *De Robespierre à Fouché*, 46.
[7]Carlyle, ed. Fletcher, 3/194. *Tape-durs* were government spies (*Vieux Cordelier*, ed. Calvet, 136n).

the documents quoted by its supporters.[1] The mendacious
Fréron adds that Robespierre always carried a pair of pistols,
with which he used to practise marksmanship in the garden,
till he became such a good shot that he remarked, one day,
'I ought to have adopted a military career'. But it is not
unlikely that this last story was suggested by the presence
of two pistols at the time of Robespierre's arrest, or by the
experiment with a quick-firing carbine, not at the rue
Saint-Honoré (where there was only a builder's yard), but
in the garden at the rue Saintonge, four years earlier.[2]

Robespierre did not often go into society. Barère says
that he was induced, with considerable difficulty, to form
one of a party at Méot's restaurant. He remained silent
during the meal, but at the end he cheered up sufficiently
to ask the names of the other guests. When he heard that
one of them was M. Loménie, ex-coadjutor of the Archbishop of Lens, he 'took his hat, and went off, without
speaking a word'.[3] This may be no more than a malicious
exaggeration: another story that has obtained currency is
apparently a pure work of fiction. In Proyart's Life of
Robespierre there is added to Le Blond's work, of which it
is in the main a reproduction, an account by 'a member of
the Convention' of a dinner-party at Mme de Chalabre's. The
guests were M. and Mme Bitaubé, Fréron, Vadier, Torné,
Ronsin, Desmoulins, and others unnamed. Robespierre
kept the company waiting, and excused his lateness by
press of business. At dinner there was a general discussion
of politics, to which he contributed very little; but his
shortest remarks were received like the replies of an oracle.
Torné and Mme de Chalabre ventured on flattering
speeches, which were coldly received: only Desmoulins
treated him naturally. This whole account has, pretty

[1]Campardon, *Tribunal révolutionnaire*, (1/342) quotes Girard (August 18, 1794)
as saying that Nicolas, Chrétien, Garnier-Launay, and others were in the habit of
accompanying Robespierre. Hamel (3/316) refers to a letter of Nicolas to Robespierre
(Corresp. 279) which has nothing to do with the subject. Esquiros (2/222) gives
David d'Angers as authority for the statement that *un fort de la halle* used to follow
Robespierre to and from the Convention, armed with a heavy stick, but that he
never knew it (Blanc 7/360). cp. 1/267, and *Vieux Cordelier*, No. 5,
[2]v. 1/221.
[3]Barère, *Mémoires* (E.T. 2/164).

obviously, been 'written round' the invitation to dinner by Mme de Chalabre in March, 1791. M. and Mme Bitaubé (a Prussian literary man and his wife) are the guests mentioned in that letter:[1] the 'small number of old friends, all good patriots', whom she will ask to meet him, is made up by the inclusion of Fréron and Desmoulins, both old school-fellows, Vadier, on friendly terms with Robespierre up to August, 1792,[2] Torné, who wrote a flattering letter to him in August, 1791,[3] and Ronsin, who asked for Robespierre's support during the elections of September, 1792.[4] Were the story true, the dinner could not have taken place in 1794, when most of these men became either Robespierre's enemies, or his victims. But it is not. The only words the narrator can remember—the flattering speeches of Torné and Mme de Chalabre—are taken verbatim from their letters, subsequently published among Robespierre's papers. All the material seems to be from the same source.[5]

No such doubt arises with regard to the authenticity of a much more life-like story. Mme Julien was the middle-aged wife of a Jacobin member of the Convention, who lived in Paris from 1790 to May, 1793, and whose letters to her son give an inimitable, because quite unconscious, picture of the bourgeois patriot point of view. 'Robespierre and his brother and sister', she writes on February 2, 1793, 'are to dine with us to-day. I shall thus make the acquaintance of that patriotic family, whose head has so many friends and so many enemies'. Robert Lindet was also invited; and a reference to the good lady's household accounts shows that the fare consisted of a chicken, a salad, bread and cheese, cider, milk, and cream—the total cost of this frugal meal being less than ten *livres*. 'I was much pleased with the Robespierre family', she reports next day. 'The sister is naïve and natural, like your aunts: she arrived two hours before her brother, and we chatted like two old women. I made her tell me about their domestic life: it is exactly like ours, simple and frugal. Her brother had as little to do with

[1]Corresp. 61.   [2]Corresp. 140.
[3]Corresp. 98.   [4]Corresp. 145.
[5]Corresp. 61, 98. Both were published in Pap. inéd. in 1828. Proyart wrote in 1850.

the 10th of August as with the 2nd of September. He is as capable of being a party leader as of catching hold of the moon. He is absent-minded, like a thinker, cold and formal, like a lawyer, but gentle as a lamb, and as sombre as Young. I see he has not our tender sensibility, but I believe he desires the good of the human race, though rather from justice than from love. For the rest, you need only see him face to face to be sure that nature never gave such attractive features to any but a noble mind'.[1]

This was before the crisis of Robespierre's struggle with the Girondins, before the access of power which brought so much trouble and suspicion into his life. His rare appearances, in the later days, give an impression of sadness and strain. Mme Carvin, the pretty tobacconist at whose shop he calls every day, reports that he speaks unhappily of the situation: 'We shall never get out of our present state (he says): I am worried to death (*bourrelé*): I'm at my wits' end' (*j'en ai la tête perdue*).[2] He is so upset by the sight of the 'food-queues', which stretch from the door of the local greengrocer's to the entrance of Duplay's yard, that Mme Duplay makes presents of butter, in his name, for the relief of her neighbours.[3]

He drops in at Maret's library in the Palais Royale, to turn over the books, and ask the news of the day. He is there with Barère on the day of Mme Elisabeth's execution, and is told the public are speaking against him. 'You see', he says, turning to Barère, 'it is always me': he had tried to save her, he added, but Collot had insisted on her death.[4]

Mossi, a Marseille bookseller, who is visiting Paris, goes one evening to the Jacobin Club, and finds himself rubbing shoulders with a pale-faced spectacled individual in a silk coat, with his hair carefully curled and powdered. Surprised at such smartness among *sansculottes*, he murmurs *Muscadin!* His neighbour draws back, pushes up his spectacles on-to his forehead, and glares at the man from Marseille. Mossi, without quite knowing why, is so alarmed that he

---

[1] *The Great French Revolution*, 298, 309.   [2] Esquiros, 2/459.   [3] A.R. 2/594.
[4] Beaulieu, *Essais historiques*, 6/10: A.R. 7/255.

slips away into the crowd. 'Who was that'? he asks. 'Robespierre'. He leaves for Marseille without a moment's delay, and it is a month before he feels his head secure on his shoulders.[1]

But fact merges insensibly into fiction. Walking one day in the country, Robespierre helps some children to pick wild roses from a hedge, and makes great friends with them; but when he asks them their name, and is told, 'Sanson', his face falls; he calls to his dog, and walks off without another word. They are nieces of the Public Executioner.[2]

So the legend grows, till the sceptical reader is not surprised to find Robespierre's occasional visits to his friends—Arthur at Bercy, Auvray at Issy, or Mme de Chalabre at Vanves—exaggerated into disreputable debauches, whilst meetings with political associates at Charenton, Maisons-Alfort, and Choisy (where his brother-in-law Vaugeois was Mayor in 1793), are represented as secret conferences of the Committee of Public Safety,[3] whose improbable plots are overheard, and communicated to Lord Granville, by the 'Dropmore spy', and whose favourite recreation it is to draw up proscription lists, 'to see how so-and-so will look under the blade of the guillotine'.[4] Robespierre is even credited with designs so ambitious as to marry the King's daughter, Mme Royale, and so heartless as to inaugurate a human skin tannery.[5] Less fantastic is the strong local tradition which credits him with having spent some part of the summer of 1794 at Rousseau's Hermitage at Montmorency; but the story that he was there on the eve of 6 Thermidor, meditating, in mystical communion with Jean-Jacques, his 'last will and testament' to an ungrateful world, bears every mark of the legend-maker's hand.[6]

XIII

The real background of Robespierre's 'Dictatorship' is best studied in his correspondence during the spring and

[1]Proyart, 212.   [2]N. and Q. series 8, 10/249.
[3]The evidence, for what it is worth, is exploited to the full in Lenôtre, 245 f.
[4]Proyart, 138.   [5]Le Blond, 307, 279.   [6]Lenôtre, 244

summer of 1794. Of the 468 letters received by him which have been published, no less than 160 belong to the last seven months of his life; but of the 78 written by him, only two: for it was dangerous to keep his writings, in the reaction that followed his fall. Most of these 160 letters deal with the personal troubles of those who had been caught up in the great net of suspicion and punishment that the government was dragging across the country. Some are from admirers or friends. Some are semi-official accounts of the state of the country. From them it is not impossible to read the condition of Robespierre's mind during the last crisis of his career.

First come the correspondents who want appointments or privileges for themselves or their friends. Lechesne has been discharged from subordinate employment under the Committee, and asks for reinstatement.[1] Aigoin, an old correspondent, and a firm friend, asks Robespierre to use his influence to forward a family arrangement for the care of their old father in Paris.[2] C. Delacroix wants a post for a relative.[3] Mlle Riquetti, Mirabeau's sister, asks the sanction of the Committee for an educational venture: she hopes to make herself useful to the Republic by giving gratuitous lessons to children in reading, writing, and music; but, more particularly, by teaching them a 'Catechism of Nature', a synopsis of which she has presented to the Convention. By way of guaranteeing her patriotism, she adds that she is a regular attendant at the Convention and at the Club, and addresses Robespierre in language which even he must have found cloying: 'No, my dear Robespierre, have no fear; I shall never desert you. Following your example and advice, I shall achieve virtue like yours. You are as steady and unwavering as the eagle that circles in the sky. How seductive your mind, and your heart! Your watchword is the love of what is good; mine is that your life may long be spared for the happiness of my beloved Convention'.[4] Had Robespierre, when he put this letter

[1]Corresp. 335.
[2]Corresp. 350; A.H. 12/33.
[3]Corresp. 356.
[4]Corresp. 377.

aside, any feeling for a great family that had been brought
so low? Duquesnoy's brother would like employment
in the army of Brest.[1] Riquier, of the Hussars, wants to
return to the front.[2] Voulland recommends an ex-postmaster
for appointment as a juror.[3] Barss, the Paris representative
of the Polish patriots, asks Robespierre to use his influence
on the Committee to obtain a favourable answer to a request.[4]
Albitte sends a testimonial in favour of the local authorities
of Briançon.[5]

Another and larger group of letters concerns persons
imprisoned, or in danger of imprisonment. Moureau, who
describes himself as an uncle of the young patriot-martyr
Viala, has been two months in prison, whilst a large deputation of local Jacobins has been waiting six weeks to give
evidence in his favour. May they be heard?[6] Dentzel asks
Robespierre to read his defence.[7] There are three more
chapters of Chabot's lamentations.[8] Massa and Dabray,
two of the seventy-three Girondins still in prison, protest
against the sealing of their effects.[9] Baudin asks for an interview, to defend himself against charges.[10] Hoche has been
arrested, and appeals to the generosity of one whom he has
always regarded as his 'guardian angel' (*génie tutélaire*);
'If my life (he says) is spared, I should have good reason to
think I owed it to your affection for patriots. If the anger of
my enemies drags me to the tomb, I shall still die blessing
the Republic and Robespierre'.[11] Another Jacobin whom a
turn of the wheel has put in prison, the ex-Minister of War,
Bouchotte, defends himself against the charge of Hébertism.[12] Loisel of Amiens is in trouble for attacking Dumont:
he asks Robespierre to put his case before the Committee
of General Security.[13] Gérard's only crime, says Harmand,
is to have written in favour of Vincent.[14] Laharpe, who
recently courted Robespierre, but has now become involved
in the charges that brought de Batz to the scaffold, is alarmed
to hear that he wishes to have copies of his works, and

[1]Corresp. 398.   [2]Corresp. 418.   [3]Corresp. 433.   [4]A.H. 5/172.
[5]Corresp. 453.   [6]Corresp. 336.   [7]Corresp. 343.   [8]Corresp. 344, 357–8.
[9]Corresp. 383, 396, 399.   [10]Corresp. 390.   [11]Corresp. 405.   [12]Corresp. 406.
[13]Corresp. 412.   [14]Corresp. 417.

suggests that he should look, for evidence of his patriotism, not in his pre-revolutionary writings, but in his tragedy of *Virginie*, his articles in the *Mercure*, or his *Lycée*, which has been much appreciated at private readings.[1] The result of Robespierre's reading was that Laharpe went to prison; whence he wrote, soon afterwards, protesting the identity of his views with Robespierre's, and eulogizing the character and policy of the man whose word could save him from civil death.[2] There are two letters from Faure of Nancy, whose anti-clerical policy had earned him a long spell of imprisonment. Congratulating Robespierre on his Presidency, he suggests that the inauguration of the worship of the Supreme Being might be accompanied by a general amnesty of prisoners; and ends, naïvely enough, by asking for six weeks leave from prison, in order to enjoy some sea-bathing.[3] Tallien, inculpated by Robespierre's speech of June 11, writes to defend his conduct at Bordeaux. He has been depicted, he says, as indulging in a luxurious and immoral life. If Robespierre will only come and see him and his old mother, still living in the same simple retreat as before the Revolution, without a sign of luxury, and not a penny the richer, he will realize the injustice of his attack.[4] Tallien was soon to have his revenge. Girault and Royer, two more of the Girondins imprisoned at La Force, protest their patriotism, and claim Robespierre's further protection.[5] The younger brother of Cécile Renault, brought back from the front as an 'accomplice' of his sister's crime, and still in prison a fortnight after the execution of his relatives, writes a cringing letter, disowning his family, and asking to be released.[6] Even more abject is the apology of Garnier-Launay, one of the organizers of the 'patriotic banquets' suppressed by the Convention on July 16. He informs his 'republican brother' that, 'thoughtlessly and unintentionally', he has been guilty of a 'grave error', for which he will

[1]Corresp. 422; R.F. 52/546.
[2]R.F. 52/546: A.R. 4/112. After Robespierre's fall, this compromising correspondence was returned to him by Courtois; and he celebrated his escape by a letter in a different tone, which described Robespierre as a 'monster', and gloated over his 'pestiferous corpse'.
[3]Corresp. 337, 427.   [4]Corresp. 432.   [5]Corresp. 435, 442.   [6]Corresp. 451.

make public apology the next day before the general assembly of his Section.[1] He knew he was in danger of being added to the next proscription-list. Finally Fernex, a member of the tribunal at Orange, writes to defend himself against charges of undue severity.[2]

Another group of correspondents have suggestions to make, which they think will interest the Committee, and secure themselves some favour. Le Chapelier, Robespierre's antagonist in the Constituent Assembly, tells his 'old friend and colleague' that he is now a whole-hearted supporter of the Republic, and submits a scheme for ruining the 'abominable' (affreux) English government.[3] Girard, deputy for l'Aude, asks for a month's leave of absence, to visit his 'respectable mother' at Narbonne. He proposes, en route, to inspect the military hospitals, revive an old salt-petre factory, and investigate the food supply. Leave was given.[4] Durand-Maillane, a prominent Moderate, has a project which he wishes to bring before the Committee; but his main purpose seems to be to flatter Robespierre's generosity towards the Catholics and the imprisoned Girondins.[5] Picard has a scheme of national defence to propose;[6] and Duchesne one for settling 'thousands of paupers' in Guiana, by way of solving the economic troubles of the Republic.[7]

The personal flattery which was a common ingredient of these letters took many forms, some of them unusual. On May 31 Robespierre received a long and rather illiterate letter from a young widow at Nantes, named Jakin, offering him her hand in marriage, with a dowry of 40,000 francs.[8] Drouhin the publisher asked leave to make an engraving of Robespierre from the portrait by Mme Guyard.[9] A letter of fulsome flattery from Besson enclosed an address from the Popular Society of Manosque.[10] Chauvet, describing himself

[1]Corresp. 462.
[2]Corresp. 468. The letter is dated 1 fructidor; but he must have heard of Robespierre's death much earlier; is it a mistake for 1 thermidor? (Michon ad loc.)
[3]Corresp. 341. For the scheme, v. Pap. inéd. 1/274; B. and R. 35/368.
[4]Corresp. 345.   [5]Corresp. 352.   [6]Corresp. 402.   [7]Corresp. 436.
[8]Corresp. 421. The name should be Jaquin? (Mathiez, G. et M. 25.)
[9]Corresp. 436, cp. 1/143.   [10]Corresp. 430.

as 'a young man of 87', commandant of a 'Company of Veterans', congratulates Robespierre on his religious policy, and calls him 'the Messiah promised by the Eternal Being, to reform everything'.[1] To Dupont, who has a favour to ask, he is 'a virtuous and upright Republican, a firm support and indestructible pillar of the French Republic'.[2] Molines of Montpelier writes to say that 'Nature has just given him a son', and that he has named him after Robespierre.[3] The same day, Dubois of Amiens, writing as an old school-fellow of Maximilien, asks for an interview. 'I want', he says, 'to refresh my eyes and heart with the sight of you; and my soul, magnetized by your republican virtues, will carry home again some of the fire which you kindle in all good republicans'.[4] An anonymous correspondent from Ville Affranchie (Lyon) writes to say that he has changed his poor opinion of Robespierre since his denunciation of Collot's terrorist policy at that place.[5]

But most of the anonymous letters, as might be expected, contain threats or abuse. One, from 'a deputy', advises Robespierre to retire into private life, if he would avoid assassination, and says there are twenty-three of his colleagues as determined as any Brutus or Scaevola to destroy him.[6] Another calls Robespierre (with unconscious prophecy of a later bearer of the title) 'Tiger', 'Hangman', and so forth.[7] A third is from a supposed confidant, who says he has money (sent him by Robespierre) and a place of refuge ready for the time when the crash comes.[8]

There may be some connexion between this last letter and a curious communication in which one Bellet, of Sene-court, consults Robespierre about a purchase of land. The writer says that he has heard indirectly that Robespierre wishes to acquire some national property in the neighbour-hood of Clermont, and offers to act on his behalf, giving as 'reference' the name of an usher in the Revolutionary Tribunal.[9] It is, however, so improbable either that Robes-

[1] Corresp. 437. [2] Corresp. 440. [3] Corresp. 448.
[4] Corresp. 449. [5] Corresp. 456. [6] Corresp. 434.
[7] Corresp. 460. [8] Corresp. 461.
[9] Corresp. 349 (not in Courtois).

pierre had money to invest in this way, or that, if he had thought it genuine, Courtois would not have included in his Report a letter so easily twisted into a charge against the Incorruptible, that perhaps the letter is a forger's clumsy attempt to implicate Robespierre in a misuse of public money.

One letter remains, which has a special interest for English readers. Benjamin Vaughan, a professional revolutionist, had, in May, 1793, followed his friend J. H. Stone into exile across the Channel, and lived under an assumed name at Passy, until discovered, imprisoned, and finally deported to Switzerland. From Geneva he wrote to Robespierre, proposing a scheme, by which Liège, the ecclesiastical Electorates, and other states on the left bank of the Rhine, should join in a federal government under French protection, reconquer their territory from the Allies, and form a buffer-state between France and Germany. This letter reached the Committee of Public Safety on the very day of Robespierre's execution. Billaud-Varennes, speaking at the Club two days later, and free to tell any lie about 'the Dictator', pretended that it proposed to partition France between Robespierre, Saint-Just, and Couthon; whilst Barère declared that it designed the dismemberment of the country, and the abandonment of Belgium and the Rhine frontier. He added, in his Memoirs, that Robespierre had been in the habit of visiting Vaughan at Passy.[1] So the legend grew.

If this correspondence is considered as a whole, the reader can hardly fail to be struck by the tone of flattery and fear in which such a large proportion of it is expressed, and the almost complete absence of those natural interests and friendly commonplaces which generally humanize even a statesman's letter-bag. It is, in fact, an abnormal, an unhealthy correspondence. Robespierre was so given up to his country, and to mankind, that he had ceased to exist for his friends.[2]

[1] Corresp. 459; A.R. 9/11.
[2] Régis Deshorties to Augustin, 30 Mess. II (A.R. 13/510).

XIV

The news which Robespierre received from the provinces, during this period, did nothing to ease his mind. Jullien has now moved to Bordeaux, whence he denounces the representative Ysabeau, and suggests that the last refuge of the fugitive Girondins should be razed to the ground.[1] Mallarmé reports food shortage and religious difficulties in the Meuse and Moselle district.[2] Delorme confirms all that Robespierre had heard before of the misconduct of the war in the Vendée, and thinks that, if hostilities continue for another three years, there will be nothing left of that unhappy country.[3] A letter from Duquesnoy shows what a hold clericalism and counter-revolution still have on the eastern part of the country in this sixth year of Revolution. Most of the local authorities are 'Moderates', the people are fanatically religious, the rich are tainted with 'aristocracy', the merchants and tradesmen ignore the 'maximum', and the frontier is infested with spies.[4] In Italy, says Augustin, as the army advances into the country, the people fly in panic, owing to stories of religious persecution, and other fables, spread by the *émigrés*.[5] Cadillot describes the industrial stagnation of the Midi;[6] whilst from Calvados, Mérouze reports a general lack of patriotism, and interest only in money-making.[7] Finally, writing from Mezières, Levasseur describes the severe measures he has been forced to take against 'fanatical, turbulent, and counter-revolutionary' clergy.[8]

The standard of revolutionary orthodoxy was doubtless higher in 1794 than it had been in 1789: but Robespierre cannot have read these reports from the provinces without feeling that there had been no corresponding improvement in revolutionary zeal. In 1789, however unenlightened the administration, there was at least a general enthusiasm for the Revolution. Since then, in proportion as the reforms introduced by the new regime had removed the grievances

---

[1]Corresp. 378, 416, 424-5, 447.
[2]Corresp. 382.   [3]Corresp. 380.   [4]Corresp. 386.   [5]Corresp. 388.
[6]Corresp. 429.   [7]Corresp. 455.   [8]Corresp. 466.

of the peasant, and afforded the townsman an opportunity of making money, revolutionary ardour had declined; whilst, by a paradox not unfamiliar at such times, the proportionate failure to satisfy these demands had produced fresh kinds of discontent. It was beginning to look as though the Jacobins were a handful of missionaries preaching a gospel unwelcome to the mass of the people.

From this point of view—had he been able to adopt it—Robespierre might have seen that both the quarrels and the crimes of the terrorists lost much of their importance. The significant fact was that France was tired of the Revolution. Those who had stood to gain by its early stages stood to lose by its later developments. Of the two classes which it had dispossessed, the rich land-owners were now its avowed enemies, whilst the city poor had not been sufficiently bribed to become its friends. Robespierre, who had made himself a political realist, in 1793, to defeat the Girondins, and in 1794, to use Jacobinism in the interests of a higher idealism, now found himself in danger of defeat by the deep and practised realism of the French people. To draw back, and to consolidate the Revolution on a basis of middle-class monopoly, was a capitulation to Dantonism such as he could never contemplate. The 'transitional period' must go on. Yet neither the quarrels of the politicians (however prominent in the press), nor Paris streets running with the blood of the guillotine, were to bring the Jacobin regime to an end, but its failure to understand the materialistic point of view of the average Frenchman. If Robespierre was beginning to realize this, it was too late. He was not destined to be one of those few leaders of revolutions who have come through the 'transitional period' alive.

CHAPTER XVII

THE MARTYR (JUNE–JULY, 1794)

I

THE last day of Robespierre's Presidency of the Convention (June 19) was also the last of his intervention in its debates, until July 26, two days before his death. At the Club, he only spoke twice between June 11 and July 9. After June 30 his comments cease to appear on the reports of the Visitatorial Board. During the week following his release from the Presidency of the Assembly (June 19–25) he signs an exceptional number of drafts at the Committee of Public Safety; then the evidence of his work there too gradually disappears. He is indeed recorded as having been present every day between July 1 and 26,[1] but his signature occurs only three times, and it is possible to think that this was one of the periods during which the register of attendances was not accurately kept. If so, the last month of Robespierre's life was spent in almost complete seclusion.

Why was this? Some of the dates are suggestive. The last days of his Presidency had seen a deliberate attempt to bring Robespierre's religious policy into disrepute.[2] A week before his virtual retirement from the Committee of Public Safety, a series of unpleasant scenes, due to the antagonism of its other members to the 'Triumvirate', had culminated (June 25) in the Committee's refusal to ratify Robespierre's decree for the arrest of the Revolutionary Committee of the *Section de l'indivisibilité*;[3] and on the following day he had been defeated in an attempt to remove Fouquier-Tinville from the post of Public Prosecutor.[4] On June 28 Saint-Just came back from the front, and was able to take over the work of the Visitatorial Board. There were thus both

[1] There are no minutes for July 12 and 22.
[3] C.P.S. 14,'511.

[2] The Théot case; v. 2/210.
[4] Mathiez, *G. et M.*, 207.

reason and opportunity for a temporary retirement from work which had become increasingly onerous and unpleasant for a tired and touchy man. If he did not entirely desert the Jacobin club, it was because that was the society most congenial to him, and the last seat of his power.

Two special considerations doubtless helped to determine Robespierre's withdrawal from public life. One was his fear of assassination; the other was the need, which every week's events made more urgent, to reconsider his position, and to think out a policy for the future.

Voluntary retirement is one of the most useful weapons in the armoury of a statesman; but it is also one of the most difficult to use. The withdrawal must be genuine—not a pretence of abandoning powers which are still exercised in another form, or under another name. It must be made at a moment when choice is perfectly free. And it demands a situation in which temporary absence is likely to increase the prestige of the absentee. It may be doubted whether even these conditions are sufficient in a time of revolution, when public attention is necessarily caught by the incident and person of the moment. Robespierre should have been warned by the example of Danton not to give his friends so good an excuse to forget him. But in any case the conditions of successful retirement were unfulfilled. Robespierre was still a deputy, though he did not speak in the House; still the chief figure at the Jacobins; still a member, and reputed the dominant member, of the Committee of Public Safety; and still, through Saint-Just, in close touch with the work of the Visitatorial Board, and of the Revolutionary Tribunal. Always cold, suspicious, and enigmatic, he seemed more dangerous when he was silent than when he spoke. The less that was known of his comings and goings, the more he was suspected of secret intrigue. Every time Simon Duplay was seen carrying home his portfolio of papers, every time it was known that Saint-Just had visited the little room off the builder's yard, the air was thick with suspicions and fears. Robespierre's was not a genuine retirement. How, indeed, could it be, when his own Prairial Law branded not only active conspiracy, but also inactive patriotism as *incivisme*?[1]

Again, Robespierre's withdrawal might have been convincing and effective, if it had taken place a month earlier—after the attempted assassination, but before the festival of the Supreme Being, the Prairial Law, the Théot affair, and the quarrels on the Committee. Then it would have been entirely voluntary, and generally regretted; now it was half forced, and welcomed by a large number of political and personal opponents.

Once more, it was not at all likely that temporary absence would increase Robespierre's prestige, or lead to a demand for his return. The crisis which had brought him into the government had passed. His special contributions to the make-up of the Committee—knowledge of parliamentary life, popularity with the crowd, and the power of formulating and presenting a programme—had grown less important to his colleagues with every month's experience of power. The Convention was subservient; programmes were rather tiresome; and it was easier to bribe or to coerce the crowd than to educate it. Robespierre was no longer indispensable. More than this; he was intent upon two lines of policy which the Committee as a whole found definitely embarrassing. The redistribution of wealth contemplated under the Laws of Ventôse was likely to alienate men of property; the cult of the Supreme Being was offensive both to Catholics and to men of philosophic conviction.

Not only, then, would Robespierre's withdrawal at this moment pass for an acknowledgment of failure, but also he could hardly hope to return to power, unless as the advocate of a new policy, or as the leader of a fresh popular movement; and both were unlikely contingencies, at this stage of the Revolution. Retirement was, in fact, a fatal mistake, Robespierre's friends forgot him: his enemies intrigued to bring about his fall.

[1]How did Robespierre's absence from duty pass uncensured? Barère's answer was that attendance at the Committee was so regular that Gossuin's decree of October 29, requiring a report to the Convention, was not enforced (R.F. 34/253).

II

Robespierre's only previous holiday, since the beginning of the Revolution, had been spent in a triumphal progress through his constituency. Now, owing partly to the political situation in Paris, but partly also to a change of feeling at Arras, this was no longer possible. Two unlucky mistakes —the quarrel between Charlotte and Augustin Robespierre, and Maximilien's weakness for the terrorist, Joseph Lebon— had fatally estranged him from his old supporters in Artois.

Elected Mayor of Arras in 1792, Lebon came to Paris as a *suppléant* deputy of the Convention in July, 1793. In August, and again in October, he did good work as a government agent in the Pas de Calais and neighbouring Departments. In the following April, when Cambrai and Landrecies were besieged, and Arras itself was threatened with attack, he was once more despatched on a mission to the same district. This time his regime was so severe that Buissart and his wife both wrote to Robespierre, begging him to intervene.[1] When Charlotte and Augustin moved to Paris in September, 1792, the house in the rue des Rapporteurs had been given up, and Maximilien had claimed exemption from taxation on the ground that he was no longer a householder; since December he had not even written to his old friends. Now, hearing that one of the persons arrested at Arras was Gabriel Leblond, whose child was a godson of his, he summoned Lebon to the capital, whilst complimenting him on 'the energy with which he had repressed the enemies of the Revolution', and telling him that it was hoped to make his work still more effective.[2] Lebon arrived in Paris, followed by a denunciation from Guffroy. 'You said the other day at the Jacobins', he wrote to Robespierre, 'that the reign of Virtue did not involve persecution; and I think you meant it. Why then do you protect this persecuting priest, who has made an end of patriotism at Arras, and has established a regime of

[1] Corresp. 385, 401.   [2] Corresp. 400.

drunkenness and crime? Unless you act quickly, and nominate a commission (to investigate his conduct), you will
become an accomplice of this horrible man, who is deceiving
you, and making the Revolution detested, by his persecution
of patriots'.[1] But Lebon, whom Robespierre's friend Lebas
considered 'worth a whole garrison of soldiers',[2] easily
exculpated himself, and was sent back to Cambrai. Not only
so: he was entrusted with the delicate mission of convoying
to Arras Charlotte Robespierre, whose quarrel with Augustin had made her presence in Paris a serious embarrassment.[3]

By this action Robespierre not only gave his sanction
to the terrorist policy which Lebon proceeded to carry
out at Arras, but also made a dangerous enemy of Guffroy,
once his colleague on the Episcopal bench at Arras, and his
collaborator in more than one affair of local politics.[4] Soon,
fresh protests from Guffroy, and a visit from Mme Buissart
herself, who apparently installed herself and her son in the
Duplays' house,[5] brought such pressure to bear, that Lebon
was at last recalled; but not till the victory of Fleurus had
made his presence in Artois no longer necessary (July 10).
The end of this complicated and rather obscure story[6] was
that Robespierre's old associates and constituents believed
him to be backing their chief persecutor; and it was even
hinted that Charlotte's journey to Arras had been designed
to end at the guillotine. The second charge was doubtless
absurd; but nothing could be less edifying than the terms
in which Augustin had written to Maximilien about a
sister whom he described as 'our greatest enemy', and 'a
woman who is the despair of us both';[7] and nothing more
likely to cause scandal and indignation than to send her
back to her home in charge of the local Inquisitor.

---

[1]Corresp. 404.   [2]Corresp. 403.   [3]v. 2/105.

[4]Guffroy had, indeed, been struck off the Jacobin Club in March (R.F. 53/371);
but his personal enmity to Robespierre seems to date from the Lebon affair.

[5]Buissart writes to her *chez Maximilien Robespierre* (Pap. inéd. 1/250).

[6]Mathiez in A.H. 1/1, is too favourable to Robespierre; the latest and most
detailed investigation of the whole affair (Jacob, *Joseph Lebon*) is as much too friendly
to Lebon as his earlier biographer (Paris, *Joseph Lebon*) was too hostile.

[7]Corresp. 423.

III

Arras was not the only quarter in which Robespierre's policy had damaged his prestige. It was the inevitable result of his pursuit of a middle path, inclining now towards the right and now towards the left, that he had made enemies in both camps. He was not specially to blame for the intrigues of priests, aristocrats, and rebels, which still kept so many Departments in a state of open or covert civil war: yet his prominence in the government made him, for many of these people, the symbol of what they were fighting against. He had done his best to crush Girondism: yet it was still a force in the country; and the gratitude which the seventy-three imprisoned deputies expressed to him for having saved their lives was nothing compared to the hatred they felt towards the man who had executed their friends, and was keeping themselves in prison. Danton was dead; but his death had brought new recruits to the banner of Indulgence, men who (for all that) were unlikely to show Robespierre a mercy he had not shown, or to allow him to patronize (as some thought he might) a movement which he had previously proscribed. Latterly, too, Robespierre's championship of the Worship of the Supreme Being had not only angered the Catholics, to whom he was little better than an atheist, but had also shown that there were still plenty of old-fashioned sceptics and anti-clericals who regarded him as a reactionary, and his attempt to nationalize religion as pandering to superstition and sacerdotalism.

These were the more obvious constituents of counter-Robespierrism. The events of the last few months had created fresh enemies. There were the patriots—for all thought themselves so—whom Robespierre's zeal for Jacobin orthodoxy had expelled from the Club. There were the deputies who, whatever Robespierre might say, believed their lives to be in danger under the Law of the 22nd Prairial. There were the officials—such of them as were still alive—who had incurred the displeasure of the Visitatorial

Board. There was the large and pitiable class of people—how large and pitiable, is not generally realized—of those whose friends and relations had been guillotined, or deported, or who were languishing in prison.[1] There were the friends with whom Robespierre had broken, the flatterers who resented the degradation of flattering him, and the rivals who were jealous of his success.

Fouché, implicated both in the massacres at Lyon and in the anti-Christian demonstrations at Nevers; Bourdon de l'Oise, who had opposed the Prairial Law, and was regarded by Payan as 'the head of the conspiracy' against the government; Tallien, accused of immoral and unpatriotic conduct at Bordeaux; and Vadier, the promoter of the Théot case—these knew themselves marked down for proscription. Collot d'Herbois, involved in the Lyon affair; Delacroix, condemned by implication on June 11; Dubois-Crancé, expelled from the Club for his conduct at Marseille; Carrier, denounced by Jullien for his crimes at Nantes, and Ysabeau, for his misconduct at Bordeaux; Delaunay, accused of intrigues against Robespierre; Garnier-Launay, the organizer of 'patriotic banquets'; Laharpe, whose books Robespierre was searching for evidences of *incivisme*; Hoche, deprived of his command; or Fernex, charged with over-severity at Orange—all of them, on the evidence of Robespierre's recent speeches or correspondence, might be counted amongst those who regarded him as a personal enemy, and saw no security but in his fall.

Among the papers included in Courtois' *Rapport* are some *Notes* written in Robespierre's own hand, which were reprinted 'to show to what a point he pushed his hatred and abuse of the deputies'. They contain denunciations of Dubois-Crancé, Delmas, Thuriot, Bourdon de l'Oise, and Léonard Bourdon.[2] The number of Robespierre's enemies may be further extended from a rather fanciful list

---

[1] Between July 11 and 26, under the Prairial Law, the Tribunal had passed 1,285 death sentences. On the usual calculation of four to a family, the number of persons deprived of husband, parent, or child, during three weeks alone, would be 3,855. At the end of July 7,800 persons were in the Paris prisons, involving 23,400 more.

[2] Courtois, *Rapport*, No. LI.

of forty-seven names given by his disciple Buonarroti: it includes, besides most of those already mentioned, Sieyès, Garnier de l'Aube, Reubell, Thirion, Merlin de Thionville, Panis, Barras, Cambon, Fréron, Bentabolle, Rovère, Lindet, Merlin de Douai, Brival, Poultier, Echasseriaux, Charlier, Dubarran, Goupilleau, Feraud, Legendre, Lacoste, Lecointre de Versailles, André Dumont, Courtois, Clausel, Ruamps, Amar, Jagot, Carnot, Barère, Voulland, Charles Duval, Bayle, Granet and Montaut.[1] Some of these had personal grievances, and some political; but it was the misfortune of Robespierre's outlook and temper that he could never discriminate between the two, so that his personal foes were driven into political opposition, and his political opponents into personal hatred; and the number of his enemies was doubled.

IV

It would be possible to consider the causes of Robespierre's fall separately, in some kind of logical order; or to classify the grievances of his enemies. But biography demands, before all else, a chronological treatment, in which the underlying causes, whether men or things, are gradually realized through their effects, as they were registered at the time in the minds of those who experienced them. It therefore seems best to take the events of the last month of Robespierre's life just as they come.

As early as April, 1794, there had been signs that certain members of the Committee of Public Safety resented Robespierre's ascendancy. 'Woe to a Republic', wrote Carnot in a report of April 1, 'in which the merit of a single man, or even his virtue, has become indispensable'.[2] Billaud-Varenne, on April 20, had spoken of Pericles in terms which were taken to refer to Robespierre: the comparison might have been flattering, had he not laid less stress upon the statesmanship of the great Athenian than

---

[1] Mathiez, *Corruption*, 275; add eighteen members of the Convention accused of financial dishonesty (*Ibid.* 277).
[2] Mathiez, 489.

upon his popularity, through which he enslaved public opinion, and set himself up as a 'sanguinary despot'.[1] To the same period belongs the first recorded quarrel between Carnot and Saint-Just, which arose out of the arrest of an agent of the Gunpowder Committee, and ended in Carnot describing both Robespierre and Saint-Just as 'contemptible dictators'.[2] The creation of the Visitatorial Board, as a monopoly of Robespierre, Saint-Just and Couthon (April 23), did nothing to mend the breach between the 'Triumvirate' and the rest of the Committee of Public Safety, whilst it created a fresh grievance for the Committee of General Security. A month later (May 22-3) had come the attempts on Robespierre's life; and no one knew better than he did that the congratulations he received on his escape were not all genuine. Rousselin's proposal of a body-guard for members of the Committee (May 25) could only make them unpopular; and where Admiral and Renault had failed, it was not at all certain that Lecointre's gang of deputies might not succeed.[3] Le Cointre, again, with Bour-don, Thériot, Montaut, and Ruamps, was heard to utter threats against the President of the Convention at the fête of the Supreme Being;[4] and public feeling at that moment was perhaps less truly expressed by the well-drilled enthu-siasm of June 8 than by the removal of the guillotine, the following day, from the west end of the Tuileries gardens to the remote Place Antoine. The Prairial Law, brought forward by Couthon on June 10, not only provoked something like a mutiny in the docile Convention, but also led to a quarrel at the Committee, where Billaud-Varenne accused Robespierre of going behind the backs of his colleagues, and Robespierre reproached the Committee for failing to give him its support. So loud (says Barère) grew the altercation, that the windows of the Committee-room had to be shut, to prevent a public scandal.[5]

[1]Mathiez, *Autour de Robespierre*, 177. Billaud's allusion was intentionally ambiguous. Saint-Just, on 9 Thermidor, accused him of comparing Robespierre with the tyrant Pisistratus.
[2]Mathiez, 497.   [3]Mathiez, 492.   [4]Baudot, in Ward, 304.
[5]R.F. 34/169.

On June 11 a deputation from the Jacobin Society of Nevers tried to dissociate itself from the anti-clerical campaign which had made the place notorious. The incident had probably been staged by Robespierre, in revenge for his own humiliation of May 12; for Fouché, who had been Chaumette's associate at Nevers, was now in the chair, and was asked for an explanation. With characteristic effrontery, he denied any knowledge of Chaumette's alleged crimes. Robespierre insisted that he had insulted the Convention's declaration on religion, and had openly preached atheism. 'The deep indignation with which Robespierre pronounced these last words', says the official report, 'was shared by his whole audience, and showed itself by threatening murmurs'.[1] Chaumette had already suffered for his indiscretions. How long could Fouché hope to go unpunished?

On June 13 Robespierre had evidence that the Admiral and Renault affairs did not stand alone; for he heard from Cellier that Lecointre had circulated an attack upon him, and was organizing a band of deputies to assassinate him in the House;[2] whilst information sent by Legendre to the Committee led to the arrest of Marcandier, an ex-employé of Roland and Desmoulins, and editor of an anti-Montagnard paper, on a charge of incitement to murder the 'modern Sulla'.[3] Hardly less significant was the fact that, in view of public protests, it was found necessary once more to move the guillotine—this time (June 14) to the Barrière du Trône, as far as possible from the centre of the capital.

Vadier's report on the Théot case, the following day—an unmistakable attack on Robespierre's religious policy—was answered by initiating the mass-executions (30 *Parlementaires*, June 14; 37 prisoners of the Bicêtre, June 16; 54 *chemises rouges*, June 17), by which the government hoped to overawe its enemies. But on the 21st the Montagne Section invited the signatures of those who had voted for

---

[1] Jac. 6/172. [2] Mathiez, 492; A.H. 8/300.
[3] A.R. 14/223; Mathiez, *Autour de Robespierre*, 182; Pap. inéd. 1/179, 183.

the Constitution of 1793—a plain hint that revolutionary Paris was tiring of the Provisional Government, and of its court-martial methods.

Meanwhile, there had been fresh quarrels in the Committee, whose members refused to ratify Robespierre's decree for the arrest of representatives of the *Section de l'Indivisibilité*,[1] and were with difficulty persuaded to quash the Théot prosecution. Once more 'the scene degenerated into an altercation, the noise of which could be heard outside the building', so that 'the Committee decided that in future it would hold its sittings on the upper floor, to be beyond the reach of indiscreet listeners'.

Robespierre's nervous reaction to these disturbing events was shown (June 24) by an outburst against the press. He complained of a recent note in the *Moniteur*, which had said, of one of his discourses, that each word was as good as a sentence, and each sentence as good as a whole speech. Whether flattery or irony, it was dangerous to be so advertised. Three days later (June 27) he returned to this theme, in a speech directed against the new conspirators. 'In London', he said, 'they denounce me to the French army as a dictator; and the same slanders are repeated in Paris. . . . In London I am caricatured, and represented as assassinating honest men; whilst libels printed in the French press by my own people depict me in the same terms. In Paris it is said that it was I who organized the Revolutionary Tribunal, for the purpose of murdering patriots and deputies: I am represented as a tyrant, and as an oppressor of the National Assembly'—at which someone in the gallery shouted, 'Robespierre, every Frenchman is on your side'. 'Truth (he goes on) is my only safeguard against crime. I desire no flattery, no partisans. My conscience protects me. I ask those citizens who hear me to remember that calumny does not spare even the purest and most innocent conduct. Betray the country cleverly enough, and in a moment the enemies of the nation back you up. Defend the cause of justice, and directly you open your mouth you are called a

[1] v. 2/228.

tyrant and a despot. You can't even appeal to public opinion without being denounced as a dictator'.

The victory of Fleurus (June 28) weakened the only respectable argument for terrorism on the Home Front, and contributed—though not so decisively as is sometimes supposed—to the public demand for a constitutional regime. Its main sequel on the Committee seems to have been a fresh quarrel between Carnot and Saint-Just over an order to Pichegru, which, had it been carried out, would have weakened Jourdan's army, and robbed him of victory. Once more (says Levasseur, who was there) the dispute became general. Billaud and Collot (who had quarrelled with Robespierre over a naval appointment) characterized him as a dictator, and he 'was seized with a fit of incredible fury', whilst 'the other members looked on him with scorn'. There was perhaps another quarrel, about the Prairial Law, on the 29th; but the details are untrustworthy, if not apocryphal. This much seems clear, that an increasing number of Robespierrists, not only amongst the leaders, but also in the party at large, believed Maximilien to be exercising an abnormal and unhealthy influence upon public policy, and feared another proscription, on the lines of that which had swept away the Girondins and the Dantonists.[1]

V

The disclosure of yet another plot—that of Rouvière, on June 30,[2] the publication of Marcandier's charges at the time of his condemnation (July 2), and a speech by Collot at the Club on July 7, in which he called for another William Tell to liberate France from its Gesslers,[3] roused Robespierre to deliver a formal attack upon the new factions (*les cabales*). This speech (July 9), though clear enough in its intention, took the form of an esoteric instruction to faithful Robespierrists on the meaning of republican virtue, and the signs by which to distinguish

[1]Mathiez, 498; Kerr, *The Terror*, 445; Buonarroti's evidence in Mathiez, *Corruption*, 283.
[2]Mathiez, 498. [3]Mathiez, *G. et M.*, 155.

between true and false patriotism. 'Of all the decrees which have saved the Republic', it declares, 'the only one which has preserved it from corruption, and freed the people from tyranny, is that which makes honesty and virtue the order of the day'. Virtue does not mean the domestic morality of a Roland or a Necker—and Necker was a tyrant in his own home—but patriotism. And what is patriotism? 'There is only one remedy', Robespierre declares, 'for all our ills: it consists in obedience to the laws of nature, which intend every man to be just, and to live a virtuous life, the foundation of all society'. There is here a series of equations. Virtue equals patriotism: patriotism equals obeying the laws of nature: obeying the laws of nature equals virtue. True, *probité* and *justice* are slipped in, to give *vertu* a moral tinge: but it is difficult to avoid the feeling that Robespierre's ideas are going round in a circle, and that patriotism pure and simple—that is, supporting the government—is the whole of his creed.

How then is one to distinguish the true from the false patriot? 'There is', he says, 'a sentiment written in the hearts of all patriots, and it is a touchstone by which they can recognize their friends. A man who is silent when he ought to speak is to be suspected: if he wraps himself in mystery, if he shows a momentary energy which soon passes away, if he limits himself to empty tirades against tyrants, and pays no heed to public morals, or to the general happiness of his fellow-citizens, he is to be suspected. When men are seen denouncing aristocrats merely as a matter of form, their own lives call for severe scrutiny. When they are heard uttering commonplaces against Pitt and the enemies of mankind, whilst at the same time they deliver covert attacks on the revolutionary government; or when, alternately moderate and extreme in their views, they are for ever denouncing and obstructing useful measures; then it is time to be on one's guard against conspiracy'.

Is there anything here that escapes from the narrow circle of the first part of the speech? Does it not all amount to saying that a good patriot is one who always supports the government, and a bad patriot one who sometimes pretends to? And is not 'the sentiment written in the hearts of all patriots' merely the flair which enabled jurymen of the Revolutionary Tribunal to convict a traitor without formal evidence, and inspired Robespierre to detect, in so many seemingly patriotic eyes, the mote of counter-revolution?

On July 11 there was a debate on Ville-Affranchie— that depopulated heap of ruins which had once been the proud and prosperous city of Lyon. Fouché, who, just a month before, had been attacked for his anti-Catholic propaganda at Nevers, was now denounced as a terrorist, and invited to exculpate himself, if he could. He was not present, but wrote, asking the Club to suspend judgment. Robespierre refused to allow this. In a second speech (July 14) he declared that he had once regarded Fouché as a patriot, but now considered him to be 'the head of the conspiracy which we have to defeat', and had his name struck off the Club. By doing so, he signed his own death-warrant. Fouché was already at work, organizing the elements of discontent: he knew now that, if he did not strike soon, he was doomed. But he felt confident of victory, and wrote to his sister at Nantes, predicting the success of his intrigues against 'the traitors'.[1]

His confidence was doubtless based on what he knew of the growing dissensions within the government. Demaillot, claiming inside knowledge of the Committee, says that several of its members, who on July 9–10 were on the point of leaving Paris—Couthon for a medical cure, Saint-Just (with Augustin Robespierre) for the front, and others on missions of various kinds—suddenly cancelled their plans and remained in the capital; whilst Saint-André, who could not stay behind, wrote from Montauban a few days later that 'a great storm was brewing'. He adds that he spoke freely to Saint-Just of Robespierre's 'weakness and indolence', and of his predilection for 'the traitor Dumas', and for Lejeune, of the Visitatorial Board; at which Saint-Just, 'with his well-known sardonic smile', remarked: 'Ronsin,

[1]Kerr, The Terror, 464.

Vincent, and others have fallen through ambition, and it will be the same with those who try to imitate them'.[1] If the first part of this story is not impossible—for matters were clearly approaching a crisis—the theory underlying the second, that Saint-Just was working against Robespierre, is unconfirmed by any trustworthy evidence, and contradicted by his conduct at Thermidor.[2]

The 'patriotic banquets' denounced by Payan on July 15, and suppressed by the Committee the next day, were a typically Parisian form of demonstration against the government, which regarded any fraternization between the front-line troops of the 'patriot' and 'aristocrat' armies as subversive of republican discipline, and as compromising the settlement it wished to achieve at its own time and in its own way. The Pille debate, the same day, showed the Jacobin Club, instigated by the head of a War department, attacking one of Carnot's nominees, and Robespierre, Carnot's colleague in the government, denouncing military despotism in terms which cannot have been welcome to the 'organizer of victory'.[3] Carnot had recently refused to carry out Robespierre's decree for refusing quarter to English or Hanoverian troops,[4] and was suspected of designs against Hanriot, the Robespierrist commandant of the National Guard. In any case, the charge of dictatorship was one which Robespierre was anxious, at all costs, to shift off his own shoulders.

VI

By the third week in July, the situation inside as well as outside the Committee was evidently coming to a head. Barère on July 20, Couthon and Augustin on the 21st, and Barère again on the 23rd, made speeches indicating fresh fears of counter-revolution, and hinting that one more faction remained to be overthrown.

The 22nd and 23rd were specially critical days. The

[1]v. Lévy-Schneider in R.F. 38/97.
[2]It is the thesis of the 'Dropmore spy', who gives much unconvincing evidence for it (Mathiez, *Conspiration*, 150).
[3]cp. Mathiez, *G. et M.*, 161. [4]v. 2/188.

subtle Barère, a born conciliator, who was grateful to Maximilien for his protection against the more violent members of the government, convinced his colleagues that they must attempt to patch up their quarrels, and to induce Robespierre to return to his place on the Committee. He might be an uncongenial ally, but he would certainly be a dangerous foe. A bargain was therefore proposed to his friends Couthon and Saint-Just. The politico-economic programme to which the 'Triumvirate' attached so much importance, and which had been inaugurated by the Laws of Ventôse, had since been held up, partly by the failure of the Committee to provide the necessary machinery, and partly by the stupidity or ill-will of the local authorities. It was now to be given a fresh impetus, by the creation of four Popular Commissions, and four Tribunals 'on circuit', which should extend to the whole country the system that the two Popular Commissions established in Paris were just beginning to apply. In return for this concession, the Triumvirate were to support the Committee in the coming struggle against the 'new conspirators'. Accordingly, on July 22 (4 Thermidor) the Committee passed the decrees creating the new Commissions: Lindet protested, but did not refuse to sign: Billaud also consented, but took the opportunity to say what some of them thought about Robespierre. The following day, Robespierre attended, by invitation, a joint meeting of the two Committees; but he came in Balaam's mood, refusing to be propitiated. Rejecting Barère's olive-branch, and the attempts of David and Saint-Just to make his return easy, he declared that the sound members of the Committees were in a minority, and attacked by name Vadier (for his Théot report), Amar (for his handling of the India Company affair), Jagot, Collot, and Billaud; and as his anger rose, he paced to and fro, glaring disdainfully through his spectacles.[1] The Committees nevertheless persisted in their conciliatory policy. The decrees of the previous day were amended, so as to give greater freedom and speed to the plan of Ventôse. Saint-

[1] Rühl, in a speech on 3 Germ. III (R.F. 13/372).

Just was commissioned to draw up a Report, in the name of the Committees, to be presented to the Convention, and agreed, out of deference to Billaud and Collot, to make no allusion in it to the cult of the Supreme Being. A decree was also signed, ordering some guns of the National Guard, which might have been used against the government, to leave Paris for the front.

There is evidence, in these measures, of a successful attempt to secure an agreed programme; and when the Committees broke up that evening, their unity, so far as the general public could judge, had been reasserted, and their prospect of weathering the coming storm immensely increased. But what of Robespierre? The turn given to the Ventôse decrees, and the entrusting of the crucial Report to his lieutenant Saint-Just, suggest that he had allowed himself to be talked round. If so, it must be supposed that he also agreed to the omission of his religious policy from the Report, and to the disarming of the National Guard, though the former was a slight upon himself, and the latter went counter to a recent resolution of the Jacobin Club. Barère, the same evening, in the Convention, and Couthon, the next day, at the Club, denied that there had ever been any serious division of opinion within the government. 'If there have been personal differences', said Couthon, 'there have been none on matters of principle. I make bold to say that the great majority of the Convention is of an exemplary purity; and I say the same of the two committees; they contain virtuous and energetic men, prepared to make the greatest possible sacrifices for the country'. The Committee of General Security, he admits, is not blameless. Its members mean well; but they are surrounded by criminals, and have committed arbitrary acts; and there are still five or six of Pitt's agents in the Convention, to whom dissensions within the Republic are more acceptable than victories at the front. So long as such dangers continue, he declares, the government will stand by the policy of Ventôse, and will at the same time endeavour to exterminate the last relics of counter-revolution. Such was the policy of the

Committees, as expounded by a close friend and accredited spokesman of Robespierre. Furthermore, as a result of these speeches, the Jacobins, on the 25th, presented an address to the Convention, in which Robespierre's favourite scape-goat, the 'foreign plot', was made responsible both for inciting the assassination of patriots, and for attributing a terrorist character to the Convention; whilst a fresh demand was made for the punishment of the new conspirators.

All this evidence goes to show that members of the Committees, including Robespierre's own supporters, believed him to have accepted the 'common front' outlined in the measures of the 23rd, and in Couthon's speech of the 24th. It is easy, therefore, to understand the consternation with which his change of front, and that of Saint-Just, was received, on the 27th. Barère, in his defence after Thermidor, claimed that the 'reconciliation' of July 22–3 was a trick to catch Robespierre. It may have been so to Billaud, whose profession of good will rang hollow; to Cambon, Ruamps, and Moise Bayle, who afterwards asserted that they had been plotting against Maximilien ever since Danton's execution; or to Carnot, whose new paper, La Soirée du Camp, was already preparing army opinion for the fall of Robespierre;[1] but Barère was as sincere as a professional 'trimmer' can be; and Robespierre was the last man to be taken in by a mere pretence. Probably, then, his original refusal represented his real mind, and he let himself be overruled, in the course of the discussion, and against his better judgement, by Couthon and Saint-Just, knowing that some members of the Committee were honest in their overtures to him, and some not. The genuine conciliators proceeded, naturally enough, to exploit their success, only to be deserted by those of their colleagues who were already working against the 'Triumvirate', and to be disowned, on second thoughts, by Robespierre himself. Perhaps if Robespierre could have honestly accepted overtures which were only half honest, all might have ended

[1] It began on July 20, and 10,000 copies were circulated daily at the expense of the Committee (Aulard, Études 1/10).

differently. His final refusal, the result of a fatal perspicuity, broke up the government, saved Fouché and Tallien, whose lives were otherwise forfeit, and inevitably destroyed himself.[1]

It would seem that at this moment there were in existence —in thought, if not in writing—three proscription lists. The first, drawn up by the reunited Committee, included Fouché and Tallien, but not Collot or Billaud. The second list, drawn up by those proscribed in the first, with the connivance of Collot, Billaud, and most of the members of the Committee of General Security, named Robespierre, Couthon, and Saint-Just. The third, drawn up in Robespierre's mind, and hinted at in the Jacobin address, was similar to the first, but included also Collot, Billaud, and perhaps Carnot.[2] To the authors of these lists, Barère's 'reconciliation' could be an amnesty, but not a treaty of peace; and the disinclination of all three parties to give the names of their intended victims is explained by the fact that, whilst speaking unanimously of conspiracy, they had in mind different conspirators.

VII

On the evening of July 25, say the legend-makers, Robespierre went for a walk, with Eléonore on his arm, and his dog by his side, and talked of God, and the immortality of the soul. The sun was setting in a red sky. 'That means (he said) a fine day to-morrow'.[3] A friend who saw him that night found him fully aware of his danger, but ready to risk his life in a supreme stroke against the traitors.[4] It was in this mood that he came to the Convention the next day, and delivered the last and most elaborate of his speeches.[5]

His hope is that, by declaring the truth, he will vindicate

[1]Mathiez, G. et M., 151, 167.
[2]Barère (Mémoires, 2/172) puts eighteen names on this list, including Tallien, Fréron, Barras, Alquier, Dubois-Crancé, Monastier, Prieur, and Cavaignac.
[3]Esquiros, 2/460.
[4]Taschereau (Kerr, The Terror, 467).
[5]It survives only in a summary report published by the Moniteur on July 29; Collot's Analyse (Moniteur, Index, 302) is even less trustworthy.

his own innocence, and that of the Revolution. As for himself, what could be more ridiculous than a charge of tyranny against one whose whole life has been given to the defence of the Assembly, and who has been the butt of every conspiracy against representative government? If he ever showed himself severe, it was against the convicted enemies of the country, whom no one would dare defend. Why is he being attacked now? Because it is alleged that the Committee is preparing a fresh proscription. Such an idea could only spring from hostile intrigue, or disordered imagination. Against all such plots, he stands for the country, and for the Convention. 'I know', he declares, 'only two parties—that of the good citizens, and that of the bad. Patriotism is not a party affair, but a thing of the heart. . . . My feeling is that, wherever one meets a man of good will, one should offer him one's hand, and press him to one's heart'. As to the charge of dictatorship, the very word is an outrage to republican ears. It is inconceivable that any Frenchman worthy of the name should covet the empty honours of a throne. Such an idea could only occur to a vile soul, destitute of virtue. For there is such a thing, he attests, in an eloquent passage, as this *vertu*, which he is never tired of eulogizing. 'There do exist pure and sensitive souls. There does exist a tender, but imperious and irresistible passion, which is at once the torment and the delight of magnanimous minds—a profound horror of tyranny, a compassionate zeal for the oppressed, a sacred love of one's country, and a love of humanity still more holy and sublime, without which a great revolution is no more than the destruction of a lesser by a greater crime. There does exist a generous ambition to found on earth the first republic in the world—an enlightened egoism, which finds pleasure in the quiet of a pure conscience, and in the ravishing spectacle of public happiness. You can feel it, at this moment, burning in your hearts; I can feel it in my own'.

Robespierre a tyrant? Rather, the enemy of all tyrants, and of every faction that might compass a despotism. 'Who am I', he asks, 'that they should accuse me so? A slave of liberty, a living martyr to the Republic, at once the enemy and the victim of crime. Every rascal insults me. The highest actions, that in others would pass for lawful, are imputed to me as an offence . . . Take away my conscience, and I am the most wretched of mortals: I cannot enjoy the rights of citizenship; I cannot even fulfil my duties as a deputy'.

'But what of all these charges?' asks Robespierre, with some reason.[1] 'For the last six weeks, at least, my so-called dictatorship has ceased to exist, and I have exercised no sort of influence upon the government. Has patriotism, during this time, found better champions? Have the factions shown more alarm? Has the country been any happier? I hope it has'. But it is evident that he does not think so. His reflections, during retirement, have been of the gloomiest tinge. 'My mind (he says), though not my heart, is beginning to despair of that Republic of Virtue whose plan I had traced out'. He is aware, too, that his life is at stake; but 'what patriot would care to go on living, when he has no more opportunity of serving and defending oppressed innocence? What motive for survival is there under a regime in which intrigue is for ever victorious over truth, in which justice is a lie, and in which the sacred interests of mankind are ousted from men's hearts by the vilest passions, and the most fantastic fears?'

At last Robespierre turns from the past, and from his personal feelings, to speak about the future, and the policy of the government. It is his last will and testament, drawn up with the frankness of a man who knows that his life is in danger. They have been told (he says) that all is well with the Republic; he denies it.[2] They have been told that the days of conspiracy are past; he fears it at this moment. They have been given pompous stories of easy victories;[3] it is not so that France will subjugate Europe,

[1] 'Let me confess how much it has astonished me, in wading through the voluminous memoirs and pamphlets of this period, to observe such universal virulence against Robespierre, coupled with such a total absence of any definite charges supported by facts' (Lewes, 331).
[2] A reference to Couthon's speech of July 24?
[3] A reference to Barère's famous Reports.

but only by the wisdom of its rulers, and by the grandeur of its national character. The foreign war may be going well, but the situation on the Home Front is more critical than ever before—finance in disorder, foreign interests neglected or betrayed, and the personnel of government deeply corrupt. This being so, the Revolutionary Tribunal must not be touched; the wide powers given to it by the Prairial Law are necessary to deal with the Protean growth of conspiracy.

What, then, are Robespierre's remedies for so many ills? 'Remember', he says to the people, 'that, unless justice alone rules in our Republic—love of equality, and love of the fatherland—liberty is a mere name. People! You are feared, you are flattered, and yet you are despised. They call you Sovereign, and they treat you as a slave. Remember that, where justice ends, there begins the arbitrary rule of officials (*les passions des magistrats*), and that the People has changed its masters without changing its final lot. Remember that there exists in your midst a gang of rascals working against public virtue, with more influence over your affairs than you have yourselves; and that, whilst they fear and flatter you as a whole, they proscribe you individually in the persons of your best citizens'. In short—and in his last paragraphs Robespierre speaks plainly enough—there is a conspiracy against public freedom; it is inspired by a body of men within the Convention, who have accomplices on the Committee of General Security; they have set this committee against the Committee of Public Safety; and some members of the latter committee too are in the plot. And the remedy? 'To punish the traitors; to change the subordinate personnel (*bureaux*) of the Committee of General Security, to purge it (*épurer*), and to subordinate it to the Committee of Public Safety; to purge that committee too; and to unify the whole government under the control of the Convention'. Perhaps (Robespierre continues) these reforms are impossible, and to propose them may only lead to his own destruction. 'But I was not made', he sadly ends, 'to govern; only to combat crime; and the time has

561

not yet arrived when men of good will can serve their country without suffering for it'.

There is little that is fresh or constructive in this eloquent but rambling discourse—a cento of ideas from a hundred previous speeches. It does not suggest that Robespierre has learnt much, in five years of Revolution, except to hate and to suspect. It offers no hope that, if his life is prolonged, he has any policy to lift the country out of the rut of 'virtue by intimidation'. It has been held that he wished to end the Terror, and to inaugurate a voluntary Reign of Virtue. Perhaps; but there is no sign of it here. The Committee is to go on—without the embarrassment of a rival body. The Tribunal is to remain—without any lessening of its powers. The Provisional Government is to continue. There is no mention of a Constitution. Robespierre is not a dictator, but the government of which he is the figure-head is nothing if not dictatorial. The charge of fresh proscriptions, ridiculed at the beginning of the speech, is fully justified by the end of it; and though no names are mentioned, enough hints are given to make it easy for Robespierre's audience to reconstruct the list that is preparing, in the offices of the Visitatorial Board, for Fouquier-Tinville's next *journée*. The speech is eloquent; but it is the eloquence of a tired and disillusioned man, the mainspring of whose life is running down. There is a programme; yet it is that of a government which has no policy save to increase the doses of a medicine which has already failed.

But the faults of the speech are more than negative. It not only shows a lack of any such strategical plan as the situation required; it also commits almost every tactical blunder possible under the circumstances. Robespierre might have enlisted the majority of the Convention, and the mass of the common people, with whom he was still the most popular politician, for a crusade to end the Terror, and to inaugurate the Constitution: instead, he identifies himself with the Provisional Government, and the Law of Prairial. Having chosen so, he might have made a bid for

the support of both committees to carry through an unpopular, if salutary policy: instead, he attacks the Committee of General Security, and demands its subordination
to that of Public Safety. Having decided for the dictatorship
of that one committee, he should at least have tried to hold
it together: instead, he flouts Barère's 'reconciliation', and
publicly criticizes, under a very thin disguise, Barère's
conduct of foreign diplomacy, Carnot's military dispositions in the capital, and the intrigues of Collot and Billaud.
Finally, having thus isolated himself from all but a few
friends on the Committees, the faithful Jacobins, and (he
still seems to have thought) the Moderates of the Convention, he goes out of his way to criticize the financial policy of
Cambon, Ramel, and Mallarmé, and to take up an intransigent attitude which might well alienate even Couthon
and Saint-Just.

The debate which followed did nothing to remove the
suspicions suggested by Robespierre's speech. When, in
answer to Billaud's protests, he said that he was not attacking the whole Committee, it was obvious that he *was* attacking some members of it. When Panis asked for an explanation of the rumour that he was to be proscribed, he took
refuge in defiant rhetoric. 'I have thrown aside my shield',
he said; 'I have exposed myself to my enemies. I have flattered no one; I have slandered no one; I fear no one'—'*And
Fouché?*'—'Why all this talk about Fouché? I don't want
to deal with him at this moment; all that is beside the point.
I am only concerned with my duty; I want no man's help or
friendship; I am not trying to win supporters; it is idle to
expect me to white-wash this or that individual. I have
done my duty: it is for others to do theirs'. When Charlier
proposed that the speech should be referred to the Committee—the furthest point in the direction of censure that
the House was prepared to go—he protested against its
being sent to 'the very persons whom I accuse'. When asked
to give their names, he would only reply, 'I stand by what I
have said', and refused to take any further part in the
debate.

VIII

The meeting of the Jacobin Club, that evening, opened stormily. Billaud and Collot disputed Robespierre's right to have the first word. They were over-ruled; but Robespierre's opening sentences were interrupted by Javogues, who shouted, 'We want no dictators here!' He proceeded to repeat all he had said in the Convention, adding at the end, if tradition is to be trusted, a peroration in which he foreshadowed his end.[1] 'Friends and Brothers', he is reported to have said, 'the speech that you have just heard is my last will and testament. My enemies, or rather, those of the Republic, are so many and so potent that I cannot hope long to escape their blows. Never have I felt so much emotion in addressing you, for I fancy I am saying farewell. Whatever may happen, my memory will always be revered in your virtuous hearts. That is enough for me. But it is not enough (he went on) for the Republic'. The Republic demands vengeance on the traitors. Now is the moment to prove your courage. 'Are you not the same Jacobins who were victorious against the threats and arms of Leopold, Brunswick, Pitt, and Coburg? The Convention has sought to humiliate you to-day by its insolent decree. Heroes of May 31, have you forgotten the way to the Convention? No, indeed! Far from having to excite your ardour, I feel that it is my duty to restrain you'—so far, at least, as to distinguish the real traitors from the rest. 'If you support me (he ends), the new traitors will share the fate of the old. If you forsake me, you will see how calmly I shall drink the hemlock'. David afterwards admitted that he was so stirred by Robespierre's eloquence that he exclaimed, 'I will drink it with you'.

These words, or others like them, were received with enthusiasm by most of Robespierre's audience, and the protests of Collot and Billaud were answered by their expulsion from the Club. There was now no course left, if

[1] It was long thought that no record had survived of the proceedings at the Jacobins on 8 and 9 Thermidor; but two journalistic accounts have been reprinted in A.H. 1/497.

the second part of Robespierre's speech was meant seriously, but to organize a rising on the lines of May 31, to overthrow the Committees, and to set up in their place either a triumvirate of Robespierre, Saint-Just, and Couthon, or a personal dictatorship. Some such plan appears to have been urged by Payan, Hanriot, Dumas, Coffinhall, and others of Maximilien's closer supporters at the Jacobins. But it seems that the militant mood soon passed, and that Robespierre ended by declaring against any immediate appeal to force. A man of words, not acts, he shrank from violence, and thought that he could still talk the Assembly round. A politician and a parliamentarian, he hoped to secure the reconstitution of the committees by a vote of the House. 'I expect no more from the Mountain', he is reported to have said, after the morning's debate; 'they think me a tyrant, and want to get rid of me: but the mass of the Assembly will listen to me'. He honestly disliked the idea of a dictatorship, and knew himself to be unfit for supreme power. On the other hand, he had so often played with the idea of martyrdom that perhaps the recklessness of his challenge may be put down to a morbid impulse towards self-immolation. If this was his desire, it was likely enough to be satisfied.

IX

There was much coming and going during the night of July 26. Fouché, Tallien, and the rest, who knew that Robespierre's triumph, with or without the Committee, meant their own destruction, were making the final preparations for to-morrow's meeting of the Convention. Prominent Moderates, such as Palasne-Champeaux, Boissy d'Anglas, and Durand-Maillane, who had hitherto looked to Robespierre for protection against the excesses of Fouché, Tallien, and their friends, must be won over by pointing to the growing number of executions, and their own danger, under the Prairial Law;[1] opposition speeches and interruptions must be organized; and plans must be made, with

[1] Durand-Maillane, *Histoire de la Convention nationale* (ed. Baudouin), 199.

the help of Collot, President of the Assembly, to prevent
Robespierre from obtaining a hearing. Meanwhile, in the
committee-room, Saint-Just was drafting the Report which
had been entrusted to him on the 23rd, and which he was to
read to the Convention the next day. Carnot, Barère, Lindet,
Lacoste, and Prieur de la Côte d'Or were there too, probably
discussing what the Committee should do, in view of Robespierre's *volte-face*, and meditating that repudiation of his
policy which was now the only way to save the government.
Soon Collot and Billaud appeared, fresh from their expulsion from the Jacobins, and indignantly accusing Saint-Just,
and 'his chief, Robespierre', as the cause of it. There
followed an altercation of a kind that was becoming
common on the Committee, and hard words were said of
the 'Triumvirate'. But Saint-Just, 'cold as marble',[1] seemed
to take no offence, and, whilst admitting that his Report
would incriminate a number of deputies, declared that he
had no intention of proposing proceedings against anyone;
he further promised to submit the draft to the Committee
before he read it in the Convention. With this arrangement
Collot and Billaud were apparently content; and they went
off to inform Fouché. Saint-Just remained at work in the
committee-room till five a.m., and then followed them out.
He had not answered the insults of his colleages ; but he
felt as though they had seared (*flêtri*) his soul.[2]

Did he, at the last moment, make up his mind to throw
in his lot with Maximilien? Had this final quarrel in the
Committee convinced him that Barère's 'reconciliation' was,
after all, a sham, that Collot and Billaud were irreconcilable,
and that Robespierre was right in believing that an appeal
to the Moderates and the masses against an unpopular and
divided Committee might yet be successful? If this change of
mind came earlier in the day, it is strange that the Committee should have been content to leave the Report in his
hands: they, at any rate, with the possible exception of
Collot and Billaud, seem to have believed that he was on
their side, until next day's events disillusioned them.

[1] B. and R. 34/39. [2] v. both his speech and his letters (Curtis, *St Just*, 281, 284).

No: it seems clear from Saint-Just's own speech that, during the evening of the 26th he was still undecided; that shaken by the attack of Collot and Billaud, he had a final interview with Robespierre during the early hours of the 27th; and that then his friend's persuasion completed his change of mind, and led to the final revision that gave such a different character to his Report.

X

On the 27th, some time before the meeting of the Assembly, the Committee sat waiting for Saint-Just, to hear his Report; but he never came. It was proposed to prevent a possible appeal to force by summoning to the Committee Hanriot, the commandant of the National Guard. While this point was being debated, a note came to Couthon from Saint-Just, saying, 'You have seared (*flétri*) my heart: I intend to open it to the Convention'. Then his indifference the night before, when accused by Collot and Billaud, had been assumed, and he had since been won over by Robespierre? In either case it meant war; and the Opposition had stolen a march on the Government. Couthon tore up the letter. 'Let us go', cried Rühl, 'and unmask the traitors, or else present our heads to the Assembly', and they all hurried into the House.[1]

Robespierre and Saint-Just—a sign of their last-minute agreement—had entered the Hall together, and it was noticed that they stood at the foot of the tribune, as though they had broken with the Mountain, and meant to rely on their right to speak to the whole House. Robespierre was still confident. 'Don't be alarmed', he had said to Duplay, as he left home for the last time; 'the mass of the Convention is pure; I have nothing to fear'. Saint-Just was probably less sure. He had with him the Report which he was to make on behalf of the Committees, reaffirming their unity, and announcing that the policy of Ventôse and Prairial was to continue. But during the night the Report had

[1] R.F. 13/372. cp. Curtis, St Just, 324.

been hurriedly altered, and might not do its work. He intended to be quite frank about his change of mind. 'Your Committees', he would say to the Assembly, 'charged me to make you a Report, and their confidence made me proud; but someone this night (*i.e. Collot or Billaud?*) has seared (*flêtri*) my soul, and I am determined to speak to none but you. I owe it to you not to be bound by the obligation that certain people (*the members of the Committees*) fancied they could impose upon me, to speak contrary to my real opinions. . . . This expectation of theirs gave me a moment's leisure in which to prepare (*by revising the Report*) to make them realize in your presence the full depth of the pit into which they themselves have fallen.' He knew, indeed, that he stood in a delicate, perhaps a dangerous situation: but, if the factions after all triumphed, it was better to die with a good conscience than to live on as an accomplice of crime. . . . After this preface, the bulk of the Report could follow as originally drafted; but the outlines of conspiracy, hitherto left vague, could be filled in with definite attacks on Collot, Billaud, Carnot, and Barère—the four members of the Committee whom Robespierre accused of having monopolized and perverted the power of the government, and of being the ring-leaders of the present plot.[1]

Such was the revised Report; and as soon as the preliminary business was over, Saint-Just stepped into the tribune, and began: 'I belong to no faction: I have come here to oppose them all.' . . . But he had only read three lines, when he was interrupted by Tallien. 'I rise', he said, 'to a point of order. The speaker claims that he belongs to no faction. No more do I. I belong to myself, and to liberty. That is why I am going to speak a home truth. What right had Robespierre yesterday, or what right has Saint-Just to-day, to talk of unity, when they isolate themselves from the Government, and do nothing but aggravate the disunion of the country? I suggest (he ended) that the veil of pretence be torn down'.

[1] The MS. of the speech was laid on the table at the time of Saint-Just's arrest; it is printed in full in B. and R. 34/6, but has been unaccountably ignored by historians. For a longer analysis, v. Curtis, *St Just*, 283.

At this there was wild and repeated applause. Then Billaud broke in, also on a point of order. Still hot from his treatment at the Club the night before, he pointed out one of his persecutors on the benches of the Mountain, and had him expelled from the House; he also attacked Saint-Just for not submitting his Report to the Committee, as he had promised to do. He then proceeded to indict Robespierre for a number of crimes. It is a curious list. This 'dictator' (he said) had appointed Lavalette, a noble, to a military command; he had declared many deputies unfit to be sent on mission into the provinces; he had misrepresented the reason for his six weeks' absence from the Committee; he had defended an employé of the Committee accused of theft; and, when Billaud first denounced Danton, he 'got up in a fury, saying that I was trying to destroy the best patriots in the country'. One would think that such evidences of Robespierre's clemency and moderation would do him good rather than harm with the majority of the Convention, whose vote was to decide his fate. But the burden of the charge was dictatorship; and Billaud was so well aware that any accusation of terrorism would recoil upon the Committee as a whole, that he could only allege acts of petty tyranny, or interferences with the course of revolutionary justice, such as might cast upon Robespierre the slur of aristocracy or Dantonism. There was a retributory fitness in such charges which masked their absurdity; and Robespierre saw his danger. He rushed towards the tribune, only to be met with the pre-arranged cry of 'Down with the tyrant!', and to find another enemy, Tallien, there before him, declaring that he had come armed with a dagger, ready, if the Convention failed to do its duty, to plunge it into Robespierre's heart. On his proposal, and to make assassination easy, the House decreed the arrest of Hanriot, the Robespierrist general. A moment later Billaud moved the seizure of Dumas, Boulanger, and Dufraise; and Delmas that of Hanriot's adjutants and aides-de-camp.

Robespierre, thus threatened and disarmed, attempted

once more to get a hearing; but his voice was drowned by cries for Barère. Barère seems to have been quite taken aback by the turn given to the proceedings. He had not, as the story goes, two speeches in his pocket, one for Robespierre, and one against him,[1] but he had come prepared to second Saint-Just's Report, and to appeal to the Convention to support the policy of the Government. His speech, far from attacking the Triumvirate, contained a warning, which Robespierre himself might have uttered, and which had in any case been made unnecessary by the arrest of Hanriot and his staff, about the dangers of a military regime. This strangely inappropriate harangue— either because he had not the wit to change it, or because he was not yet sure which way the fight would go—he pronounced, as though nothing unexpected were occurring; and the House humoured him by passing a decree and proclamation dealing with the speculative dangers of a royalist revolt. In his Memoirs Barère says that, during this speech, Robespierre fell into such convulsions of anger that his brother feared he would attempt personal violence against the speaker. But, in fact, there was nothing in the speech to cause him a moment's emotion.[2]

As soon as this interlude was over, Vadier resumed the baiting of Robespierre, and charged him with defending the Dantonists, drafting the Prairial Law, imprisoning the *Section de l'Indivisibilité*, attacking the Committee of General Security, quashing the Théot case—here he introduced the famous letter, which he had either kept back or fabricated for the occasion[3]—and spying upon the deputies. As the spiteful old man became more and more anecdotal, Tallien interrupted him with a demand that the debate should be brought back to the point. 'I could do that well enough myself', remarked Robespierre, and made as though he would speak; but once more he was shouted down. Tallien reiterated the charge about the *Section de*

[1] Esquiros 2/461.
[2] Barère, *Mémoires*, 2/178. Michelet's view is that Barère was trying to save Robespierre by distracting his enemies (9/309).
[3] v. 2/212.

l'Indivisibilité. 'That's a lie!' cried Robespierre. His angry gaze rested a moment on his old supporters of the Mountain; some turned away their heads, but others remained unmoved, and the majority answered his look defiantly. He had expected no less, and turned from them to the main body of the House. 'It is to you', he was heard to say, 'that I address myself; for you are honest men, and not brigands'. Amid violent interruptions he appealed to the chair. 'For the last time, President of Assassins, I demand the right to speak'. This was a critical moment. In the uproar that followed, Thuriot replaced Collot in the chair, and said that Robespierre must wait his turn. There were cries of 'No, No!' from many who resented the 'rigging' of the debate, and he tried once more to make himself heard. It was his last chance. But his voice failed him. 'It's Danton's blood that's choking him', taunted Garnier. 'Is it Danton, then', said Robespierre, 'that you are avenging?' and it was a fair retort, considering that he had just been charged with trying to save Danton's life.[1]

In the renewed uproar Louchet at last proposed the arrest of Robespierre. At first—so uncertain was the issue—only a few voices supported him; but soon the cry was taken up all over the House: 'Vote! Vote!' Loseau seconded the motion. Augustin stood up. 'I am as much to blame as my brother', he said; 'I share his virtues: I would share his fate. I claim to be included in the charge against him'. This was perhaps designed as a last appeal to the better feelings of the House, and a few members seemed to be affected by it; but most shrugged their shoulders, indifferent to his generosity. When Robespierre tried to improve the occasion, he could not make himself heard, and apostrophized the chair in vain. 'President', demanded Charles Duval, 'is an individual to be allowed to dictate to the Convention?' 'He has done it too long', said someone; and, 'How difficult it is', remarked Fréron, 'to strike down a tyrant!' 'Arrest both brothers!' shouts Loseau. Billaud, to

---

[1] *C'est donc Danton que vous voulez venger?* The usual version (Lacretelle's), 'Cowards, why did you not defend him?' misses the point.

clinch the matter, produces fresh charges, which he believes
Robespierre cannot deny: he had, for instance, accused the
Committee of wishing to disarm the citizens ('What I said',
objects Robespierre, 'was that there were some scoundrels
. . .'), and he had charged the Government with pulling
down monuments consecrated to the Supreme Being ('I
was partly responsible for that', interjects Couthon). But
this line of attack led nowhere, and the House was growing
impatient. 'Vote on the arrest!' cried a number of members.
So at last it was put to the vote, and carried unanimously.
Thereupon the whole House rose in their places, and the
roof rang with cries of *Vive la Liberté!* and *Vive la République!* . . . 'The Republic!' Robespierre bitterly exclaimed,
'it is lost, for brigands have won the day!' When Fréron
began to talk of freedom, and the fatherland, he tried once
more to interrupt; and when Collot remarked that the
Robespierrists had planned another May 31st, he shouted,
'It's a lie!' They were his last words. As a final indignity,
he was forced to descend to the bar of the House, and
there, along with his brother, Saint-Just, Couthon, and
Philip Lebas, was arrested, and taken away.[1] Orders were
also given to place a seal on his papers.

He was dumbfounded by the attitude of the House.
Like a mountain walker who has lost his bearings in a mist,
and finds himself emerging into country which should be
familiar, but which (until he realizes he has gone astray) he
quite fails to recognize; so the Convention seemed to
Robespierre, who had not calculated upon its sudden
hostility, an Assembly that he had never seen before. The
experience unnerved him, and numbed his mind, so that,
in the hours that followed, he was unable to make the
decisions that might still have saved his life.

XI

There was no such hesitation among the eighty-one
members of the General Council of the Commune, who, as

[1] Esquiros (2/464), on the authority of Lebas' family, says that Philip's coat-tails
were torn off in the attempt of his friends to prevent his joining Robespierre.

soon as they heard of the arrest of the Robespierrists, met at the Hôtel de Ville (at 5.30 p.m.). They at once took active steps against the Committees and the Convention. Although no preparations had been made, as on August 10, or May 31, for an organized insurrection, they had foreseen the possibility of an appeal to arms. Orders were soon despatched all over the city. The barriers were closed, the tocsin rung, and the Sections invited to support and keep in touch with the Council. The sectional authorities and officers of the National Guard were ordered to attend at the Town Hall, and to take an oath of allegiance to the Commune. Cannon were commandeered from such Sections as were able and willing to supply them. A proclamation was issued, calling upon the people to re-enact August 10 and May 31, and to overthrow the 'criminals' who were persecuting Robespierre, the author of 'the consoling principle of the existence of the Supreme Being', Saint-Just, 'the apostle of virtue', Lebas, who 'brought victory to the arms of the Republic', Couthon, 'who has only the body and the head of a living man, but they burn with patriotic ardour', and the younger Robespierre, who 'presided over the victorious army of Italy'. Finally, an Executive Committee, consisting of Payan, Coffinhall, Lerebours, Arthur, and others, was appointed to carry out these measures, and to deal with such emergencies as might arise.[1] Hanriot was entrusted with the military dispositions; and the governors of the Paris prisons were instructed to refuse any prisoners sent them by the Convention.

These decisions, the usual preliminaries of a popular rising, were reported to the Jacobin Club, which (at 7 p.m.) declared itself in permanent session, and, during the night, sent three deputations to the Commune, expressing its determination to conquer or to die.[2] Many of the Council's orders were, however, either countermanded by the Committees, or disregarded by the Sections; and some of the latter, with their detachments of the National Guard, remained faithful throughout to the Convention. In-

[1] Pap. inéd. 3/293.   [2] A.H. 1/503.

deed, it soon became apparent that the Commune could no longer count on such popular support as had given it victory two years, or even twelve months before. By ten o'clock in the evening twenty-seven out of the forty-eight Sections had sent commissioners to ask for instructions from the Commune, and thirteen had also supplied troops for the defence of the Town Hall; but the rest thought it prudent to make no move; and several of them subsequently declared for the Convention. The zeal for liberty which had prompted Robespierre to support the independence of the Sections now reacted fatally upon his own fortunes.

Meanwhile (at about 7 p.m.) Hanriot, defying the decree for his arrest, had set out with a few men to rescue the Robespierrist leaders. He found them in the rooms of the Committee of General Security, where they had been dining after their defeat; but, instead of releasing them, he let himself be overpowered, and put under arrest; then, for greater security, Robespierre was sent in a *fiacre* to the Luxembourg prison, Augustin to Saint-Lazare, and subsequently to La Force, Lebas (after going home to witness the sealing of his effects) to the same place, Couthon to the Bourbe, and Saint-Just to the Écossais.

When news of Hanriot's arrest reached the Commune, Coffinhall was despatched (about 9 p.m.) to the Tuileries, and found no difficulty in releasing him: indeed, had they seized the opportunity, the communal troops might then and there have dispersed the Convention, which had reassembled at seven o'clock for its evening session, and was still irresolute and unarmed.

Soon afterwards news reached the Assembly that the arrested deputies were at large again. Robespierre, refused imprisonment at the Luxembourg, had asked to be taken to the municipal police-station at the Mairie: he had been seen hurrying from his cab, pale and exhausted, holding a white handkerchief to his mouth; and the members of the Mayor's staff had embraced him, saying, 'You are among friends'.[1] Augustin, released from La Force, came to the

[1]Lenôtre, 289.

Town Hall, and made a speech to the Commune, saying that he had been arrested, not by the Convention, but by 'the cowards who had been plotting for the last five years'. Soon afterwards he was joined by Saint-Just, and by Lebas, who had stayed behind to take leave of his wife. Couthon could not be persuaded to leave his prison till one o'clock in the morning, when he received a message signed by Robespierre and Saint-Just saying that the patriots were proscribed, that the whole people was in revolt, and that it would be treasonable of him not to join his colleagues.[1] Robespierre himself, though a deputation was sent to the Mairie reminding him that 'he did not belong to himself, but to the country, and to the people', had hesitated for some time to break prison, and to join what had now become a revolt against the Government.[2] He still hoped to avoid violence, and to keep on the right side of the law— his own Prairial Law, which showed no mercy to rebels; and he seems to have thought that the fair hearing refused to him by the Convention might yet be won, as it had been by Marat, from the Revolutionary Tribunal, the last strong-hold of his influence.[3]

XII

But now the Convention intervened, and with deadly effect. When, after a short adjournment, it met again (at 7 p.m.) it was in a more dangerous position than its members appear to have realized. There were, indeed, 'movements of indignation' when Bourdon de l'Oise announced 'a rumour that the Paris Commune and the Jacobins were co-operating to organize an insurrection'; for this step does not seem to have been anticipated by the one side any more than it was premeditated by the other; but the speaker proceeded to make light of the danger. Matters were felt to be more serious when Merlin described how he had been arrested by Hanriot; though he went on to say that, with the help of some citizens of the *Section de*

---

[1]B. and R. 34/76.
[2]Pap. inéd. 3/293. Mathiez, *Autour de Robespierre*, 220.   [3]B. and R. 34/41.

la Montagne, the tables had been turned, and Hanriot arrested instead: and it was determined to summon the authorities of the Commune and Department to the bar of the House. Thereafter the evening passed in futile speeches, and decrees of arrest, until Billaud made the alarming announcement that a company of rebel *canonniers* was attacking the Tuileries, and being met by force of arms, whilst Robespierre was at large, and had joined his supporters at the Hôtel de Ville. The spectators in the hall and galleries at once rushed out to join in the fight, and the Committees met to consider what should be done. A little later it was announced that the attack of the communal troops had been successful, and that Hanriot had been released. In this crisis—for now the Robespierrists had not only an army, but also a general—fear gave the Committees courage. Robespierre and his friends were declared *hors la loi*— 'outlaws', to be taken dead or alive, and to be executed without trial. Barras, with six deputies to help him, was put in command of the military forces at the disposal of the Convention. Barère, in the name of the Committee, which he at last judged to be the winning side, made a speech condemning the insurrection, and carried resolutions annulling the orders given by the Commune, and outlawing all the authors of the attack on the Convention. Steps were also taken to secure the Camp des Sablons, whose cadets were believed to be under Robespierrist influence, and the Paris prisons, which might soon be needed for the internment of the traitors. These measures had a good effect. Barras, after going a round of the streets, came back to report that the people were on the side of the Assembly.

Meanwhile, at the Town Hall (at about 1 a.m.),[1] Robespierre, Couthon, Saint-Just, and Lebas had presented themselves before the General Council of the Commune, where they were received with loud applause, and had then joined the Executive Committee, in an adjoining room, to forward the insurrection. Appeals were hurriedly issued to the Sections. Warrants of arrest were directed against the

[1] Mathiez (*Autour de Robespierre*, 218) thinks Robespierre had been there since 10.30 or 11.

leaders of the Convention. A proclamation was addressed to the armies in the name of the French people. And to Robespierre's own *Section des Piques*, which (it was one of the ironies of the situation) could not be trusted to support him, a letter was sent in these terms: 'Courage, patriots of the Pikes Section! Liberty is winning the day! Those men whose constancy made them feared by the traitors have already been released. Everywhere the people is showing itself worthy of its reputation. The rallying-point is the Commune, where the brave Hanriot will carry out the orders of the Executive Committee which has been set up to save the country'. This letter, which still survives,[1] is signed, '*Lerebours, Legrand, Louvet, Payan, Ro*'—Robespierre's signature stands alone, below the flourish with which the letter ends; and it is incomplete. As the letter was addressed to his own Section, it may have been thought expedient for him to add his name, although he was not a member of the Committee; and some scruple or accident may have prevented his signing in full. There are, at any rate, good reasons against the more popular hypothesis, that he was in the act of writing his name when the soldiers of the Convention burst into the room, and that the stains which can still be traced on the paper were made by his blood.[2]

But all this took time, and time was on the side of the Convention. The communal troops in the square outside the Town Hall, tired, hungry, doubtful to whom they owed allegiance, and disheartened by inaction, gradually dispersed. The public proclamation of the decree of outlawry by members of the Convention in each of the Sections decided such of them as were still wavering to withdraw their support from the rebels: one of these was the *Section des Piques*. By two o'clock in the morning of the 28th, Barras and Léonard Bourdon felt strong enough to march upon the Hôtel de Ville. Bourdon, advancing by the quays,

[1] It is in the Carnavalet Museum.
[2] Mathiez (*Autour de Robespierre*, Ch. 10); the argument turns on the wording of the letter, and the time of its dispatch. Robinet (R.F. 15/255) prints the original form of the letter, and its numerous corrections, from which he argues that Robespierre had fallen into *un désordre cérébral étrange*.

found the Place de Grève deserted, and the Town Hall itself, to guard against surprise, blazing with lights.[1] A part of his forces, using Hanriot's pass-word, and shouting *Vive Robespierre!* gained an entry into the room where the Executive Committee were at work. They made no attempt to defend themselves. Saint-Just, disdaining flight, let himself be taken where he stood. Augustin climbed out of a window, took off his shoes, and tried to escape along a cornice overlooking the square; but slipped, fell upon the heads of those below, and was picked up with a broken thigh, nearly dead.[2] Hanriot tried to escape by a window at the back, and was found later, lying injured upon a heap of manure in an inner court of the building. The crippled Couthon, in his flight, fell downstairs, and cut his head open.[3] Lebas, whose friends had provided him with a pair of pocket pistols, used one of them to blow his brains out. Robespierre turned the other upon himself, but missed his aim, and fell across the table at which he was sitting, with a shattered jaw. The rest of the Committee, and such members of the General Council as were still in the building, were seized without resistance.

Augustin was carried in a chair to the committee-room of the Section de la Commune, and, after being examined by doctors,[4] sent on to the Committee of General Security. Couthon, unconscious, was taken on a stretcher to the Hospice de l'Humanité. Robespierre, laid on a plank, and covering his shattered face with his right arm, was carried down the great staircase which Louis XVI had mounted, just five years before, to give his blessing to the Revolution. At its foot a crowd had gathered. Someone lifted the arm that hid his face. 'He's not dead', remarked one; 'he's still warm'. 'He makes a handsome king, doesn't

[1]The full moon described by historians, and depicted by artists, is a fiction (N. and Q. 10th Series, 4/286). So is the midnight rain (Lenôtre, 312).
[2]He fell over forty feet onto the head of a man who subsequently applied to the government for assistance, on the ground that his injuries rendered him unable to earn his living (R.F. 61/238).
[3]The doctors who examined him in hospital reported a deep cut below the *bosse frontale gauche* (R.F. 18/464).
[4]Their report is given in B. and R. 34/87.

he?' jeered another. 'Even if he were Caesar', said a third, 'he should be thrown into the gutter'. But the carriers would not let him be touched, and held his head as high as they could, to keep a little life in him. And so they set off for the Tuileries.

The first news of these events seems to have reached the Convention through a member of the Revolutionary Committee of the Section de la Montagne, who announced that the Town Hall had fallen, and that Robespierre was being brought back on a stretcher. Charlier, from the chair, said, 'The dastard Robespierre is here; you do not wish him to be brought in?' There were cries of 'No, No!' from all parts of the House; and Thuriot declared that it would be a shame to spoil a good day's work by defiling the Convention with the body of a tyrant. The proper place for it, he said, was the Place de la Révolution.[1] The Committees should be instructed to arrange for a speedy execution. Soon afterwards Léonard Bourdon entered the Hall, amidst loud applause, accompanied by a gendarme named Médal. He described the assault on the Town Hall, and the capture of the rebel leaders. Médal proudly claimed to have shed the blood of traitors.[2]

XIII

Rejected by the Convention, Robespierre was brought on his plank, by some artillerymen and armed citizens, to the rooms occupied by the Committee of Public Safety. Here they laid him on the table in the ante-room (*salle d'audience*), and placed a deal box containing some scraps of army bread under his head, to serve as a pillow. For nearly an hour he remained in a state of torpor, and looked as though he was at the point of death. At last he opened his eyes. Blood was flowing freely from the wound on the left side of his lower jaw, which was fractured, and the cheek was pierced by a bullet-hole. His shirt was blood-stained; he had no hat, and no cravat; though he still wore his blue coat

---

[1] Where the guillotine was set up next day.
[2] B. and R. 34/75, 82. For the claim of Médal (or Méda, as he is generally called) to have shot Robespierre, v. Lenôtre, 296.

and nankeen breeches, his white cotton stockings had fallen down to his ankles.[1] About three or four o'clock it was noticed that he held in his hand a small white leather bag, inscribed in front, '*Au Grand-Monarque, Lecourt, fourbisseur du roi et de ses troupes, rue Saint-Honoré, pres celle des Poulies, à Paris*, and on the back, *à M. Archier*.[2] He used this bag to wipe away the coagulated blood that ran from his mouth. The citizens standing round watched his every movement, and some of them gave him bits of paper, in place of linen, which he applied to the same purpose, using his right hand, and leaning on his left elbow. Two or three times he was treated to hard words by certain of the bystanders, particularly by a gunner from his own part of France, who abused him with military brutality for his treachery and wickedness. About ten o'clock a surgeon who happened to be in the courtyard of the Palais National was called in to dress his wounds. Keeping Robespierre's mouth open with a key, he found that the left jaw-bone was fractured, took out two or three loose teeth, bound up the wound, and placed a bowl of water by his side.[3] This Robespierre used from time to time, and wiped away the blood which filled his mouth with scraps of paper, doubled up, and applied with his right hand. Then, when no one was paying much attention, to him, he sat up, pulled up his stockings, slid off the table with a rapid movement, and threw himself into a chair. As soon as he was seated, he asked for water, and clean linen. During the whole time that he had lain on the table, since regaining consciousness, he had fixed his eyes on those surrounding him, especially the employees of the Committee, whom he knew by sight. He often raised his eyes to the ceiling; but, apart from a few spasmodic movements, the noticeable thing all the time was the absence of any sign of suffering (*une grande impassibilité*), even at the moment when his wound was being

[1] Michelet (9/353) was told by General Petiet, who had the story at first hand, that an employé in Carnot's office unbuckled Robespierre's garters for him, and pulled down his stockings; and that Robespierre, grateful for this kindness, said, with old-fashioned courtesy, *Je vous remercie, Monsieur*.

[2] The narrator thought the details worth noting, as suspicious of royalism?

[3] The doctor's report is in B. and R. 34/90.

dressed, which must have caused intense pain. His complexion, always livid, wore the pallor of death.[1]

At nine o'clock Couthon and Gobault[2] were brought in, both on stretchers, and set down at the foot of the main staircase of the building. There the bearers in charge of them stood by, whilst a police commissioner and an officer of the National Guard reported to Billaud, Barère, and Collot, who were now in the Committee-room, what they had done. These three men drafted a warrant for the immediate transfer of Robespierre, Couthon, and Gobault to the Conciergerie; and this order was at once carried out by the citizens to whom the custody of the three conspirators had been entrusted.[3] Someone remembered in after life how, as a school-boy, he had seen Robespierre put down for a few minutes' rest near the Quai des Lunettes; how a crowd collected, and hooted the wounded man; and how he turned his bandaged head towards the noise, and shrugged his shoulders.

Saint-Just and Dumas, too, were brought as far as the ante-room of the Committee, and then taken straight on by their escort to the Conciergerie. It was said that Saint-Just, noticing a copy of the Rights of Man that hung in the Hall, remarked ironically: 'To think that I made that!'

Arriving at the prison, Robespierre was pushed into a cell, until the Court should be ready for him. It is said that he made signs for a pen and paper; the gaoler refused, and it was never known what he wished to write. In the afternoon the twenty-two outlaws appeared before the Revolutionary Tribunal. Robespierre and his brother, Couthon and Hanriot, were carried in on stretchers; amongst the rest were Saint-Just, Payan, Simon, Dumas, who had presided over that very court the day before, and Lescot-Fleuriot, the mayor of Paris. When the last appeared, Fouquier-Tinville, not to sentence a friend, gave up his

---

[1]B. and R. 34/92. It is added that Robespierre's colleagues on the Committee insulted him, struck him, and spat in his face, and that the clerks pricked him with their knives (*ibid*. 34/94). This seems inconsistent with the rest of the story.

[2]Or Gobeau, Deputy Public Prosecutor, and a member of the Commune.

[3]Another unlikely tradition records that Robespierre struck one of the men who was carrying him.

place as Public Prosecutor to his deputy. The proceedings, in any case, were of no account. The accused men had only to be identified, and handed over to the executioner. About six o'clock they were placed in three carts—Hanriot and Augustin in the first, Robespierre and Dumas in the second, Couthon in the third, and driven out of the prison.

In order to advertise a Government victory, the guillotine had been moved back, for this occasion, to the Place de la Révolution, and the slow procession moved, for an hour, through the centre of the capital—along the rue Saint-Honoré, past the Palais Royal, and the Jacobin Club, to the west end of the Tuileries gardens—amidst the largest and gayest crowd that Paris had seen since Robespierre himself led the procession of the Supreme Being past that same spot six weeks before. Opposite the Duplays' house, it is said, a halt was called; women danced at the entrance to the builder's yard; and an urchin with a broom sprinkled the closed shutters with blood: but, if so, their insults were wasted, for the Duplay family were already in prison.

Couthon was the first beheaded, Robespierre the last but one. He lay for half an hour on the ground, exhausted by hunger and loss of blood, his torn coat knotted round his bare shoulders, hearing the cheers of the crowd, and the thud of the falling blade: half conscious, he was at last hustled up the steps, and strapped to the board: the executioner, to bare his neck, stripped the bandage from his jaw; and all his eloquence ended in an irrepressible cry of pain.

CONCLUSION: THE MAN

I

Robespierre's body was thrown into a common grave in the Parc Monceau[1]: Barras' story, that it was buried in the Madeleine cemetery with that of Louis XVI, and mistaken for it afterwards, deserves no more credit than the journalistic report of the discovery of his remains by some workmen digging the foundations of a house in Les Batignolles seventy years later.[2]

The 'Incorruptible', correct to the last, had left no debts. His effects were sold by auction in the Palais Royale, early in 1796, and fetched 38,601 *livres*—something over £100.[3] The national representatives, as Marat had long ago pointed out, were cheap at eighteen *livres* a day; and declarations made by outgoing members of the Convention showed that few of them were the richer for their four years of public service.[4]

A committee of the Convention was set up to examine Robespierre's papers, and those of his 'accomplices'. Its report, drawn up by the deputy Courtois, and laid before the House in January, 1795, took the form of a rhetorical indictment of the dead 'Dictator', supported by selected and sometimes mishandled extracts from his memoranda and correspondence.[5] It was by now agreed, amongst those of Maximilien's party who had brought about or survived his fall, that he should be the scape-goat of their offences; whilst anti-Jacobin journalists castigated, in a hundred virulent pamphlets, *la queue de Robespierre*.

There was never greater need to placate, or to divert, public feeling. The wholesale execution, on the day following Robespierre's death, of the leaders of the Commune,

---

[1] Alger, *Paris*, 476.   [2] N. and Q. 3rd series, 5/11. cp. Hamel's opinion, R.F. 57/355.
[3] A few uncertain relics have been preserved: a lock of hair, and a tricolour rosette, in the Carnavalet Museum; a silk and velvet *gilet*, in black, blue, white, and red, with figures and republican mottoes; a coffee-pot; a watch; a shaving dish.(A.R.2/378.)
[4] R.F. 32/474.   [5] v. 1/xx.

showed too clearly that the dead man's 'tyranny' had been one of moderation, not of excess, and that the party which had succeeded in overturning him had no intention of relinquishing power, or of relaxing the Terror. What had begun as a private feud was now becoming a political revolution. The temporary alliance between the anti-Robespierrists on the Committees and the Moderates in the Assembly was to be turned against the Jacobin club and the Commune. The Girondists were to be recalled, and one more attempt made to stabilize the Revolution in the hands of the propertied middle class. The political indifference which was by now the temper of the majority rendered most of this plan feasible; but in one respect it met with unexpected opposition. The policy of the guillotine had gradually to be abandoned. Seeing that no attempt was made to stop the daily batch of executions on the evening of the 9th Thermidor, and that over a hundred persons were guillotined on the 11th and 12th, it can hardly be supposed that any promise had been made by the anti-Robespierrist leaders that there should be an end of the executions. Considering the outbreak of anti-Jacobin massacres in the provinces, and the apathy of the people of Paris, it seems equally hazardous to assume that public opinion, outside the families of the victims, was pressing for an end of bloodshed. It is more likely that fear—an ever-present motive in time of revolution—was once more the deciding factor. The surviving Jacobins, deprived, by their own act, of the support of the Commune, and disowned by the Sections, were not strong enough to carry on the regime of intimidation, whilst the Girondins could not very well demand, or the Moderates sanction, the use of Prairial Law justice, which they had agreed to denounce, even against its authors. So it must suffice to re-invoke 'revolutionary justice' against a few 'criminals' whom no one could be found to defend, such as Carrier and Fouquier-Tinville—both enemies of Robespierre; or against Babeuf, an 'enemy of society' itself; to be content with the deportation to Cayenne—a sentence hardly lighter than death—of

Billaud and Collot; and then to put away the guillotine. The last demonstration in honour of terrorism was the 'pantheonisation' of Marat, in September, 1794; the first gesture of the anti-terrorist regime was his 'de-pantheonisation' in January, 1795. In May of that year the Revolutionary Tribunal was abolished; in June the very word 'revolutionary' was banned; and the last act of the dying Convention on October 26 was to rename the Place de la Révolution—the site of the guillotine—Place de la Concorde.

II

It is unfortunate, for a fair judgement of Robespierre, that most of the descriptions of him handed down by historians came originally from men who, either by conviction or by policy, were his enemies, and that they were first published at a time when it was fashionable to blacken his memory. Nevertheless, it is possible to reconstruct a sufficiently lifelike figure from descriptions which, however prejudiced, are at any rate contemporary.

Robespierre was a short man, not more than five feet three inches tall. Of slight build, he carried a small head on broad shoulders, and walked briskly along, holding himself rather stiffly, as though on guard against the nervous spasms which occasionally twisted his neck and shoulders, and showed themselves in the clenching of his hands, the twitching of his features, and the blinking of his eye-lids. His hair, naturally of a light chestnut colour, was carefully curled and powdered. His broad, rather flat face, short nose, weak green-blue eyes, and pale pock-marked complexion, sometimes lost their smug mildness in a harsh utterance, or a dangerous glance, of feline ferocity. He dressed neatly, almost foppishly, in a fashion that protested against republican carelessness; and the black suit of the lawyer was soon replaced by a striped or dark blue tail-coat, with high collar, wide lapels, and large buttons, worn with undemocratic breeches, and stockings of Lyon silk; on his head, a three-cornered hat; and always, when reading, a pair of 'preservers' (spectacles), which he was in the habit of pushing up onto his forehead—a disconcerting gesture—when he wished to look anyone in the face. His habitual expression seemed to his friends melancholy, and to his enemies arrogant; sometimes he would laugh with the immoderateness of a man who has little sense of humour; sometimes the cold look softened into a smile of ironic and rather alarming sweetness.

As a speaker, he had learnt to soften the tones of a normally rough and shrill voice, and to moderate his Artois accent; but his utterance remained weak; and his power as a speaker even in his eloquent moments, lay less in the manner of his delivery, than in the seriousness of what he had to say, and the deep conviction with which he said it. With all the tricks, and more than his share of the commonplaces of the rhetorical tradition of the eighteenth century, as he had studied it at College, and practised it at the bar, Robespierre was able to sway the professional and shop-keeping audiences of the Jacobin Club as no other politician of his time could do. There is nothing absolute in eloquence; it is the art of using words to create opinions or acts; and it is judged by its success in producing an intended effect upon a given audience. Robespierre would have been as unconvincing in the House of Commons as a Welsh revivalist in a University church: but in the Assembly, or in the tribune of the Jacobin Club, he was one of the world's great orators.

III

Robespierre's detractors have been prodigal with the charge of hypocrisy. But a hypocrite is one who professes to be something which he knows he is not, the pretender to a title to which he is aware he has no claim. Robespierre can be represented as a hypocrite only by those who cannot or will not understand the real state of his mind. If anything is certain about him, it is that he was not so much anxiously trying to reconcile, as triumphantly certain that he had succeeded in reconciling, apparent opposites—belief in liberty with a policy of intimidation, love of the people with a suspicious distrust of individuals, dislike of the death penalty with wholesale executions, hatred of militarism with a national war, and a belief in an overruling Providence with a vindictive and merciless Inquisition into the conduct of his associates. His conscience may have been twisted, but it was all of one piece. He may have unconsciously cheated himself: he never consciously cheated others. Honest as to principles he never questioned, he was equally honest as to the exceptions that made them inapplicable. A stupider man would have died for liberty, or peace; a cleverer man would have become a mere opportunist. Robespierre, guided by something lower than logic, but higher than the instinct of self-preservation, kept himself intact and incorrupt, nearer than any other man to the brain and heart of the Revolution.

Most of what was good in him may be summed up in three words—Democrat, Prophet, and Puritan. He sincerely believed, all his life, in the wisdom and goodness of the common people; believed in it at a time when the fashion was to look for enlightenment and virtue from above, not from below; and believed in it, not as a consoling phrase from the pulpit, but as a political axiom, issuing in manhood franchise, equal justice, and the administration of property as a trust for the poor. Again, as he clung to his first principles of liberty and equality, even at moments when, for the best of reasons, he was forced to compromise them, so he refused to be diverted by the opportunism of government from pursuing his vision of a republic founded on virtue and sustained by religion; and the crowd, not understanding what he meant, but feeling that there was something fine afoot, climbed nearer to the summit of the Revolution than the cynics who sneered at him as a wordy ideologue. Puritanism is never popular, particularly in the country of Calvin; and there was an unpleasantly Genevan flavour in Robespierre's moral preaching and practice. But this, which might have been intolerable in a peaceful society, was forgiven, in a time of commotion and civil war, for the consistency with which 'the Incorruptible' stood out against temptations of money and office which were corrupting every rank of political power. 'He was a man of purity and integrity', confessed Barère on his death-bed, 'a true and sincere republican'.[1] 'No one knows better than I', said Souberbielle, 'how sincere, how disinterested, how absolute was his devotion to the republic'.[2]

Such were the qualities which won for Robespierre the admiration, and sometimes almost the worship, of people who knew him only by his public reputation, or by his speeches. In the more difficult sphere of private relationship, with its often drastic revaluations of character, respect for Robespierre's principles was balanced, if not outweighed, by dislike of his personal qualities. A cramped and unhappy childhood, a professional career impeded by prejudice and tactlessness, and a political experience of almost ceaseless opposition and intrigue, had left him, by the time he tasted power, jealous, suspicious, and vindictive. He was not a coward; but his caution in face of danger, and his underhand methods of attacking an enemy, had the appearance of it. He was not naturally cruel or bloodthirsty; but patriotism and Puritanism made him ruthless in the shedding of blood. He was no wicked tyrant, oppressing for personal ends, but that much more dangerous character, the conscientious Inquisitor, torturing the body that he might save the soul. Many such have been kindly men, who returned from a *séance* of rack and thumb-screw feeling that their work had been well done, and faced the world with a smile. Robespierre, said Lakanal, 'was a man full of good qualities, and gifted above all with great sweetness of character' (*douceur*);[3] and an old man visited by Hamel in 1866 still remembered 'the distinction of his manners, his extreme politeness, and his affability'.

IV

This, it may well be said, is the portrait of a man framed for opposition, and out of place in government; and Robes-

[1]Esquiros, 2/472.   [2]Poumiès de la Siboutie, *Souvenirs*, 27.
[3]A.R. 4/231.

pierre himself was sadly aware of it. The story of his life has recently been described as 'a study in deterioration'; and there is some justification for this view in the obvious contrast between Robespierre's professions of 1789 and his acts of 1794. But the change that came about was not due to the surrender of any of the citadels of conviction or character, but to intentional, and, as he supposed, temporary withdrawals of the front line, 'for strategical purposes'. He did not believe less in liberty, because he muzzled the anti-patriot press; nor more in capital punishment, when he urged the execution of the king. He had, no doubt, a lawyer's flair for justifying evasions of the law, and applied it to moral problems in such a way as to give rise to the suspicion of casuistry; but it would not be fair to charge him with anything so crude as the belief that the end justifies the means. Intimidation was, to him, not merely a cause of virtue, but its inseparable counterpart; and virtue not merely an effect of intimidation, but its living fruit. It was his original creed that the common people—that is, the classes least corrupted by wealth and power—are essentially wiser and better than their 'superiors'. His aim was to give them power and wealth, but not in sufficient quantities to infect them with the consequential disease. To secure this, virtue must be led by the hand, government checked by safeguards, and breaches of the law relentlessly punished. There was, in this scheme of life, no before and after, no separation of means and end, no probationary or transitional period. The Robespierrian Utopia was all of one piece. Such inconsistencies as might appear, during the approach to it, were due to the atmosphere in which it was forced to grow, not to any inherent weakness. The thing itself was as single and sincere as the mind and character of its author. If, then, there was 'deterioration', it was not because Robespierre turned aside from some heavenly vision that he had once enjoyed, but because, clinging to it all his life, he was driven to clothe it in the forms of maturer experience, to re-express the ideas of 1789 in the language of 1794. This does not mean that he never expected to be able to do away with terrorism; for, though he had moods of pessimism in which he doubted whether the interests of the rulers would ever be identified with those of the ruled, there were other times when he hoped, by popular education, good laws, and liberal institutions, to bring the Revolution to a happy issue, in a virtuous and enlightened republic. But he did not often put such hopes on record; he left no Political Testament; and it is uncertain how far he felt himself able to look ahead.

v

Statesmanship implies more than political idealism. Robespierre had something of Mazzini in his outlook: had he anything of a Cavour's insight into the realities of a political situation? If his advice had been taken in 1789–90, and the Declaration of Rights had been embodied in a really democratic constitution, would there have come about such an alliance between the king and the people as might have saved the throne, and defeated the counter-revolution? It is more than doubtful. The middle classes were right in their belief that the common people were unfit for political power; and Robespierre himself was to find that it was one thing to champion their rights in Opposition, and quite another thing to hold them to their duties in the government of the country. Again, if Robespierre's advice had been followed in 1791–92, could France either have kept out of war, or have waged it more successfully? He was right in foreseeing defeat, and in dreading a military dictatorship; but his policy of distrust, and his insistence that military commands should go to patriots rather than proved soldiers, had a sinister effect upon the discipline and efficiency of the army. The six weeks' dictatorship of the Commune in 1792, a foretaste of Robespierre's ideal state, produced, along with a genuine outburst of patriotic fervour, an unscrupulous rigging of the elections, and an abominable series of massacres. In the matter of the king's trial and execution Robespierre showed a clear-sightedness and ruthlessness which lacked only one thing

—the certainty that he was not aiming at merely a party success, but at an act of national justice. The overthrow of the Gironde in June, 1793—another stroke of Robespierrian policy—was necessary for the safety of the country, and the proscription of the party leaders which followed was justified by their resort to civil war; but it is hard not to lay part of the blame, for all this bitterness, upon the inquisitorial methods of the Jacobin 'purge', which made it increasingly difficult for anyone to work for the country, unless he belonged to the straitest sect of Robespierrism. When, finally, Robespierre found himself the reputed head of a dictatorial committee, his statesmanship was put to the supreme test—and failed. For a year, indeed, the country was more effectively organized and disciplined than by any ruler between Louis XIV and Napoleon. But it was done at a terrible cost. An ignorant and provocative foreign policy gave the Revolution the habit of war, and increased the danger of Robespierre's own bugbear, a military dictatorship. Terrorism, the weak man's remedy for disorder, became a drug the strong man could not do without, till it destroyed just those elements of virtue and good sense to which Robespierre had hoped to appeal; whilst the failure of Jacobinism to provide an economic programme ruined its credit with the common people, and rendered it helpless in face of a vulgar coup d'état. Robespierre was never a dictator, and part of his failure must be put down to personal qualities which made him unfit for leadership or power; but there is enough evidence that he was at once too visionary, too narrow-minded, and a man of too little worldly experience or tact to be a statesman.

VI

Where, then, did his greatness lie? In the thoroughness with which he embodied the main ideas and experiences of the Revolution, from the enthusiastic liberalism of 1789, through the democratic aspirations' of 1792, to the disciplined disillusionment of 1794. At every turn of events he was there, ready, like a Greek chorus, with appropriate comments; ready, like a Jewish prophet, with denunciation and warning; ready also, like any demagogue, with flattery of the people, and promises of a political millennium. Through it all, he was as sincere, as solemn, and as self-questioning as his master, the model of Jacobinism, Jean-Jacques Rousseau; fundamentally impracticable, perhaps, as he had been; and an unwilling example of the ultimate savagery of an appeal to the laws of nature.

More than this. Robespierre's place in history hardly rests upon anything that he was, or thought, or said, except in so far as he was impersonating the Revolution. However pure his conduct, and pleasant his manners, his personality was cold and unattractive. However eloquent his speeches, they seldom went outside the commonplaces of republican oratory; they contain ideas which have borne fruit in later reforms and revolutions, but they provide little permanent food for thought. The praise that might justly be accorded to the one republican leader who professed to identify government with the rule of morality is silenced by the reflection that he also identified it with the regime of the Revolutionary Tribunal, and of the guillotine. But so long as the French Revolution is regarded, not as the 'suicide of the eighteenth century', but as the birth of ideas that enlightened the nineteenth, and of hopes that still inspire our own age; and so long as its leaders are sanely judged, with due allowance for the terrible difficulties of their task; so long will Robespierre, who lived and died for the Revolution, remain one of the great figures of history.

THE EVIDENCE

I

ROBESPIERRE'S own writings consist of poems, essays, pleadings, speeches, articles, official documents, private letters, and notes.

The poems, all Juvenilia, have been recovered from various sources, and reprinted by Deprez and Lesueur, *Oeuvres complètes de Maximilien Robespierre, I. Oeuvres littéraires*, (1910).

The essays have been reprinted by Deprez and Lesueur in the same edition.

The pleadings have been collected and printed both by Barbier and Vellay, *Oeuvres complètes de Maximilien Robespierre* (1910), and by Lesueur (same title, 1912): they are summarily described in Paris, *La Jeunesse de Robespierre*.

The speeches can be read in the *Procès-verbaux* of the Assemblies, in the files of the *Moniteur*, in the more fragmentary reports of other journals, and in accounts of the proceedings of the Jacobin Club (Aulard, *La Société des Jacobins*, 1889–97). The most important of them were printed as *brochures*, after delivery, and can be found in collections of revolutionary literature—thirty-seven are in the British Museum, and five in the Bodleian. Selections have been reprinted by Vermorel, *Oeuvres de Robespierre* (1865), Morse Stephens, *Orators of the French Revolution* (1892), and Vellay, *Discours et Rapports de Robespierre* (1908).

Robespierre's articles are to be found in the journals he edited—*Défenseur de la Constitution* (1792), and *Lettres à ses commettans* (1792): files of both are in the British Museum.

Official documents written, signed, or annotated by Robespierre occur in the correspondence and resolutions of the Committee of Public Safety (Aulard, *Recueil des Actes du Comité de Salut Public*, 1889–99), and the papers studied by

593

THE EVIDENCE

Ording (*Le Bureau de police du Comité de Salut Public*, 1930). Some further references occur in Lacroix, *Actes de la Commune de Paris pendant la Révolution* (1894–1909), and Charavay, *L'Assemblée électorale de Paris* (1890–5).

Michon, *Correspondance de Maximilien et Augustin Robespierre* (1926), collected for the first time most of the known letters of Robespierre and his brother, and summarized those of his correspondents. For critical notes on this edition, v. Thompson, *The French Revolution*, etc. (1935).

The so-called *Carnet de Robespierre*—a small notebook found among his effects—was reprinted in facsimile by Motteroz (1920?), and with a critical commentary by Mathiez, *Robespierre Terroriste* (1921); in the same volume is a reprint, with critical commentary, of the *Notes* Robespierre wrote for Saint-Just's *Rapport* against the Dantonists.

Recueil des œuvres de Maximilien I. Robespierre et de pièces pour servir à son histoire, par J. W. Croker (1819), is the general title of the eleven volumes of *brochures* in the British Museum (907. f. 1) containing the part of Croker's collection concerning Robespierre. More papers of the same kind will be found under F.R. 375 (6 items), F. 166–7 (38 items) and F. 849–58 (112 items).

Robespierriana of all kinds—sometimes reprints of his writings—have accumulated in the files of the *Annales Révolutionnaires*, later *Annales Historiques*, ever since 1908; and some others can be found in the *Révolution Française*, *Revue Historique de la Révolution Française*, and other journals.

Two facts—the destruction of Robespierre's papers, as compromising documents, which went on under the anti-Jacobin reaction of 1794–9, and, to a lesser extent, under the Napoleonic and Bourbon regimes that followed;[1] and the encouragement given by the *Société des Études Robespierristes*, during the past twenty-seven years, to the publication of any sort of *document inédit* bearing on Robespierre, make it unlikely that much of value remains to be unearthed amongst the French archives.

[1] Hamel (ed. 1862, 1/365, note) says the MSS. of most of Robespierre's speeches were destroyed by Simon Duplay in 1815.

II

Of the many bibliographies, catalogues, and collections of material dealing with the French Revolution, the following have been found of special value for the study of Robespierre: Buchez and Roux, *Histoire parlementaire de la Révolution française* (40 vols., 1834); Aulard, *Recueil des actes du comité de Salut public* (12 vols., 1889–99); Aulard, *La société des Jacobins* (6 vols., 1889–97); Tourneux, *Bibliographie de l'histoire de Paris pendant la Révolution* (1890–1913); Tourneux, *Les sources bibliographiques de l'histoire de la Révolution française* (1898); Caron, Brière and Caron, Caron and Stein (three series), *Repertoire méthodique de l'histoire moderne et contemporaine de France* (1898–); Tuetey, *Repertoire des sources bibliographiques de l'histoire de Paris pendant la Révolution* (1889); Fortescue, *List of the contents of the three collections of books, pamphlets, and journals in the British Museum relating to the French Revolution* (1899); Schmidt, *Les sources de l'histoire de France depuis* 1789 (1907); Caron, *Manuel pratique pour l'étude de la Révolution française* (1912); Cahen and Guyot, *L'oeuvre législative de la Révolution* (1913); Kuscinski, *Dictionnaire des Conventionnels* (1916).

III

All books dealing with the Revolution or Robespierre have to be read with one eye on the personal and political background of their authors. They are therefore put here in chronological order, and grouped under the periods into which the study of the subject can most easily be divided. Help has been found, in this connexion, in Thierry, *Lettres sur l'histoire de France* (1820); Frederick Harrison, *Historians of the French Revolution* (1883, reprinted in *The Choice of books*, 1886); Flint, *The Philosophy of History* (1893); Jullian, *Historiens français du XIXe siècle* (1896); Aulard, *Les premiers historiens de la Révolution française* (in *Études et Leçons sur la Révolution française*, 6e série, 1910); Acton, *The Literature of the Revolution* (Appendix to *Lectures on the French Revolution*, 1910); and Gooch, *History and Historians of the Nineteenth Century* (1931).

The aim of this bibliography is (1) to call attention to all books and articles dealing primarily with Robespierre, and to such general histories of the Revolution as are of special importance for the study of his career; and (2) to indicate, where it seems worth while to do so, the general character of these books, and their attitude towards Robespierre.

IV

Between 1789 and 1799 history was being made more rapidly than it could be written. The closing down of academies, schools, and *salons*, the distaste for what was traditional or authoritative, and the demand for political propaganda, turned literature into journalism, eloquence into rhetoric, and critical taste into the facile abuse or applause of the time-server. Such attempts as were made to produce a history of the Revolution either failed to keep pace with events, or were distorted by partisanship. It became not uncommon for the editors of serial works, whose earlier pages had blessed the reforms of the National Assembly, to fill their later volumes with vituperation of Robespierre and the Jacobin regime; whilst others attempted, not without difficulty, to dissociate the Revolution from revolutionists of whom they could no longer approve. Meanwhile, of the making of *brochures* there was no end—printed speeches, projects of legislation, papers (hardly yet distinguishable from pamphlets), and pasquinades. Press laws were passed, but the press remained free; and there was no effective check upon what one man might write about another, except the fear of what he might write in reply.

In most of these literary *genres* Robespierre—a writer and speaker whom circumstances and a mistaken ambition thrust into politics—was persistent and painstaking. When he fell, his memory bore the odium of more crimes than he had committed; and political literature contains nothing meaner or more vile than the anti-Jacobin pamphlets by ex-Jacobin authors which Croker collected from the lumber-rooms of Restoration booksellers.

The scanty elements of autobiography in Robespierre's speeches and writings will be noticed as they occur; they do not in fact tell us very much about him. The same may be said of the ephemeral pamphlets bearing on controversies about Robespierre's conduct during his life-time, or disputing, soon after his death, his character and career. Hardly any of them contain historical evidence which can be trusted, or corroborated.

There remain, however, from these early years, a certain number of historical or biographical sources of real value.

The *Histoire de la Révolution de* 1789, by 'Deux Amis de la Liberté,' began to appear in 1791. Vol. 7, describing the end of the Constituent Assembly (September 1791), came out in 1792. Then there was a long pause, and when Vol. 8 appeared, in 1797, the editors were found to have changed their view of the Revolution. Robespierre's followers are now 'brigands' or 'conspirators', comparable only to Catiline or Cartouche (8/137); and Robespierre himself, after an early career not unsympathetically described (12/7), becomes an arch-villain, who sets himself to crush all rivals (8/295), spends disreputable week-ends in the country (13/300), dreams of nothing but bloodshed, and plans to decimate the population—another Nero, 'the most ferocious cannibal, the most monstrous scoundrel to whom nature ever gave birth'. This view influenced Michelet and Carlyle, both of whom used the book. Michelet had a high opinion of Vol. 1, and derived from it his opinion (2/308) that Robespierre failed as an orator in the Constituent Assembly—a notion which coloured his whole psychological interpretation, and has become a commonplace among later historians.

Vie secrette et curieuse de M. J. Maximilien Robespierre, etc., by Du Perron, (Paris, Prévost, An. II) is bitterly hostile, but includes a personal description of Robespierre which is of some interest.

The history of Robespierre, political and personal (2nd ed., London, 1794), an anonymous English work, full of the wildest nonsense, ends with *A brief sketch of the Person, Life, and Manners of Robespierre*, based on information 'from a person who knew him', which is apparently taken from the *Vie secrette* above.

A German work, *Maximilian Robespierre in seinem Privatleben geschildert von einem Gefangenen in Pallast Luxemburg* (Berlin, 1794) professes to be translated from a *Vie privée de Robespierre* published in Paris in May, 1794, and sold out within a day of publication. This work was described and partly translated by Avenel in *L'Amateur des Autographes* (July 16, 1863), and was used, in this form, by Cabanés, *Robespierre intime* (*Cabinet secret de l'histoire*, 3/391). Its credibility can be judged from the fact that it represents Robespierre, as a boy of 8–10, going with his mother, 'an uncommonly pretty woman', to visit her brother Damiens, who was awaiting execution for his attempt to assassinate Louis XV, and whose fate made Maximilien an anti-royalist. The legend that Robespierre was a relation of Damiens was, it is generally agreed, invented by the royalist press: in any case Damiens was executed in 1757, a year before Robespierre was born.

The popular *Histoire de la conjuration de Maximilien Robespierre* (it went through many editions, and was translated into several languages) was one of a series of anti-Jacobin works published by C. F. L. Ventre de la Toulouse, *dit* Galart de Montjoie, editor of the Catholic Royalist journal *L'Ami du Roi*. He wrote with the animus of a proscript and an exile. Taine's judgement that, when his evidence can be confirmed, it deserves credit, is the most that can be said for him.

On January 5, 1795, the deputy Courtois read to the Convention his *Rapport fait au nom de la commission chargée de l'examen des papiers trouvées chez Robespierre et ses complices*. It was subsequently printed, by order of the Convention, and remained for many years a storehouse of anti-Robespierrist propaganda. It was not until the publication

of *Papiers inédits trouvés chez Robespierre, Saint-Just, etc.,
supprimés ou omis par Courtois* (Paris, 1828) that it was
generally realized how dishonestly Courtois had done his
work. A comparison of the two versions shows that, out of
the first bundle (*liasse*) of 10 papers Courtois printed
eight, out of the second (56) 17, out of the third (49) 42—
most of these were anonymous letters of flattery or abuse,
equally useful for his argument; out of the fourth (62) 11—
here he omits the military mission of Saint-Just and Lebas;
out of the fifth (35) 25—including a number of letters from
spies; out of the sixth (34) 24—spies again; out of the seventh
(46) 14; out of the eighth (30) 12; and all of the ninth, viz.
15. Thus, out of a total of 377 documents, Courtois only
printed 153; and these were chosen so as to give colour to
the rhetorical indictment of Robespierre with which
his *Rapport* began. Not only so: in more than one instance
he altered the text of his documents to Robespierre's
disadvantage; instances will be found below (v. pp. 1/257n,
2/33n, 207).

The most important bibliographical problem bearing on
the life of Robespierre is that of the authorship of a rare
work called *La Vie et les Crimes de Robespierre, surnommé le
Tyran; depuis sa naissance jusq'à sa mort. Ouvrage dedié à Ceux
qui commandent et à Ceux qui obéissent. Par M. le Blond de
Neuvéglise. Colonel d'Infanterie légere.* (Augsbourg, 1795:
for title-page, v. Frontispiece). It has hitherto been held,
on the authority of Barbier, who had it from the Count
de Firmas-Periès (v. Quérard, *Supercheries*, sub *Le Blond*),
that *Le Blond de Neuvéglise* was a pseudonym for a certain
Abbé L. B. Proyart (1743–1808), whose nephew, the Abbé
J. M. Proyart (1803–88), reissued the book, with omissions and additions, as *La Vie de Maximilien Robespierre*,
at Arras in 1850. But a careful comparison of the two books
shows (1) that Le Blond de Neuvéglise cannot have been the
Abbé Proyart, (2) that his work can be exactly dated, (3)
that he was an independent witness, whose evidence as to

Robespierre's early life, at least, is of considerable value, and (4) that the omissions and additions made by the later Abbé Proyart gave the edition of 1850 a tendency which the book did not originally possess.

(1) The author of *La Vie et les Crimes de Robespierre* is a Catholic and a Royalist, but not a priest; for he is a soldier (pp. 343, 368), who has emigrated, leaving behind a wife and children (p. 344). (2) He quotes Courtois' *Rapport*, which appeared in January, 1795 (p. 334); he knows of the exclusion of Cambon from the Finance Committee, on April 3 (p. 197); but Fouquier-Tinville, though convicted, has not yet been guillotined—May 7 (p. 98). The book was therefore written late in April or early in May, 1795. (3) The author made use of information supplied to him by the Abbé Proyart; the fact that he always puts such passages in the third person, and the way in which he refers to his informant (*M. L'Abbé Proyart . . . ne désavouera pas ce que nous allons rapporter à ce sujet*, p. 41) are conclusive. Add that when he was himself present he uses the first person, as (for instance) on the occasion of Robespierre's speech of welcome to Louis XVI (p. 48). The writer, then, was in close touch with Louis-le-Grand: he was also sufficiently behind the scenes at Arras to quote a private letter from Robespierre to *une Personne de sa Province* (p. 135), and to obtain particulars of his wardrobe in May, 1789, from Mme Marchand's maid, who packed his bag (p. 81). (4) The chief changes in Le Blond's book made by Proyart in 1850 are these. He adds the particulars, so beloved by sentimental biographers, about Robespierre's pet birds, and his dog *Brount* (p. 4); he adds a story, taken from his uncle's book, *Louis XVI, sa Vie et ses Vertus*, about Robespierre's lack of clothes while at College (p. 22); he corrects the *L'Anguillette* of Le Blond's story (p. 77) into *Lantilette*, but misses the point by omitting the reference to Dubois de Fosseux (p. 40; cp. his omission of an abusive note about this man in Le Blond, p. 59); he adds further stories about Desmoulins from his uncle's *Louis XVI* (p. 51); he inserts an account of Fouquier-Tinville's execution (p. 55),

and of Hébert's (p. 56); he omits a long paragraph accusing Robespierre of duplicity (p. 63, Le Blond, 107); he adds an attack, as a priest might, upon Jacobin iconoclasm (p. 72), but tones down Le Blond's royalist extravagances in the account of the king's trial (p. 84); he inserts, as a description of Robespierre's room at Humbert's, in the rue de Saintonge, a passage from Barbaroux's memoirs describing a visit to Robespierre's room at the Duplays, in the rue Saint-Honoré (p. 112); he expands Le Blond's modest account of Robespierre's country house into a story of disreputable orgies (p. 117, cp. further details, p. 138); he omits two of Le Blond's 'tallest' stories—the execution of Bousmard's parrot (p. 247), and the human skin tannery (p. 279); as well as a long account of Robespierre's intention to marry Madame Royale (p. 238); and he adds, at the end of the book, fresh descriptions of Robespierre's death from other sources, and, in place of Le Blond's *Conclusion*, Pelletan's *Portrait de Robespierre*. The general effect of these changes is to substitute for the local antagonisms of the Arras officer the ecclesiastical prejudices of the Arras priest; to bring the book up to date, by omitting references to by-gone issues, and adding accounts of well-known events; and to replace discredited legends about Robespierre by domestic details more in the taste of 1850.

'Le Blond de Neuvéglise' was, therefore, a real man—a member, it can hardly be doubted, of that Le Blond family which played a large part in Arras affairs during the Revolution; not Gabriel Le Blond, for one of whose children Robespierre himself acted as godfather (Corresp. 439), nor his brother the General; for both of them, however anti-Jacobin they became, remained Revolutionists; but perhaps another brother, who took his name from a family property at Neuvéglise, south-west of Ypres, who emigrated in 1792, but kept in touch with Arras affairs, talked over 'old days' with his friend Proyart, and hoped, by this publication, to work up counter-revolution amongst Catholic-royalist exiles.

Some of this remains guess-work; but uncertainty as

to the exact authorship of the book does not detract from its value as the first serious biography of Robespierre, written by a man who was in close touch with Maximilien's native town, his college, his tutor, and his friends.

The comparative trustworthiness of Le Blond will be realized when his account of Robespierre is compared with that of some further contemporary historians. In 1796 F. X. Pagés, who had brought out, three years before, a poem in ten cantos celebrating the fall of the Gironde, published a *Histoire secrète de la Révolution française* (an English translation appeared the same year) recanting his earlier views, and attributing to Robespierre a 'base envy, engendered by the consciousness of his inferior abilities', and 'a desire of reigning solitary sovereign over ruins and carcases' (p. 60). In Fantin des Odoards' *Histoire philosophique de la Révolution* (1796)—a royalist work largely based on Girondist memoirs —Robespierre is represented as a leader of the Cordeliers Club, and Mirabeau, who died in April, 1791, as one of the authors of the prison massacres in September, 1792. Prudhomme's *Histoire générale et impartiale des erreurs, des fautes, et des crimes commis pendant la Révolution française* (1796–7) is a six-volume indictment of the Revolution, in which Robespierre's misdeeds are swallowed up in elaborate statistics of the number of *châteaux* burnt, of persons driven to madness or suicide, of victims of war, of starvation, and so forth, between 1789 and 1795. Desessarts' popular *Précis historique de la vie, des crimes, et du supplice de Robespierre* (1797, followed by various translations and new editions) is sufficiently characterized by its title. Finally, this stratum of anti-Jacobin history was explored, for the benefit of English readers, by John Adolphus, whose *Biographical Memoirs of the French Revolution* (2 vols. 1799) were praised by Croker as the best English work before his own, but were in fact based upon such inferior authorities (e.g., in the case of Robespierre, Montjoie) that they are of little historical value.

Between 1800 and 1815 the Napoleonic censorship of history—all the more effective because directed by a man who understood and appreciated historical studies—encouraged the production of chronological summaries, in which the Empire appeared as the climax of the French Monarchy, and frowned on any attempt to rehabilitate the Revolution. Though he was in the habit of saying—and he spoke from personal knowledge—that Robespierre was by no means the worst of the Jacobin leaders, Napoleon would not tolerate any public defence of a regime, the fear of whose return was one of the chief supports of his own. Thus denied the free study of its own age, history found an outlet in a Catholic romantic reconstruction of the Middle Ages; Michaud's *Histoire des Croisades* and Chateaubriand's *Les Martyrs* became the school in which Michelet learnt a new approach to the Revolution.

Four histories of the Revolution published during this period were more than superficial chronicles. De Moleville's *Histoire de la Révolution de France* (1800), enlarged from his *Mémoires secrètes* of 1793, and subsequently extended by Delisle de Salle (in English, *Annals of the French Revolution*), is nothing more than an immense counter-revolutionary pamphlet; but the author admits Robespierre as the one exception to his thesis that the revolutionary leaders were in the pay of the Court. Lacretelle's *Histoire de la Révolution française* (begun in 1801, but taking final form in 1824–6) is a hostile account of the three revolutionary Assemblies by a Deist who turned Catholic, a liberal constitutionalist who became a royalist, and a Girondin who lived to serve under Louis XVIII. Beaulieu, always a royalist, put together his personal reminiscences, and quotations from the *Moniteur*, into *Essais historiques sur les causes et les effets de la Révolution française* (1801–3). The only value of these two works lies in the occasional relics of eye-witness they enshrine.

On the other hand, Toulongeon, *Histoire de la France depuis la Révolution de* 1789 (1801–10), was the first historian to attempt a sober and impartial account of the facts, such as might help extremists to understand one another; he was also the first to quote his sources, document his narrative, and distinguish between first and second-hand evidence. His account of Robespierre's rise and fall is as reasonable and impartial as, at that date, anyone dared make it.

In 1802 a certain Pierre Villiers, who described himself as *ancien capitaine de Dragons*, and said that most of his papers had been destroyed in a police raid on 18 Fructidor, An. IV, entrusted a friend with the publication of what was left; and they appeared the same year, under the title of *Souvenirs d'un Deporté, pour servir aux Historiens, aux Romanciers, aux Compilateurs d'Ana, aux Folliculaires, aux Journalistes, aux Feseurs de tragédies, de comédies, de vaudevilles, de mélodrames, et de pantomimes dialoguées.* Neither the sub-title, nor the mystification of the *Avis au public*, nor the character of the book, which is a haphazard collection of insipid and faintly indecent stories and verse, inspires much faith in the trustworthiness of its author. Yet the book contains a few pages (pp. 1–6, 19, 43, 87) about Robespierre which bear the stamp of originality and truth. Villiers states that for seven months of the year 1790 he used to visit Robespierre's rooms in the rue Saintonge, and act as his secretary; and he gives some particulars of his life at that time which are of the highest value. A copy of this very rare book, from Lord Acton's collection, is in the University Library at Cambridge.

VI

The return of peace, the removal of the Napoleonic censorship, and the influence of the romanticists, made the fifteen years following Waterloo a spring-time of French historical studies. It is also due to this period that the history of the Revolution began to be written—and continued to be

written—with an eye to contemporary politics; it was not
without intention that Thiers or Mignet recalled the
revolutionary scenes of 1789 on the eve of those of 1830.
As the Bourbon regime declined from the constitutionalism
of Louis XVIII into the reactionism of Charles X, historians
of the Revolution once more experienced the change from
Girondism to Jacobinism, and there were the beginnings
of a rehabilitation of Robespierre.

Mme de Stael, whose *Considérations sur les principaux
événements de la Révolution française* appeared in 1818—
two years after her death—was the first writer to popularize
the idea that the Revolution 'went wrong' after 1791.
She had met Robespierre at her father's house in 1789, and
continued to regard him as an austere fanatic, who won
leadership by his singleness of purpose, and lost it by thirst
for power (ed. Treuttel, 1820, 2/130).

The great works of Thiers (*Histoire de la Révolution française*, 10 vols, 1823–7), and Mignet (*Histoire de la Révolution
française depuis 1789 jusqu'à 1814*, 1824) had one origin and
one purpose—to show that the Revolution was essentially
a national movement, and that its extravagances and
crimes were due to the opposition of the royalist party.
Constitutionalism was represented for the first time (always
with an eye on Charles X), as counter-revolution. Thiers,
owing to the obscurity surrounding his early collaboration
with Bodin, and his careless use of authorities, deserves a
little of the abuse poured on him by Croker (*Essay* 1), but
Mignet is generally accounted a judicious and honest
writer. His Robespierre, though commendable as an anti-
royalist, is actuated by jealousy and ambition. Owing to his
inferior talents he was late in becoming a leader—a great
advantage in a revolution. But he was destroyed by his
passion for power.

Amongst the crowd of smaller works which came out
during these years, a biographer of Robespierre will notice
Méda's *Précis historique des événements qui se sont passés dans*

le soirée du 9 thermidor (1825), defending the author's claim to have shot Robespierre; an article by Nodier in the *Revue de Paris* (1829) on Robespierre as an orator; and another by Deschiens, in his *Bibliographie des journaux* (1829), afterwards published in book form, entitled *Opinion sur Robespierre*, which restated for the first time Napoleon's suggestion that Robespierre was put to death as a Moderate, who attacked the extremists, and opposed the Terror.

The so-called *Mémoires authentiques de Maximilien Robespierre*, whose publication (2 vols, 1830) coincided with the end of this period, is a 'manifest fabrication' (Croker, 299) by Charles Reybaud, containing a few scraps of authentic material, and a number of extracts from the *Moniteur*, ending in September, 1791. It is of no historical value.

VII

The revolution of 1830 was largely the work of historians. The new king, Louis Philippe—ex-Jacobin, ex-*émigré*, son of a regicide, and cousin of the prince his father had condemned to death—was himself a historical monument, and under his patronage unprecedented opportunities were provided for a new generation of historians. Michelet's *Précis de l'Histoire moderne* (1827) proclaimed, too, a new method, combining the romantic approach of Chateaubriand with Vico's search for the animating ideas, and Herder's insistence on the physical background of history. Besides, it was now possible to study the Revolution freely and sympathetically, to collect its relics, to question its survivors, and to fight over again the battle between the Mountain and the Gironde. As 1830 moved towards 1848, and the Government once more became reactionary, the experiences of 1815–30 were renewed; but whereas Thiers and Mignet need only recall the constitution of 1791 to overturn a Bourbon who had forgotten nothing and forgiven nothing, Michelet and Blanc must justify Jacobinism and the Republic of 1793 against an Orléans who was trying to forget everything since 1791. Towards one belief all the historians of these eighteen years converged—that the Revolution was a national event, springing out of the soil and homes of France; its virtues French virtues, and its faults French faults. Meanwhile other countries—England, following Croker, and Germany, Niebuhr—took up the study of a period which they were at last able to disentangle from the toils of the Napoleonic Empire.

Revolutionary studies were immensely helped by the publication, between 1834 and 1838, of Buchez and Roux's *Histoire parlementaire de la Révolution française*, in forty volumes—less a history than a huge repertory of documents, but influenced throughout by Buchez's belief that the Revolution was the climax of Christian civilization, Jacobinism its gospel, and Robespierre its apostle (v. Prefaces to Vols. 1 and 40). For Robespierre, the re-trial of his case after Thermidor (Vols. 33–4) is specially important, and some of his papers are reprinted in Vol. 35.

Simultaneously with Buchez's work, a first attempt was made to collect and publish the *Oeuvres de Maximilien Robespierre* (2 vols. 1832, 3 vols. 1840–2), by Laponneraye, who had just suffered imprisonment for delivering a course of Sunday lectures to working men on the Revolution. This edition contained none of Robespierre's writings before 1789, and not all of them afterwards; but it was a significant gesture, and started a definite movement for his rehabilitation.

Three years later Laponneraye made himself responsible for a publication which has roused much controversy—*Mémoires de Charlotte Robespierre* (1835); in the second edition *sur ses deux frères* was added to the title. The violence with which Croker (*Essays*, p. 300) assailed the authenticity of these memoirs seems a little forced. The pretence that Robespierre's sister, who died in 1834, had left the completed MS. to Laponneraye for publication is transparent enough, and the style is Laponneraye's own: but there is no reason to doubt that he obtained most of his material in

the course of conversations with Charlotte; or that the
sentimentality with which it is clothed was as much that of
the repentant sister (cp. the language of her will; *Charlotte*,
116) as of the enthusiastic disciple. However this may be,
these *Mémoires* are our only authority for many details of
Robespierre's personal and domestic life.

Another admirer of Robespierre whose reminiscences
helped to revise the public estimate of him was Buonarroti,
a fellow-conspirator of Babeuf. Bronterre O'Brien, who
knew him, and used his writings, remembered seeing 'that
brave and venerable old man, at the advanced age of
seventy-eight, shed tears like a child at the mention of
Robespierre's name' (*Dissertation and Elegy*, 7). 'If the political doctrines comprised in Robespierre's Declaration of
Rights', he writes, 'and in the discourses which Robespierre
delivered in his last days, are viewed in juxtaposition with
the purity of his morals, his devotedness, his courage, his
modesty, and his rare disinterestedness, we are forced to
render a brilliant homage to so lofty a wisdom' (*History of
Babeuf's Conspiracy*, English translation, 1836); and the same
view characterizes his *Observations sur Maximilien Robespierre* (in *La Fraternité*, Sept. 17, 1842 ; reprinted in
R.H.R.F. 1912/476).

The same year O'Brien published the first volume of
his own *The Life and Character of Maximilian Robespierre*,
but was forced to discontinue the work owing to a 'dark,
cruel, and systematic private and public persecution,' on
the part of the English middle class, who feared, he thought,
his exposure of their 'System of fraud and murder.' For
O'Brien's later work, v. p. xxxvi.

English middle-class opinion found, at this time, a
serious and long-winded exponent in Sir A. Alison, whose
*History of Europe from the commencement of the French Revolution
to* 1815 came out in fourteen volumes between 1833 and 1842.
More critical in his elaborate marginal references, and
copious extracts from documents, than in his use of sources,

Alison makes no secret of his views: the French Revolution illustrates the perils of political innovation, the law of nature by which social evils, running to excess, purge themselves out of the body politic ('The same principle which drove the government of Robespierre through the Reign of Terror to the ninth of Thermidor impelled Napoleon to the snows of Russia and the rout of Waterloo'), and the overruling design of Providence, expressed in Bossuet's words, *Les hommes agitent, mais Dieu les meue.*

A less popular but more formidable champion of English middle-class views of the Revolution was J. W. Croker, whose reviews of French works on the period, contributed to the *Quarterly Review* between 1823 and 1853, were reprinted in 1857 as *Essays on the early period of the French Revolution.* Croker not only knew more about the Revolution than any other Englishman of his day, and was a diligent collector of the 48,000 pamphlets which place the British Museum second only to the Bibliothèque Nationale as a store-house of Revolutionary literature; but he also had a knowledge of parliamentary life which enabled him to expose the party intrigues and electoral devices of the revolutionary leaders. His essay on *Robespierre* (1835) is shrewder in its detailed judgements than in its wider generalizations; but it suggests that, intending simply to curse, the writer gradually realized that Robespierre was a psychological problem, and ended, not indeed by blessing, but by pitying: 'obscure and unaccountable as the whole of Robespierre's later conduct was, we repeat our inclination to believe that the chief cause of his fall was his being suspected of an intention of returning to some system of decency, mercy, and religion' (p. 420). The essay is still well worth reading.

The year 1837 saw the publication of one of the most famous, and (for English readers) most influential of all histories of the French Revolution. Critics of Carlyle (e.g. Acton, *Lectures on the French Revolution*, 358; Alger, *Paris in* 1793-4, Appendix D; Aulard, Preface to French edition of 1912) are agreed that his historical insight and dramatic sense triumphed over an inadequate study of authorities. His Robespierre—'that anxious, slight, in-effectual-looking man, under thirty (*but he was thirty-one*), in spectacles; his eyes (were the glasses off) troubled, care-ful; with upturned face, snuffing dimly the uncertain future times; complexion of a multiplex atribiliar colour, the final shade of which may be the pale sea-green;' 'most consistent, incorruptible of thin acrid men'—'acrid, implacable-impo-tent; dull-drawling, barren as the Harmattan wind'—is a cruelly life-like caricature. Unfortunately, Carlyle's failure to see the constructive side of the Revolution (but compare the views expressed in *Chartism*, 1839), and the passion which led him not to 'investigate much more about it, but to splash down what I know in large masses of colours, that it may look like a smoke and flame conflagration in the distance, which it is' (letter to Mrs. Carlyle, 1836), blinded him to most of what is important in Robespierre.

Ten years later, on the eve of the Revolution of 1848, and with an eye to the Republic which he was sure would follow, Lamartine wrote his *Histoire des Girondins* (1847)—a work in which feeling so distorts fact that Dumas ironically congratulated its author on having lifted history to the level of romance (Acton, 347). In this apotheosis of Republican virtue, Robespierre stood for Utopia: the pity was that the kind guest of the Duplays (of whom Lamartine heard from Mme Lebas) let himself become a tyrant and a terrorist—a Marius instead of a Cato—and so disqualified himself as an idol in 1848. The only type of revolutionism (Lamartine reckoned) fit for popular consumption was Girondism.

Esquiros, in his *Histoire des Montagnards*, the same year, set himself to answer Lamartine. To him the influence of the Girondins was transitory, that of the Jacobins permanent;

the *Montagne* was the Mount Sinai of the new order, from which, 'amid thunder and lightning, are revealed' (by the mouth of Moses-Robespierre), 'the oracles of transfigured humanity'.

The most learned and critical rehabilitation of Robespierre and Jacobinism that this period produced came from Louis Blanc, whose *Histoire de la Révolution française* (1847–) treated the Revolution as the climax of an age-long movement from Authority to Individualism, which itself culminated in a transition to Rousseauistic Fraternity. Of this creed Robespierre, an intellectual fanatic, whose faith and political foresight outweighed his crimes, was the apostle. In his portrait of the man, Blanc owed much to the reminiscences of Souberbielle, the Duplays' doctor, and to hitherto unpublished letters of Robespierre.

Meanwhile Michelet, the greatest national historian, had escaped from the glamour of Rome and the Middle Ages to proclaim (in *Le Peuple*, 1846) his belief in the undying unity and patriotism of the French people; and the approach of the Revolution of 1848 threw him into a passionate study of 1789. 'The unbelievable happiness of finding the story, after sixty years, so vivid and so exciting swelled my heart with a heroic joy, and the paper on which I wrote seemed impregnated with my tears' (Preface of 1868). 'From the first page to the last (he wrote) there is one hero, and one only—the People' (9/361). As the People's mood changes, so does its regard for Robespierre. In 1789 he is the diligent and austere lawyer who forces himself upon the attention of the Assembly. Soon he wins the support of the Jacobins, the women, and the priests; later, that of the provincial landlords. In the spring of 1791 he takes Mirabeau's place, and leads the Opposition; in the autumn he recreates and controls the Jacobin club. His position there, and his popularity as an incorruptible democrat, outweigh his pacifism in 1792, and his accusations of conspiracy in 1793. He is destroyed only when he becomes the dictator and terrorist of 1794, the author of the (to Michelet) offensive *Culte de l'Être Suprème* (Preface to Vol. 7). This view has, upon the whole, held the field, between the extremists who have either admired or detested everything that Robespierre did or said.

The controversies of the ten years before 1848 brought many smaller writers into the field for the defence or attack of the Jacobin leader. It will be enough to enumerate, as works of secondary importance: Schultze ('Wahrheitsfreund'), *Robespierre, mit Bezeihung auf die neueste Zeit* (1837); Elsner, *Maximilien Robespierre, Dictator von Frankreich* (1838); Rabbe, *Robespierre* (*Biographie universelle et portative*, 1838); Nodier, *Robespierre* (*Dictionnaire de la conversation*, 1838); Vieillard, *Notice sur Robespierre* (*Encyclopédie des gens du monde*, 1844); Guillot, *Maximilien Robespierre et Monsieur Thiers* (*Revue indépendante*, 1845); Gallois, *Étude sur Robespierre considéré comme journaliste* (*Histoire des journaux et journalistes de la Révolution française*, 1845–6); Reinier, *Robespierre* (*Dictionnaire encyclopédique de France*, 1845); Anon., *Histoire de Robespierre* (1846); Pont, *Sur Maximilien Robespierre* (*Le Haro*, Caen, 1847, answering Guillot); Travers, *Maximilien Robespierre* (*Journal*, Caen, 1847, answering Pont); Bergonnioux, *Robespierre* (1847); Pelletan, *Portraits de Robespierre et de Marat* (*La Presse*, 1848, answering Esquiros); Pillet, *Le Robespierre de M. de Lamartine* (1848); and a *Journal de la réforme sociale*, entitled *Le Robespierre*, of which four numbers were published in Paris in 1848.

VIII

Between 1848 and 1870 the constitutional reaction from republicanism towards Bonapartism, if not Bourbonism, suggested the idea, which may have got some help from *The Origin of Species* (1859), that the national development tended to 'revert to type'. But this notion, admirable as a clue to the past, was a dangerous argument to apply to the future.

If Napoleon could justify his regime as true to the French liking for Liberal Dictatorships, so could his opponents justify rebellion against him as true to the *frondeur* tradition of 1649, 1789, 1830, and 1848. If a tendency towards kings was French, so was a tendency towards regicide. If the Revolution was an integral part of the national history, Jacobinism was an integral part of the Revolution. If Napoleon was a French liberator, so was Robespierre. The interest aroused in Robespierre by Laponneraye, Buchez, and Louis Blanc was carried almost to excess in the years following 1848. His speeches were collected and published; details of his family and youth were disinterred; his biography was written in English and Italian; he became the subject of a German tragedy. Finally Hamel, collecting every fact that could be learnt about him, composed not so much a Life as a panegyric, and did his best to prohibit, for the future, all secular study of a canonized saint.

The period opens with an English work. George Henry Lewes, the spiritual ancestor of our amateur philosophers, was led to write *The Life of Maximilian Robespierre* (1849) by interest in the Revolution of 1848. He relied mainly on Lamartine, Michelet, and Louis Blanc, the last of whom lent him some hitherto unpublished letters of Robespierre. Avoiding extremes either of praise or blame, he represented the man as a political fanatic—'honest, self-denying, and consistent', but also 'cowardly, relentless, pedantic, unloving, intensely vain, and morbidly envious'; one who 'has not left the legacy to mankind of one grand thought, nor the example of one generous and exalted action' (394–7).

A year later Villiaumé at last published the results of long investigation and meditation. His *Histoire de la Révolution française* (1879) attempted to rehabilitate Marat as Robespierre's collaborator, and as the author of most of the beneficent acts of the Revolution.

Lodieu's *Maximilien Robespierre*, published at Arras the same year, contained thirty pages of biography, and a hundred of *considérations*, showing how Lamartine had failed to do Robespierre justice. This was the book which roused the Abbé Proyart to re-edit, in his uncle's name, Le Blond's *La vie et les crimes de Robespierre* (v. p. xxi).

A weightier reply to the apologists for Jacobinism, inspired by Garat's Memoirs, and by the coup d'état of 1851, was Barante's *Histoire de la Convention Nationale*—the work of 'a more or less liberal Orléanist, who has no sympathy with the democracy of the Year II' (Aulard, *Etudes*, 7/218), and who sees, in the overthrow of the republic of 1848, the condemnation of that of 1793. Robespierre, whom Garat compared to Jesus, was a despot who died because he dared not end the Terror.

The *Geschichte des Revolutionszeit* of von Sybel (1853–; English and French translations), whilst anticipating de Tocqueville's view of French history (Acton, 369), studied the Revolution, for the first time, in its relation to European history as a whole. To von Sybel, as to Louis Blanc, the revolutionary movement of 1789 fell into line with the disciplined progress of the modern world from authority to freedom; but it was carried to extremes of violence and immorality, became purely destructive, and therefore ended in military despotism and international reaction. In such a scheme, political personalities count for little, and the fall of Robespierre is described 'as an episode in the partition of Poland' (Acton).

In *L'Ancien régime et la Révolution* (1857; English translations) de Tocqueville began his impeccable study of French society on the eve of the Revolution; but the sequel, which was to compare it with post-revolutionary society, was never written. If he had described the Jacobin regime, he would doubtless have seen in it an instance of French political atavism; had he drawn Robespierre, it would have been in the attitudes of a Louis XIV.

In 1857 Bronterre O'Brien followed up his unfinished *Life and character of Robespierre* (p. xxx) with *An Elegy on the death of Robespierre*, a poem in twenty parts, in honour of 'the greatest reformer and legislator the world has yet

known:' two years later he included this in a larger publication, *A dissertation and elegy on the life and death of the immortal
Maximilian Robespierre*, together with 'notes in elucidation'
of both compositions, which included a *Life of Robespierre* in
sixteen chapters, down to the end of the Constituent
Assembly.

It was left to Hamel to consummate the work of Robespierre's admirers in his *Histoire de Robespierre* (1862).
Collecting, with immense diligence and devotion, every
tradition or document that bore on his subject, and professing complete impartiality, frankness, and criticism of his
sources (Preface to Vol. I), he is yet so carried away by his
enthusiasm for the Revolution of 1848, by his indignation
with attacks upon his grandfather's friend, Saint-Just, and
by the charms of rhetorical hero-worship, that every word
and act of Robespierre is viewed in a distorting glass, and
each detail added only serves to make the whole picture less
trustworthy.

It was not unnatural that Hamel's uncritical eulogy of
Robespierre should be followed by a reaction.

Quinet was, like Michelet, a democrat, whose lectures
(at the Collège de France in 1841–5) helped to bring about
the Revolution of 1848: unlike Michelet, he believed that
religion was the basis of social and political reform, and in
his *La Révolution* (1865) attributed the failure of the Revolution to its refusal to break with the Catholic Church, and
to put Protestantism in its place (1/163). Robespierre's
solution—a civic religion à la Rousseau—he could not
accept; and was puzzled by Robespierre himself, inclining
to the view that he was a mere talker, who shrank from
personal dictatorship (2/293, 310).

Vermorel's *Oeuvres de Robespierre*, a selection from the
speeches, with a historical introduction (1865), was accused
by Hamel of *dénigrement systématique* of his hero.

*La Jeunesse de Robespierre, et la convocation des États-
Généraux dans l'Artois*, by J. Paris (1870, based on articles in

Mémoires de l'Académie d'Arras, 1869) is the most important contribution made to the study of Robespierre's early career. Based on long research into local archives, it provides an indispensable documentation; and the fact that the author had as a colleague the Abbé J. M. Proyart (v. p. xxi), and to some extent drew on his uncle's reminiscences, (v. Fleischmann, Introduction to *Mémoires de Charlotte Robespierre*) does not seriously detract from the importance of his book.

Of minor works during this period, attention may be called to: Dinaux, *La Société des Rosati à Arras* (1850)—an account of the Poetry Club to which Robespierre belonged; Opitz, *Robespierre's Triumph und Sturtz* (1850); Chabot, *Ce bon Monsieur de Robespierre!!!*, with the motto, *Lecteur, ne pleurez pas son sort, Car, s'il vivait, tu serais mort*; Grille, *La Fleur des Pois—Carnot et Robespierre* (1853); Jorry, *Les hommes de la Terreur* (1854); Maggiolo, *Robespierre* (1856); Mélicocq (La Fons, Baron de), *La famille Robespierre et ses armoiries* (*Archives du Nord de la France*, 1858, 3e série, 6/72); von Ising, *Robespierre: ein Trauerspiel* (1859); and Quérard, *Robespierre* (*La France littéraire*, 1859–64),—summing him up as 'the French Caligula.'

IX

The disasters of 1870–1871 took the heart out of historical apologists, whether for Bonapartism or republicanism: it only remained for Taine, turning from anatomy to history, to dissect the dead body of the Revolution, and enumerate the symptoms of the national disease. Martin's level-headed survey did something to redress the balance, and towards the end of the period Sorel, taking up von Sybel's work, described in a masterly way the international relations of the whole revolutionary epoch, which was by this time being seriously studied abroad.

In his *History of English Literature* (1863) Taine had disputed Carlyle's view of the People in revolution; his experience of the Paris Commune brought him round to it, and he entered on the study of the events of 1789 with a conviction, as passionate as Michelet's, that the People was the villain of the piece. But whereas Michelet threw himself romantically into every mood of his characters, Taine had fixed a formula for them all: 'his Danton is a savage, his Robespierre a pedant, his Marat a lunatic, his Napoleon a *condottieri*, and the Revolution a fit of alcoholic frenzy' (Jullian, *Historiens français du XIXe siècle*, cxxvi). Consequently the part of his great work dealing with the Revolution—*Les origines de la France contemporaine*, Vol. 4, *La Révolution* (1876)—is more a pathological study than an impartial analysis of the facts.

Ch. d'Héricault's *La Révolution de Thermidor* (1878) is, as the sub-title says, a study of *Robespierre et le Comité de Salut Public*, based partly upon fresh sources, and treated in great detail; but the upshot is a portrait of Robespierre not unlike the conventional one that the author claims to reject: he is a man who aims at personal power by following every turn of public opinion, and by destroying every rival who gets in his way. At the same time, his policy, like the course of the Revolution, becomes increasingly constructive and governmental: even the Terror was an attempt to preserve the work of the Revolution (52–3). This book anticipates much modern work (e.g. by Mathiez, Lenôtre, and Kerr) upon the causes of the fall of Robespierre.

When Henri Martin, in the course of his long survey of French history, reached the *Histoire de France depuis* 1789 (1878), he had come to regard the troubles of those times as part of a series of births and deaths, advances and retreats, ending in the final achievement of national liberty by the Third Republic. Asking himself why the Revolution of 1789 had failed, he answered that, if the Republic had been declared in 1791, before the outbreak of war, it might have survived—a view which justifies the implicit, though not the expressed, policy of Robespierre during the winter of 1791-2.

Sorel was a friend of Taine, but trained in law instead of medicine, and viewing history, not from a laboratory bench, but from the windows of the Quai d'Orsay. His *L'Europe et la Révolution Française* (8 vols., 1885-) is set out with so much art that it hides a certain conventionality of mind. His Robespierre is a foil to Danton, obscure where Danton was lucid (too lucid for a revolution), austere where Danton was immoral; but at bottom 'one of those shallow and empty souls who become famous in history because they are, for a moment, the puppets of fate' (3/511). This is too easy a view; and overlooks characteristics which had puzzled, and were to puzzle, more inquisitive minds.

The minor works of this period include several of more than usual importance: Morley, *Robespierre* (in *Critical Miscellanies*, Vol. I, 1877)—a brilliant and suggestive study, in which Robespierre is represented as essentially a speaker, driven into action through fear of being left behind—a Parisian Cicero; Brunnemann, *Maximilien Robespierre* (1880); Kolisch, *Marie-Antoinette, Mirabeau, Robespierre* (1880); Lecesne, *Arras sous la Révolution* (1882); and Schumm, *Maximilien Robespierre* (1885)—a Catholic-monarchist corrective to the panegyric of Hamel and Brunnemann.

Amongst articles dealing with Robespierre during this period are:

1878. Tarbouriesh, *Une anecdote révolutionnaire* (Revue Gascogne, 19/535)—Robespierre's execution.

1879. Dubois, *Deux apologistes de Gresset en 1785* (Mem. Acad. Amiens, 3/5/1).

1882. Nodier, *Recherches sur l'éloquence révolutionnaire* (R.F. 2/779).

1884. Advielle, *Les portraits de Robespierre et de Lebon au Musée Carnavalet* (R.F. 6/822, 915).

1886–1914

1885. Mallet du Pan, *Le Comité de Salut Public, La Convention, et les Jacobins* (R.F. 7/259); *Certificat de remise à Robespierre de la medaille du* 10 *août* (R.F. 8/723); Bernard, *Quelque spoésies de Robespierre* (R.F. 9/97, 396).

X

The organization of historical studies in France, where it has probably been better done than in any other country (Jullian, cxxiv) was definitely directed to the study of the French Revolution by the appointment of Alphonse Aulard to a Lectureship founded by the Paris Municipal Council in 1886. From that date until the eve of the Great War he composed or edited a series of important books which influenced all subsequent workers in the same field. The only aspect of the Revolution that he tended to ignore —its social-economic background—was enthusiastically taken up, first, by Jean Jaurès, who induced the Government to make a grant, from 1905 onwards, towards the publication of documents bearing on the economic side of the Revolution; and then by Albert Mathiez, who, starting as a follower of Aulard, founded in 1907–8 an independent, and increasingly hostile society and magazine, devoted to a socialistic and Robespierrist interpretation of the Revolution. Both Aulard and Mathiez formed schools of investigators: libraries were ransacked, and documents published at such a rate that constructive work on a large scale became increasingly difficult. But, for the first time, historians were able to feel that they had their hand on the real pulse of the People in revolution; and foreigners, not only in England and Germany, but also in Italy, Scandinavia, Russia, and America, were able to study, from the original documents, problems to which they found analogies in their own national history.

So many books have to be mentioned during this period that it will be best to classify them, rather arbitrarily, according to their importance for the study of Robespierre.

First, certain works of primary importance.

Aulard's *La Société des Jacobins* (6 vols. 1889–97) reprinted, with a historical and critical Introduction, all that seemed important in the papers and reported proceedings of the Jacobin Club. It is indispensable for a study of Robespierre's activities there.

Aulard's *Recueil des Actes du Comité de Salut Public* (12 vols. 1889–99) did the same for the papers of the Committee of Public Safety, and is equally indispensable.

Morse Stephens, *A History of the French Revolution* (2 vols. 1891) was the first English attempt to use part, at least, of the new evidence in a general history of the Revolution. Learned and sensible, it remained unfinished, ending in 1793. The same author's *Orators of the French Revolution* (2 vols. 1892) reprinted, with biographical and critical comments, a selection from the speeches of the revolutionary leaders.

Aulard's *Études et Leçons sur la Révolution française*, of which nine series appeared between 1893 and 1924, were reprints of articles on all aspects of the Revolution from *La Révolution française*, of which he was editor, and from other periodicals. They contain a good many articles dealing directly or indirectly with Robespierre.

Lord Acton's *Lectures on the French Revolution*, delivered at Cambridge between 1895 and 1899, were published posthumously in 1910. Written when Aulard was only beginning his work, and when it was still possible to say that 'in a few years all will be known that ever can be known' (372–3), but by a man whose insight and experience outweighed many authorities, these Lectures are of lasting value. Acton's judgement on Robespierre illustrates his limitations —'the most hateful character in the forefront of history since Machiavelli reduced to a code the wickedness of public men.'

In 1896 appeared Vol. VIII, *La Révolution française*, of the *Histoire générale* edited by Lavisse and Rambaud. Most of it was written by Aulard, and has the authority of his wide knowledge. 'Aulard's narrative is not complete, and lacks detail; but it is intelligent and constructive beyond all others, and shows the standard that has been reached by a century of study' (Acton, 372).

Aulard's *Histoire politique de la Révolution française* (1901) is a masterly synthesis of all that could be learnt, particularly from the new collections of official documents, as to the 'origins and development of democracy and the republic' (sub-title) between 1789 and 1804. To Aulard, Robespierre is the champion of the People, whose 'sincerity, perfect honesty, and austerity earned him the title of The Incorruptible' (422), but who changed his political colour with that of popular opinion, made an idol of his own virtues, and defeated his highest ends by *ses rancunes éternelles, inexorables*.

The *Histoire socialiste de la Révolution française*, by Jaurès (5 vols. 1901–4; new edit. by Mathiez, 8 vols. 1922) views the Revolution as the first stage in the progress of European society from economic bondage to spiritual liberty—the second beginning in 1848, and the third in 1871 (1/25). To Jaurès, Robespierre, though a democrat and a libertarian, is an arid, short-sighted leader, 'a strange mixture of optimism and pessimism—optimism as regards the moral worth of the People, pessimism as regards the equal distribution of property'; for whilst he deplored poverty, he would do nothing to destroy the monopoly of wealth (3/400). Here Jaurès anticipates the later Russian repudiation of Robespierre and Jacobinism. His book, especially the early volumes, remains a richly documented and often eloquent appreciation of the social-economic aspects of the Revolution.

Vol. 8 of the Cambridge Modern History, *The French Revolution* (1904), by Montagu and Moreton Macdonald, follows the usual plan of Acton's great compilation—something between expert and popular treatment, continuous history and detached essays. The standpoint is that of an enlightened conservatism.

Prince Kropotkin's *Velikaya Frantsuzskaya Revolyntsiya* (*La Grande Révolution*, 1789–1793; published in French, English, and German, 1909; not in Russian till 1917) summed up the work of Michelet, Blanc, and Jaurès in a vivid and interesting sketch, which, moreover, applied to France, for the first time, ideas learnt in Russia, and from the practice of revolution, about the land question, the class-struggle, and the necessary failure of a movement which aims at the economic benefit of individuals, not of communities (E.T., 2/562-2). In Kropotkin's view, Robespierre already tends to become what he is in present-day Russian thought, a typical *petit bourgeois*, the product rather than the author of a policy, who rises and falls with the economics of Jacobinism.

At the end of this period (1911) Madelin, skimming the cream off the new knowledge of the Revolution, brought Carlyle up to date in his dramatic *La Révolution française* (English translation, 1916). It is the work of a receptive emotional mind, influenced by a study of Fouché to see the shadier aspects of revolutionary politics, and by admiration for Napoleon to regard the Empire as the logical outcome of the Revolution. Robespierre becomes a self-conscious, self-centred, 'infallible pontiff' (381), an Inquisitor, who dies as the victim of a 'palace revolution' (430). Madelin's later *Histoire politique de la nation française* (1926) shows, by the small proportion of space allotted to the Revolution, that he regards it as little more than an aberration in the monarchical course of French history from Louis XIV to Napoleon.

Books of secondary importance during this period are: Bravo, *Robespierre: cronica dramatica del Terror*, 1887; Juste, *Robespierre* (1887); Barbier, *Les Rosati* (1888); *The contemporary history of the French Revolution* (1889)—a convenient compilation from the *Annual Register*; Kleinschmudt, *Characterbilder aus der französische Revolution* (1889); Strada, *Robespierre et la révolution de l'humanité* (1890); Bax, *The Story of the French Revolution* (1890)—originally written for *Justice*, and including an attack on Robespierre, in the Russian manner, as 'a *petit bourgeois*, a Philistine to the backbone, who desired a republic of *petit bourgeois* virtues, with himself at the head, and was prepared to wade through a sea of blood for the accomplishment of his end' (v); Toft, *Statskoupet den 9 thermidor aar II—Robespierre's Fald* (1890); Bernard, *Quelques poésies de Robespierre* (1890); Barbier, *Lettres inédites d'Augustin Robespierre à Antoine Buissart* (1890–1); Welschinger, *Le livret de Robespierre* (in *Le Roman de Dumouriez*, 1890); Sardou, *Thermidor* (1891)—a play attacking the Terror, which led to a debate in the French Chamber, and to a speech by Clemenceau declaring the Revolution to be a *bloc*, which one must accept or reject as a whole; Eckhardt, *Figuren und Ansichten der Pariser Schreckenzeit* (1893)—with a careful but rather hostile portrait of Robespierre; Lenôtre, *Chez Robespierre* (*Paris Révolutionnaire*, 1894)—one of this author's over-imaginative reconstructions; Gros, *Le comité de Salut Public de la Convention nationale* (1894)—useful for Robespierre's work on the Committee; Sardou, *La maison de Robespierre* (1895)—an important contribution to an unimportant controversy; Cabanès, *Robespierre intime* (*Le cabinet secret de l'histoire*, Vol. 3, 1897); Bleibtrau, *Von Robespierre zu Buddha* (1899); Brink, *Robespierre and the Red Terror* (1899); Stéfane-Pol, *Autour de Robespierre: le conventionnel Le Bas* (1901)—with important details of Robespierre's life at the Duplays', drawn from the reminiscences of Mme Le Bas; Belloc; *Robespierre: a study* (1901)—the author's reactions to Hamel's *Histoire de Robespierre*; reissued in 1927 without any use of later evidence; Alger, *The Fall of Robespierre* (Chap. xi of *Paris in 1789–94*, a store of curious information, 1902); de Poli, *Maximilien Robespierre, héraldiste* (1903); Salvemini, *La Rivoluzione francese, 1789–92* (1905)—a standard Italian work, ending with Valmy; the second edition influenced by Jaurès; Robespierre represented as the champion of the People (205); Alméras, *Les dévotes de Robespierre* (1905)—an anti-Robespierrist study of the Théot case; Stéfane-Pol, *De Robespierre à Fouché* (1906); Schmidt, *Pages choisies des grands republicains—Robespierre* (1907); Savine and Bournand, *Le 9 thermidor* (1907); Vellay, *Discours et Rapports de Robespierre* (1908)—a convenient selection; Peise, *Quelques vers*

623

de Maximilien Robespierre (1909); Fleischmann, *Robespierre et les femmes* (1909; English translation, misnamed *Robespierre and the women he loved,* 1913); Warwick, *Robespierre and the French Revolution* (1909)—the third volume of a trilogy beginning with Mirabeau and Danton; Buffenoir, *Les portraits de Robespierre* (1910)—*the* authority on this subject; Clerget, *Robespierre destructeur de la première République* (1910); Fleischmann, *Charlotte Robespierre et ses Mémoires* (1910)—an indispensable but badly produced edition of the Memoirs, with additional matter; Deprez, *Oeuvres complètes de Maximilien Robespierre* (1910)—begun under the auspices of the Société des Études Robespierristes, this ended after publishing *Les Oeuvres littéraires* (3 fascicules) and *Les oeuvres judiciaires* (4 fascicules); Barbier and Vellay, *Oeuvres complètes de Maximilien Robespierre* (1910)—begun in connexion with the *Revue historique de la Révolution française,* it never got beyond Vol. I, *Oeuvres judiciaires,* 1782–9; *Revue des curiosités révolutionnaires*—a special issue devoted to Robespierre (1910); Lesueur, *Oeuvres complètes de Maximilien Robespierre* (1912)—planned by the Société des Études Robespierristes, its publication suspended by the war; Clauzel, *Études humaines: fanatiques: I. Maximilien Robespierre* (1912) —of little historical value; e.g. Chap. I is constructed round the mistaken idea that Robespierre was nicknamed *Le romain*; Godard, *Le procès du 9 thermidor* (1912).

Amongst articles dealing with Robespierre during this period are:

1887. *Notes et souvenirs de Courtois* (R.F. 11/806, 922, 998).

1888. Robinet, *Robespierre aux archives* (R.F. 15/255)—his signature on the night of 9 Thermidor. *Un pamphlet sur Robespierre en 1791* (R.F. 15/457).

1890. Aulard, *Le Comité de Salut Public* (R.F. 18/5, 125, 232, 434, 19/27).

1891. Pagart d'Hermansart, *Le paratonnerre de Saint-Omer* (L'Indépendant du Pas de Calais, August 25–7). Ganderax, *A propos de Thermidor* (Revue bleue, 47/324). Aulard, *Le culte de l'Être Suprême* (R.F. 21/5, 134, 226, 307).

1892. *Robespierre et Méda* (R.F. 22/400). Aulard, *Le club des Jacobins* (R.F. 23/106).

1894. Dubov, *Les conventionnels poètes*: Robespierre (Revue bleue, 4/1/812).

1895. Métin, *Les origines du Comité de Sûreté Générale* (R.F. 28/257, 340). Guillaume. *Le personnel du Comité de Sûreté Générale* (R.F. 28/124, 219). *Fragonard et Robespierre* (R.F. 28/278, 462). Hamel, *La Maison de Robespierre* (R.F. 29/193, 380).

1896. Sallier, *Robespierre, ses principes, son système politique* (R.Q.H. 60/135). Aulard, *La politique religieuse du Comité de Salut Public* (R.F. 30/97, 31/9). Charavay, *Robespierre jeune et Bouchotte* (R.F. 30/549).

1897. Aulard, *Le bureau du club des Jacobins* (R.F. 31/415) —names of officials.

1898. Bonnal de Ganges, *Robespierre dictateur* (Rev. Mond. cath. 134/21). Albalat, *Une psychologie de Robespierre* (N.R. 111/19, 286). *Quelques mots sur Robespierre* (Carn. H. 2/880). *Les descendants de Robespierre* (Int. des Cherch. et Cur. 5/37, 278, 491, 576. 754, 868, 38/14).

1899. Bonnal de Ganges, *Robespierre et Carrier en Vendée* (Rev. Mond. Cath. 6/22/122). *La sœur de Marat et la sœur de Robespierre* (Ch. Med. 6/623, 701). Coyecque, *La Maison de Robespierre* (Bull. Soc. Paris, 26/36). Téo, *Le Club Breton* (R.F. 36/385).

1900. *Relation de l'exécution de Robespierre* (Int. des Cherch. et Cur. 41/181). Zagoulaief, *La mort de Robespierre* (Rev. Britannique, 1/5, 174; 2/5, 181). Lévy-Schneider, *Les démêlés dans le Comité de Salut Public* (R.F. 38/97). Guillaume, *Le personnel du Comité de Salut Public* (R.F. 38/297).

1901. Daux, *Dictature de Robespierre et les mystiques révolutionnaires* (R.H. 79/224)—the Théot case. Mathiez, *Catherine Théot* (R.F. 40/481).

1902. *L'hymne à l'Être Suprême* (R.F. 43/347, 44/13, 45/130, 259, 47/543).

1904. *Louis XVIII et Robespierre* (Int. des Cherch. et Cur. 49/719). Pilon, *La jeunesse sentimentale de Robespierre* (Rev. bleue, 5/1/154). Pinson, *Fête célébrée en souvenir de la chute de*

Robespierre, 1797 (Rev. Hist. Versailles 1904, 316). Aulard, *Le Comité de Salut Public et les biens nationaux* (R.F. 46/514, 47/62).

1906. *Notes oratoires de Robespierre* (R.F. 50/451).

1908. Mathiez, *Un portrait de Robespierre* (A.R. 1/27), Barbier, *Le flambeau de Provence et la chandelle d'Arras* (A.R. 1/33). Lévi, *Robespierre dans le théâtre allemand* (A.R. 1/38). *Robespierre aux Rosati* (A.R. 1/90). Buffenoir, *Les portraits de Robespierre* (A.R. 1/244, 457, 641, 2/55, 220, 377). *Les Lettres inconnues de Robespierre* (A.R. 1/300). *Robespierre à l'Assemblée constituante* (A.R. 1/482). *La popularité de Robespierre en 1791* (A.R. 1/487). Lévi, *Autour du 10 août, 1793* (R.F. 55/236).

1909. Vellay, *Robespierre et le procès du paratonnerre* (A.R. 2/25, 201). *Une maladie de Robespierre* (A.R. 2/82). *Robespierre en l'An IV* (A.R. 2/84). *Guffroy contre Robespierre en 1789* (A.R. 2/243). Mathiez, *Robespierre et la déchristianisation* (A.R. 2/321, 513). *Un entretien avec M. Hamel* (R.F. 57/355).

1910. Pelissier, *Robespierre et une femme* (R.H.R.F. 1/45, 240). Vellay, *Mémoires de Charlotte Robespierre* (R.H.R.F. 1/110, 254, 436, 571). Madelin, *La dictature de Robespierre* (R.D.M. 6/1/867). Vellay, *Robespierre et Buzot en 1791* (R.H.R.F. 2/253). Atalone, *Un oeuvre de jeunesse de Robespierre* (Marches de l'Est. 1911, 300). Bart, *Une légende sur Robespierre* (Rev. Cur. Rev. 2/200, 230)—the story of Suzanne Ferber. Rudler, *Robespierre dans la correspondance de Benjamin Constant* (A.R. 3/92). *Fausse légende sur la famille de Robespierre* (A.R. 3/103). *Robespierre chez Duplay* (A.R. 3/106). Mathiez, *Robespierre et le culte de l'Être Suprême* (A.R. 3/209). Fleischmann, *Charlotte Robespierre et Guffroy* (A.R. 3/321). Mathiez, *La politique de Robespierre et le 9 Thermidor expliqués par Buonarroti* (A.R. 3/481). Fribourg, *Le Club des Jacobins en 1790* (R.F. 58/507, 59/52, 129).

1911. *Robespierre apprécié par Mme Julien* (A.R. 4/93). *Robespierre et Talleyrand* (A.R. 4/102). Letaconnoux, *Un portrait inconnu de Robespierre* (A.R. 4/206). *Un témoignage sur Robespierre* (A.R. 4/231). Vermale, *Leconte de Lisle et Robespierre* (A.R. 4/289). Fleischmann, *Le Masque mortuaire de Robespierre* (A.R. 4/601). Lévy, *Le robespierrisme en 1849* (A.R. 4/654). *Charlotte Robespierre et la réaction thermidorienne* (R.F. 60/344).

1912. Marcel, *Contribution à l'iconographie de Robespierre* (A.R. 5/37). *Un arrière grand oncle de Robespierre* (A.R. 5/88). *Robespierre et le Comité de Salut Public* (A.R. 5/89). Lesueur, *Généalogie de la famille de Robespierre* (A.R. 5/237). Lesueur, *Robespierre et Charles Michaud* (A.R. 5/325). Vermale, *Danton, Robespierre, Comte, et Aulard* (A.R. 5/625). *Ouvrard et Robespierre* (A.R. 5/692).

1913. Grasilier, *Un secrétaire de Robespierre: Simon Duplay* (R.H. 114/117). Lesueur, *Un médaillon inédit de Robespierre* (A.R. 6/87), Mathiez, *Les divisions de la Montagne* (A.R. 6/209). Marat, *Défense de Robespierre en 1792* (A.R. 6/392). Mathiez, *La politique sociale de Robespierre* (A.R. 6/551). Lesueur, *Comment Robespierre composa l'éloge de Gresset* (A.R. 6/635).

XI

The immediate effects of the Great War upon the study of the French Revolution were the loss of life among historians, especially the younger men, the representatives of new ideas; the breaking off of undertakings, such as editions of Robespierre's works, begun before 1914; the disorganization of studies, e.g. through failure to produce or to take in periodicals; the distraction of interest and funds from scholarship and research to controversy and propaganda; and still more serious, both during and after the war, the suppression, in some countries, of independent thought and free enquiry. It is too soon to estimate the results of all this, or to assess the general trend of revolutionary studies since 1918; but two influences are obvious— that of Mathiez, and that of Marxism—the one idolizing Robespierre, and finding the essence of the Revolution in a kind of state socialism; the other rejecting Robespierre and his ideas as *petit bourgeois*, and finding, to some extent in Marat, but more fully in Babeuf, the beginnings of communism and the proletarian revolution.

Lukin, *Maksimilian Robesper* (*Maximilian Robespierre*, 1919)—described by the author as 'a scientific popular work, based on original documents', deals with Robespierre's career under the three Assemblies, with special attention to agrarian and economic questions. The heading of the Introduction—'Contradictoriness of class interests at the outset of the Revolution'—indicates the modern Russian point of view.

Sagnac and Pariset, *La Révolution* (1789–92 by Pariset, 1793–9 by Sagnac, in *Histoire de France contemporaine*, ed. Lavisse, 1920) is the most complete, impartial, and well-arranged narrative produced since the war, with discussions of disputed points, and full bibliographies.

Mathiez, *Robespierre Terroriste* (1921) contains two papers expounding Mathiez's view of Robespierre, and critical editions of two essential documents—the *Carnet*, and the *Notes* for Saint-Just's report on the Dantonists.

Mathiez, *La Révolution française* (1922, English translation, 1926) sums up his detailed studies of the subject in a closely-packed narrative, showing intimate knowledge of parties and personalities, stress on social-economic factors, and Robespierrist sympathy. The best account hitherto given of the inner history of the Revolution.

Zacker, *Robesper* (*Robespierre*, 1925)—a short biography, but illustrative of the Russian Marxian standpoint, to which the class-struggle and the economic motive are all-important, and Robespierre is '*petit bourgeois* in his ideas and his activity, just as he is *petit bourgeois* in his personal life' (91)—the representative of a party which fails, and is cast aside, as soon as its economic limitations became a drag on the wheel of proletarian progress.

Michon's edition of the *Correspondance de Maximilien et Augustin Robespierre* (1926) prints all Robespierre's known letters, and summarizes those of his correspondents. The work is indispensable to the study of Robespierre, but might have been better done, and requires considerable addenda and corrigenda: cp. p. xvi.

Lenôtre, *Robespierre et la Mère de Dieu* (1926, English

translation, *The rise and fall of Robespierre*, 1927) is the most ambitious attempt of the anti-Robespierrist school to provide an alternative to Mathiez's account of his fall, special stress being laid on the Théot case.

Kerr, *The Reign of Terror* (1927) is a detailed study of the last phase of Jacobinism, and of the fall of Robespierre, by an American follower of Mathiez.

Mazzuchelli, *Robespierre* (1930) is a competent Italian biography, using some of the new material, especially for the early life of Robespierre.

Lefebvre, Guyot, and Sagnac, *La Révolution française* (1930). A comprehensive history, from a modernized Sybel-Sorel standpoint, with a concluding section on *The French Revolution and European civilization*, by Sagnac.

Ording, *Le bureau de police du Comité de Salut Public* (1930) is a study of a little-known aspect of Robespierre's work in connexion with the Terror, essential for a judgement on his responsibility for it.

Somerset Ward, *Robespierre: a study in degeneration* (1934) attempts to interpret Robespierre's life psychologically, as an instance of the perversion of high faculties by wrong choices. The writer makes use, for the first time in English, of much of the new material, especially for Robespierre's early life.

Villat. *La Révolution et l'Empire* (I. *Les Assemblées révolutionuaires*, 1936) is valuable for its *Notes* discussing disputed points.

Walter, *Robespierre* (I. *La montée vers le pouvoir*, 1936) is the first attempt of a modern French historian to write a critical life of Robespierre ; and it incorporates some new documents.

Books of secondary importance for the study of Robespierre, in this period are:

Mathiez, *Études Robespierristes*, I. *La Conspiration de l'étranger* (1917), II. *La corruption parlementaire sous la Terreur* (1918)—both containing papers on Robespierre; Webster,

The French Revolution (1919)—interpreting it as an Orléanist conspiracy; Bourgin, *Die französische Revolution* (*Weltgeschichte*, Vol. 8, 1922)—translated from the French; Elton, *The revolutionary idea in France* (1923)—raising the question whether Robespierre was the founder of modern socialism; Hentig, *Robespierre: Studien zur Psychopathologie des Machttriebes* (1924); Bainville, *Histoire de France* (1924)—includes a monarchist view of the Revolution; Vingtrinier, *La contre-révolution, 1789–91* (1924–5)—a careful study of an aspect of the Revolution hitherto neglected; Mathiez, *Autour de Robespierre* (1925)—reprinting articles on persons with whom Robespierre had dealings; Brachvogel, *Robespierre* (1925); Zacker, *9 Termidora* (*Le 9 thermidor*, 1926); Bradby, *A short History of the French Revolution* (1926)—a competent narrative, using modern knowledge; Barthou, *Le neuf thermidor* (1926)—anti-Robespierrist; Mathiez, *La vie chère et le mouvement social sous la Terreur* (1927)—important for Robespierre's relations with the *Enragés*; Gaxotte, *La Révolution française* (1928, English translation)—Catholic-royalist; Thompson, *Leaders of the French Revolution* (1928) —with a short study of Robespierre; Gottschalk, *The Era of the French Revolution* (1929)—an interesting survey of 1715–1815, by Mathiez's most expert American follower; Duplay, *Robespierre amant de la Patrie* (1929)—a romance, by a descendant of Robespierre's host; Lecomte, *Au chant de la Marseillaise: Danton et Robespierre* (1929); Laski, *The Socialist tradition in the French Revolution* (1930); Duplay, *Robespierre chez les Duplay* (1930); Whitham, *A biographical history of the French Revolution* (1930); Mathiez, *Girondins et Montagnards* (1930)—contains several essays bearing on Robespierre; Hazen, *The French Revolution* (1932); Gershon, *The French Revolution and Napoleon* (1934); Sieburg, *Robespierre* (1935)—in the popular 'screen' style; Renier, *Robespierre* (1936); Korngold, *Robespierre* (1936); Michon, *Robespierre et la guerre révolutionnaire* (1937).

Amongst articles dealing with Robespierre during this period are:

1914. Mathiez, *Les divisions dans les Comités de gouvernement* (R.H. 118/70). Lesueur, *Les origines et la fortune de la famille de Robespierre* (A.R. 7/179). Mathiez, *Robespierre jeune en Franche-Comté* (A.R. 7/309, 8/79).

1916. Mathiez, *Robespierre et l'armée* (A.R. 8/131). Rouanet, *Robespierre d'après les comptes rendus parlementaires en 1789* (A.R. 8/336). Bergounioux, *Robespierre* (A.R. 8/405). *La popularité de Robespierre en 1789* (A.R. 8/720).

1917. Mathiez, *Robespierre et Benjamin Vaughan* (A.R. 9/1). Rouanet, *Robespierre et le journal 'L'Union'* (A.R. 9/145). Mathiez, *Fouquier-Tinville et Robespierre* (A.R. 9/239). Combet, *Les arrêtés de Robespierre jeune* (A.R. 9/314). Mathiez, *Babeuf et Robespierre* (A.R. 9/370). Rouanet, *Les séances de la Constituante* (A.R. 9/433, 610, 10/162, 289, 11/62, 195). Lintilhac, *Dans la salle du Manège* (R.F. 70/289).

1918. Mathiez, *Le carnet de Robespierre* (A.R. 10/1). *Documents sur Robespierre et sa famille* (A.R. 10/400).

1919. Rouanet, *Michelet et la légende antirobespierriste* (A.R. 11/28). *Robespierre jugé par Napoléon* (A.R. 11/116). *Nouveaux témoignages sur Catherine Théot* (A.R. 11/388). *Le testament de Charlotte Robespierre* (A.R. 11/535). Lévi, *Saint-Just et Robespierre* (R.F. 72/387).

1920. Mathiez, *Robespierre et Aigoin* (A.R. 12/33). Vermale, *Joseph le Maistre et Robespierre* (A.R. 12/117). Mathiez, *Robespierre terroriste* (A.R. 12/177). Michon, *Robespierre et le guerre* (A.R. 12/265). Hardy, *Robespierre et la question noire* (A.R. 12/357). *Charlotte Robespierre et le 9 thermidor* (A.R. 12/502).

1921. Durieux, *Thermidor* (R.F. 74/150).

1922. *Un témoignage de Bonaparte sur Robespierre* (A.R. 14/60). Mathiez, *Les intrigues contre Robespierre en 1794* (A.R. 14/223).

1923. Chabaud, *Robespierre Defenseur de Marseille* (A.R. 15/113). Mathiez, *L'opposition entre les Girondins et les Montagnards* (A.R. 15/177). *L'hommage d'Arras à Robespierre* (A.R. 15/441).

1924. Mathiez, *Robespierre et Joseph Le Bon* (A.H. 1/1). Michon, *La maison de Robespierre* (A.H. 1/64). Mathiez,

Défense de Robespierre (A.H. 1/97). Dommanget, *Robespierre et les cultes* (A.H. 1/193). Mathiez, *Robespierre à la commune le 9 thermidor* (A.H. 1/289). Michon, *Les séances des 8 et 9 thermidor* (A.H. 1/497).

1925. Stein, *Louis-le-Grand* (R.Q.H. 102/134). *La succession des frères Robespierre* (A.H. 2/172). *Le " Courrier français " de Philadelphie et la mort de Robespierre* (R.F. 78/74).

1926. Michon, *La maison de Robespierre* (A.H. 3/217). Mathiez, *Le Comité de Salut Public et le complot de l'étranger* (A.H. 3/305). *Robespierre et la réunion d'Avignon* (A.H. 3/583). *Comptes rendus des séances des Jacobins, 1791* (R.F. 79/151).

1927. Mathiez, *Le 'Neuf Thermidor' de M. Barthou* (A.H. 4/1). Mathiez, *Le Robespierre de M. Lenôtre* (A.H. 4/97). Mathiez, *Les séances des 4 et 5 thermidor* (A.H. 4/193). Mathiez, *L'affaire Legray* (A.H. 4/305).

1928. Héritier, *Robespierre, ou le ' Saint ' de la Démocratie* (R.Q.H. 109/313). *Robespierre franc-maçon?* (A.H. 5/62). *Le portrait de Robespierre par Godefroy* (A.H. 5/63). Mathiez, *Les décrets de Ventôse* (A.H. 5/193). Mathiez, *Notes inédites de Blanqui sur Robespierre* (A.H. 5/305). *Le capitaine Linde chez Robespierre* (A.H. 5/457).

1929. Mathiez, *La Révolution française et la théorie de la dictature* (R.H. 161/304). Mathiez, *Robespierre et Vergniaud* (A.H. 6/113, 217). Mathiez, *Robespierre et le procès de Catherine Théot* (A.H. 6/392). Vaillandet, *Les séances des Jacobins* (A.H. 6/551).

1930. Bouchemakine, *Le neuf thermidor* (A.H. 7/401).

1931. Lefebvre, *La rivalité du Comité de Salut Public et du Comité de Sûreté générale* (R.H. 167/366). Vaillandet, *Robespierre et les Jacobins de Versailles* (A.H. 8/49). *Les souvenirs de Robespierre à Châlons* (A.H. 8/159). Walter, *Le problème de la dictature jacobine* (A.H. 8/515). *Robespierre et le Gironde au deux Septembre* (R.F. 85/152).

1932. *Un secrétaire de Robespierre* (A.H. 9/163, 462).

1933. Mansuy, *Robespierre vu de Pologne* (A H. 10/222). Eude, *La Commune robespierriste* (A.H. 10/412, 11/323, 528, 12/132). Thompson, *l'organisation du travail du Comité de Salut Public* (A.H. 10/454). *Le buste de Robespierre à Arras*

(A.H. 10/481). Lefebvre, *Discours sur Robespierre* (A.H. 10/492).

1934. *Un petit cousin de Robespierre* (A.H. 11/250). Lemoine, *L'origine du club des Jacobins* (R.F. 87/17).

1935. Kerr, *Robespierre et le jeune Millingen* (A.H. 12/38). Eude, *Buissart et Robespierre* (A.H. 12/460).

1936. Vermale, *Sur le portrait de Robespierre par Barnave* (A.H. 13/63). Contamine, *A propos d'un mémoire de Robespierre* (A.H. 13/167).

XII

Thus, for 140 years, historical opinion about Robespierre and the Revolution has swung to and fro, under the impulse of personal predilection, or political passion. But two steadying influences have gradually come into action—the publication of original sources, and freedom of historical study. The first of these cannot be taken away; the second may be withdrawn, but only for a time. If, at the present moment, intensive and specialized study of the Revolution goes on side by side with superficial and semi-fictional popularization; if impartial judgment of the revolutionary leaders has to contend against distorting propaganda; yet there is a growing consensus of informed opinion, establishing conclusions which will not easily be upset. Such conclusions seem to be: that the French Revolution was not the work of a class or of a clique, but of the whole nation; that all its stages must be judged as parts of a single movement; that the men who, from time to time, were thought to direct this movement, did little more than follow it; and that Robespierre, in particular, owed his repute to the thoroughness with which he realized, expounded, and embodied the revolutionary spirit of the French people.

BIBLIOGRAPHICAL NOTE

Half a century has elapsed since J. M. Thompson's biography first appeared. It is some measure of his scholarly rigour and clarity of thought that this remains today not merely a viable biography but the most accessible introduction to Robespierre's career. Of course, given Thompson's mastery of the documentation, the staying-power of his book is due in part to the fact that no documents of any great significance have been uncovered since he wrote, with the single exception of the early piece published by N. Berthe and M. de Langre (eds), *Les Droits et l'Etat des Bâtards* (Arras, 1971). The evidence is, however, now much better displayed in the scholarly edition published by the *Société des Etudes Robespierristes: Oeuvres Complètes de Maximilien Robespierre* (10 vols. Paris, 1910-67).

Nonetheless, no reader of this biography can remain unaware that fifty years of historical writing have profoundly modified the interpretation of the context in which Thompson placed his study. At the same time, there have appeared other important biographies of Robespierre to which the reader needs to refer.

As far as the context immediately relevant to a biography of Robespierre is concerned, the most significant historiographical development has been in the area of the popular and radical movements. The landmark publications are undoubtedly A. Soboul, *Les Sans-Culottes Parisiens en l'an II* (Paris, 1958); G. Rudé, *The Crowd in the French Revolution* (Oxford, 1959); R. C. Cobb, *Les Armées Révolutionnaires* (2 vols. Paris, 1961-63). In addition, one may consult some collected essays of Soboul and Cobb respectively in A. Soboul, *Paysans, Sans-Culottes et Jacobins* (Paris, 1966) and R. C. Cobb, *Terreur et Subsistances* (Paris, 1965) as well as R. C. Cobb, *The Police and the People* (Oxford, 1970) and R. B. Rose, *The Making of the Sans-Culottes* (Manchester, 1983).

It is not simply that this work has introduced the popular

movement into the mainstream of interpretation of the Revolution far beyond anything of which Thompson could have been aware. For the purposes of a biography of Robespierre, these publications reshape some of the important questions whch it must address. The whole question of how the Terror originated and to what purposes it was directed now look rather different. Moreover, both Soboul and Cobb provide considerable material for understanding the faction struggles (Hébertism and Dantonism) during the Terror. Finally, this work poses acutely the question of the historical function of jacobinism and its relationship to the popular movement.

Like many other historians, Albert Soboul saw Robespierre as the true spokesman of jacobin radicalism and thus also of the 'official' interpretation of the Terror. He viewed Robespierre as epitomizing the problems of jacobinism which, in its dealings with the popular movement, he saw as caught in the contradiction between its bourgeois assumptions and its radical, democratic principles. He expressed this view in two important articles: 'Robespierre et les Sociétés Populaires', *Annales historiques de la Révolution française,* 1958 and 'Robespierre et la Formation du Gouvernement Révolutionnaire', *Revue d'histoire moderne et contemporaine,* 1958, (both reprinted in his *Paysans, Sans-Culottes et Jacobins* pp. 223–256). A summary of his view is contained in A. Soboul, *Portraits de Révolutionnaires,* ed. C. Mazauric (Paris, 1986), pp. 223–42 ('Robespierre ou les Contradictions du Jacobinisme').

Other elements crucial to a biography of Robespierre have received uneven attention. The early history of radicalism in the Revolution (that is to say, the kind of world with which Robespierre had many connections) has been explored as yet in only a rather fragmentary fashion. Among recent work, there are interesting perspectives in G. Kates, *The 'Cercle Social', the Girondins and the French Revolution* (Princeton, 1985) and J. R. Censer, *Prelude to Power* (Baltimore, 1976). Michael Kennedy, *The Jacobin Clubs in the French Revolu-*

ution (Princeton, 1982. Second volume forthcoming) contains a great deal of material from all over France. Robespierre's position in the debate over war was examined shortly after Thompson's biography appeared by G. Michon, *Robespierre et la Guerre Révolutionnaire* (Paris, 1937). A useful general survey of the coming of the war, but one which does not elaborate much our understanding of the debates and constraints inside revolutionary France, is to be found in T. C. W. Blanning, *The Origins of the French Revolutionary Wars* (London, 1986).

The struggle between the Girondins and the Montagnards has attracted consistent attention. Possibly the best material on this subject and on the politics of the early Convention is to be found in M. J. Sydenham, *The Girondins* (London, 1961) and A. Patrick, *The Men of the First French Republic* (Baltimore, 1972). In this context, K. M. Baker, *Condorcet: From Natural Philosophy to Social Mathematics* (Chicago, 1975) provides an excellent parallel to a biography of Robespierre – another typical product of the eighteenth-century educated elites who ended up in opposition to Robespierre. Much more disappointing is A. Soboul (ed.), *Actes du Colloque Girondins et Montagnards* (Paris, 1980) which adds little that is substantial. Utterly disappointing is A. Soboul (ed.), *Actes du Colloque Robespierre* (Paris, 1967) which is entirely devoted to perceptions of Robespierre.

Finally, although considerable advances have been achieved in the understanding of many aspects of the Terror, there is still reluctance to attack some central themes. In particular, the great committees of government have proved difficult to study. The Committee of General Security has yet to be properly analysed. As for the Committee of Public Safety, R. R. Palmer, *Twelve Who Ruled* (Princeton, 1941) has not really been replaced (M. Bouloiseau, *Le Comité de Salut Public* (Paris, 1962) is competent but slim) although it is showing its age. From the point of view of biography, the great problem is that it is almost impossible to determine beyond a superficial level the roles played by individuals in this collegial government. However, for the final act in Robespierre's life, one can look with profit at R. Bienvenu (ed.), *The Ninth of Thermidor: The Fall of Robespierre* (New York, 1968) and M. Lyons, 'The 9 Thermidor Crisis', *European Studies Review*, 1975.

As for Robespierre himself, some detailed aspects have been explored in articles. J. L. Shulim, 'The Youthful Robespierre and His Ambivalence towards the Ancien Regime', *Eighteenth-Century Studies*, 1972, adds a necessary interpretative gloss for any reader of the first two chapters of Thompson's biography. However, most attention has been directed at Robespierre's ideas. One substantial discussion is to be found in two articles by Alfred Cobban, who was principally interested in Robespierre's relationship with Rousseau and the whole question of democratic sovereignty: A. Cobban, 'The Political ideas of Maximilien Robespierre during the Period of the Convention', *English Historical Review* 1946, and 'The Fundamental Ideas of Robespierre', *English Historical Review* 1948 (both reprinted in A. Cobban, *Aspects of the French Revolution* (London, 1968), pp. 136–91). Another way of looking at this can be found in N. Hampson, *Will and Circumstance* (London, 1983). In addition to these materials, the reader can consult Françoise Theuriot, 'La Conception Robespierriste du Bonheur', *Annales historiques de la Révolution française* 1968, which emphasizes (perhaps too much) the closeness of Robespierre's ideas to those of the sans-culottes. There is also a suggestive brief article by Jean Deprun, 'A la Fête Suprême: Les "Noms Divins" dans deux discours de Robespierre', *Annales historiques de la Révolution française* 1972, which seeks to place Robespierre's speeches at this event within a double eighteenth-century current of both jesuit and philosophe thought. Indeed, the anti-religious compaign which preoccupied Robespierre during the Terror has received considerable attention since Thompson's time: see especially M. Vovelle, *Religion et Révolution* (Paris, 1976).

Since Thompson, other biographers have been attracted to

Robespierre. At root, the attraction of this subject is not so much the evidently dominant role he played in the Revolution, as the mysterious quality which, all biographers agree, is to be found in a man who revealed so little of himself and yet personified (or 'impersonated' as Thompson has it) the Revolution to so many contemporaries and to subsequent generations. He personified it to such a degree that he appears to contain within himself all the contradictions of an event that was simultaneously libertarian and tyrannical, lofty and base, idealistic and pragmatic. To an unusual degree, therefore, Robespierre imposes upon his biographers a resolution of their own attitude to the Revolution and some kind of selection of what they deem to be its most significant characteristics (whether positive or negative), which they will discover in Robespierre. Biographies of Robespierre diverge widely despite the common ground of documentary material.

The closest biography to Thompson's, both in time (first published in 1936) and in its insistence on grounding the work in a close reading of the documents, is G. Walter, *Robespierre* (2 vols. Paris, 1936–39; revised 'definitive' edition 1961). Among the biographies published in France since the war, the most interesting are J. Massin, *Robespierre* (Paris, 1956) and M. Gallo, *Robespierre, Histoire d'une Solitude* (Paris, 1968). The former is a clear and competent biography proceeding from a marxist analysis; the latter is a Freudian psycho-biography which remains interesting despite a fair dose of naivety.

The most interesting recent biographies of Robespierre have been in English. In some ways the most honest of them (without thereby imputing deliberate dishonesty to the others) is N. Hampson. *The Life and Opinions of Maximilien Robespierre* (London, 1974). Hampson displays all the contradictions in his own attitude to Robespierre and, through him, to the Revolution by refusing to synthesize his ambivalence into a conventional, discursive analysis. Instead, most of the book is presented as a discussion between three figures representing different mind-sets in their reactions to evidence presented by a fourth figure, the 'narrator'. For someone who has familiarized himself or herself with the subject (possibly by reading Thompson's biography) there are strong insights to be found in this book; for others, it can make extraordinarily aggravating reading. There is, however, one chapter of analysis in the conventional mode devoted to Montagnard politics in the Convention, which is the best available text on that subject.

G. Rudé, *Robespierre* (London, 1975) displays no such ambivalence. Rudé presents Robespierre as the champion of popular sovereignty, a democrat who came as close to fighting for the people's rights as was possible in a man caught in a social condition and in a century which precluded any realization that wage-earners had particular problems of their own. This volume also contains a useful historiographical discussion.

The most recent good study of Robespierre is D. P. Jordan, *The Revolutionary Career of Maximilien Robespierre* (New York, 1985). Jordan escapes some of the problems of a biographer by confining himself largely to an intellectual biography. He is concerned essentially to work out from Robespierre's words what his attitudes were and how they evolved during the Revolution. This is perhaps the sharpest portrait of how Robespierre came both to identify himself and be identified with the Revolution, to be seen as the incarnation of its moral fire and to be vulnerable to accusation of cant and tyranny. What it lacks is the sense of Robespierre as pragmatic politician, manoeuvring in the daily play of intrigue and manipulation that were also one reality of the Revolution.

Colin Lucas

APPENDIX

Portraits of Robespierre

THE main authority for Robespierre's portraits is H. Buffenoir, whose articles in A.R. 1/244, 457, 641, 2/55, 220, 377, were republished as *Les portraits de Robespierre* in 1908. Further research has from time to time added fresh items. References will be found below.

But it must be noted that Buffenoir's enthusiasm made him too ready to accept, as portraits of Robespierre, pictures which, to the ordinary eye, bear little resemblance to one another; and that no critical treatment of the whole subject has yet been attempted. The following list must therefore be regarded as provisional.

1 An oil painting by J. Boze, exhibited at the *Exposition, Paris et la Révolution,* in 1931; reproduced in Ward (27) as representing Robespierre at the age of 17. It looks much younger; there is no resemblance to the later portraits; the dress is not that of a poor scholar; and why should Boze have painted Robespierre then? (½ length, ¾ left, frizzed hair, and *queue*; dark coat with high collar, white stock, arms crossed.)

2 An oil painting by Boilly, done at Arras in 1783, when Robespierre was 24. It belonged to the family, and was purchased for the Carnavalet Museum (where it is now) at the Dancoisne sale in Paris about 1900. It is reproduced in Buffenoir (frontispiece) and above (½ length, ¾ left, powdered hair, pointed collar, stock, lace *jabot*, coat with 4 large buttons, right hand in waistcoat with small buttons).

3 The picture in the Saint-Albin collection described by Michelet (2/257), and Lewes (53) with the inscription *Tout pour mon amie*; said to be the earliest portrait of Robespierre. Should belong to much the same date as No. 2.

4 An oil painting by Danloux, done at Arras in 1789 (aet. 27) and showing Robespierre (?) in the dress of a deputy to the States-General; in a private collection. (¾ length, full face, frizzed hair, right hand holding hat under left arm, left hand on sword-hilt, black frock-coat and waistcoat.) It looks too

young (Robespierre was 31 in 1789), and bears no resemblance
to later portraits.

5 An anonymous oil painting in the Carnavalet Museum, per-
haps of 1789 ($\frac{1}{2}$ length, life size; striped coat; *gilet* and *jabot*);
reproduced in Jaurès, 1/233.

6 An engraving by Fiesinger, after Guèrin, 1789 (?), v. N. and
Q., 4th Series, 5/341, 432.

7 A silhouette of 1790–1 (?) attributed by Rabbe to Fragonard.
v. R.F. 38/256, 470, 39/278, 382, 462: the upshot of the discussion is that it does not represent Robespierre.

8 An anonymous oil painting of 1790–1 (?) in a private collection. v. A.R. 2/387 (head and shoulders, full face; puce coat,
large *revers*, high collar, white cravat and *jabot*).

9 A pastel by Mme Guyard, shown in the Salon of 1791; since
lost. This is the portrait referred to in Corresp 5.8.(1/143 above).

10 A pastel by J. Boze, shown in the Salon of 1791; said to have
belonged to Albertine Marat; since lost. v. R.H.R.F. 3/131,
and 1/144 above.

11 An anonymous crayon drawing in three colours, of 1791 (?),
reproduced in A.R. 1/248.

12 An anonymous pastel of 1791 (?) belonging to C. Vellay.

13 A medallion of 1791 by Chinard of Lyon. v. A.R. 1/457. cp.
one reproduced in Buffenoir (60), from his own collection.

14 A miniature by Pajou, 1791 (? 1797) in the Carnavalet Museum.

15 A tinted drawing, from M. George Duruy's collection, inscribed *Croquis d'après nature, à une séance de la Convention*, and
with the note *les yeux verts, la teint pâle, habit nankin rayé vert,
jabot blanc rayé bleu, cravatte blanche rayée rouge*. Commonly
attributed to Gérard, and supposed to be a preliminary sketch
for No. 16. Reproduced as such in Barras' *Mémoires*, A.R.
15/441, and elsewhere. Aulard, reviewing Buffenoir (R.F.
60/157), points out that the inscription is not in Gérard's
hand, nor in that of his mistress. ($\frac{1}{2}$ length, full face, spectacles
on forehead, other details as above.) v. above.

16 An oil painting by F. Gérard, which hung in the Duplays'
salon, and was destroyed by fire in 1815. (Full length.)

17 A painting (?) by David, 1792 (?), in dress and theatrical pose
of a deputy; said to have been done, like No. 16, for the
Duplays. Is this the portrait described by A. de Ligny as
being in the possession of the Prince de Ligne (A.R. 10/696)?

18 An oil painting by Lefèvre, 1792, from E. Hamel's collection,

now in the Carnavalet Museum. (¾ length, sitting, ¾ face right, holding book open on knees; curled hair, dark coat, white *jabot* and waistcoat, lace cuffs.) Interesting, rather sinister, in bad condition. Reproduced in Buffenoir (32).

19 An engraving by Chrétien after Fouquet, 1792.

20 An anonymous oil painting of 1793 (?) given by Clemenceau to the Carnavalet Museum. (¾ right, blue coat, with red and white *revers*, knotted cravat.)

21 An anonymous water colour (?) of 1793 (?) representing Robespierre in his room at the Duplays; in H. Buffenoir's collection. Reproduced in Buffenoir (36) and above.

22 An oil painting (?) of 1793 (?) by Ducreux (?) in the collection of M.G.C-L.; supposed to have been shown at the Salon of 1793.

23 An engraving by Kugner, 1793, with title *Robespierre unter den Jacobinen*.

24 An oil painting by Greuze, 1794, bought at Lord Lonsdale's sale, and now in Lord Rosebery's collection. Reproduced in Dayot, *La peinture française au 18ᵉ siécle*, Belloc, Ward, and above. A fine portrait, but is it Robespierre?

25 An oil painting by Bouteville, in England (?); engraved by Jones, in 1794, as *Robbespierre*. (Robespierre as a school-boy, head and shoulders, side face left, plain coat and shirt; attractive, but it might be anyone.) The engraving is reproduced by Buffenoir (16).

26 An oil painting by Fragonard, 1794, reproduced in A.R. 1/257. (Nearly full face, in damaged condition.) Is it Robespierre?

27 An oil painting (?) signed *Diogg, P.*, 1794, now at Arcueil-Cachan. Reproduced in A.R. 5/37, and Hayes, *Irishmen in the French Revolution* (217), who thinks it shows an Irish strain in Robespierre. But the dress and hair are unlike him.

28 A pen and ink sketch by P. Grandmaison, done in the Convention on July 27 (9 Thermidor), 1794. (Head, side-face left.) From the Charavay collection. Reproduced in Buffenoir (118), and above.

29 A sketch in Indian ink, Mess. II, belonging to Mlle Louise Lévi, described in A.R. 2/387.

30 Robespierre's death-mask, 1794. For discussions of the claims of various masks to be authentic, v. A.R. 1/244, 2/391, 4/426, 601. Probably they are all fakes. One is reproduced in Buffenoir (74), who believes it authentic. Another in Dayot, *La Révolu-*

tion françiase (319). Another in Cabanés, *Les indiscrétions de l'histoire*, 5/357, showing a curious likeness to Lenin.

31 An anonymous pastel, in M. Buffenoir's collection, reproduced by him (2). (Head and shoulders, side-face right, *queue*, high stock, coat with dark collar patterned waistcoat open at throat.)

32 A lithograph, from a picture attributed to David, in M. Buffenoir's collection, and reproduced by him (10). (Full length, tail-coat, sash, breeches, boots; Robespierre making a speech. MS. on desk right, background of citizens behind barrier.)

33 An anonymous oil-painting from the collection of Arsène Houssaye, now in M. Buffenoir's collection; shown at the Galérie Georges Petit in 1893. (Head and shoulders, side-face right, in oval frame, dark coat with three buttons, knotted stock.) Interesting, but not Robespierre's eyes. Reproduced in Buffenoir (20).

34 An anonymous miniature, perhaps by Ducreux. (Head and shoulders, ¾ face right, in oval frame.) Not like Robespierre. Reproduced in Buffenoir (22).

35 An anonymous oil painting from Dr. H. D.'s collection, reproduced in Buffenoir (26). (Head and shoulders, ¾ face right: not the least like Robespierre.)

36 An anonymous oil painting from M. Buffenoir's collection, reproduced by him (28). (½ length, sideface right, head stiffly thrown back, huge stock, collar, and *jabot*.) Almost a caricature.

37 An anonymous oil painting in the Carnavalet Museum. (Head and shoulders, ¾ face left, hair brushed back, high stock, big *jabot* and collar, with striped *revers*, in square frame.) Has the cat-like look; v. above.

38 An anonymous painting. (Head, in oval, with square frame, ¾ face left, very faded.) Reproduced in Buffenoir (34).

39 A sketch by Gros, almost a caricature, from nature, from M. Georges Cain's collection. Reproduced (very small) in Buffenoir (38).

40 A sketch by Pajou (?) belonging to M. Martin-Schrameck. (Head and shoulders, side face left, curled hair, ribboned *queue*.) Reproduced in Buffenoir (42). Not like Robespierre.

41 A sketch by J. Boze (?) left by Albertine Marat to the Bibliothèque Nationale. (½ length, ¾ face left.) Not much like Robespierre.

Appendix

42 A crayon drawing in two colours, by J. Boze (?), in the Versailles Museum. (Head and shoulders, side face left.) Like No. 40, but idealized.

43 An engraving by Beljambe, from Gros, reproduced by Buffenoir (86) from his collection. (Head and shoulders, side-face right, in oval, above pediment, with inscription *La loi et le roi*.) Previous to August, 1792.

44 An engraving by Gautier, after Bonneville from Buffenoir's collection, and reproduced by him (94). Also an English engraing b y Chapman. (Head and shoulders, side-face left.) Like No. 42, but more life-like.

45 An anonymous oil painting belonging to the *Société archéologique 'La Cité'*. (Head and shoulders, full face, blue coat, white cravat, *jabot*.) Like No. 8, but not so good. v. A.R. 2/387.

46 An oil painting by David (?), or Doucre, given by M. Nadar to the Musée de Longchamp at Marseille in 1898, and reproduced in A.R. 4/206. Wrong in almost every particular, but not unlike No. 27.

47 An anonymous painting, in England (?), known only in Egleton's engraving. Belonged to J. B. Jarman (?).

48 A drawing of Robespierre and his dog 'Brount', described in A.R. 2/391.

49 A print by Godefroy (Geoffroy?) of 1794 (?), belonging to G. Laurent. v. A.H. 5/63.

INDEX

INDEX

INDEX

INDEX

Devienne, 33
Dictatorship, 241, 288, 319, 449
Diderot, 139 n.
Didier, 185
Diederichsen, 463
Dietrich, 199
Dillon, T., 141, 233, 238; A., 472 n.
Dinaux, 606
Directoire du département de Paris, 201, 210, 247, 257, 278, 295
Discours sur les subsistances, 297
Dodun, Mme, 437
Dolivier, 240
Doppet, 232
Doraison, 342
Douai, 120, 392
Droit d'affiche, 130
Droit de chasse, 75, 79
Droit de grâce, 169
Droit de triage, 78
'Dropmore spy', 457 n., 531, 554 n.
Drouet, 348 n.
Drouhin, 144, 535
Dubois d'Amiens, 8, 536
Dubois de Fosseux, 21, 26–7, 29, 110 n., 342
Dubois-Crancé, 113, 202, 329, 415, 546
Dubuisson, 44, 83, 321, 323, 431
Duchesne, 535
Dufourny, 240, 303, 473, 482
Dufraise, 569
Dumas, 421, 515–6, 553, 565, 569, 581–2
Dumas de Labrousse, 155
Dumesnil, 7
Dumont, André, 406–7, 414, 420, 533
Dumont, Étienne, 51–2
Dumouriez, 212–5, 244, 285, 317–8, 320–5, 329–30, 335, 338, 384, 403, 433, 466–8
Dunkirk, 415
Dupaty, 14, 26
Duperrey, 381
Du Perron, 597
Duplain, 235
Duplessis, 65, 144, 474
Duplay family, 187, 251, 265, 292, 363, 417, 526, 582; Maurice, 178, 182, 294, 418, 516, 527; Madame, 179, 182–3 f., 186, 292–3, 458, 516, 530; Eléonore, 29, 527, 558; Sophie, 183; Victoire, 183; Elisabeth (Mme Lebas), 183–4, 418, 526–7; J. M., 179, 183, 186; Simon, 179, 184, 513 n., 516, 541
Dupont, 35, 62, 536
Duport, Adrien, 60, 68, 73, 96, 134, 149, 156–7, 164, 226, 465
Duport-Dutertre, 8

Duquesnoy, 428, 458, 533, 538
Durand-Maillane, 350, 535, 565
Duroy, 484
Durut, 17–8, 21
Dussaulx, 208
Dutard, 346
Duvignau, 109

E

Eckhardt, 623
École centrale d'expériences, 200
Education, 355, 365, 375, 380
Elections, 264, 268
Elisabeth, Madame, 530
Éloge de Dupaty, 26, 95
Éloge de Gresset, 24
Elsner, 612
Elton, 629
Émigrés, 191, 202, 269, 313, 315–6, 322
Enclosures, 78
England, 101, 107, 164, 207, 302, 314, 319, 326, 425–6, 435, 447–8, 500
Enragés, 316, 378, 380–1, 396, 409, 428, 437–8, 459
d'Enthieuloye, 7, 12
Entretiens du Père Gerard, 398 n.
d'Espagnac, 437, 463
Esquiros, 610
Étampes, 240
l'Être Suprême, 430, 488–9
Eugene IV, Pope, 1
Evrard, Simonne, 403
Exmes, 517

F

Fabre d'Églantine, 245, 262 n., 272, 437, 442–4, 454, 463–5, 489
Faubourg Saint-Antoine, 229
Fauchet, 399
Fauré, 406, 420, 422, 534
Fayau, 471
Fédéralisme, 89, 125, 283, 365
Fédérés, 246, 250, 254–6, 285–6, 289
Félix, 414
Fénelon, 180
Fernex, 535, 546
Ferrières, 14–5
Fersen, 157
Fête of Federation, 98, 177
Fête de la Liberté, 220
Fête de la Loi, 240
Fête de la Nature, 503 n.
Fête de l'Être Suprême, 503–4
Feuillants, 164–5, 189, 198, 266
Feuille de Salut Public, 398, 427
Flachet, 408
Fleischmann, 624

651